Alan J. Hu   Moshe Y. Vardi   (Eds.)

Computer Aided Verification

10th International Conference, CAV'98
Vancouver, BC, Canada, June 28 – July 2, 1998
Proceedings

D1324339

 Springer

Springer

Berlin
Heidelberg
New York
Barcelona
Budapest
Hong Kong
London
Milan
Paris
Singapore
Tokyo

Preface

This volume contains the proceedings of the Tenth International Conference on Computer-Aided Verification (CAV'98), held June 28 – July 2 at the University of British Columbia. The CAV conferences are dedicated to the advancement of the theory and practice of computer-assisted formal analysis methods for software and hardware systems. The conference covers the spectrum from theoretical results to concrete applications and has traditionally drawn contributions from both researchers and practitioners in both academia and industry. This year is no exception. We accepted 33 research papers out of 98 submissions and 10 short tool papers out of 19 submissions. Rounding out the program are a set of invited papers.

Given the practical and industrial aspects of CAV, we are very proud of the support we receive from industry. We would like to thank the following generous and forward-looking companies for their sponsorship of CAV'98:

Cadence Design Systems

Chrysalis Symbolic Design

Dassault Aviation

Fujitsu Ltd.

Hewlett-Packard

IBM Research

Intel

Lucent Technologies

Mentor Graphics

Motorola

NEC USA

Prover Technology (Logikkonsult)

Rockwell Collins

SGS-Thomson Microelectronics

Siemens

Sun Microsystems

Synopsys

Verisity

Verysys

The conference program was selected by the program committee: Martin Abadi (DEC SRC, USA), Rajeev Alur (Univ. of Pennsylvania, USA), Ahmed Bouajjani (VERIMAG, France), Jerry Burch (Cadence Labs, USA), Olivier Coudert (Synopsys, USA), Werner Damm (Oldenburg University, Germany), David Dill (Stanford University, USA), Limor Fix (Intel, Israel), Patrice Godefroid (Bell Labs, USA), Mike Gordon (Cambridge University, Great Britain), Orna Grumberg (The Technion, Israel), Alan Hu, co-chair (Univ. of British Columbia, Canada), Daniel Jackson (MIT, USA), Bengt Jonsson (Uppsala University, Sweden), Kim Larsen (Aalborg University, Denmark), Ken McMillan (Cadence Labs, USA), Doron Peled (Bell Labs, USA), Carl Pixley (Motorola, USA), Amir Pnueli (Weizmann Institute, Israel), Carl Seger (Intel, USA), Natarajan Shankar (SRI International, USA), Joseph Sifakis (VERIMAG, France), Prasad Sistla (Univ. of Illinois, Chicago, USA), Fabio Somenzi (Univ. of Colorado, Boulder, USA), Moshe Vardi, co-chair (Rice University, USA), and Yaron Wolfsthal (IBM, Israel).

The following additional reviewers also helped in the evaluation of submitted papers: Parosh Abdulla, Roy Armoni, Tamarah Arons, Eugene Asarin,

Series Editors

Gerhard Goos, Karlsruhe University, Germany
Juris Hartmanis, Cornell University, NY, USA
Jan van Leeuwen, Utrecht University, The Netherlands

Volume Editors

Alan J. Hu
The University of British Columbia, Department of Computer Science
2366 Main Hall, Vancouver, BC, V6T 1Z4, Canada
E-mail: ajh@cs.ubc.ca

Moshe Y. Vardi
Rice University, Department of Computer Science
P.O. Box 1892, Houston, TX 77251-1892, USA
E-mail: vardi@cs.rice.edu

Cataloging-in-Publication data applied for

Die Deutsche Bibliothek - CIP-Einheitsaufnahme

Computer aided verification : 10th international conference ;
proceedings / CAV '98, Vancouver, BC, Canada, June 28 - July 2,
1998. Alan J. Hu ; Moshe Y. Yardi (ed.). - Berlin ; Heidelberg ; New
York ; Barcelona ; Budapest ; Hong Kong ; London ; Milan ; Paris ;
Santa Clara ; Singapore ; Tokyo : Springer, 1998
    (Lecture notes in computer science ; Vol. 1427)
    ISBN 3-540-64608-6

CR Subject Classification (1991): F.3, D.2.4, D.2.2, F.4.1, B.7.2, C.3, I.2.3

ISSN 0302-9743
ISBN 3-540-64608-6 Springer-Verlag Berlin Heidelberg New York

© Springer-Verlag Berlin Heidelberg 1998
Printed in Germany

Typesetting: Camera-ready by author
SPIN 10637540   06/3142 – 5 4 3 2 1 0   Printed on acid-free paper

Andrea Asperti, Adnan Aziz, Clark Barrett, Ilan Beer, Shoham Ben-David, Sergey Berezin, Roderick Bloem, Juergen Bohn, Bernard Boigelot, Dragan Bosjnatsjki, Olivier Bournez, Alex Brodsky, Stephen Brookes, Glenn Bruns, Paul Caspi, Judy Crow, David Cyrluk, Mads Dam, Dennis Dams, Juergen Dingel, Cindy Eisner, Henrik Ejersbo Jensen, Amy Felty, Martin Fraenzle, Ranan Fraer, Danny Geist, Boris Ginsburg, Leonid Glukhovski, Susanne Graf, Efim Gukovsky, Viktor Gyuris, Gary Hachtel, Alan Hartman, Henrik Huldgaard, Hardi Hungar, Norris Ip, Amitai Irron, Radhakrishnan Jagadeesan, Jae-Young Jang, Somesh Jha, Bernhard Josko, Gila Kamhi, Sagi Katz, Shmuel Katz, Yonit Kesten, Kaare Kristoffersen, Andreas Kuehlmann, Orna Kupferman, Yassine Lakhnech, Avner Landver, Karen Laster, Jorn Lind-Nielsen, Sela Mador-Haim, Bozga Maler, Monica Marcus, Will Marrero, Stephan Melzer, Stephan Merz, Kim Milvang-Jensen, Marius Minea, Faron Moller, In-Ho Moon, Laurent Mounier, David Notkin, Sam Owre, Paul Pettersson, Sriram Rajamony, Rajeev Ranjan, Kavita Ravi, Michel Raynal, Yoav Rodeh, Roni Rosner, Sitvanit Ruah, John Rushby, Mark Sauer, Elad Shahar, Dafna Sheinwald, Tom Shiple, Ze'ev Shtadler, Ofer Shtrichman, Michael Siegel, Vigyan Singhal, Gal Siton, Jens Skakkebaek, Arne Skou, Mandayam Srivas, Martin Steffen, Ulrich Stern, Jeffrey Su, Serdar Tasiran, Gadi Taubenfeld, Stavros Tripakis, Shmuel Ur, Koen van Eijk, Carsten Weise, Derek Williams, Gunnar Wittich, Pierre Wolper, Howard Wong-Toi, Han Yang, Wang Yi, Sergio Yovine. We would like to thank all of the reviewers for their time and expertise.

The steering committee consists of the founders of the conference: Edmund Clarke (Carnegie Mellon University, USA), Robert Kurshan (Bell Labs, USA), Amir Pnueli (Weizmann Institute, Israel), and Joseph Sifakis (VERIMAG, France). We thank them and last year's conference chair Orna Grumberg (Technion, Israel) for their helpful advice.

Finally, on the logistical side, the conference was held at UBC with the cooperation of the Computer Science Department and the Center for Integrated Computer Systems Research (CICSR). We thank CICSR Director Rabab Ward for sanctioning UBC's hosting of the conference. Computing Facilities Manager John Demco orchestrated computer access for the conference. The UBC Conference Center staff Melanie Kelleher, Brenda Kiernan, and Karen Read were invaluable in planning local arrangements. Holly Mitchell provided indispensable secretarial support. We thank them for their time and energy.

Vancouver, British Columbia
Houston, Texas

Alan J. Hu
Moshe Y. Vardi

April 1998

Table of Contents

Invited Papers

Regular Papers

Tool Papers

Synchronous Programming of Reactive Systems*

A Tutorial and Bibliography

Nicolas Halbwachs

Verimag, Grenoble - France
email: Nicolas.Halbwachs@imag.fr

1 Reactive Systems

The term "reactive system" was introduced by David Harel and Amir Pnueli [HP85], and is now commonly accepted to designate permanently operating systems, and to distinguish them from "transformational systems" — i.e., usual programs whose role is to terminate with a result, computed from an initial data (e.g., a compiler). In a transformational program, either, we distinguish it in a more restrictive way, distinguishing between "interactive" and "reactive" systems:

- Interactive systems permanently communicate with their environment, but at their own pace. They are able to synchronize with their environment, i.e., make it wait. Operating systems or databases are typical interactive systems are not purely interactive.

Reactive systems, in our meaning, have to react to an environment which cannot wait. Typical examples appear when the environment is a physical process. The specific features of reactive systems have been pointed out many times [Ha93,BCG88,Ber89]:

- In contrast with interactive systems, they are generally intended to be deterministic.
- Their description involves concurrency, for several different reasons:
  1. They run in parallel with their environment.
  2. They are often conducted on distributed architectures, for reasons of speed, fault-tolerance or physical distribution requirements.
  3. Most of the time, it is convenient to describe them as a set of concurrent processes.

  Cases (2) and (3) must be distinguished: in the latter case, concurrency is nothing but a description facility, we call it logical concurrency. Generally it has nothing to do with physical concurrency involved in case (2), and is not submitted to the same constraints.

- They are submitted to critical reliability requirements. In fact, most critical systems either are reactive, or contain reactive parts.

---
*This work has been partially supported by the ESPRIT-LTR project "SYRF".

†Verimag is a joint laboratory of Université Joseph Fourier (Grenoble I), CNRS and INPG.

Synchronous Programming of Reactive Systems*
A Tutorial and Commented Bibliography

Nicolas Halbwachs

Vérimag**, Grenoble – France
e-mail: `Nicolas.Halbwachs@imag.fr`

1   Reactive Systems

The term *"reactive system"* was introduced by David Harel and Amir Pnueli [HP85], and is now commonly accepted to designate permanently operating systems, and to distinguish them from *"transformational systems"* — i.e, usual programs whose role is to terminate with a result, computed from an initial data (e.g., a compiler). In synchronous programming, we understand it in a more restrictive way, distinguishing between *"interactive"* and *"reactive"* systems:

Interactive systems permanently communicate with their environment, but at their own speed. They are able to synchronize with their environment, i.e., making it wait. Concurrent processes considered in operating systems or in data-base management, are generally interactive.

Reactive systems, in our meaning, have to react to an environment which cannot wait. Typical examples appear when the environment is a physical process. The specific features of reactive systems have been pointed out many times [Hal93,BCG88,Ber89]:

- In contrast with most interactive systems, they are generally intended to be *deterministic*.
- Their description involves *concurrency*, for several different reasons:
  1. They run in parallel with their environment;
  2. They are often implemented on distributed architectures, for reasons of speed, fault-tolerance, or physical distribution requirements;
  3. Most of the time, it is convenient to describe them as sets of concurrent processes.

  Cases (2) and (3) must be distinguished. In the later case, concurrency is nothing but a description facility; we call it *logical concurrency*. Generally, it has nothing to do with *physical concurrency* involved in case (2), and is not submitted to the same constraints.
- They are submitted to critical reliability requirements. In fact, most critical systems either are reactive, or contain reactive parts.

---

* This work has been partially supported by the ESPRIT-LTR project "SYRF".
** Verimag is a joint laboratory of Université Joseph Fourier (Grenoble I), CNRS and INPG

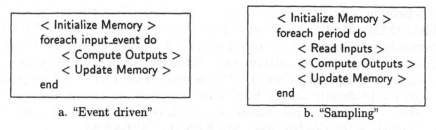

a. "Event driven"   b. "Sampling"

Fig. 1. Execution schemes for reactive systems

2 Synchronous Programming

All control engineers know a simple way to implement a reactive system by a single loop, of the form shown by Fig. 1.a. This program scheme is *"event driven"* since each reaction is triggered by an input event.

Fig. 1.b shows an even simpler and more common scheme, which consists in periodically sampling the inputs. This *"sampling"* scheme is mainly used in numeric systems which solve, e.g., systems of differential equations. These two schemes do not deeply differ, but they correspond to different intuitive points of view. In both cases, the program typically implements an *automaton*: the states are the valuations of the memory, and each reaction corresponds to a transition of the automaton. Such a transition may involve many computations, which, from the automaton point of view, are considered *atomic* (i.e., input changes are only taken into account between two reactions). This is the essence of the synchronous paradigm, where such a reaction is often said to *take no time*. An atomic reaction is called an *instant* (logical time), and all the events occurring during such a reaction are considered *simultaneous*.

Now, automata are useful tools — from their simplicity, expressive power, and efficiency —, but they are very difficult to design by hand[1]. Synchronous languages aim at providing high level, modular, constructs, to make the design of such an automaton easier. The basic construct that all these languages provide, is a notion of synchronous concurrency, inspired by Milner's synchronous product [Mil81,Mil83]: in the sampling scheme, when automata are composed in parallel, a transition of the product is made of *"simultaneous"* transitions of all of them; in the event-driven scheme, some automata can stay idle, when not triggered by events coming either from the environment or from other automata. In any case, when participating in such a compound transition, each automaton considers the outputs of others as being part of its own inputs. This *"instantaneous"* communication is called the *synchronous broadcast* [BCG88,Ber89,BB91]. The important point is that, in contrast with the asynchronous concurrency considered in asynchronous languages like ADA [ADA83,Coh96], this synchronous product can preserve *determinism*, a highly desirable feature in reactive systems design.

There are two fields where this synchronous model has been used for years:

---

[1] Consider, e.g., scanners and parsers, and the usefulness of tools like LEX and YACC!

In synchronous circuit design, it is the usual model of communicating Mealy machines (FSM). Most hardware description formalisms (e.g., [Bli90,CLM91]) are naturally synchronous, or contain a significant synchronous subset [Per93]. As a matter of fact, the compilation and verification of synchronous programs borrow many techniques from circuit CAD. However, while hardware description languages can be directly used to describe the data part of a circuit, they are of little help in designing complex hardware controllers. This explains the success of synchronous imperative languages, like ESTEREL, in this field.

In control engineering, high level specification formalisms are often *data-flow* synchronous formalisms, inherited from earlier analog technology: differential or finite-difference equations, block-diagrams, analog networks. Interpreted in a discrete world, these models can be formalized using the data-flow paradigm [Kah74,AW85,PP83]. However, these formalisms are seldom used as programming languages, and automatic code generation is not available. On the other hand, more imperative languages used for programming automatic controllers (e.g., Sequential Function Charts [LM93,AG96]) generally follow the same cyclic execution scheme.

3 Synchronous Languages

[Hal93,IEE91] are general references on synchronous languages.

Statecharts [Har87] is probably the first, and the most popular, formal language designed in the early eighties for the design of reactive systems. However, they were proposed more as a specification and design formalism, rather than as a programming language. Many features (synchronous product and broadcast) of the synchronous model are already present in Statecharts, but determinism is not ensured, and many semantic problems were raised [vdB94]. Almost at the same time, three programming languages were proposed by French academic groups:

- ESTEREL[2] [BCG88,BS91,BG92,Ber93,Ber98] is an imperative language developed at the "Ecole des Mines" and Inria, in Sophia Antipolis.
- SIGNAL[3] [LGLL91,BL90] and LUSTRE[4] [HCRP91,CPHP87] are data-flow languages, respectively designed at Inria (Rennes) and CNRS (Grenoble). SIGNAL is more "event-driven", while LUSTRE mainly corresponds to the "sampled" scheme.

Also, following the formal definition of the synchronous model, a purely synchronous variant of the Statecharts was proposed: ARGOS[5] [Mar92]. The ideas of ARGOS are currently used as a basis for a graphical version of ESTEREL, named SYNCCHARTS[6] [And96], proposed at the University of Nice.

---

[2] see http://www.inria.fr/meije/esterel/esterel-eng.html
[3] see http://www.inria.fr/Equipes/EPATR-eng.html
[4] see http://www.imag.fr/VERIMAG/SYNCHRONE/lustre-english
[5] see http://www-verimag.imag.fr/SYNCHRONE/argonaute-english.html
[6] see http://www.inria.fr/meije/esterel/syncCharts/

4

In this section, we use simple examples to give a flavor of the programming styles in LUSTRE and ESTEREL.

3.1 Overview of the synchronous data-flow language Lustre

LUSTRE is based on the synchronous data-flow model, i.e., on a synchronous interpretation of block-diagrams. A block diagram may be viewed as a network of operators (or as a system of equations, see opposite) running in parallel at the rate of their inputs.

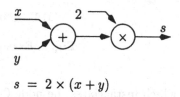

$$s = 2 \times (x + y)$$

The synchronous interpretation of such a description consists in considering each variable as taking a value at each cycle of the program. According to this interpretation, the above description means: "*at any cycle n, $s_n = 2 * (x_n + y_n)$*".

A LUSTRE program defines its output variables as functions of its input variables. Each variable or expression E denotes a function of discrete time, giving its value E_n at each "instant" n. Variables are defined by means of equations: an equation "X=E", specifies that the variable X is always equal to expression E.

Expressions are made of variable identifiers, constants (considered as constant functions), usual arithmetic, boolean and conditional operators (considered as applying pointwise to functions) and only two specific operators: the "previous" operator — which refers to the previous value of its argument — and the "followed-by" operator — which is used to define initial values: If E and F are LUSTRE expressions, so are "pre(E)" and "E -> F", and we have at any instant $n > 0$:

- $(pre(E))_n = E_{n-1}$, while $(pre(E))_0$ has the undefined value *nil*.
- $(E\ \text{->}\ F)_n = F_n$, while $(E\ \text{->}\ F)_0 = E_0$.

For instance, if x_n, y_n denote the respective values of x and y at "instant" n, the equation "z = 0->(pre(x) + y)" means that the initial value z_0 of z is 0, and that, at any non initial instant n, $z_n = x_{n-1} + y_n$.

A LUSTRE program is structured into *nodes*: a node is a subprogram defining its output parameters as functions of its input parameters. This definition is given by an unordered set of equations, possibly involving local variables. Once declared, a node may be freely instanciated in any expression, just as a basic operator.

As an illustration, Figure 2 shows an extremely simple node describing a counter: it receives two integer inputs, init and incr, and a boolean input, reset. It returns an integer output, count, which behaves as follows: at the initial instant and whenever the input reset is true, the output is equal to the current value of the input init. At any other instant, the value of count is equal to its previous value incremented by the current value of incr. One can make use of this node elsewhere, for instance in the equation

mod5 = Counter(0, 1, pre(mod5)=4);

```
node Counter (init, incr: int; reset: bool)
     returns (count: int);
let
     count = init ->    if reset then init
                        else pre(count)+incr;
tel
```

cycle nr.	0	1	2	3	4	5	6	7
reset	ff	ff	ff	ff	tt	ff	ff	ff
init	0	0	0	0	10	0	0	0
incr	1	1	1	1	1	1	2	2
count	0	1	2	3	10	11	13	15
pre(count)	nil	0	1	2	3	10	11	13

(a) Program   (b) Behavior

Fig. 2. Example of LUSTRE program: A counter

which instanciates the node Counter, with 0 and 1 as constant initial and increment values, and resets it whenever the previous value of its output is 4. The variable mod5 is then the cyclic sequence of integers modulo 5.

So, through the notion of node, LUSTRE naturally offers hierarchical description and component reuse. Data traveling along the "wires" of an operator network can be complex, structured informations.

From a temporal point of view, industrial applications show that several processing chains, evolving at different rates, can appear in a single system. LUSTRE offers a notion of boolean clock, allowing the activation of nodes at different rates.

3.2 Overview of the synchronous imperative language Esterel

Being an imperative language, ESTEREL looks more familiar at first glance, since it provides usual constructs, like assignments, sequences, loops, ... However, its synchronous semantics makes this apparent friendliness somewhat deceiptive: one must keep in mind that, apart from a few statements that explicitly take time (e.g., "await $<$ signal $>$"), most ESTEREL statements are conceptually *instantaneous*, i.e., are executed in the same reaction than other statements that sequentially precede or follow them in the program.

ESTEREL provides a lot of constructs that we cannot present in detail. We only comment a small example, which is a speed supervisor (see Fig. 3): the program is intended to measure the speed of a vehicle, and to detect when this speed exceeds a maximum bound.

Fig. 3.a describes a speedometer: it is an ESTEREL *module*, receiving two *signals*, Second and Meter, which occur, respectively, whenever the vehicle has travelled for 1 meter and a second has elapsed. It emits a valued signal Speed, carrying the current value of the speed, an integer, measured in m/s. The *body* of the module is an infinite loop (lines 4–13) which initializes a local variable Distance — that will measure the number of Meters received within a Second — and enters a "do ... upto Second" construct (lines 6–10). This construct executes its body — a loop incrementing Distance on every occurrence of Meter (lines 7–9) —, until being interrupted by the next occurrence of the signal Second. So, on the first occurrence of Second following the entering in the global loop, the "do ... upto Second" statement is terminated and the counter Distance contains

1 module Speedometer:	1 module SpeedSupervisor:
2 input Second, Meter;	2 input Second, Meter;
3 output Speed : integer in	3 output TooFast in
4 loop	4 signal Speed : integer in
5 var Distance := 0 : integer in	5 [run Speedometer
6 do	6 ||
7 every Meter do	7 every Speed do
8 Distance := Distance+1	8 if ?Speed > MaxSpeed
9 end every	9 then emit TooFast
10 upto Second;	10 end if
11 emit Speed(Distance)	11 end every
12 end var	12]
13 end loop	13 end signal
14 end module	14 end module
(a)	(b)

Fig. 3. A speed supervisor in ESTEREL

the number of Meters received during this time. The signal Speed, carrying the value of Distance, is simultaneously emitted (line 11), and the loop is entered again for a new Second. So, the signal Speed is emitted *exactly* each Second.

Fig. 3.b shows the speed supervisor, which makes use of the Speedometer module. Here the input signals are Second and Meter, and the output is a signal TooFast that is emitted whenever the speed excceeds the bound MaxSpeed. A local signal Speed is used to transmit the result of the speedometer. Within the scope of this signal, the speedometer is instanciated[7], through the run construct (line 5), in parallel with a process comparing the speed to the bound: this process is triggered whenever the speedometer emits a Speed signal, whose current carried value ?Speed is compared with the bound, with the possible effect of emitting the signal TooFast.

4 Compilation of Synchronous Languages

This section is an overview of the various approaches related to the compilation of synchronous languages into sequential or distributed code. Beforehand, we have to tackle a static semantic problem, which is specific to synchronous languages: *causality*.

4.1 Causality analysis

Generally speaking, the problem of causality comes from the fact that not all synchronous programs have a unique, deterministic meaning. In the data-flow model,

---

[7] In the run statement, the parameters of the Speedometer module could have been renamed.

this problem has a very simple statement, since it boils down to the well known problem of *combinational loops* in synchronous circuits [Mal93,Kau70,Sto92]: consider the following LUSTRE equations:

$$(a)\ x = \text{not } x \qquad (b)\ y = y \qquad (c)\ z = (z*z + 1.0)/2.0$$
$$(d)\ u = \text{if } c \text{ then } v \text{ else } w;\ v = \text{if } c \text{ then } w \text{ else } u$$

Case (a) is clearly a nonsense: the equation doesn't have any solution. Case (b) can be viewed as non deterministic, since y can have any value. Case (c) is an equation with one and only one solution ($z=1$), but solving such implicit algebraic equations is clearly unfeasible, in general. Case (d) can be disputed: apparently, u depends on v, that depends on u, so there is a combinational loop. Now, whatever be the value of the condition c, this loop is semantically cut.

In data-flow languages, all these situations are quite unnatural — because the user keeps the data dependences in mind — and generally easy to avoid. This is why, in LUSTRE, all the preceding examples are rejected by the compiler. However, in imperative languages like ESTEREL, ARGOS, or Statecharts, it is extremely easy to write programs with apparent causality problems — i.e., where, in some states, the presence of a signal seems to depend on itself —, to which users want to give meaning. More precise criteria must be applied to identify really problematic programs. Most of the various semantics that have been proposed for Statechart [vdB94] differ from each other by the way these problems are solved.

Let's go further into these problems, by means of some ESTEREL examples (see Fig. 4), taken from [Ber95]. A simple way of examining the correctness of these examples is by considering all the cases of presence/absence of signals: we want to have one (reactivity) and only one (determinism) consistent solution, for each configuration of input signals. For the module P1 of Fig. 4, either O is present, in which case the else part of the "present ... else ..." statement is not executed, so O is not emitted, and O is not present; this assumption is not consistent; or O is absent, the else part is executed, so O is emitted, and the assumption is again violated. This module doesn't have any consistent behavior. In fact, this example shows exactly the same kind of inconsistency as the equation "O = not O" in LUSTRE. Consider now the module P2 of Fig. 4. If we assume that O is present, the then part of the "present ... then ..." statement is executed, so O is emitted, and our assumption is satisfied. Now, assuming that O is absent, O is not emitted, and our assumption is satisfied again. Here, we have two consistent behaviors, it is a case of non determinism similar to the LUSTRE equation "O = O". The module P3 is a similar case of non determinism, showing that the problem can result from dependence paths of arbitrary length. For P4, if I is present, the first process in the parallel construct emits S, and the presence of S makes the second process to emit O. Conversely, if I is absent, neither S nor O is emitted. So P4 is correct; it corresponds to the LUSTRE fragment "S = I ; O = S", which doesn't show any loop. The case of P5 is more questionable: the first process in the parallel seems to be non deterministic (like in P2). Now, if we assume that O1 is present, we find that the second process in

```
module P1:              module P2:              module P3:
output O;               output O;               output O1, O2;
    present O               present O               present O1 then emit O2 end
        else emit O             then emit O         ||
    end present             end present             present O2 then emit O1 end
end module              end module              end module


module P4:
input I;
output O;                                       module P5:
    signal S in                                 output O1, O2;
        present I then emit S end                   present O1 then emit O1 end
    ||                                          ||
        present S then emit O end                   present O1 then
    end signal                                          present O2 else emit O2 end
end module                                          end present
                                                end module
```

Fig. 4. Causality problems in ESTEREL

the parallel doesn't have any behavior (like in P1). So, P5 has one and only one consistent behavior, where neither O1 nor O2 is emitted.

All the semantics proposed for synchronous languages reject modules P1, P2, and P3, and accept P4. The *Boolean causality* considered in [HM95], analyzes the problem in classical logic, and accepts also P5, since it has one and only one solution. The *constructive causality* [SBT96,Ber95] rejects P5, because the only solution doesn't have a constructive explanation, by means of causes and effects. Moreover, the constructive causality has been shown [SBT96] to coincide with *electric stability*: a constructively causal circuit will stabilize whatever be the traversal delays of its gates.

Causality problems are an obstacle to separate compilation and distributed code generation. Several authors[8] [Bou91,BdS96,Bon95] propose a weakenning of the synchronous communication, to get round these problems.

4.2 Sequential code generation

The straightforward way for compiling a data-flow synchronous language like LUSTRE into sequential code, is by generating a single loop, after conveniently sorting the equations according to their dependences. Sequential code generation from an imperative language like ESTEREL is less obvious: in the compilers ESTEREL-V2 and -V3 [BCG88,BG92], the control part of the program was compiled into an explicit automaton, representing the control structure of the code. This approach has also been applied to LUSTRE [CPHP87], with on-the fly minimization (by bisimulation) of the automaton [BFH+92,HRR91]. The explicit automaton is a very efficient implementation — since the whole internal synchronization of the program is computed at compile time —, with the drawback

---

[8] See also http://www.inria.fr/meije/rc/rc-project.html.

of possibly involving an exponential expansion of the code size. This is why it is now generally abandonned for single loop compilation. However, it played a central role in the development of verification tools.

The single loop code generation for ESTEREL was a side-effect of the development of a silicon compiler [Ber92] (see §4.5): compiling ESTEREL into circuits is mainly a translation into a data-flow network, which can be easily implemented by a single loop program. The ESTEREL-V4 and -V5 compilers [Ber95] are based on this principle.

About the compilation of synchronous imperative languages into data-flow networks, let us mention also the translation of ARGOS [MH96] into the DC common format (see §4.3) and the REGLO tool [Ray96] which produces recognizers (in LUSTRE) for regular expressions.

4.3 Common formats

The LUSTRE, SIGNAL, and ESTEREL compilers were developed in tight cooperation. In order to share common tools, and to make the languages integration easier, common formats were defined and used as intermediate codes in the compilers: the OC ("object code") format [PS87] was used to encode explicit automata in the earlier versions of the compilers. Another format [CS95], named DC/DC+ (for "declarative code") is used now to encode implicit automata, at the equational level.

4.4 Distributed code generation

Compiling synchronous languages into code for distributed architectures is obviously a challenge. In [ML94], techniques are proposed to separate a clocked data-flow networks into sub-networks independent enough to be sperately compiled into processes. The SYNDEX tool [LSSS91] can be used to schedule the resulting tasks on various architectures, and to study adjust the performances of the resulting system. Another approach is presented in [CGP94,CG95], which starts from the sequential code produced by the standard compilers, and from distribution directives given by the user; it consists of (1) replicating the code on each site of the architecture, (2) simplifying the code on each site according to its assigned role, and (3) adding communications along simple bounded FIFOs, to ensure both communication and synchronization.

4.5 Silicon compiling

Compiling synchronous programs into circuits is also an important goal, particularly in a codesign approach. Synchronous data-flow languages are very close to hardware description languages (HDLs), and their compilation to circuits is quite easy (see, e.g., [RH91]). The translation into circuits of ESTEREL was a much more difficult task, but the result is more interesting, since ESTEREL is of much higher level than usual HDLs for describing controllers. The translation proposed in [Ber92] is structural, and must be completed by deep optimizations, using both standard CAD tools [SSL+92], and specific techniques [STB96,STB97] that take advantage of knowledge coming from the structure of the source code.

5   Verification of Synchronous Programs

Since synchronous programming is mainly devoted to the field of critical embedded systems, the formal verification of synchronous programs is a particularly important goal. By chance, it can take advantage of some specific features of the application field and of the synchronous model:

- Experience shows that critical properties that must be verified are generally *simple, safety* properties. By "simple properties", we mean logical dependency relations between events, in contrast with deep arithmetic properties. As a consequence, these properties can often be model-checked on an abstraction of the program [Hal94], the most natural of which is the control automaton generated by the earlier versions of the compilers (see §4.2).
- The control automaton, being obtained as a synchronous product, is generally much smaller that models obtained by asynchronous composition (no interleaving, no need for partial orders, ...).
- The transition relation is a *vectorial function*, which allows particularly efficient BDD-based techniques [CBM89a] to be applied for the symbolic construction of the reachable state space.
- Thanks to the synchronous model, a specific approach can be applied to express safety properties by means of *synchronous observers*, i.e., special programs possibly written in the same language as the program under verification.

The verification methods for synchronous programs are all based on the control automaton.

Reduction methods have been applied [dSR94], mainly to automata compiled from ESTEREL: using the tools AUTO/AUTOGRAPH [RdS90] reduced views of the automaton can be obtained and compared.

Other methods are based on *model-checking* [QS82,CES86], and mainly symbolic model-checking [CBM89b,BCM+90]. TEMPEST [JPV95] is a model-checker of temporal logic formulas dedicated to ESTEREL. SIGALI [LDBL93] model-checks SIGNAL programs, using the symbolic resolution of SIGNAL *clocks* constraints.

The tool LESAR [HLR92] is a symbolic, BDD-based, model-checker of LUSTRE programs; it is based on the use of *synchronous observers*, to describe both the property to be checked and the assumptions on the program environment under which these properties are intended to hold: an observer of a safety property is a program, taking as inputs the inputs/outputs of the program under verification, and deciding (e.g., by emitting an *alarm*

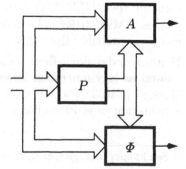

signal) at each instant whether the property is violated. Running in parallel the program, P, an observer Φ of the desired property, and an observer A of the assumption made about the environment one has just to check that either the alarm signal of Φ is never emitted (property satisfied) or the alarm signal of A is emitted (assumption violated), which can be done by a simple traversal of the reachable states of the compound program. Besides this only need of considering reachable states (instead of paths) this specification technique has several advantages:

- observers are written in the same language as the program under verification;
- observers are *executable*; they can be tested, or even kept in the actual implementation (redundancy, autotest).

Notice that, with an asynchronous language, observers would have to be explicitly synchronized with the program under verification, with the risk of changing its behavior. For an application of this technique, see also [WNT96].

Taking into account some numerical aspects — in particular delay counting — is considered in [HPR97], using abstract interpretation techniques [CC77]. In [LHR97], observers and abstract intepretation are used for verifying parameterized networks of synchronous processes.

6 Other Related Topics

[Le94] is an interesting comparative study of formal description techniques, including synchronous languages. This section lists some other works related to synchronous programming.

Program testing will remain a validation technique complementary to formal verification. The automatic testing of synchronous programs is studied in [MHMM95,TMC94,OP94,NRW98].

Integration of synchronous/asynchronous aspects: In general, only some parts of a complex system can be suitably described in the synchronous model. The language ELECTRE [CR95] is devoted to the synchronous control of asynchronous tasks. CRP [BSR93] allows ESTEREL modules to be composed asynchronously.

Combination of formalisms: Data-flow and imperative synchronous languages are complementary, and several attempts have been made, either to combine them [JLRM94], or to introduce imperative concepts in data-flow languages [RM95,MR98]. The most advanced work on combining synchronousa languages is probably the "SYNCHRONIE WORKBENCH[9]", developed at GMD.

Higher order data-flow languages: Data-flow synchronous languages can be viewed as lazy functional languages working on infinite sequence. "Lucid synchrone" [Cas93,CP95,CP96] is a higher order extension of LUSTRE, where the synchronous execution (bounded memory) is preserved.

---

[9] See http://set.gmd.de/EES/synchronie/swb.html.

Aknowledgements: I hope all prominent contributors to synchronous languages have been properly cited. However, the theses on the subject are not referenced, because most of them are written in French. Nevertheless, I would like to aknowledge the significant contribution of the following students[10]:

> P. Amagbégnon, M. Belhadj, J.-L. Bergerand, R. Bernhard, C. Bodennec, F. Boniol, A. Bouali, B. Chéron, L. Cosserat, E. Coste-Maniere, P. Couronné, B. Dutertre, X. Fornari, D. Gaffé, G. Gherardi, A. Girault, G. Gonthier, A.-C. Glory, M. Jourdan, V. Lecompte, B. Le Goff, D. Lesens, D. L'Her, O. Mafféis, H. Marchand, C. Mazuet, F. Mignard, J.-P. Paris, I. Parissis, J. Plaice, C. Ratel, P. Raymond, A. Ressouche, F. Rocheteau, V. Roy, J.-B. Saint, T. Shiple, J.-M. Tanzi, H. Toma, D. Weber

References

[ADA83]   ADA. *The Programming Language* ADA *Reference Manual.* LNCS 155, Springer Verlag, 1983.

[AG96]   C. André and D. Gaffé. Proving properties of GRAFCET with synchronous tools. In *IEEE-SMC'96, Computational Engineering in Systems Applications,* Lille, France, July 1996.

[And96]   C. André. Representation and analysis of reactive behaviors: a synchronous approach. In *IEEE-SMC'96, Computational Engineering in Systems Applications,* Lille, France, July 1996.

[AW85]   E. A. Ashcroft and W. W. Wadge. LUCID, *the data-flow programming language.* Academic Press, 1985.

[BB91]   A. Benveniste and G. Berry. The synchronous approach to reactive and real-time systems. *Proceedings of the IEEE,* 79(9):1270–1282, September 1991.

[BCG88]   G. Berry, P. Couronné, and G. Gonthier. Synchronous programming of reactive systems, an introduction to ESTEREL. In K. Fuchi and M. Nivat, editors, *Programming of Future Generation Computers.* Elsevier Science Publisher B.V. (North Holland), 1988. INRIA Report 647.

[BCM+90]   J.R. Burch, E.M. Clarke, K.L. McMillan, D.L. Dill, and J. Hwang. Symbolic model checking: 10^{20} states and beyond. In *Fifth IEEE Symposium on Logic in Computer Science, Philadelphia,* 1990.

[BdS96]   F. Boussinot and R. de Simone. The SL synchronous language. *IEEE Transactions on Software Engineering,* 22(4):256–266, April 1996.

[Ber89]   G. Berry. Real time programming: Special purpose or general purpose languages. In *IFIP World Computer Congress,* San Francisco, 1989.

[Ber92]   G. Berry. Esterel on hardware. *Philosophical Transactions Royal Society of London,* 339:217—248, 1992.

[Ber93]   G. Berry. Preemption and concurrency. In *Proc. FSTTCS 93,* Lecture Notes in Computer Science 761, pages 72–93. Springer-Verlag, 1993.

[Ber95]   G. Berry. The constructive semantics of esterel. Draft book available by ftp at ftp://ftp-sop.inria.fr/meije/esterel/papers/constructiveness.ps.gz, 1995.

---

[10] Of course, most of them are no longer students!

[Ber98]   G. Berry. The foundations of Esterel. In C. Stirling G. Plotkin and M. Tofte, editors, *Proof, Language and Interaction: Essays in Honour of Robin Milner*. MIT Press, 1998.

[BFH+92]   A. Bouajjani, J.-C. Fernandez, N. Halbwachs, P. Raymond, and C. Ratel. Minimal state graph generation. *Science of Computer Programming*, 18:247–269, 1992.

[BG92]   G. Berry and G. Gonthier. The Esterel synchronous programming language: Design, semantics, implementation. *Science of Computer Programming*, 19(2):87–152, 1992.

[BL90]   A. Benveniste and P. LeGuernic. Hybrid dynamical systems theory and the SIGNAL language. *IEEE Transactions on Automatic Control*, 35(5):535–546, May 1990.

[Bli90]   Blif-MV: An interchange format for design verification and synthesis. Technical report, Berkeley Logic Synthesis Group, 1990.

[Bon95]   F. Boniol. Synchronous communicating reactive processes. In *2nd AMAST Workshop on Real-Time Systems*, Bordeaux, June 1995.

[Bou91]   F. Boussinot. Reactive C: An extension of C to program reactive systems. *Software Practice and Experience*, 21(4):401–428, 1991.

[BS91]   F. Boussinot and R. de Simone. The ESTEREL language. *Proceedings of the IEEE*, 79(9):1293–1304, September 1991.

[BSR93]   G. Berry, R. K. Shyamasundar, and S. Ramesh. Communicating reactive processes. In *Proc. 20th ACM Conf. on Principles of Programming Languages, POPL'93*, Charleston, Virginia, 1993.

[Cas93]   P. Caspi. Lucid synchrone. In *International Workshop on Principles of Parallel Computing (OPOPAC)*, November 1993.

[CBM89a]   O. Coudert, C. Berthet, and J. C. Madre. Verification of sequential machines using boolean functional vectors. In L. J. M. Claesen, editor, *Formal VLSI Correctness Verification*. North-Holland, November 1989.

[CBM89b]   O. Coudert, C. Berthet, and J. C. Madre. Verification of synchronous sequential machines based on symbolic execution. In *International Workshop on Automatic Verification Methods for Finite State Systems, Grenoble*. LNCS 407, Springer Verlag, 1989.

[CC77]   P. Cousot and R. Cousot. Abstract interpretation: a unified lattice model for static analysis of programs by construction or approximation of fixpoints. In *4th ACM Symposium on Principles of Programming Languages, POPL'77*, Los Angeles, January 1977.

[CES86]   E. M. Clarke, E. A. Emerson, and A. P. Sistla. Automatic verification of finite-state concurrent systems using temporal logic specifications. *ACM TOPLAS*, 8(2), 1986.

[CG95]   P. Caspi and A. Girault. Execution of reactive distributed systems. In *EURO–PAR'95 Stockholm*, volume 966 of *LNCS*. Springer Verlag, August 1995.

[CGP94]   P. Caspi, A. Girault, and D. Pilaud. Distributing reactive systems. In *Seventh International Conference on Parallel and Distributed Computing Systems, PDCS'94*, Las Vegas, USA, October 1994. ISCA.

[CLM91]   E. M. Clarke, D. E. Long, and K. L. McMillan. A language for compositional specification and verification of finite state hardware controllers. *Proceedings of the IEEE*, 79(9):1283–1292, September 1991.

[Coh96]   N. H. Cohen. ADA *as a second langguage*. McGraw-Hill Series in Computer Science, 1996.

[CP95]   P. Caspi and M. Pouzet. A functional extension to LUSTRE. In *Eighth International Symp. on Languages for Intensional Programming, ISLIP'95*, Sidney, May 1995.

[CP96]   P. Caspi and M. Pouzet. Synchronous Kahn networks. In *Int. Conf. on Functional Programming, Philadelphia*. ACM SIGPLAN, May 1996.

[CPHP87]   P. Caspi, D. Pilaud, N. Halbwachs, and J. Plaice. LUSTRE: a declarative language for programming synchronous systems. In *14th ACM Symposium on Principles of Programming Languages, POPL'87*, Munchen, January 1987.

[CR95]   F. Cassez and O. Roux. Compilation of the ELECTRE reactive language into finite transition systems. *Theoretical Computer Science*, 144, June 1995.

[CS95]   C2A-SYNCHRON. The common format of synchronous languages – The declarative code DC. Technical report, Eureka-SYNCHRON Project, October 1995.

[dSR94]   R. de Simone and Annie Ressouche. Compositional semantics of ESTEREL and verification by compositional reductions. In *CAV'94*, Stanford, June 1994.

[Hal93]   N. Halbwachs. *Synchronous programming of reactive systems*. Kluwer Academic Pub., 1993.

[Hal94]   N. Halbwachs. About synchronous programming and abstract interpretation. In B. LeCharlier, editor, *International Symposium on Static Analysis, SAS'94*, Namur (Belgium), September 1994. LNCS 864, Springer Verlag.

[Har87]   D. Harel. Statecharts: A visual approach to complex systems. *Science of Computer Programming*, 8(3), 1987.

[HCRP91]   N. Halbwachs, P. Caspi, P. Raymond, and D. Pilaud. The synchronous dataflow programming language LUSTRE. *Proceedings of the IEEE*, 79(9):1305–1320, September 1991.

[HLR92]   N. Halbwachs, F. Lagnier, and C. Ratel. Programming and verifying real-time systems by means of the synchronous data-flow programming language LUSTRE. *IEEE Transactions on Software Engineering, Special Issue on the Specification and Analysis of Real-Time Systems*, September 1992.

[HM95]   N. Halbwachs and F. Maraninchi. On the symbolic analysis of combinational loops in circuits and synchronous programs. In *Euromicro'95*, Como (Italy), September 1995.

[HP85]   D. Harel and A. Pnueli. On the development of reactive systems. In *Logic and Models of Concurrent Systems*, NATO *Advanced Study Institute on Logics and Models for Verification and Specification of Concurrent Systems*. Springer Verlag, 1985.

[HPR97]   N. Halbwachs, Y.E. Proy, and P. Roumanoff. Verification of real-time systems using linear relation analysis. *Formal Methods in System Design*, 11(2):157–185, August 1997.

[HRR91]   N. Halbwachs, P. Raymond, and C. Ratel. Generating efficient code from data-flow programs. In *Third International Symposium on Programming Language Implementation and Logic Programming*, Passau (Germany), August 1991. LNCS 528, Springer Verlag.

[IEE91]   Another look at real-time programming. *Special Section of the Proceedings of the IEEE*, 79(9), September 1991.

[JLRM94]   M. Jourdan, F. Lagnier, P. Raymond, and F. Maraninchi. A multiparadigm language for reactive systems. In *5th IEEE International Conference on Computer Languages*, Toulouse, May 1994. IEEE Computer Society Press.

15

[JPV95] L. J. Jagadeesan, C. Puchol, and J. E. Von Olnhausen. Safety property verification of ESTEREL programs and applications to telecommunication software. In P. Wolper, editor, *7th International Conference on Computer Aided Verification, CAV'95*, Liege (Belgium), July 1995. LNCS 939, Springer Verlag.

[Kah74] G. Kahn. The semantics of a simple language for parallel programming. In *IFIP 74*. North Holland, 1974.

[Kau70] W. H. Kautz. The necessity of closed loops in minimal combinatorial circuits. *IEEE Trans. on Computers*, pages 162–164, 1970.

[LDBL93] M. Le Borgne, Bruno Dutertre, Albert Benveniste, and Paul Le Guernic. Dynamical systems over Galois fields. In *European Control Conference*, pages 2191–2196, Groningen, 1993.

[Le94] C. Lewerentz and Th. Lindner (eds.). *Case Study "Production Cell": a Comparative Study in Formal Software Development*. FZI-Publikation 940001, ISSN 0944-3037, Forschungszentrum Informatik, Karlsruhe, 1994.

[LGLL91] P. LeGuernic, T. Gautier, M. LeBorgne, and C. LeMaire. Programming real time applications with SIGNAL. *Proceedings of the IEEE*, 79(9):1321–1336, September 1991.

[LHR97] D. Lesens, N. Halbwachs, and P. Raymond. Automatic verification of parameterized linear networks of processes. In *24th ACM Symposium on Principles of Programming Languages, POPL'97*, Paris, January 1997.

[LM93] P. LeParc and L. Marcé. Synchronous definition of Grafcet with Signal. In *IEEE SMC'93*, 1993.

[LSSS91] C. Lavarenne, O. Seghrouchni, Y. Sorel, and M. Sorine. The SynDEx software environment for real-time distributed systems design and implementation. In *European Control Conference, ECC'91*, July 1991.

[Mal93] S. Malik. Analysis of cyclic combinational circuits. In *ICCAD'93*, Santa Clara (Ca), 1993.

[Mar92] F. Maraninchi. Operational and compositional semantics of synchronous automaton compositions. In *CONCUR'92*, Stony Brook, August 1992. LNCS 630, Springer Verlag.

[MH96] F. Maraninchi and N. Halbwachs. Compiling Argos into boolean equations. In *Formal Techniques in Real-Time and Fault Tolerant Systems (FTRTFT)*, Uppsala (Sweden), September 1996. LNCS 1135, Springer Verlag.

[MHMM95] M. Müllerburg, L. Holenderski, O. Maffeis, and M. Morley. Systematic testing and formal verification to validate reactive programs. *Softaware Quality Journal*, 4(4):287–307, 1995.

[Mil81] R. Milner. On relating synchrony and asynchrony. Technical Report CSR-75-80, Computer Science Dept., Edimburgh Univ., 1981.

[Mil83] R. Milner. Calculi for synchrony and asynchrony. *TCS*, 25(3), July 1983.

[ML94] O. Maffeis and P. Le Guernic. Distributed implementation of SIGNAL: scheduling and graph clustering. In *3rd Internationl Symposium on Formal Techniques in Real-Time and Fault-Tolerant Systems*. LNCS 863, Springer Verlag, September 1994.

[MR98] F. Maraninchi and Y. Rémond. Mode-automata: About modes and states for reactive systems. In *European Symposium on Programming, ESOP'98*, Lisbon, April 1998.

[NRW98] X. Nicollin, P. Raymond, and D. Weber. Automatic testing of reactive programs. In preparation 1998.

[OP94]   F. Ouabdesselam and I. Parissis. Testing synchronous critical software. In *5th International Symposium on Software Reliability Engineering (IS-SRE'94)*, Monterey, USA, November1994.

[Per93]   D. Perry. *VHDL*. McGraw-Hill, 1993.

[PP83]   N.S. Prywes and A. Pnueli. Compilation of nonprocedural specifications into computer programs. *IEEE Transactions on Software Engineering*, SE-9(3), May 1983.

[PS87]   J. A. Plaice and J-B. Saint. The LUSTRE-ESTEREL portable format. Unpublished report, INRIA, Sophia Antipolis, 1987.

[QS82]   J. P. Queille and J. Sifakis. Specification and verification of concurrent systems in CESAR. In *International Symposium on Programming*. LNCS 137, Springer Verlag, April 1982.

[Ray96]   P. Raymond. Recognizing regular expressions by means of dataflows networks. In *23rd International Colloquium on Automata, Languages, and Programming, (ICALP'96)* Paderborn, Germany. LNCS 1099, Springer Verlag, July 1996.

[RdS90]   V. Roy and R. de Simone. Auto and Autograph. In R. Kurshan, editor, *International Workshop on Computer Aided Verification*, Rutgers (N.J.), June 1990.

[RH91]   F. Rocheteau and N. Halbwachs. Implementing reactive programs on circuits, a hardware implementation of LUSTRE. In REX *Workshop on Real-Time: Theory in Practice, DePlasmolen (Netherlands)*, pages 195–208. LNCS 600, Springer Verlag, June 1991.

[RM95]   E. Rutten and F. Martinez. SIGNALGTI, implementing task preemption and time interval in the synchronous data-flow language SIGNAL. In *7th Euromicro Workshop on Real Time Systems*, Odense (Denmark), June 1995.

[SBT96]   T. R. Shiple, G. Berry, and H. Touati. Constructive analysis of cyclic circuits. In *International Design and Testing Conference IDTC'96*, Paris, France, 1996.

[SSL+92]   E. Sentovich, K. J. Singh, L. Lavagno, C. Moon, R. Murgai, A. Aldanha, H. Savoj, P. R. Stephan, R. K. Brayton, and A. L. Sangiovanni-Vincentelli. SIS: a system for sequential circuit synthesis. Technical report memorandum nr. ucb/erl m92/41, University of California at Berkeley, 1992.

[STB96]   E. Sentovich, H. Toma, and G. Berry. Latch optimization in circuits generated from high-level descriptions. In *ICCAD'96*, November 1996.

[STB97]   E. Sentovich, H. Toma, and G. Berry. Efficient latch optimization using incompatible sets. In *34th Design Automatio Conference*, June 1997.

[Sto92]   L. Stok. False loops through resource sharing. In *ICCAD'92*, Santa Clara (Ca), 1992.

[TMC94]   P. Thevenod-Fosse, C. Mazuet, and Y. Crouzet. On statistical testing of synchronous data flow programs. In *1st European Dependable Computing Conference (EDCC-1)*, pages 250–67, Berlin, Germany, 1994.

[vdB94]   M. von der Beeck. A comparison of Statecharts variants. In *FTRTFT*. LNCS 863, Springer Verlag, 1994.

[WNT96]   M. Westhead and S. Nadjm-Tehrani. Verification of embedded systems using synchronous observers. In *FTRTFT'96*, Uppsala, September 1996. LNCS 1135.

Ten Years of Partial Order Reduction

Doron Peled*

Bell Laboratories

Abstract. Checking the properties of concurrent systems is an ever growing challenge. Along with the development of improved verification methods, some critical systems that require careful attention have become highly concurrent and intricate. Partial order reduction methods were proposed for reducing the time and memory required to automatically verify concurrent asynchronous systems. We describe partial order reduction for various logical formalisms, such as LTL, CTL and process algebras. We show how one can combine partial order reduction with other efficient model checking techniques.

1 Introduction

An important progress in formal verification was the introduction of model checking of finite state systems [6, 8, 36]. It allowed systems of certain types to be verified in a completely automatic way. Other techniques soon accompanied the basic model checking algorithms, allowing bigger and more complicated systems to be verified. Yet, it has been a constant challenge to verify concurrent systems with many independent components. The number of different states, representing the different values assigned to the variables of such systems, rapidly grows with the number of concurrent components. With the rapidly growing telecommunication and hardware industry, faster and cheaper computers became available; as a result, concurrent systems became more customary.

A seminal progress in attacking the intricacy of large concurrent systems was achieved by the use of binary decision diagrams (BDDs) [3, 4]. This data structure allows an efficient representation of states, such that certain logical operations can be performed on sets of states, rather than on a state-by-state basis. Symbolic model checking using BDDs was used to analyze systems with an impressively large number of states. The success of symbolic model checking was demonstrated mainly in verifying hardware systems. It was observed that BDDs tend to represent hardware circuits in a rather compact way. As a result, automatic verification technology has started to be integrated with hardware development and new industrial tools have been developed.

Even with the introduction of BDDs and symbolic model checking, software verification is still a challenging task. Concurrent programs tend to be less structured than hardware, as the basic units of software are cheaper to produce (e.g.,

---

* This survey was written while the author was visiting Carnegie Mellon University School of Computer Science Pittsburgh, PA 15213-3891, USA. Author's current address: Bell Laboratories, 700 Mountain Ave. Murray Hill, NJ 07974, USA

compare manufacturing a new adder circuit to writing a procedure for summing).
An important difference between hardware and software is their mode of execution. Hardware is usually executed synchronously: all enabled concurrent units
make progress at the same time, synchronized by some global clock. Software is
usually executed asynchronously: concurrent units may execute independently
and the result would be the same whether they execute simultaneously, or one
at a time in any order.

Partial order reduction techniques [1, 5, 9, 12, 13, 14, 15, 17, 21, 23, 32, 33,
37, 38, 39, 40, 42] are based on this latter observation. Most formalisms, including logics such as LTL or CTL, and many process algebras, model the execution
of concurrent systems as interleaved sequences, i.e., a total order between the occurrences of transitions. Thus, concurrently executed transitions create multiple
executions that differ from each other only by their relative order of appearance.
Since this order is usually uninteresting, or unobservable, most specifications do
not distinguish between such executions. However, the existence of such different executions may contribute considerably to the state space explosion. Partial
order reduction attempts to exploit the cases where the specification does not
make such a distinction and allow performing model checking on smaller state
spaces, based on a smaller number of executions.

2   Partial Order Reduction

A *finite transition system* is a fivetuple (S, S_0, T, AP, L) where S is a finite set
of *states*, $S_0 \subseteq S$ are the *initial states*, T is a finite set of *transitions* such that
each transition $\alpha \in T$ is a partial function $\alpha : S \mapsto S$, AP is a finite set of
propositions and $L : S \mapsto 2^{AP}$ is the *assignment function*. An *execution* is an
alternating sequence of states and transitions $s_0\alpha_0 s_1\alpha_1 \ldots$ such that $s_0 \in S_0$,
and for each $i \geq 0$, $s_{i+1} = \alpha_i(s_i)$. Without loss of generality, we assume that
an execution is always infinite. For each execution ξ we can define the following
sequences:

- The states sequence $st(\xi) = s_0 s_1 s_2 \ldots$.
- The transitions sequence $tr(\xi) = \alpha_0 \alpha_1 \alpha_2 \ldots$.
- The propositions sequence $pr(\xi) = L(s_0)L(s_1)L(s_2) \ldots$.

A *segment* is a finite or infinite contiguous part of an execution.

A transition $\alpha \in T$ is *enabled* from a state s if $\alpha(s)$ is defined. That is, α can
be applied to s, obtaining some successor state $s' = \alpha(s)$. Denote by $enabled(s)$
the set of states that are enabled from s. States based model checking techniques (including automata based algorithms) perform a search, often a depth
first search (DFS), to explore the state space of the transition system. Then,
some verification algorithms are applied to the state space. (In practice, these
algorithms are usually applied to the state space *during* its construction. We defer the treatment of such on-the-fly algorithms to a later subsection.) The main
principle of partial order reduction is to find a subset of the enabled transitions
$ample(s) \subseteq enabled(s)$ that are used to generate the successors of a state s.

By choosing the subset of enabled transitions carefully, the correctness of the checked property (or the existence of a counterexample) is preserved between the full state space and the reduced one. It is important to notice that partial order reduction avoids generating the full state space, and constructs directly the reduced one.

Partial order reduction is based on several observations about the nature of concurrent computations and specification formalisms. The first observation is that concurrently executed transitions are often commutative. This is formalized in the definition of independence.

Definition 1. An *independence relation* $I \subseteq T \times T$ is symmetric and antireflexive. For each pair of independent transitions $(\alpha, \beta) \in I$ and state $s \in S$ such that $\alpha, \beta \in enabled(s)$, the following hold:

- $\alpha \in enabled(\beta(s))$ and $\beta \in enabled(\alpha(s))$. That is, independent transitions cannot disable each other.
- $\alpha(\beta(s)) = \beta(\alpha(s))$. That is, executing two enabled independent transition in any order result in the same global state.

Denote $D = (T \times T) \setminus I$. If $(\alpha, \beta) \in D$, we say that α and β are *dependent*. A refinement of this definition, allowing the independency between pairs of transitions to vary from state to state, can be used to further improve partial order reduction [13, 20] and will not be discussed here.

Consider a state s and two enabled independent transitions α and β. Let $r = \alpha(\beta(s))$. Then also $r = \beta(\alpha(s))$. If the specification only mentions the first and last states, there is no need to include both α and β in $ample(s)$. Otherwise, we need to consider the possibility that $L(\alpha(s))$ and $L(\beta(s))$ can be different from each other, and can even be distinct from $L(s)$ or $L(\alpha(\beta(s)))$.

A second observation is that in many cases, only a few of the transitions can change, when executed, the truth values of the propositional variables [40].

Definition 2. A transition $\alpha \in T$ is *invisible* if for each $s, s' \in S$ such that $s' = \alpha(s)$, $L(s) = L(s')$.

When deciding the invisibility of a transition α is hard, one can conservatively assume that α is visible.

When a pair of independent transitions α, β are enabled at s and *at most one* of them is visible, we have one of the following cases:

α is invisible. $L(s) = L(\alpha(s))$, $L(\beta(s)) = L(\alpha(\beta(s)))$.
β is invisible. $L(s) = L(\beta(s))$, $L(\alpha(s)) = L(\beta(\alpha(s)))$.
α, β invisible. $L(s) = L(\alpha(s)) = L(\beta(s)) = L(\alpha(\beta(s)))$.

In each one of these cases, there is at most one change when progressing from s to $r = \alpha(\beta(s))$. The difference between executing α before β or β before α in the first two cases amounts to stuttering, as defined below. Typical specifications cannot distinguish between two executions that are equivalent up to stuttering. This allows eliminating either α or β from $ample(s)$.

Definition 3. The *stutter removal operator* ♯ applied to a propositions sequence ρ results in a sequence $\sharp(\rho)$ where each consecutive repetition of labeling is replaced by a single occurrence. Two propositions sequences σ, ρ are *equivalent up to stuttering* if $\sharp(\sigma) = \sharp(\rho)$. This is denoted by $\sigma \equiv_\sharp \rho$.

For example, if $AP = \{p, q\}$, the finite sequences $\sigma = (p)(p, q)(p, q)(q)(q)(p, q)$ and $\rho = (p)(p)(p, q)(p, q)(q)(p, q)$ are stuttering equivalent since $\sharp(\sigma) = \sharp(\rho) = (p)(p, q)(q)(p, q)$.

In the following sections we present reductions for several formalisms. In each case, the reduction is represented by a set of constraints that need to be enforced on selecting $ample(s)$ for a given state s. When $ample(s) = enabled(s)$, we say that s is *fully expanded*.

2.1 Reduction for LTL

Linear temporal logic (LTL) cannot distinguish between two stuttering equivalent sequences when disallowing the nexttime operator ('$\bigcirc$'). It is in fact argued that specifications *should* be closed under stuttering equivalence [24] and proved that LTL without the nexttime operator is exactly as expressive as stuttering closed first order monadic logic properties [34]. The following conditions for selecting the set $ample(s)$ when generating a reduced state space are based on DFS. We use the fact that during DFS, reaching a state that is already on the search stack implies closing a cycle. The partial order reduction generates a reduced state space such that for each execution in the full state space, there is a stuttering equivalent sequence in the reduced one.

C1 [13, 19, 32, 37] For every segment[2] starting from the state s, a transition that is dependent on some transition in $ample(s)$ cannot be executed before a transition from $ample(s)$.

To understand Condition **C1**, consider a suffix of an execution σ, starting at s. There are two possible cases:

Case 1. α is the first transition from $ample(s)$ on σ. Then, α is independent of all the transitions that precedes it on σ. By applying Definition 1 repeatedly, all the transitions on σ prior to α can be commuted with α, obtaining a segment σ'.

Case 2. No transition in $ample(s)$ occurs on σ. Then any $\alpha \in ample(s)$ is independent of all the transitions of σ. By Definition 1, one can form a segment σ' by executing α and then the transitions of σ.

Condition **C1** is quite abstract. Implementing it takes into account the particular mode of execution, e.g., shared variables, asynchronous or synchronous message passing [13, 14, 17, 40]. Consider for example an execution model with asynchronous message passing. Then the reduction can be implemented by searching

---

[2] Notice that the segment mentioned in **C1** are not necessarily constructed in the reduced state space.

for a set E of transitions belonging to a single process P. These transitions can be executed at the current location of P. To guarantee Condition **C1**, there should be no other transition α of type *receive* or *send*, originating at the same location of P and disabled due to an empty or full communication queue, respectively. The reason is that α is then dependent on the transitions in E (since $E \cup \{\alpha\}$ belong to the same process). By executing a sequence of independent transitions of other processes that end with a *send* or *receive* transition, respectively, α may become enabled.

In order for $pr(\sigma)$ and $pr(\sigma')$ will be stuttering equivalent (for both of the above cases) we enforce the following condition:

C2 [33] If s is not fully expanded then all of the transitions in $ample(s)$ are invisible.

Expanding $ample(s)$ from s instead of $enabled(s)$ can defer the execution of a transition $\beta \in enabled(s) \setminus ample(s)$. (Notice that β remains enabled in any state $\alpha(s)$ for $\alpha \in ample(s)$.) With only Conditions **C1** and **C2**, a transition can be deferred forever along a cycle. This may result in ignoring an execution that is not represented in the reduced state space by another stuttering equivalent execution, and can consequently lead to incorrect verification result. The following condition guarantee that no transition would be deferred forever.

C3 [32] If s is not fully expanded then for no transition $\alpha \in ample(s)$ it holds that $\alpha(s)$ is on the search stack.

There are different alternatives for condition **C2**, for example, Valmari [37] presented an algorithm for the following condition:

C3i For every cycle in the reduced state space there is at least one fully expanded node.

Another possibility is

C3ii [42] If a cycle contains a state where some transition $\alpha \in T$ is enabled, then it must also contain some state where α is taken.

It can be easily shown that **C3** implies **C3i**, which in turn implies **C3ii**. Using a stronger condition instead of a weaker one is less general and can be understood as an implementation of the weaker condition. When restricting the specification to safety properties, the following condition is sufficient:

C3iii [16] For at least one of the transitions $\alpha \in ample(s)$, $\alpha(s)$ is not on the search stack.

2.2 Reduction for CTL

The model for temporal logics such as CTL or CTL* is a branching structure. Even without the nexttime operator (the nexttime operator in these logics is usually written as 'X'), two structures can have corresponding stuttering equivalent sequences but still be distinguished as they have different branching points. Thus, for branching temporal logics, we require that the partial order reduction generates a reduced state space that is *stuttering bisimilar* [2] to the full state space. Two states s and s' are related if the following conditions hold:

1. $L(s) = L(s')$,
2. for each infinite sequence σ starting from s there exists an infinite sequence σ' starting from s' such that σ and σ' can be partitioned into infinitely many finite blocks of consecutive states $B_0 B_1 \ldots$ and $B_0' B_1' \ldots$, respectively and the states in B_i are stuttering bisimilar to the states in B_i' for each $i \geq 0$, and
3. similarly, for each sequence σ' from s' there exists a blockwise matching path σ from s.

It is shown in [2] that CTL and CTL* without the nexttime operator cannot distinguish between stuttering bisimilar structures. Stuttering bisimilarity between the full and reduced state space is achieved by adding the following constraint:

C4 [9] If s is not fully expanded, then *ample*(s) contains exactly one transition.

2.3 Reduction for process algebra

The focus in process algebras is on the branching structure of states and the execution of transitions. The model for various process algebras usually impose labeling the transitions rather than the states. A transition labeled with τ is considered invisible, regardless of its effect on the state. Process algebras are usually based on simulation relations. Such relations associate corresponding pairs of states that have similar branching structure. Stuttering bisimulation was discussed above. Other relations for which we can apply partial order reduction are *branching bisimulation* [11, 29] and *weak bisimulation* [28].

The conditions **C1–C4** can be applied to produce a reduced structure that is branching bisimilar [9] and thus also weak bisimilar. One concern is that in process algebras transitions are often nondeterministic. To allow nondeterminism in partial order reduction, one can reformulate Condition **C4** as follows:

C4i [40] If s is not fully expanded, then *ample*(s) consists of one deterministic transition.

Thus, nondeterministic transitions are allowed in ample sets of nodes that are fully expanded.

2.4 Reduction under fairness

In many systems, the execution of concurrent components is constrained by some fairness assumption. For example, it is natural to require that if a concurrent process *can* execute some transition, independently of other processes, then it is eventually allowed to do so. Model checking under fairness is modified to check whether the fair executions satisfy the given specification [25].

For partial order reduction, the following 'weak' fairness (or 'justice' [26]) assumption is quite natural:

F if an operation α is enabled from some state of an execution, then some operation that is dependent on α must appear later in this execution.

The reduction is based now on the following equivalence relation between sequences:

Definition 4. Given an independence relation I, two finite transitions sequences u and v are *trace equivalent* [27], denoted $u \equiv_{tr} v$, if there exists a sequence $u = w_1, w_2, \ldots, w_n = v$ such that for each $1 \le i < n$, there exists some $x, y \in T^*$ and independent transitions $(\alpha, \beta) \in I$ such that $w_i = x\alpha\beta y$ and $w_{i+1} = x\beta\alpha y$.

Thus, $u \equiv_{tr} v$ iff v can be obtained from u by repeatedly commuting adjacent transitions. The trace equivalence relation can be extended to infinite traces in the following way: $u \equiv_{tr} v$ iff for every finite prefix u' of u there exists a finite prefix v' of v such that $u'w \equiv v'$ for some sequence $w \in T^*$. The symmetric condition, replacing u with v, must also hold.

In fact, the origin of the term 'partial order reduction' is due to the use of trace equivalence. One can view trace equivalence as a partial order semantics. Consider the events obtained by taking the *occurrences* of transitions in an execution, e.g., the first appearance of α denoted $\langle \alpha, 1 \rangle$ and the second denoted $\langle \alpha, 2 \rangle$. Now, consider a partial order between occurrences of transitions on a trace equivalence class. (It can be easily checked that all trace equivalent sequences have the same occurrences.) Then define the order $\prec$ between occurrences such that $e_1 \prec e_2$ when e_1 preceded e_2 on all the equivalent sequences. This order can easily be checked to be a partial order, i.e., asymmetric, irreflexive and transitive. Occurrences that can appear in both orders in different equivalent sequences are unordered by $\prec$ and are considered concurrent.

Consider the case where the checked property φ is closed under trace equivalence. That is, it cannot distinguish between two executions by having $\sigma \models \varphi$ and $\rho \not\models \varphi$, while $tr(\sigma) \equiv_{tr} tr(\rho)$. Assuming **F**-fairness, **Case 2** of Section 2.1 cannot happen. Then it is sufficient to apply Conditions **C1** and **C3**; the obtained reduced state space includes at least one sequence for each trace equivalence class.

Checking that an LTL property is closed under trace equivalence [35] may be unnatural: LTL usually refers to the states, whereas trace equivalence relates executions according to their executed transitions. Instead, it is possible to connect trace equivalence to stuttering equivalence, supplying a condition that guarantees that every pair of sequences σ and ρ such that $tr(\sigma) \equiv_{tr} tr(\rho)$ satisfies that $st(\sigma) \equiv_{\sharp} st(\rho)$. One way to enforce this is by requiring the following:

D1 [32] Extend the dependency relation D to include every pair of visible transitions.

It is important to note that the fairness assumption is still defined with respect to the original dependency relation and not the extended one. Extending the dependency relation limits the reduction. One way to relax Condition **D1** is to write the checked property, when possible, as a boolean combination $\varphi = \bigwedge_i \bigvee_j \varphi_{i,j}$. We can refine visibility such that $vis(\alpha, p)$ for $\alpha \in T, p \in AP$ holds when the truth value of p may change by executing α. Then we require the following:

> **D2** [32] Extend the dependency relation D to include every pair of transitions α, β such that $vis(\alpha, p)$ and $vis(\beta, q)$, and p, q both appear in some boolean component $\varphi_{i,j}$.

Weaker definitions, which require fewer dependencies to be added, appear in [18, 30].

Checking a property φ under a fairness condition that is stronger than **F**, e.g., strong fairness [26], can be done in the following way. The fairness condition is writen as a formula ψ, and dependencies are added to D according to **D2** (or a variant of it) as if the property $\psi \rightarrow \varphi$ is checked. However, the checked property is still φ, while the model checking algorithm checks the executions that satisfies ψ. Model checking algorithms that assume various fairness constraints appear in [25]. Typically, ψ is written as a large boolean combination, containing predicates related to the enabledness and execution of each transition. Thus, using Condition **D1** instead of **D2** would not result in any reduction.

2.5   On-the-fly model checking

In practice, model checking does not include a separate stage where the full or reduced state space is first generated before it is being analyzed. The analysis of the state space can coincide with its construction [7, 22, 41]. With this *on-the-fly* approach, if a counterexample is found, there is no further need to complete the construction of the state space. This observation has a potential of considerably reducing the memory size and time required for the verification. One way of performing on-the-fly model checking is to represent the state space as an automaton $\mathcal{A}$, recognizing the executions of the checked system. The checked property φ is also represented as an automaton. In fact, one generally uses an automaton $\mathcal{B}$ that accepts the sequences that do not satisfy φ (by a direct translation of $\neg\varphi$) [10, 41]).

The intersection of $\mathcal{A}$ and $\mathcal{B}$ is an automaton recognizing executions of the system that do not satisfy the specification. Such executions exist iff the property φ is not satisfied by the system, and can be presented as counterexamples. Specifically, with on-the-fly model checking one can combine the following [33, 39]:

- the construction of an automaton $\mathcal{A}$ that corresponds to the *reduced* state space,
- the intersecting with the automaton $\mathcal{B}$, and
- checking for the emptiness of the intersection.

The crucial change from the off-line partial order reduction presented in Section 2.1 is with respect to Condition **C3**. The cycles found during an on-the-fly construction are cycles of the automaton for $A \cap B$, rather than of the state space automaton A. It can be shown [33] that relativizing **C3** to these cycles, i.e., fully expanding a state when it closes a cycle in the intersection of A and B, still preserves the correctness of the algorithm. In fact, in the intersection, cycles are going to be larger (they may include several iterations of the cycles of the state space, coupled with different values for the property automaton). On the other hand, since the reduced state space, as represented by the automaton A, contains fewer executions, some of the counterexamples may not be included, deferring the discovery of a counterexample.

2.6 Symbolic model checking

By combining various verification techniques, one may obtain the benefits offered by each one of them separately. Obvious candidates for such a combination are partial order reduction and symbolic model checking. The main problem is that the former is usually implemented using a DFS procedure that handles one state at a time, while the latter is described using a fixpoint computation that involves many states at the same time. This effects Condition **C3** (or one of its variants). One proposal for changing this condition for symbolic model checking is that the fixpoint computation can be seen as a breadth first search (BFS) [1]. With each successive fixpoint approximation, a new layer of states with further distance from the original ones are discovered. The cycle closing condition can then be relativized to BFS by pessimistically assuming that states in a new layer that also appeared in previous layers are closing a cycle [5].

Another solution is based on the observation that each cycle of the state space must be composed of several local cycles of the separate concurrent processes. The local structures of the processes are analyzed and at least one transition from each local cycle is selected. The selected transitions are called *sticky transitions*, and the following condition is imposed:

C3iv [23] If s is not fully expanded then no transition $\alpha \in ample(s)$ is sticky.

It can easily shown that Condition **C3iv** implies **C3ii**. With this new condition, the need to find when a cycle is closed during the state space exploration is eliminated. One can in fact combine Conditions **C3iv** with **C2** as follows:

C2+3 If s is not fully expanded then no transition $\alpha \in ample(s)$ can be sticky or visible.

Sticky transitions decrease the reduction and thus their number need to be minimized. One observation is that there are some dependencies between local cycles of different processes. If one local cycle includes only local operations and receiving messages, another local cycle that includes sending messages must also be included to form global cycle of the state space. Similarly, if one local cycle only decreases the value of a variable, a local cycle of another process that increases it is also needed to complete a global cycle. Thus, local cycles that change some resource in a monotonic way can be exempted from the search for sticky transitions (but not at the same time with cycles that change it in the complementary way).

2.7   Reducing visibility

Experimental results [17] show that the reduction decreases rapidly with the number of visible transitions. One way to reduce the effect of visibility on partial order reduction is to let it dynamically decrease while checking the specification [21]. We will illustrate this with an example. Suppose that the property to be checked is $\varphi = \Box(p \to \Box q)$. The negation of the property is $\neg\varphi = \Diamond(p \wedge \Diamond \neg q)$. Once the automaton $\mathcal{B}$ constructed for $\neg\varphi$ has encounted a state where p holds, it may concentrate on checking $\Diamond\neg q$.

In this case, one may start the reduction by considering visible transitions with respect to all the propositions that appear in the formula. In this case, the relevant propositions are $\{p, q\}$. Then, once p occurs, we can then reduce the visible transitions to those that can affect the truth value of q, which is the only proposition that appears in $\Diamond\neg q$. Those transitions that can effect p but not q can now be considered invisible. An LTL translation algorithm that produces an automaton $\mathcal{B}$ that allows monotonically reducing the set of visible transitions as $\mathcal{B}$ executes appears in [10].

Acknowledgement The author would like to thank Marius Minea for carefully reading the paper and many useful comments.

References

1. R. Alur, R.K. Brayton, T.A. Henzinger, S. Qadeer, and S.K. Rajamani, Partial order reduction in symbolic state space exploration. In *Proceedings of the Conference on Computer Aided Verification (CAV'97)*, Haifa, Israel, June 1997.
2. M.C. Browne, E.M. Clarke, O. Grümberg, Characterizing finite Kripke structures in propositional temporal logic, *Theoretical Computer Science* 59 (1988), Elsevier, 115–131.
3. R.E. Bryant, Graph-based algorithms for boolean function manipulation, IEEE Transactions on Computers, C-35(8), 1986, 677–691.
4. J.R. Burch, E.M. Clarke, K.L. McMillan, D.L. Dill, L.J. Hwang, Symbolic model checking: 10^{20} states and beyond, Information and Computation, 98 (1992), 142–170.
5. C.T. Chou, D. Peled, Verifying a model-checking algorithm, *Tools and Algorithms for the Construction and Analysis of Systems*, LNCS 1055, Springer, 1996, Passau, Germany. 241–257.
6. E.M. Clarke, E.A. Emerson, Design and synthesis of synchronous skeletons using branching time temporal logic, *Logic of Programs*, Yorktown Heights, NY, LNCS 131, Springer, 1981, 52–71.
7. C. Courcoubetis, M.Y. Vardi, P. Wolper, M, Yannakakis, Memory-efficient algorithms for the verification of temporal properties, *Formal methods in system design* 1 (1992) 275–288.

8. E.A. Emerson, E.M. Clarke, Characterizing correctness properties of parallel programs using fixpoints, Automata, Languages and Programming, LNCS 85, Springer, 1980, 169–181.

9. R. Gerth, R. Kuiper, W. Penczek, D. Peled, A partial order approach to branching time logic model checking, ISTCS'95, *3rd Israel Symposium on Theory on Computing and Systems*, IEEE press, 1995, Tel Aviv, Israel, 130-139. A full version was accepted to *Information and Computation*.

10. R. Gerth, D. Peled, M.Y. Vardi, P. Wolper, Simple on-the-fly automatic verification of linear temporal logic, *PSTV95, Protocol Specification Testing and Verification*, Chapman & Hall, 1995, Warsaw, Poland, 3–18.

11. R.J. van Glabbeek, W.P. Weijland, Branching time and abstraction in bisimulation semantics, *Information Processing 89*. Elsevier Science Publishers, 1989, 613–618.

12. P. Godefroid. Using partial orders to improve automatic verification methods. In Proc. *2nd Workshop on Computer Aided Verification*, LNCS 531, Springer, New Brunswick, NJ, 1990, 176–185.

13. P. Godefroid, D. Pirottin, Refining dependencies improves partial order verification methods, *5th Conference on Computer Aided Verification*, LNCS 697, Elounda, Greece, 1993, 438–449.

14. P. Godefroid, D. Peled, M. Staskauskas, Using partial order methods in the formal validation of industrial concurrent programs, 1996, ISSTA'96, *International Symposium on Software Testing and Analysis*, ACM Press, San Diego, California, USA, 261-269.

15. P. Godefroid, P. Wolper, A Partial approach to model checking, *6th Annual IEEE Symposium on Logic in Computer Science*, 1991, Amsterdam, 406–415.

16. G.J. Holzmann, P. Godefroid, D. Pirottin, Coverage preserving reduction strategies for reachability analysis, Proc. 12th Int. Conf on Protocol Specification, Testing, and Verification, INWG/IFIP, Orlando, Florida, 1992, 349–363.

17. G.J. Holzmann, D. Peled, An improvement in formal verification, *7th International Conference on Formal Description Techniques*, Berne, Switzerland, 1994, 177–194.

18. S. Jha, D. Peled, Generalized stuttering equivalence for linear temporal logic specification, Submitted for publication.

19. S. Katz, D. Peled, Verification of distributed programs using representative interleaving sequences, *Distributed Computing* 6 (1992), 107–120. A preliminary version appeared in Temporal Logic in Specification, UK, 1987, LNCS 398, 21–43.

20. S. Katz, D. Peled, Defining conditional independence using collapses, Theoretical Computer Science 101 (1992), 337-359, a preliminary version appeared in *BCS–FACS Workshop on Semantics for Concurrency*, Leicester, England, July 1990, Springer, 262–280.

21. I. Kokkarinen, A. Valmari, D. Peled, Relaxed visibility enhances partial order reduction, CAV'97, June 1997, Israel, LNCS 1254, 328–339.

22. R.P. Kurshan. *Computer-Aided Verification of Coordinating Processes: The Automata-Theoretic Approach.* Princeton University Press, Princeton, New Jersey, 1994.

23. R.P. Kurshan, V. Levin, M. Minea, D. Peled, H. Yenigün, Static partial order reduction, 345–357, 1997.

24. L. Lamport, What good is temporal logic, in R.E.A. Mason (ed.), *Information Processing '83: Proc. of the IFIP 9th World Computer Congress,*, Paris, France, North-Holland, Amsterdam, 1983, 657–668.

25. O. Lichtenstein, A. Pnueli, Checking that finite-state concurrent programs satisfy their linear specification, Proceedings of the 11th Annual Symposium on Principles of Programming Languages. ACM Press, 1984, 97–107.

26. Z. Manna, A. Pnueli, How to cook a temporal proof system for your pet language. Proceedings of the Symposium on Principles on Programming Languages, Austin, Texas, 1983, 141-151.
27. A. Mazurkiewicz, Trace theory, *Advances in Petri Nets 1986*, Bad Honnef, Germany, LNCS 255, Springer, 1987, 279-324.
28. R. Milner, *A calculus of communicating system*, LNCS, Springer, 92.
29. R. de Nicola, F. Vaandrager, Three logics for branching bisimulation, *Logic in Computer Science '90*, IEEE, 1990, 118-129.
30. D. Peled, On projective and separable properties, *Theoretical Computer Science*, 186(1-2), 1997, 135-155.
31. D. Peled, A. Pnueli, Proving partial order properties, *Theoretical Computer Science*, 126(1994), 143-182.
32. D. Peled, All from one, one for all, on model-checking using representatives, *5th Conference on Computer Aided Verification*, Greece, 1993, LNCS, Springer, 409-423.
33. D. Peled, Combining partial order reductions with on-the-fly model-checking. *Formal Methods in System Design* 8 (1996), 39-64. A preliminary version appeared in *Computer Aided Verification 94*, LNCS 818, Springer, Stanford, USA, 377-390.
34. D. Peled, Th. Wilke, Stutter-invariant temporal properties are expressible without the nexttime operator, *Information Processing Letters* 63 (1997), 243-246.
35. D. Peled, Th. Wilke, P. Wolper, An algorithmic approach for checking closure properties of ω-Regular Languages, *CONCUR'96, 7th International Conference on Concurrency Theory*, Piza, Italy, LNCS 1119, Springer, August 1996, 596-610. A full version accepted to *Theoretical Computer Science*.
36. J.P. Quielle, J. Sifakis, Specification and verification of concurrent systems in CESAR, Proceedings of the 5th International Symposium on Programming, 1981, 337-350.
37. A. Valmari, Stubborn sets for reduced state space generation, *10th International Conference on Application and Theory of Petri Nets*, Bonn, Germany, 1989, LNCS 483, Springer, 491-515.
38. A. Valmari, A stubborn attack on state explosion. *Formal Methods in System Design*, 1 (1992), 297-322.
39. A. Valmari, On-the-fly verification with stubborn sets, Proceedings of CAV '93, 5th International Conference on Computer-Aided Verification, Elounda, Greece, LNCS 697, Springer 1993, pp. 397-408.
40. A. Valmari, Stubborn set methods for process algebras, *POMIV'96, Partial Orders Methods in Verification*, American Mathematical Society, DIMACS, Princeton, NJ, USA, 1996, 213-232.
41. M.Y. Vardi, P. Wolper, An automata-theoretic approach to automatic program verification, *1st Annual IEEE Symposium on Logic in Computer Science*, 1986, Cambridge, England, 322-331.
42. B. Willems, P. Wolper, Partial-order methods for model-checking: from linear time to branching time, *11th Annual IEEE Symposium on Logic in Computer Science*, New Brunswick, NJ, USA, 1996, 294-303.

An ACL2 Proof of Write Invalidate Cache Coherence

J Strother Moore[1]

Department of Computer Sciences
The University of Texas at Austin
Austin, TX 78712-1188
moore@cs.utexas.edu

Abstract. As a pedagogical exercise in ACL2, we formalize and prove the correctness of a write invalidate cache scheme. In our formalization, an arbitrary number of processors, each with its own local cache, interact with a global memory via a bus which is snooped by the caches.

1 Ongoing Industrial Applications of ACL2

The ACL2 theorem proving system is finding use in industrial-scale verification projects. Two significant projects which have been reported previously are

- the mechanical verification of the floating-point division microcode for the AMD-K5^{TM}[6], and
- the ACL2 modeling of the Motorola CAP digital signal processor and its use to prove that a pipeline hazard detection predicate was correct and that several DSP microcode applications were correct [1].

The abstract of a recent talk given by David Russinoff of Advanced Micro Devices, Inc., summarizes the current AMD work with ACL2:

Formal design verification at AMD has focused on the elementary arithmetic floating point operations, beginning with the **FDIV** and **FSQRT** instructions of the AMD-K5^{TM} processor, and continuing with the **FADD**, **FSUB**, **FMUL**, **FDIV**, and **FSQRT** instructions of the AMD-K7^{TM} processor, which is currently under development.

Design-level mathematical models of all of these operations have been rigorously proved to comply with behavioral specifications derived from IEEE Standard 754 and the Intel Pentium Family User's Manual. Every step of each proof (with one minor exception in the case of **FSQRT**) has been formally encoded in the logic of ACL2 and mechanically checked with the ACL2 prover.

In this talk, we shall briefly describe the results of this project:
- a reusable general theory of floating point representation, rounding, and logical operations on bit vectors;
- an automatic translator from AMD's RTL language (essentially a subset of Verilog) to ACL2;

- several design flaws that were exposed by our analysis and ultimately corrected after surviving extensive testing;
- the proofs of correctness of the operations listed above.

This monumental work is reported in [8]. To corroborate the ACL2 RTL translation, AMD executed the ACL2 translation on a test suite of 80 million floating point problems and compared the results to their standard RTL simulation. The bugs found by Russinoff's proofs were not uncovered by this extensive test suite.

ACL2 is being used to model microprocessors at several industrial sites. For example, at Rockwell-Collins, Inc., ACL2 is being used experimentally to provide an executable model of JEM1, the world's first silicon Java Virtual Machine [2].

In addition, [9] describes an ACL2 model of a microprocessor with multiple, out-of-order instruction issue with a reorder buffer, speculative execution and exceptions. Proofs are being done to relate this model to a more conventional ISA model. While this work is not industrial scale, the microprocessor is more complicated than many academic models studied.

Finally, ACL2 is being used at EDS, Inc., in the verification of "renovation rules" used in COGEN 2000^{TM}, an in-house, proprietary suite of tools used at EDS CIO Services to renovate legacy COBOL code that is not "Year 2000 compliant." Roughly speaking, the problem is how to use given fixed-width data fields to encode the dates in a 100-year window so that commonly used relations are correctly and efficiently implemented. Matt Kaufmann, in [4], describes how he used ACL2 to verify that certain rules were correct. In fact, he describes an environment in ACL2 that can be used conveniently to verify newly proposed transformation rules and to simplify date manipulation expressions.

2 What is ACL2?

"ACL2" stands for "A Computational Logic for Applicative Common Lisp." The logic is both an applicative programming language and a first order mathematical logic[5]. Technically, the programming language is an extension of a subset of applicative Common Lisp. In addition, "ACL2" is the name we use for the implemented system[1]. The system provides an execution environment for the programming language and a theorem proving environment for the logic.

The theorem prover's behavior is determined by rules in its data base. The rules are determined by the theorems the system has proved already. The user can guide the system to deep proofs by presenting it with an appropriate sequence of lemmas to prove. The user is not responsible for soundness, since no rule can be entered into the system's data base until it (or more accurately, its corresponding formula) has been proved as a theorem.

Collections of definitions and theorems can be assembled into "books." The user can instruct the system to include a book into the data base, thereby adding all the (non-local) rules contained in the book. Books thus provide both a scoping mechanism and a way to take advantage of the work of others.

3 A Write Invalidate Cache Example

In the rest of this paper we present a formal model of a write invalidate cache scheme and prove it correct. Write invalidate schemes are known not to scale efficiently to large numbers of processors. But this is a simple problem that is familiar to many readers. Furthermore, at first sight, it may not seem to lend itself to Common Lisp modeling. By choosing this example, we hope to arose the reader's curiosity while illustrating ACL2.

Our model is based on the discussion on page 658 of [3]. Our model includes an arbitrary number of processors, each with its own local cache connected via a bus to one global memory. Fundamentally, a cache is a table of "cache lines", each of which is associated with an address and contains a value and a flag indicating whether the cache line is valid – i.e., whether the value for the given address is consistent with the value assigned by the global memory. Each processor can send its cache read and write requests, receiving some response. The cache's behavior on a read request depends on whether it contains a valid cache line for the requested address. If it does, it responds with the associated value. If it does not, the cache sends a read request on the bus, waits for the reply, constructs a new cache line containing the resulting value, and then responds to the processor with the value obtained from memory. The cache's behavior on a write request is to update (or create) the appropriate cache line, send a write request on the bus, and respond to the processor with the value written. All caches snoop the bus. Read requests are ignored. Write requests cause the other caches to invalidate the corresponding cache line, if any. We model the read/write actions of the individual processors as interleaved atomic actions.

To specify this system we construct a cache-free model in which the interleaved actions are played directly against the global memory. We prove that the response to every read/write action is the same in the two models. The proof requires less than 10 seconds on a Sun Ultra 2 (177 MHz).

For pedagogical purposes, we have divided our work on this problem into three books, discussed in turn below. These books are available at http://www.-cs.utexas.edu/users/moore/publications/write-invalidate-cache/index.html.

4 Utilities

In the "utilities" book we define some generic functions and predicates for dealing with problems of this sort. Fundamental to our formalization is the notion of an *association list*. Each element in an association list (or *alist*) is a pair consisting of a *key* and a *datum*. The key is said to be *bound* to the datum. If no key in an alist is bound twice, we say the alist has *unique keys*. The function **fetch** fetches the datum associated with a key in an alist. The function **deposit** binds a given key to a given datum in a given alist.

A *memory* is an alist binding addresses to values.

A *cache* is an alist binding addresses to pairs of the form (*value flag*). Such pairs are called *lines*. A line is said to be *valid* if *flag* is on. A cache is *ok* with respect to a memory if every valid cache line has as its value the value of the corresponding address in the memory.

A *named cache* is a processor identifier and a cache. In a slight abuse of terminology, we call a list of such pairs simply a *caches* list. Note that a caches list is itself an alist in which each key is a processor identifier and each datum a cache.

An *event* is a pair consisting of a processor identifier and an action. We call the processor identifier of an event the *agent*. An *action* is a list either of the form (READ *addr*) or (WRITE *addr* *val*). A list of events is *appropriate* with respect to a caches list if each agent has an associated cache, i.e., if the set of agents of the events is a subset of the keys of the caches list.

The concepts mentioned above are formalized with functions named appropriately. To save space we do not exhibit those definitions here.

The "utilities" book contains fifteen theorems relating these concepts in various ways. Most of the theorems tell us how the various concepts are affected by deposits. For example,

```
(defthm  cache-okp-deposit2
   (implies (and (cache-okp cache mem)
                 (unique-keysp cache))
            (cache-okp (deposit addr (list any nil) cache)
                       (deposit addr val mem)))) .
```

Informally, this theorem tells us that if *cache* is ok with respect to *mem* (i.e., every line with a true flag contains the correct value), and the cache has unique keys, then invalidating the (first) line for *addr* produces a cache that is ok with respect to a memory in which *addr* has been changed. We do not mention the others but they are stated entirely in terms of the concepts enumerated above, plus ACL2 primitives.

ACL2 requires less than 4 seconds to admit all the definitions and prove all the theorems in the "utilities" book. This is called *certifying* the book. No hints are required, but the order in which the theorems are proved is important.

5 Cache System

In the "system" book, we define our model of the write invalidate cache system. A cache system state, *csys*, is a pair consisting of a caches list and a memory. We say that *p* is a processor of *csys* if *p* is bound in the caches list of *csys*. We define a *good cache system state* with

```
(defun good-csysp (csys)
   (and (unique-keysp (caches csys))
        (every-cache-unique-keysp (caches csys))
        (every-cache-okp (caches csys) (mem csys)))) .
```

The semantics of an action by a processor on its cache and the memory is formalized by

```
(defun do-action (action cache mem)
  (let ((op (car action))
        (addr (cadr action))
        (val (caddr action)))
    (case op
      (READ
        (let* ((line (fetch addr cache))
               (oldval (car line))
               (validp (cadr line)))
          (cond
            ((and line validp)
             (mv oldval cache nil))
            (t (let ((memval (fetch addr mem)))
                 (mv memval
                     (deposit addr (list memval t) cache)
                     (list 'READ addr)))))))
      (otherwise ; WRITE
        (mv val
            (deposit addr (list val t) cache)
            (list 'WRITE addr val))))))
```

This function returns three results packaged together using ACL2's "multiple
values" facility. The first of the three values is the response to the processor.
The second is the new version of the local cache. The third is the message sent
to the bus. We now paraphrase the definition above. Recall that an action is
of the form (READ *addr*) or (WRITE *addr val*). Consider first the case where
the operation is READ. If the cache has the corresponding line and it is valid,
then respond with the value, do not change the cache, and send no message.
Otherwise, respond with the value from memory, change the cache accordingly,
and send the READ request on the bus. (In an implementation, they are done in
the opposite temporal order, but that is not relevant here.) In the case where
the operation is a WRITE, respond with the written value, change the cache
accordingly and send the WRITE request on the bus.

Here is how a cache snoops the bus:

```
(defun snoop (msg cache)
  (cond
    ((null msg) cache)
    (t (let ((op (car msg))
             (addr (cadr msg)))
         (case op
           (READ cache)
           (otherwise ; WRITE
             (let* ((line (fetch addr cache))
                    (val (car line))
                    (validp (cadr line)))
               (cond ((and line validp)
                      (deposit addr
                               (list val nil)
```

```
                              cache))
                    (t cache)))))))))) .
```

We can paraphrase this: If there is no message on the bus, do not change the cache. If the message is a READ, do not change the cache. Otherwise (the message is a WRITE), if the cache contains a lined marked valid, invalidate it.

We similarly define (new-mem *msg mem*) to describe how memory changes in response to a message on the bus.

Here is how the system state, *csys*, is changed by a single *action* performed by a processor *p*.

```
(defun step-csys (p action csys)
  (let ((cache (fetch p (caches csys))))
    (mv-let (response cache' msg)
            (do-action action cache (mem csys))
            (mv response
                (csys (deposit p
                               cache'
                               (snoop-others p
                                             msg
                                             (caches csys)))
                      (new-mem msg (mem csys)))))))
```

This function returns two values. The first is the response of *p*'s cache to the action. The second is a modified system state. We compute this as follows. First, do the action on *p*'s cache, obtaining three results which are bound to the variables *response*, *cache'* and *msg*, respectively.[1] The first is the response of the cache to the action, the second is the new cache for *p*, and the third is the message sent to the bus. The modified system state is then built with csys from a modified list of caches and a modified memory. The modified list of caches is obtained by letting the other caches snoop the message and then depositing *p*'s new cache into the *p* slot. The modified memory is obtained via new-mem. We leave the simple subroutine snoop-others to the reader; it calls snoop on every cache in the caches except *p*'s.

Finally, here is how we run a sequence of events.

```
(defun run-csys (events csys)
  (cond ((endp events) nil)
        (t (let ((p (car (car events)))
                 (action (cadr (car events))))
             (mv-let (response csys')
                     (step-csys p action csys)
                     (cons (cons p response)
                           (run-csys (cdr events) csys')))))))
```

Recall than an event consists of a processor identifier and an action. The function above returns a history of every processor that performed an action and the

---

[1] In this paper we sometimes use primed variable names, as in *cache'*. ACL2 does not permit such names. Our actual text uses a caret instead of a prime.

response to the action. It should be obvious how this is done: If the list of events is empty, return the empty list. Otherwise, step the system once with the indicated processor and action. Obtain two values, a response and a new state. Pair the processor and its response and cons that pair onto the result of running the rest of the events on the new state.

Also in this book we prove two key theorems. Both are invariants about the state, say *csys'*, produced as the second value by **step-csys** on some state *csys*. The first invariant is that if *csys* is a good state then so is *csys'*. The second invariant is that if *events* is appropriate with respect to the caches in *csys*, it is appropriate with respect to those in *csys'*. One can regard our formalization and proof of these invariants as simple discipline: if a system is thought to enjoy an invariant, say so and prove it. In fact, we use both invariants in our correctness proof below.

ACL2 requires the user to state seven lemmas to lead it to the proofs of these two invariants. ACL2 uses less than 4 seconds to certify the **"system"** book.

6 Correctness

To specify what it is for the cache system to be correct, we define a model in which the processors interact directly with the memory. In this cache-free model, the state is simply the memory. An action evokes a response from memory and possibly changes memory, as described by the two values returned by the following function.

```
(defun step-mem (action mem)
  (let ((op (car action))
        (addr (cadr action))
        (val (caddr action)))
    (case op
      (READ (mv (fetch addr mem) mem))
      (otherwise ; WRITE
       (mv val (deposit addr val mem)))))))
```

If the action is a READ, the response is the associated value in the memory and no change is visited upon the memory. If the action is a WRITE, the response is the value written and the memory is changed by depositing that value at the associated address.

To run a sequence of events against a memory we use:

```
(defun run-mem (events mem)
  (cond ((endp events) nil)
        (t (let ((p (car (car events)))
                 (action (cadr (car events))))
             (mv-let (response mem')
                     (step-mem action mem)
                     (cons (cons p response)
                           (run-mem (cdr events) mem'))))))) .
```

36

The correctness of the cache system is given by

```
(defthm cache-system-correct
  (implies (and (good-csysp csys)
                (appropriate-eventsp events (caches csys)))
           (equal (run-csys events csys)
                  (run-mem events (mem csys)))))) ,
```

which may be paraphrased as follows. Suppose *csys* is a good cache system state and every agent in *events* is a processor in the system. Then running *events* in the cache system *csys* produces the same history of processor/responses as running the same *events* in the simple shared memory model, starting from the initial memory in *csys*.

We now illustrate how to interact with ACL2 to lead it to interesting proofs. The main idea is to use ACL2 to help us decide how to proceed. We start by asking it to prove the conjecture above, without actually expecting it to succeed! However, it is helpful when trying prove theorems about functions like **run-csys** and **run-mem** to "disable" the two step functions, **step-csys** and **step-mem**, because they introduce case analysis and make the failed proof attempt hard to decipher. By "disable" we mean to attempt the proof without using the definitions of those two functions. This will help us identify what we need to prove about them. We similarly disable **good-csysp** during the proof attempt.

The proof attempt proceeds by an induction on the structure of *events*. In the inductive step, the variable *csys* above is replaced by the cache system state returned as the second value of **step-csys**. The two previously mentioned invariants in the **"system"** book are sufficient to relieve the **good-csysp** and **appropriate-eventsp** hypotheses of the induction hypothesis. Nevertheless, the proof attempt runs on for many seconds and eventually starts causing a lot of garbage collections. We abort the proof attempt and really look at the output for the first time.

A subgoal near the beginning of the aborted proof attempt reads[2]

```
(IMPLIES (AND ...
              (GOOD-CSYSP CSYS)
              (BOUND P (CACHES CSYS))
              ...)
         (EQUAL (MV-NTH 0 (STEP-CSYS P ACTION CSYS))
                (MV-NTH 0 (STEP-MEM ACTION (MEM CSYS))))) .
```

A little further down is another subgoal with similar hypotheses and the conclusion:

```
(EQUAL (RUN-MEM EVENTS
                (MEM (MV-NTH 1 (STEP-CSYS P ACTION CSYS))))
       (RUN-MEM EVENTS
                (MV-NTH 1 (STEP-MEM ACTION (MEM CSYS))))) .
```

---

[2] In the actual output, the variable EVENTS3 is used for P and EVENTS5 is used for ACTION. We have changed the names to make the formulas more suggestive.

These two subgoals suggest the need for the following two lemmas.

```
(defthm  mv-nth-0-step-csys
  (implies (and (good-csysp csys)
                (bound p (caches csys)))
           (equal (mv-nth 0 (step-csys p action csys))
                  (mv-nth 0 (step-mem action (mem csys)))))) .
```

and

```
(defthm  mv-nth-1-step-csys
  (implies (and (good-csysp csys)
                (bound p (caches csys)))
           (equal (mem (mv-nth 1 (step-csys p action csys)))
                  (mv-nth 1 (step-mem action (mem csys)))))) .
```

What do these two formidable looking conjectures say? The first hypothesis of each lemma requires that *csys* be a good cache system state. The second hypothesis requires that *p* be one of the processors in *csys*. The two lemmas equate a left-hand side term with a right-hand side term. To read the left-hand sides, it is helpful to know that `mv-nth` is the ACL2 function used to retrieve a value from a "multiple values" tuple. Also, recall that `step-csys` returns two values, the response of the processor's cache to an action and a new cache system state, while `step-mem` returns the cache-free response and the new memory. But now it is easy to interpret the two lemmas. The first says that the response of processor *p*'s cache to an action is the same as memory's response. The second says that the memory produced by the cache system is that of the simple system.

These two lemmas are easy to prove, by expanding the definitions of the two step functions and using the results in the `"utilities"` book.

With these two lemmas in the data base, ACL2 proves the correctness theorem. ACL2 requires less than 2 seconds to certify the `"correctness"` book. The total time to certify all three books is 9.05 seconds.

7   Conclusions

The simplicity of this example hides several important observations. First, we are talking here about an "infinite state" system: there are an arbitrary number of processors, a cache can be arbitrarily large, addresses and data values are arbitrarily large, and the memory is arbitrarily large. The proof is made *easier* by these infinities, not harder.

Second, interaction with the theorem prover helps the informed user find proofs. Here is some advice for the new user. Simple theorems are usually proved quickly. Keep ACL2 on a "short leash." Either it succeeds within a few seconds or it should be aborted. Treat the first response as "yes, I believe the fact you just told me." Treat the second as "no, I don't believe it." In the case of a "no," look at the output to determine what obvious fact you know that ACL2 does not. Sometimes you will think "But I've already told it this fact!" Most likely, you did, but it is unable to use that "old" fact because some hypothesis could not be relieved or some term does not actually match. Given what you've told it, what is it missing? Once you realize what ACL2 is missing, formulate the new fact as a lemma and get ACL2 to say "yes" by continuing this dialog. When the system says "yes" to the lemma, return to the original conjecture again and see if ACL2 agrees with it now. Unfortunately, the ACL2 interface does not make it at all obvious that such a structured dialog is being conducted. We illustrate this dialog approach in the source files for these books, available on the web.

Third, the proof described here takes virtually no time. The "bottleneck," if there is one, is the time it takes the user to model the cache system and explain why it is correct. To the extent that the explanation is simple, the proof is simple and quick. In this case, the explanation is simple: The cache system is always in a good state with appropriate events. These are the two invariants in the **"system"** book. Furthermore, in such a state, the response and new memory produced by an action in the cache system are the same as those produced by the simple system. These are the two lemmas noted in the **"correctness"** book. These facts are obvious to anyone familiar with the design. Stating them requires familiarity with the language of ACL2 and the user's own model of the cache system. Their proofs are easily constructed by the dialog method described above.

References

1. B. Brock, M. Kaufmann, and J S. Moore. ACL2 Theorems about Commercial Microprocessors. In *Proceedings of Formal Methods in Computer-Aided Design (FM-CAD'96)*, M. Srivas and A. Camilleri (eds.), Springer-Verlag, November, 1996, pp. 275–293.
2. D. A. Greve and M. M. Wilding Stack-based Java a back-to-future step", Electronic Engineering Times, Jan. 12, 1998, pp. 92.
3. J. Hennessy and D. Paterson, *Computer Architecture A Quantitative Approach, Second Edition*, Morgan Kaufmann Publishers, Inc., San Francisco, 1996.
4. M. Kaufmann. ACL2 Support for Verification Projects. In *15th International Conference on Automated Deduction (CADE)* (to appear, 1998).
5. M. Kaufmann and J S. Moore. An Industrial Strength Theorem Prover for a Logic Based on Common Lisp. In *IEEE Transactions on Software Engineering* **23**(4), April, 1997, pp. 203–213.
6. J S. Moore, T. Lynch, and M. Kaufmann. A Mechanically Checked Proof of the Correctness of the Kernel of the AMD5$_K$86 Floating-Point Division Algorithm, *IEEE Transactions on Computers* (to appear). See URL http://devil.ece.utexas-.edu:80/~lynch/divide/divide.html for a preliminary draft.
7. J S. Moore. Symbolic Simulation: An ACL2 Approach. 1998. (submitted for publication)
8. D. M. Russinoff. A Mechanically Checked Proof of IEEE Compliance of the Floating Point Multiplication, Division, and Square Root Algorithms of the AMD-K7^{TM} Processor URL http://www.onr.com/user/russ/david/k7-div-sqrt.html.
9. J. Sawada, W. Hunt, Jr., Processor Verification with Precise Exceptions and Speculative Execution, *Computer Aided Verification 1998*, Lecture Notes in Computer Science, Springer Verlag, 1998 (to appear).

Transforming the Theorem Prover into a Digital Design Tool: From Concept Car to Off-Road Vehicle

David Hardin, Matthew Wilding, and David Greve

Advanced Technology Center
Rockwell Collins
Cedar Rapids, IA 52498 USA
{dshardin, mmwildin, dagreve}@collins.rockwell.com

Abstract. As digital designs grow evermore complex and design cycles become ever shorter, traditional informal methods of design verification are proving inadequate. Design teams are increasingly turning to formal techniques to address this "verification crunch". The theorem prover, with its emphasis on establishing correctness, is arguably the dream design verification tool; however, theorem provers are rarely used in digital design. Much like automotive industry "concept cars", theorem provers provide a compelling vision of the future, but in the real world of industrial design they have proven to be difficult to drive and expensive to maintain. We suggest ways that the theorem prover "concept cars" of today can be adapted to become the "off-road vehicles" necessary to negotiate the rough-and-tumble terrain of digital design in the 21st century.

1 Introduction

The relentless march of semiconductor process technology over the last thirty years has given engineers exponentially increasing transistor budgets at constant recurring cost. This has encouraged increased functional integration onto a single die, as well as increased architectural sophistication of the functional units themselves. In CPU design, we have seen integration of memory management units, floating point units, cache, etc., as well as increased word length, pipelining, superscalar execution, and other architectural enhancements in the CPU core itself. Higher-end CPU designs now routinely encompass ten million transistors. Additionally, the lifetimes of designs are decreasing – Intel Pentium production lasted only two years – thus pressuring engineers to reduce design cycle time.

The increased scope of a typical digital chip design project, coupled with the desire for decreased cycle time, has caused design teams to increase in both size and number. It is not uncommon for a large company to be engaged in the design of several generations of a product simultaneously, with large teams of engineers working on each generation.

Not surprisingly, this rough-and-tumble environment has led to a number of uncaught design flaws. The most famous of these flaws is the Intel Pentium FDIV bug, although it is hardly alone; the errata sheet for a modern microprocessor may have more than one hundred entries.

Obviously, traditional simulation-based design verification has not kept up with the scale or pace of modern digital design. Increasingly, designers speak of a "verification crunch", and many design teams have looked to formal verification methods for help. Refutation-based techniques such as model checking are currently in use in a number of locations, and have been effective in finding some bugs. However, engineers aspire to create perfect designs; a verification tool that could establish that a design faithfully implements its specification would be ideal. In addition, the mere act of creating an unambiguous specification would have enormous benefit to the designers of the multiple upwardly compatible generations of a product, as well as to the user community.

Such correctness tools exist, in the form of theorem provers such as PVS [14] and ACL2 [10]. These tools have been used in the verification of industrial-scale designs [6, 5, 11, 12, 2, 15] but have not enjoyed much mainstream use. The reasons for the lack of success of theorem provers include:

- Insufficient automation
- Inefficient executability of formal models
- Lack of integration with the engineering environment
- Unfamiliar syntax and semantics
- Lack of support for digital design languages (e.g., VHDL, Verilog)
- Lack of infrastructure for reasoning about digital design (e.g., bitvectors)
- Sometimes gaping holes in basic mathematical libraries
- Speed, especially as a function of model size

To make an automotive analogy, theorem provers are much like "concept cars" that provide a compelling vision of the future but are difficult to drive and expensive to maintain in the real world. What is needed is an "off-road vehicle" to negotiate the rough-and-tumble terrain of digital design. In the next sections, we describe adaptations of theorem prover technology that can transform the theorem prover into a real-world digital design tool, such as might be used during our group's recent development of the JEM1 [9, 18]. We are currently evaluating many of these adaptations in the Rockwell Collins engineering design environment, using real development projects as our testbed.

2 Increasing Automation

Mistakes in proof development and changes to system design and specification are inevitable for real verifications. It is crucial that proofs we construct about our systems be robust in the face of changes. Large programming projects use software engineering techniques to make software robust despite inevitable changes. So too must large machine-checked proof projects use techniques to develop robust proofs. We've learned this lesson the hard way by building fragile proofs. For example, in the AAMP-FV verification effort a change was made in the formal model related to memory address decoding [11]. This change caused every previously-constructed instruction correctness proof to fail although the change had little to do with the substance of most of the proofs.

We are working toward more robust proofs by relying on automated proof techniques. An important advance in this area is the interpreter style of proofs that has been used in a variety of verification projects, including [1, 3, 4, 13, 16]. This approach involves specifying the semantics of a computer system with an interpreter and deriving symbolic results using automatic reasoning. We have adapted this approach for use in PVS [17] and believe that its usefulness transcends the particularities of different theorem proving systems.

3   Achieving Efficient Execution of Formal Models

It is often the case when proving theorems about computer systems that one is faced with an expression composed entirely of functions and constants. Perhaps the word in memory pointed to by the PC is an "add" instruction, or the carry flag holds, or the microcode uses the bit mask 0xFFFF. Proofs about *executable* functions are often easier to construct because function execution can be used to simplify expressions.

Using executable functions in specifications has another, easily overlooked, advantage. An issue that arises in formal verification work is the validation of the processor model used to support the reasoning. Model validation is crucial to ensure that formal analysis applies to the actual machine. Function execution provides an avenue for model validation. Model inspections can be enhanced by using the model to execute test vectors and comparing the results to the result of running the tests on the actual processor. Examples of this approach include the 68020 verification work [4], FM9001 verification [6], and Russinoff's recent floating-point verification work [15].

We are investigating how a model of a processor can be crafted that is amenable to formal microcode analysis and supports efficient simulation. We want the formal model to be validated by having microcode developers use it. We are using ACL2 for this work because its logic is a real programming language – an applicative subset of Common Lisp – that we hope can support our simulation needs. Our initial results seem promising: a prototype processor model written in ACL2 runs at about 90% of a similar model written in C with some optimizations we have developed [7].

The integration of simulator and analysis models has several advantages beyond simpler proofs and model validation. There is potential for the integration of symbolic simulation results into the development cycle. We are experimenting with this using a PVS-based symbolic simulation system that we have developed [8]. The availability of symbolic results may enable us to perform regression tests of designs more effectively. We hope in the longer term that our creation and use of formally analyzable models will allow us ultimately to verify formally aspects of our designs.

4 Integrating with the Engineering Environment

We are currently integrating formal models as "engines" into an existing development and debugging environment, replacing existing simulator artifacts written in C. Ultimately, we would like to have only one design artifact that can be used for synthesis, simulation, and formal analysis. In our experience, it is not difficult to teach a competent engineer to use formal languages such as PVS or ACL2 to describe digital systems, but we would rather avoid the time spent and errors introduced by manual translation of the design.

Hardware description languages such as VHDL and Verilog are commonly used for synthesis, but do not produce very efficient simulators, and do not have a formal basis. Recent work by Mark Bickford at ORA, however, promises to bridge the gap between VHDL and formal analysis [2]. An intriguing additional feature of the ORA toolset is its ability to excise an element of the design, and produce new VHDL with the element removed.

5 Improving the Hardware Reasoning Infrastructure

Many of the pioneering efforts in the use of theorem provers for industrial-scale digital design verification suffered from the lack of basic infrastructure needed to reason about hardware. For example, much effort in the AAMP-FV effort [11] was spent on developing an efficient bitvector library for PVS.

Engineers do not have much patience for proving basic mathematics facts in order to get their work done. We note for example that although ACL2 provides many benefits over Nqthm, there appears to be less automatic support for basic arithmetic. The research community could do a great service here by consolidating the basic work that has already been done, and making it part of the standard distributions for the various theorem provers.

6 Improving Speed and Scalability

The industrial theorem proving projects using PVS that we have undertaken at Rockwell Collins have all managed to tax its capabilities, especially as the size of the model grows, or the number of repetitions of a model execution increases. The highly automated, GRIND-heavy operations that we tend to employ in order to promote proof robustness appear to be atypical of most PVS users. However, the PVS developers have stepped up to the challenge, and delivered marked improvements in performance and scalability over the past year. We look forward to further improvements in areas such as rewriting speed as this tool continues to develop.

7 Conclusions

At Rockwell Collins, we are currently exploring ways in which formal models can improve our computer system development work. The proofs of correctness offered by theorem provers are an important capability, and we have discovered other cost-effective benefits of formal model development, including creation of unambiguous specifications, use of formal models as efficient simulators, integration of symbolic results into the design process, and use of symbolic results to aid regression testing. In the long term we hope to verify formally the most difficult aspects of our designs as part of the basic design cycle.

References

1. William R. Bevier, Warren A. Hunt Jr., J Strother Moore, and William D. Young. An approach to systems verification. *Journal of Automated Reasoning*, 5(4):411–428, December 1989.
2. Mark Bickford and Damir Jamsek. Formal specification and verification of VHDL. In Mandayam Srivas and Albert Camilleri, editors, *Formal Methods in Computer-Aided Design – FMCAD*, volume 1166 of *Lecture Notes in Computer Science*. Springer-Verlag, 1996.
3. Robert S. Boyer and J Strother Moore. Mechanized formal reasoning about programs and computing machines. In R. Veroff, editor, *Automated Reasoning and Its Applications: Essays in Honor of Larry Wos*. MIT Press, 1996.
4. Robert S. Boyer and Yuan Yu. Automated proofs of object code for a widely used microprocessor. *Journal of the ACM*, 43(1):166–192, January 1996.
5. Bishop Brock, Matt Kaufmann, and J Strother Moore. ACL2 theorems about commercial microprocessors. In Mandayam Srivas and Albert Camilleri, editors, *Formal Methods in Computer-Aided Design – FMCAD*, volume 1166 of *Lecture Notes in Computer Science*. Springer-Verlag, 1996.
6. Bishop C. Brock and Jr. Warren A. Hunt. The DUAL-EVAL hardware description language and its use in the formal specification and verification of the FM9001 microprocessor. *Formal Methods in System Design*, 11(1):71–104, July 1997.
7. David Greve, Matthew Wilding, and David Hardin. Efficient simulation using a simple formal processor model. Technical report, Rockwell Collins Advanced Technology Center, April 1998. (submitted for publication).
8. David A. Greve. Symbolic simulation of the JEM1 microprocessor. Technical report, Rockwell Collins, Inc., Cedar Rapids, IA, 1998. (submitted for publication).
9. David A. Greve and Matthew M. Wilding. Stack-based Java a back-to-future step. *Electronic Engineering Times*, page 92, January 12, 1998.
10. M. Kaufmann and J S. Moore. An industrial strength theorem prover for a logic based on Common Lisp. *IEEE Transactions on Software Engineering*, 23(4):203 – 213, April 1997.
11. Steven P. Miller, David A. Greve, Matthew M. Wilding, and Mandayam Srivas. Formal verification of the AAMP-FV microcode. Technical report, Rockwell Collins, Inc., Cedar Rapids, IA, 1996.
12. Steven P. Miller and Mandayam Srivas. Formal verification of the AAMP5 microprocessor: A case study in the industrial use of formal methods. In *WIFT'95: Workshop on Industrial-Strength Formal specification Techniques*, Boca Raton, FL, 1995. IEEE Computer Society.
13. J Strother Moore. *Piton – A Mechanically Verified Assembly-Level Language*. Kluwer Academic Publishers, 1996.
14. S. Owre, N. Shankar, and J. M. Rushby. *User Guide for the PVS Specification and Verification System (Beta Release)*. Computer Science Laboratory, SRI International, Menlo Park, CA, February 1993.

15. David M. Russinoff. A mechanically checked proof of IEEE compliance of the floating point multiplication, division, and square root algorithms of the AMD-K7 processor. Available at www.onr.com/user/russ/david/, January 28 1998.
16. Matthew Wilding. A mechanically verified application for a mechanically verified environment. In Costas Courcoubetis, editor, *Computer-Aided Verification - CAV '93*, volume 697 of *Lecture Notes in Computer Science.* Springer-Verlag, 1993.
17. Matthew M. Wilding. Robust computer system proofs in PVS. In C. Michael Holloway and Kelly J. Hayhurst, editors, *LFM97: Fourth NASA Langley Formal Methods Workshop.* NASA Conference Publication, 1997. (http://atb-www.larc.nasa.gov/Lfm97/).
18. Alexander Wolfe. First Java-specific MPU rolls. *Electronic Engineering Times,* page 1, September 22, 1997.

A Role for Theorem Proving in Multi-Processor Design

Albert J. Camilleri

Hewlett-Packard Company, 11000 Wolfe Rd, Cupertino, CA 94179
ac@cup.hp.com

1 Overview

The role of theorem proving in industry is far from obvious. Especially in the absence of critical requirements such as safety or security, many of the potential advantages it offers, such as the power of expressibility and thorough analysis, can be quickly outweighed by the disadvantages of long interaction times and demands for high levels of expertise.

At Hewlett-Packard we have been using theorem proving as part of our verification arsenal for several years [1], constantly searching for new ways of fitting it into our verification methodology with the goal of improving design quality without adversely affecting time to market. In [1] we describe a *lightweight* style of specification to facilitate quick analysis and proof. We advocate using theorem proving not as an end in itself, but as a means to an end, focussing on analysis, and feedback to designers, rather than on delivering proof as an ironclad guarantee. We still favour this approach, and we have continued to build on it and the specification style described.

One way of addressing some of the shortcomings of theorem proving is to use it alongside other verification techniques, invoking the true power of the theorem prover only where necessary and using alternative techniques where they are more efficient. In [3], a hybrid approach of theorem proving and model checking is used to verify *liveness* for a commercial, symmetric multi-processor. Liveness properties of Runway based multiprocessors [2] are analysed by means of theorem proving because of the large number of queues and dependencies involved in the model, while fairness, inherently a property concerning finite state machine descriptions, is efficiently addressed using model checking.

2 Fitting Theorem Proving into the Design Cycle

Currently, at the Cupertino Systems Laboratory of Hewlett-Packard, theorem proving is being used selectively to verify various aspects of multi processor design. The commercial schedules and pressures do not permit a full scale, hierarchical verification effort using theorem proving. Indeed, simulation technology is still considered the most efficient verification technique for most parts of the designs, so

46

careful selection of problems is done to decide which aspects need to be formally checked, and of those, which require theorem proving.

There are currently no sweeping generalizations that can be made to define a general purpose methodology advocating where best to apply theorem proving. Some rules of thumb can be provided, however, regarding criteria to look for when considering theorem proving. These are best presented by means of a simplified view of a typical VLSI design cycle, as illustrated in Figure 1.

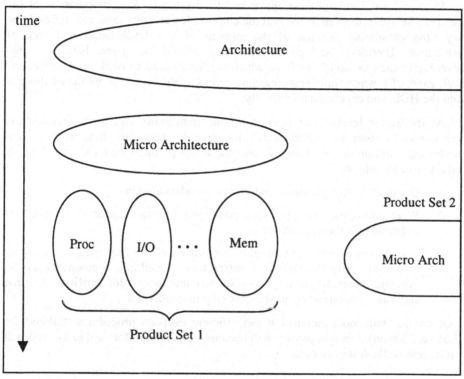

Figure 1. A Simplified View of the VLSI, Pre-silicon Design Cycle.

The diagram depicts the definition of computer *architecture* as the first stage in the design cycle. Architectures are intended to last a relatively long time (over 10 years, say) so they are often intentionally loosely defined and partially specified. They are aimed at providing a framework for the definition of several products as defined by their *micro-architectures*; the next phase in the design cycle. Micro-architectures define the chip sets, topology, protocols and requirements for a set of products to ensure the correct functionality of the system with respect to the architecture. For example, protocols for coherency, flow-control and ordering would be included in a micro-architecture.

Theorem proving plays a natural role during these early stages of the design cycle because of its ability to deal with partial specifications, its expressiveness at very high levels of abstraction and its ability to handle system-level (multiple-chip) complexity which often causes state explosion for model checking or infeasibly long simulation runs.

The third phase in the design cycle shown above involves the definition of the individual chips (such as microprocessors, I/O adapters, memory interface chips, etc.). They are defined and implemented once the micro-architecture is reasonably stable, and are typically done by means of synthesizable hardware description languages (often referred to as the RTL, or register-transfer level).

In an industrial environment, quick and timely feedback to designers is of the essence. The use of theorem provers at the chip implementation level can currently be very time consuming because of the amount of low level detail and lack of abstraction. Therefore, serious consideration should be given here to other technologies such as model checkers, which we have found to work very well at this level, especially when finite state machine representations can be extracted directly from the HDL, and checked automatically.

At the higher levels of abstraction of the architecture and micro-architecture, even though theorem proving can play a natural role, interaction time with theorem provers can still remain a problem. To overcome this problem we have tended to use at least three techniques:

1. Use of a lightweight specification style as advocated in [1].

2. When appropriate, doing pen and paper proof for quick analysis to avoid the overhead of a theorem prover [4].

3. Use of theorem proving as a 'glue' for other methods, e.g. using the theorem prover to verify the high-level interaction of multiple components and to generate invariants (or implementation requirements) for verification of the separate components by model checking or simulation.

Of course, with more automation and efficient decision procedures (tailored for VLSI verification), theorem provers will become more straightforward to use and will require less methodological care.

3   Conclusions

Overall, at this stage, theorem provers are still a long way from becoming a standard design tool. They require expertise and good judgment both on how to use them as well as where. They have, however, unique abilities for verification not present in other verification techniques. For now, they remain a tool for experts, but if carefully deployed, they can be used to increase confidence in today's designs.

References

1. Bainbridge S., Camilleri A., Fleming R., 'Theorem Proving as an Industrial Tool for System Level Design', in *Theorem Provers in Circuit Design,* Stavridou V., Melham T., Boute R. (eds.), North-Holland, 1992, pp. 253-274, Proceedings of the IFIP TC10/WG 10.2 International Conference, Nijmegen, 22-24 June 1992.

2. Bryg W., Chan K., Fiduccia N., 'A High-Performance, Low-Cost Multiprocessor Bus for Workstations and Midrange Servers', *Hewlett-Packard Journal,* 47 (1), February 1996.

3. Camilleri, A., 'A Hybrid Approach to Verifying Liveness in a Symmetric Multi-Processor', in *Theorem Proving in Higher Order Logics,* Gunter E., Felty A. (eds.), Springer-Verlag, 1997, pp. 49-69, Proceedings of the 10th International Conference, New Jersey, 19-22 August 1997.

4. Corella F., Shaw R., Zhang C., 'A formal proof of absence of deadlock for any acyclic network of PCI buses', in *Computer Hardware Description Languages and their Applications,* Chapman & Hall, 1997, Proceedings of the 13th International Conference.

A Formal Method Experience at Secure Computing Corporation

John Hoffman and Charlie Payne

Secure Computing Corporation
{john_hoffman,charlie_payne}@securecomputing.com

Abstract. We discuss the formal methods efforts for LOCK6, a secure operating system. We emphasize how the process of formal methods fit into the development process as a whole, and discuss the lessons learned from our experience.

1 Introduction

In this paper we discuss the formal methods efforts performed on the development effort of LOCK6, a secure operating system partially developed under contract to the U.S. Government. We describe from a high level the high assurance processes used, the motivations behind these processes, and the lessons we learned during the experience.

LOCK6 was an effort to create a new highly secure operating system, with a POSIX compliant interface. While the system itself has been deployed, the assurance component of the work was not completed because the original customer stopped funding for the project, and the new customer was not interested in funding the remaining assurance tasks. The reasons behind the original customer dropping funding were unrelated to the formal methods involved with the project.

The basic design of LOCK6 incorporated much of the operating system technology developed at Secure Computing over the past 10 years. Some of these technologies include the LOCK operating system [Say89], an operating system developed as a proof of concept that an operating system could be formally proved correct. Another collection of technologies were developed in the DTOS program, and some of its spinoff programs [Min95, FM93, Cor97, Fin96, CL98]. The primary goal of DTOS was to incorporate strong security mechanisms into the Mach micro kernel. Many of the architectural concepts and formal modeling techniques developed on DTOS were directly incorporated into the LOCK6 effort.

The primary goal of the LOCK6 effort was to create a B3+ operating system. B3 is defined in the Trusted Computing Security Evaluation Criteria [Cen85] (also known informally as the Orange Book). For a product to achieve B3 status, it has to have the following assurance evidence:

1. a complete formal model of the security policy
2. an informal model of the system

3. convincing arguments (informal proofs) that the model satisfies the security policy

4. evidence that the system model matches the system implementation

For LOCK6, the "+" in B3+ refers to additional additional assurance tasks that we performed. We created a formal model of the system suitable for performing a noninterference analysis. Noninterference is a characterization of a multi-level secure system. More accurately, it is a characterization of a model of a multi-level secure system. A model that satisfies noninterference is a model that contains no information flows from higher classification levels to lower classification levels. Noninterference was a large driver in the formal methods effort. Noninterference requires a detailed model because noninterference is not closed under refinement [McL94]. Consequently if anything is left out of the model, it could potentially be used as a means to illicitly downgrade information between levels. Thus, all error codes and all passed parameters need to be included in the model. We completely specified the operating system interface in the LOCK6 modeling efforts.

Developing an operating system to go through a B3 TCSEC evaluation requires a great deal of documentation. The five primary areas of assurance documentation developed for LOCK6 include a formal security policy model, an informal system model, a formal system model, informal proofs that the models satisfy the security policy, and evidence that the models correspond to the code. A significant effort was made to minimize the amount of documentation produced. A primary goal in our software development process is for the assurance evidence to be a byproduct of the development process. On previous projects at Secure Computing this was not the case. Assurance analysts would work largely independently of the designers, and have a parallel set of documentation. Later in the paper we will describe in more detail the five main areas of assurance documentation and how these documents fit into the development process.

The lessons learned from our experience are common and summarized below.

1. Formalizing natural language statements find mistakes and ambiguities.
2. Tightly linking the development and assurance processes is very beneficial.
3. Modeling is a significantly different skill from programming.
4. Table-based specifications are easy to grasp.
5. Good tools are important.
6. Good means of inter-team communication are necessary.

2 The System Architecture and Assurance Documents

2.1 Basic System Architecture

The basic architecture of LOCK6 has a Supervisor that provides interprocess communication (IPC), virtual memory, hardware interrupt, thread, and process management services. It is the only component to execute in privileged mode on the processor. Servers executing in unprivileged mode provide device, file system, network, security, audit and logging services. Each of these servers has an interface that is built upon the IPC services provided by the Supervisor. One advantage of this approach is that with different servers operating in isolated address spaces, we are guaranteed that the servers can only interact through the IPC interface. No "back door" (accidental or intentional) manipulation of global data structures can occur. This removes one of the major concerns in secure system development.

2.2 Formal Security Policy Model

The formal security policy model describes at a high level what it means for the system to be secure. The basic policy was a multi-level secure (MLS) policy [Cen85] that included noninterference [FHOT89, Rus92, Fin90], with a mandatory non-hierarchical access control policy (aka Type Enforcement [BK85]), incorporated RBAC [SCFY96, Hof97] (Role based Access control) and also included Unix mode bits.

The policy is first specified in English as requirements that are incorporated into the requirements database tool used for the project. The security policy is essentially a requirements document for the system, and the database tool is used to track all requirements. Thus, the security policy requirements are all fed directly into the requirements documents for the system, and the security policy is written at the same time the system requirements documents are written.

Writing security policies is as difficult as writing any requirements document. In addition, for various programmatic reasons, the policy we wrote had many different authors. We found formalizing the policy a very useful exercise. Formalizing requirements helps to resolve the ambiguity inherent in English specifications. Our formalization effort caused numerous changes to the English when we realized how ambiguous it was and how many disagreements there were as to the meaning. Unambiguous English is of course impossible to write, but the process of formalizing the policy assisted in its clarification. For a point of reference, the English version of the policy was 100 pages long, and the English with the PVS formalizations interspersed was 150 pages long.

Placing requirements directly from the policy into the requirements process was first attempted at SCC in the LOCK6 effort. Most security requirements as written are untestable (e.g. No high level process shall be able to send data to a low level process unless it has special permission). Allocating this requirement through appropriate parts of the system raised visibility of these security requirements to developers. And the usual requirements traceability process made it easier to determine if the security requirements had been satisfied. This was a significant cultural shift for the testing staff, to accept requirements that may be untestable.

2.3 Informal Model

The informal model is an English statement of the interface of the operating system as seen by a client process. The model is a finite state machine, that contains an abstraction of the system data structures. All parameters are specified for each system call. All possible return values are completely described in a stylized English and tabular format.

The model was created by developers with assistance from assurance personnel as part of the detailed design process of the system. The portion of the informal model that corresponded to each server was directly incorporated into the design documentation for the component, and was maintained by the appropriate developer. The model emulated the system design, in that each component was a stand-alone model. All 180 entry points into the operating system were modeled, with the informal model running roughly 500 pages long.

Putting developers in charge of the informal model greatly facilitated communication between the teams. One of the techniques we used to facilitate developer buy-in was to use a table-based approach. We found tables generally easier to read and understand than a more functionally oriented specification. An unfortunate consequence of our table based approach was that the tools we used to maintain the document were too cumbersome. LaTeX was used as the document production system, and the tables were too complicated to easily edit. In the future we intend to adopt better documentation strategies to facilitate this portion of the process.

Because we had developer buy-in, the developers owned the informal model. Developer ownership meant the model was maintained better than in the past, in part because it was used extensively by the developers. Inclusion of the model in the design documentation meant that while the document was larger than it may have been in the past, it reduced the redundancy between model and design, and consequently reduced the overall size of the documentation. This is one case where having a detailed model sufficient for noninterference greatly facilitated the process.

Developers found abstraction difficult to grasp, and defining detailed guidelines for how to abstract the model proved to be quite difficult. Having a model with significant abstraction would have made the model less useful for developers, who used the model as a reference during debugging. The informal model was the best description of the system outside of the code itself, and was a very effective means of communication between teams who needed to quickly understand the detailed operations of the entry points. Many developers found that the act of creating the model clarified the design. It forced them to think through the design completely, much as formalizing the policy helped clarify the security requirements.

2.4 Formal Model

The formal model is the informal model translated into a formal language.

Once the informal model was complete and agreed upon by developers and the assurance group, the developers began coding and the assurance group began formalizing the model. If ambiguity was found in the informal model, the design was checked and (if it existed) the code was reviewed. If the behavior of the system was appropriate, a bug report was filed against both the informal and formal models to reflect the behavior of the system. If the system behavior was incorrect or undesirable, then a bug report was filed against the code. The entire model was written in PVS [Owr95, Owr93]. We made extensive use of subtyping within PVS. Typechecking the specifications found many of the common specification errors of incomplete bounds checking, and missed cases. However, few of these cases were missed in the code.

The basic framework of the formal model utilized SCC's composability framework [Cor97] began as part of the DTOS program, and was later extended as part of the Composability program. This framework borrows heavily from the Abadi-Lamport work [AL93] and allows the modeler to specify several different "components" (in our case, servers) that interact through an interface (in our case, IPC). Initially we had intended the supervisor to be modeled as another server. This created problems, because each server uses IPC to supply an interface to other servers and client processes. Thus, there were essentially two different layers of abstraction residing simultaneously in the model. This caused confusion among developers examining the model and among testers who needed to create test harnesses for the system. We began to address this problem using refinement techniques. We started to create a high level abstraction of IPC that could be invoked by the other servers in modeling their outcalls, and interfaces.

Much of the formal model was complete when the funding for the project was cut. It was quite a large model; on the order of 15K lines of specification. The large size was due to two significant factors: the size of the interface, and the level of detail in the model. One of the design goals of LOCK6 was to create a POSIX compliant interface. POSIX supports a rather robust collection of operations, and while we were able to push a significant portion of the POSIX processing into clients (who made use of libraries), the interface was still quite extensive. Since we wrote our specifications to support a noninterference analysis, all inputs, outputs, and error codes had to be specified. This made both the informal and formal models quite large, and potentially impossible to analyze. It should be noted however, that PVS is quite good at proving state invariants, and we believe that all of the invariant proofs necessary for a thorough analysis of the system would have been executed with a minimum of human interaction. This would have added a great deal of confidence to the otherwise informal proofs.

It is interesting to note how small a role the formal tools has played in this discussion. Good tools are crucial, and we found PVS to be a good tool if the user has sufficient sophistication. But much of the work associated with this development and formal methods effort went into aspects that were completely independent of the tool set. It is interesting to note also that experience with previous generations of verification environments made signing up for complete formal proofs appear much riskier than we now believe it would have been. PVS is a very robust system and has a number of features that cause us to believe that we would have been able to successfully formally prove many of the statements we had originally intended to prove informally. These features include the ability to create proof strategies, and the ability to automatically rerun proofs.

2.5 Formal Model Based Testing

Formal model-based testing is an orange book requirement for A1 systems (A1 systems are considered more secure than B3 systems). In this testing, the code is tested against a formal design level model to ensure the model and the system are consistent. Formal model-based testing checks that all required behaviors are exhibited, and that no undesirable behaviors occur.

Due to the cut in funding we were unable to complete the formal model based testing. However, we did create a process and tested it on some of the smaller components of the system. Test cases were developed from the tables in the informal model. Each test case was translated into a PVS theorem, and proven. Each test case was also translated into code, and a test harness was created to dump the server data structures before and after the test ran. These data structures were then compared to ensure only the appropriate portions changed.

We found the model to code correspondence to be difficult to establish. Although our model was detailed, the code had far more detail than the model. Separating the PVS analysis from the code testing allows the two activities to proceed in parallel. This was very useful since the implementation was changing far more rapidly than the model. The informal model proved to be more readily understandable to the testers than the formal model, and it was easier to create the test cases from. We also found that specific proof strategies were needed to allow us to repeatedly rerun the proofs. PVS has many high level powerful proof commands, but often ran quite slow on our specifications. Some modest customization of these proof commands created significant improvements in performance.

3 Conclusions

Some of the lessons learned by our recent (albeit incomplete) effort in formal methods showed us that developer buy in and ownership is crucial. The LOCK6 assurance effort was on track to complete under budget once the funding was cut. A critical reason was that developers owned the informal model and used it. Thus it was in their interest to keep it maintained and current. The bug tracking and fixing process was set up such that changes to the informal model spawned change requests to the formal model. It was therefore possible to always know the delta between the informal and formal models. This is something that in previous programs had been quite difficult.

Useful incorporation of formal methods into software development requires a very mature development process. Extensive and detailed communication must occur between many different teams, and these communication channels must be very clearly defined and rigorously followed in order to avoid extensive rework and confusion. This is perhaps not too surprising, since it has been long been argued in the community that formal methods only make sense in a mature environment.

We did not work hard enough to add additional abstraction to the formal model. The formal model was at too low a level of detail to make it analyzable.

However, having the detail in the informal model was important for developers and testers. They could use the document to understand the exact logical conditions that caused their error returns. If we had abstracted these out of the informal model, the developers would not have found it as useful. What was needed was a clear criteria for how to abstract error messages in the formal model without abstracting out potential covert channels. Moreover, it is imperative that the mapping between the models be clear and easy to follow. Often different people are required to maintain the specifications, and since a typical transition could take two or three pages to completely describe, the specification needed to match the informal model in an obvious way to facilitate comprehension and maintenance.

Although little testing was performed to verify the correctness of the formal model, we had developed tooling to perform the testing. The basic process was that test cases were developed from the informal model and coded into the system. From each test case a PVS theorem was defined, and then proved. The proof of most test cases was very similar. It was our intention to develop PVS proof strategies that would prove the majority of these theorems.

As with code, specification conventions are important. It makes reading specifications by different authors easier to read, and increases the flexibility of staffing and loading.

In summary, even though some of our processes are 10 years old, there always seems to be significant opportunities for improvement.

References

[AL93]   Martin Abadi and Lesli Lamport. Conjoining specifications. Technical Report 118, Digital Equipment Corporation, Systems Research Center, December 1993.

[BK85]   W.E. Boebert and R.Y. Kain. "A Practical Alternative to Hierarchical Integrity Policies". In *Proceedings of the 8th National Computer Security Conference*, pages 18–27, October 1985.

[Cen85]   National Computer Security Center. Department of Defense Trusted Computer System Evaluation Criteria. Technical report, US National Computer Security Center, NCSC, Fort Meade, Maryland, 1985.

[CL98]   Michael Carney and Brian Loe. A comparison of methods for implementing adaptive security poli cies. In *Seventh USENIX Security Symposium Proceedings*, pages 1–14, San Antonio, TX, January 1998. USENIX Association.

[Cor97]   Secure Computing Corporation. DTOS Composability Study. Technical report, 1997. http://www.securecomputing.com/randt/HTML/technical-docs.html.

[FHOT89]   Todd Fine, Thomas Haigh, Richard O'Brien, and Dana Toups. Noninterference and Unwinding for LOCK. In *Proceedings of Computer Security Foundations Workshop II*, pages 22–28, Franconia, NH, Jun 1989. IEEE.

[Fin90]   Todd Fine. Constructively Using Noninterference to Analyze Systems. In *IEEE Symposium on Security and Privacy*, pages 162–169, Oakland, CA, May 1990.

[Fin96]   Todd Fine. A framework for composition. In *Proceedings of the Eleventh Annual Conference on Computer Assurance*, pages 199–212, June 1996.

[FM93]   Todd Fine and Spencer E. Minear. Assuring Distributed Trusted Mach. In *Proceedings IEEE Computer Society Symposium on Research in Security and Privacy*, pages 206–218, May 1993.

[Hof97]   John Hoffman. Implementing RBAC on a Type Enforced System. In *Proceedings of the Thirteenth Annual Computer Security Applications Conference*, pages 158–163, 1997.

[McL94]   John McLean. A general theory of composition for trace sets closed under selective interleaving functions. In *Proceedings of the IEEE Symposium on Security and Privacy*, Oakland, CA, May 1994.

[Min95]   Spencer E. Minear. Providing policy control over object operations in a mach based system. In *Fifth USENIX Security Symposium Proceedings*, pages 141–156, Salt Lake City, UT, June 1995. USENIX Association.

[Owr93]   Owre, Shankar and Rushby. The PVS Specification Language (Beta Release). User Manual, SRI International Computer Science Laboratory, 333 Ravenswood Avenue, Menlo Park, CA 94025-3493, June 1993. http://www.csl.sri.com/reports/pvs-language.dvi,ps.Z.

[Owr95]   Owre, Shankar, Rushby, Crow and Srivas. A Tutorial Introduction to PVS. User Manual, SRI International Computer Science Laboratory, 333 Ravenswood Avenue, Menlo Park, CA 94025-3493, June 1995. http://www.csl.sri.com/sri-csl-fm.html.

[Rus92]   John Rushby. Noninterference, Transitivity, and Channel-Control Security Policies. Technical Report CSL-92-02, SRI International Computer Science Laboratory, 333 Ravenswood Avenue, Menlo Park, CA 94025-3493, December 1992. http://www.csl.sri.com/csl-92-2.html.

[Say89]   Sami Saydjari. LOCK Trek: Navigating Uncharted Space. In *Proceedings of the IEEE Symposium on Security and Privacy*, Oakland, CA, 1989.

[SCFY96]   Ravi Sandhu, Edward Coyne, Hal Feinstein, and Charles Youman. Role-based access control models. *IEEE Computer*, 29(2):38–47, February 1996.

Formal Methods in an Industrial Environment

Jorge R. Cuéllar

Siemens AG
Corporate Technology ZT SE 4
Otto-Hahn-Ring 6
D-81739 Munich, Germany
Jorge.Cuellar@mchp.siemens.de

Industrial applications of formal techniques may be divided roughly in two types:

- *Consultant Service.* A formal method team inside or outside the company acts as a consultant to the engineering group responsible for the design. This is the most common type of application of formal methods in industry found in the literature and to a certain extent it is usual at Siemens.
- *Ready to use tools.* The formal method group only *provides* tools, training and support, while the design or verification task itself is planned and realized by the group of engineers responsible for the design. They use the formal method tools increasingly as a routine part of their development process, in very the same way as they use editors, compilers, simulation tools or data bases. This is turning to be the most common situation within Siemens, with about two thirds of the formal methods group dedicated to the development of tools and interfaces to the different design languages and to the established development tools in the application domains.

The formal methods group has successfully developed the tools CVE (Circuit Verification Environment) and SVE (System Verification Environment), which are used within the business divisions of Siemens as *ready to use tools*. They provide interfaces to quite a few languages, in particular to SDL (used at the divisions public networks, private networks, and others), HiGraph and AWL (both used in particular at the automation divisions), and hardware description languages such as VHDL, Verilog or EDIF. Existing programs (not: abstract versions of them) are used directly as input to application specific compilers that generate automatically finite state machine representations. The specified properties and assumptions about the environment (physical process, other system components) are formulated in customised, user-friendly specification languages and are translated internally into temporal logic and/or finite state machines. The model checking algorithms verify whether the given properties hold or, if not, generate a counter example trace. This counter example is transformed to a trace at the application level and presented to the user in their usual environment. For instance, in HiGraph (a new programming tool for the Siemens Automation Systems Simatic), the user can animate the counter example sequence in a graphical debugging environment or view it in a textual form.

Let us briefly look at concrete application examples and present some figures. The tools (see [8]) have been applied for instance to programs developed by Siemens customers controlling components in several production lines, for example drilling stations for the production of automobile engines. These HiGraph program sizes range between 1000 and 3000 LOCs and contain several hundred boolean variables. Also we would like to mention the verification of protocol software in mobile phones produced by Siemens (see [12]). Each mobile phone contains an implementation of the highly complex GSM protocol. Typically, the number of reachable states of the models generated range between 10^7 and 10^{13}. Other examples include ISDN Protocols (network signaling for public switching networks or call processing for the private branch exchange HICOM), of 600 pages and 110 kLOCs of SDL Code, respectively. Applications in HW design include the areas of consumer electronics, industrial automation, telecommunication, and multiprocessor systems. There, ASICS with up to a million gates are routinely automatically compared.

The rest of the formal methods team is on the one hand acting as a consultant group within the corporation and, on the other hand, developing tools that, we hope, will be eventually used by the business divisions on their own. Their activities center around DES (supervising control of discrete event system, [2, 11]), synchronous languages (in particular SCSL, synchronous control specification language, a new language closely related to TLT [5], [6] and CSL [9]), abstract state machines (formerly evolving algebras, see [1]), and theorem proving, see [13] and [3, 4]. This last activity is being currently reduced, due mostly to the poor acceptance of the methods by the engineers. The DES Tools could be used by the engineers to synthesise controllers for automation systems, or to check their consistency (for instance, the "non-blocking" property). Synchronous Languages ([7]) are very interesting because they provide a higher abstraction level that in general is easier to verify than a conventional, sequential solution. There are quite efficient compilation techniques for synchronous languages. Within the ESPRIT project SACRES ([10]), we are applying the SVE model checker to synchronous programming languages such as SIGNAL and Statemate, and supporting several industrial case studies in the aerospace and automotive industries. ASMs are currently successfully used for the *documentation* of the design process.

Formal Methods for the design or verification of HW or SW systems is an emerging technique in industry. As with *any other* new methodology, the decision to use it is driven by considerations of benefits, costs, efficiency and risks: for instance,

- *Are the benefits of the new methodology clear to managers and engineers?* For most formal methods the answer is *yes*. Indeed, the benefits of using formal methods to validate/verify the correctness of the product are easy to explain: Existing software products may fail and the costs due to their malfunctioning is high. Formal methods have demonstrated success in specifying, designing and verifying industrial systems.
- *Do the benefits of the new method exceed the costs of converting to it?* This is somewhat difficult to determine. If the new method implies a drastic change in the established design flow, the costs will probably be high or unpredictable. For instance, a design or verification methodology based on estab-

lishing a sequence of design descriptions at different abstraction levels, linked together by a formal refinement notion, is found to be difficult. This is even true in the case of a finite-state setting with Model Checking and worse for the theorem-proving approach. The situation is that high level descriptions are not used further in the current design flow. The construction and maintenance of the consistency mapping of abstract descriptions with the actual system is a not trivial task, poorly supported with tools and costly in time and effort.

– *Can you estimate the risks?* For most formal methods, that require a change in the design process: the answer is *no*.

In order for a formal method to be used in a given, typical industrial environment, the following criteria should be met:

– the method must handle examples of industrial size, at reasonably low levels of abstraction,
– the costs in terms of effort, time, etc. should be less or comparable to the ones in the existing design process,
– the method should be accepted by engineers who do not have a strong background in logic, and
– the technique must be easily integrated into the existing design flow.

Most of these criteria favour the Model Checking approach.

References

1. ASM-Bibliography. http://www.eecs.umich.edu/gasm/. WWW page.
2. B. A. Brandin, "The Real Time Supervisory Control of an Experimental Manufacturing Cell", IEEE Transactions on Robotics and Automation, Vol. 12, No. 1, February 1996, pp. 329-342.
3. H. Busch. A Practical Method for Reasoning About Distributed Systems in a Theorem Prover. In *Higher Order Logic Theorem Proving and its Applications - 8th International Workshop, Aspen Grove, UT, USA, Proceedings*, pages 106–121. Springer-Verlag, LNCS 971, September 1995.
4. H. Busch. Proving Liveness of Fair Transition Systems. In J. v. Wright, J. Grundy, and J. Harrison, editors, *Theorem Proving in Higher Order Logics: 9th International Conference, TPHOL'96*, volume 1125 of *LNCS*, pages 77–92. Springer-Verlag, August 1996.
5. J. R. Cuéllar and I. Wildgruber. A TLT Solution. In J.-R. Abrial, E. Börger, and H. Langmaak, editors, *Formal Methods for Industrial Applications. Specifying and Programming the Steam Boiler*, volume 1165 of *LNCS*, pages 165–183. Springer-Verlag, 1996.
6. Jorge Cuéllar, Dieter Barnard, and Martin Huber. Rapid Prototyping for an Assertional Specification Language. *TACAS'96, LNCS 1055*, March 1996.
7. N. Halbwachs. *Synchronous Programming of Reactive Systems*. Kluwer, 1993.
8. M. Hölzlein, Th. Filkorn, P. Warkentin, and M. Weiss. Eine Verifikationskomponente für HiGraph. Volume 1397 of *VDI-Berichte*. VDI-Verlag, Düsseldorf, 1998.

9. Klaus Nökel and Klaus Winkelmann. The FZI Production Cell Case Study: A distributed solution using TLT. In *Formal Development of Reactive Systems: Case Study Production Cell*, volume 891 of *LNCS*. Springer-Verlag, 1995.
10. Sacres Esprit Project. http://www.ilogix.co.uk/ilogix/sacres.html. WWW home page.
11. P. J. Ramadge and W. M. Wonham, "The Control of Discrete-Event Systems", IEEE Proceedings, Vol. 77, No. 1, January 1989, pp. 81-98.
12. Franz Regensburger and Aenne Barnard. Formal Verification of SDL Systems at the Siemens Mobile Phone Department. In *TACAS 1998*, Lecture Notes in Computer Science. Springer-Verlag, 1998.
13. Karl Stroetmann. SEDUCT — a proof compiler for first order logic. In Manfred Broy and Stefan Jänichen, editors, KORSO: *Methods, Languages, and Tools for the Construction of Correct Software*, volume 1009 of *Lecture Notes in Computer Science*, pages 299–316. Springer Verlag, 1995.

On Checking Model Checkers

Gerard J. Holzmann
gerard@research.bell-labs.com

Bell Laboratories, Murray Hill, NJ 07974, U.S.A.

Abstract. It has become good practice to expect authors of new model checking algorithms to provide not only rigorous evidence of the algorithms correctness, but also evidence of their practical significance. Though the rules for determining what is and what is not a good proof of correctness are clear, no comparable rules are usually enforced for determining the soundness of the data that is used to support the claim for practical significance. We consider here how we can flag the more common types of omission.

1 Introduction

Most of us will have experienced the phenomenon that a 'Friday afternoon discovery' falls apart when reconsidered more carefully in the early morning light. Not all compelling ideas are logically sound, not all sound ideas are also relevant, and few ideas that survive these two filters can actually make a significant difference in practice. One could say that the purpose of science is to help us perform this filtering process in a reliable and systematic manner. We know how to discover the logical flaws in our reasoning, to filter out the ideas that are not correct. ¨To intercept the ideas that are (perhaps temporarily) not relevant, we rely on program committees, editorial boards, and grant committees. That leaves practical significance.

How do we convince ourselves that an idea can have practical impact? This is, of course, not a new problem, and it is not without solution. What makes this problem of interest is that its solution is so seldomly used.

In this paper we will look at experiments that are meant to demonstrate practical significance and critique them. Drawing examples for this purpose from the literature would make for a far too enjoyable paper. The strawman example used here is therefore strictly made-up for this purpose.

2 A Strawman Algorithm

Let us look at a simple example of a proposed improvement of the search algorithm used in the model checker SPIN. SPIN implements an on-the-fly procedure for LTL model checking that is based on explicit state enumeration by a nested depth-first search, as detailed in, for instance, [6]. The improvement we will consider here is to perform a semi-stateless search, maintaining only the depth-first stack as a temporary holding place for visited states, but no statespace. This was called a *stack-search* or *Type 3* algorithm in the taxonomy of [3].

2.1 Correctness and Relevance

The correctness of the algorithm follows from the fact that a classic depth-first search will visit all the states in a graph that are reachable from given start node, independent of whether the reached nodes are marked as visited or not. If the marking is used, the successors of each reachable state are expanded only once. If no marking is used this may happen more than once, but the search is still guaranteed to terminate. Since SPIN's model checking procedure relies only on reachability, its scope is unaffected by such a change. Furthermore, SPIN's partial order reduction strategy [5] can be expected to reduce the overhead introduced by possibly multiple visits to the same states.

The new algorithm is meant to reduce the memory requirements of a search. Memory is reduced to the requirements for the stack alone. In many cases, the maximum depth of the stack needed to traverse a graph is considerably smaller than the number of nodes in that graph. It is possible, though, that all reachable states appear in a single execution sequence, and hence would all appear in sequence on the stack. Even in this case we can expect a small memory savings because we avoid the need for the hashtables that are normally used to store the states that are removed from the stack.

2.2 Practical Value

We now have a description of a new algorithm, a persuasive argument for its logical correctness and relevance. With that, we have arguably passed two of the three filters. Next, we will try to show that the algorithm is also of practical value.

The data from a comparison of the behavior of the algorithm compared to a standard search is given in Table 1. The test data is for SPIN models of a leader election protocol [2], the classic alternating bit protocol [1], and a model of the X.21 protocol, e.g., [10], all verified using partial order reduction [5] combined with either a standard search algorithm, or the stack search algorithm using only the depth-first search stack but no statespace to store previously visited states.

Application	Standard Search		Stack Search		Ratio (see text)	
	States	Depth	States	Depth	Memory	Time
Alternating Bit	11	9	11	9	0.45	1.0
Leader Election	108	125	108	125	0.54	1.0
X21 model	29	21	79	31	0.42	2.7

Table 1. Comparison between Standard Search and Stack Search

With a conventional storage discipline, using hashed table-lookup, the memory requirements for the standard search are determined by the number of states reached plus the maximum depth of the stack. In the stack search it is determined only by the latter. The entry in the one-before last column is therefore calculated as the ratio of the number of states reached with the stack search and the sum of the number of states reached in the standard search and the depth of the stack. For the relative time requirements, the ratio given in the last column is calculated as the number of states visited in the stack search divided by the number of states visited in the standard search. In both cases, a ratio less than one indicates a gain, and a ratio greater than one indicates overhead.

The focus in evaluating the stack search method is on the amount of overhead it could introduce in revisits to old states, that are avoided in the standard algorithm. The measurements in Table 1 indicate that it is indeed not unusual for the stack to gather all the reachable states in a single execution: in two of the three tests performed this phenomenon is observed. The measurements also show that the concern about the overhead introduced by the stack search is less serious than feared: in the first two tests the overhead was absent. Only in the third test did the overhead cause the number of states reached that is reported to increase.

2.3   Test Quality

The measurements appear to confirm the central assumption about the behavior of the new algorithm. But do they really? In most cases we cannot judge the validity of a conclusion by other means, as in this case, so we have to rely on the data. But even if we could not tell by other means that the conclusion was invalid, could we at least see that the experiments reported here do not constitute a valid test of the stack search algorithm? We can. The strawman demonstration above indeed has many flaws.

- **Reproducibility** We have not stated how the experiments were performed. Can a peer reproduce the results given the data? Are all the models used in the public domain and accessible to colleagues? Which system was used to perform the experiments? How was the standard search modified into a stack search, or was a new search engine written from scratch for these experiments?
- **Test Selection** How were the tests chosen? Are the results representative? What precautions were taken to make sure that this is so? What would trigger worse behavior? Is it predictable in which cases we get good and in which cases we get bad behavior from the new algorithm? Is the mechanism that accounts for the outcome of the tests fully understood and reported?
- **Scope and Controls** The test provides isolated data points, but does not give the context needed to properly interpret them. Can the parameter that was changed between the two algorithms also be varied more gradually? (The parameter is arguably the number of states that is saved in a statespace cache, and it could be varied from all to none.) The test fails to provide all results for the controlled parameter.

- **Interpretation** Is the data clearly separated from the tester's interpretation? In the example, the computation of the ratios from the last two columns in Table 1 conceals the real measurements of memory and time. How can we be sure that no data was lost or accidentily misrepresented? Note that in a standard search the stack only needs to maintain a pointer to a state that appears elsewhere in the statespace. The cost of maintaining a stack in the standard search, therefore, is less than in a stack search. The memory ratios in Table 1, therefore, are probably too optimistic.

A rigorous testing procedure has the same purpose as a formal correctness proof: it is intended to help us catch bugs in our reasoning. Without any discipline or controls, we are generally motivated to collect only supporting evidence for the quality of a proposed new algorithm. A meaningful test asks us to go against our best judgement and to undertake a targeted attempt scrutinize the validity of our work. A meaningful test is, in a way, the documentation of a serious, scrupulously objective, verifiable, and hopefully failed, attempt to **find fault** with our work. Clearly, the data reported in Table 1 has none of these qualities.

3   The Test Hypothesis

A good test is not the random collection of data from measurements: it is a targeted attempt to check a specific claim, or *hypothesis*. In model checking applications the hypothesis is typically about the relative performance of algorithms. The hypothesis should be specific enough that it can predict the outcome of the measurements before they are done. The prediction must be specific enough that it can clearly distinguish random luck in the outcome of a test from a match of the theory.

So where does the hypothesis itself come from? It can be based on a critical insight into the nature of a prior algorithm, or, it can be based on measurements, which, in this case only, are more or less randomly performed. The first type of measurements are not 'tests' since they are not intended to test anything in particular. There is a fundamental difference between a *measurement* and a *test*. [1]

- **Measurements** are intended to collect empirical data without bias. The data generally suggests a hypothesis that can explain the data that was obtained. The quality of such a hypothesis is determined by its predictive power: the hypothesis should predict the outcome of a new set of tests in which some parameter is changed. The hypothesis should also firmly identify specific results as a contradiction to the hypothesis itself, which, if observed, would cause the hypothesis itself to fall. That is: in advance of new experiments it should be possible to identify clearly what specific results would contradict the hypothesis itself.

---

[1] In this paper we use the term *experiment* if either a *measurement* or a *test* is meant.

- **Tests** are meant to challenge the hypothesis. They are intended to be a serious attempt to determine if results that would contradict the hypothesis can be obtained [8, 9]. They are **not** attempts to further support the hypothesis: that support is already available in the data that inspired the hypothesis to begin with.

We frequently tend to use a *measurement* when a *test* is called for. The sample measurements for the stack search algorithm are an example of such an omission.

What are the properties of a true test? A test can offer support for a hypothesis by recording the outcome of a serious attempt to discover contradictions to the results it predicts or implies. In a sense, a test therefore is intended to work just like a model checker: it attempts to find a counter-example to a correctness claim, and from its failure to do so we may draw some tentative (though rarely definitive) conclusions.

We can only test a hypothesis if it can indeed be contradicted: Popper's classic criterion for distinguishing a scientifically meaningful statement [8, 9] from a non-scientific one. A good test, then, must have the following identifiable components:

- **Hypothesis** – The hypothesis is based on easily obtainable supporting data, which are obtained by more or less random, but certainly unbiased, measurements. The hypothesis must have a predictive power and should, if it can survive meaningful challenges, provide insight or knowledge. The hypothesis can, for instance, postulate a specific cause of complexity in model checking applications. Removing that cause then should result in a visible reduction of the complexity. The failure to observe such a relation would contradict the hypothesis.
- **Test Setup** – A clear description of how the tests were performed with sufficient detail that the tests can be repeated, and *challenged*, by peers.
- **Test Data** – The test data must give an uninterpreted description of the results of a series of controlled experiments that are meant to seriously and thoroughly challenge the validity of the hypothesis.
- **Interpretation** – Data and the interpretation of data must be clearly separated, so that in principle it would be possible for peers to reach different conclusions based on the same raw data. The interpretation concludes whether the hypothesis survived or failed the tests, or it could conclude that the outcome is inconclusive and requires a different set of challenges.

To evaluate the validity of a conclusion drawn from the tests, all four pieces of the test description are generally needed.

4 Application

Let us now return to the stack search example and test its performance, rather than measure it. We can take the data from Table 1 as an initial set of measurements. We now first describe a motivation for a hypothesis to be tested, and then the hypothesis itself.

Motivation – The statespace used in a reachability analysis can be seen as a way to optimize the search process by preventing the renewed exploration of the successors of previously explored states. Partial order reduction reduces the number of times that previously explored states are revisited, and therefore the reliance on the statespace is also diminished. The statespace increases the memory requirements in order to decrease the time requirements of the search. By examining the properties of a stack search in combination with partial order reduction, we can check if this trade-off needs to be re-assessed.

Hypothesis – The stack search saves memory over a standard search, at the expense of potentially increasing the time requirements. A larger increase in time requirements is predicted to be correlated with a larger decrease in memory requirements. Specifically, reductions in memory requirements of one order of magnitude or more are predicted to be linked to an increase in the time requirements by no more than an order of magnitude.

This hypothesis fails if, for instance, we can establish that there are cases where the stack search uses more memory than the standard search, or (more likely) if we can show that in a set of reasonable applications a reduction in memory of less than an order of magnitude is combined with an increase of time by more than an order of magnitude.

Test Setup – In the following, a "standard search" is the classic depth-first search algorithm with both a search stack and a statespace. The search stack contains (pointers to) states on the path that leads from the initial system state to the currently explored state. The statespace is assumed here to be implemented with hashed table-lookup. A "stack search" is the same algorithm that operates without the statespace store. This can be implemented, at least for the purposes of the tests that follow, by adapting the statespace storage routine (`hstore` in SPIN) to pretend that states that were found in the statespace store (and outside the search stack) where newly created. The Appendix shows the specific code fragment that is modified for these tests.

To test the hypothesis, we will first check if we really understand the mechanism that controls the tradeoff between the two resources that are at stake here: memory and time. We will try to create a simple model for which the stack search algorithm is predicted to perform optimally, giving memory savings without time penalty. We will also try to create a model for which the stack search should exhibit worst case performance, giving minimal memory reduction in return for maximal time penalty. To accomplish this we must (according to the hypothesis) control the number of revisits to previously visited states. If we can avoid revisits entirely we should observe best case performance, if we can secure a maximally connected statespace, or something close to it, we should observe worst case performance. The Appendix gives the PROMELA source for the two models that were used to trigger *best case* and *worst case* performance.

Data – Table 2 gives the results of the experiments performed with the best and worst case test models as input. Instead of given estimated ratios for the time requirements, we give memory use in Megabytes, and seconds of runtime measured on an 180 MHz SGI workstation, with 64 Mbytes of memory. For the memory requirements of a stack search the amount of memory used for the state space is subtracted from the amount of memory that is reported (see Appendix).

Application	Standard Search				Stack Search			
	States Reached	Depth Max.	Memory Mbyte	Time Sec.	States Reached	Depth Max.	Memory Mbyte	Time Sec.
Best Case	2047	30	1.25	0.09	2047	30	0.14	0.10
Worst Case	124	20	1.25	0.06	23,694,800	20	0.15	218.89

Table 2. Best and Worst Case Performance of Stack Search Algorithm

Interpretation – The memory reduction achieved is not as large as might be expected, because of a small overhead that goes to unrelated data structures used in the model checking process. The time penalty for the best case test is negligible, but for the worst case test it is beyond the maximum predicted by the hypothesis. We will consider these first two tests to be inconclusive and defer judgement until we can determine how likely it is to observe best or worst case performance in average practical applications.

Additional Tests – Performing extra tests is complicated by the fact that it is somewhat rare to find a larger application that can be run to completion with the stack search algorithm, so severe is the runtime overhead. A runtime overhead of three orders of magnitude, for instance, turns one minute of runtime into one day. Five orders of magnitude overhead, turns one minute into three months. This restricts us to only relatively small models to gather more data. The test results for three realistic applications for which the stack search does complete within a reasonable amount of time are given in Table 3.

Application	Standard Search				Stack Search			
	States Reached	Depth Max.	Memory Mbyte	Time Sec.	States Reached	Depth Max.	Memory Mbyte	Time Sec.
Ring (Appendix)	466	18	1.25	0.10	16,469,100	18	0.14	251.32
URP model [4]	1,363	146	1.35	0.13	26,018,900	146	0.15	1080.58
DTP model [4]	16,459	526	3.30	0.63	79,308,200	549	0.20	1562.81

Table 3. Additional Tests of the Stack Search Algorithm

Interpretation – The hypothesis as it was formulated for these tests has failed. The additional experiments show an increase of runtime well beyond what is allowed by the hypothesis. A reduction in memory use of approximately one order of magnitude is paired with an increase of runtime by more than an order of magnitude in all tests, except the one test that was deliberately constructed to behave well.

To explain these results, we can observe that the stack search is really a special case of a caching strategy with a zero-size cache. With shrinking cache size the depth-first search incurs exponentially rising costs. It is known [4] that when state caching is used in combination with a partial order reduction strategy, the exponential effect sets in for smaller cache sizes, but does not disappear. To understand and measure these effects more precisely we could now add a parameter to our test implementation of the stack search method, that denies the presence of a state in the statespace only with a certain test-controlled probability. The above experiments, however, will suffice for the purposes of this paper.

5 Conclusion

Many papers on model checking algorithms contain a section with experimental data. We have considered how, in an ideal world, such a section would be written.

A well-known dictum says: *"A program without a specification cannot be proven correct; it can neither be right nor wrong."* We can paraphrase this as: *"A test without a hypothesis cannot succeed or fail."* For a test to be able to succeed, it must also be able to fail, and either result can be of interest. But to succeed or fail, a test needs to have a precisely stated purpose. The purpose of a well-designed test is not to confirm, but to *challenge* our presumptions.

It is not hard to see the value of a self-imposed obligation to render a formal proof of correctness of even a trivially correct (sic) algorithm. Imposing more rigor in conducting a demonstration of practical significance similarly has the benefit of protecting us from occasionally misleading ourselves.

The occurrence of bugs is of course not restricted to algorithms or implementations. They can also appear in formal proofs and in the experiments we perform to demonstrate practical significance. That's the bad news. The good news is: bugs don't like rigor.

> *"Bugs are by far the largest and most successful class of entity, with nearly a million known species. In this respect, they outnumber all the other known creatures four to one.*
> Prof. Snopes' *"Encyclopedia of Animal Life"*, as quoted in [7], p. 31.

6 Appendix

Test Setup – The experiments reported in this paper were performed with SPIN version 3.2.0 (`http://netlib.bell-labs.com/netlib/spin/`). The results should be similar for most other versions of SPIN. A small discrepancy in the numbers of reached states is possible for some older versions of SPIN, due to the recent revision of the partial order reduction strategy described in [6].

Stack Search Implementation – The search algorithm from the `pan.c` model checkers generated by SPIN on a `spin -a model` command was modified to imitate a stack search algorithm by editing the `pan.c` file with the following script.

```
/bin/ed pan.c
/match outside stack/
s/.*/tmp-> tagged = (S_A)?V_A : (depth + 1); Lstate = tmp; return 0;/
w pan.c
q
```

The change is designed to be conservative, being slightly more efficient than a true implementation of a stack search algorithm, which would have to recreate and store every previously visited state on each new visit. In the version of the algorithm tested, the previously created state is preserved, but returned to the stack when revisited, by resetting its **tagged** field to a non-zero value.

Best Case Test – The following PROMELA program attempts to trigger best-case performance in the stack search, by minimizing the number of revisits.

```
#define N 10
byte a; chan q = [N] of { byte, byte };
active [2] proctype T() { do :: atomic { a < N - > q!a, _pid; a + + } od }
```

Worst Case Test – The matching attempt to trigger worst case performance, by maximizing the number of revisits.

```
#define N 4
byte a;
active [N] proctype T() { do :: a = (a + 1)%N :: break od }
```

Ring Protocol – The following is the PROMELA source for the ring protocol, that was used for the measurements reported in Table 3.

```
#define N 6
chan ring[N] = [1] of { byte };
active [N] proctype node() { ring[(_pid + 1)%N]!1; ring[_pid]?1 }
```

References

1. Bartlett, K.A., Scantlebury, R.A., and Wilkinson, P.T. A note on reliable full-duplex transmission over half-duplex lines, *Comm. of the ACM*, Vol. 12, No. 5, 260-265.
2. Dolev, D., Klawe, M., and Rodeh, M., An O(n log n) unidirectional distributed algorithm for extrema finding in a circle, *Journal of Algorithms*, Vol 3., 1982, pp. 245-260.
3. Holzmann, G.J., Algorithms for automated protocol verification, *AT&T Technical Journal*, Vol. 69, No. 2, Feb. 1990, pp. 32-44.
4. Godefroid, P., Holzmann, G.J., and Pirottin, D., State Space Caching Revisited, *Formal Methods in System Design.* Vol. 7, No. 3, Kluwer Academic Publ., 1995, pp. 1-15.
5. Holzmann, G.J., and Peled, D. An improvement in formal verification, *Proc. Formal Description Techniques, FORTE94*, Chapman & Hall, pp. 197-211, October 1994.
6. Holzmann, G.J., Peled, D., and Yannakakis, M., On Nested Depth First Search, *The Spin Verification System*, pp. 23-32. American Mathematical Society, June 1996.
7. Van der Linden, P., *Expert C programming*, Prentice Hall, 1994.
8. Popper, K.R., *Logic of scientific discovery.* Basic Books. original 1934, revised edition 1959.
9. Popper, K.R., *Conjectures and refutations: the growth of scientific knowledge.* Basic Books, 1962.
10. West, C.H., and Zafiropulo, P. Automated validation of a communications protocol: the CCITT X.21 recommendation, *IBM J. Res. Develop.*, Vol. 22, No. 1, pp. 60-71.

Finite-State Analysis of Security Protocols

John C Mitchell

Dept. Computer Science, Stanford University, Stanford, CA, 94305
mitchell@cs.stanford.edu   http://www.stanford.edu/~jcm

Abstract. Several approaches have been developed for analyzing security protocols. These include specialized logics that formalize notions such as secrecy and belief, special-purpose automated tools for cryptographic protocol analysis, and methods that apply general theorem-proving or model-checking tools to security protocols. This short document, written to accompany the author's invited lecture, provide background information and references on finite-state methods that use standard model-checking tools.

1   Introduction

A variety of protocols based on cryptographic primitives have been used to protect access to computer systems and to protect transactions over the internet. Two well-known examples are the Kerberos authentication scheme [KNT94,KN93], used to manage encrypted passwords on clusters of interconnected computers, and the Secure Sockets Layer [FKK96], used by internet browsers and servers to carry out secure internet transactions. Handshake or initialization protocols are often used to establish secret session keys for subsequent encrypted communication. These protocols also generally try to establish or confirm the identity of participants. Since a protocol used to establish secure communication may transmit secret keys across the network, correctness of such a protocol is essential for system security.

Over the past decade or two, a variety of methods have developed for analyzing and reasoning about protocols that use cryptographic primitives. The recognized approaches include specialized logics such as BAN logic [BAN89], special-purpose tools designed for cryptographic protocol analysis [KMM94], and theorem proving [Pau97] and model-checking methods using general purpose tools [Low96,Mea96,MMS97,Ros95,Sch96]. While specialized logics and methods have proven successful in many situations, the focus of this paper is the use of conventional logics and analysis methods. One reason is that a summary of methods based on conventional logics and formalisms necessarily involves explicit discussion of the modeling assumptions used to treat cryptographic primitives and security goals. Although modeling assumptions that are common to theorem proving and model checking will be discussed, finite-state methods will be emphasized since another CAV '98 lecture is expected to focus on theorem-proving methods.

In general, software and hardware verification involve establishing that a system design meets some specification. Depending on the level of verification, the specification may be a detailed description of precise inputs and expected resulting behavior, or may simply require that certain undesirable conditions do not occur. The main challenge, and the main property distinguishing verification from "checked execution," lies in some form of quantification over possible inputs and possible internal choices. We naturally want a system to perform correctly for any reasonable or anticipated input, and in spite of any variations in factors such as network transfer rates or the order in which tasks or processes might be scheduled. In many contexts, factors outside of our control are modeled nondeterministically, meaning that we want the specification to be satisfied even when the system operates in the most unlucky manner imaginable.

In security analysis, a system must not only behave correctly when internal events occur in an unlucky order, but also when a malicious adversary interferes with the operation of the system. From a general point of view, this might be viewed only as a matter of degree: a concurrent system must behave well when the scheduler is "malicious" and a cryptographic protocol must behave correctly when messages may be "maliciously" blocked, stored, altered and replayed. However, in practice, this is a significant matter of degree. A simple authentication protocol with only three steps leads to a nondeterministic system with over $500,000$ states when a malicious intruder is added and two sessions are allowed to be carried out simultaneously [MMS97].

From a scientific point of view, the most significant problem in analyzing security protocols is accurate modeling of the malicious adversary (also referred to as the *intruder*). Generally speaking, the more detailed model, the more difficult the analysis and the more useful the results. Most current approaches, however, use essentially the same basic model of network communication and adversary capabilities. This model, largely derived from [DY81], provides a reasonable balance between tractability and insight into the behavior of protocols. However, since many reasonable attacks are not modeled within this common framework, it is likely that at least one branch of future research will focus on more detailed intruder models. The eventual goal would be to bring protocol analysis closer to the common intruder assumptions used in cryptography, which allow probabilistic attacks and incorporate complexity-theoretic assumptions (see, e.g., [Lub96,MvV97]). Other directions for further research involve improved proof methods, more efficient and expressive tools that take advantage of particular properties of cryptographic protocols, and methods that combine theorem proving with finite-state methods or specialized decision procedures.

2 Outline of a general approach

We have analyzed a range of protocols [MMS97,MSS98] using the verification tool Murφ [DDHY92], which does an optimized form of exhaustive search of finite-state nondeterministic systems. This work follows a general methodology that is similar to the approach used in CSP model checking [Low96,Sch96] of cryptographic protocols. In outline, this approach uses the following sequence of steps:

1. *Formulate the protocol.* If the protocol is described in detail, then this generally involves simplifying the protocol by identifying the key steps and primitives. On the other hand, formal analysis requires a more detailed description of the behavior of protocol participants than the high-level descriptions sometime seen in the literature. For example, the common notation

$$A \rightarrow B : \{n\}_K$$
$$B \rightarrow A : \{n+1\}_K$$

   specifies that Alice send a number n to Bob, under encryption by key K, and Bob returns $n + 1$ encrypted in the same way. However, this notation does not clearly specify what Bob will do in response to a message other than $\{n\}_K$. In order to analyze the effects of a malicious adversary, we need to understand the way that each participant will respond to any possible message.

2. *Add an adversary to the system.* It is commonly assumed that the network is under control of the adversary and that the adversary has the following capabilities:
   - overhear any message and prevent a message from reaching the intended recipient if desired,
   - decompose a message comprised of several fields into parts and decrypt any field for which the intruder has already obtained the encryption key,
   - remember all parts of all messages that have been intercepted or overheard,
   - generate messages and send them to any other protocol participant. Generated messages may be composed of any combination of initial intruder knowledge about the system and data obtained by overhearing or intercepting messages.

   The simplest way to model an adversary of this form is by a process that maintains a set of "known" data and chooses nondeterministically between possible actions at each step. While this provides an extremely limited range of possible attacks (with virtually no computation of attack messages), many protocol errors can be identified in this way. However, since there may be many possible intruder messages at each point, the state space may become very large. One relevant optimization is to eliminate useless messages from the adversary description (as discussed below).

3. *State the desired correctness condition.* Typical correctness conditions are related to authentication and secrecy. For example, if a server S enters a state in which it commits to open a session with client C, then C must have previously requested a session with S. We also specify that each datum that is initially secret remains secret. We have generally found it easy to state correctness conditions, but we have no reason to believe that there are no protocols where this step could prove subtle.

4. *Run the protocol* for some specific choice of system size parameters. Speaking very loosely, systems with 4 or 5 participants (including the adversary) and 3 to 5 intended steps in the original protocol (without adversary) are easily analyzed in minutes of computation time using a modest workstation. Doubling or tripling these numbers, however, may cause the system to run for many hours, or terminate inconclusively by exceeding available memory.

5. *Experiment with alternate formulations and repeat.* In examples which are found to be incorrect, it can be informative to repair the detected errors, either by strengthening the protocol or redirecting the efforts of the adversary. In cases where a protocol appears correct, it may be useful to investigate the consequences of strengthening the adversary, possibly by revealing some of the "secret" information to see how robust the protocol is to partial breaches of security.

In the general approach used by our group and other researchers, a protocol adversary is allowed to nondeterministically choose among possible actions. This is a convenient idealization, intended to give the adversary a chance to find an attack if there is one. At the same time, the set of messages an adversary may use to interfere with a protocol is severely limited. For example, an adversary cannot send a message with random data, for example, even though it is certainly possible for an attacker to send randomly chosen data in practice. Another limitation is that a nondeterministic setting does not allow us to analyze probabilistic protocols. Some of the advantages of probabilistic encryption, for example, are enumerated in [GM84].

3 Discussion

General-purpose finite-state analysis tools have proven useful for analyzing cryptographic or security-related protocols. The main challenges that arise are:

- State-space explosion, as with other tools,
- Subtleties involving formalization of the adversary or adversaries, and
- Subtleties involving properties of the encryption primitives, which may be modeled as completely secure black-box primitives, or primitives with other algebraic or "malleability" [DDN91] properties.

Formulating the adversary can be complex and can consume close to half of the time required to prepare a Murφ description of a protocol. There are two main challenges in formulating an adversary to a protocol:

- Formalize the "knowledge" of the adversary, as a function of some initial conditions and the set of messages an adversary has observed up to that point in the run of the protocol. By "knowledge," we mean set of possible entries that an adversary may insert in each message field.
- Select a finite set of possible adversary actions at any point in the run of the protocol, using the knowledge the adversary has at that point.

The first activity is more conceptual; the later involves pragmatic considerations.

For the protocols we have examined, we have characterized the knowledge of the adversary as simply the union of some set of initial data, such as public keys and the names of participants, and the data obtained by overhearing any message sent from one participant to another. This is relatively straightforward, given the message format and the assumption that an encrypted message may be decrypted only if the adversary knows the associated key. In particular, the initial data is finite (and small) and the data remembered from previous communication is also finite (and small), keeping us within the domain of finite-state systems. For adversaries of this form, we believe it will be possible to generate some or all of the adversary description automatically from formulations of other parts of the system.

With more subtle cryptographic assumptions, it becomes more difficult to model the adversary accurately. For example, if we want to allow the adversary to transmit $\{n{\cdot}i\}_K$, on the basis of seeing only $\{n\}_K$, for small integers $i = 1, 2, 3$, say, then we currently have to specify this explicitly in our intruder description. (Using the terminology of [DDN91], this change in the cryptographic assumption gives us a *malleable* encryption function, of which RSA is a specific example.) Moreover, we either have to model the message content as an integer and perform multiplication, or model the message content as a pair and put both n and i into the message. In any case, we must keep the state space small if the analysis is to remain practical.

The second general intruder consideration is that while we may want to run the protocol against the most capable, most nondeterministic adversary possible, this may cause the analysis to run more slowly, or consume more space, than desirable. While we have not had to weaken the adversary for complexity reasons, we have found it useful to optimize the adversary using information about the set of messages that other participants will actually accept. For example, suppose the receiver of a message computes a checksum and discards any message without the correct checksum. Then an unoptimized non-deterministic adversary may generate messages that do not have a correct checksum. However, these messages would have no effect on the protocol, if every other participant would reject them. Therefore, we can improve the running time and space of the analysis by rewriting the adversary to avoid generating these useless messages. Depending on the size and complexity of the system, we have found this sort of optimization to alter the size of the state space by one to several orders of magnitude. Therefore, we consider it a useful direction to explore automatic optimization of the adversary.

Acknowledgments: Thanks are due to Martin Abadi, David Dill, Cynthia Dwork, Stephen Freund, Li Gong, Mark Mitchell, John Rushby, Ulrich Stern, Vitaly Shmatikov and many others for helping me learn about security and for their efforts in carrying out work mentioned here.

References

[BAN89]   M. Burrows, M. Abadi, and R. Needham. A logic of authentication. *Proceedings of the Royal Society, Series A*, 426(1871):233–271, 1989. Also appeared as SRC Research Report 39 and, in a shortened form, in ACM Transactions on Computer Systems 8, 1 (February 1990), 18-36.

[DDHY92] D. L. Dill, A. J. Drexler, A. J. Hu, and C. H. Yang. Protocol verification as a hardware design aid. In *IEEE International Conference on Computer Design: VLSI in Computers and Processors*, pages 522–5, 1992.

[DDN91]   D. Dolev, C. Dwork, and M. Naor. Non-malleable cryptography (extended abstract). In *Proc. 23rd Annual ACM Symposium on the Theory of Computing*, pages 542–552, 1991.

[DY81]   D. Dolev and A. Yao. On the security of public-key protocols. In *Proc. 22nd Annual IEEE Symp. Foundations of Computer Science*, pages 350–357, 1981.

[FKK96]   A. Freier, P. Karlton, and P. Kocher. The SSL protocol version 3.0. `draft-ietf-tls-ssl-version3-00.txt`, November 18 1996.

[GM84]   S. Goldwasser and S. Micali. Probabilistic encryption. *J. Computer and System Sciences*, 28:281–308, 1984.

[KMM94]   R. Kemmerer, C. Meadows, and J. Millen. Three systems for cryptographic protocol analysis. *J. Cryptology*, 7(2):79–130, 1994.

[KN93]   J.T. Kohl and B.C. Neuman. The Kerberos network authentication service (version 5). Internet Request For Comment RFC-1510, September 1993.

[KNT94]   J.T. Kohl, B.C. Neuman, and T.Y. Ts'o. *The evolution of the Kerberos authentication service*, pages 78–94. IEEE Computer Society Press, 1994.

[Low96]   G. Lowe. Breaking and fixing the Needham-Schroeder public-key protocol using CSP and FDR. In *2nd International Workshop on Tools and Algorithms for the Construction and Analysis of Systems*. Springer-Verlag, 1996.

[Lub96]   M. Luby. *Pseudorandomness and Cryptographic Applications*. Princeton Computer Science Notes, Princeton University Press, 1996.

[Mea96]   C. Meadows. Analyzing the Needham-Schroeder public-key protocol: a comparison of two approaches. In *Proc. European Symposium On Research In Computer Security*. Springer Verlag, 1996.

[MMS97]   J.C. Mitchell, M. Mitchell, and U. Stern. Automated analysis of cryptographic protocols using Murφ. In *Proc. IEEE Symp. Security and Privacy*, pages 141–151, 1997.

[MSS98]   J.C. Mitchell, V. Shmatikov, and U. Stern. Finite-state analysis of SSL 3.0. In *Proc. Seventh USENIX Security Symposium*, pages 201–216, 1998. Preliminary version presented at DIMACS Workshop on Design and Formal Verification of Security Protocols, September 1997; distributed on workshop CD.

[MvV97]   A.J. Menzes, P.C. van Oorschot, and S.A. Vanstone. *Handbook of Applied Cryptography*. CRC Press, 1997.

[Pau97]   L.C. Paulson. Proving properties of security protocols by induction. In *10th IEEE Computer Security Foundations Workshop*, pages 70–83, 1997.

[Ros95]   A. W. Roscoe. Modelling and verifying key-exchange protocols using CSP and FDR. In *CSFW VIII*, page 98. IEEE Computer Soc Press, 1995.

[Sch96]   S. Schneider. Security properties and CSP. In *IEEE Symp. Security and Privacy*, 1996.

Integrating Proof-Based and Model-Checking Techniques for the Formal Verification of Cryptographic Protocols

Dominique Bolignano

Dyade, B.P.105 78153 Le Chesnay Cedex France, Dominique.Bolignano@dyade.fr

Abstract. We discuss the advantages and limitations of the main proof-based approaches to the formal verification of cryptographic protocols. We show possible routes for addressing their limitations by combining them with model-checking techniques. More precisely we argue that proof-based techniques can be used for providing a general framework, model-checking techniques for mechanization and invariant techniques for bringing precise understanding of protocol strengths and weaknesses.

1 Introduction

Three different basic research directions have been adopted for the formal verification of cryptographic protocols: one is based on the use a specific modal logic (e.g. a logic of authentication); another is based on the use of general purpose formal methods; the third is uses of model-checking techniques [13, 11]. The two first approaches use proof-based techniques for the verification phase.

We believe that neither of these approaches provides a complete solution to the verification problem, and we try here to discuss the benefits of integrating the various techniques, taking general formal methods based techniques as a framework. As an illustration we use the integration achieved for this purpose in [6]. Of course the adequacy of the integration clearly depends on the objectives that are assigned to the use of formal methods. In the following discussion we basically assume, based on our experience in applying formal methods in the design of large secure systems, that no potentially unsafe approximation or simplification should be allowed, neither in the modelization of the protocol, nor in the expression of properties, or in the verification itself. We further believe that verification should be a vehicle to bringing precise understanding of the protocol strengths and weaknesses. We argue that these objectives are not necessarily conflicting with automatization.

Typical modal logic approaches such as the BAN logic [7] provide a very elegant way of proving authentication properties, but the modeling is in some way wired and corresponds to a high level of abstraction. They are thus the most efficient when the objective of the verification is to identify major flaws (as opposed to proving the absence of flaws). Some other modal logics have been proposed to achieve more precision, but this is often done at the expense of a loss in conciseness or simplicity (see [3] for a more detailed discussion).

Model checking techniques on the other hand perform a verification on a finite model. The verification is thus automatic. Typically this model is not the specification itself but only corresponds to an abstraction of the specification. As a result, nothing can be formally inferred from the verification when it is successful. To this respect they are very similar to modal logic approaches. A discussion on this issue can be found in [6]. As compared to BAN-like modal logics they provide more automatization capabilities. But since the verification is a black-box process it also provides less insight into the precise understanding of the strength and weaknesses of a protocol.

The use of general purpose formal methods has the advantage of relying on largely used techniques. The main approaches are the approach of Kemmerer [12] based on the formal specification language Ina Jo, the approach of Chen and Glicor [9] also based on the Ina Jo specification language, but using the BAN logic [7] to model belief, Bieber's approach [2] based on the formal specification language B and finally the approach of Meadows [14], based on communicating processes and which builds upon the approach of Millens [15] and the approach of Dolev and al. [10]. More recently two other approaches have been presented. The first approach defined in [3] uses general purpose formal methods as a frame-work but it also relies on abstract interpretation and model-checking techniques for achieving automatization, while the second one [16] is a pure proof-based technique which, as we will see, imposes a few constraints.

The main challenge with general purpose formal methods is to achieve precision and conciseness at the same time. It is also of prime importance to achieve significant automatization to keep the approach efficient and workable. An added but very important potential benefit of formal methods is to provide a very precise understanding of the protocol design issues (weaknesses, strengths, hypotheses, etc.). We will use three of the most recent accounts on these issues [14], [16] and [6], and use the formalism proposed in the latter one as a means of illustration of our discussion.

2 Formalizing the Protocol

Following the approach of [3] we first have to identify the different principals involved in a protocol. Principals receive messages at one end and emit other messages at another end. Some principals will be considered to be "trustable" (i.e. to work according to their role in the protocol) and some not. Communication media are typically considered to be non-trustable, because messages can usually be intercepted, replayed, removed, or created by intruders. We will consider that this is the case in the following discussion. The set of untrustable principals is modeled as a single (black box) agent which is called the "external world" or, more concisely, the intruder. The intruder is modeled as a principal that may know some data initially and that will store and try to decrypt all data passed to him and thus in particular all information circulating on the communications media. The intruder will also be able to encrypt data to create new messages that will be sent to mislead other principals. But the intruder will be able to decrypt and encrypt data only with keys he knows. This modeling will in particular allow us to determine at any time which data are potentially known to the intruder under the chosen "trustability" hypothesis. The same protocol can be studied in terms of many different hypotheses. According to [3], the knowledge of the intruder is formalized as a set of data components. Data components range over domain C and sets of data components over domain S. Data components can be basic data, which may be cryptographic keys which take their values in domain KA (for asymmetric keys) or KS (for symmetric ones), or other basic data which take their values in domain D. Data components can also be obtained by composition using the pair operator which takes some data c_1 and some c_2 and returns the pair (c_1, c_2), or by encryption of some data c using key k which is noted c_k. The domains S and C are formalized as:

$$\boxed{\begin{aligned} S &= C \cup S | \emptyset \\ C &= C_K | (C,C) | B \end{aligned}} \quad \boxed{\begin{aligned} B &= K | D \\ K &= KA | KS | K^{-1} \end{aligned}}$$

modulo a few axioms[1] ($\cup$ is for example an ACUI operator with neutral $\emptyset$).

For illustration purposes, we use the Needham-Schroeder protocol which allows two principals, A and B, to perform mutual authentication. The protocol is initiated by one of the principals. This principal is A in our case. The protocol requires the use of a certification authority, S, in order to distribute public keys to principals requesting them. The protocol is composed of seven message exchanges between A, B and S: (1) $A \to S : (A,B)$; (2) $S \to A : (K_B, B)_{K_S^{-1}}$; (3) $A \to B : (N_A, A)_{K_B}$; (4) $B \to S : (B,A)$; (5) $S \to B : (K_A, A)_{K_S^{-1}}$; (6) $B \to A : (N_A, N_B)_{K_A}$; (7) $A \to B : (N_B)_{K_B}$.

It is assumed here that the principals A and B both know the public key K_S, and that S knows the public keys K_A and K_B. The keys K_A^{-1}, K_B^{-1}, K_S^{-1} are the corresponding private keys. They are respectively known by A, B and S, and only by them. N_A and N_B are fresh nonces.

The two first messages can for example be read as follows : (1) A sends a message to S to tell him or her that he or she is the principal A and wants to start an authentication procedure with B; no encryption is used; (2) S replies to the request by sending A the public key K_B of B; this message is encrypted with the private key K_S^{-1} which S is the only one to know and which thus authenticates the producer.

The formal specification of the protocol consists in the description of the role of each trustable agent and is given as a set of atomic actions. Sending and reception of a message are not synchronous. Consequently the transmission of a message is considered as two atomic actions, one for sending and one for receiving. Our modeling of the NS protocol will thus distinguish 14 different kinds of atomic actions. These actions will be identified using the labels drawn from $\mathcal{L} = \{1a, 1s, 2s, 2a, 3a, 3b, ..., 7a, 7b\}$. Each of the 14 labels n_X of $\mathcal{A}$ stands for one action: principal X sends or receives message n.

---

[1] See [3] for a more precise definition.

The system is defined as a pair (s_0, r) where s_0 is the initial global state, and r is a relation binding the global state before applying an action to the global state after applying the action. The relation r is defined using a predicate or logic formula p, defined on $(\mathcal{S} \times (\mathcal{L} \times \mathcal{C}) \times \mathcal{S})$ where the domain for global states $\mathcal{S}$ is the Cartesian product, $\mathcal{S}_A \times \mathcal{S}_B \times \mathcal{S}_S \times \mathcal{S}_I$, of local state domains, i.e. $\mathcal{S}_A$, $\mathcal{S}_B$ and $\mathcal{S}_S$ for the three trustable principals, A, B and S, and $\mathcal{S}_I$ for the intruder. By definition $p(s, (l, m), s')$ is true if and only if the global state s is modified into s' upon firing the action labelled l for sending or receiving of message m. The set $\mathcal{S}_I$ is the domain S of data components defined in the previous section. Intuitively the state of the intruder is the set of data components that have been listened to on the communication line and that the intruder may use to build new messages. The state of a trustable principal is defined as an aggregate or a tuple describing the value of each local state variable. Here the states for the three trustable principals are defined as the following aggregates:

$S_A =$		$S_B =$	
slave	: Principal	master	: Principal
n_a	: Nonce	n_a	: Nonce
n_b	: Nonce	n_b	: Nonce
k_b	: K	k_A	: K
nonces	: set of Nonce	nonces	: set of Nonce
at	: ProgramAddress	at	: ProgramAddress
$S_S =$			
key	: Principal $\to$ K		
at	: ProgramAddress		

Fields *at* are used in each state to hold the value of the abstract program counter for the algorithm executed by the corresponding principal. The field *slave* is used by principal A to store the identifier of the supposed requested principal. The field *master* is used in the same way to store the identifier of the supposed requester. The public and private keys of A, B, and S which are constant values will be noted $K_A, K_B, K_S, K_A^{-1}, K_B^{-1}$ and K_S^{-1}.

The predicate $p((s_A, s_B, s_S, s_I), (l, m), (s'_A, s'_B, s'_S, s'_I))$ that formalizes the protocol is defined as the disjunction of 14 predicates, i.e. one for each atomic action (1) $action(s_a.at, 1a, s'_a.at) \wedge s'_i = s_i \cup (A, s'_a.slave)$; (2) $action(s_s.at, 1s, s'_s.at) \wedge (d_1, d_2)$ $known\_in$ s_i; (3) $action(s_s.at, 2s, s'_s.at) \wedge s'_i = s_i \cup (s_s.key(d_3), d_3)$; (4) $action(s_a.at, 2a, s'_a.at) \wedge (s'_a.k_b, s_a.slave)_{K^{-1}} known\_in s_i$; (5) $action(s_a.at, 3a, s'_a.at) \wedge s'_i = s_i \cup (s'_a.n_a, A)_{s_A.K_b} \wedge s'_a.n_a \notin s_a.nonces \wedge s'_a.nonces = s_a.nonces \cup \{s'_a.n_a\}$; (6) $action(s_b.at, 3b, s'_b.at) \wedge (s'_b.n_a, s'_b.master)_{K_B} known\_in(s_i)$; (7) $action(s_b.at, 4b, s'_b.at) \wedge s'_i = s_i \cup (B, s_b.master)$; (8) $action(s_s.at, 4s, s'_s.at) \wedge (d_4, d_5) known\_in s_i$ (9) $action(s_s.at, 5s, s'_s.at) \wedge s'_i = s_i \cup (s_s.key(d_6), d_6)_{K^{-1}}$; (10) $action(s_b.at, 5b, s'_b.at) \wedge (s'_b.k_a, B)_{K_S^{-1}} known\_in s_i$; (11) $action(s_b.at, 6b, s'_b.at) \wedge s'_i = s_i \cup (s_b.n_a, s'_b.n_b)_{s_B.K_A} \wedge s'_b.n_b \notin s_b.nonces \wedge s'_b.nonces = s_b.nonces \cup \{s'_b.n_b\}$; (12) $action(s_a.at, 6a, s'_a.at) \wedge (s_a.n_a, s'_a.n_b)_{K_A} known\_in(s_i)$; (13) $action(s_a.at, 7a, s'_a.at) \wedge s'_i = s_i \cup (s_a.n_a)_{s_A.K_B}$; (14) $action(s_b.at, 7b, s'_b.at) \wedge$

$(s_b.n_b)_{K_B}$ *known_in* s_i, where by convention state variables that are not explicitly changed are supposed to be unchanged. Predicate *action* is used to specify sequencing constraints, i.e. control structure for each role. Here we assume that A (resp. B) is repeating an infinite loop $1a, 2a, 3a, 6a, 7a$ (i.e. $1b, 3b, 4b, 5b, 6b, 7b$). This complete formalization can be found in [3].

The first action (i.e. 1_A) describes A sending a pair composed of the identification of A and of the identification of the principal *id* for which the public key is requested. Each sending of a message m increases the knowledge of the intruder, i.e. $s_i' = s_i \cup m$. The value of *id* is not constrained in any way. This allows A to request any public key he wishes. The second action (i.e. 1_S) describes S receiving a pair of data. This pair can be the pair just sent by A or any pair of data known by the intruder. The second situation is meaningful if this can go undetected by A: here, there is no particular checking other than on the form of the message. Receiving a message m does not change the state of the intruder (i.e. $s_i' = s_i$), but the message should be deducible from the knowledge of the intruder (i.e. m *known_in* s_i). The third action (i.e. $2s$) describes S sending a pair composed of the public key of d and of the identifier d stored previously. The fourth action (i.e. 2_A) implicitly specifies that the received message is to be signed using K_s^{-1}.

Describing the protocol with as much accuracy as required is a quite difficult problem for modal logic approaches where the problem is known as the idealization problem: the modelization of the protocols requires some abstraction or adaptation of the protocol at hand in order to fit within the chosen logical framework. This problem is difficult to avoid as the formalism has to satisfy at the same time conflicting logical and practical properties.

The situation is less problematic for proof-based approaches relying on general purpose formal methods, because the logical constraints imposed by these formalisms are much weaker: it is typically possible and easy in these approaches to use as many variables as required, to describe control or sequencing constraints. The main problem is that the use of these features has a very negative impact on the size and automatization of the proof process.

Most recent approaches based on general purpose formal methods [14], [3] and [16] allow for the description of the protocol at a level of detail that is comparable to the approach illustrated here. The two main differences concern the way the intruder is modeled and the way the control structure of the protocol is described.

The intruder knowledge is here implictly modeled and axiomatized once for all, whereas in other approaches such as [14] the internal behavior of the intruder needs to be explicitly formalized and analyzed. This is typically done by describing the actions that the intruder can perform to exploit data. Paulson's approach lies somewhat in between (intruder actions are still explicitly modeled but some already proven theorems can be used during the verification).

Control structure is specified in the previous section by the means of the *action* predicate and the presence in the principal states of a control field, namely the *at* field. It is thus for example possible, by just changing the definition of the *action* predicate to specify a version of the same protocol that would allow for multi-session either for the master (i.e. *A* is allowed to start a new session before having completed a previous one), the slave or the both of them. But adding such a control structure adds more complexity and this has a cost when proof-based techniques are used. Thus in most approaches, such as Paulson's one or Meadows's one, this control structure is not specified which basically amounts to specifying a multi-session version of the protocol (i.e. taking the *action* predicate to be defined as *true* in our approach). Of course if the multi-session version works, it is likely that a single version will also work, but the converse is not true.

The situation is similar for modal logics: the control structure is wired in the formalism. Parallel multi-role for trusted principals is not supported by most modal logics. It is supported in [17], but it is then the only possible choice.

3 Expressing security properties

The way security properties are expressed is an even greater area of differentiation among various approaches. In this section we briefly present the approach described in [6]. In this approach a security property is described using a *filtering function* characterizing the visible actions and an automaton specifying the required sequencing of these visible actions. The filtering allows to focus on any particular session and on the relevant actions expected for this session: unexpected actions or actions carrying non coherent values will be abstracted away, and the security property can be more concisely and more simply expressed on remaining actions, which are called the visible actions. The automaton is to express constraints on visible actions. Here we consider one of the security properties expressed in [3] and referred to as the master authentication property. This property is expressed using the following filtering function:

$$ff_{N_a}\left(\left((s_a, s_b, s_s, s_i), (l, msg), (s'_a, s'_b, s'_s, s'_i)\right)\right) =$$
$$3a \text{ if } l = 3a \wedge s'_a.slave = B \wedge s'_a.n_a = N_a$$
$$3b \text{ if } l = 3b \wedge s'_b.master = A \wedge s'_b.n_a = N_a$$
$$6b \text{ if } l = 6b \wedge s_b.master = A \wedge s_b.n_a = N_a$$
$$6a \text{ if } l = 6a \wedge s_a.slave = B \wedge s_a.n_a = N_a$$
$$\varepsilon \text{ otherwise}$$

This filtering function uses here only one parameter, N_a, which intuitively stands for a nonce characterizing the particular session of interest. This function identifies four visible actions, 3a, 3b, 6b, 6a, which correspond to the situation where the action is fired with the correct session parameter (e.g. the master is going through action 3a, believes he is talking to *B* and uses the nonce that characterizes the particular session of interest). The automaton just states that the visible action should be seen (by the global observer) always in the same order: 3a, 3b, 6b, 6a. The automaton thus corresponds to the regular expression $3a\ 3b\ 6b\ 6a$

By definition the property is satisfied iff $\forall x.\forall t.t \in T \Rightarrow \widetilde{ff}_x(t) \in P$ where $\widetilde{ff}$ is the extension of ff to traces, T is the set of possible traces and P is the prefix closure of the language recognized by the automaton. Thus, if for some trace t of T, it is possible for the slave to answer to A using the correct nonce N_a, but in believing that he is talking to another (potentially corrupted) principal C with A not being aware of this (even after receipt of message 6) then we have $\widetilde{ff_x}(t) = 3a\ 6a$ which is not a prefix of $3a\ 3b\ 6b\ 6a$. This is exactly the situation for the flaw described in [3] for the same protocol (but for another authentication property). This property is then transformed automatically into a very simple invariant property. This invariant can be proven using proof-based techniques or can be automated as will be seen in the next section.

The problem of precisely expressing security properties using a modal logic is very similar to the problem of describing a protocol with adequate precision: basic modal operators are typically not general enough to cover all potential needs (e.g. the expression of freshness). But the problem is even more complex for more elaborate properties that are found in electronic commerce protocols and no modal logic has yet be proposed for this class of cryptographic protocols.

For general purpose formal methods the situation is quite different. Very few approaches laid down the basis for expressing sophisticated security properties: most approaches only provide for the expression of confidentiality; only a few provide for the expression of authentication properties; the first attempt to express more elaborate properties such as those found in electronic commerce was done in [4] using the approach just illustrated; another tentative has just been presented very recently in [8]. We nevertheless believe that the use of a filtering function and of an automaton as illustrated previously could be adapted to fit with most approaches. The only negative side-effect being that it would then possibly conflict with the corresponding proof automatization.

4 Bringing automatization

Now that we have discussed the ability to describe the protocols and security properties with adequate accuracy, we consider automatization of the verification. Most general purpose formal methods based approaches use proof-techniques for bringing some automatization: term-rewriting based techniques are for example used in Meadow's approach, and induction in Paulson's approach. As discussed in the previous section, using such an automatization has the drawback of puting some constraints on the formalization itself. Here we show that the various features used in the previous section (control structures, variables, etc.) do not necessarily prevent automatization.

Following [5] we first define an abstraction function $h : B \to B_0$ where B is the set of basic data (keys, nonces, numbers and identifiers), and B_0 is a finite subset of B which is to be proposed by the user when willing to verify a particular property. In practise this comes down to selecting a few values of interest (a few keys, a few nonces, etc.) and defining h to leave these values unchanged (i.e. $h(x) = x$) and to collapse other elements into one representative for each basic type, i.e. one for keys, one for nonces, etc. An abstract interpretation based technique is then applied where the abstraction function is derived from h and the verification is performed in an automatic and safe way using model-checking techniques on the abstract model. An algorithm is also provided for trying to compute the abstract model and the abstract properties in an automatic way. In fact the algorithm tries to prove that the same specification can be used for both the general protocol and its finite abstraction. The algorithm may fail to show that a particular sub-expression meets the associated sub-goal. In this situation, which is very rare in practice the user should then either prove manually using a proof tool that the problematic sub-expression indeed meets an automatically generated proof-obligation, or should provide a new sub-expression by himself.

With the current protocol specification the algorithm will in fact fail for action 3a and 6b on sub-expressions $s'_a.n_a \notin s_a.nonces$ and $s'_b.n_b \notin s_b.nonces$. We first notice that the algorithm would succeed for the first sub-expression if the value of $s'_a.n_a$, let us say a, would be such that $\hat{h}^{-1}(a) = \{a\}$. This is clearly not always true, but we can easily notice that $s'_a.n_a \notin s_a.nonces$ is the equivalent to $(s'_a.n_a = N_a \wedge s'_a.n_a \notin s_a.nonces \vee s'_a.n_a \neq N_a \wedge s'_a.n_a \notin s_a.nonces)$ and can thus be replaced by the weaker proposition $s'_a.n_a = N_a \wedge s'_a.n_a \notin s_a.nonces \vee s'_a.n_a \neq N_a$. The problem is similar with the second sub-expression and is handled in the same way. The algorithm then completes on this revised version. By construction, the specification of the abstract model is thus identical to the specification of the protocol itself but for the two relations describing the actions 3a and 6b. The new relation for 3a is for example $action(s_a.at, 3a, s'_a.at)$ $\wedge s'_I = s_I \cup (s'_a.n_a, A)_{s_A.K_b} \wedge s'_a.n_a = N_a \wedge s'_a.n_a \notin s_a.nonces \vee s'_a.n_a \neq N_a \wedge s'_a.nonces = s_a.nonces \cup \{s'_a.n_a\}$.

The same algorithm is then applied to the authentication property and succeeds without any user intervention. Now we are in a position to verify the abstract property on the abstract model using model-checking techniques. The verification succeeds[2]. Since the abstraction is safe, we can conclude that the protocol also meets the expressed authentication property. Typically since only a few distinct keys, nonces and identifiers need to be distinguinshed to prove a particular property on a given protocol, the number of states used during the verification is very small according to model-checking standards (a few hundred for current real life protocols). Thus by integrating model-checking techniques it is possible to automatize a significant part of the verification process without any compromise on the precision of the protocol modeling and of security property expression. By keeping to pure proof-based techniques this would have been very difficult to achieve if not impossible.

---

[2] In fact the verification shows that B can apparently repeat the sequence of visible action 3b 6b more that once. This is due to the fact that the abstraction function transforms nonces in a way that does not preserve freshness property of nonces generated by B. It would be easy to avoid this situation by revisiting h to distinguish one more nonce, let say N_b. But this situation is clearly not problematic from the master perspective: what is important is that B answers at least once in a coherent manner. Thus we could as an alternative revisit the automaton by allowing a few more transitions that seem acceptable. This is what we assume in the following to simplify presentation.

5 Bringing understanding into the protocol design

The verification process can be used to generate a set of reachable global states, G. This set is very small according to model-checking standards but it is quite big for human standards. The verification thus does not provide a lot of insight into understanding in a very precise manner protocol correctness. We believe that this understanding is very important in many respects. First the verification is based on some hypotheses, and it is of prime importance to understand the precise impact of each one. Of course it is still possible to do the verification for all set of possible hypotheses but the number of such combinations is typically too big. Second, bringing such insight is very useful for designing or improving the protocol itself. It is furthermore a way of assessing the adequacy of the modeling of the protocol.

In order to achieve this, it is suggested in [6] to transform the abstract model by applying a second abstraction. The main advantage of the second model is that it is much easier to understand. This bears some similarities with the situation using invariant proof-based techniques: an invariant does not need to be precise enough to characterize the set of reachable states; it should be only precise enough for the proof to work.

For this we proceed as follows : (1) for each trustable principal x we propose a set $E^x = \{E_1^x, E_2^x, ..., E_{n_x}^x\}$ such that $\bigcup_{E_i^x \in E^x} \subseteq L_x$ where L_x is the set of reachable states for principal x; (2) we propose a finite set $S_i = \{s_i^1, s_i^2, ..., s_i^{n_i}\}$ where each element of S_i is some potential intruder knowledge (i.e. a value drawn from domain S); (3) we finally identify a subset G' of $E^{x_1} \times E^{x_2} \times ... \times E^{x_n} \times S_i$ where $\{x_1, x_2, ..., x_n\}$ is the set of trustable principals (i.e. $\{A, B, S\}$ for the protocol at hand) such that for each reachable global state $(s_{x_1}, s_{x_2}, ..., s_{x_n}, s_i)$ of G there exists a corresponding element $(E_{x_1}, E_{x_2}, ..., E_{x_n}, s_i')$ of G' where $s_{x_1} \in E_{x_1}, s_{x_2} \in E_{x_2}, ..., s_{xn} \in E_{x_{n1}}$ and $s_i \subseteq s_i'$. Intuitively, G' which has to be a very small set in order to achieve its objective, represents in a structured way the basic dependence between local states. The similarity with an invariant is more then just apparent and is discussed in [6].

Each subset $E_1^x, E_2^x, ..., E_{n_x}^x$ of E^x can be described by extension or more likely by intension. A particularly concise way is to characterize each of them using two logic formulae that apply respectively on states and transitions. The generated subset is then by definition the one that can be reached from the set of states characterized by the first logic formula without firing transitions drawn from a set of transitions characterized by the second one. Here for example we propose to use three subsets for A and three for B. For A we have (1) the subset of states characterized by $s_a.at = 71 \wedge s_a.nonces = \{N\}^3$, and $l = 3a \wedge s_a'.slave = B \wedge s_a'.n_a = N_a$; (2) the subset characterized by $s_a.at = 36 \wedge s_a.nonces = \{N, N_a\} \wedge (s_a.slave = B \wedge s_a.k_b = K_b) \wedge s_a.n_a = N_a$ and $l = 6a \wedge s_a'.slave = B \wedge s_a'.n_a = N_a$; (3) and the subset characterized by $s_a.at = 67 \wedge s_a.nonces = \{N, N_a\} \wedge (s_a.slave = B \wedge s_a.k_b = K_b) \wedge s_a.n_a = N_a \wedge s_a.n_b = N$ and $false$.

---

[3] Label nm stands by convention for the control point of principal x between the firing of action n_x and m_x (e.g. 71 is the control point of A between 7a and 1a).

For B we have the subset characterized by the state condition $s_b.at = 73 \wedge$ $s_b.nonces = \{N\}$, and $l = 3b \wedge s_b'.n_a = N_a$; the subset characterized by the state condition $s_b.at = 36 \wedge s_b.nonces = \{N\} \wedge s_a.n_a = N_a$, and $l = 6b$; and a third subset characterized by the state condition $s_b.at = 67 \wedge s_b.nonces = \{N\} \wedge (s_b.master = A \wedge s_b.k_a = K_a) \wedge s_a.n_a = N_a$ and $false$. The three first sets of states will be called respectively A_1, A_2, A_3 and the three other ones B_1, B_2, B_3. For the intruder we use three different knowledge values $s_i^1 = K_s \cup K_c^{-1} \cup (K_a, A)_{K_s^{-1}} \cup (K_b, B)_{K_s^{-1}} \cup (K_c, C)_{K_s^{-1}} \cup N$, $s_i^2 = s_i^1 \cup N \cup (N_a, A)_{K_b}$ and , $s_i^3 = s_i^2 \cup (N_a, N)_{K_a}$.

The set G' is $\{(A_1, B_1, s_i^1), (A_2, B_1, s_i^2), (A_2, B_2, s_i^2), (A_2, B_3, s_i^3), (A_3, B_3, s_i^3)\}$. The initial state of the abstract model is corresponding to (A_1, B_1, s_i^1). All moves from states corresponding to this element lead to states that are still associated to the same element, but for the visible action $3a$, which leads to an element corresponding to (A_2, B_1, s_i^2): the intruder knowledge has increased by $(N_a, A)_{K_b}$; principal A is just after the sending of visible action $3a$; it cannot proceed because he would need some data of the form $(N_a, n)_{K_a}$, but the intruder is unable to produce such a value (either by replay or construction). The only possible move is the visible action $3b$ which leads to a state corresponding to (A_2, B_2, s_i^2). The only possible move now is visible action $6b$ which leads to the sending of $(N_a, N)_{K_a}$ and to a state corresponding to (A_2, B_3, s_i^3). Now moves either lead to a state that corresponds to the same element (A_2, B_3, s_i^3), either a visible action $6a$ is performed and the new states that is reached corresponds to (A_3, B_3, s_i^3) and all subsequent moves lead to states that correspond to the same object.

The element of G' thus represent the five different phases that correspond to a particular session. This number would have been unchanged also in the event where a more discriminating abstraction function had been changed in the previous step (i.e. an abstraction function distinguishing one more nonce). For each of the five phases the element of G' precisely characterize the corresponding global states. A simple invariant expressed as the disjunction of five different sub-formulae could in fact be derived from this set. Another benefit here is that the correctness of the invariant can be checked automatically by using model-checking techniques.

6 Conclusion

Thus we have tried to show that by integrating various verification techniques it is possible to achieve at the same time automatization and precision in modeling. In particular we have used modal logic style to achieve conciseness in the description of the intruder knowledge, general purpose formal methods for providing a general framework and for applying abstract interpretation techniques, and model-checking based techniques for automatizing the verification process. Finally we have used a second abstraction to achieve better understanding of the protocol design. But the formalism that is used here is in some way over-killing: it is typically possible to verify the same properties using model-checking techniques or alternatively using pure proof-based techniques, filtering functions are more general then required, etc. The main objectives here was to show that the various objectives were achievable within a same framework. This framework is currently used for the verification of large protocols. We nevertheless believe that there is some room and need for designing a more dedicated formalism (i.e. typically a modal logic) that would achieve the same needs. This formalism would be more elegant and its theoretical properties could be studied more easily.

References

1. J.R. Abrial. The B-method for large software specification, design and coding. In *VDM'91*. Springer Verlag, 1991.
2. P. Bieber and N. Boulahia-Cuppens. Formal development of authentication protocols. In *BCS-FACS sixth Refinement Workshop*, 1994.
3. D. Bolignano. Formal verification of cryptographic protocols. In *Proceedings of the third ACM Conference on Computer and Communication Security*, 1996.
4. D. Bolignano. Towards the Formal Verification of Electronic Commerce Protocols. In *Proceedings of the 10 th IEEE Computer Security Foundations Workshop*. IEEE, June 1997.
5. D. Bolignano. Towards the Mechanization of Cryptographic Protocol Verification. In *Proceedings of the 9th International Conference on Computer-Aided Verification (CAV'97)*, June 1997.
6. D. Bolignano. Using abstractions for automatizing and simplifying the verification of cryptographic protocols. Technical report, Dyade, 1998.
7. M. Burrows, M. Abadi, and R. Needham. A logic of authentication. *ACM Transactions on Computer Systems*, 8, 1990.
8. P. Syverson C. Meadows. A formal specification of requirements for payment transactions in the set protocol. In *Finacial Cryptography*, 1998.
9. P.C. Chen and V.D. Gligor. On the formal specification and verification of a multiparty session protocol. In *Proceedings of the IEEE Symposium on Research in Security and Privacy*, 1990.
10. D. Dolev and A. Yao. On the security of public key protocols. *IEEE Transactions on Information Theory*, IT-29(2):198–208, 1983.
11. G.Leduc, O. Bonaventure, E. Koerner, L. Léonard, C. Pecheur, and D. Zanetti. Specification and verification of a ttp protocol for the conditional access to services. In *Proceedings of the 12th Workshop on the Application of Formal Methods to System Development (Univ Montreal)*, 1996.
12. R.A. Kemmerer. Analyzing encryption protocols using formal verification techniques. In *IEEE Journal on Selected Areas in Communications*, volume 7(4), 1989.
13. G. Lowe. An attack on the needham-schroeder public-key protocol. In *Information Processing Letters*, 1995.
14. C. Meadows. Applying formal methods to the analysis of a key management protocol. In *Journal of Computer Security*, 1992.
15. J. K. Millen, S.C. Clark, and S.B. Freedman. The interrogator: Protocol security analysis. *IEEE Transactions on Software Engineering*, 13(2), 1987.
16. L. Paulson. The inductive approach to verifying cryptographic protocols. *J. Computer Security*, 1998.
17. E. Snekkenes. Roles in cryptographic protocols. In *Proceedings of the IEEE Symposium on Research in Security and Privacy*, pages 105–119. IEEE, 1992.

Verifying Systems with Infinite but Regular State Spaces

Pierre Wolper, Bernard Boigelot*

Université de Liège
Institut Montefiore, B28
B-4000 Liège Sart-Tilman, Belgium
{pw,boigelot}@montefiore.ulg.ac.be

Abstract. Thanks to the development of a number of efficiency enhancing techniques, state-space exploration based verification, and in
particular model checking, has been quite successful for finite-state systems. This has prompted efforts to apply a similar approach to systems
with infinite state spaces. Doing so amounts to developing algorithms for
computing a symbolic representation of the infinite state space, as opposed to requiring the user to characterize the state space by assertions.
Of course, in most cases, this can only be done at the cost of forgoing
any general guarantee of success. The goal of this paper is to survey a
number of results in this area and to show that a surprisingly common
characteristic of the systems that can be analyzed with this approach is
that their state space can be represented as a regular language.

1 Introduction

If a system is finite-state, its set of reachable states can, at least in theory, always
be computed. The sometimes "theoretical" nature of this possibility comes from
the fact that, even for simple systems, finite state spaces can be much too large
to be computed with any realistic amount of resources. This is not surprising
since, for instance, state reachability for a concurrent system is a PSPACE-
complete problem. In spite of such rather discouraging complexity results, much
effort has been devoted to making state-space exploration practically feasible.
These efforts have been quite successful and techniques such as symbolic verification [BCM+92] or partial-order methods [Val92, WG93] are quite effective
and tools based upon them are in regular use.

For infinite-state systems, even the theoretical possibility of exploring the
state space disappears. Indeed, except for severely restricted classes of systems,
most problems about reachable states become undecidable. This has long been
taken as evidence that infinite-state systems had to be handled by "assertional"
methods in which the user is requested to characterize the system behavior by
logical assertions, the validity of which is then established by a formal proof.
However, undecidability only excludes perfectly general algorithmic solutions,

---

* "Chargé de Recherches" (Post-Doctoral Researcher) for the National Fund for Scientific Research (Belgium).

not solutions that work on restricted cases or for which termination is not guaranteed. Note that this situation is to some extent similar to the one for finite-state systems. Indeed, in the latter case high complexity excludes always efficient algorithmic solutions, but years of experimental work have confirmed the existence of solutions that work perfectly well on many practically relevant instances.

Work on the algorithmic verification of infinite-state systems has thus proceeded in two directions. The first is the study of classes of infinite-state systems that are decidable, e.g. [BS95, FWW97]. In general such classes are somewhat artificial and practical examples of systems that fall within them are hard to find. There are fortunately exceptions to this rule, for instance timed automata [AD94], which have been used as the basis of exploited verification tools. The second direction is to consider a larger class of systems, but to be satisfied with a semi-algorithmic solution, i.e., an algorithmic solution that is allowed to give up or run forever on some instances.

In this paper, we will consider examples of both categories in the context of closed systems whose infinite state space originates from the possibility of executing arbitrarily long computations with unbounded data. The focus on closed systems is typical of many verification approaches and allows us to use a simple semantical model. Furthermore, by eliminating the possibility of reading arbitrarily large values, it restricts the source of the infinite number of states to arbitrarily long computations. We will also limit our focus to the problem of computing a representation of the set of reachable states of the system. Indeed, this allows the verification of many properties of the state space such as reachability of a given state or truth of an invariant. Furthermore, once the reachable states can be computed, other verification problems can often also be solved. For instance, model checking for linear-time safety properties reduces to reachability, and model checking of general linear-time temporal properties reduces to repeated reachability [VW86].

The first class of systems we will consider are finite-state systems with one pushdown stack. This is a decidable class for which the state space can always be algorithmically computed. Concretely, we will show that a finite-automaton representation of reachable states (control state and stack content) can simply and easily be computed [FWW97]. Next, we will turn to finite-state systems communicating through unbounded message queues. This is an undecidable class and thus only semi-algorithmic solutions are possible. The approach we will consider represents queue contents by finite automata and focuses on cycles in the control graph in order to finitely generate infinite state spaces [BW94, BG96, BGWW97].

The last class of systems we will consider is that of finite-state systems augmented with a number of integer variables. The traditional way to represent sets of integer values is to use arithmetic constraints. Here, we will turn to an alternative representation with potential computational advantages: finite automata operating on the binary (or in general base-r) encodings of integer vectors. This representation is as expressive as Presburger arithmetic, but is much more computationally oriented, just like BDDs [Bry92] are a computationally-oriented representation of Boolean functions. With this representation, the effect of repeating a cycle of linear operations can often be computed and, furthermore, a natural characterization of cycles for which this computation is possible has been given [Boi98].

2 Modeling Infinite-State Systems

We consider systems that can be modeled as *extended automata*, i.e., state machines with a finite control and possibly infinite data. In most cases, an extended automaton will be obtained from a higher level representation of the system, for instance a concurrent program. The class of systems that can be modeled by extended automata is thus quite large.

An extended automaton A is a tuple $(C, c_0, M, m_0, Op, \Delta)$, where

- C is a finite set of *control locations*;
- M is a (possibly infinite) *memory domain*;
- $Op \subseteq 2^{M \to M}$ is a set of *memory operations*;
- $\Delta \subseteq C \times Op \times C$ is a finite set of *transitions*;
- c_0 is an *initial control location*, and m_0 is an *initial memory content*.

A *state* of A is an element of $C \times M$, i.e., a pair (c, m) composed of a control location c and a memory content m. The initial state is (c_0, m_0). A state (c', m') is *directly reachable* from a state (c, m) if there exists a transition $(c_1, \theta, c_2) \in \Delta$ such that $c_1 = c$, $c_2 = c'$ and $m' = \theta(m)$. For this, we use the notation $(c, m) \Rightarrow (c', m')$. Furthermore, we denote by $\Rightarrow^*$ the reflexive and transitive closure of $\Rightarrow$. A state (c', m') is *reachable from* a state (c, m) if $(c, m) \Rightarrow^* (c', m')$. The *reachable states* of A are those that are reachable from the initial state.

The main problem we will address in subsequent sections is that of computing a representation of the set of reachable states of various classes of extended automata.

3 Pushdown Systems

A pushdown system is a system composed of a finite control associated with an unbounded stack over a finite alphabet Σ. Such a system can be modeled by a *pushdown automaton*, i.e., an extended automaton $A = (C, c_0, M, m_0, Op, \Delta)$ whose memory domain $M = \Sigma^*$ is the set of all the potential *stack contents*, and whose set of memory operations Op contains the two *stack operations* a_+ and a_- for every $a \in \Sigma$. These operations are defined by $a_+(w) = wa$ and $a_-(wa) = w$ for every $w \in \Sigma^*$ (the value of $a_-(w)$ is not defined if w does not end with the symbol a).

It is known (see for instance [Cau92]) that the set of reachable states of a pushdown automaton is regular, or more precisely, that for each control location $c \in C$, the memory contents $m \in M$ for which (c, m) is a reachable state form a regular set. In [FWW97], a very simple construction of a finite automaton accepting the possible stack contents for each control location is given and is shown to be implementable in $O(n^3)$, n being the size of the pushdown automaton. This construction is the following. Given a stack alphabet Σ and a pushdown automaton $A = (C, c_0, M, m_0, Op, \Delta)$ over Σ, one constructs the *reachability automaton* of A, which is the finite-state automaton $A_r = (Q_r, \Sigma_r, \Delta_r, q_r^0, F_r)$ such that

- The set of states Q_r is identical to C;
- The input alphabet Σ_r is identical to Σ;
- The transition relation $\Delta_r \subseteq Q_r \times (\Sigma_r \cup \{\varepsilon\}) \times Q_r$ is the smallest relation that satisfies the following conditions, where Δ_r^* denotes the reflexive and transitive closure of Δ_r, and ε denotes the empty word:
  - If $(q, a_+, q') \in \Delta$, then $(q, a, q') \in \Delta_r$, and
  - If $(q, a_-, q') \in \Delta$ and $(q'', a, q) \in \Delta_r^*$, then $(q'', \varepsilon, q') \in \Delta_r$;
- The initial state q_r^0 is c_0;
- All the states are accepting, i.e., we have $F_r = Q_r$.

The relation between A and A_r is given by the following theorem.

Theorem 1. *A state (q, w) is reachable in a pushdown automaton A if and only if the state q is reachable in the reachability automaton A_r through the word w.*

In other words, the stack contents with which a control location c is reachable are exactly the words accepted by A_r when c is taken as the unique accepting state. It follows that A_r represents exactly and effectively the set of reachable states of A. The automaton A_r can then be used to check properties of the system than are reducible to reachability properties. Furthermore, in [FWW97] it is shown how repeated reachability and hence temporal logic model checking can be handled with related constructions.

4   Queue Systems

A queue system is a system composed of a finite control together with one or several unbounded FIFO channels (also called queues) containing elements of finite alphabets. It is a very common model of distributed systems communicating through unbounded queues. Such a system can be modeled by a *queue automaton*, which is an extended automaton $A = (C, c_0, M, m_0, Op, \Delta)$ satisfying the following.

- The memory domain M is of the form $\Sigma_1^* \times \Sigma_2^* \times \cdots \times \Sigma_n^*$, where $n > 0$ represents the *number of queues* of A, and each Σ_i is the finite *queue alphabet* of the i-th queue of A (this queue is usually denoted q_i). For simplicity, we assume that the different queue alphabets are distinct. Each element $(w_1, \ldots, w_n)$ of M associates a content w_i to each queue q_i of the system and is called a *queue-set content*.
- The set of memory operations Op contains the two *queue operations* $q_i!a$ and $q_i?a$ for each queue q_i and symbol $a \in \Sigma_i$. The *send* operation $q_i!a$ is defined by $(q_i!a)(w_1, \ldots, w_n) = (w_1, \ldots, w_{i-1}, w_i a, w_{i+1}, \ldots, w_n)$. The *receive* operation $q_i?a$ is defined by $(q_i?a)(w_1, \ldots, w_{i-1}, aw_i, w_{i+1}, \ldots, w_n) = (w_1, \ldots, w_n)$ (this operation is not defined if the content of q_i does not start with the symbol a).

Unsurprisingly, computing the set of reachable states of a queue automaton, or more precisely, a finite and effective representation of this set, is in general impossible. It is indeed well known that queue automata for which there is more than one symbol in at least one queue alphabet can simulate arbitrary Turing machines.

This does not, however, exclude partial algorithmic approaches to computing the set of reachable states of queue systems. One such approach relies upon the concept of *meta-transition* introduced in [BW94] and applied to queue systems in [BG96]. A meta-transition is a derived transition that in one step generates a potentially infinite set of states. Precisely, a meta-transition is a triple (c, f, c'), where $c, c' \in C$ are the *origin* and the *destination* locations and $f : M \to 2^M$ is the *memory function* of the meta-transition. The memory function must be such that, for every set $U \subseteq C \times M$ of reachable states of A, its *image* $U' = \{(c', m') \mid (\exists m \in M)((c, m) \in U \wedge m' \in f(m))\}$ by the meta-transition only contains reachable states. A particular class of meta-transitions are the *cycle* meta-transitions. These correspond to the arbitrarily repeated execution of a given cycle in the control graph (C, Δ) of A. The origin and destination locations of a cycle meta-transition are thus the origin of the cycle. Its memory function maps any memory content m to the set of values that can be obtained by applying any number of times the sequence of operations σ labeling the cycle. In other words, the memory function of a cycle transition computes the image of memory contents by the closure σ^* of the sequence of operations of the cycle.

To compute the reachable states of a queue automaton, one can thus proceed by augmenting the automaton with a finite set of meta-transitions and then exploring the state space of the augmented automaton. By the definition of meta-transitions, this state space is guaranteed to be identical to the one of the original automaton. While exploring the augmented automaton, one follows both transitions and meta-transitions, each time expanding the set of known reachable states. The search terminates when a stable set is obtained. Of course, there is no guarantee that this will eventually happen, but the fact that a meta-transition can produce in one step an infinite number of states makes termination possible, even when the number of reachable states is infinite.

Applying this method requires the ability to represent possibly infinite sets of states, and to perform operations on represented sets. Since queue automata have a finite control, a simple idea consists of associating to each control location a set of corresponding queue-set contents represented with the help of a specific representation system. The *Queue Decision Diagram, or QDD* [BG96], is such a symbolic representation system. It relies on an *encoding scheme* which maps every queue-set content $(w_1, \ldots, w_n)$ onto the concatenation $w_1 \cdot w_2 \cdots w_n$ of the individual queue contents. Given a set $U \subseteq M$ of queue-set contents, a QDD A representing U is simply a finite-state automaton accepting all the encodings of the elements of U.

Of course, QDDs cannot represent all the subsets of M. The following theorem, which appears in [BGWW97], characterizes exactly the sets of queue-set contents that can be represented by a QDD.

Theorem 2. *A set $U \subseteq M$ is representable by a QDD if and only if it can be expressed as a finite union of Cartesian products of regular languages over the queue alphabets.*

A positive point of QDDs is that they can easily be manipulated algorithmically. First, computing the union, intersection, complement and difference of sets represented as QDDs simply amounts to performing the corresponding operation over finite-state automata. This is a consequence of the fact that the encoding scheme that has been chosen maps every queue-set content onto a unique and unambiguous word over $\Sigma_1^* \cdot \Sigma_2^* \cdots \Sigma_n^*$. Second, it has been shown in [BG96] that one can always compute the effect of a transition of a queue automaton on a set represented as a QDD:

Theorem 3. *Let $U \subseteq M$ be a set represented by a QDD. Given a queue q_i and a symbol $a \in \Sigma_i$, one can compute QDDs representing the sets $(q_i!a)(U)$ and $(q_i?a)(U)$.*

In order to compute the set of reachable states of a queue automaton with the help of QDDs, one must also be able to add meta-transitions to the automaton. Selecting cycles that are suitable for meta-transitions can be done thanks to the following result, which appears in [BGWW97] and is proved in [Boi98].

Theorem 4. *Given a queue automaton A and a cycle in its control graph (C, Δ) labeled by the sequence of operations $\sigma \in Op^*$, it is decidable whether the closure σ^* preserves the representable nature of sets of queue-set contents, i.e., whether $\sigma^*(U)$ is always representable by a QDD whenever U is representable by a QDD.*

Note that in particular, the necessary and sufficient condition presented in [BGWW97] implies that for every sequence σ in which the queue operation only involves a single queue, σ^* always preserves the representability of sets of queue-set contents.

The fact that a meta-transition preserves representability is not sufficient. One also needs to be able to effectively compute its effect. The required result is given by the following theorem.

Theorem 5. *If $\sigma \in Op^*$ is a sequence of queue operations such that $\sigma^*(U)$ is representable for every representable set $U \subseteq M$, then one can compute a QDD representing $\sigma^*(U)$ given a QDD representing U.*

An algorithm implementing this computation is presented in [Boi98].

5 Linear Integer Systems

A linear integer system is a system composed of a finite control together with one or several unbounded integer variables on which linear operations are performed. Such a system can be modeled by a *linear integer automaton*, which is an extended automaton $A = (C, c_0, M, m_0, Op, \Delta)$ satisfying the following.

- Its memory domain M is $\mathbf{Z}^n$, where $n > 0$ represents the *number of variables* of A (these variables are usually denoted $x_1, x_2, \ldots, x_n$). Each element $(v_1, \ldots, v_n)$ of M is called a *variable-set content* and associates one value v_i to each variable x_i of the system.
- Its set of memory operations Op contains all functions $M \to M$ of the form $P\mathbf{x} \le \mathbf{q} \to \mathbf{x} := T\mathbf{x} + \mathbf{b}$, where $P \in \mathbf{Z}^{m \times n}, \mathbf{q} \in \mathbf{Z}^m, m \in \mathbf{N}, T \in \mathbf{Z}^{n \times n}$ and $\mathbf{b} \in \mathbf{Z}^n$. The linear system $P\mathbf{x} \le \mathbf{q}$ is the *guard* of the operation and expresses a condition that must be satisfied by the variable vector $\mathbf{x} = (x_1, \ldots, x_n)$ for the operation to be defined. The linear transformation $\mathbf{x} := T\mathbf{x} + \mathbf{b}$ is the *assignment* of the operation and expresses the transformation undergone by the variable values when the operation is performed.

It is well known that linear integer systems that have at least two variables can simulate two-counter machines and are therefore as expressive as Turing machines. As a consequence, one cannot in general compute the set of reachable states of a linear integer automaton.

One can however follow the same semi-algorithmic approach as in Section 4, adding meta-transitions to the system and then exploring the resulting augmented linear integer automaton. This requires the ability to represent possibly infinite subsets of $\mathbf{Z}^n$, to apply linear operations to represented sets (for computing the effect of a transition), and to apply the repetition of linear operations to represented sets (for computing the effect of meta-transitions).

There are many ways of representing sets of integer vectors, but we will adopt an automaton-based representation that is far from new since it can be found in [Büc60], but has only recently been investigated as a potentially usable representation [WB95, BC96, BBR97, BRW98]. It consists of representing the elements of the vector in binary (or some other base) and then viewing the result as a word. Sets of vectors thus become languages and can be recognized by finite automata.

Precisely, given an integer vector $\mathbf{v} = (v_1, \ldots, v_n)$ and an integer *base* $r > 1$, one encodes each positive component v_i as a finite word $a_{p-1}a_{p-2}\cdots a_0$ over the alphabet $\{0, \ldots, r-1\}$, such that $v_i = \sum_{i=0}^{p-1} a_i r^i$. If $v_i < 0$, then the encoding of v_i consists of the last p digits of the encoding of $r^p + v_i$ (the number $r^p + v_i$ is called the r's *complement* of v_i). The number of digits p is not fixed, but chosen identical for each v_i and such that $-r^{p-1} \le v_i < r^{p-1}$. An encoding of $\mathbf{v}$ is then obtained by grouping together the digits that share the same position in the encodings of the v_i. The encoding of $\mathbf{v}$ can be viewed either as a tuple of words of identical length over the alphabet $\{0, \ldots, r-1\}$, or as a single word over the alphabet $\{0, \ldots, r-1\}^n$. The latter corresponds to simultaneously reading all digits at a given position and is the one we adopt. Every vector in $\mathbf{Z}^n$ has an infinite number of possible encodings, the length of the shortest being determined by the component with the highest magnitude.

Example 1. A representation of the vector $(3, -1)$ in base 2 is $(0011, 1111)$ or $(0, 1)(0, 1)(1, 1)(1, 1)$.

Given a set $U \subseteq \mathbf{Z}^n$ of vectors, a *Number Decision Diagram, or NDD* [WB95, Boi98] representing U is simply a finite-state automaton accepting all the encodings of all the elements of U. The following results, due to Büchi [Büc60], Cobham [Cob69] and Semenov [Sem77], characterize precisely the sets of integer vectors that can be represented by NDDs:

Theorem 6. *A set $U \subseteq \mathbf{Z}^n$ is representable by an NDD in a base $r > 1$ if and only if it can be defined in the first-order theory $\langle \mathbf{Z}, +, \leq, V_r \rangle$, where V_r is a function that maps every nonzero integer onto the highest power of r dividing it.*

Theorem 7. *A set $U \subseteq \mathbf{Z}^n$ is representable by an NDD in any base if and only if it can be defined in Presburger arithmetic, i.e., in the first-order theory $\langle \mathbf{Z}, +, \leq \rangle$.*

An important corollary of Theorem 7 is that any vector transformation that can be expressed in Presburger arithmetic can be applied to sets of integer vectors represented as NDDs. In particular, one can always compute the image of such a set by any linear operation that belongs to Op. It is thus possible to compute the effect of a transition of a linear integer automaton on a set of variable-set values represented as an NDD.

In order to compute the set of reachable states of a linear integer automaton with the help of NDDs, one must also be able to add meta-transitions to the automaton. Selecting cycles that are suitable for meta-transitions can be done thanks to the following result, which is proved in [Boi98].

Theorem 8. *Given a sequence $\sigma \in Op^*$ of linear integer operations without guards, it is decidable whether the closure σ^* preserves the representable nature of sets of integer vectors. Moreover, if σ^* preserves the representable nature of sets of integer vectors, then any sequence σ' obtained by adding guards to the operations composing σ is such that $(\sigma')^*$ preserves the representable nature of sets of integer vectors.*

Very roughly, the criterion under which a sequence of linear operations preserves representability is that the eigenvalues of the matrix corresponding to the transformation defined by the sequence are same-order roots of a power of the base used for the representation.

Computing the effect of a meta-transition on a represented set of variable-set values can be done thanks to the following result, which is fully developed in [Boi98].

Theorem 9. *If $\sigma' \in Op^*$ is a sequence of linear integer operations such that the corresponding guardless linear integer operation σ has a closure that preserves the representable nature of sets of integer vectors, then one can compute an NDD representing $(\sigma')^*(U)$ from σ' and an NDD representing $U \subseteq \mathbf{Z}^n$.*

6   Conclusions

For many years, there has been a dichotomy in verification approaches: algorithmic methods for finite-state systems, proof-based methods for infinite-state systems. This dichotomy has not been absolute, but when algorithmic methods have been proposed for infinite-state systems, it has usually been for restricted classes for which most problems are decidable. For instance, much research has been devoted to Petri nets, which sit interestingly close to the limit of decidability [EN94].

Most of the results presented in this paper are linked to a different starting point: consider undecidable classes, but be satisfied with partial algorithmic solutions. There are two strong reasons for doing so. The first is that for a verification approach to be usable in an industrial setting it has to be supported by tools that do most of the work. Hence, methods that at least attempt to provide results without user intervention are essential. The second reason is that there is little practical benefit from focusing on decidable classes of systems. Indeed, the high complexity of all meaningful verification problems has as consequence that, even for perfectly decidable classes, solutions are anyway only partial from a practical point of view. No verification tool is guaranteed to succeed on any but the most trivial instances and, often, the only way to know if a tool can handle a particular instance is to run the tool. Since the ideas presented in this paper lead to tools for infinite-state systems with a perfectly similar behavior, there is no reason to, a priori, doubt their acceptability for practical use. The determining factor will be how often they succeed on the program instances for which verification is indeed needed.

Another central theme of this paper is the importance of well-adapted representation systems for sets of values. In the finite-state case, BDDs have provided a substantial boost to the success of verification methods. The intuition underlying this paper is that representation methods with similar characteristics will be crucial to the success of verification techniques for infinite-state systems. With respect to this, the finite automaton, which has already proven its use for developing finite-state verification algorithms [VW86, BVW94], though probably not the ultimate solution, might again be a very fruitful starting point.

References

[AD94]   R. Alur and D. Dill. A theory of timed automata. *Theoretical Computer Science*, 126(2):183–236, 1994.

[BBR97]   B. Boigelot, L. Bronne, and S. Rassart. An improved reachability analysis method for strongly linear hybrid systems. In *Proc. 9th Int. Conf.on Computer Aided Verification*, volume 1254 of *Lecture Notes in Computer Science*, pages 167–178, Haifa, June 1997. Springer-Verlag.

[BC96]   A. Boudet and H. Comon. Diophantine equations, Presburger arithmetic and finite automata. In *Proceedings of CAAP'96*, number 1059 in Lecture Notes in Computer Science, pages 30–43. Springer-Verlag, 1996.

[BCM+92] J.R. Burch, E.M. Clarke, K.L. McMillan, D.L. Dill, and L.J. Hwang. Symbolic model checking: 10^{20} states and beyond. *Information and Computation*, 98(2):142–170, June 1992.

[BG96]   B. Boigelot and P. Godefroid. Symbolic verification of communication protocols with infinite state spaces using QDDs. In *Proceedings of Computer-Aided Verification*, volume 1102 of *Lecture Notes in Computer Science*, pages 1–12, New-Brunswick, NJ, USA, July 1996. Springer-Verlag.

[BGWW97] B. Boigelot, P. Godefroid, B. Willems, and P. Wolper. The power of QDD's. In *Proc. of Int. Static Analysis Symposium*, volume 1302 of *Lecture Notes in Computer Science*, pages 172–186, Paris, September 1997. Springer-Verlag.

[Boi98] B. Boigelot. *Symbolic Methods for Exploring Infinite State Spaces*. PhD thesis, Université de Liège, 1998.

[BRW98] B. Boigelot, S. Rassart, and P. Wolper. On the expressiveness of real and integer arithmetic automata. to appear in Proc. ICALP'98, 1998.

[Bry92] R.E. Bryant. Symbolic boolean manipulation with ordered binary-decision diagrams. *ACM Computing Surveys*, 24(3):293–318, 1992.

[BS95] O. Burkart and B. Steffen. Composition, decomposition and model checking of pushdown processes. *Nordic Journal of Computing*, 2(2):89–125, 1995.

[Büc60] J. R. Büchi. Weak second-order arithmetic and finite automata. *Zeitschrift Math. Logik und Grundlagen der Mathematik*, 6:66–92, 1960.

[BVW94] O. Bernholtz, M.Y. Vardi, and P. Wolper. An automata-theoretic approach to branching-time model checking. In *Computer Aided Verification, Proc. 6th Int. Workshop*, volume 818 of *Lecture Notes in Computer Science*, pages 142–155, Stanford, California, June 1994. Springer-Verlag. full version available from authors.

[BW94] B. Boigelot and P. Wolper. Symbolic verification with periodic sets. In *Computer Aided Verification, Proc. 6th Int. Conference*, volume 818 of *Lecture Notes in Computer Science*, pages 55–67, Stanford, California, June 1994. Springer-Verlag.

[Cau92] D. Caucal. On the regular structure of prefix rewriting. *Theoretical Computer Science*, 106:61–86, 1992.

[Cob69] A. Cobham. On the base-dependence of sets of numbers recognizable by finite automata. *Mathematical Systems Theory*, 3:186–192, 1969.

[EN94] J. Esparza and M. Nielsen. Decidability issues for Petri nets – a survey. *Bulletin of the EATCS*, 52:245–262, 1994.

[FWW97] A. Finkel, B. Willems, and P. Wolper. A direct symbolic approach to model checking pushdown systems (extended abstract). Presented at Infinity'97 (Bologna), Electronic notes in theoretical computer science, August 1997.

[Sem77] A. L. Semenov. Presburgerness of predicates regular in two number systems. *Siberian Mathematical Journal*, 18:289–299, 1977.

[Val92] A. Valmari. A stubborn attack on state explosion. *Formal Methods in System Design*, 1:297–322, 1992.

[VW86] M.Y. Vardi and P. Wolper. An automata-theoretic approach to automatic program verification. In *Proceedings of the First Symposium on Logic in Computer Science*, pages 322–331, Cambridge, June 1986.

[WB95] P. Wolper and B. Boigelot. An automata-theoretic approach to presburger arithmetic constraints. In *Proc. Static Analysis Symposium*, volume 983 of *Lecture Notes in Computer Science*, pages 21–32, Glasgow, September 1995. Springer-Verlag.

[WG93] P. Wolper and P. Godefroid. Partial-order methods for temporal verification. In *Proc. CONCUR '93*, volume 715 of *Lecture Notes in Computer Science*, pages 233–246, Hildesheim, August 1993. Springer-Verlag.

Formal Verification of Out-of-Order Execution Using Incremental Flushing

Jens U. Skakkebæk[1], Robert B. Jones[1,2], and David L. Dill[1]

[1] Computer Systems Laboratory, Stanford University, Stanford, CA 94305, USA
{jus,dill}@cs.stanford.edu
[2] Strategic CAD Labs, Intel, JFT-104, 2111 NE 25th Ave., Hillsboro, OR 97124, USA
rjones@ichips.intel.com

Abstract. We present a two-part approach for verifying out-of-order execution. First, the complexity of out-of-order issue and scheduling is handled by creating an in-order abstraction of the out-of-order execution core. Second, *incremental flushing* addresses the complexity difficulties encountered by automated abstraction functions on very deep pipelines. We illustrate the techniques on a model of a simple out-of-order processor core.

1 Introduction

Formal verification of microprocessor designs using theorem proving aims at proving that a processor model behaves as defined by an *instruction-set architecture* (ISA). The ISA captures the programmer-level view of the machine. This approach requires an *abstraction function* that relates the state of the processor model with the corresponding state of the ISA. Finding this abstraction function manually for pipelined designs is tedious and time consuming. In response, Burch and Dill devised an approach that automatically generates the abstraction function by *flushing* the implementation state [3]. The technique has been extended to dual-issue and super-scalar architectures [7, 2, 15].

While formal verification techniques exist for pipelined and super-scalar architectures, experience verifying out-of-order architectures is minimal. The distinct features of out-of-order architectures challenge existing verification approaches. First, the extended instruction parallelism in out-of-order architectures results in many complex interactions between executing instructions. This greater complexity makes it very difficult to devise an abstraction function. Second, large (≥ 40 element) buffers are used to record and maintain the program order of instructions. Burch and Dill's automated pipeline flushing approach does not work for out-of-order architectures in practice because the number of cycles required to empty the buffer completely is so large. The logical formulas are too complex to manipulate in proofs and often too complex even to construct.

We present a two-part approach that deals with the out-of-order scheduling logic and the in-order buffering mechanisms separately. First, the implementation is modified to derive an in-order abstraction. These modifications bypass the out-of-order logic and result in instructions executing in order. By exploiting domain-specific knowledge, we are able to establish a functional equivalence relation between the out-of-order implementation and the abstraction. The second step of our technique shows that the in-order abstraction is functionally equivalent to the ISA. This is accomplished via a technique introduced in this paper that we call *incremental flushing*, based on the Burch-Dill automatic flushing approach and the self-consistency technique of Jones *et al.* [8]. Incremental flushing reduces the verification complexity associated with flushing lengthy pipelines. This technique is also applicable to verification of other deeply-pipelined hardware designs, not just out-of-order microarchitectures.

We have created a simple model of an out-of-order execution core that we use to illustrate our approach. Although our example is not representative of industrial-scale designs, it captures essential features of out-of-order architectures: large queuing buffers, resource allocation within the buffers, and data-path scheduling of execution resources. However, using the techniques presented here, we were able to verify it using the Stanford Validity Checker (SVC) [1]. In particular, we have verified its correctness for any (reasonable) scheduling algorithm.

2 Related Work

Sawada and Hunt's theorem-proving approach uses a table of history variables, called a *micro-architectural execution trace table* (MAETT) [14, 13]. The MAETT is an intermediate abstraction that contains selected parts of the implementation as well as extra history variables and variables holding abstracted values. It includes the ISA state and the ISA transition function. A predicate relating the implementation and MAETT is found by manual inspection and proven by induction to be an invariant on the execution of the implementation. In our approach, the intermediate abstraction does not include the ISA state, but is closer to the implementation in abstraction level. This minimizes the manual work needed to find the relation between the implementation and abstraction. We then use an incremental flushing technique to automatically generate the abstraction function, significantly reducing the manual work required to relate the intermediate abstraction to the ISA.

Damm and Pnueli generalize an ISA specification to a non-deterministic abstraction [4]. It is then verified that the implementation satisfies the abstraction by manually establishing and proving the appropriate invariants. They have applied their technique to the Tomasulo algorithm [5], which has out-of-order instruction completion. In contrast, our out-of-order model features in-order retirement. In our approach, the intermediate abstraction executes instructions in-order. Damm and Pnueli's abstraction represents all possible instruction sequences which observe dataflow dependencies. Applying their method to architectures with in-order retirement would require manual proof by induction that the intermediate abstraction satisfies the ISA. We automate this proof by incremental flushing.

Henzinger *et al.* use Tomasulo's algorithm to illustrate a method for manually decomposing the proof obligation [6]. They provide abstract modules for parts of the implementation. These modules correspond to implementation internal transactions. Similar to our approach, the abstractions are invariants on the implementation and are extended with auxiliary variables. Again, our approach automates part of the abstraction process.

McMillan model checks the Tomasulo algorithm by manually decomposing the proof into smaller correctness proofs of the internal transactions that together form one step of execution [11]. Furthermore, he uses symmetry reduction technique to extend the proof to a large number of execution units. Our proofs are also decomposed into properties of internal transactions. In contrast to an automated model checking approach, our theorem-proving based method is able to handle internal buffers of arbitrary size.

Incremental flushing is related to the distributed systems work of Katz [10]. His formalization deals with atomic, concurrent transactions which can be reordered into a more convenient form for formal analysis—without affecting the soundness of the final result. However, the framework of distributed transactions cannot be directly applied to verification microprocessor architectures where the control logic dictates the sequencing of internal transactions.

3 Preliminaries

The desired behavior of a processor is defined by an *instruction-set architecture* (ISA). The ISA represents the programmer-level view of the machine where instructions execute sequentially. The ISA for our example is shown in Figure 1a. The simple state

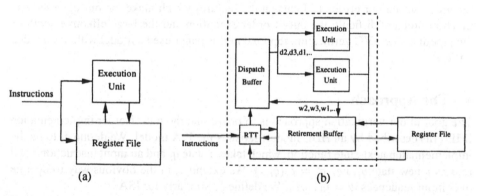

Fig. 1. (a) The simple ISA model. (b) Instruction flow in our out-of-order execution core IMPL.

consists of a register file (RF), while the next-state function is computed with an execution unit (EU) that can execute any instruction. The ISA also accepts a bubble input that leaves the state unchanged. Note that our ISA model does not include a program counter or memory state—as these are also omitted from our simplified out-of-order model.

Modern processors do not implement the ISA in this manner, because the performance would be abysmal. In out-of-order architectures, instructions are fetched, decoded, and sent to the execution core in program order. Internally, however, the core executes instructions out-of-order, as allowed by data dependencies. This allows independent instructions to execute concurrently. Finally, instruction results are written back to architecturally-visible state (the register file) in the order they were issued.

Consider our example out-of-order execution core (IMPL) shown in Figure 1b. The architectural register file (RF) contains the current state of the ISA-defined architectural registers. When an instruction is *issued*, new entries are allocated in both the dispatch and retirement buffers, and the register translation table (RTT) entry for the logical register corresponding to the instruction destination is updated. The RTT is used to locate the instruction's source data. Instructions are *dispatched*, possibly out-of-order, from the dispatch buffer (DB) to individual execution units when their operands are ready and an execution unit is available. When an instruction finishes execution, the result is *written back* to the retirement buffer (RB). This data is also bypassed into the DB for instructions awaiting that particular result. Finally, the RB logic must ensure that instruction results are *retired* (committed to architectural state) in the original program order. When an RB entry is retired, the RTT is informed so that the logical register entry corresponding to the instruction's destination can be updated if necessary. IMPL also accepts a special bubble flushing input in place of an instruction. Intuitively, a bubble is similar to a NOP instruction but does not affect any state or consume any resources after being issued.

We have made significant simplifying assumptions in our processor model: instructions have only one source operand, and only one issue and one retire can occur each cycle. Our model is out-of-order because the execution units have variable latency. We also omit a "front-end" with fetch, decode, and branch prediction logic. Omitting these features allowed our efforts to focus on the features which make the out-of-order verification problem difficult: the out-of-order execution and the large effective depth of the pipeline. The SVC verification reported in this paper used a model with unbounded buffers.

4 The Approach

The goal of our verification approach is to prove that the out-of-order implementation IMPL (as described by an HDL model) satisfies the ISA model. We define δ_i to be the implementation next-state function, which takes a state q_i and an input instruction i and returns a new state q_i', i.e., $q_i' = \delta_i(q_i, i)$. We extend δ_i in the obvious way to operate over input sequences $w = i_0 \ldots i_n$. We define δ_s similarly for ISA.

Let σ be a *size* function that returns the number of currently executing instructions, i.e., those that have been issued but not retired. We require that $\sigma(q_i^\circ) = 0$ for an initial implementation state q_i°. We define an instruction sequence w to be *completed* iff $\sigma(\delta_i(q_i^\circ, w)) = 0$, i.e., all instructions have been retired after executing w. We use the projection function $\pi_{\text{RF}}(q_i)$ to denote the register file contents in state q_i. For clarity in presentation, we define $q_{i1} \stackrel{\text{RF}}{=} q_{i2}$ to be $\pi_{\text{RF}}(q_{i1}) = \pi_{\text{RF}}(q_{i2})$, and we will sometimes use $\stackrel{\text{RF}}{=}$ when the projection π_{RF} is redundant on one side of the equality.

The overall correctness property for IMPL with respect to ISA is expressed as:
Correctness *For every completed instruction sequence w and initial state q_i°,*

$$\delta_i(q_i^\circ, w) \stackrel{\text{RF}}{=} \delta_s(\pi_{\text{RF}}(q_i^\circ), w).$$

That is, the architecturally visible state in IMPL and ISA is identical after executing any instruction sequence that retires all outstanding instructions in the implementation. This is the same commuting property used by several approaches, including [3]. Note that because our model is only an execution core, we are only checking the correctness of the register file. A (future) verification of a more complete processor model could check the program counter and memory.

We verify the correctness property by dealing with the out-of-order and in-order parts of IMPL separately. First, we derive an in-order intermediate abstraction (ABS) from IMPL. We then establish an equivalence relation between ABS and IMPL. In the second step, we demonstrate functional equivalence between ABS and ISA. By transitivity of equality of the final register file values, this establishes functional equivalences between IMPL and ISA.

5 First Step: Functional Equivalence of IMPL and ABS

ABS is derived directly from IMPL by removing the "out-of-orderness" while preserving the in-order buffering mechanism (Figure 2). In ABS, the DB has been removed: instructions are executed immediately upon issue. However, the results are queued and not written to architectural state until later. In the ABS model for this paper, instructions are issued, executed, and written into an annotated RB in one clock. The write-only annotated state in the RB contains some of the information lost with the DB removal and aids in finding invariants. ABS accepts the same `bubble` input as IMPL. We add an extra input to ABS called the *retirement flag* that signals when to retire the oldest instruction. ABS thus has more possible behaviors than IMPL: while instruction results are computed immediately in ABS, they may be buffered indefinitely in the annotated RB before being committed to architectural state.

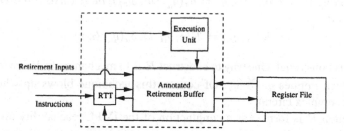

Fig. 2. Instruction flow in the intermediate abstraction.

We must prove that IMPL is a *refinement* of ABS. We define δ_a to be the ABS next-state function, which takes an initial state q_a and a pair consisting of an input instruction i and a Boolean-valued retirement input r, and returns a new state q_a', i.e., $q_a' = \delta_a(q_a, \langle i, r \rangle)$. The retirement input r indicates in each step of execution whether or not to retire a result. A retirement input r is *allowed* by a state q_a and input i iff r never tells ABS to retire an instruction when one is not waiting. Note that it is allowable for r to *not* retire a waiting instruction. We extend the definition of δ_a to sequences of instruction inputs w and retirement inputs $w_r = r_0 \ldots r_n$ such that $q_a' = \delta_a(q_a, \langle w, w_r \rangle)$[1].

We define states q_i of IMPL and q_a of ABS to be *consistent* when $q_i \stackrel{\text{RF}}{=} q_a$. We must demonstrate that:

---

[1] The pair of sequences $\langle w, w_r \rangle$ is easily derived from the corresponding sequence of pairs $\langle i_0, r_0 \rangle, \ldots, \langle i_n, r_n \rangle$.

Impl-ABS Refinement *For every completed instruction sequence w and every pair of consistent initial states q_i°, q_a°, there exists a sequence of retirement inputs w_r allowed by q_a° and w such that*

$$\delta_i(q_i^\circ, w) \overset{RF}{=} \delta_a(q_a^\circ, \langle w, w_r \rangle).$$

We prove that IMPL is a refinement of ABS by induction: we show that for each step that IMPL makes, there exists an ABS step such that the register files are identical. Forcing ABS to retire instructions in lock step with IMPL is straightforward. ABS retirement inputs are generated from an oracle which observes whether or not the IMPL is retiring an instruction and instructs ABS to do the same thing. We establish $q_i \overset{RF}{=} q_a$ by proving a stronger property. We derive a relation $\mathcal{R}$ between IMPL and ABS states such that: $\mathcal{R}(q_i, q_a) \Rightarrow (q_i \overset{RF}{=} q_a)$. We demonstrate that $\mathcal{R}$ is a *simulation relation* [9]:

Proof Obligation 1 (IMPL-ABS Equivalence)

1. *(Base Case) For every initial implementation state q_i°, there exists an initial ABS state q_a°, such that:*

$$\mathcal{R}(q_i^\circ, q_a^\circ).$$

2. *(Induction Step) For every instruction i, for every pair of consistent initial states q_i°, q_a°, and for every instruction sequence w and retirement sequence w_r with resulting states $q_i = \delta_i(q_i^\circ, w)$, $q_a = \delta_a(q_a^\circ, \langle w, w_r \rangle)$, there exists a retirement input r such that*

$$\mathcal{R}(q_i, q_a) \Rightarrow \mathcal{R}(\delta_i(q_i, i), \delta_a(q_a, \langle i, r \rangle)).$$

Deriving $\mathcal{R}$ is non-trivial. One way to construct $\mathcal{R}$ is to mechanically derive the weakest invariant which implies $q_i \overset{RF}{=} q_a$. Of course, this technique blows up when applied directly to a complex circuit.

The relation $\mathcal{R}$ is formed as a conjunction of the IMPL reachability invariant, the ABS reachability invariant, and assertions relating the IMPL state with the ABS state. The difficulties associated with deriving invariants are ubiquitous. We used an *ad hoc* collection of domain-specific techniques we found to be quite effective. The process of deriving and proving the reachable-state invariant for IMPL was simplified by recognizing that the out-of-order mechanism in a given cycle consists of a number of *transactions*—each of which operate on only part of IMPL state. In IMPL, these are *issue, dispatch, writeback,* and *retire*. The ABS reachability invariant is easily derived from the IMPL reachability invariant, because ABS is essentially a simple IMPL. Some IMPL state is not present in ABS, and other IMPL state has been renamed and is now part of the annotated RB.

We added *link assertions* which relate partially executed instructions in the DB and RB of IMPL to their counterparts in the annotated RB of ABS. The link assertions ensure that the partially executed instructions in the implementation always have the correct value or the information needed (pointers or data) to eventually compute the correct value. Run times and memory usage for proving the proof obligations on our example are reported in Section 7.

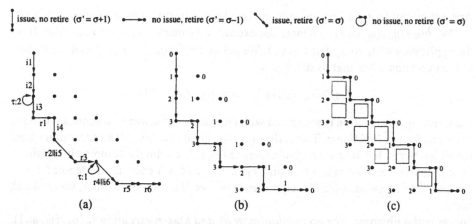

Fig. 3. (a) A *Max-n* execution ε_n. (b) An equivalent non-diagonal execution $\varepsilon_{\hat{n}}$. (c) An equivalent *Max-1* execution ε_1. Labels *in* and *rn* denote the issue and retirement of instruction number n. The label $rn\|in$ denotes simultaneous issue and retire. $\tau : n$ is a shorthand for n cycles where in each cycle, bubbles are issued and nothing is retired. The numbers indicate the sizes of each state. The squares indicate the distance between $\varepsilon_{\hat{n}}$ and ε_1.

6 Second Step: Functional Equivalence of ABS and ISA

In this section, we introduce incremental flushing, and use it to prove that ABS satisfies ISA. Formally, we desire to establish that:

ABS-ISA Equivalence *For every completed instruction sequence w, initial ABS state q_a°, and sequence of retirement inputs w_r allowed by w and q_a°:*

$$\delta_a(q_a^\circ, \langle w, w_r \rangle) \stackrel{\text{RF}}{=} \delta_s(\pi_{\text{RF}}(q_a^\circ), w).$$

ABS contains an annotated RB that queues instruction results before they are committed to architectural state. Recall that the Burch-Dill abstraction function *flushes* an implementation (by inserting bubbles) for the number of clock cycles necessary to completely expose the internal state. In the case of a simple five-stage pipeline, only five steps are required to complete the partially executed instructions. Following this approach with our model would compare a potentially full annotated RB with the ISA model. The Burch-Dill flushing technique would unroll ABS to the depth of the annotated RB, resulting in a logical expression too large for the decision procedure to check.

Our *incremental flushing* approach overcomes this unmanageable complexity. Instead of flushing the entire pipeline directly, a set of smaller, inductive flushing steps is performed. Taken together, these proof obligations imply the monolithic flushing operation. To illustrate, consider the graphical presentation of three different *executions* of ABS in Figure 3. We define the *execution* of a system as the sequence of states that the system passes through when executing a given pair of input sequences $\langle w, w_r \rangle$. For instance, the execution shown in Figure 3a is a result of executing the input sequence:

$$\langle i_1, \text{F} \rangle, \langle i_2, \text{F} \rangle, \langle \text{bubble}, \text{F} \rangle, \langle i_3, \text{F} \rangle, \langle \text{bubble}, \text{T} \rangle, \langle i_4, \text{F} \rangle,$$
$$\langle i_5, \text{T} \rangle, \langle \text{bubble}, \text{T} \rangle, \langle \text{bubble}, \text{F} \rangle, \langle i_6, \text{T} \rangle, \langle \text{bubble}, \text{T} \rangle, \langle \text{bubble}, \text{T} \rangle$$

Apart from self-loops, edges are only traversed when instructions are issued or retired.

We use $\varepsilon(q_a, \langle w, w_r \rangle)$ to denote the execution (sequence of states) resulting from the application of δ_a to q_a and $\langle w, w_r \rangle$. We define $last(\varepsilon(q_a, \langle w, w_r \rangle))$ as the last state of the execution. Note that by definition:

$$last(\varepsilon(q_a, \langle w, w_r \rangle)) = \delta_a(q_a, \langle w, w_r \rangle).$$

Each state in an execution is associated with the number of active instructions—defined earlier as the *size* function σ. This is illustrated in Figure 3c. We call an execution where for all states $\sigma \leq n$ a *Max-n* execution (denoted ε_n). Accordingly, completely serialized executions with at most one outstanding element are *Max-1* executions (denoted ε_1).

Our verification of ABS-ISA equivalence proceeds in two steps. First, we establish that:

Incremental Flushing *For every initial state q_a° and Max-n execution $\varepsilon_n(q_a, \langle w, w_r \rangle)$, there exists $\langle w^1, w_r^1 \rangle$ (derived from w, w_r by reordering issues and retires) and a corresponding Max-1 execution $\varepsilon_1(q_a, \langle w^1, w_r^1 \rangle)$ such that:*

$$last(\varepsilon_n(q_a^\circ, \langle w, w_r \rangle)) = last(\varepsilon_1(q_a^\circ, \langle w^1, w_r^1 \rangle)).$$

A *Max-1* execution is derived from a *Max-n* execution by reordering the issues and retires. This notion is based on the concept of *self-consistency*: execution results should be equivalent for certain classes of inputs [8]. The final results of *Max-n* and *Max-1* executions will be identical if we can prove inductively that reordering issue and retires for distinct instructions does not change the resulting state. Section 6.1 details the proof obligations for this step.

The second ABS-ISA verification step shows that all *Max-1* executions produce the same result as the ISA model.

Max-1 ABS-ISA Equivalence *For every initial state q_a°, and for every Max-1 execution ε_1 corresponding to an instruction sequence w^1 and allowed retirement sequence w_r^1:*

$$last(\varepsilon_1(q_a^\circ, \langle w^1, w_r^1 \rangle)) \stackrel{\text{RF}}{=} \delta_s(\pi_{\text{RF}}(q_a^\circ), w).$$

Proving this is much simpler than the original problem of directly proving ABS-ISA equivalence, since only one instruction is present in ABS at a time. The proof is carried out by induction on the length of instruction sequences, as described in Section 6.2.

6.1 Incremental Flushing

Space limitations prevent us from presenting the complete proofs justifying the incremental flushing approach. We will, however, state the verification steps and resulting proof obligations. We also include a proof sketch for the inductive step of incremental flushing.

The incremental flushing proof step can be split up into three proof obligations, as illustrated in Figure 4a-c. Recall that δ_a takes a state, an input, and a retirement input flag. We use T and F for the values of the retirement input flag, where T forces ABS to retire an instruction, and F prevents it from doing so. The first proof obligation demonstrates the independence of inserting and removing elements from the system:

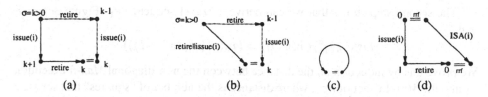

Fig. 4. (a) Proof Obligation 2, the nodes are labeled with their sizes. (b) Proof Obligation 3. (c) Proof Obligation 4. (d) Proof Obligation 5, the ISA induction step.

Proof Obligation 2 (Reordering Step) *For every reachable state q_a s.t. $\sigma(q_a) \geq 1$, and for every input i:*

$$\delta_a(\delta_a(q_a, \langle i, \text{F} \rangle), \langle \text{bubble}, \text{T} \rangle) = \delta_a(\delta_a(q_a, \langle \text{bubble}, \text{T} \rangle), \langle i, \text{F} \rangle).$$

In other words, we must show that the relative order of retirement and issue is immaterial for distinct instructions. The next proof obligation requires that simultaneous issue and retirement of distinct instructions yields the same result as a sequential retirement and issue:

Proof Obligation 3 (Parallel Correctness) *For every reachable state q_a s.t. $\sigma(q_a) \geq 1$, and for every input i:*

$$\delta_a(q_a, \langle i, \text{T} \rangle) = \delta_a(\delta_a(q_a, \langle \text{bubble}, \text{T} \rangle), \langle i, \text{F} \rangle).$$

The final proof obligation illustrates that bubble inputs without retirement do not change ABS state:

Proof Obligation 4 (Correctness of Self-Loops) *For every reachable state q_a:*

$$\delta_a(q_a, \langle \text{bubble}, \text{F} \rangle) = q_a.$$

Taken together, these three proof obligations establish the *Incremental Flushing* step of our verification, i.e., that every *Max-n* execution has a functionally equivalent *Max-1* execution. We next give a brief sketch of the proof.

Proof Sketch: We assume the three Proof Obligations shown above and must show that for every *Max-n* execution ε_n there exists a corresponding *Max-1* execution ε_1 such that

$$last(\varepsilon_n(q_a^\circ, \langle w, w_r \rangle)) = last(\varepsilon_1(q_a^\circ, \langle w^1, w_r^1 \rangle)).$$

We perform the proof in two steps, as illustrated in Figure 3. Given an execution ε_n (Figure 3a) we first show that we can construct a "non-diagonal" execution $\varepsilon_{\hat{n}}$ (Figure 3b) from ε_n that does not have any diagonals nor self-loops, and such that

$$last(\varepsilon_n(q_a^\circ, \langle w, w_r \rangle)) = last(\varepsilon_{\hat{n}}(q_a^\circ, \langle \hat{w}, \hat{w}_r \rangle)).$$

This is proved by induction on the length of ε_n. We use Proof Obligation 3 to replace any diagonal edge with horizontal and vertical edges. Proof Obligation 4 is used to remove the self-loops.

The second step shows that we can derive a *Max*-1 sequence ε_1 (Figure 3c) such that

$$last(\varepsilon_{\hat{n}}(q_a^\circ, \langle \hat{w}, \hat{w}_r \rangle)) = last(\varepsilon_1(q_a^\circ, \langle w^1, w_r^1 \rangle)).$$

We prove this by induction on the distance between the non-diagonal *Max-$\hat{n}$* execution $\varepsilon_{\hat{n}}$ and the *Max*-1 execution ε_1, where distance is the number of "squares" that separate the two executions. For example, eight squares separate the executions in Figures 3b and 3c. We repeatedly apply Proof Obligation 2, "folding" the *Max-$\hat{n}$* execution $\varepsilon_{\hat{n}}$ back to the corresponding *Max*-1 execution ε_1. This is possible because the input sequences resulting in ε_n and $\varepsilon_{\hat{n}}$ are completed (defined in Section 4). Each folding is a reordering of independent retires and issues.
End Proof Sketch.

Note that each folding is a rewrite of the execution. It is easy to see that Proof Obligations 2–4 together are a confluent (Church-Rosser) set of rewrite rules, where the *Max*-1 execution is the unique normal form.

6.2 *Max*-1 ABS-ISA Equivalence

The final verification step is to show that all *Max*-1 executions of ABS are functionally equivalent with ISA. We can divide the *Max*-1 execution up into issue-retire fragments that are simple "steps" in the graphical illustration. The proof is a simple induction on the number of these fragments, comparing the execution and retirement of an arbitrary instruction from an arbitrary ABS *Max*-1 state with the result that is retired by ISA. This is illustrated in Figure 4d. Formally:

Proof Obligation 5 (ABS-ISA Induction) *For every initial IA state q_a° and every instruction i:*

$$\delta_a(\delta_a(q_a^\circ, \langle i, \text{F} \rangle), \langle \text{bubble}, \text{T} \rangle) \stackrel{\text{RF}}{=} \delta_s(\pi_{\text{RF}}(q_a^\circ), i).$$

Because we have previously shown that a functionally equivalent *Max*-1 execution can be derived from an arbitrary *Max-n* execution, this step completes the proof of ABS-ISA equivalence.

7 Results

We have mechanically checked Proof Obligations 1-5 for our models using the Stanford Validity Checker (SVC). The three models (IMPL, ABS, and ISA) and the proof obligations were written in a Lisp-like HDL. The proof formulas were constructed by symbolically simulating the models in Lisp. SVC was invoked through a foreign-function interface to decide the validity of the formulas. SVC's built-in support for linear arithmetic was used to model buffer pointers for the IMPL, RB, and ABS annotated RB. We also extended SVC with special read and write updates to support the writeback to the associative memory in the dispatch buffer.

The total CPU run times and number of case splits required are enumerated in Figure 5. The number of case splits is a rough indicator of the relative complexity of the simplified formula.

IMPL-ABS Verification	IMPL Reach. Inv. CPU (sec)	Case Splits	IMPL-ABS CPU (sec)	Case Splits
Base Case	1.9	10	0.7	4
Issue	454.8	26,214	130.9	18,686
Dispatch	49.1	12,036	163.3	45,828
Writeback	35.0	842	42.1	4,426
Retire	29.5	8,392	307.0	59,474

(a)

ABS-ISA Verification	CPU (sec)	Case Splits
ABS Inv.	222.2	48,440
Obl. 2	37.6	530
Obl. 3	26.2	2
Obl. 4	7.0	2
Obl. 5	17.8	14

(b)

Fig. 5. (a) SVC run-times and number of case splits required for Proof Obligation 1, specified for each IMPL transaction. (b) SVC run-times and case splits for the verification of ABS. All runs performed on a 200-MHz Intel Pentium Pro system running Redhat Linux.

8 Discussion

Our work addresses two of the major problems in symbolic verification of out-of-order processor designs: the complexity of the out-of-order scheduling logic and the deep effective length of the pipeline. While our IMPL example is far simpler than an actual out-of-order implementation, it is representative of the architectural features which make out-of-order verification difficult for existing techniques.

There is still much work to be accomplished in addressing the complexity limitations encountered by formal methods on practical industrial designs. As these problems are solved, we expect that our approach will be directly applicable. We also anticipate that the incremental flushing approach will find use in a wide variety of verification problems involving very deep pipelines, such as digital-signal processing.

We are currently formalizing the incremental flushing theory in the PVS theorem prover [12]. For each new design, PVS will automatically instantiate the proof obligations and pass them to SVC for automatic verification.

Acknowledgments

We thank Mark Aagaard, Tom Melham, and Carl Seger for reading drafts of this paper. They each provided detailed and helpful feedback.

The second author is supported at Stanford by an NDSEG graduate fellowship. The other authors are partially supported by DARPA under contract number E276. Insight about the difficulties associated with verifying pipelined processors was developed while the third author was a visiting professor at Intel's Strategic CAD Labs in the summer of 1995.

References

1. C. Barrett, D. L. Dill, and J. Levitt. Validity checking for combinations of theories with equality. In *FMCAD '96*, volume 1166 of *LNCS*, pages 187–201, Stanford, CA, USA, November 1996. Springer-Verlag.
2. J. R. Burch. Techniques for verifying superscalar microprocessors. In *DAC*, pages 552–557, Las Vegas, Nevada, USA, June 1996. ACM Press.

3. J. R. Burch and D. L. Dill. Automatic verification of microprocessor control. In David L. Dill, editor, *CAV*, volume 818 of *LNCS*, pages 68–80, Stanford, California, USA, June 1994. Springer-Verlag.
4. W. Damm and A. Pnueli. Verifying out-of-order executions. In H.F. Li and D.K. Probst, editors, *CHARME '97*, pages 23–47, Montreal, Canada, October 1997. Chapman & Hall.
5. J. L. Hennessy and D. A. Patterson. *Computer Architecture: A Quantitative Approach*. Morgan Kaufmann, 1990.
6. T. A. Henzinger, S. Qadeer, and S. K. Rajamani. You assume, we guarantee: Methodology and case studies. Technical report, Electronics Research Lab, Univ. of Californaia, Berkeley, CA 94720, 1998.
7. R. B. Jones, D. L. Dill, and J. R. Burch. Efficient validity checking for processor verification. In *ICCAD'95*, November 1995.
8. R. B. Jones, C.-J. H. Seger, and D. L. Dill. Self-consistency checking. In *FMCAD '96*, volume 1166 of *LNCS*, pages 159–171, Stanford, CA, USA, November 1996. Springer-Verlag.
9. B. Jonsson. On decomposing and refining specifications of distributed systems. In J. W. de Bakker, W.-P. de Roever, and G. Rozenberg, editors, *Stepwise Refinement of Distributed Systems. Models, Formalisms, Correctness.*, volume 430 of *LNCS*, pages 361–385, Mook, The Netherlands, May-June 1989. Springer-Verlag.
10. S. Katz. Refinement with global equivalence proofs in temporal logic. In D. A. Peled, V. R. Pratt, and G. J. Holzmann, editors, *Partial Order Methods in Verification*, volume 29 of *DIMACS, Series in Discrete Mathematics and Theoretical Computer Science*, pages 59–78, Princeton, NJ, USA, 1996. Amer. Math. Society.
11. K. McMillan. Verification of an implementation of Tomasulo's algorithm by compositional model checking. Appears in this volume.
12. S. Owre, S. Rajan, J. M. Rushby, N. Shankar, and M. K. Srivas. PVS: Combining specification, proof checking, and model checking. In R. Alur and T.A. Henzinger, editors, *CAV '96*, volume 1102 of *LNCS*, pages 411–414, New Brunswick, NJ, July/Aug 1996. Springer-Verlag.
13. J. Sawada and W. A. Hunt. Processor verification with precise exceptions and speculative execution. Appears in this volume.
14. J. Sawada and W. A. Hunt. Trace table based approach for pipelined microprocessor verification. In Orna Grumberg, editor, *CAV '97*, volume 1254 of *LNCS*, pages 364–375, Haifa, Israel, June 1997. Springer-Verlag.
15. P. J. Windley and J. R. Burch. Mechanically checking a lemma used in an automatic verification tool. In *FMCAD'96*, pages 362–376, November 1996.

Verification of an Implementation of Tomasulo's Algorithm by Compositional Model Checking

K. L. McMillan

Cadence Berkeley Labs
2001 Addison St., 3rd floor
Berkeley, CA 94704-1103
mcmillan@cadence.com

Abstract. An implementation of an out-of-order processing unit based on Tomasulo's algorithm is formally verified using compositional model checking techniques. This demonstrates that finite-state methods can be applied to such algorithms, without recourse to higher-order proof systems. The paper introduces a novel compositional system that supports cyclic environment reasoning and multiple environment abstractions per signal. A proof of Tomasulo's algorithm is outlined, based on refinement maps, and relying on the novel features of the compositional system. This proof is fully verified by the SMV verifier, using symmetry to reduce the number of assertions that must be verified.

1 Introduction

We present the formal design verification of an "out-of-order" processing unit based on Tomasulo's algorithm [Tom67]. This and related techniques such as "register renaming" are used in modern microprocessors [LR97] to keep multiple or deeply pipelined execution units busy by executing instructions in data-flow order, rather than sequential order. The complex variability of instruction flow in "out-of-order" processors presents a significant opportunity for undetected errors, compared to an "in-order" pipelined machine where the flow of instructions is fixed and orderly. Unfortunately, this variability also makes formal verification of such machines difficult. They are beyond the present capacity of methods based on integrated decision procedures [BD94], and are not amenable to symbolic trajectory analysis [JNB96].

This paper was inspired by Damm and Pnueli, who recently presented a pencil-and-paper proof of an implementation of Tomasulo's algorithm [DP97]. This proof is in two stages, first refining a sequential specification to an intermediate model based on partially ordered executions, and then refining this model to the implementation. The proof presented here has several advantages over this earlier work. First, it is conceptually simpler, since we refine the specification directly to the implementation, with no intermediate step, and no need to reason about second-order objects such as sets or partial orders. Second, the proof here is fully mechanically checked, using a verifier based on symbolic model checking. Although in principle, the proof of [DP97] can be carried out in a higher order prover such as PVS [ORSS94], this would require considerable elaboration. Here, the use of model checking to handle the details of the proof allows the proof to be presented here in the same form in which it is actually presented to the verifier. Third, the implementation here is at the bit level, meaning that it can be either synthesized automatically into gates and latches, or compared directly to a manual implementation by combinational equivalence checking methods [KSL95]. The disadvantage of the present proof is that it applies to only a given fixed configuration of the implementation. However, the proof is easily reverified for any desired configuration.

The compositional system used to construct the proof is similar in principle to the work of Abadi and Lamport [AL93], in that it allows the use of environment assumptions in a cyclic manner. As in [AL95], the proof relies on refinement maps. However, there are several distinctions. First, the system allows the use of synchronous processes with zero delay (*i.e.*, combinational logic), whereas [AL93] uses interleaving processes. Second, whereas in [AL95], the refinement maps are functions from implementation state to specification state, here maps in either direction may be used (though they are mostly in the opposite direction, from specification to implementation). They are expressed as processes within the system, and may be one-to-many. Third, all of the lemmas here are verified by model checking, rather than by manual proof or automated proof assistants. Hence, the degree of automation is greater (though far from complete).

Two techniques here are novel relative to previous work in compositional model checking. The first is the compositional rule, which is more general than those of [AH96, McM97] in that it allows the conjunction of multiple environment processes constraining the same signal, while still allowing cyclic environment reasoning. This ability is key to decomposing the proof of Tomasulo's algorithm. Second, the verification system exploits symmetry to reduce the number of proof obligations that need to be verified. This is key to the tractability of proof checking in the present example.

In this article, we begin with a brief overview of the compositional system and its implementation in the SMV model checking tool [McM93] (section 2). Then we introduce an implementation of Tomasulo's algorithm, and prove its correctness w.r.t. an executable specification within the compositional system (section 3). Finally, we show how SMV uses symmetries to reduce proof obligations to a tractable number (section 4), and conclude with some observations and areas for future work (section 5).

2 Proof framework

In this section, we briefly sketch the compositional system and its implementation as part of the SMV verifier.

A compositional system Let S be a finite set of *signals*, and V be a finite set of *values*. A *model* is a function $\pi : S \to \mathbb{N} \to V$ assigning an infinite sequence of values to each signal. A *process* is a predicate on models. It constrains the value of exactly one signal as a function of other signals, with either zero delay (a gate) or unit delay (a latch). A gate p is a predicate of the form: for all $t \geq 0$,

$$\sigma_p(t) \in f(\gamma_1(t) \ldots \gamma_k(t))$$

where $\sigma_p, \gamma_1 \ldots \gamma_k$ are signals, and f is a function $V^k \to 2^V$. That is, the set of possible values of σ_p at time t is a function of signals $\gamma_1 \ldots \gamma_k$ at time t. A latch

p is a predicate of the form

$$\sigma_p(t) \in \begin{cases} v_0 & ; t = 0 \\ f(\gamma_1(t-1)\ldots\gamma_k(t-1)) & ; t > 0 \end{cases}$$

That is, v_0 is the set of possible initial values of σ_p, and f gives the set of possible values of σ_p as a function of signals $\gamma_1\ldots\gamma_k$ one time unit earlier. We assume the functions f never return the empty set.

Composition of processes in this system is simply conjunction. That is, the composition of two processes p_1 and p_2 is $p_1 \wedge p_2$. Now, suppose we are given two sets of processes: a specification P and an implementation Q, and we would like to prove $(\bigwedge Q) \Rightarrow (\bigwedge P)$. That is, the composition of the implementation processes implies the composition of the specification processes. Using a "compositional" approach, we would verify each component of P independently, using some small subset of Q. For example, we might prove that $q_1 \Rightarrow p_1, q_2 \Rightarrow p_2, \ldots$ and thus avoid the complexity of considering all of the processes at once. Often, however, this approach fails, as each process q_i functions correctly only given some constraints on its "environment". Absent these constraints, it will not satisfy its part of the specification, hence the compositional proof will fail.

As observed in [AL93], we must typically assume that process q_2 satisfies some specification p_2 to prove that q_1 satisfies p_1, and *vice versa*. This apparent circularity can be broken by induction over time. That is, let the notation $p \uparrow^\tau$ stand for $\forall t \leq \tau.\ p$, or "p holds up to time $t = \tau$". We can soundly reason as follows, by induction on τ:

$$\frac{p_1 \uparrow^{\tau-1} \Rightarrow p_2 \uparrow^\tau \qquad p_2 \uparrow^\tau \Rightarrow p_1 \uparrow^\tau}{\forall t.\ (p_2 \wedge p_1)}$$

In the base case, when $\tau = 0$, note that $p_1 \uparrow^{\tau-1}$ is a tautology. Hence, we have $p_2 \uparrow^0$, and thus $p_1 \uparrow^0$, $p_2 \uparrow^1$, $p_1 \uparrow^1$ and so on. By reasoning inductively, we use each process's specification as the environment of the other, avoiding circularity. In general, given a well-founded order $\prec$ on P, when proving $p \uparrow^\tau$ we assume $p' \uparrow^\tau$ if $p' \prec p$ and $p' \uparrow^{\tau-1}$ otherwise. This rule of inference is stated formally in the following meta-theorem. We use $\mathcal{E}_p$ to stand for the environment of p and Z_p to stand for those processes which may be assumed with "zero delay" when proving p:

$$Z_p = Q \cup \{p' \in P : p' \prec p\}$$

Note that p itself may be in $\mathcal{E}_p$, but by definition, $p \notin Z_p$. Now, letting a set of processes stand for the conjunction of its components, and Z_p^c stand for the complement of Z_p, we have:

Theorem 1. *For all $p \in P$, let $\mathcal{E}_p \subseteq P \cup Q$. If, for each $p \in P$,*

$$(\mathcal{E}_p \cap Z_p) \uparrow^\tau \wedge (\mathcal{E}_p \cap Z_p^c) \uparrow^{\tau-1} \Rightarrow p$$

is valid, then $(\forall t.\ Q) \Rightarrow (\forall t.\ P)$ is valid.

Proof. Let $\sqsubset$ be the lexical order s.t. $(t, i) \sqsubset (t', i')$ iff $t < t'$ or $t = t'$ and $i \prec i'$. Then $p_i(t)$ holds by induction over $\sqsubset$.

Note that this rule allows us to assume that some environment process p_j holds for all times from 0 to τ when proving that p_i holds at $\tau + 1$ (or τ itself in the zero delay case). This allows us to take into account reachability from the initial state, using model checking techniques. Thus, the technique is quite different from proving mutually inductive invariants, as is typically done using theorem provers. Also, though the rule is similar to [AL93] in that it allows the cyclic use of environment assumptions, it differs in that it applies to synchronous processes that can have zero delay (as opposed to their interleaving, unit delay model). Other systems based on synchronous processes, such as [Kur94, GL94], do not allow cyclic assumptions. Further, the above rule allows environment assumptions to contain the conjunction of many processes constraining the same signal, whereas [McM97, AH96] do not. This ability is key to the proof presented here of Tomasulo's algorithm, in that it allows for case analysis.

Implementation in SMV In the SMV implementation of the above system, a "process" is an assignment of an expression to a signal (where the parameter t is implicit). Syntactically, a gate is written in this form:

```
signal := expression;
```

while a "latch" appears thus:

```
init(signal) := expression1;
next(signal) := expression2;
```

Here, $\text{init}(\sigma)$ stands for $\sigma(0)$ and $\text{next}(\sigma)$ stands for $\sigma(t+1)$. Assignments are grouped into named collections called "layers", as follows:

```
layer <name> : { <assignment1> <assignment2> ... }
```

Within a layer, a given signal may be assigned only once. Thus, an assignment (*i.e.* process) can be uniquely identified by a signal-layer pair, which is written `signal//layer`. The environment for proving a given specification component is determined by statements of the form

```
using signal1//layer1 prove signal2//layer2;
```

The well-founded order $\prec$ is determined automatically in most cases. SMV assumes that an assumption about signal σ_1 should be used to prove an assertion about σ_2 with zero delay only when there is some actual zero-delay dependency path from σ_1 to σ_2. In order to guarantee a well-founded order, however, there must be no zero-delay path from σ_2 to σ_1. This leaves an ambiguity in the case of assignments to the same signal, or to two signals on a zero-delay cycle. To resolve this, the user can enter declarations of the form

```
layer1 refines layer2;
```

indicating that `layer1` assignments should precede `layer2` assignments in the order. SMV then determines for each environment component whether it is in Z_p, and hence whether it is assumed up to τ or $\tau - 1$ when proving $p \uparrow^\tau$.

Verification by model checking The actual verification of each specification component p is done by symbolic model checking [BCM+92, McM93]. This topic is mainly beyond the scope of this article. However, for the reader familiar with these methods, we outline one possible (but highly simplified) implementation, the understanding of which is not material to what follows. Briefly, the conjunction of the zero-delay environment assumptions ($\mathcal{E}_p \cap Z_p$) is translated into a symbolically represented Kripke model (S_0, R_0, I_0). Here S_0 is a state invariant term derived from the gates, R_0 is a symbolic transition relation and I_0 is an initial condition (the latter two deriving from the latches). Similarly, the unit-delay environment assumptions $(\mathcal{E}_p \cap Z_p^c)$ are translated into a model (S_1, R_1, I_1), and p is translated into (S_p, R_p, I_p). Then our proof goal:

$$(\mathcal{E}_p \cap Z_p) \uparrow^\tau \wedge (\mathcal{E}_p \cap Z_p^c) \uparrow^{\tau-1} \Rightarrow p$$

is true iff the Mu-Calculus formula

$$(I_0 \wedge I_1 \wedge \mu H. (A \vee B \vee \operatorname{Img}^{-1}(R_0 \wedge R_1, H))) \vee (I_0 \wedge S_0 \wedge \neg(S_p \wedge I_p))$$

is empty, where $A = \operatorname{Img}^{-1}(R_0, S_0 \wedge \neg S_p)$, $B = \operatorname{Img}^{-1}(R_0 \wedge \neg R_p, S_0)$ and $\operatorname{Img}^{-1}(R, S)$ the the inverse image of S w.r.t. R. This formula can be evaluated using symbolic model checking methods, and a counterexample trace generated if the result is nonempty.

Auxiliary variables Often it is necessary to introduce auxiliary variables either as part of a specification, or part of the proof (as introduced by Owicki and Gries [OG76]). The definitions of these variables (or signals in our case) can be assumed, provided they are a "conservative extension". Formally, this means that if $\mathcal{S}_A$ is the set of auxiliary signals, Q is the implementation, and A is the set of auxiliary signal definitions, then $Q \Rightarrow \exists \mathcal{S}_A.(Q \wedge A)$. That is, for every implementation behavior, there exists a feasible valuation of the auxiliary signals. In this case, if we can prove that $Q \wedge A \Rightarrow P$, then we infer that $Q \Rightarrow \exists \mathcal{S}_A.P$. The following conditions are sufficient to ensure conservative extension:

1. Every signal in $\mathcal{S}_A$ has a unique assignment in A,
2. No assignment in Q refers to any signal in $\mathcal{S}_A$, and
3. There are no zero-delay cycles in A

In the SMV system, auxiliary variables are declared with the keyword **abstract**. The system guarantees that the above three conditions are met. As we will see, auxiliary variables allow us to use recorded history information in compositional proofs. We can then use these variables to express abstractions of the actual implementation variables. Used in specifications, they also allow us to express any regular-language property, which otherwise would not be possible.

3 Verifying Tomasulo's algorithm

In this section, we introduce Tomasulo's algorithm, and show how a proof of correctness can be constructed in the foregoing framework and mechanically checked using symbolic model checking. The proof is based on auxiliary variables and refinement maps. These maps can be viewed as an interpretation of the intended semantics of the various components of the implementation state.

Tomasulo's algorithm We consider here a pipelined arithmetic unit Q, executing a stream of operations on a register file. Tomasulo's algorithm allows execution of instructions in data-flow order, rather than sequential order. This can increase the throughput of the unit, by avoiding pipeline stalls. Each pending instruction is held in a "reservation station" until the values of its operands become available, then issued "out-of-order".

The flow of instructions is pictured in figure 1. Each instruction, as it arrives, fetches its operands from a special register file. Each register in this

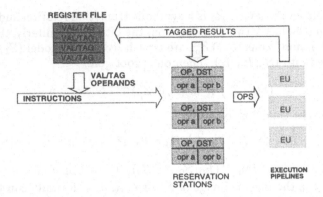

Fig. 1. Flow of instructions in Tomasulo's algorithm

```
stallout := {0,1};
if(~stallout)
  switch(opin){
    ADD_OP : {
      opr_a := r[srca];  opr_b := r[srcb];
      res := opr_a + opr_b;
      next(r[dst]) := res;
    }
    RD_OP : {
      dout := r[srca];
    }
    ...
```

Fig. 2. Specification code (partial).

file holds either an actual value, or a "tag" indicating the reservation station that will produce the register value when it completes. The instruction and its operands (either values or tags) are stored in a reservation station (RS). The RS watches the results returning from the execution pipelines, and when a result's tag matches one of its operands, it records the value in place of the tag. When the station has the values of all of its operands, it may issue its instruction to an execution pipeline. When the tagged result returns from the pipeline, the RS is cleared, and the result value, if needed, is stored in the destination register. However, if a subsequent instruction has modified the register tag, the result is discarded, since its value in a sequential execution would be overwritten.

The arithmetic unit also has instructions that read register values to an external output and write values from an external input, and has a "stall" output, indicating that an instruction cannot be executed because either there is no available RS, or the value of the register to be read is not yet available.

Verification approach The specification is a machine P that executes instructions in order as they arrive, and stalls nondeterministically. A fragment of the SMV code is shown in figure 2. Our goal is to prove that implementation Q implies specification P, with internal variables S_A projected. That is, $Q \Rightarrow \exists S_A . P$.

We introduce auxiliary variables for each RS, and refinement maps relating the specification state, auxiliary variables and implementation state. Finally we verify these relations using the compositional rule. We thus decompose the proof into "lemmas" small enough to be verified by model checking.[1]

Auxiliary variables We begin this decomposition by introducing new state components. When an RS is loaded with an instruction, we record the actual values of the instruction operands and result, according to the specification machine. In SMV we have:

```
if(~stallout & IS_PIPE_OP){
    next(hist[st_choice].opr_a) := opr_a;
    next(hist[st_choice].opr_b) := opr_b;
    next(hist[st_choice].res) := res;
}
```

where hist is the array of auxiliary variables, and st_choice is the reservation station to which the arriving instruction is assigned. Because these are auxiliary variables, we cannot refer to them in the implementation. However, we can use them in refinement maps that specify components of the implementation state.

Refinement maps The first refinement map states that if a given implementation register holds a value (and not a tag), then that value must equal the "real" register value in the specification machine. In SMV, we write:

```
layer map1 :
  forall(i in REG)
    if(~ir[i].resvd) ir[i].val := r[i];
```

where ir is the implementation register file, and resvd is a bit indicating that the register holds a tag. The second maps states that, if a register holds a tag, the actual register value must equal the result of the indicated RS (an auxiliary variable):

```
forall(i in REG)
  layer  map2[i] :
    forall(j in TAG)
      if(ir[i].resvd & ir[i].tag = j){
        st[j].valid := 1;
        hist[j].res := r[i];
      }
```

Here, st is the RS array, valid is a bit indicating the station is full. The third map defines the "producer/consumer" relation between RS's. It states that if station j holds an operand value, then that value is the actual operand value. Otherwise, if station j is waiting for an operand from station k, then the result value of k is the actual operand value of j. This is the statement in SMV for the "a" operand (the "b" operand is similar):

```
forall(j in TAG)
  layer map3a[j] :
    if(st[j].valid){
      if(st[j].opr_a.valid) st[j].opr_a.val := hist[j].opr_a;
      else hist[j].opr_a.tag].res := hist[j].opr_a;
    }
```

[1] The implementation and part of the proof text are omitted here for space reasons. See http://www-cad.eecs.berkeley.edu/~kenmcmil for their complete text.

Note here that opr_a, the "a" operand field of the RS, has three subfields: valid indicates that the value is available, val is the value, and otherwise, tag is the tag. The final map states that, if a value returns on the result bus with a tag j, then it must be the actual result of RS j:

```
forall (j in TAG)
  layer map4[j] :
    if(pout.tag = j & pout.valid) pout.val := hist[j].res;
```

Here, pout is the result bus, which has three fields: valid, indicating a result is present, tag, indicating a reservation station, and val, the result value.

Compositional proof Now we give the environment for proving each of the above maps. The compositional system allows us to use any map as an assumption when proving another, even in an apparently circular manner, while ensuring that the proof is inductively sound. The flow of this proof roughly follows the progress of an instruction through the machine, as follows:

1. map2: For each pair i, j if register i contains tag j, then the result of RS j must be the actual value of register i. This is verified using only the implementations of register i and RS j.
2. map3 ("else" case): For each pair j, k, if RS j holds tag k as an operand, then the result value of k is the operand value of j. This is verified using map2 and the implementations of RS's j and k.
3. map3 ("if" case): The operand values obtained by RS j are always correct. Since operand values may come from the register file or the result bus, we need to assume both map1 (for all registers) and map4. Since map4 gives the result bus value in terms of the RS results, we also need map3 for each RS result. We also use the implementation of RS j.
4. map4: Result bus values tagged j match RS j's result. To guarantee the operands used are correct we use map3. We also use the execution pipeline, RS j (including auxiliary vars) and the specification ALU.
5. map1: Values in implementation register i are correct. We use map4 and map3 (for each RS result) to prove this.

Note, for example, the circularity in steps 3–5. Also note that, with other refinement maps as the "environment", each of the maps is verified using the implementations of at most two registers or RS's, leaving the others as free variables. This addresses the state explosion problem and makes the verification by model checking tractable. The general principle is to break the proof down into lemmas relating pairs of array elements, rather than considering entire arrays.

As an example, consider the producer/consumer lemma (map3). We want to show that when RS j holds tag k as an operand, the result value of k must be the operand value of j. Suppose that an instruction is loaded into RS j, with register i as its source operand, and suppose that register i holds tag k. Now, map2 states that the result of station k (hist[k].res) is in fact the correct value for register i (r[i]). It follows that at the next time the operand of j will be equal to the result of k (which is what we are trying to prove). The behavior of the reservation stations guarantees that this will continue to be true as long as station j holds tag k, since neither station can change until a result value for tag k returns on the result bus.

We don't need to spell out the above reasoning, however. To verify the lemma, we just apply model checking, assuming map2 holds between RS k and all registers i. In SMV, this is expressed as follows (for the "a" operand):

```
using hist[k].res//map2[i] prove hist[k].res//map3a[j];
```

If there are n registers, then in checking the lemma we are actually using a simultaneous conjunction of $n + 1$ assignments to hist[k].res. One is the definition of this signal as an auxiliary variable and the others are maps that give its value as a function of each specification register. This allows us to prove the correctness of station k relative to each register i as a separate case, then to combine these cases to prove our lemma. The ability to use multiple assignments to the same signal in the environment is thus key to the tractability of the proof.

Verification by model checking As mentioned earlier, the SMV system translates each refinement map verification problem into a symbolic model checking problem. BDD-based methods are then used to either verify the map or produce a counterexample. A counterexample can indicate either that the map doesn't hold, or that insufficient environment assumptions were used.

Note that, using model checking, we can only verify a fixed finite configuration of the processor. For example, with 32-bit data, 16 registers, 16 RS's, and one four-stage execution pipeline with one operation (integer addition) the total model checking time (to verify all the refinement maps and the unit outputs) is 92 seconds, running on a 266MHz Pentium II processor, and a total of 52454 OBDD nodes used.[2]

Several factors make the verification tractable. First, by stating refinement maps and choosing environments appropriately, the number of state variables is reduced to a tractable level. One important factor in this process is "bit slicing". That is, for most of the data-related refinement maps, we treat each bit of the data path separately. This is done automatically by SMV, which prunes away those parts of the model which have no influence on the property being verified. The only exception is the verification of the execution pipeline, in which there are clearly dependencies between data bits.

4 Exploiting symmetry

The final important factor is the exploitation of symmetry. Notice that several of the refinement maps have an instance for each register/station or station/station pair (and also for each bit of the data path, if we use bit slicing). The number of lemmas to be proved is thus on the order of $R \times S \times B$ or $S \times S \times B$, where R is the number of registers, S is the number of stations and B is the number of bits. However, by exploiting symmetry we can reduce this to a small number of representative cases. Space allows only a brief synopsis of this technique here.

---

[2] In fact, the verification of the processor as described here fails, due to a design error. A register bypass is needed to handle the case when an instruction arrives exactly at the moment one of its operands is returning on the result bus. This requires the addition of a one-line refinement map, not described here. The verification time given is for the corrected version. Note also that if floating point arithmetic were used, more elaborate techniques would be required to verify the arithmetic at the bit level. Arithmetic verification, however, is beyond the scope of this work.

Scalarsets in SMV To express symmetries, the SMV language has been augmented with scalarset types, as used in the Murphi language [ID96]. A scalarset is a finite type, whose use is restricted such that a program's semantics is invariant under permutations of elements of the type. A scalarset type is introduced by a declaration such as:

```
scalarset TAG 0..15;
```

which creates a type called TAG with 16 values. Although these values are nominally in the range 0..15, no constants of a scalarset type may occur in the program. Values of scalarset type may appear only in certain symmetric constructions:

1. Two expressions of the same scalarset type may be compared for equality.
2. The index type of an array may be a scalarset. Subscripts applied to the array must be of the same type. For example, if x is of type TAG and z of type array TAG of boolean, then one could write z[x], but not z[0].
3. In a forall statement of the form:

    ```
    forall (i in type) { <statements> }
    ```

    the type may be a scalarset. The semantics of this statement is the conjunction of statements for all i in type.[3]
4. Any commutative/associative operator may be applied as a "reduction operator" over a scalarset type. For example we can take the conjunction of the elements of z as follows:

    ```
    &[ z[i] : i in TAG]
    ```

    Similarly, a "comprehension expression" can be formed over a scalarset type. For example, this expression {i : i in TAG, z[i]} denotes the set of values i in the type TAG such that z[i] is true.

Symmetry reduction technique The meaning of each of the above constructs is unchanged if we exchange the roles of any pair of elements of a scalarset type. As a result, the overall program semantics is invariant. So, if we have two assertions p_1 and p_2, such that one is obtained from the other by some permutation of scalarset values, then p_1 holds iff p_2 holds. Hence we need only verify p_1. SMV uses this fact in the following way: given a parameterized class of assertions to prove, SMV chooses a representative set of instances of the class, such that any instance can be reduced to one in the set by permuting scalarset values. For example, suppose that an arbiter is to acknowledge exactly one user of a resource, and that type "user" is a scalarset. The assertion mutex[i][j] states that users i and j are not acknowledged at the same time, if $i \neq j$. Here, two representative cases, mutex[0][0] and mutex[0][1], suffice. All cases where $i = j$ reduce to the former, while all cases where $i \neq j$ reduce to the latter. In general, if we have k parameters of a given scalarset type, then no more than $k!$ instances are required, regardless of the type's size.

In the case of Tomasulo's algorithm, we have three scalarset types: REG, TAG and BIT, corresponding to registers, RS's, and bits of the data path, respectively. The "producer/consumer" lemma, for example, is a class of proof obligations of the form:

---

[3] As an aside for those familiar with Murphi, the use of a forall construct rather than an iterative for loop as in Murphi simplifies the rules for scalarsets, since there is no need to check for possible "side effects" between loop iterations.

```
hist[k].res[i]//map3a[j]
```

where j and k are tags, and i is a bit index, stating that when RS j points to RS k, bit i of k's result is bit i of j's operand. There are $R^2 \times B$ instances to prove, which reduce to two representatives: `hist[0].res[0]//map3a[0]` and `hist[1].res[0]//map3a[0]`. If there are 16 RS's and 32 bits, then a factor of 8192/2 in run time is saved.

Symmetry breaking In the case of Tomasulo's algorithm, the symmetry of the scalarset types is broken in several places. For example, the arithmetic unit breaks the symmetry of the data path bits, and the logic that selects an RS for the arriving instruction breaks the tag symmetry. Assignments that break the symmetry of a scalarset can be introduced with a declaration such as the following:

```
breaking (BIT)
   res := opr_a + opr_b;
```

which defines the adder function in the specification. The system ensures that a symmetry reduction over a given scalarset type is not performed when an assignment breaking that type's symmetry is used in the "environment". This allows us to localize the effect of symmetry breaking. For example, since the "producer/consumer" lemma does not depend on the adder function, we can still make use of the bit symmetry when proving it.

5   Conclusion

We have seen that it is possible using compositional model checking methods to formally verify an out-of-order processor. This was done by a direct refinement from specification to implementation, without need of an infinite-state intermediate abstraction or reasoning about partial orders. This refutes the claim in [DP97] that such an intermediate level is needed to give a concise statement of the refinement relation. In fact, the proof was possible even though the processes in the compositional system are not only finite-state, but are not even first-order expressive (much less regular-language expressive).

The proof itself is not automatic. Substantial human insight was required to decompose the proof into lemmas about small collections of state components. However, we note that the proof is at least textually short – substantialy shorter than the implementation – and that the refinement maps are a fairly natural representation of the function of the various machine components. Also note that other processor architectures (such as "in-order-completion" machines) are strictly more deterministic in their scheduling than Tomasulo's algorithm. Thus, it might be possible to reuse the present proof by refining Tomasulo's algorithm to various other architectures, and thereby save the effort of verifying them "from scratch".

There are several areas in which the present work could be extended or improved. First, the processor is unrealistic in that it has no provision for "exceptions" (caused, for example by, interrupts, arithmetic errors, or mispredicted branches). It would be useful to know, for example, if one could use a similar technique to verify a processor using "snapshots" or some other technique to roll back the processor state after an exception. Second, the verification of Tomasulo's algorithm should in principle be independent of the actual arithmetic functions used, since they have no effect on the scheduling of instructions.

If the present techniques were integrated with the uninterpreted function calculus techniques of [BD94], then the arithmetic unit might be modeled by an uninterpreted function symbol, allowing the problem of arithmetic verification to be separated. Third, note that this work and [DP97] only deal with the issue of safety and not of liveness (*i.e.*, a processor that always stalls would meet the specification). The compositional framework presented here cannot handle liveness properties (in fact, Abadi and Lamport [AL93] show that liveness assertions cannot be used as cyclic environment assumptions). The proof could, perhaps, be undertaken using assume/guarantee style temporal reasoning, which is also supported by SMV.

References

[AH96]   R. Alur and T. A. Henzinger. Reactive modules. In *11th annual IEEE symp. Logic in Computer Science (LICS '96)*, 1996.

[AL93]   M. Abadi and L. Lamport. Composing specifications. *ACM Trans. on Prog. Lang. and Syst.*, 15(1):73–132, Jan. 1993.

[AL95]   M. Abadi and L. Lamport. Conjoining specifications. *ACM Trans. on Prog. Lang. and Syst.*, 17(3):507–534, May. 1995.

[BCM+92] J. R. Burch, E. M. Clarke, K. L. McMillan, D. L. Dill, and L. J. Hwang. Symbolic model checking: 10^{20} states and beyond. *Information and Computation*, 98(2):142–70, Jun. 1992.

[BD94]   J. R. Burch and D. L. Dill. Automatic verification of pipelined microprocessor control. In *Computer-Aided Verification (CAV '94)*. Springer-Verlag, 1994.

[DP97]   W. Damm and A. Pnueli. Verifying out-of-order executions. In D. Probst, editor, *CHARME '97*. Chapman & Hall, 1997. To appear.

[GL94]   O. Grümberg and D. E. Long. Model checking and modular verification. *ACM Trans. Programming Languages and Systems*, 16(3):843–871, 1994.

[ID96]   C.N. Ip and D.L. Dill. Better verification through symmetry. *Formal Methods in System Design*, 9(1-2):41–75, Aug. 1996.

[JNB96]   A. Jain, K. Nelson, and R. E. Bryant. Verifying nondeterministic implementations of deterministic systems. In *Formal Methods in Computer-Aided Design (FMCAD '96)*, pages 109–25, 1996.

[KSL95]   A. Kuehlmann, A. Srinivasan, and D. P. LaPotin. Verity – a formal verification program for custom CMOS circuits. *IBM J. of Research and Development*, 39(1–2):149–65, Jan.–Mar. 1995.

[Kur94]   R. P. Kurshan. *Computer-Aided Verification of Coordinating Processes*. Princeton, 1994.

[LR97]   D. Leibholz and R. Razdan. The alpha 21264: a 500 mhz out-of-order execution microprocessor. In *Digest of Papers, COMPCON Spring 97*, pages 28–36, 1997.

[McM93]   K. L. McMillan. *Symbolic Model Checking*. Kluwer, 1993.

[McM97]   K. L. McMillan. A compositional rule for hardware design refinement. In *Computer Aided Verification (CAV'97)*, pages 24–35, 1997.

[OG76]   S. Owicki and D. Gries. Verifying properties of parallel programs. *Comm. ACM*, 19(5):279–85, May 1976.

[ORSS94] S. Owre, J. M. Rushby, N. Shankar, and M. K. Srivas. A tutorial on using PVS for hardware verification. In *Theorem Provers in Circuit Design (TPCD '94)*, pages 258–79. Springer, 1994.

[Tom67]   R. M. Tomasulo. An efficient algorithm for exploiting multiple arithmetic units. *IBM J. of Research and Development*, 11(1):25–33, Jan. 1967.

Decomposing the Proof of Correctness of Pipelined Microprocessors*

Ravi Hosabettu[1], Mandayam Srivas[2] and Ganesh Gopalakrishnan[1]

[1] Department of Computer Science, University of Utah, Salt Lake City, UT 84112,
hosabett,ganesh@cs.utah.edu
[2] Computer Science Laboratory, SRI International, Menlo Park, CA 94025,
srivas@csl.sri.com

Abstract. We present a systematic approach to decompose and incrementally build the proof of correctness of pipelined microprocessors. The central idea is to construct the abstraction function using *completion functions*, one per unfinished instruction, each of which specifies the effect (on the observables) of completing the instruction. In addition to avoiding term-size and case explosion problem that limits the pure *flushing* approach, our method helps localize errors, and also handles stages with iterative loops. The technique is illustrated on a pipelined and a superscalar pipelined implementations of a subset of the DLX architecture. It has also been applied to a processor with out-of-order execution.

1 Introduction

Many modern microprocessors employ radical optimizations such as superscalar pipelining, speculative execution and out-of-order execution to enhance their throughput. These optimizations make microprocessor verification difficult in practice. Most approaches to mechanical verification of pipelined processors rely on the following key techniques: First, given a pipelined implementation and a simpler ISA-level specification, they require a suitable abstraction mapping from an implementation state to a specification state and define the correspondence between the two machines using a commutative diagram. Second, they use symbolic simulation to derive logical expressions corresponding to the two paths in the commutative diagram which will then be tested for equivalence. An automatic way to perform this equivalence testing is to use ground decision procedures for equality with uninterpreted functions such as the ones in PVS. This strategy has been used to verify several processors in PVS [5, 4, 15]. Some of the approaches to pipelined processor verification rely on the user providing the definition for the abstraction function. Burch and Dill in [3] observed that the

---

* This work was done in part when Ravi Hosabettu was visiting SRI International in summer 1997. The work done by the authors at University of Utah was supported in part by DARPA under Contract #DABT6396C0094 (Utah Verifier) and NSF MIP MIP−9321836. The work done by the authors at SRI International was supported in part under NASA Contract NAS1−20334 and ARPA Contract A721/NAG 2−891.

effect of flushing the pipeline, for example by pumping a sequence of NOPs, can be used to automatically compute a suitable abstraction function. Burch and Dill used this *flushing approach* along with a validity checker [9, 1] to automate effectively the verification of pipelined implementations of several processors.

The pure flushing approach has the drawback of making the size of the abstraction function generated and the number of examined cases impractically large for deep and complex superscalar pipelines. To verify a superscalar example using the flushing approach, Burch [2] decomposed the verification problem into three subproblems and suggested a technique which required the user to add some extra control inputs to the implementation and set them appropriately to construct the abstraction function. He also had to fine-tune the validity checker used in the experiment requiring the user to help it with many manually derived case splits. It is unclear how the decomposition of the proof and the abstraction function used in [2] can be reused for verifying other superscalar examples. Another drawback of the pure flushing approach is that it is hard to use for pipelines with indeterminate latency, which can arise if the control involves data-dependent loops or if some part of the processor, such as memory-cache interface, is abstracted away for managing the complexity of the system.

In this paper, we propose a systematic methodology to modularize as well as decompose the proof of correctness of microprocessors with complex pipeline architectures. Called the *completion functions* method, our approach relies on the user expressing the abstraction function in terms of a set of completion functions, one per unfinished instruction. Each completion function specifies the *desired effect* (on the observables) of completing the instruction. Notice that one is not obligated to state *how* such completion would actually be attained, which, indeed, can be very complex, involving details such as squashing, pipeline stalls, and even data dependent iterative loops. Moreover, we strongly believe that a typical designer would have a very clear understanding of the completion functions, and would not find the task of describing them and constructing the abstraction function onerous. In addition to actually gaining from designers' insights, verification based on the completion functions method has a number of other advantages. It results in a natural decomposition of proofs. Proofs build up in a layered manner where the designer actually debugs the last pipeline stage first through a verification condition, and then uses this verification condition as a rewrite rule in debugging the penultimate stage, and so on. Because of this layering, the proof strategy employed is fairly simple and almost generic in practice. Debugging is far more effective than in other methods because errors can be localized to a stage, instead of having to wade through monolithic proofs.

1.1   Related Work

Levitt and Olukotun [10] use an "unpipelining" technique for merging successive pipeline stages through a series of behavior preserving transformations. While unpipelining also results in a decomposition of the proofs, their transformation is performed on the implementation whereas completion functions are defined based on the specification. Their method has the disadvantage that the implementation is verified against itself in the initial steps and that their transformations can get complex for superscalar processors and processors with out-of-order execution. Cyrluk's technique in [6], which has also been applied to a superscalar processor, tackles the term-size and case explosion problem by lazily "inverting the abstraction mapping" to replace big implementation terms with smaller specification terms and using the conditions in the specification terms to guide the proof. Our method contains the complexity of the proof by decomposing the proof of the commutative diagram one stage at a time in a fashion that is closer to the user's intuition about the design. Park and Dill have used aggregation functions [12], which are conceptually similar to completion functions, for distributed cache coherence protocol verification. In [13], Sawada and Hunt used an incremental verification technique to verify a processor with out-of-order execution which we have reverified using our approach. We describe the differences in section 4.5.

2   Correctness Criteria for Processor Verification

The completion functions approach aims to realize the correctness criterion (used in [13, 3]) expressed in Figure 1(a), in a manner that proofs based on it are modular and layered as pointed out earlier.

Figure 1(a) requires that every sequence of n implementation transitions which start and end with *flushed* states (i.e., no partially executed instructions) corresponds to a sequence of m instructions (i.e., transitions) executed by the specification machine. I_step is the implementation transition function and A_step is the specification transition function. The projection extracts only those implementation state components visible to the specification (i.e. the observables). This criterion is preferred over others that have been used to verify pipelined processors because it corresponds to the intuition that a real pipelined microprocessor starting at a flushed state, running some program and terminating in a flushed state is emulated by a specification machine whose starting and terminating states are in direct correspondence through projection. This criterion can be proved by induction on n once the *commutative diagram* condition shown in Figure 1(b) has been proved on a single implementation machine transition. This inductive proof can be constructed once, as we have demonstrated in [8], for arbitrary machines that satisfy the conditions described in the next paragraph. In the rest of the paper, we concentrate on verifying the commutative diagram condition.

Intuitively, Figure 1(b) states that if the implementation machine starts in an arbitrary reachable state impl_state and the specification machine starts in a corresponding specification state (given by an abstraction function ABS), then after executing a transition their new states correspond. ABS must be chosen so that for all flushed states fs the *projection condition* ABS(fs) = projection(fs) holds. The commutative diagram uses a modified transition function A_step', which denotes zero or more applications of A_step, because an implementation

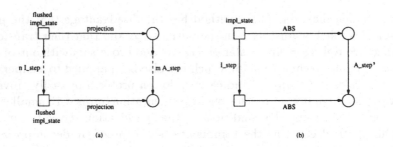

Fig. 1. Pipelined microprocessor correctness criteria

transition from an arbitrary state might correspond to executing in the specification machine zero instruction (*e.g.*, if the implementation machine stalls due to pipeline interlocks) or more than one instruction (*e.g.*, if the implementation machine has multiple pipelines). The number of instructions executed by the specification machine is provided by a user-defined *synchronization* function on implementation states. One of the crucial proof obligations is to show that this function does not always return zero. One also needs to prove that the implementation machine will eventually reach a flushed state if no more instructions are inserted into the machine, to make sure that the correctness criterion in Figure 1(a) is not vacuous. In addition, the user may need to discover *invariants* to restrict the set of `impl_state` considered in the proof of Figure 1(b) and prove that it is closed under `I_step`.

3   The Completion Functions Approach

One way of defining `ABS` is to use a part of the implementation definition, modified, if necessary, to construct an explicit *flush* operation [3, 2] to flush the pipeline. The completion functions approach is based on using an abstraction function that is behaviorally equivalent to flushing but is *not* derived operationally via flushing in our basic approach[1]. Rather, we construct the abstraction function as a composition (followed by a projection) of a sequence of *completion functions* that map an implementation state to an implementation state. Each completion function specifies the *desired effect* on the observables of completing a particular unfinished instruction in the machine leaving all non-observable state components unchanged. The order in which these functions are composed is determined by the program order of the unfinished instructions. The conditions under which each function is composed with the rest, if any, is determined by whether the unfinished instructions ahead of it could disrupt the flow of instructions for example, by being a taken branch or by raising an exception. Observe that one is not required to state how these conditions are actually realised in the implementation. Any mistakes, either in specifying the completion functions or

---

[1] Later we discuss a hybrid scheme extension that uses operational flushing.

in constructing the abstraction function, might lead to a false negative verification result, but never a false positive.

Consider a very simple four-stage pipeline with one observable state component **regfile** which is shown in Figure 2. The instructions flow down the pipeline with every cycle in order with no stalls, hazards etc. updating the **regfile** in the last stage. (This is unrealistically simple, but we explain how to handle these artifacts in subsequent sections.) The pipeline can contain three unfinished instructions at any time, which are held in the three sets of pipeline registers labeled IF/ID, ID/EX, and EX/WB. The completion function corresponding to an unfinished instruction held in a set of pipeline registers (such as ID/EX) defines how the information stored in those registers are combined to complete that instruction. In our example, the completion functions are **C_EX_WB**, **C_ID_EX** and **C_IF_ID**, respectively. Now the abstraction function, whose effect should be to flush the pipeline, can be expressed as a composition of these completion functions as follows (we omit **projection** here as **regfile** is the only observable state component):

```
ABS(impl_state) = C_IF_ID(C_ID_EX(C_EX_WB(impl_state)))
```

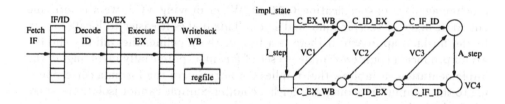

Fig. 2. A simple four stage pipeline and decomposition of the proof under completion functions

This definition of the abstraction function leads to a decomposition of the proof of the commutative diagram for **regfile** as shown in Figure 2, generating the following series of verification conditions, the last one of which corresponds to the complete commutative diagram.

```
VC1: regfile(I_step(impl_state)) = regfile(C_EX_WB(impl_state))
VC2: regfile(C_EX_WB(I_step(impl_state))) =
          regfile(C_ID_EX(C_EX_WB(impl_state)))
VC3: regfile(C_ID_EX(C_EX_WB(I_step(impl_state)))) =
          regfile(C_IF_ID(C_ID_EX(C_EX_WB(impl_state))))
VC4: regfile(C_IF_ID(C_ID_EX(C_EX_WB(I_step(impl_state))))) =
          regfile(A_step(C_IF_ID(C_ID_EX(C_EX_WB(impl_state)))))
```

I_step executes *partially* the instructions already in the pipeline as well as a newly fetched instruction. Given this, VC1 expresses the following fact: since regfile is updated in the last stage, we would expect that after I_step is executed, the contents of regfile would be the same as after completing the instruction in the EX/WB registers.

Now consider the instruction in ID/EX. I_step executes it partially as per the logic in stage EX, and then moves the result to the EX/WB registers. C_EX_WB can now be used to complete this instruction. This must result in the same contents of regfile as completing the instructions held in sets EX/WB and ID/EX of pipeline registers *in that order*. This is captured by VC2. VC3 and VC4 are constructed similarly. Note that our ultimate goal is to prove only VC4, with the proofs of VC1 through VC3 acting as "helpers". Each verification condition in the above series can be proved using a *standard strategy* that involves expanding the outermost function on the both sides of the equation and using the previously proved verification conditions (if any) as rewrite rules to simplify the expressions, followed by automatic case analysis of the boolean terms appearing in the conditional structure of the simplified expressions. Since we expand only the topmost functions on both sides, and because we use the previously proved verification conditions, the sizes of the expressions produced during the proof and the required case analysis are kept in check.

The completion functions approach also supports *incremental* and *layered* verification. When proving VC1, we are verifying the writeback stage of the pipeline against its specification C_EX_WB. When proving VC2, we are verifying one more stage of the pipeline, and so on. This makes it easier to locate errors. In the flushing approach, if there is a bug in the pipeline, the validity checker would produce a counterexample—a set of formulas potentially involving *all* the implementation variables—that implies the negation of the formula corresponding to the commutative diagram. Such a counterexample cannot isolate the stage in which the bug occurred.

Another advantage of using completion functions is that their definition, unlike that of flush operation, is not dependent on the latency of the pipeline. Hence our method is applicable even when the latency of the pipeline is indeterminate, which can happen if, for example, the pipeline contains data-dependent iterative loops or when the implementation machine has non-determinism. The proof that the implementation eventually reaches a flushed state can be constructed by defining a measure function that returns the number of cycles the implementation takes to flush and showing that the measure decreases after a transition from a non-flushed state.

A disadvantage of the completion functions approach is that the user must explicitly specify the definitions for these completion functions and then construct an abstraction function. In a later section, we describe a hybrid approach to reduce the manual effort involved in this process.

4 Application of Our Methodology

In this section, we explain how to apply our methodology to verify three examples: a pipelined and a superscalar pipelined implementations of a subset of the

DLX processor [7] and a processor with out-of-order execution. We describe how to specify the completion functions and construct an abstraction function, how to handle stalls, speculative fetching and out-of-order execution, and illustrate the particular decomposition and the proof strategies we used. The DLX example was verified in [3] using the flushing approach, the superscalar DLX example was verified in [2] and the processor with out-of-order execution was verified in [13]. Our verification is carried out in PVS [11]. The detailed implementation, specification as well as the proofs for all these examples can be found at [8]. The manual effort spent on developing the proofs for the processor with out-of-order execution was less than two person weeks. The first two examples were verified while developing our methodology and took about two person months, which also included the time to learn PVS.

4.1 DLX Processor Details

The specification of this processor has four state components: the program counter pc, the register file regfile, the data memory dmem, and the instruction memory imem. The processor supports six types of instructions: load, store, unconditional jump, conditional branch, alu-immediate and a 3-register alu instruction. The ALU is modeled using an uninterpreted function. The memory system and the register file are modeled as stores with read and write operations.

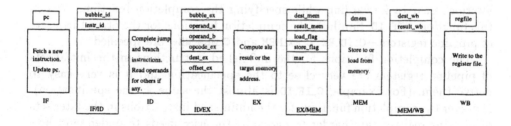

Fig. 3. Pipelined implementation

The implementation uses a five stage pipeline as shown in Figure 3. There are four sets of pipeline registers holding information about the partially executed instructions in 15 pipeline registers. The intended functionality of each of the stages is also shown in the figure. The implementation uses a simple "assume not taken" prediction strategy for jump and branch instructions. Consequently, if a jump or branch is indeed taken (br_taken signal is asserted), then the pipeline squashes the subsequent instruction and corrects the pc. If the instruction in the IF/ID registers is dependent on a load in the ID/EX registers, then that instruction will be stalled for one cycle (st_issue signal is asserted), otherwise the instructions flow down the pipeline with every cycle. No instructions are fetched in the cycle where stall_input is asserted. The implementation provides forwarding of data to the instruction decode unit (ID stage) where the operands are read. The details of forwarding are not shown in the figure.

4.2 Specifying the Completion Functions

The processor can have four partially executed instructions at any time, one each in the four sets of pipeline registers shown. We associate a completion function with each such instruction. We need to identify how a partially executed instruction is stored in a particular set of pipeline registers—once this is done, the completion function for that unfinished instruction can be easily derived from the specification.

Consider the set IF/ID of pipeline registers. The intended functionality of the IF stage is to fetch an instruction (place it in instr_id) and increment the pc. The bubble_id register indicates whether the instruction is valid or not. (It might be invalid, for example, if it is being squashed due to a taken branch). So in order to complete the execution of this instruction, the completion function should do nothing if the instruction is not valid, otherwise it should update the pc with the target address if it is a jump or a taken branch instruction, update the dmem if it is a store instruction and update the regfile if it is a load, alu-immediate or alu instruction according to the semantics of the instruction. The details of how these are done can be gleaned from the specification. This function is not obtained by tracing the implementation, instead, the user directly provides the intended effect. Also note that we are not concerned with load interlock or data forwarding while specifying the completion function. We call this function C_IF_ID. Similarly the completion functions for the other three sets of pipeline registers—C_ID_EX, C_EX_MEM and C_MEM_WB—are specified.

The completion functions for the unfinished instructions in the initial sets of pipeline registers are very close to the specification and it is very easy to derive them. (For example, C_IF_ID is almost the same as the specification). However the completion functions for the unfinished instructions in the later sets of pipeline registers are harder to derive as the user needs to understand how the information about the instruction is stored in the various pipeline registers but the functions themselves are much simpler.

4.3 The Decomposition and the Proof Details

Since the instructions flow down the pipeline in order, the abstraction function is defined as a simple composition of these completion functions as :

    projection(C_IF_ID(C_ID_EX(C_EX_MEM(C_MEM_WB(impl_state)))))

The synchronization function returns zero if either st_issue or stall_input or br_taken is true, otherwise it return one.

The Decomposition. The decomposition we used for regfile for this example is shown in Figure 4. The justification for the first three verification conditions is similar as in Section 3. There are two verification conditions corresponding to the instruction in the IF/ID registers. If st_issue is true, then that instruction is not issued, so C_IF_ID ought not to be applied in the upper path in the commutative diagram. VC4_r requires us to prove this under condition P1 = st_issue. VC5_r is for the case when the instruction is issued, so it should be proved under condition P2 = NOT st_issue. Observe that st_issue also appears as a disjunct in the synchronization function and hence in A_step' too. Finally, VC6_r is the verification condition corresponding to the final commutative diagram for regfile.

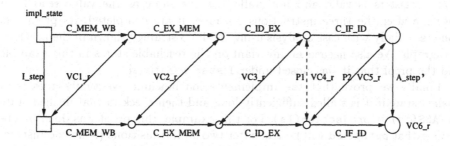

Fig. 4. The decomposition of the commutative diagram for regfile

The decomposition used for a particular observable depends on the pipeline stage where that observable is updated. For example, the first verification condition for dmem states that dmem(C_MEM_WB(impl_state)) = dmem(impl_state) since dmem is not updated in the last stage of the pipeline. Other verification conditions are exactly identical to that of regfile. Finally, the decompositions we used for pc and imem had three and two verification conditions, respectively.

The Proof. The proof is organized into three phases: first that of generating and proving certain rewrite rules, second that of proving the verification conditions and other lemmas and invariants (if needed) using these rewrite rules and third that of proving the other proof obligations mentioned in section 2.

For each register in a particular set of pipeline registers, we need a rewrite rule that states that the register is unaffected by the completion functions of the unfinished instructions ahead of it. For example, for bubble_ex, the rewrite rule is bubble_ex(C_EX_MEM(C_MEM_WB(impl_state))) = bubble_ex(impl_state). All these rules can be generated and proved automatically by rewriting using the definitions of the completion functions. We then defined a PVS strategy that makes these rules, and the definitions and the axioms from the implementation and the specification (leaving out a few on which we do case analysis), as rewrite rules.

Now, the proof strategy for proving all the verification conditions is similar— use the PVS strategy described above to setup the rewrite rules, setup the previously proved verification conditions as rewrite rules, **expand** the outermost functions on both sides, use the PVS command **assert** to do the rewrites and simplifications by decision procedures, then perform case analysis with the PVS strategy (apply (then* (repeat (lift-if)) (bddsimp) (ground))). Some verification conditions (like VC4_r) needed the outermost function to be expanded on only one side and some were slightly more involved (like VC6_r) needing case analysis on the various terms introduced by expanding A_step'.

The proof above needed a lemma expressing the correctness of the feedback logic. With completion functions, we could state this succinctly as follows: the value read in the ID stage by the feedback logic (when the instruction in the IF/ID registers is valid and not stalled) is the same as the value read from **regfile** after the three instructions ahead of it are completed. Its proof was done essentially with case analysis using the PVS strategy shown in the previous paragraph. We also needed an invariant on the reachable states in this example and the proof that it was closed under I_step was trivial.

Finally we prove that the implementation machine eventually goes to a flushed state if it is stalled sufficiently long and then check in that flushed state **fs, ABS(fs) = projection(fs)**. For this example, this proof was done by observing that **bubble_id** will be true after two stall transitions (hence no instruction in the IF/ID registers) and that this "no-instruction"-ness propagates down the pipeline with every stall transition. Also, we prove that the synchronization function does not always return zero which was straightforward.

4.4 Application to Superscalar DLX Processor

The superscalar DLX processor [2] is a dual issue version of the DLX processor. Both the pipelines have similar structure as Figure 3 except that the second pipeline only executes **alu-immediate** and **alu** instructions. In addition, the processor has one instruction buffer location.

Specifying the completion functions for the various unfinished instructions was similar to the DLX example. A main difference was how the completion functions of the unfinished instructions in the IF/ID registers and the instruction buffer (say the instructions are **i, j, k** and completion functions are C_i, C_j and C_k respectively) are composed to handle the speculative fetching of instructions. These unfinished instructions could be potential branches since the branch instructions are executed in the ID stage of the first pipeline. So while constructing the abstraction function, we compose C_j (with C_i(...rest of the completion functions in order...)) only if instruction i is not a taken branch and then compose C_k only if instruction j is not a taken branch too. We used a similar idea in constructing the synchronization function. The specification machine would not execute any new instructions if any of the instructions **i, j, k** mentioned above is a taken branch. It is very easy and natural to express these conditions using completion functions since we are not concerned with when exactly the branches are taken in the implementation machine. However, in the pure flushing approach, even the synchronization function will have to be much more complicated—having to cycle the implementation machine for many cycles [2].

Another difference between the two processors was the complex issue logic here which could issue zero to two instructions per cycle. We had eight verification conditions on how different instructions get issued or stalled/move around. The proofs of all the verification conditions again used very similar strategies. The synchronization function had many more cases in this example and the previously proved verification conditions were used many times over.

4.5 Application to a Processor with Out-of-order Execution

We have applied our approach to an out-of-order execution processor that was verified in [13]. This processor has three execution units—a multiplier, an adder and a load/store unit—sharing the write-back stage. This situation represents a structural hazard which is resolved by the issue logic by not issuing instructions such that two may simultaneously be in the write-back stage. We prove an invariant on the issue logic that this hazard is resolved properly and then build the proof of the commutative diagram in the various cases. Formulating the verification conditions in these various cases was similar as in the earlier examples. The interesting case is the following scenario of out-of-order completion. An add instruction takes one cycle in the execution unit while a mult takes three cycles. So, an add instruction, issed after a mult instruction, can complete before it. However, the processor would issue such an add instruction only if its destination register is different from that of the mult instruction issued earlier. We use this fact to reorder the completion functions of the add and the mult instructions into the the order used by the abstraction function.

In [13], Sawada and Hunt construct an intermediate abstraction of the implementation machine using a table that represents the (infinite) trace of all executed instructions up to the present time. They achieve incrementality by postulating and proving individually a large set of invariant properties about this intermediate representation, from which they derive the final correctness proof. The main difference of our approach is that the incremental nature of the proof in our case arises from the way we construct our abstraction function and the decomposition of the proof of the commutative diagram that it leads to. This decomposition is to a large extent independent of the processor design. Our approach also has the advantage that the amount of information the user needs to specify is significantly less than their method. For example, we require just a few simple invariants on the reachable states and do not need to construct an explicit intermediate abstraction of the implementation machine.

4.6 Hybrid Approach to Reduce the Manual Effort

In some cases, it is possible to *derive* the definitions of some of the completion functions automatically from the implementation to reduce the manual effort. We illustrate this on the DLX example.

The implementation machine is provided in the form of a typical transition function giving the "new" value for each state component. Since the implementation modifies the regfile in the writeback stage, we take C_MEM_WB to be

new_regfile which is a function of dest_wb and result_wb. To determine how
C_EX_MEM updates the register file from C_MEM_WB, we perform a step of symbolic
simulation of the non-observables in the definition of C_MEM_WB, that is, replace
dest_wb and result_wb in its definition with their "new-" counterparts. Since
the MEM stage updates dmem, C_EX_MEM will have another component modifying dmem which we simply take as new_dmem. Similarly we derive C_ID_EX from
C_EX_MEM through symbolic simulation. For the IF/ID registers, this gets complicated on two counts: the instruction there could get stalled due to a load
interlock, and the forwarding logic that appears in the ID stage. So we let the
user specify this function directly. We have done a complete proof using these
completion functions. The details of the proof are similar. An important difference here is that the invariant that was needed earlier was eliminated.

While reducing the manual effort, this way of deriving the completion functions from the implementation has the disadvantage that we are verifying the
implementation against itself. This contradicts our view of these as *desired* specifications and negates our goal of incremental verification. To combine the advantages of both, we could use a hybrid approach where we use explicitly provided
and symbolically generated completion functions in combination. For example,
we could derive it for the last stage, specify it for the penultimate stage and
then derive it for the stage before that (from the specification for the penultimate stage) and so on.

5 Conclusions

We have presented a systematic approach to modularize and decompose the proof
of correctness of pipelined microprocessors and shown its generality by applying
it to three different processors. The methodology relies on the user expressing
the cumulative effect of flushing in terms of a set of completion functions, one
per unfinished instruction. This method results in a natural decomposition of the
proof based on the individual stages of the pipeline and allows the verification
to proceed incrementally overcoming the term-size and case explosion problem
of the flushing approach. While this method increases the manual effort on the
part of the user, we found the knowledge required in specifying the completion
functions, constructing the abstraction function and formulating the verification
conditions is close to the designer's intuition about how the pipeline works.

One of our future plans is to build a system that uses PVS or a part of it as a
back-end to support the methodology presented. Besides automating parts of the
methodology, this system would help the user interactively apply the rest of the
process. We would also like to see how our approach can be extended to verify
more complex pipeline control that uses reorder buffers or other out-of-order
completion techniques. Other plans include testing the efficacy of our approach
for verifying pipelines with data dependent iterative loops and asynchronous
memory interface.

Acknowledgements We would like to thank John Rushby and David Cyrluk
for their feedback on earlier drafts of this paper.

References

1. Clark Barrett, David Dill, and Jeremy Levitt. Validity checking for combinations of theories with equality. In Srivas and Camilleri [14], pages 187–201.

2. J. R. Burch. Techniques for verifying superscalar microprocessors. In *Design Automation Conference, DAC '96*, June 1996.

3. J. R. Burch and D. L. Dill. Automatic verification of pipelined microprocessor control. In David Dill, editor, *Computer-Aided Verification, CAV '94*, volume 818 of *Lecture Notes in Computer Science*, pages 68–80, Stanford, CA, June 1994. Springer-Verlag.

4. D. Cyrluk, S. Rajan, N. Shankar, and M. K. Srivas. Effective theorem proving for hardware verification. In Ramayya Kumar and Thomas Kropf, editors, *Theorem Provers in Circuit Design (TPCD '94)*, volume 910 of *Lecture Notes in Computer Science*, pages 203–222, Bad Herrenalb, Germany, September 1994. Springer-Verlag.

5. David Cyrluk. Microprocessor verification in PVS: A methodology and simple example. Technical Report SRI-CSL-93-12, Computer Science Laboratory, SRI International, Menlo Park, CA, December 1993.

6. David Cyrluk. Inverting the abstraction mapping: A methodology for hardware verification. In Srivas and Camilleri [14], pages 172–186.

7. John L. Hennessy and David A. Patterson. *Computer Architecture: A Quantitative Approach*. Morgan Kaufmann, San Mateo, CA, 1990.

8. Ravi Hosabettu. PVS specification and proofs of the DLX, superscalar DLX examples and the processor with out-of-order execution, 1998. Available at http://www.cs.utah.edu/~hosabett/pvs/processor.html.

9. R. B. Jones, D. L. Dill, and J. R. Burch. Efficient validity checking for processor verification. In *International Conference on Computer Aided Design, ICCAD '95*, 1995.

10. Jeremy Levitt and Kunle Olukotun. A scalable formal verification methodology for pipelined microprocessors. In *Design Automation Conference, DAC '96*, June 1996.

11. Sam Owre, John Rushby, Natarajan Shankar, and Friedrich von Henke. Formal verification for fault-tolerant architectures: Prolegomena to the design of PVS. *IEEE Transactions on Software Engineering*, 21(2):107–125, February 1995.

12. Seungjoon Park and David L. Dill. Protocol verification by aggregation of distributed actions. In Rajeev Alur and Thomas A. Henzinger, editors, *Computer-Aided Verification, CAV '96*, volume 1102 of *Lecture Notes in Computer Science*, pages 300–310, New Brunswick, NJ, July/August 1996. Springer-Verlag.

13. J. Sawada and W. A. Hunt, Jr. Trace table based approach for pipelined microprocessor verification. In Orna Grumberg, editor, *Computer-Aided Verification, CAV '97*, volume 1254 of *Lecture Notes in Computer Science*, pages 364–375, Haifa, Israel, June 1997. Springer-Verlag.

14. Mandayam Srivas and Albert Camilleri, editors. *Formal Methods in Computer-Aided Design (FMCAD '96)*, volume 1166 of *Lecture Notes in Computer Science*, Palo Alto, CA, November 1996. Springer-Verlag.

15. Mandayam K. Srivas and Steven P. Miller. Applying formal verification to the AAMP5 microprocessor: A case study in the industrial use of formal methods. *Formal Methods in Systems Design*, 8(2):153–188, March 1996.

Processor Verification with Precise Exceptions and Speculative Execution

Jun Sawada[1] and Warren A. Hunt, Jr.[2]

[1] Department of Computer Sciences, University of Texas at Austin
Austin, TX 78712, USA
E-mail: sawada@cs.utexas.edu
[2] IBM Austin Research Laboratory
11400 Burnet Road MS/9460, Austin, TX 78758, USA
E-mail: whunt@austin.ibm.com

Abstract. We describe a framework for verifying a pipelined micro-processor whose implementation contains precise exceptions, external interrupts, and speculative execution. We present our correctness criterion which compares the state transitions of pipelined and non-pipelined machines in presence of external interrupts. To perform the verification, we created a table-based model of pipeline execution. This model records committed and in-flight instructions as performed by the micro-architecture. Given that certain requirements are met by this table-based model, we have mechanically verified our correctness criterion using the ACL2 theorem prover.

1 Introduction

We have studied the verification of a pipelined microprocessor whose implementation contains speculative execution, external interrupts and precise exceptions. The verification of pipelined microprocessors has been studied[1, 12, 6, 13], but complicated features, such as exception mechanisms, are often simplified away from the implementation model. Several verified microprocessor designs contain exception mechanisms[4, 11]; however, they contain only one kind of exception and require only a few cycles before exception handling starts. Modern micro-processors have multiple exception types, which can occur simultaneously in its pipeline. Correct handling of an exception requires synchronizing and saving the machine state, which may take many clock cycles. This synchronization process may itself cause further exceptions.

Modern processors often execute a large number of instructions speculatively using branch prediction mechanisms. The processor has to keep track of these instructions correctly so that speculatively executed instructions following a mis-predicted branch have no side-effect. Also speculatively executed instructions may themselves cause exceptions, which may need to be ignored.

* This research was supported in part by the Semiconductor Research Corporation under contract 97-DJ-388.

To investigate these issues, we designed a processor model which can speculatively execute instructions and simultaneously detect multiple exceptions while executing instructions out-of-order. This machine has been specified at the instruction-set architecture level and micro-architecture level. We discuss the machine specification in Sect. 2.

Previously, we used a correctness criterion for verifying a pipelined microprocessor which did not contain exceptions[10]. In Sect. 3, we have extended this correctness criterion to permit the verification of a design containing speculative execution and external interrupts.

We have modeled the behavior of our processor using an intermediate model, called a MAETT, which records all executed instructions. This model, given in Sect. 4, presents an abstraction of the behavior of our pipelined design on speculative execution and exceptions. Using this model, we wrote an invariant condition that meets several requirements, and show that these requirements are strong enough to prove the correctness criterion. The proof has been carried out with ACL2 theorem prover[9]. A brief proof sketch is given Sect. 5. The verification of the invariant condition is in progress.

2   Hardware Specifications

Our processor model has been specified at two levels: its micro-architecture (MA) and its instruction-set architecture (ISA). At the ISA level, we only describe the states of the components visible to the programmer, which are shown as shaded boxes in Fig. 1. We specify the ISA behavior with an instruction interpreter function ISA-step(), which takes a current ISA state and an external interrupt input and returns the state after executing a single instruction. At the MA level, we describe the behavior of all components shown in Fig. 1. The behavioral function MA-step() takes a current MA state and its external inputs, and returns the state after one clock cycle of execution. The ISA model is a non-pipelined machine specification while the MA model is pipelined.

Our ISA model implements eleven instructions, each in a different instruction class. For instance, ADD is the only integer operation instruction. For the purpose of our investigation, parameters such as the number of instructions, registers, and the register width are not critical. The ISA specification describes the action for external interrupts and internal exceptions. When an exception occurs, the processor saves some states in special registers, switches to supervisor mode, and jumps to the address specific to the exception type.

The MA specification gives an abstract description of the complete design shown in Fig. 1, as well as the exception mechanism, branch prediction unit, and memory-write buffers. It fetches and commits instructions in program order, but it has the capability to issue up to three instructions to the execution units simultaneously and does execute instructions in an out-of-order manner. The machine can hold as many as 15 instructions in the pipeline, and 12 instructions can be speculatively executed.

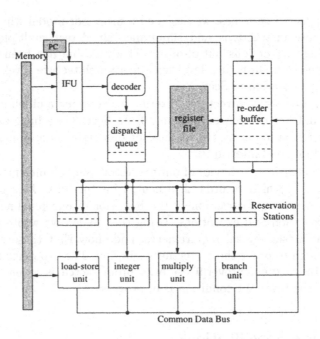

Fig. 1. Block Diagram of Our Pipeline Machine Design

Instructions are executed as follows. A fetched instruction is decoded and dispatched to an appropriate reservation stations, where the instruction waits for its operands. Once an instruction has all necessary values, it is issued to the corresponding execution unit, and the result is written to the re-order buffer[7]. Finally, instructions are committed in program order. Committing is the point where the instruction actually takes its effect. Speculatively executed instructions may reach the re-order buffer, but are only committed if appropriate.

Our MA deals with four types of exceptions: fetch errors, decode errors, data access errors, and external interrupts. The first three exceptions have internal causes, and they are called *internal exceptions*. All exceptions are *precise*; that is, the correct machine state is saved so that the executed program can be restarted from the point where the exception occurred. To achieve this, our machine satisfies the following properties for precise exceptions:

1. All instructions preceding an exception must complete their operation.
2. All partially executed instructions following an exception must be abandoned with no side-effect.

The machine may take a large number of machine cycles before it actually starts exception handling, because the first condition requires completion of partially executed instructions that precede the exception in program order. The re-order buffer is used to sort out the instructions to be completed from those to be abandoned[5]. If multiple exceptions are detected in the pipeline, only the earliest exception in program order is processed. Our MA design does not contain any imprecise exceptions, and we have not considered the verification a processor with imprecise exceptions.

3 Correctness Criterion

Our verification objective is to show that the MA design correctly executes instructions as specified by the ISA. Various ways to show the equivalence between the two levels have been presented. Burch and Dill verified pipelined designs using a correctness criterion that involves pipeline flushing[2]. Although this criterion with flushing has been extended to cover superscalar processors[3, 14], it does not address speculative execution and external exceptions.

We previously used the correctness criterion shown as diagram (a) in Fig. 2 to verify a pipelined design[10]. This diagram compares two paths. The lower path runs the MA design for an arbitrary number of clock cycles from a flushed pipeline state MA_0 to another flushed state MA_n, which causes m ISA instructions to be executed. By stripping off states not visible to the programmer, we can project MA_n to ISA_m. The upper path first projects MA_0 to an initial ISA state ISA_0 and then runs the ISA specification for m cycles to get the final state ISA_m. By comparing ISA_m obtained by following the different paths, we can check whether the MA design conforms to the ISA specification.

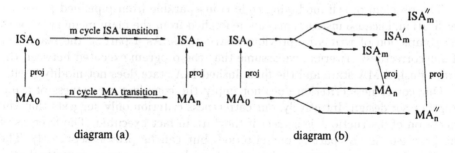

Fig. 2. Correctness Diagrams

In a correctly implemented MA design, speculatively executed instructions after a mispredicted branch should have no side-effect on the programmer visible state. This can be checked by verifying diagram (a), because the ISA executes instructions one-by-one. The correctness diagram shows that instructions are executed correctly independently of how branches are predicted.

Let us consider how internal exceptions affect the diagram. The ISA specification describes the machine behavior for internal exceptions; it specifies what states are stored in special registers, what the next PC value is, and so on. We want to show the MA design implements this action correctly, but we also want to check it implements precise exceptions. Since the ISA specification executes instructions one-by-one, it captures the requirements for precise exceptions given in Sect. 2. The correct behavior on multiple exceptions in the pipelined MA is also implied by the ISA specification, because it always processes exceptions in program order. These are our reasons to claim that verifying diagram (a) demonstrates precise handling of internal exceptions, as well as the correct action on exceptions. We do not check how exceptions are handled by exception handlers, since this is a software verification problem[11].

External exceptions make the problem more complicated. The ISA specification function $ISA\text{-}step()$ takes an external interrupt signal as its argument, and describes the action of an external interrupt as it does for internal exceptions. The problem is that the non-determinism introduced by the external signal can lead to different final ISA states, as shown in diagram (b). The commutative diagram holds only for the ISA state transitions which interrupt the same instructions as the MA does. Since supplying different environments to the MA will cause different instructions to be executed and interrupted, we need to find the corresponding ISA sequence for each MA state sequence with different input signals.

> **Correctness Criterion:** For an arbitrary MA execution sequence from a flushed state MA_0 to another flushed state MA_n, there exists a corresponding ISA execution sequence from ISA_0 to ISA_m. This sequence executes and interrupts the same instructions as occur in the MA execution sequence, and satisfy $ISA_0 = proj(MA_0)$ and $ISA_m = proj(MA_n)$.

The problem of self-modifying code is inseparable from pipelined processor verification, because instructions can be fetched from the main memory prior to the completion of writes by previous instructions. As a part of the statement of our correctness criterion, we assume that the program executed between the initial flushed MA state and the final flushed MA state does not modify itself.

Our correctness criterion does not imply the complete correctness of a microprocessor design. Intuitively, our correctness criterion only suggests that the execution of instructions is correct if they are in fact executed. The liveness of the processor is not part of our criterion, but can be proven separately. The criterion suggests that external interrupt signals are processed correctly, but it does not guarantee that all the interrupt signals actually interrupt the machine. For a real time system, we may further want to show that the processor responds to an external signal in a bounded amount of time.

4 MAETT for Speculative Execution and Exceptions

We have extended our Micro-Architectural Execution Trace Table ($MAETT$)[10] to model the behavior for speculative execution, internal exceptions and external interrupts. A MAETT is an abstraction of an MA state, which contains redundant information that makes it straitforward to specify machine invariants.

A MAETT is a list whose entries correspond to either a committed or in-flight instruction. Each entry represents an instruction with a data structure whose fields are shown in Table 1. A MAETT records all instructions that are executed from the initial MA state, and the size of a MAETT is unbounded. A MAETT grows as more instructions are fetched, and shrinks when speculatively executed instructions are abandoned. Instructions are recorded in the ISA execution order. The MAETT corresponding to a flushed MA state contains only committed instructions.

In the rest of the paper, we write $(I_1, \ldots, I_l)$ to designate a MAETT which records instructions $I_1, \ldots, I_l$. $ISA_0 \xrightarrow{I_1} ISA_1 \xrightarrow{I_2} \cdots \xrightarrow{I_l} ISA_l$ designates an ISA state sequence that executes instructions $I_1, \ldots, I_l$. The arrow labeled with I_i means state ISA_{i-1} changes to ISA_i under the action of I_i. Since each MAETT entry contains the ISA states before and after executing the corresponding instruction, it is easy to reconstruct the ISA state sequence $ISA_0 \xrightarrow{I_1} \cdots \xrightarrow{I_l} ISA_l$ from a MAETT $(I_1, \ldots, I_l)$.

Field name	Brief description
ID	Identity of I_i.
word	Instruction word.
stg	Current pipeline stage of I_i.
robe	Reorder buffer entry where I_i is stored.
modify?	Flag to show whether I_i is a modified instruction.
speculative?	Flag to show whether I_i is speculatively executed.
br-predict?	Outcome of branch prediction if I_i is a conditional branch.
exintr?	Flag to show whether I_i is interrupted.
pre-ISA	ISA_{i-1}, i.e., ISA state before executing I_i.
post-ISA	ISA_i, i.e., ISA state after executing I_i.

Table 1. Data structure for representing an instruction.

We define a MAETT step function *MAETT-step*() to simulate the MA state transition. *MAETT-step*() takes the current MA state, its corresponding MAETT, and external inputs, and returns a new MAETT representing the MA state one cycle later.

Each clock cycle, a MAETT is updated in concert with the MA state transition. Suppose the current MAETT is $(I_1, \ldots, I_l)$. If the MA fetches a new instruction I_{l+1}, *MAETT-step*() returns an extended MAETT $(I_1, \ldots, I_l, I_{l+1})$. The fields of each in-flight instruction are modified to reflect its progress in the pipeline.

When the MA abandons instructions following a mispredicted branch or an exception, MAETT entries corresponding to these instructions are eliminated. Figure 3 shows branching of an ISA state transition sequence due to an external interrupt. If instruction I_i is not interrupted, state ISA_{i-1} changes to ISA_i. If I_i is interrupted, it changes to ISA_i'. Before an external interrupt occurs, the MA executes instructions along the normal execution path, and the MAETT contains instructions $(I_0, \ldots, I_i, I_{i+1}, \ldots, I_k)$, and looks like MAETT (a). When an exter-

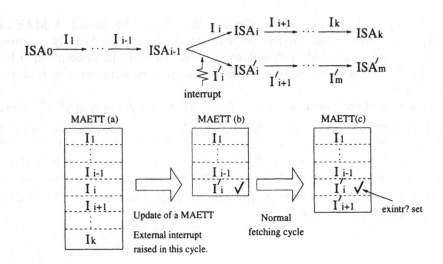

Fig. 3. Branching of ISA state sequence on an external interrupt. Corresponding MAETTs are also shown.

nal interrupt signal is received, the MA design starts synchronizing the machine and picks an instruction to be interrupted. If the interrupted instruction is I_i, instructions $I_i, \ldots, I_k$ are abandoned. When this happens, *MAETT-step*() eliminates the abandoned instruction and returns $(I_0, \ldots, I_{i-1}, I'_i)$, which is shown as MAETT (b). *MAETT-step*() replaces I_i with I'_i, whose **post-ISA** field contains ISA'_i and **exintr?** flag is set to record the fact that I'_i was where the interrupt occurred. By the time we reach the final MA state, the MAETT will contain a history of instructions that shows where the interrupts occurred. From the MAETT, we can easily reconstruct the ISA execution sequence that satisfies the commutative diagram of our correctness criterion. Similarly, we use the MAETT to model speculative execution and internal exceptions.

5   Invariants Conditions and Correctness Criterion

We have defined various invariant properties about our pipeline implementation. Instead of discussing a complete list of invariant properties and techniques to define them, we present the minimum requirements that our invariant condition should satisfy, and we give a sketch of the proof of our correctness criterion using them.

In the following argument, we assume that MT_k is the MAETT representing an MA state MA_k, and MT_k contains l instructions $I_1, \ldots, I_l$. MT_k essentially represents the ISA transitions $ISA_0 \xrightarrow{I_1} \cdots \xrightarrow{I_l} ISA_l$, by storing ISA states in fields **pre-ISA** and **post-ISA**.

We defined an invariant condition as $Inv(MT_k, MA_k)$ that should satisfy following requirements.

Requirement 1. *If $Inv(MT_k, MA_k)$ holds and MA_k is a flushed pipeline state, then every instruction I_i in MT_k is committed.*

A mispredicted conditional branch and an error-causing instruction will eventually cause instructions to be abandoned. $MAETT\text{-}speculative?(MT_k)$ is a predicate to check whether MT_k contains such an uncommitted mispredicted branch or an uncommitted error-causing instruction. The program counter in MA_k should correctly point to the next instruction I_{l+1} to be fetched by ISA_l, unless it is fetching instructions speculatively.

Requirement 2. *If $Inv(MT_k, MA_k)$ holds and $MT_k = (I_1, \ldots, I_l)$, then*

$$\neg MAETT\text{-}speculative?(MT_k) \Rightarrow MA\text{-}pc(MA_k) = ISA\text{-}pc(ISA_l).$$

Results of instructions are written back to the register file when the instructions commit.

Requirement 3. *If $Inv(MT_k, MT_k)$ is true and I_{i+1}, $i < l$, is the first uncommitted instruction in $MT_k = (I_1, \ldots, I_l)$, then*

$$MA\text{-}regs(MA_k) = ISA\text{-}regs(ISA_i).$$

Requirement 4. *If $Inv(MT_k, MA_k)$ is true and I_{i+1}, $i < l$, is the first memory store instruction whose memory write is not completed, then*

$$MA\text{-}mem(MA_k) = ISA\text{-}mem(ISA_i).$$

Requirement 5. *For an arbitrary flushed initial state MA_0 and its MAETT MT_0, $Inv(MT_0, MA_0)$ holds.*

We must show that the invariant condition $Inv()$ is preserved during MAETT updates; however, if self-modified code is executed, the pipelined MA may not work correctly with respect to ISA specification. To characterize this problem, we defined a predicate $commit\text{-}self\text{-}modified\text{-}inst\text{-}p(MT)$ to check whether any instruction in MT is self-modified and also committed. Our invariant is preserved only when there is no such instruction. The machine can speculatively execute self-modified instructions, if they are eventually abandoned and have no effect on the programmer visible state.

Requirement 6. *Suppose MA_{k+1} and MT_{k+1} are the next MA state and next MAETT, that is:*

$$MA_{k+1} = MA\text{-}step(MA_k, Inputs_k),$$
$$MT_{k+1} = MAETT\text{-}step(MT_k, MA_k, Inputs_k).$$

Then

$$Inv(MT_k, MA_k) \Rightarrow Inv(MT_{k+1}, MA_{k+1}) \lor commit\text{-}self\text{-}modified\text{-}inst\text{-}p(MT_{k+1}).$$

Requirements 5 and 6 assure that $Inv()$ is true for all reachable states. Requirements 2, 3 and 4 constrain the relation between an MA state and the ISA state sequence represented by its MAETT. An example of this relation is shown in Fig. 4. Let us assume that, at the state MA_i, instruction I_0 is committed, I_1 is waiting for its memory operation to complete, I_2 and I_3 are being executed, and I_4 is not fetched yet. Requirement 2 implies that the program counter in MA_i is equal to that of ISA_4, because it should point to instruction I_4 in both states. Examples of Requirement 3 and 4 are also shown in the figure; the register file in MA_i is equal to the register file in ISA_2, and the memory of MA_i is equal to the memory in ISA_1. If all instructions $I_0, \ldots, I_5$ are committed, then the skewed dashed lines align to relate the final MA state and the final ISA state.

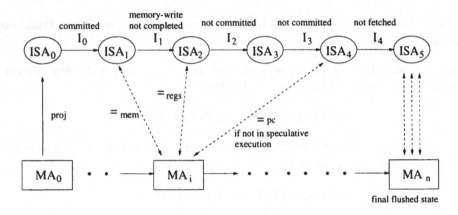

Fig. 4. Relations between MA and ISA sequences.

Checking the first five requirements is easy, since they don't involve a state transition of MA. However, checking Requirement 6 takes extensive analysis of MA state transitions, and this is where the actual verification activity of the hardware design takes place. In the rest of this section, we summarize the proof of our correctness criterion, assuming that $Inv()$ satisfies Requirement 6.

From Requirements 2, 3 and 4 and the definition of $MAETT\text{-}speculative?()$, it is straight forward to get the following lemma.

Lemma 1. *Suppose that invariant condition* $Inv(MA_n, MT_n)$ *holds, and every instruction* I_i *in* $MT_n = (I_1, \ldots, I_m)$ *is committed, then*

$$proj(MA_n) = ISA_m.$$

Lemma 2. *Let* MA_0 *be a flushed MA state,* MA_n *be the state after* n *MA transitions, and* MT_n *be the MAETT of* MA_n. *Then*

$$\neg commit\text{-}self\text{-}modified\text{-}inst\text{-}p(MT_n) \Rightarrow Inv(MT_n, MA_n).$$

Proof. Although a MAETT trace grows and shrinks, committed instructions are never removed from a MAETT. So any instruction in the intermediate MAETT MT_i for $i < n$ is also in the final MAETT MT_n. This implies

$$\neg commit\text{-}self\text{-}modified\text{-}inst\text{-}p(MT_n) \Rightarrow \neg commit\text{-}self\text{-}modified\text{-}inst\text{-}p(MT_i).$$

Hence, if $commit\text{-}self\text{-}modified\text{-}inst\text{-}p(MT_n)$ is false, we can combine Requirement 5 and 6 and get $Inv(MT_n, MA_n)$ by induction. ◇

Corollary 3. *If MAETT MT_n does not contain any modified instructions, then $Inv(MT_n, MA_n)$ is true.*

From Requirement 1, Lemma 1 and Corollary 3, we get the following theorem.

Theorem 4. *Suppose MA_0 is a flushed MA state and $ISA_0 = proj(MA_0)$. After n cycles of MA state transitions with arbitrary input sequence Inputs, we arrive at another flushed MA state $MA_n = MA\text{-}stepn(MA_0, Inputs, n)$. Then there exists a corresponding ISA transition sequence $ISA_0 \xrightarrow{I_1} \cdots \xrightarrow{I_m} ISA_m$, and if this sequence is not self-modifying, then $proj(MA_n) = ISA_m$.*

The ISA sequence $ISA_0 \xrightarrow{I_1} \cdots \xrightarrow{I_m} ISA_m$ can be constructed by calculating the MAETT of state MA_n with MAETT step function $MAETT\text{-}step()$.

The proof of Theorem 4 has been mechanically checked with ACL2 theorem prover. At this point, we have not yet completed the verification of Requirement 6. As pointed out earlier, the real verification problem is finding and verifying the invariant conditions. A merit of using the MAETT is that it helps us to define various pipeline invariants. For example, one invariant is that instructions are dispatched and committed in the ISA execution order. This is nicely defined as a recursive function over the list of instructions in a MAETT. We have verified 6 out of 18 invariant conditions of $Inv()$. So far, this verification process found three bugs in the design, even though the design had been simulated.

Our proof presented here reduces the problem of checking the correctness criterion to the problem of verifying our requirements. In this sense, what we have presented here is a framework for verifying a microprocessor. Our requirements are strong enough to prove our correctness criterion, since we have carried out the mechanical proof by assuming only those conditions. This suggests the possibility that we can reuse the structure of the proof for other hardware designs which satisfy these requirements, even though the construction of $MAETT\text{-}step()$ and the verification of the requirements are design dependent.

6 Conclusion

We have described a framework for verifying pipelined machine designs at the micro-architectural level. Our correctness criterion compares MA state transitions between two flushed states to the corresponding ISA state transitions. We discussed why our correctness criterion implies correct speculative execution and precise exceptions. The non-determinism at the ISA level introduced by external interrupts requires us to dynamically construct corresponding ISA transitions. This construction is done by modeling the execution of the MA design with a MAETT, which is essentially a history of committed and in-flight instructions. We defined an invariant condition that satisfies several requirements, and proved our correctness criterion under the assumption that the invariant conditions are preserved during MA state transitions. The proof has been mechanically checked by the ACL2 theorem prover. We have shown that our requirements are strong enough to carry out the proof.

We are currently verifying the invariant condition. We also would like to check whether an external interrupt is guaranteed to be processed. In our MA design, some external interrupts are dropped because internal exceptions have higher priority or because multiple interrupts are received within too short of an interval. It is an open question whether the MAETT model can help us to prove properties such as that an isolated external interrupt is guaranteed to be serviced.

References

1. Bishop C. Brock and Warren A. Hunt, Jr. Formally Specifying and Mechanically Verifying Programs for the Motorola Complex Arithmetic Processor DSP. In *1997 IEEE International Conference on Computer Design*, IEEE Computer Society. pp. 31–36, October 13–15, 1997.
2. J. R. Burch, D. L. Dill. Automatic Verification of Pipelined Microprocessor Control, Computer Aided Verification, Lecture Notes in Computer Science 818, Springer Verlag, pages 68-80, 1994.
3. J. R. Burch. Techniques for verifying superscalar microprocessors. In Design Automation Conference, June 1996.
4. M. Coe. Results from Verifying a Pipelined Microprocessor, Master's Thesis, University of Idaho, 1994.
5. H. G. Cragon. Memory Systems and Pipelined Processors, Jones and Bartlett Publishers, Inc., 1996.
6. D. Cyrluk. Microprocessor verification in PVS: A methodology and simple example, Technical Report SRI-CSL-93-12, SRI Computer Science Laboratory, Dec. 1993.
7. J. Hennessey, D. Patterson. Computer Architecture a Quantitative Approach, Morgan Kaufmann Publishers, Inc., 1996.
8. W. A. Hunt, Jr., B. Brock. A Formal HDL and Its Use in the FM9001 Verification. In C.A.R. Hoare and M.J.C. Gordon, editors, Mechanized Reasoning and Hardware Design, pages 35-48. Prentice-Hall International Series in Computer Science, Englewood Cliffs, N.J., 1992.
9. M. Kaufmann, J S. Moore. ACL2: An Industrial Strength Version of Nqthm, Proceedings of the Eleventh Annual Conference on Computer Assurance (COMPASS-96), pages 23-34 , IEEE Computer Society Press, June 1996.
10. J. Sawada, W. Hunt, Jr. Trace Table Based Approach for Pipelined Microprocessor Verification, Computer Aided Verification, Lecture Notes in Computer Science 1254, Springer Verlag, pages 364-375, 1997.
11. M. Srivas, M. Bickford. Formal Verification of a Pipelined Microprocessor, IEEE Software, pages 52-64, September 1990.

12. M. K. Srivas, S. P. Miller. Formal Verification of a Commercial Microprocessor, Technical Report SRI-CSL-95-12, SRI Computer Science Laboratory, July 1995.
13. S. Tahar, R. Kumar. Formal Verification of Pipeline Conflicts in RISC Processors, Proc. European Design Automation Conference (EURO-DAC94), Grenoble, France, IEEE Computer Society Press. pages 285-289, September 1994.
14. P. J. Windley, J. R. Burch. Mechanically Checking a Lemma Used in an Automatic Verification Tool, Formal Methods in Computer-Aided Design, Lecture Notes in Computer Science 1166, Springer Verlag, pages 362-376, 1996.

Symmetry Reductions in Model Checking *

E. M. Clarke[1] and E. A. Emerson[2] and S. Jha[1] and A.P. Sistla[3]

[1] School of Computer Science, Carnegie Mellon University, Pittsburgh, PA
[2] Department of Computer Science, University of Texas, Austin, TX
[3] Department of Electrical Engg and Computer Science, University of Illinois,
Chicago, IL

Abstract. The use of symmetry to alleviate state-explosion problems
during model-checking has become a important research topic. This paper investigates several problems which are important to techniques exploiting symmetry. The most important of these problems is the *orbit
problem*. We prove that the orbit problem is equivalent to an important
problem in computational group theory which is at least as hard as the
graph isomorphism but not known to be *NP*-complete. This paper also
shows classes of commonly occurring groups for which the orbit problem
is easy. Some methods of deriving symmetry for a shared variable model
of concurrent programs are also investigated. Experimental results providing evidence of reduction in state space by using symmetry are also
provided.

1 Introduction

Temporal Logic Model Checking is a technique for determining whether a temporal logic formula is valid in a finite state system $M = (S, R, L)$, where S is
the state space, R is the state transition relation, and L is a function that labels
states with sets of atomic propositions [4]. Such a structure is usually called a
Kripke structure and may have an enormous number of states because of the
state explosion problem. A system with n boolean state variables can have a
state space which is exponential in n. An efficient Model Checking procedure
tries to reduce the number of states that are actually explored [2, 4]. Recently,
techniques which exploit the inherent symmetry of the system while performing
model checking have become quite popular [3, 6, 11].

Basically, the idea of exploiting symmetry is the following: given a Kripke
Structure $M = (S, R, L)$, a symmetry group G is a group acting on the state
set S that *preserves* the transition relation R, G partitions the state set S into
equivalence classes called *orbits*. A quotient model M_G is constructed that contains one or more representative from each orbit. The state space S_G of the

* Clarke and Jha's research was supported in part by NSF Grant no. CCR-8722633 and
SRC Contract 92-DJ-294; Emerson's research was supported in part by NSF grant
no. CCR-941-5496 and SRC grant no. 388-DP-97; Sistla's research was supported in
part by NSF grants CCR-9623229 and CCR-9633536.

quotient model will, in general, be much smaller than the original state space S. This makes it possible to verify much larger structures.

This paper investigates several problems associated with exploiting symmetry. For example, given a group G and two states s and s', the *orbit problem* asks whether s and s' are in the same orbit. Determining whether two states are in the same orbit is at the core of any model checking procedure exploiting symmetry. We prove that the orbit problem is equivalent to an important problem in computational group theory. We explore ways of deriving symmetries of shared variable concurrent programs. Since the orbit problem in its full generality is quite hard, this paper also shows that the orbit problem is easy for certain commonly occurring groups and provides alternative techniques which do not require solving the orbit problem. We have also built a model-checker called SYMM which allows the user to specify the symmetries of the model and then uses the symmetries to perform efficient model-checking. Few of these problems were considered in [3, 6]. The results provided in this paper represent significant advances over those presented in [3, 6]. Although the paper only presents results for asynchronous composition of processes, all the results do extend to synchronous composition of processes but are not presented here because of lack of space. Complete details will be provided in the full version of the paper.

Our paper is organized as follows: In Section 2 we introduce a shared variable model. Section 3 gives a technique to derive symmetries of shared variable programs. Section 4 investigates the complexity of the orbit problem. Section 5 investigates some special classes of the orbit problem. Experimental results on an arbiter example are shown in section 6. Section 7 concludes with some interesting future directions. Due to space limitations we have not presented the background material here. For background on group theory the reader is referred to [9]. For general background on symmetry groups and model-checking see [3, 6].

2 A Shared Variable Model of Computation

We adopt the model of computation from [6]. A *shared variable program* is defined with the state sets and the transition relation as follows:

- $S = Loc^I \times D^V$ is the finite set of *states*, with Loc a finite set of individual process *locations*, I the set of process indices, and V is a finite set of shared *variables* over a finite *data domain* D.
- $R \subseteq S \times S$ which represents the transitions of the system.

For convenience, each state $s = (s', s'') \in S$ can be written in the form $(\ell_1, \ldots, \ell_n, v = d, \ldots, v' = d')$ indicating that processes $1, \ldots, n$ are in locations $\ell_1, \ldots, \ell_n$, respectively and the shared variables $v, \ldots, v'$ are assigned data values $d, \ldots, d'$, respectively.

Next, we define a labeling function for a shared variable program. The set of *terms* are expressions of the form l_i ($i \in I$) and $v = d$ ($v \in V$ and $d \in D$). The set of atomic propositions AP are constructed from the set of terms by the logical connectives $\wedge$ and $\neg$. Given an atomic proposition $p \in AP$ and a state $s \in S$, the satisfaction relation $s \models p$ is defined in the following way:

$s \models l_i$ iff the i-th process in the state s is in location l_i.

$s \models (v = d)$ iff the shared variable v has the value d in the state s.

$s \models f \wedge g$ iff $s \models f$ and $s \models g$.

$s \models \neg f$ iff $s \not\models f$.

Given a shared variable program, we can construct a corresponding Kripke Structure $M = (S, R, L)$ (S and R were defined before) by constructing the following labeling function $L : S \to 2^{AP} : p \in L(s) \Leftrightarrow s \models p$.

In practice, for ordinary model checking, M is the Kripke Structure corresponding to a finite state *concurrent program* $\mathcal{P}$ of the form $\|_{i=1}^n K_i$ consisting of processes $K_1, \ldots, K_n$ running in parallel. Each K_i may be viewed as a finite state transition graph with node set *Loc*. An arc from node ℓ to node ℓ' may be labeled by a guarded command $B \to A$. The guard B is an atomic proposition that can inspect shared variables and local states of "accessible" processes. A is a set of *simultaneous assignments* to shared variables $v := d \| \cdots \| v' := d'$. When process K_i is in local state ℓ and the guard B evaluates to *true* in the current global state, the program $\mathcal{P}$ can nondeterministically choose to advance by firing this transition of K_i which changes the local state of K_i to be ℓ' and the shared variables in V according to A. Thus the arc from ℓ to ℓ' in K_i represents a *local transition* of K_i denoted by $\ell : B \to A : \ell'$.

The Kripke structure $M = (S, R, L)$ corresponding to $\mathcal{P}$ is thus defined using the obvious formal operational semantics. First, the set of (all possible) states S is determined from $\mathcal{P}$ because it provides us with the set of local (i.e., individual process) locations *Loc*, process indices I, variables V, and data domain D. For states $s, t \in S$, we define $s \to t \in R$ iff $\exists i \in I$ such that the process K_i can cause s to move to t, denoted by $s \to_i t$ iff $\exists i \in I$ $\exists$ local transition $\tau_i = \ell_i : B_i \to A_i : m_i$ of K_i which *drives* $s = (s', s'')$ to $t = (t', t'')$; i-th component of s' equals ℓ_i, the i-th component of t' equals m_i, all other components of s' equal the corresponding component of t', predicate $B_i(s) = true$, and $t'' = A_i(s'')$. $A_i(s'')$ is constructed from s'' by replacing the values of the shared variables according to the simultaneous assignment statement A_i. The labeling function L is defined as before. Notice that we use asynchronous composition in the definition given here. Analogous definition can be given for synchronous composition. All the results given in the paper hold for synchronous composition, but are not stated because of lack of space.

3 Deriving Symmetry

This section analyzes how one can derive symmetry for shared variable programs introduced in the previous section. Intuitively, if one has a graph G whose nodes corresponds to processes and the processes communicate over the edges of G, an automorphism of the graph G should manifest itself into a symmetry of the underlying structure [3, 6]. Succinctly speaking, *structural symmetry introduces symmetry in the model* [3](cf. [5]). This section proves that for certain cases one can derive the symmetry of the model from the topology of the system. Given a concurrent program $\mathcal{P} = \|_{i=1}^{n} K_i$, we build a hypergraph $HG(\mathcal{P})$. Under certain restrictions, we prove that each automorphism of $HG(\mathcal{P})$ is also a symmetry of the underlying Kripke Structure M. A restricted version of the theorem already appeared in [6]. There the authors assumed that all processes are isomorphic and the variables are only shared between two processes. The new and more general version of the theorem, presented here, can handle a broader class of systems. For example, an arbiter which maintains a global shared variable (indicating who has the resource) can now be accomodated.

Let $\mathcal{P} = \|_{i=1}^{n} K_i$ be a concurrent program. In this section the index set is $I = [n]$. Each shared variable v is subscripted by the set of indices of the processes which access that shared variable. For example, if x is accessed by processes 1, 4, and 5, we write x as $x_{\{1,4,5\}}$. Notice that each shared variable is uniquely determined by its name and subscript, but we allow shared variables to have the same name as long as their subscripts are different. For example, $x_{\{1,2\}}$ and $x_{\{3,4\}}$ are allowed. A permutation $\pi \in S_n$ acts on the variables in a natural manner, i.e., $\pi(x_w) = x_{\pi(w)}$. A permutation π acting on $[n]$ is called *consistent* if and only if for every shared variable x_w, $x_{\pi(w)}$ is a variable as well. This means that we only allow permutations which map shared variables to shared variables.

We define how a consistent permutation π acts on states, atomic propositions, and processes. Let π be a consistent permutation.

- Given a state $s = (l_1, \cdots, l_n, v_{w_1} = d_1, \cdots, v_{w_k} = d_k)$, the state $\pi(s)$ is defined as follows: i-th process is in location $l_{\pi(i)}$ in the state $\pi(s)$, and the shared variable $v_{\pi(w)}$ in the state $\pi(s)$ has the same value as the variable v_w in the state s.
- Let $p \in AP$ be an atomic proposition. $\pi(p)$ is recursively defined as follows: $\pi(f \wedge g) = \pi(f) \wedge \pi(g)$, $\pi(\neg f) = \neg \pi(f)$, $\pi(l_i) = l_{\pi(i)}$, and $\pi(v_w = d) = (v_{\pi(w)} = d)$.
- Given a simultaneous assignment $A = (v_{w_1} = d_1 \| \cdots \| v_{w_k} = d_k)$, define $\pi(A)$ as the following simultaneous assignment: $v_{\pi(w_1)} = d_1 \| \cdots \| v_{\pi(w_k)} = d_k$
- Given a process K_i, the process $\pi(K_i)$ is constructed in the following manner: $l : B \to A : l'$ is a transition in K_i iff $l : \pi(B) \to \pi(A) : l'$ is a transition in $\pi(K_i)$.

Definition 1. A *colored hypergraph* with n vertices and k colors is a 3-tuple $H = ([n], E, L)$ such that $E \subseteq 2^{[n]}$ is the *edge set*, and $L : [n] \to [k]$ is the *coloring function* which colors each node with one of the k colors. A permutation π acting on $[n]$ is called an *automorphism* of the hypergraph H iff the following two conditions hold:

For all $1 \leq i \leq n$, $L(i) = L(\pi(i))$.
$w \in E$ iff $\pi(w) \in E$.

The group of automorphisms of the hypergraph H is denoted by $Aut(H)$.

Given a process K_i, let $\tau(K_i)$ be the *type* of that process. For example, if process K_i is an instance of MODULE m [14], then $\tau(K_i) = m$. Next, we define the concept of isomoprhism between two processes. Let $\Gamma(K_i)$ be the set of indices r such that there exists a shared variable x_w such that $\{i, r\} \subseteq w$. Intuitively, if $r \in \Gamma(K_i)$, then K_i and K_r share some variables. $\Gamma(K_i)$ is called the *neighborhood* of K_i. We require that $i \in \Gamma(K_i)$, i.e., a process is in its own neighborhood. We say that $K_i \cong K_j$ if and only if for every consistent permutation π such that $\pi(i) = j$ and such that for all $r \in \Gamma(K_i)$, $\tau(K_r) = \tau(K_{\pi(r)})$ it is the case that $\pi(K_i) = K_j$ and vice versa. Many times the condition $K_i \cong K_j$ can be checked by checking that $\pi(K_i) = K_j$ with respect to all permutations π that map i to j and that map elements in $\Gamma(K_i)$ to elements in $\Gamma(K_j)$ and that satisfy local consistency conditions (i.e. x_w is a variable iff $x_{\pi(w)}$ is a variable for cases where $i \in w$); this property can be checked efficiently.

Definition 2. Given a concurrent program $\mathcal{P} = \|_{i=1}^{n} K_i$, define the *corresponding* colored hypergraph $HG(\mathcal{P}) = ([n], E, L)$ in the following manner:

- $w \in E$ iff there exists a shared variable with subscript w.
- Partition the processes $K_1, \cdots, K_n$ into equivalence classes induced by the relation $\cong$. Let $c_1, \cdots, c_k$ be the k equivalence classes. The coloring function L is defined as follows: $L(i) = r$ iff the process K_i is in the equivalence class c_r.

Theorem 3. Let $HG(\mathcal{P})$ be the hypergraph corresponding to the program $\mathcal{P} = \|_{i=1}^{n} K_i$. Let M be the Kripke Structure corresponding to $\mathcal{P}$. Given these conditions, $Aut(HG(\mathcal{P})) \leq Aut(M)$.

4 Complexity of the Orbit Problem

In this section we assume that the state space of our system is given by assignments to n boolean state variables $x_1, \cdots, x_n$. Therefore, the state space is isomorphic to B^n (where $B = \{0, 1\}$). We assume that the symmetry group $G \leq S_n$ acts on B^n in the natural way: a permutation σ maps a vector $(z_1, \cdots, z_n)$ to $(z_{\sigma(1)}, \cdots, z_{\sigma(n)})$. The orbit problem is at the core of any method exploiting symmetry [3, 6, 12, 11]. The orbit problem asks whether two states s and s' (which in this case are two 0-1 vectors of size n) are in the same orbit, i.e., there exists a permutation $\sigma \in G$ such that $s' = \sigma(s)$. In [3] it was proved that the graph isomorphism problem can be reduced to the orbit problem. Therefore, the orbit problem is atleast as hard as the graph isomorphism problem. Here we show that the orbit problem is equivalent to the problem of finding a set stabilizer of a set Y in a coset (we call this problem SSC). Since the graph isomorphism problem can be reduced to SSC [8], this result subsumes the result which appeared in [3]. Moreover, SSC (and hence the orbit problem) is equivalent to several important problems in computational group theory, which are harder than graph isomorphism, but not known to be NP-complete. Proofs of most the theorems are based on techniques introduced in [13].

The Orbit Problem (OP): Given two 0-1 vectors x and y of size n and a group $G \leq S_n$, does there exist a permutation $\sigma \in G$ which maps x to y, i.e., $y = \sigma(x)$.

Set Stabilizer in a coset (SSC): Given a set $Y \subseteq [n]$, let $G \leq S_n$ be a group and $\gamma \in S_n$ be a permutation. The problem is to find whether there exists $\sigma \in G\gamma$ which *stabilizes* the set Y, i.e., $\sigma(Y) = Y$.

Constructive Set Stabilizer in a coset $(CSSC)$: Given a set $Y \subseteq [n]$, let $G \leq S_n$ be a group and $\gamma \in S_n$ be a permutation. The problem is to find whether there exists $\sigma \in G\gamma$ which stabilizes the set Y, i.e., $\sigma(Y) = Y$ and if yes, to exhibit such a σ.

Lemma 4. The problems SSC and $CSSC$ are polynomially equivalent.

Theorem 5. The problems OP and SSC are polynomially equivalent.

In general, the SSC problem is harder than *graph isomorphism* [8]. Conditions under which SSC can be solved in polynomial time are discussed in [8, 13]. In [8] it is proved that the *Coset Intersection Emptiness* problem stated below is polynomially equivalent to several important problems in computational group theory.

Definition 6. Coset Intersection Emptiness (CIE) Given the groups $A, B \leq S_n$ by generating sets and given a permutation $\pi \in S_n$, test whether $A\pi \cap B$ is empty.

Theorem 7. The set stabilizer in a coset problem (SSC) is polynomially equivalent to **CIE**.

Therefore, using the previous theorems one can deduce that OP is polynomially equivalent to **CIE** and hence several problems in computational group theory.

4.1 The Constructive Orbit Problem

Modeling states by boolean variables, in some cases, is too cumbersome and detailed. For example, consider the shared variable program introduced in Section 2. Let $\mathcal{P} = \|_{i=1}^{n} K_i$ be a concurrent program which does not have shared variables. Let the size of the set of locations Loc be k. In this case, a typical state in $\mathcal{P}$ is given by a vector of size n whose elements are integers between 1 and k, i.e., the space $[k]^n$. Permuting the processes K_i amounts to permuting the corresponding integers in that state. A symmetry group $G \leq S_n$ acts on the space $[k]^n$ in the following way: a permutation $\sigma \in G$ maps $(x_1, \cdots, x_n)$ to $(x_{\sigma(1)}, \cdots, x_{\sigma(n)})$.

Given a symmetry group G, one frequently needs a *representative function* $\xi : S \to S$ [3, 6, 11] (S is the state space of the system) which has the following properties:

- s and $\xi(s)$ are in the same orbit.
- If s and s' are in the same orbit, then $\xi(s) = \xi(s')$.

Such a representative function is used during state exploration in [3, 6, 11]. The need to find such a representative function motivates the following problem.

Definition 8. The Constructive Orbit Problem (COP)**:** Given a group acting on $[n]$ and vector $x = (x_1, \cdots, x_n)$ find the lexicographically least element (or lex-least element for short) in the orbit of x (the group G permutes the indices of x)

Notice that if one can solve COP in polynomial time, one can construct the representative function ξ. Given a state x, $\xi(x)$ is simply the lex-least element in its orbit. In [1] it is proved that the problem is NP-hard. The paper also shows that for certain special groups COP can be solved in polynomial time. Actually, for our purposes it is enough to find a canonical element from each orbit.

5 Working Around the Orbit Problem

Results of section 4 prove that the Orbit problem and the Constructive Orbit Problem are quite hard in its full generality. In this section we discuss two possible techniques which will help circumvent the complexity of the orbit problem.

1. We prove that for a large class of groups, which occur commonly in practice, the orbit problem can be easily solved. This means that if the symmetries are restricted to this class of groups, the orbit problem can be easily solved.
2. We also describe an approach that uses multiple representatives from each orbit rather than just one. This approach is partcularly useful for symbolic model checking [3].

The ensuing subsections outline these approaches.

5.1 Easy Groups

Notice that if a group $G \le S_n$ has polynomial size, COP for G can be solved in polynomial time by exhaustive enumeration. For example, a rotation group acting on set of size $[n]$ has order n. Therefore, for the rotation group one can solve COP in linear time. The lemma given below states that if COP can be solved in polynomial time for two disjoint groups J and K, then COP can be solved in polynomial time for their direct product.

Lemma 9. Let G be a disjoint product of J and K. If COP for J and K can be solved in polynomial time, then COP for G can be solved in polynomial time.

The next lemma is similar to the previous one but refers to wreath products.

Lemma 10. Let $G = J \wr K$ be the wreath product of J and K. The group J, K, G act on the sets $[n], [m], [nm]$ respectively. If COP for J, K can be solved in polynomial time, then COP for G can be solved in polynomial time.

Lemma 11. Let S_n be the full symmetric group acting on the set $[n]$. The *COP* problem for S_n can be solved in polynomial time.

Proof: Given a vector $x = (x_1, \cdots, x_n)$, the lex-least element of x under the group S_n can be obtained by sorting the elements x_i. $\square$

In practice, symmetries are given as a set of transpositions. For example, in a system which has the star topology, the two outer processes can be switched. The lemma given below states that if the group is only generated by transpositions, then *COP* for it can be solved in polynomial time.

Lemma 12. Let G be a permutation group acting on the set $[n]$. Assume that G is generated by a set of transpositions S. The *COP* problem for G can be solved in polynomial time.

This means that during model-checking if one restricts to the class of groups mentioned above, exploiting symmetry is relatively easy. Hence while exploiting symmetry one should try to work with these easy groups.

5.2 Multiple Representatives

Multiple Representatives were discussed in [3]. The account given here is much cleaner and general. Assume that we are given a Kripke Structure $M = (S, R, L)$ and a symmetry group G of M. Let $C \subseteq G$ be an arbitrary set of permutations which is *inverse closed*, i.e., $\pi \in C$ implies that $\pi^{-1} \in C$. We also assume that the identity permutation e is in C. Let $Rep \subseteq S$ be a set of *representatives* which satisfies the following requirements:

1. Every orbit of S under the action of G has a non-empty intersection with Rep.
2. Given an $s \in S$, there exists a $\sigma \in C$ such that $\sigma(s) \in Rep$.

Let $M_{Rep} = (Rep, R_{Rep}, L_{Rep})$, where R_{Rep} and L_{Rep} are defined as follows:

- We have that $(r_1, r_2) \in R_{Rep}$ iff there exists $s \in S$ and $\sigma \in C$ such that $(s, r_2) \in R$ and $\sigma(s) = r_1$.
- $L_{Rep}(r) = L(r)$.

The *representative relation* $\xi \subseteq S \times Rep$ is defined as follows: $(s, r) \in \xi$ iff there exists a $\sigma \in C$ such that $\sigma(s) = r$. Notice that $R_{Rep} = \eta^{-1} \circ R$.

Theorem 13. let $M = (S, R, L)$ be a Kripke structure, G be a *symmetry group* of M, and h be a CTL^* formula. If G is an invariance group for all the atomic propositions p occurring in h, then for all r such that $(s, r) \in \xi$

$$M, s \models h \Leftrightarrow M_{Rep}, r \models h$$

A natural question to ask is: how does one choose *Rep* given a set of polynomial size C? One natural choice of *Rep* is given below:

$$r \in Rep \Leftrightarrow \forall(\sigma \in C)(r \geq \sigma(r))$$

where $\leq$ represents the lexicographical ordering on the 0-1 vectors. It is easy to check that *Rep* has the required properties. Also notice that given an $s \in S$ and $r \in Rep$ one can decide the following questions in polynomial time?

1. Is s a representative, i.e., $s \in Rep$?
2. Is $(s, r) \in \xi$?

First we argue that the choice of C is very important on how much reduction is achieved. For example, let us consider the case when $C = G^{[1,k]}$. In this case we will only permute the first indices k indices of the states. Therefore if there exists an orbit $\Theta \subseteq S$ which does not involve these k indices, then $\Theta \subseteq Rep$, i.e., the whole orbit has to be represented. We need a way of choosing C such that we have uniform savings across all orbits of S in G. One possibility is to take a subgroup $H \leq G$ such that $[G : H]$ is polynomial in n. Let B be the full right traversal of H in G. Let C be the inverse closure of B. The subgroup H can be chosen in many ways and its choice will depend upon the structure of the system being verified. One choice is as follows: Fix a set $I = \{i_1, \cdots, i_k\} \subseteq [n]$ of size k. Let H be the pointwize stabilizer of I in G. The *pointwise stabilizer* of I in G is the following group:

$$\{\sigma \in G \mid \forall(i \in I)(\sigma(i) = i)\}$$

Notice that $[G : H] \leq n^k$. The subgroup H and its full traversal in G can be found in polynomial time [7].

6 Empirical Results

Using the multiple representatives theory presented in section 5.2 we have built a symbolic model checker called SYMM. The tool SYMM has a language based on the shared variable model of computation described earlier. It allows the user to give *CTL* specifications. The tool also provides the facility for the user to give symmetries of the system. We have verified several examples using our tool. Here we describe our results for an arbiter example. In this arbiter, each module has a priority number. While competing for the bus, modules with higher priority number are given preference. Among competing modules with the same priority number, the winner is decided non-deterministically. Winner is the module which wins the competing phase. The arbitration cycle (which results in a winner) has six phases. We give a brief overview of these phases. The interested reader is referred to the IEEE Futurebus standard for a more detailed account [10].

Phase 0: In this phase modules decide to compete for the bus.
Phase 1: Noticing that a competition phase is about to begin, other modules might decide to compete.

Phase 2: In this phase a winner (called the *master elect*) is selected from the set of competing modules. Winner is selected according to the rules described earlier.

Phase 3: Other modules check that the master elect had the highest priority number among the competing modules. If this is not the case, modules assert an error. If an error has not occurred, this phase continues until the master of the bus relinquishes its control. In this phase a module with higher priority than the master elect might start a new arbitration cycle. This is called *deposing* the master elect.

Phase 4: In this phase the current master of the bus might inhibit transfer of control of the bus to the master elect. If the master relinquishes its control over the bus, the arbitration cycle moves to the last phase.

Phase 5: In this phase the master elect gets control of the bus. This phase is called the *transfer of tenure* phase.

There are three boolean variables in each module which ensures the proper sequencing of the phases in an arbitration cycle. The internal state of the module depends on the outcome of the arbitration cycle and is shown below.

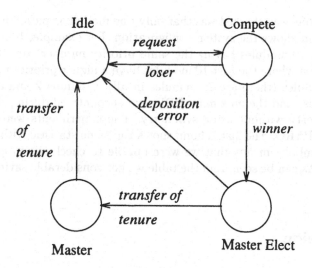

Fig. 1. States of the Arbiter

Notice that two modules with the same priority number can be permuted without changing the behavior of the system. Formally, the permutation corresponding to exchanging two modules with the same priority number is a symmetry of the system. However, two modules with different priority numbers cannot be exchanged. In the table given below the first column shows the configuration of the system. Assume that we have m sets of n modules (denoted by $\{M_{1,1}, \cdots, M_{1,n}\}, \cdots, \{M_{m,1}, \cdots, M_{m,n}\}$). Moreover, the priority numbers of two modules $M_{j,l}$ and $M_{r,t}$ are the same iff $j = r$, or they belong to the same set. In this case the set of representatives *Rep* is the set of states where the first module from a particular set is always chosen master elect. The set C contains all the transpositions of the form $\sigma_{i,l} = ((i,1),(i,l))$ $(1 \leq i \leq m$ and $1 \leq l \leq n)$ and their products. The transposition $\sigma_{i,l}$ corresponds to exchanging modules $M_{i,1}$ and $M_{i,l}$. It is easy to see that C is inverse closed. Moreover, given an arbitrary state s there exists a representative state $r \in Rep$ and $\sigma \in C$ such that $\sigma(s) = r \in Rep$. Consider a state s where $M_{j,l}$ is the master elect. In this case $\sigma_{i,l}(s)$ is the state where $M_{j,1}$ is the master elect. Hence all conditions for applying the multiple representative theory are satisfied. The table of experimental results is shown below.

System Config	Time	BDD size	Time (Symm)	BDD size (Symm)
10m	163.41	369,705	37.04	27,671
12m	487.56	921,034	43.12	36,135
10m10m	1171.85	932,429	126.17	73,514
12m12m	-	-	198.195	93,094

The property that was checked was that only one module is picked master elect. The first column shows the system configuration. For example, 10m is the configuration with 10 modules having the same priority number. 10m10m denotes the configuration where the first 10 modules have a higher priority number than the last 10 modules (there are 20 modules in all). Columns 2 and 3 shows the time (in seconds) and the maximum BDD size encountered during checking the temporal property without using symmetry. The experiments were run on an Sun ULTRA SPARC. The last column shows the same statistic with using symmetry. The symbol - means that we were unable to check the property in the time allowed. As can be seen from the table we get considerable savings by using symmetry.

7 Conclusion

In this paper we investigated various problems associated with exploiting symmetry in model checking. We also provided ways of deriving symmetry for shared variable concurrent programs. An important research problem will be to take some existing hardware description languages and derive symmetry information statically from the system descriptions written in that language. Ideas presented in section 3 are applicable in this context. This paper also makes connection between exploiting symmetry in model checking and computational group theory. An important research direction will be to use some of the powerful techniques available in the computational group theory literature in the model checking domain. It will be also very useful to apply some of the symmetry ideas on industrial size examples.

158

References

1. L. Babai and E. Luks. Canonical labeling of graphs. In *Proceedings of the 15th ACM STOC*, 1983.
2. J. R. Burch, E. M. Clarke, K. L. McMillan, D. L. Dill, and L. J. Hwang. Symbolic model checking: 10^{20} states and beyond. 98(2):142–170, June 1992.
3. E. Clarke, R. Enders, T. Filkorn, and S. Jha. Exploiting symmetry in temporal logic model checking. *Formal Methods in System Design*, 9(1/2):77–104, 1996.
4. E. M. Clarke, E. A. Emerson, and A. P. Sistla. Automatic verification of finite-state concurrent systems using temporal logic specifications. *ACM Trans. Prog. Lang. Syst.*, 8(2):244–263, Apr. 1986.
5. P. Curie. Sur la symétrie dans les phénomènons physiques, symétrie d'un champ électrique magnétique. *J. Physics (3rd, ser.)*, 3:393–415, 1894.
6. E. Emerson and A. Sistla. Symmetry and model checking. *Formal Methods in System Design*, 9(1/2):105–130, 1996.
7. M. Furst, J. Hopcroft, and E. Luks. Polynomial-time algorithms for permutations groups. In *Proceedings of the 21st Annual Symposium on Foundations of Computer Science*, 1980.
8. C. Hoffman. *Group Theoretic Algorithms and Graph Isomorphism*, volume 697 of *Lecture Notes in Computer Science*. Springer-Verlag, Berlin, 1982.
9. T. Hungerford. *Algebra*. Springer-Verlag, 1980.
10. IEEE Computer Society. *IEEE Standard for Futurebus+—Logical Protocol Specification*, Mar. 1992. IEEE Standard 896.1-1991.
11. C. Ip and D. Dill. Better verification through symmetry. *Formal Methods in System Design*, 9(1/2):41–76, 1996.
12. K. Jensen. Condensed state spaces for symmetrical coloured petri nets. *Formal Methods in System Design*, 9(1/2):7–40, 1996.
13. E. Luks. Permutation groups and polynomial-time computation. In *Workshop on Groups and Computation*, volume 11 of *Dimacs*. American Mathematical Society, Oct. 1991.
14. K. L. McMillan. *Symbolic Model Checking: An Approach to the State Explosion Problem*. PhD thesis, Carnegie Mellon University, 1992.

Structural Symmetry and Model Checking

Gurmeet Singh Manku[1] and Ramin Hojati[2] and Robert Brayton[3]

[1] IBM Almaden Research Center (manku@almaden.ibm.com)
[2] University of California at Berkeley and HDAC Inc. (hojati@hdac.com)
[3] University of California at Berkeley (brayton@ic.berkeley.edu)

Abstract. A fully automatic framework is presented for identifying symmetries in structural descriptions of digital circuits and CTL* formulas and using them in a model checker. The set of sub-formulas of a formula is partitioned into equivalence classes so that truth values for only one sub-formula in any class need be evaluated for model checking. Structural symmetries in net-list descriptions of digital circuits and CTL* formulas are formally defined and their relationship with the corresponding Kripke structures is described. A technique for automatic identification of structural symmetries is described that requires computation of the automorphism group of a suitable labeled directed graph. A novel fast algorithm for this problem is presented. Finally, experimental results are reported for BLIF-MV net-lists derived from Verilog.

1   Introduction

Temporal model checking algorithms [CES86,BCL+94] typically explore the states of a non-deterministic finite state machine that represents the system under scrutiny. A major bottleneck is the exponential number of states that need be explored. This is commonly known as *State Space Explosion*. Among the techniques being developed for countering this problem are partial order methods, abstraction, compositional approaches, and symmetry reductions. Symmetries abound in hardware circuits, distributed algorithms and concurrent programs.

Emerson and Sistla [ES96] and Clarke *et al* [CEFJ96] show how symmetries in Kripke structures and CTL* formulas allow the construction of a smaller sized *quotient* structure such that the formula need be verified only for the quotient. In both works, symmetries are specified by hand by the designer. Emerson and Sistla [ES95] have developed theory for using symmetries with fairness constraints. Gyuris and Sistla [GS97] have developed an on-the-fly model checker that utilizes symmetries under fairness. Emerson, Jha and Peled [EJP97] have combined partial orders and symmetries. Symmetries have also been shown to speedup transistor-level verification [PB97].

Ip and Dill [ID96] use symmetries for speeding up verification of safety properties using explicit techniques for designs specified in a guarded command language. They propose augmentation of the language itself by introducing a new data type with syntactic constraints for sets of fully symmetric variables called *scalarsets*. A major drawback of scalarsets is that important and standard specification languages such as Verilog and VHDL cannot be modified easily.

Our work is distinguished from previous work on several counts. First, we provide a framework for identifying symmetries *automatically*. Second, we formalize the notion of *structural symmetries* in net-list descriptions, show how they relate to those in Kripke structures and present effective algorithms for automatically identifying them. Third, we show how *symmetries in the formula* itself can be used with or without quotient structures to expedite model checking.

2 Preliminaries

Kripke Structures: Let AP be a set of atomic propositions. A *Kripke structure* over AP is a triple $M = (S, R, K)$, where S is a finite set of *states*, $R \subseteq S \times S$ is a *transition relation* that is *total*, i.e. $(\forall s \in S)(\exists t \in S)((s, t) \in R)$, and $K : S \to 2^{AP}$ is a *labeling function*. Let states in S be encoded such that there is a 1-1 mapping from S into 2^L for some L. Then K is a multi-output boolean function $K : 2^L \to 2^{AP}$.

Temporal Logic CTL* is the set of strings S generated by the two productions $S \to \langle AP \rangle \mid \neg S \mid S \vee S \mid E(\mathcal{P})$ and $\mathcal{P} \to S \mid \neg \mathcal{P} \mid \mathcal{P} \vee \mathcal{P} \mid X\mathcal{P} \mid \mathcal{P}U\mathcal{P}$, where $\langle AP \rangle$ denotes any proposition $p \in AP$, S denotes a set of *state formulas*, and $\mathcal{P}$ denotes a set of *path formulas*. If $M = (S, R, K)$ is a Kripke structure, $(M, s \models f)$ denotes that the state formula f is true for state $s \in S$. Similarly, $(M, \psi \models g)$ denotes that path formula g is true for path ψ. See [CEFJ96] for a formal definition of $\models$ using this notation.

We say that two CTL* formulas are *logically equivalent* if their truth values are identical for every state in any Kripke structure. We say that two CTL* formulas are *structurally equivalent* if they also have isomorphic parse trees. Intuitively, the second formula is the same as the first one written in a structurally different way due to the commutativity of some operators.

Model Checking Problem: *Given a set of atomic propositions AP, a Kripke structure $M = (S, R, K)$, a CTL* formula f and a set of initial states $I \subseteq S$, does every state in I satisfy f?* Clarke, Emerson and Sistla [CES86] presented the first algorithm for CTL model checking using explicit state space exploration. A Binary Decision Diagrams based symbolic model checker that can handle more than 10^{120} states on some pipelined circuits has been described by Burch *et al* [BCL$^+$94].

Permutation Groups: A permutation π is a bijective mapping $\pi : S \to S$ defined over a finite non-empty set S. We denote the action of π on an element $s \in S$ by πs. We use $H \leq G$ to denote that H is a subgroup of G. We denote the intersection of G_1 and G_2 by $G_1 \cap G_2$, which itself is a group. For a set $T \subseteq S$, we define $\pi T = \{s \mid s = \pi t \text{ where } t \in T\}$. This overloads operator π but buys us notational convenience. For a set $X \subseteq S$, such that $\pi X = X$, we use $\pi_{<X>} : X \to X$ to denote the restriction of π to X.

Definition of $\bowtie$ Operator: Let G denote a permutation group over $S_1 \cup S_2$ such that $(\forall \pi \in G)((\pi S_1 = S_1) \wedge (\pi S_2 = S_2))$. Let H denote a permutation group over $S_2 \cup S_3$ similarly. Then $G \bowtie H$ is defined to be a permutation group over $S_1 \cup S_3$ such that $\pi \in G \bowtie H$ if and only if there exist $g \in G$ and $h \in H$ such that $(\forall s \in S_1)(gs = \pi s)$, $(\forall s \in S_3)(hs = \pi s)$ and $(\forall s \in S_2)(gs = hs)$.

3 Symmetric Sub-formulas

Let $M = (S, R, K)$ be a Kripke structure with 2^L states. Let $\pi : L \to L$ be a permutation. It induces a permutation $\Pi : 2^L \to 2^L$ naturally. Let π be such that Π is an automorphism of the directed unlabeled graph (S, R). The set of all such π forms a group, which we denote by $Aut_M L$. Later, we consider a Kripke structure M having additional labels drawn from a set $X \supseteq AP$. The new labels can be looked upon as a mapping $K' : 2^L \to 2^X$. When $X = AP$, $K' = K$.

Consider a permutation $\pi : L \cup X \to L \cup X$ such that $(\pi L = L)$ and $(\pi_{<L>} \in Aut_M L)$ and $(\forall x \in 2^L)(\forall y \in 2^{AP})((K'(x) = y) \Leftrightarrow (K'(\pi x) = \pi y))$. The set of all such permutations π forms a group which we denote by $Aut_M L \cdot X$.

For $s \in S$ and $\pi \in Aut_M L \cdot AP$, let πs denote the state obtained by applying π to the encoding of s. For any path ψ in M, let $\pi\psi$ denote the path obtained by applying π to every state in ψ. For a CTL* formula f defined on AP, let πf denote the formula obtained by replacing every occurrence of $p \in AP$ by πp.

Theorem 1. *For a Kripke structure $M = (S, R, K)$ and a permutation $\pi \in Aut_M L \cdot AP$, $((M, s \models f) \Leftrightarrow (M, \pi s \models \pi f))$ and $((M, \psi \models g) \Leftrightarrow (M, \pi\psi \models \pi g))$ for any state $s \in S$, any path ψ in M, any CTL* state formula f and any CTL* path formula g.* $\square$

Theorem 1 can be proved by induction using the identities $(\pi(\neg f) = \neg(\pi f))$, $(\pi(f \vee g) = \pi f \vee \pi g)$, $(\pi(Xf) = X(\pi f))$, $(\pi(Eg) = E(\pi g))$ and $(\pi(g_1 U g_2) = \pi g_1 U \pi g_2)$. A detailed proof can be found in [Man97]. For a Kripke structure M and CTL* formula f defined on AP, let SF denote the set of all sub-formulas of f, including any atomic propositions in AP that occur in f. Recall the definitions of logical and structural equivalence from Section 2. For a subgroup $G \leq Aut_M L \cdot AP$, we define a relation $\approx^G \subseteq SF \times SF$ as $(\forall f_1, f_2 \in SF)((f_1 \approx^G f_2) \Leftrightarrow (\exists \pi \in G)(\pi f_1 \text{ and } f_2 \text{ are logically equivalent}))$. We also define a relation $\approx_s^G$ the same way as $\approx^G$ but replacing logical equivalence by structural. The following theorem is immediate.

Theorem 2. *For $G \leq Aut_M L \cdot AP$, the relations $\approx^G$ and $\approx_s^G$ are equivalence relations, with $\approx^G$ inducing a partition coarser than that induced by $\approx_s^G$.* $\square$

3.1 Applications

First, consider two sub-formulas g and h in the same equivalence class. Let $\pi \in Aut_M L \cdot AP$ be a witness that transforms h into g. If the truth value of h has been evaluated for all states in S, the truth value for g is immediately available. In a symbolic technique, the BDD for g can be computed from that for h by variable substitution corresponding to π. Second, having proved the correctness of a CTL* formula f, one can use Theorem 1 to generate new formulas whose truth value is already known by producing a non-trivial $\pi \in G$ and constructing πf. A model checker can present new formulas to a designer in a controlled fashion using an interactive user interface. Third, it will be clear that identification of symmetric sub-formulas contributed to savings on top of quotient structures that we describe in Section 4.

3.2 Computing Equivalence Classes

Given $G \leq Aut_M L \cdot AP$ and a CTL formula f, how do we find two sub-formulas g and h such that $g \approx^G h$?* This is a computationally hard problem even if f is a simple boolean formula without path operators or temporal quantifiers [AT96]. If we replace $\approx^G$ by $\approx_s^G$, the problem is as hard as graph isomorphism [Man97]. We outline a technique that can identify symmetric sub-formulas if the symmetry in the specification is reflected in the formula as well, which is true in practice.

For a CTL* formula f, let SF denote the set of sub-formulas of f, including all atomic propositions that occur in f. Consider the group consisting of permutations π : $AP \rightarrow AP$ such that f and πf are structurally equivalent. Every permutation in this group implicitly defines a permutation on the set $AP \cup SF$. We denote this group by $Aut_f\ AP \cdot SF$. Let $G \leq Aut_M\ L \cdot AP$. Let $H \leq Aut_f\ AP \cdot SF$. Recall the definition of $\bowtie$ from Section 2. We see that the group $G \bowtie H$ is well defined. We define a relation $\approx_s^{G \bowtie H} \subseteq SF \times SF$ as $(\forall f_1, f_2 \in SF)((f_1 \approx_s^{G \bowtie H} f_2) \Leftrightarrow (\exists \pi \in G \bowtie H)(\pi f_1$ and f_2 are structurally equivalent)). This is an equivalence relation. In general, the partition induced by $\approx_s^{G \bowtie H}$ is finer than that induced by $\approx_s^G$ for $G = Aut_M\ L \cdot AP$.

In Section 5, we will show how $G \leq Aut_M\ L \cdot AP$, $H \leq Aut_f\ AP \cdot SF$ and $G \bowtie H$ can all be computed automatically. The representation for $G \bowtie H$ would allow us to easily identify the partitions induced by $\approx_s^{G \bowtie H}$ and produce witnesses that transform one sub-formula into another.

4 Quotient Structures

We now develop a theory of symmetries for Kripke structures, extending those developed by Clarke *et al* [CEFJ96] and Emerson and Sistla [ES96]. Let $M = (S, R, K)$ be a Kripke structure with 2^L states. Let $G \leq Aut_M\ L \cdot X$ for some set of labels $X \supseteq AP$. Let two states s and t in S be related if there exists $\pi \in G$ such that $\pi s = t$. This defines an equivalence relation, partitioning S into equivalent sets called *orbits*. We denote the orbit of a state $s \in S$ by $[s]_G$. We pick a state from each orbit to obtain a set of representatives and define a function $\xi_G : S \rightarrow S$ such that each state is mapped to the representative of the orbit it belongs to. ξ_G is not unique. The results in this paper hold for any ξ_G. For a Kripke structure $M = (S, R, K)$ and $G \leq Aut_M\ L \cdot X$ for some set of labels X, the *quotient structure* is defined as $M_G = (S_G, R_G, K_G)$, where $S_G = \{[s]_G \mid s \in S\}$, $R_G = \{([s]_G, [t]_G) \mid (s, t) \in R\}$ and $K_G([s]_G) = K(\xi_G(s))$. The fundamental result in [CEFJ96] is captured by the following theorem:

Theorem 3. *[CEFJ96] For a Kripke structure $M = (S, R, K)$ and a group $G \leq Aut_M\ L \cdot AP$, if $(\forall \pi \in G)(\forall p \in AP)(\pi p = p)$, then for any CTL* formula f, it is true that $(\forall s \in S)((M, s \models f) \Leftrightarrow (M_G, [s]_G \models f))$.* □

Application of Theorem 3 requires that the truth value of every atomic proposition be invariant under every permutation in G. In the extreme case, we could have $AP = L$, giving each state a unique label and making G trivial. Emerson and Sistla [ES96] present a generalization of Theorem 3. However, their theory is built for Kripke structures derived from systems of communicating isomorphic processes, the set of atomic propositions being the set of shared variables. In our terminology, it amounts to assuming $AP = L$ and a single initial state. We now develop a generalization of their result so that it is applicable to Kripke structures derived from net-list descriptions.

For a CTL* formula f, let MPS be the set of its maximal propositional sub-formulas. Let f_{MPS} be the multi-output boolean function $2^{AP} \to 2^{MPS}$. We define $Aut_f \, AP \cdot MPS = \{\pi : AP \cup MPS \to AP \cup MPS \mid \pi \text{ is a permutation}, \pi AP = AP, \pi MPS = MPS, (\forall y \in MPS)(\pi y = y) \text{ and } (\forall x \in 2^{AP})(f_{MPS}(x) = f_{MPS}(\pi x))\}$. This set forms a group. For $G \leq Aut_M \, L \cdot AP$ and $H \leq Aut_f \, AP \cdot MPS$, the group $G \bowtie H$ is well defined.

Theorem 4. *For $G \leq Aut_M \, L \cdot AP$ and $H \leq Aut_f \, AP \cdot MPS$, it is true that*
$$(\forall s \in S)((M, s \models f) \Leftrightarrow (M_{G \bowtie H}, [\![s]\!]_{G \bowtie H} \models f))$$

Proof. The crux lies in showing that $G \bowtie H \leq Aut_M \, L \cdot X$, where $X = MPS$. Then replacing labels of M by labels corresponding to evaluations of sub-formulas in MPS allows a straightforward application of Theorem 3 to get the desired result. $\square$

To construct the quotient, we require $G \bowtie H$, for which we present an automatic procedure in the next section. Once we have constructed $G \bowtie H$, how do we use it to expedite model checking? A detailed exposition can be found in [ES96,CEFJ96]. Briefly, we need to compute the canonical state function $\xi_{G \bowtie H}$ and modify the model checker so that it canonicalizes every state encountered during state space traversal. See [Man97] for a summary of known results for computing $\xi_{G \bowtie H}$. Theorem 4 can be further extended along the lines of *Auto f* in [ES96] by introducing an additional set of labels corresponding to all sub-formulas that have E, X or U as the topmost operator. Although we omit the theorem from this paper, we note that computation of the corresponding $G \bowtie H$ can still be automated.

5 Structural Symmetries

In Section 3.2, we saw how knowledge of groups $G \leq Aut_M \, L \cdot AP$ and $H \leq Aut_f \, AP \cdot SF$ would help us partition sub-formulas of a CTL* formula f into equivalence classes. In Section 4, we saw how knowledge of the same group G but a different $H \leq Aut_f \, AP \cdot MPS$ would allow us to construct quotient structures. In both the cases, we need to compute $G \bowtie H$. We now describe how G, H and $G \bowtie H$ can be computed automatically from net-lists of digital circuits and CTL* formulas, with no assistance from the designer. We have chosen BLIF-MV [B+91] as a representative structural hardware description language.

5.1 Characterizing a BLIF-MV Circuit

We model a BLIF-MV circuit as a five tuple $\mathcal{C} = \langle \mathcal{I}, \mathcal{O}, \mathcal{L}, \mathcal{T}, \mathcal{S} \rangle$, consisting of a set of primary input ports $\mathcal{I}$, a set of primary output ports $\mathcal{O}$, a set of latches $\mathcal{L}$, a set of tables $\mathcal{T}$ and a set of interconnection signals $\mathcal{S}$. Intuitively, $\mathcal{C}$ is a big black-box with I/O ports (primary inputs and outputs) consisting of smaller black boxes (tables and latches) whose I/O ports are interconnected with signals.

A table $T \in \mathcal{T}$ has input ports $i_1^T, i_2^T, \ldots$ and output ports $o_1^T, o_2^T, \ldots$. With each output o_i^T, we associate a function f_i^T that takes the ordered tuple $\langle i_1^T, i_2^T, \ldots \rangle$ as its argument. In general, f_i^T is non-deterministic, as allowed by BLIF-MV. See the figure below for a BLIF-MV table description. A latch $L \in \mathcal{L}$ has two input ports i_1^L, i_2^L and one output port o_1^L. The second input port specifies the initial value for the latch.

Let $P_{sink} = P_{in}^T \cup P_{in}^L \cup \mathcal{O}$, where $P_{in}^T = \bigcup_{T \in \mathcal{T}} \{i_1^T, i_2^T, \ldots\}$, $P_{in}^L = \bigcup_{L \in \mathcal{L}} \{i_1^L\}$. Let $P_{source} = P_{out}^T \cup P_{out}^L \cup \mathcal{I}$, where $P_{out}^T = \bigcup_{T \in \mathcal{T}} \{o_1^T, o_2^T, \ldots\}$ and $P_{out}^L = \bigcup_{L \in \mathcal{L}} \{o_1^L\}$. Thus P_{sink} is the set of primary outputs and input ports of tables and latches, except those for initial values for latches. And P_{source} is the set of all primary inputs and all output ports of tables and latches.

Each port is associated with a domain. Let $dom(p)$ denote the domain of any port $p \in P_{sink} \cup P_{source}$. For $o_j^T \in P_{out}^T$, let the function $f_j^T(i_1^T, i_2^T, \ldots)$ be the boolean function specified in its table that corresponds to the output produced at o_j^T. This function takes an ordered list of input ports as its arguments. It could be non-deterministic. The interconnection signals $\mathcal{S}$ simply define a relation $S_{ext} \subseteq P_{source} \times P_{sink}$. Also define $S_{int} = \bigcup_{T \in \mathcal{T}} (\{i_1^T, i_2^T, \ldots\} \times \{o_1^T, o_2^T, \ldots\}) \bigcup_{L \in \mathcal{L}} (i_1^L, o_1^L)$. Thus S_{int} captures the internal dependencies of input and output ports within a latch or a table. And S_{ext} captures the *external* dependencies between primary inputs, primary outputs and I/O ports of tables and latches.

```
.table a b c -> carry
.default 0
1 1 - 1
1 - 1 1
- 1 1 1
```

A *structural symmetry* of $\mathcal{C}$ is an automorphism $\pi : P_{sink} \cup P_{source} \to P_{sink} \cup P_{source}$ of the directed unlabeled graph $(P_{sink} \cup P_{source}, S_{int} \cup S_{ext})$ that satisfies the following constraints: (a) $(\forall \mathcal{X} \in \{P_{in}^T, P_{out}^T, P_{in}^L, P_{out}^L, \mathcal{I}, \mathcal{O}\})(\pi \mathcal{X} = \mathcal{X})$, (b) $(\forall p \in P_{sink} \cup P_{source})(dom(p) = dom(\pi p))$, and (c) $(\forall o_j^T \in P_{out}^T)(f_j^T(i_1^T, i_2^T, \ldots) = f_{j'}^{T'}(i_{1'}^{T'}, i_{2'}^{T'}, \ldots))$ where $(o_{j'}^{T'} = \pi o_j^T)$, $(i_{1'}^{T'} = \pi i_1^T)$, $(i_{2'}^{T'} = \pi i_2^T)$, $\ldots$. It follows from the first two conditions that vertices corresponding to a table get mapped to vertices of another table with the same number of I/O ports such that their domains match. Condition (c) stipulates that even the functionality of the two tables should match modulo π. It may be verified that the set of structural symmetries forms a group.

How are structural symmetries in $\mathcal{C}$ related to symmetries in some Kripke structure M? For a circuit $\mathcal{C}$, there exists a Kripke structure $M = (S, R, K)$ with 2^L states and the set of atomic propositions AP. The set L corresponds to the latches. The set AP corresponds to outputs in $\mathcal{O}$. The function K represents the boolean predicate on latches that generate outputs. We assume that the outputs in $\mathcal{C}$ do not depend on the inputs i.e. $\mathcal{C}$ defines a Moore machine. However, we note that the basic ideas developed in this paper can be extended to Mealy machines also. For a structural symmetry π, let $\pi_C : L \cup AP \to L \cup AP$ denote the permutation naturally induced by π. Let $Aut_C \ L \cdot AP$ denote the set of all such permutations. $Aut_C \ L \cdot AP$ forms a group.

Theorem 5. $Aut_C \ L \cdot AP \leq Aut_M \ L \cdot AP$. $\qquad\qquad\square$

Although we used BLIF-MV terminology to formalize the notion of structural symmetries, we believe that our definition is general enough to be applicable to gate level descriptions like those expressible in EDIF, Verilog and VHDL.

5.2 Graphs for BLIF-MV Circuits

One problem with the definition of structural symmetries in the previous section is that the third condition cannot be expressed in purely graph theoretic terms. However, we can augment the graph so that there is a 1-1 correspondence between structural symmetries and automorphisms of the graph. This allows us to leverage results from computational group theory developed for identifying graph automorphisms.

First, label each vertex in $P_{sink} \cup P_{source}$ with its domain. Next, substitute each subgraph corresponding to a table by a graph similar to the one shown in the adjoining figure. The new nodes are *internal* to the table and are labeled with the corresponding table entries.

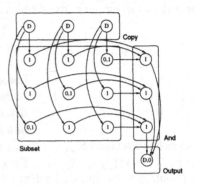

Let A_C denote the labeled directed graph so constructed. For an automorphism π of A_C, let $\pi_A : L \cup AP \rightarrow L \cup AP$ denote the 1-1 mapping naturally defined by π. Let $Aut_C \ L \cdot AP$ denote the set of all such permutations. It can be verified that Theorem 5 still holds. A detailed proof can be found in [Man97], which also shows how multiple-output tables, the "=" construct [B+91], pseudo inputs and other special cases can be handled. The size of the graph is linear in the size of the *flattened* BLIF-MV description.

Here are two interesting theoretical questions: First, is every group possible? Let $G \subseteq Aut_M \ L \cdot AP$. Computation of the canonical state requires $G_{<L>}$, the restriction of G to L, as input. Is there any group $G_{<L>}$ that does not correspond to any BLIF-MV circuit? If so, we can focus on the remaining groups to solve the canonical state problem. However, the answer is negative [Man97]. Second, how hard is it to identify scalarsets? A scalarset is an automorphism of the graph A_C such that the automorphism can be written as a product of disjoint transpositions. Note that A_C is not an arbitrary directed graph. It has been derived from a valid BLIF-MV circuit. See [Man97] for a simple proof that the problem is as hard as graph isomorphism.

5.3 Graphs for CTL* Formulas

To compute $H \leq Aut_f \ AP \cdot SF$, draw the parse tree for the formula f. Label each internal node with the operator it represents. The leaf nodes correspond to propositions in AP. For each internal node labeled *Until*, introduce two new nodes labeled *Left* and *Right*. Replace the edge between *Until* and its left operand by two edges: one from *Until* to *Left* and one from *Left* to the left operand. Replace the edge between *Until* and its right operand similarly. Collapse all leaf nodes representing tha same $p \in AP$ into a single node. Label these nodes with a common color, say *White*. Introduce a new set of nodes, one for every $p \in AP$, labeled identically with a new color, say *Black*. Draw an edge from a *White* node to a *Black* node if they correspond to the same atomic proposition. Let A_f denote the graph we constructed. It is clear that the nodes of A_f, except those labeled *Left* or *Right*, are in 1-1 correspondence with elements of $AP \cup SF$. For every automorphism of the graph A, let π denote its restriction to nodes corresponding to $AP \cup SF$. The set of all such π forms a group, which we denote by $Aut_{A_f} AP \cdot SF$.

Theorem 6. $Aut_{A_f} AP \cdot SF \leq Aut_f AP \cdot SF$. $\qquad\qquad$ □

To compute $H \leq Aut_f AP \cdot MPS$, first identify MPS, the set of maximal propositional sub-formulas of f. For each $g \in MPS$, construct its parse tree. Label each internal node with the operator it corresponds to. Collapse all leaf nodes which correspond to the same $p \in AP$ into a single node. Label them identically with a new color, say *White*. Introduce a new node for every proposition $p \in AP$, all labeled identically with a new color, say *Black*. Draw an edge from every *White* node to a *Black* node if they correspond to the same atomic proposition p. Re-label each root node corresponding to some $g \in MPS$, with a distinct new color. Let $\bar{A}_f$ denote the graph we constructed. Let $\pi : AP \cup MPS \rightarrow AP \cup MPS$ denote the permutation corresponding to the restriction of some automorphism of $\bar{A}_f$ to vertices corresponding to AP and MPS. The labels of $\bar{A}_f$ ensure that $\pi AP = AP$ and $(\forall g \in MPS)(\pi g = g)$. The set of all such π forms a group, which we denote by $Aut_{\bar{A}_f} AP \cdot MPS$.

Theorem 7. $Aut_{\bar{A}_f} AP \cdot MPS \leq Aut_f AP \cdot MPS$. $\qquad\qquad$ □

5.4 Computing $G \bowtie H$

One approach is to compute the groups G and H separately and then compute $G \bowtie H$ using group-theoretic algorithms. G need be computed only once for a given circuit. However, computing group intersections is as hard as graph isomorphism [Hof80], though polynomial time algorithms do exist for special cases.

A simpler approach is to join the two graphs corresponding to G and H together by drawing an edge between every pair of vertices that correspond to the same $p \in AP$ in both the graphs. The key to correctness lies in the fact that the sets of labels in the two graphs, except for the vertices corresponding to AP, are mutually exclusive.

5.5 The Big Picture

Given a BLIF-MV circuit C, a CTL* formula f and a set of initial states I, we first compute sets of symmetric sub-formulas of f, as defined in Section 3, by constructing the graphs A_C and A_f, described in Section 5.2 and Section 5.3 respectively, joining them as described in Section 5.4 and solving the graph automorphism problem for the resulting graph. The data structure for representing graph automorphisms allows identification of partitions of sub-formulas of f easily. We then compute $H \leq Aut_f AP \cdot MPS$ by constructing the graph $\bar{A}_f$ described in Section 5.3, joining it with A_C as described in Section 5.4 and solving the graph automorphism problem for the resulting graph. This would give us generators for the group $G \bowtie H$, from which we compute $\xi_{G \bowtie H}$. Finally, we feed the sets of symmetric sub-formulas and the function $\xi_{G \bowtie H}$ to a modified model checker that canonicalizes states during state space traversal and uses Theorem 2 to avoid computing truth values for all sub-formulas. After having evaluated the truth value of f for all initial states, the modified model checker can start offering new formulas to the designer, whose truth value can easily be deduced, as described in Section 3.1.

6 Computing Automorphisms

Let us first breeze through a set of definitions. Consider a directed labeled graph $A = (V, E)$ with n vertices and m edges. A **bipartition** P defined over V is a set of ordered pairs $\cup_{1 \leq i \leq k}\{(V_i, W_i)\}$, where (a) $\cup_{1 \leq i \leq k} V_i = \cup_{1 \leq i \leq k} W_i = V$, (b) $(\forall i.1 \leq i \leq k)(|V_i| = |W_i| \neq 0)$, and (c) $(\forall j.1 \leq i < j \leq k)(V_i \cap V_j = W_i \cap W_j = \phi)$. The set of edges of a graph or its labeling function play no role in the definition. A bipartition P is a **unipartition** if $(\forall i.1 \leq i \leq k)(V_i = W_i)$. It is simply a partition of the set of vertices V into disjoint non-empty sets. A bipartition $Q = \cup_{1 \leq i \leq q}\{V_i^Q, W_i^Q\}$ is a **refinement** of another bipartition $P = \cup_{1 \leq i \leq p}\{V_i^P, W_i^P\}$ if they are defined over the same set of vertices V and $(\forall i.1 \leq i \leq q)(\forall j.1 \leq j \leq p)((V_i^Q \cap V_j^P = \phi) \vee (V_i^Q \subseteq V_j^P \wedge W_i^Q \subseteq W_j^P))$. We denote this relationship by $Q \preccurlyeq P$. We also say that P is coarser than Q and that Q is finer than P. The relation $\preccurlyeq$ is reflexive and transitive. Two bipartitions $P = \cup_{1 \leq i \leq p}\{(V_i^P, W_i^P)\}$ and $Q = \cup_{1 \leq i \leq q}\{(V_i^Q, W_i^Q)\}$ are **compatible** if $(\forall i.1 \leq i \leq p)(\forall j.1 \leq j \leq q)(|V_i^P \cap V_j^Q| = |W_i^P \cap W_j^Q|)$. The **intersection** of two compatible bipartitions P and Q is defined as $P \wedge Q = \cup_{1 \leq i \leq p, 1 \leq j \leq q}\{(V_i^Q \cap V_j^P, W_i^Q \cap W_j^P)\} - \{(\phi, \phi)\}$, which itself is a bipartition. Let $A = (V, E)$ be a directed labeled graph with labeling function c. A bipartition P is an **automorphism** of A if (a) $(\forall i.1 \leq i \leq k)(|V_i| = |W_i| = 1)$, (b) $(\forall v, w \in V)(\forall i.1 \leq i \leq k)((v \in V_i \wedge w \in W_i) \Rightarrow (c(v) = c(w)))$, and (c) $(\forall v, v', w, w' \in V)(\forall i.1 \leq i \leq k)(\forall j.1 \leq j \leq k)((v, v') \in E \Leftrightarrow (w, w') \in E)$. The set of all automorphisms of A forms a group. We denote it by $Aut\ A$. A bipartition P is **consistent** with an automorphism if there exists an automorphism P' of A such that $P' \preccurlyeq P$. For notational convenience, we will denote both a vertex $v \in V$ and a singleton set $\{v\}$ by simply v. This allows us to write a set like $\{(\{u\}, \{v\})\}$ as (u, v). The following lemmas are immediate:

Lemma 1. *If P, Q and R are bipartitions of A such that $P \preccurlyeq Q$ and $P \preccurlyeq R$, then Q and R are compatible and $P \preccurlyeq Q \wedge R$.*

Lemma 2. *Let U_{max} be a unipartition such that two vertices of A lie in the same set iff they have the same label. Then, U_{max} is consistent with every automorphism of A.*

Lemma 3. *Let U_{min} be a unipartition such that two vertices u and v lie in the same set if and only if $(\exists \pi \in Aut\ A)(\pi u = v)$. Then, U_{min} is consistent with every automorphism of A and is the finest such unipartition.*

Lemma 4. *If P is a bipartition such that $P \in Aut\ A$ and $(u, v) \in P$, then $P \preccurlyeq \{(succ(u), succ(v)), (V - succ(u), V - succ(v))\}$, where $succ(x) = \{y \mid (x, y) \in E\}$.*

Lemma 5. *If P is a bipartition such that $P \in Aut\ A$ and $(u, v) \in P$, then $P \preccurlyeq \{(pred(u), pred(v)), (V - pred(u), V - pred(v))\}$, where $pred(x) = \{y \mid (y, x) \in E\}$.*

We tackle the following problem: *Given a bipartition P for a directed labeled graph $A = (V, E)$, produce an automorphism of A consistent with P, if one exists.*

```
SEARCH_AUTOMORPHISM(Graph A, Bipartition P)
   Compute U_max;
   U = REFINE (U_max);
   if (COMPATIBLE (P,U))
      P = P ⋏ U;
   else return 0;
   return BRANCH_AND_BOUND(A, P, φ);


BRANCH_AND_BOUND (Graph A, Bipartition P, PairSet S)
   while ((∃u, v ∈ V)((u,v) ∈ P ∧ (u,v) ∉ S))
      S = S ∪ (u,v);
      Q = (succ(u), succ(v)) ∪ (V − succ(u), V − succ(v));

      if (COMPATIBLE (Q, P))
         P = P ⋏ Q;
      else return 0;

      Q = (pred(u), pred(v)) ∪ (V − pred(u), V − pred(v));

      if (COMPATIBLE (Q, P))
         P = P ⋏ Q;
      else return 0;
   if (SET_COMPLETE(A, S))
      return 1;

   (v, W) = CHOOSE_VICTIM (P);
   foreach (w ∈ W)
      P' = P − (V, W) ∪ (v, w) ∪ (V − v, W − w)
      S' = S;
      if BRANCH_AND_BOUND (A, P', S')
         return 1;
   return 0;
```

Fig. 1. Algorithm for finding an automorphism, given graph A and bipartition P.

6.1 Branch and Bound Algorithm

Pseudo-code for the algorithm is given in Figure 1. We start with U_{max}, as defined in Lemma 2, since U_{max} is consistent with every automorphism of A. Ideally, we should start with U_{min}, as it is the finest such partition. However, computing U_{min} itself is as hard as graph isomorphism [vL90]. Therefore, we compute an approximation U such that $U_{min} \preccurlyeq U \preccurlyeq U_{max}$ using REFINE, which we describe in detail in Section 6.2. U is consistent with every automorphism of A. Having computed U, we check whether P and U are compatible. If not, then from Lemma 1, P is not consistent with any automorphism of A; the algorithm terminates. If P and U are compatible, we compute their intersection $P \curlywedge U$. From Lemma 1, any automorphism consistent with P and U has to be consistent with $P \curlywedge U$. Finally, we invoke BRANCH_AND_BOUND.

The Bounding Step is the *while* loop in BRANCH_AND_BOUND is the bounding step. From Lemma 4, we conclude that if $(u,v) \in P$ and if an automorphism is consistent with P, then it has to be consistent with $Q = \{(succ(u), succ(v)), (V - succ(u), V - succ(v))\}$ as well. From Lemma 1, we conclude that P and Q must be compatible and that the automorphism must be consistent with $P \curlywedge Q$ as well. A similar argument holds for $Q = \{(pred(u), pred(v)), (V - pred(u), V - pred(v))\}$ also. If P and Q are non-compatible, BRANCH_AND_BOUND terminates.

The bounding step also helps to refine P by computing $P \curlywedge Q$, which in turn might generate new singleton pairs $(u,v) \in P$. Intuitively, the *implications* of mapping u to v are getting *propagated*. The set S remembers such pairs (u,v), thereby avoiding duplicate work. The *while* loop terminates when no such pairs remain. At this point, all pairs in P which have size one, lie in S. The function SET_COMPLETE checks whether all vertices in V have found their way into S. If so, we have discovered an automorphism. Otherwise, it is time to branch.

The Branching Step: CHOOSE_VICTIM first selects a pair (V, W) in P such that $|V| \neq 1$ using some heuristic. It then selects a vertex $v \in V$ using another heuristic and returns (v, W). The choice of v and W is important for at least two reasons. First, small sized W implies fewer branches to explore. Second, branches that lead to dead ends need be avoided. Our implementation is not fancy: we simply choose the smallest sized W available, breaking ties arbitrarily; our choice of $v \in V$ is also arbitrary. Having chosen v and W, we try to discover $w \in W$ such that v maps to w in some automorphism of A. To this end, we compute $P' = P - (V, W) \cup (v, w) \cup (V - v, W - w)$ and invoke BRANCH_AND_BOUND. Clearly, if all choices of w fail, there is no automorphism consistent with P and the function terminates unsuccessfully.

Lemma 6. *For a directed graph $A = (V, E)$, a bipartition $P = \cup_{1 \leq i \leq n}\{(V_i, W_i)\}$ is an automorphism of A if and only if (a) $(\forall i.1 \leq i \leq n)(|V_i| = |W_i| = 1)$, (b) $P \preccurlyeq U_{max}$, and (c) $(\forall i.1 \leq i \leq n)(\forall v, w \in V)((v \in V_i \wedge w \in W_i) \Rightarrow (P \preccurlyeq \{(succ(v), succ(w)), (V - succ(v), V - succ(w))\}$* $\qquad \square$

Proof of Correctness: Condition (a) is verified by SET_COMPLETE before termination. Condition (b) is true because SEARCH_AUTOMORPHISM computes $P \curlywedge U$ where $U \preccurlyeq U_{max}$. Condition (c) is checked for each vertex pair in the *while* loop. The entire algorithm simply verifies Condition 3 for vertex pairs generated by the branching step.

Time Complexity: Testing compatibility and computing intersection of two bipartitions require $O(n)$ time. Computing U_{max} is trivial. From Figure 1, it might appear that each level of recursion is required to store its own copy of P and S. However, this can be obviated by remembering set boundaries at each recursion level and quickly merging subsets when backtracking. Our implementation uses only nine arrays of size n, apart from the usual adjacency lists for edges. If we never backtrack and if the size of sets returned by CHOOSE_VICTIM is bounded by a constant, our implementation runs in $O(m + n)$ time.

6.2 Refinement

REFINE computes a unipartition U such that $U_{min} \preccurlyeq U \preccurlyeq U_{max}$. Why is refinement useful? First, it might generate singleton pairs whose implications can be propagated immediately in the bounding step. Second, by shrinking the sizes of pairs of sets, fewer branches may have to be explored later. Ideally, if a graph has no non-trivial automorphisms, all sets in U should be singleton.

A unipartition U can also be looked upon as a function that computes the same value for two vertices if they lie in the same set. Some such functions that satisfy $U_{min} \preccurlyeq U$ are easy to compute. The intersection of two such functions $U_1 \curlywedge U_2$ is also guaranteed to be at least as coarse as U_{min}. Such functions are called *vertex invariants* [FH+83]. Some vertex invariants that can be computed in $O(m + n)$ time are the in-degree and out-degree of vertices, the set of degrees of vertices incident at a vertex and the set of degrees of vertices which a vertex is incident upon. See [Man97] for references to articles that describe other vertex invariants that are more expensive to compute.

An important trick is to treat a unipartition U as a labeling function and use it to refine itself. For a vertex v, let U' compute the set of labels of vertices incident upon v. Then U' is a vertex invariant such that $U_{min} \preccurlyeq U'$ [FH+83]. U can be refined by computing $U \curlywedge U'$ in $O(m + n)$ time repeatedly. At most $n - 1$ iterations are required. In practice, a few iterations suffice.

6.3 The Automorphism Group

It is possible to produce *all* the automorphisms by continuing the search even after discovering the first one. Since their total number could be exponential in n, we need a succinct representation of *Aut A*. A detailed description of an algorithm for computing *Aut A*, that draws ideas from computational group theory and uses the algorithm in Figure 1 as a backbone, is given in [Man97]. We omit its discussion from this paper as it is yet to be implemented.

We initially experimented with a software package called GAP [Gap], which offers a graph automorphism program called *nauti* [McK90] based on one of the earliest such programs written by McKay [McK81]. It is natural to ask: Why write another graph automorphism program? Existing packages are general purpose and carry around a lot of baggage. We found GAP to be slow. We can exploit a lot of structure in the graphs we construct. For a detailed description of several other motivating reasons see [Man97].

7 Experimental Results

We implemented the algorithm in Figure 1 to convince ourselves that our modeling of the circuit is sufficient to allow discovering symmetries. As it stands, it is useful when a circuit verifier suspects that certain symmetries exist in the circuit at hand. She can ratify it by providing a bipartition using her intuition and running our algorithm.

Example	n	m	C	C_1	C_2	C_f	*iter*
ctlp20	4920	6740	15	34	51	246	7
ping-pong	288	378	11	25	39	144	7
z4ml	527	929	5	14	19	108	4
4-arbit	3158	4000	19	52	105	3110	60

Example	*back-track*	*maxset*	*numchoices*
ctlp20	0	20	19
ping-pong	0	2	1
z4ml	8	4	21

Starting with a Verilog description, we obtain a BLIF-MV description using a compiler called v12mv written by Cheng [CYB93]. The BLIF-MV description is *flattened* using a standard VIS command. The flattened circuit along with a bipartition is fed to our program which first generates a suitable labeled directed graph, then refines the labels and finally runs the branch and bound algorithm. We identified symmetries in all the examples in the second table. ctlp20 solves the dining philosophers problem for 20 philosophers. It has a cyclic group. ping-pong has a fully symmetric system of size 2. z4ml is a combinational circuit whose inputs constitute three sets of fully symmetric variables. We tabulate n, m and C, the number of vertices, edges and colors respectively, in the initial graph. Since refinement impacts the running time of the algorithm greatly, we also tabulate the number of colors after successive refinement steps. C_1 denotes the number of colors after the in-degree and out-degrees have been used as vertex invariants. C_2 denotes the number of colors after the set of in-degrees of fan out vertices and the set of out-degrees of fan out vertices have been used as vertex invariants. C_f denotes the final number of colors after iterative refinement. The number of iterations is listed under *iter*. We also list the number of times our branch and bound algorithm had to backtrack, the number of times CHOOSE_VICTIM was invoked and the maximum size of the set returned by this routine. Our algorithm runs in linear time if we never backtrack and if the size of sets returned by CHOOSE_VICTIM is bounded. The table shows that the two conditions are almost satisfied.

References

[AT96]   M. AGRAWAL AND T. THIERAUF. The Boolean Isomorphism Problem. In *Proc. Symp. on Foundations of Computer Science*, pp. 422–430, October 1996.

[B+91]   R. K. BRAYTON ET AL. BLIF-MV: An Interchange Format for Design Verification and Synthesis. Technical Report UCB/ERL M91/97, UC Berkeley, November 1991.

[BCL+94] J. R. BURCH, E. M. CLARKE, D. E. LONG, K. L. MCMILLAN, AND D. L. DILL. Symbolic Model Checking for Sequential Circuit Verification. *IEEE Tran. on Comp. Aided Design of Integrated Circuits and Sys.*, 13(4):401–424, April 1994.

[CEFJ96] E. M. CLARKE, R. ENDERS, T. FILKORN, AND S. JHA. Exploiting Symmetry in Temporal Logic Model Checking. *Formal Meth. in Sys. Design*, 9(1/2):77–104, 1996.

[CES86]   E. M. CLARKE, E. A. EMERSON, AND A. P. SISTLA. Automatic Verification of Finite-State Concurrent Systems Using Temporal Logic Specifications. *ACM Transactions on Programming Languages and Systems*, 8(2):244–263, 1986.

[CYB93]   S.-T. CHENG, G. YORK, AND R. K. BRAYTON. VL2MV: A Compiler from Verilog to BLIF-MV, October 1993.

[EJP97]   E. A. EMERSON, S. JHA, AND D. PELED. Combining Partial Order and Symmetry Reductions. In *Proc. TACAS 97*, pp. 19–34, April 1997.

[ES95]   E. A. EMERSON AND A. P. SISTLA. Utilizing Symmetry when Model Checking under Fairness Assumptions: An Automata-theoretic Approach. In *Proc. CAV 95*, pp. 309–324, July 1995.

[ES96]   E. A. EMERSON AND A. P. SISTLA. Symmetry and Model Checking. *Formal Meth. in Sys. Design*, 9(1/2):105–131, 1996.

[FH+83]   G. FOWLER, R. HARALICK, ET AL. Efficient Graph Automorphism by Vertex Partitioning. *Aritificial Intelligence*, 21:245–269, 1983.

[Gap]   GAP: Groups, Algorithms and Programs, Version 3, Release 4. Available via ftp from ftp.math.rwth-aachen.de, directory /pub/gap.

[GS97]   V. GYURIS AND A. P. SISTLA. On-the-Fly Model Checking under Fairness that Exploits Symmetry. In *Proc. CAV 97, Haifa, Israel, June 1997*, pp. 232–243, 1997.

[Hof80]   C. M. HOFFMAN. On the Complexity of Intersecting Permutation Groups and its Relationship with Graph Isomorphism. Technical Report 4/80, Institüt for Informatik und Praktische Mathematik, Christian-Albrechts-Universität Kiel, 1980.

[ID96]   C. N. IP AND D. L. DILL. Better Verification Through Symmetry. *Formal Meth. in Sys. Design*, 9(1/2):41–76, 1996.

[Man97]   GURMEET SINGH MANKU. Structural Symmetries and Model Checking. Master's thesis UCB/ERL M97/92, University of California at Berkeley, 1997. Available as http://www-cad.eecs.berkeley.edu/~manku/papers/ms.ps.gz.

[McK81]   B. D. MCKAY. Practical Graph Isomorphism. In *Proc. Tenth Manitoba Conf. on Numerical Math. and Computing, Winnepeg, 1980, vol 1*, pp. 45–87, 1981.

[McK90]   B. D. MCKAY. Nauty Users Guide (Version 1.5). Technical Report TR-CS-90-02, Computer Science Department, Australian National University, Australia, 1990.

[PB97]   M. PANDEY AND E. BRYANT. Exploiting Symmetry when Verifying Transistor-Level Circuits by Symbolic Trajectory Evaluation. In *Proc. CAV 97, Haifa, Israel, June 1997*, pp. 244–255, 1997.

[vL90]   J. VAN LEEUWEN. Graph Algorithms. In *Algorithms and Complexity*, volume A of *Handbook of Theoretical Computer Science*, pp. 525–631. Elsevier Science, 1990.

Using Magnetic Disk Instead of Main Memory in the Mur φ Verifier

Ulrich Stern and David L. Dill

Computer Science Department, Stanford University,
Stanford, CA 94305
{uli, dill}@cs.stanford.edu

Abstract. In verification by explicit state enumeration a randomly accessed state table is maintained. In practice, the total main memory available for this state table is a major limiting factor in verification. We describe a version of the explicit state enumeration verifier Murφ that allows the use of magnetic disk instead of main memory for storing almost all of the state table. The algorithm avoids costly random accesses to disk and amortizes the cost of linearly reading the state table from disk over all states in a given breadth-first level. The remaining runtime overhead for accessing the disk is greatly reduced by combining the scheme with hash compaction. We show how to do this combination efficiently and analyze the resulting algorithm. In experiments with three complex cache coherence protocols, the new algorithm achieves memory savings factors of one to two orders of magnitude with a runtime overhead of typically only around 15%.

1 Introduction

Modern digital systems often have components that run concurrently. Interactions among these components are a notorious source of design errors. Conventional verification methods based on hand-generated test vectors and pseudo-random simulation are not capable in practice of finding all of these problems. Programs that exhaustively enumerate all reachable states of a part of the system (or an abstraction of the system), however, have been shown to be very effective at detecting bugs that are missed by other means. The reachability analysis in these formal verification tools can be performed using two different methods: the states can be explicitly enumerated, by storing them individually in a table, or a symbolic method can be used, such as representing the reachable state space with a binary decision diagram (BDD) [1].

In many applications, such as directory-based cache coherence protocols, BDD-based reachability analysis exhibits close to worst-case behavior. In such situations, reasonably efficient explicit enumeration can save a factor of 50 or more in space, because the size of the state table is the product of the number of reachable states and the number of bits to represent each state, while a BDD requires almost one node per bit per reachable state, and each node is approximately 20 bytes.

Recently, several techniques have been developed that allow significantly more complex systems to be handled using explicit state enumeration, especially when the techniques are used in combination. These techniques follow two different approaches. First, state reduction methods have been developed that aim at reducing the size of the reachability graph while ensuring that system errors will still be detected. Examples are exploiting symmetries, utilizing reversible rules, and employing repetition constructors [8], as well as partial order techniques [11]. These methods directly tackle the main problem in reachability analysis: the very large number of reachable states of most systems. The second approach aims at exploring a given reachability graph in the most efficient manner, minimizing memory usage and runtime (both of which are limiting factors in verification). Examples are bitstate hashing [5], hash compaction [17, 14], and parallelizing the state space search [16].

In this paper, we describe a technique that reduces the main memory requirements of the state table maintained in explicit state enumeration. The state table eventually holds all reachable states of the system being verified unless an error is detected. In addition, the state table is typically randomly accessed, in which case the use of magnetic disk for this table incurs a huge runtime penalty and hence main memory is required to store this table. In practice, the total main memory available for the state table is a major limiting factor in verification.

We describe a version of the explicit state verifier Murφ [4] that allows the use of magnetic disk instead of main memory for storing almost all of the state table, at the cost of only a small runtime overhead. The algorithm is based on the observation that when a breadth-first search is used to enumerate the state space, a newly generated state does not need to be checked against the state table immediately; in fact, one can postpone the checking until an entire level of the breadth-first search has been explored and then check all states in that level together by *linearly* reading the table from disk. This scheme avoids costly random accesses to disk and amortizes the time for accessing the full table on disk over all states in a given search level.

The remaining runtime overhead for accessing the disk can be greatly reduced by combining the new scheme with hash compaction. Hash compaction stores only hash signatures instead of full state descriptors in the state table. The resulting memory savings of typically two orders of magnitude and the resulting reduced disk access times come at a certain price; there is now a small probability that the verifier misses the error states of the system and incorrectly claims that an erroneous system is correct (i.e., produces a false positive). We derive an upper bound on this probability in the combined scheme and show that, e.g., 6-byte signatures are typically sufficient to reduce the bound to 0.1%.

One might be concerned about the reliability of a "probabilistic verifier" that can miss errors with a small probability. For several reasons, however, this concern is unjustified. First, the probability of missing an error due to hash compaction should not be confused with the probability of the very same error not occurring when running or simulating the system for a long time. The former probability is guaranteed to be very small even in situations where the latter is high. Second, it is typically necessary to scale down or simplify a system of industrial size to make it amenable to formal verification, which also results in some probability of missed errors. In comparison to this probability, which cannot even be approximated, the probability of missed errors due to hash compaction seems negligible. Third, when re-running a probabilistic verifier with independent hash functions, the resulting probability of missed errors is the product of the probabilities in the two runs, which allows making the probability of missed errors arbitrarily small. For a more detailed explanation of why it is safe to use a probabilistic verifier see Sect. 1.3.1. in [13].

We ran experiments using the new scheme on three complex cache coherence protocols (SCI [7], DASH [10], and FLASH [9]), varying the ratio of the number of states stored on disk to the states in main memory. We call this ratio the *memory savings factor*. (The additional memory savings due to hash compaction are not taken into account here.) For example, with a memory savings factor of 50, the new scheme slowed down verification by an average of only 20% on an SGI Indy and an average of only 29% on a Sun UltraSPARC. In fact, the algorithm is shown to work well if the reachability graph of the system under verification has a small diameter, which is true for virtually all systems that have been studied with Murφ.

The algorithm presented in this paper was inspired by a scheme devised by Roscoe that allows the use of magnetic disk in explicit state enumeration [12]. His scheme seems more complicated than ours since it is based on an algorithm for sorting without randomly accessing memory. Also, one can show with a simple analysis that his scheme would induce a high runtime overhead. (He has not reported any empirical data about his scheme.) In addition, the file merging used in his scheme doubles the memory requirements of the state table on disk. A detailed comparison of the two algorithms is given in [13].

This paper is organized as follows. Section 2 provides background on explicit state enumeration and magnetic disk speed. The new algorithm that enables the use of magnetic disk instead of main memory for storing almost all of the state table is described and analyzed in Sect. 3. Results running the algorithm are reported in Sect. 4. Finally, Sect. 5 gives some concluding remarks.

2 Background

2.1 Explicit State Enumeration

In explicit state enumeration, the automatic verifier tries to examine all reachable states from a set of possible start states. Either breadth-first or depth-first search can be employed for the state enumeration process. Both the breadth-first and the depth-first algorithms are straightforward.

Two data structures are needed for performing the state enumeration. First, a state table stores all the states that have been examined so far and is used to decide whether a newly-reached state is old (has been visited before) or new (has not been visited before). Besides the state table, a state queue holds all active states (states whose successors still need to be generated). Depending on the organization of this queue, the verifier does a breadth-first or a depth-first search.

2.2 Magnetic Disk Speed

The speed of a magnetic disk depends strongly on the way it is accessed. When linearly accessing a large file on disk, we have measured a read transfer rate of typically 3 MB/s and a write transfer rate of typically 1.5–2 MB/s. The seek time for a random access, however, is typically 10 ms. Thus, to read, say, a single word randomly from disk requires almost four orders of magnitude more time than to read one in the course of a linear access.

3 Explicit State Enumeration Using Magnetic Disk

3.1 The Basic Algorithm

The basic algorithm for explicit state enumeration using magnetic disk is given in Figure 1 and is described in the following paragraph. Note that the algorithm maintains two state tables: one in main memory and one on disk. The state queue and the disk table will be accessed only sequentially; the main memory table will be accessed randomly.

The state enumeration is started by calling SEARCH(). First, the startstates are generated and inserted into the main memory table by calling INSERT(). The search loop generates the successors for all states in the state queue and also inserts these successors into the main memory table. When the state queue becomes empty, the algorithm calls CHECKTABLE(), which determines those states in the main memory table that are new and inserts them into the state queue. Note that CHECKTABLE() linearly reads the disk table to sort out old states, and eventually clears the main memory table. Further note that if there is sufficient space in the main memory table, the algorithm will call CHECKTABLE() exactly once for each breadth-first level of the search; otherwise, if the main memory table fills up (because some breadth-first levels have too many states), CHECKTABLE() will also be called from within the INSERT() routine.

3.2 Estimating the Overhead

We now estimate the runtime overhead incurred by accessing the magnetic disk in our algorithm. Let k_i denote the number of states in the disk table when it is read for the ith time and assume that it is read a total of t times during the state space search. Note that $k_1 = 0$ since the disk table is empty the first time it is read. The total number of states read from disk is $\sum_{i=1}^{t} k_i$. This sum has its smallest possible value if the main memory table never fills up completely, as in this case the disk table is read exactly once for each breadth-first level (plus once for the successors of the states in the last level). In this case, $t = d + 2$,

```
var      // global variables
  M: hash table;       // main memory table
  D: file;             // disk table
  Q: FIFO queue;       // state queue

SEARCH()      // main routine
begin
  M := ∅; D := ∅; Q := ∅;      // initialization
  for each startstate s₀ do      // startstate generation
    INSERT(s₀);
  end
  do                             // search loop
    while Q ≠ ∅ do
      s := dequeue(Q);
      for all s' ∈ successors(s) do
        INSERT(s');
      end
    end
    CHECKTABLE();
  while Q ≠ ∅;
end


INSERT(s: state)      // insert state s in main memory table
begin
  if s ∉ M then begin
    insert s in M;
    if full(M) then
      CHECKTABLE();
  end
end


CHECKTABLE()      // do old/new check for main memory table
begin
  for all s ∈ D do      // remove old states from main memory table
    if s ∈ M then
      M := M − {s};
  end
  for all s ∈ M do      // handle remaining (new) states
    insert s in Q;
    append s to D;
    M := M − {s};
  end
end
```

Fig. 1. Explicit State Enumeration Using Magnetic Disk

where d denotes the diameter of the reachability graph. Since this diameter is typically quite small, the disk table will only be read a small number of times. (We shall see the diameters of some complex example protocols in Sect. 4.)

In an instance of the SCI protocol, for example, the (minimum) total number of states read from disk is $2.64 \cdot 10^7$. With 124 bytes per state and a disk bulk transfer rate of 3 MB/s, this would result in a runtime overhead of at least 1091 s. Comparing this value to the verification time (723 s) of the conventional algorithm on, for example, an UltraSPARC, yields a runtime overhead of at least 151 %. This overhead, however, can be reduced by combining the new algorithm with hash compaction.

Note that if a conventional verifier with randomly accessed state table runs out of main memory and is forced to do swapping, each checking of a newly generated state might require a seek. In fact, if the state table is much larger than the available main memory, we can assume that each checking does require a seek. For the above instance of the SCI protocol, $2.97 \cdot 10^6$ such seeks would be performed, resulting in a runtime overhead of $2.97 \cdot 10^4$ s, or 4108 %, assuming 10 ms per seek and verification on the above UltraSPARC.

3.3 Combining with Hash Compaction

Hash compaction reduces the memory requirements of the state table by storing (only) hash signatures instead of full state descriptors in this table. The resulting memory savings come at the price of a small probability, say, 0.1%, that the verifier incorrectly claims that an erroneous system is correct. For complex verification problems, hash compaction has achieved memory reduction factors of two orders of magnitude. Note that by reducing the number of bytes stored per state, hash compaction also reduces the time to read the disk table.

Figure 2 shows the new INSERT() and CHECKTABLE() routines when using hash compaction. Note that signatures are used for both main memory table M and disk table D; full state descriptors, however, need to be stored in the state queue Q, since successors cannot be generated from a signature. In the INSERT() routine, first the signature is calculated from the state descriptor with a hash function. Then, state descriptor and signature are stored in the state queue, while only the signature is stored in the main memory table. The state queue will hold two types of states: unchecked states (i.e., states for which it has not yet been checked whether they are 'old' or 'new') and states that are known to be 'new.' The two types of states partition the state queue into two parts and thus an implementation need only store the position of the border between the two parts.

The CHECKTABLE() routine first deletes all 'old' states from the main memory table, and then checks for all unchecked states in the queue whether they are 'old' or 'new.' While the 'old' states are deleted from the queue, the 'new' ones are appended to the disk table. Note that the checking of the state queue can be done by linearly reading the unchecked part of the queue. When storing the signatures separately from the state descriptors in a second queue, the algorithm need only (linearly) read the unchecked part of this small second queue. This

```
INSERT(s: state)      // insert s in main memory table and state queue
begin
   h := hash(s);      // calculate signature
   if h ∉ M then begin
      insert h in M;
      insert (s, h) in Q;
      if full(M) then
         CHECKTABLE();
   end
end

CHECKTABLE()      // do old/new check for main memory table
begin
   for all h ∈ D do      // remove old states from main memory table
      if h ∈ M then
         M := M − {h};
   end
   for all unchecked (s, h) ∈ Q do   // remove old states from state queue
      if h ∈ M then                   // and add new states to disk table
         append h to D;
         M := M − {h};
      else
         Q := Q − {(s, h)};
   end
end
```

Fig. 2. INSERT() and CHECKTABLE() routines when using hash compaction

results in a significant improvement, because as shown in [13], the state queue can become quite large in practice.

The new algorithm has another nice property: states are inserted into the disk table in the order of their exploration. This property enables using the scheme proposed in [15] to store the information needed for error trace generation in a file, which contains for each reachable state a record with two elements – the state's signature and the position (in the file) of the record of the state's predecessor. Since the disk table already contains each state's signature, additional storage is only required for the values for the positions of each state's predecessor. These values can be stored in a separate file to avoid slowing down accesses to the disk table.

3.4 Analysis of the Combined Scheme

The following analysis yields an upper bound on the probability of false positives, i.e., on the probability that the verifier incorrectly claims that an erroneous system is correct. This probability will be denoted by p_{om}.

As in [15], one can show that

$$p_{om} \leq 1 - \prod_{i=2}^{t} p_{k_i - 1} \; ,$$

where p_k denotes the probability that there is no omission (identical signature) when inserting a new state into a state table with a total of k states in main memory and on disk, and k_i denotes the number of states in the disk table when it is read for the ith time. We assume that the hash function yields signatures distributed uniformly over $\{0, \ldots, l-1\}$. (Universal hashing [2], used in Murφ, can be shown to distribute at least as well as uniformly. In addition, by choosing the hash function at random when the verifier is started, universal hashing distributes well $independently$ of the system under verification.) Thus, the probability p_k can be bounded as $p_k \geq 1 - k/l$. Hence,

$$p_{om} \leq 1 - \prod_{i=2}^{t}(1 - \frac{k_i - 1}{l}) \; . \tag{1}$$

This formula can be used by the verification tool to calculate (and report) a bound on the probability of false positives.

Next, we derive a formula for an approximate bound on the probability of false positives, in order to estimate the number of bits needed for the signatures. For p_{om} to become small, it has to hold that $\sum_{i=2}^{t} k_i \ll l$. Then, using $e^x \approx 1+x$ for $|x| \ll 1$, one can approximate the right-hand side of (1) as $\sum_{i=2}^{t}(k_i - 1)/l$. Assuming linear growth of the disk table, i.e., $k_i \approx n\,i/t$, where n denotes the number of reachable states, and a moderately large t, an approximate bound $\tilde{P}_{om}$ on the probability of false positives can be derived, namely

$$\tilde{P}_{om} = \frac{n\,t}{2\,l} \; .$$

Table 1 gives values for $\tilde{P}_{om}$ assuming $n = 10^9$ reachable states while varying the number of bits b for the signatures ($l = 2^b$) and the number of times t the disk table is read. The diameters of the systems we examined were typically quite small (less than 100) and similarly were the numbers of times the disk table was read. Note that 6-byte signatures yield an approximate bound $\tilde{P}_{om}$ on the order of 0.1% for the chosen values of n and t.

In comparison to the main memory version of hash compaction [15], the disk version needs approximately two times the number of bits b for the signatures. This increase is due to the fact that in the disk version a newly reached state is compared against almost all of the states in the state table, while in the main memory version it is compared against only a few of the states in the table. Since the memory savings factor achievable with the new scheme is typically one or two orders of magnitude, however, the doubling of the size of the signatures amounts to an insignificant penalty.

Table 1. Approximate bounds $\tilde{P}_{\mathrm{om}}$ on the probabilities of false positives for $n = 10^9$

	t		
b	200	500	1000
40	9.1%	23%	45%
48	0.036%	0.089%	0.18%

4 Results on Sample Protocols

Figures 3 and 4 show the measured slowdown of the new scheme on an Indy and on an UltraSPARC, for instances of the SCI, DASH, and FLASH protocols. Some parameters of these instances are shown in Table 2. The protocols were scaled to provide interesting data and yet prevent the process of running the examples from becoming too time-consuming. The slowdown graphs show that the main memory requirements of the Murφ verifier can be reduced by one or two orders of magnitude with only a small increase in runtime.

Table 2. Example protocols

protocol	reachable states	bytes/ state	diameter	conventional scheme's runtime	
				Indy	UltraSPARC
SCI	1179 942	124	46	1437s	723s
DASH	254 937	532	64	2429s	1287s
FLASH	1021 464	136	45	2739s	2500s

The slowdown for the new algorithm was calculated relative to the most recent release (3.0) of Murφ, which was optimized for running in main memory. In fact, the disk version of Murφ is based on this main memory version of Murφ, which also contains symmetry reduction (which was employed in the above experiments). We have only partially optimized the disk version; in particular, the code for the main memory table, which is used much more often in the disk version than in the main memory version, could probably be optimized.

For our slowdown measurements, we did not reduce the size of the main memory; instead, we reduced the size of the main memory table to yield the desired memory savings factors. There was usually main memory left for the Unix file system buffer cache, which had not been disabled, since it turned out to not be feasible to disable it. Thus, the measured slowdowns might actually be smaller than the slowdown in the case when the verifier is really running out of main memory. Estimating the minimum slowdown from the amount of data read from disk, however, shows that the measured slowdown is typically higher than this minimum slowdown. Hence, the effect of the buffer cache cannot have had a dominating impact on our measurements.

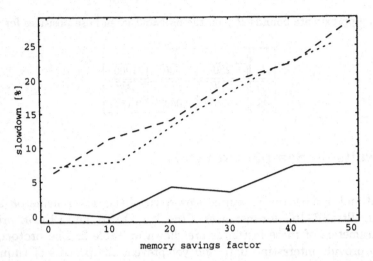

Fig. 3. Slowdown for the SCI (*dotted*), DASH (*solid*), and FLASH (*dashed*) protocols, calculated from the average runtime over three runs on an Indy

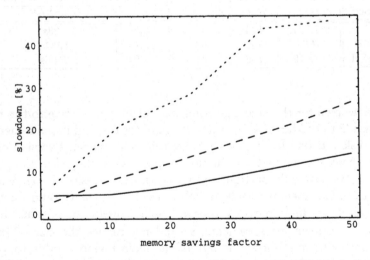

Fig. 4. Slowdown for the SCI (*dotted*), DASH (*solid*), and FLASH (*dashed*) protocols, calculated from the average runtime over eight runs on an UltraSPARC

5   Conclusions and Future Research

This paper describes a version of the explicit state enumeration verifier Murφ that allows the use of magnetic disk instead of main memory for storing almost all of the state table, at the cost of a small runtime overhead. The algorithm avoids slow random accesses to disk and amortizes the time for linearly reading the state table from disk over all states in a given breadth-first level. The remaining runtime overhead for accessing the disk is greatly reduced by combining the scheme with hash compaction. In experiments with three complex cache coherence protocols, the new algorithm achieved memory savings factors of one to two orders of magnitude with a runtime overhead of typically only around 15%. Hence, the algorithm can be used to tackle more complex problems or to run large verification jobs on a local workstation instead of a dedicated verification machine with a huge main memory.

The algorithm described could also be used in other explicit state verification tools like SPIN [6]. In addition, the algorithm is compatible with all three state reduction techniques in Murφ [8], with hash compaction, and with the parallel version of Murφ [16]. The algorithm is also compatible with Peled's partial order method [11], which had been assumed to require depth-first search, but was recently shown to also work with breadth-first search [3], on which the new scheme is based. This recent finding suggests that other partial order methods might also work with breadth-first search.

For checking liveness properties, all currently known efficient algorithms require a (modified) depth-first search of the state space. Hence, the new scheme is not directly compatible with these algorithms. Two other recent techniques that allow bigger state spaces, the most advanced version of hash compaction [15] and the parallel version of Murφ [16], however, also require a breadth-first search. Hence, checking liveness properties with a breadth-first style algorithm seems to be an interesting area for future research.

Acknowledgments

We would like to thank Ben Verghese for explaining some details of the Unix file system buffer cache to us and Ravi Soundararajan for his comments on a draft of this paper.

This work was supported in part by the Defense Advanced Research Projects Agency through NASA contract NAG-2-891 and a scholarship from the German Academic Exchange Service (DAAD-Doktorandenstipendium HSP-II). The views and conclusions contained in this document are those of the authors and should not be interpreted as representing the official policies, either expressed or implied, of the Defense Advanced Research Projects Agency, NASA, or the US Government.

References

1. J. R. Burch, E. M. Clarke, K. L. McMillan, and D. L. Dill. Sequential circuit verification using symbolic model checking. In *27th ACM/IEEE Design Automation Conference*, pages 46–51, 1990.

2. J. L. Carter and M. N. Wegman. Universal classes of hash functions. *Journal of Computer and System Sciences*, 18(2):143–54, 1979.

3. C.-T. Chou and D. Peled. Formal verification of a partial-order reduction technique for model checking. In *Tools and Algorithms for the Construction and Analysis of Systems. 2nd International Workshop*, pages 241–57, 1996.

4. D. L. Dill. The Murφ verification system. In *Computer Aided Verification. 8th International Conference*, pages 390–3, 1996.

5. G. J. Holzmann. On limits and possibilities of automated protocol analysis. In *Protocol Specification, Testing, and Verification. 7th International Conference*, pages 339–44, 1987.

6. G. J. Holzmann and D. Peled. The state of SPIN. In *Computer Aided Verification. 8th International Conference*, pages 385–9, 1996.

7. *IEEE Std 1596-1992, IEEE Standard for Scalable Coherent Interface (SCI)*.

8. C. N. Ip. *State Reduction Methods for Automatic Formal Verification*. PhD thesis, Stanford University, 1996.

9. J. Kuskin, D. Ofelt, M. Heinrich, J. Heinlein, R. Simoni, K. Gharachorloo, J. Chapin, D. Nakahira, J. Baxter, M. Horowitz, A. Gupta, M. Rosenblum, and J. Hennessy. The Stanford FLASH multiprocessor. In *21st Annual International Symposium on Computer Architecture*, pages 302–13, 1994.

10. D. Lenoski, J. Laudon, K. Gharachorloo, W.-D. Weber, A. Gupta, J. Hennessy, M. Horowitz, and M. S. Lam. The Stanford DASH multiprocessor. *Computer*, 25(3):63–79, 1992.

11. D. Peled. Combining partial order reductions with on-the-fly model-checking. In *Computer Aided Verification. 6th International Conference*, pages 377–90, 1994.

12. A. W. Roscoe. Model-checking CSP. In *A Classical Mind, Essays in Honour of C. A. R. Hoare*. Prentice-Hall, 1994.

13. U. Stern. *Algorithmic Techniques in Verification by Explicit State Enumeration*. PhD thesis, Technical University of Munich, 1997.

14. U. Stern and D. L. Dill. Improved probabilistic verification by hash compaction. In *Advanced Research Working Conference on Correct Hardware Design and Verification Methods*, pages 206–24, 1995.

15. U. Stern and D. L. Dill. A new scheme for memory-efficient probabilistic verification. In *Joint International Conference on Formal Description Techniques for Distributed Systems and Communication Protocols, and Protocol Specification, Testing, and Verification*, pages 333–48, 1996.

16. U. Stern and D. L. Dill. Parallelizing the Murφ verifier. In *Computer Aided Verification. 9th International Conference*, pages 256–67, 1997.

17. P. Wolper and D. Leroy. Reliable hashing without collision detection. In *Computer Aided Verification. 5th International Conference*, pages 59–70, 1993.

On-the-Fly Model Checking of RCTL Formulas

Ilan Beer, Shoham Ben-David, Avner Landver

IBM Science and Technology
Haifa Research Laboratory
Haifa, Israel
landver@vnet.ibm.com

Abstract. The specification language $RCTL$, an extension of CTL, is defined by adding the power of regular expressions to CTL. In addition to being a more expressive and natural hardware specification language than CTL, a large family of $RCTL$ formulas can be verified on-the-fly (during symbolic reachability analysis). On-the-fly model checking, as a powerful verification paradigm, is especially efficient when the specification is false and extremely efficient when the computation needed to get to a failing state is short. It is suitable for the inherently gradual design process since it detects a multitude of bugs at the early verification stages, and paves the way towards finding the more complex errors as the design matures. It is shown that for every erroneous finite computation, there is an $RCTL$ formula that detects it and can be verified on-the-fly. On-the-fly verification of $RCTL$ formulas has moved model checking in IBM into a different class of designs inaccessible by prior techniques.

1 Introduction

CTL Model-Checking [CE81a] [CE81b] is the procedure of deciding whether a given model satisfies a given CTL formula (we use the term *model* to denote a finite, closed, non-deterministic state machine). The main problem of model checking in general is the state explosion problem. That is, the number of states in the model grows exponentially with the number of state variables and therefore, very quickly, models become too large to be model checked. Symbolic model checking, using BDD's, was suggested by McMillan who wrote the model checker SMV [McM93]. SMV has made model checking applicable to real life designs. Nevertheless, the state explosion problem is still the greatest concern of model checking.

Another major concern related to CTL model checking is the specification language. CTL is difficult to use for most users, and requires a new way of thinking about hardware design. The tree of computations is not a natural idea for most hardware designers which tend to think more in terms of a single computation. In addition, even the expert CTL user might have great difficulties expressing some properties in bare CTL.

In this paper we define the specification language $RCTL$ which is an extension of CTL. This extension was motivated by the need of the users for tools to express hardware properties that are difficult to express in CTL. A very common property template is the following: "at the end of every finite computation that agrees with a given <computation-description>, p must be true". In $RCTL$, a <computation-description> is represented by a regular expression R and the syntax of the above template is $\{R\}(p)$. Using regular expressions to describe sets of computations is a powerful and intuitive way of thinking.

Even though the original motivation for introducing $RCTL$ was its expressive power and ease of use, it was also realized that $RCTL$ has a large subset that can be verified on-the-fly. (In this paper, the term on-the-fly is used for error detection during symbolic reachability analysis.) Let M be a model and let R be a regular expression that represents an erroneous computation of M (computation that contradicts the requirements on M). Let $\mathcal{A}(R)$ be a finite automaton that runs with M and enters the state $match_R$ only if the model M performs a computation that agrees with R. The specification "M has no computations that agree with R" is equivalent to

$$M \times \mathcal{A}(R) \models AG(\neg match_R)$$

This check can be performed on-the-fly as described in [Lon93] and in [EM95]. That is, in the process of reachable state space computation, one checks whether $\mathcal{A}(R)$ enters the state $match_R$. If it does, then model checking is stopped and the above specification fails, otherwise model checking is stopped when the entire reachable state space is computed and the specification passes. There is no need to compute the transition relation for the entire reachable state space, neither to apply model checking algorithms to verify the specification. This is an enormous saving, and the only price is the extra automaton $\mathcal{A}(R)$. Since the number of states in $\mathcal{A}(R)$ is linear in the length of R, and since $\mathcal{A}(R)$ does not influence M ($\mathcal{A}(R)$ is a satellite), in our experience this price is negligible with respect to the benefits of on-the-fly model checking. Our experience also shows that well over 80% of the formulas needed for a typical hardware design can be verified with the above on-the-fly method.

The results of this paper were implemented in 1995 in RuleBase [BBEL], which is an IBM model checker based on SMV. RuleBase reads formulas in $RCTL$ and decides whether it is possible to verify them on-the-fly. Formulas that can not be verified on-the-fly are evaluated using the original CTL model checking algorithm. A large number of errors were detected by RuleBase using on-the-fly verification, usually much faster than they would have been detected with the original algorithm. In many cases, errors were detected that would have been missed by original CTL model checking since that run would not have been completed due to memory explosion. On-the-fly verification of $RCTL$ formulas has moved model checking in IBM into a different class of designs inaccessible by prior techniques.

Translating formulas into state machines is not a new idea. Tableau construction for LTL model checking was given in [LP85]. A different algorithm was presented in [VW86] . In [CGH97], LTL model checking is performed using a tableau construction and running within SMV. Tableau construction for $ACTL$ is presented in [GL94]. In all these referenced works, the construction of the tableau is exponential in the length of the formula. In [CYF94] it is shown how to translate a specific CTL formula into an FSM in order to save run-time, on-the-fly verification is not mentioned there and no other CTL formulas are discussed. Using regular expressions for specifications is discussed in [Wol81] (for LTL) and in [IN97] (for CTL).

The rest of the paper is organized as follows. In the next section we define the specification language $RCTL$. In section 3, we introduce a significant subset of $RCTL$ and show how its formulas can be verified on-the-fly. Section 4 includes some experimental results, and section 5 concludes the paper.

2 Definition of RCTL

In this section we define Regular CTL ($RCTL$) which is an extension of CTL. Let AP be a non-empty finite set of atomic propositions that includes all the signals of the model under discussion, and the constants $true$ and $false$. Let B be the collection of all boolean expressions over AP. Notice that, modulo logical equivalence, B is finite. For every regular expression R let $\mathcal{L}(R)$ be the language of R over the alphabet B. Let ϵ denote the empty word.

In $RCTL$ regular expressions are used to specify sets of non-empty finite computations. Let M be a model (finite, closed, non-deterministic state machine). We say that the computation $s_0, s_1 \ldots, s_n$ of M belongs to $\mathcal{L}(R)$ when there is a word $b = b_0 b_1 \ldots b_n$ over B such that $b \in \mathcal{L}(R)$ and for every $0 \leq i \leq n$, $(M, s_i) \models b_i$.

The following two definitions are needed before we define $RCTL$. First we define the operation $\sim$ between any two regular expressions. Informally, $Q^\sim R$ is a regular expression whose language consists of all words that are a result of taking a word from $\mathcal{L}(Q)$ and a word from $\mathcal{L}(R)$ and concatenating them with an overlap by "anding" the last letter of the former with the first letter of the latter.

Definition 1. Let Q, R, U, V, W be regular expressions and let $q, r \in B$. We define the regular expression $Q^\sim R$ by:

1. If $Q = \emptyset$ or $R = \emptyset$, then $Q^\sim R = \emptyset$
2. If $Q = Uq$ and $R = rV$, then $Q^\sim R = U(q \wedge r)V$
3. If $Q = UV^*$, then $Q^\sim R = UV^*V^\sim R + U^\sim R$
4. If $Q = U(V + W)$, then $Q^\sim R = UV^\sim R + UW^\sim R$
5. If $R = U^*V$, then $Q^\sim R = Q^\sim UU^*V + Q^\sim V$
6. If $R = (U + V)W$, then $Q^\sim R = Q^\sim UW + Q^\sim VW$

For example, if $Q = q$ and $R = p * P$, then

$$Q^\sim R = (q \wedge p)(p*)P + q^\sim P$$

Next, we define the operator $\mathcal{S}$ that determines, for every non-empty regular expression R, whether $\epsilon \in \mathcal{L}(R)$ or not. That is, $\mathcal{S}(R) = 1$ if and only if $\epsilon \in \mathcal{L}(R)$.

Definition 2. Let Q and R be non-empty regular expressions over B, and $p \in B$.

1. $\mathcal{S}(p) = 0$
2. $\mathcal{S}(QR) = \mathcal{S}(Q) \wedge \mathcal{S}(R)$
3. $\mathcal{S}(R^*) = 1$
4. $\mathcal{S}(Q + R) = \mathcal{S}(Q) \vee \mathcal{S}(R)$

We are now ready to define $RCTL$. The specification language $RCTL$ is an extension of CTL where to the usual CTL temporal operators ($AX, EX, AU, EU, \ldots$) we add infinitely many new temporal operators, one for each regular expression over B. Roughly, for every regular expression R we add the temporal operator $\{R\}()$ and the meaning of $\{R\}(\psi)$ is the following. For every computation $\pi \in \mathcal{L}(R)$, ψ is true in the last cycle of π.

Definition 3. $RCTL$ is the smallest superset of CTL that is closed under all boolean and temporal operators of CTL and in addition satisfies the following condition:

- If $\psi \in RCTL$ and R is a non-empty regular expression over B such that $\mathcal{S}(R) = 0$, then $\{R\}(\psi) \in RCTL$

To formally define the semantics of $RCTL$ we'll need the following. It is well known that for every regular expression R there exists a non deterministic finite automaton with no ϵ-transitions, $\mathcal{A}(R)$, such that $\mathcal{L}(R) = \mathcal{L}(\mathcal{A}(R))$. The number of states in $\mathcal{A}(R)$ is linear in the length of R. For the purposes of what is presented in this paper, $\mathcal{A}(R)$ has the following properties. The input to $\mathcal{A}(R)$ is a stream of elements of B which should be viewed as a computation of M. $\mathcal{A}(R)$ has a match state and a no match state denoted by $match_R$ and no_match_R. The only transitions out of $match_R$ and no_match_R are into no_match_R. The set of initial states is denoted by $\mathcal{I}_R$.

We also need a variant of $\mathcal{A}(R)$ denoted by $\mathcal{A}^s(R)$. It has an additional initial state $idle_R \in \mathcal{I}_R$. The only transition into $idle_R$ is from $idle_R$ itself and there are transitions out of $idle_R$ into every initial state. $\mathcal{A}^s(R)$ has the ability to start its action in the middle of the word (computation) and ignore the prefix of that word simply by staying in $idle_R$ for an arbitrary number of cycles.

Next, the semantics of $RCTL$ is defined in the following manner. For every $\psi \in RCTL$ we define $\mathcal{T}(\psi) \in CTL$ and $\mathcal{E}(\psi)$ which is a collection of automata such that for every model M

$$M \models \psi \iff M \times \Pi(\mathcal{E}(\psi)) \models \mathcal{T}(\psi)$$

We need $\mathcal{E}(\psi)$ because the expressive power of $RCTL$ is larger than that of CTL. This is demonstrated by the $RCTL$ formula

$$\{true((true)(true))^*\}(p)$$

which expresses the fact that p is true in every even cycle. It is well known that this fact can not be expressed in CTL. In the following definition, for every regular expression Q^* ($Q \notin B$) that appears in ψ we'll add the automaton $\mathcal{A}^s(Q)$ to $\mathcal{E}(\psi)$.

Let us define the CTL formula $\mathcal{T}(\psi)$ and the set $\mathcal{E}(\psi)$ for a given $RCTL$ formula ψ. This is done by the following recursive procedure.

Procedure 4 *Initialize $\mathcal{E}(\psi) = \emptyset$. Let R be a non-empty regular expression with $\mathcal{S}(R) = 0$. Let OP_1 be any of the usual unary CTL temporal operators and let OP_2 be any of the usual binary CTL temporal operators. Let $\varphi, \rho \in RCTL$.*

1. $T(\neg\varphi) = \neg T(\varphi)$ and $\mathcal{E}(\neg\varphi) = \mathcal{E}(\varphi)$
2. $T(\varphi \vee \rho) = T(\varphi) \vee T(\rho)$ and $\mathcal{E}(\varphi \vee \rho) = \mathcal{E}(\varphi) \cup \mathcal{E}(\rho)$
3. $T(OP_1(\varphi)) = OP_1(T(\varphi))$ and $\mathcal{E}(OP_1(\varphi)) = \mathcal{E}(\varphi)$
4. $T(OP_2(\varphi,\rho)) = OP_2(T(\varphi), T(\rho))$ and $\mathcal{E}(OP_2(\varphi,\rho)) = \mathcal{E}(\varphi) \cup \mathcal{E}(\rho)$
5. $T(\{R\}(\varphi))$ and $\mathcal{E}(\{R\}(\varphi))$ are given by the following definition

Definition 5. Let P, Q and R be non-empty regular expressions, $\varphi \in RCTL$ and $p \in B$. Let $idle_P$ denote the statement "$\mathcal{A}^s(P)$ is in the state $idle_P$" and similarly for $match_P$.

1. (a) $T(\{p\}(\varphi)) = \neg(p \wedge \neg T(\varphi))$
   (b) $\mathcal{E}(\{p\}(\varphi)) = \mathcal{E}(\varphi)$
2. (a) $T(\{pP\}(\varphi)) = \begin{cases} \neg(p \wedge EX(\neg T(\{P\}(\varphi)))) & \text{if } \mathcal{S}(P) = 0 \\ \neg(p \wedge (\neg T(\varphi) \vee EX(\neg T(\{P\}(\varphi))))) & \text{otherwise} \end{cases}$
   (b) $\mathcal{E}(\{pP\}(\varphi)) = \mathcal{E}(\{P\}(\varphi))$
3. (a) $T(\{p^*\}(\varphi)) = \neg(E[pUp \wedge \neg T(\varphi)])$
   (b) $\mathcal{E}(\{p^*\}(\varphi)) = \mathcal{E}(\varphi)$
4. (a) $T(\{p^*P\}(\varphi)) = \begin{cases} \neg(E[pU\neg T(\{P\}(\varphi))]) & \text{if } \mathcal{S}(P) = 0 \\ \neg(E[pU((p \wedge (\neg T(\varphi)) \vee (\neg T(\{P\}(\varphi)))))]) & \text{otherwise} \end{cases}$
   (b) $\mathcal{E}(\{p^*P\}(\varphi)) = \mathcal{E}(\{P\}(\varphi))$
5. (a) $T(\{P^*\}(\varphi)) = T(\{P^\sim idle_P(\neg idle_P)^*(match_P \vee idle_P)^\sim P + P\}(\varphi)) \wedge T(\varphi)$
   (b) $\mathcal{E}(\{P^*\}(\varphi)) = \{\mathcal{A}^s(P)\} \cup \mathcal{E}(\varphi)$
6. (a) $T(\{P^*Q\}(\varphi)) = T(\{P^\sim idle_P(\neg idle_P)^*(match_P \vee idle_P)^\sim Q + Q\}(\varphi))$
   (b) $\mathcal{E}(\{P^*Q\}(\varphi)) = \{\mathcal{A}^s(P)\} \cup \mathcal{E}(\{Q\}(\varphi))$
7. (a) $T(\{P + Q\}(\varphi)) = T(\{P\}(\varphi)) \wedge T(\{Q\}(\varphi))$
   (b) $\mathcal{E}(\{P + Q\}(\varphi)) = \mathcal{E}(\{P\}(\varphi)) \cup \mathcal{E}(\{Q\}(\varphi))$
8. (a) $T(\{(P + Q)R\}(\varphi)) = T(\{PR\}(\varphi)) \wedge T(\{QR\}(\varphi))$
   (b) $\mathcal{E}(\{(P + Q)R\}(\varphi)) = \mathcal{E}(\{PR\}(\varphi)) \cup \mathcal{E}(\{QR\}(\varphi))$

Let us emphasize that at the entrance to procedure 4 it is checked that all regular expressions R that appear in ψ satisfy $\mathcal{S}(R) = 0$ (otherwise it is an error). So, for example, $\{P^*\}(\varphi)$ can appear only during the recursion as a sub formula, but is not a legal $RCTL$ formula on its own.

Notice that item 5 and 6 should be invoked only when $P \notin B$, otherwise items 3 and 4 are sufficient. The subset of $RCTL$ that allows the $*$ operation to be applied only to boolean expressions is in fact equal to CTL. For every formula ψ in this subset, $\mathcal{E}(\psi) = \emptyset$ and T is a mapping into CTL such that for every model M

$$M \models \psi \iff M \models T(\psi)$$

The main reason for preferring $RCTL$ over CTL as an hardware specification language is not its theoretical expressive power but rather its practical expressive power (i.e. ease of use).

The following formula is an example of $RCTL$ relative ease of use.

$$AG(\{wb^*a(v^*r + v^*wb^*r)\}(d))$$

The CTL version of this formula is

$$AG(\neg(w \wedge (EX(E[bU(a \wedge (EX(((E[vU(r \wedge \neg d)]) \wedge$$
$$(E[vU(w \wedge (EX(E[bU(r \wedge \neg d)])))])))])))))]))))$$

Sugar is the RuleBase specification language [BBEL]. Many useful Sugar operators are easily defined in $RCTL$. The formula φ *until* p (weak until) means that on all paths, φ is true until p is true, but p could be false forever (in which case φ stays true forever). In $RCTL$, φ *until* p is expressed by

$$\{\neg p^* \neg p\}(\varphi)$$

The $next\_event(p)(\varphi)$ operator states that on all paths, in the next cycle in which p is true, φ is also true. On the paths where p is never true, nothing is being claimed. In $RCTL$, $next\_event(p)(\varphi)$ is expressed by

$$\{\neg p^* p\}(\varphi)$$

Notice that by definition 5, both φ *until* p and $next\_event(p)(\varphi)$ can be expressed in CTL.

3   On-The-Fly Model Checking of RCTL formulas

In order to model check a CTL formula, SMV computes the transition relation of the model and then applies the CTL model checking algorithm to determine the truth value of the given CTL formula. Since the computation of the transition relation on the entire state space is often too costly, an option exists in SMV to first compute the reachable state space (this is an iterative process where at every iteration only the partial transition relation on the new states is needed), then compute the transition relation only on the full reachable state space, and finally apply the CTL model checking algorithm. According to our experience, this three stage SMV computation is by far more efficient for most hardware designs. In many examples, the tasks of computing the transition relation on the full reachable state space and applying the model checking algorithm are the bottlenecks of the whole process. In all examples they consume a significant part of the space and time resources that are needed for model checking.

If a CTL formula has the form $AG(p)$, where $p \in B$, a better technique can be used [Lon93, EM95]. Note that an $AG(p)$ formula states that p is true in every reachable state of the model. Therefore, to disprove this formula, it is sufficient to find one state in which p is false. Let S be the set of states where p is false.

All that one needs to do is to check, after every iteration of the reachable state space analysis, whether the intersection of S with the reachable state space computed so far is empty. If it is not empty, the process is stopped and $AG(p)$ is false, otherwise, the process continues and is terminated when the entire reachable state space has been computed, and in this case, the formula $AG(p)$ is true.

Thus, there is no need to compute the full transition relation, neither to apply the model checking algorithm. This saves significant space and time resources. Furthermore, since this check is done "on-the-fly", in the cases where the formula fails, only a portion of the reachable states space is computed, saving even more space and time.

Experience shows that in the beginning stages of the design/verification process, most of the formulas that fail, fail quickly, and a short computation is needed to demonstrate the error in either the design or the specification. As the design process progresses, longer and longer computations are needed to reveal errors. This makes the on-the-fly approach very attractive. It finds a large number of easy bugs (in the specification or design) very quickly in the beginning and works harder, as the design/verification matures, to find the more complex errors. Unfortunately, in real life CTL model checking, most of the formulas do not have this desired form of $AG(p)$.

To overcome this limitation, and in order to apply the on-the-fly method to a larger class of formulas $\mathcal{F} \subset RCTL$ (formally defined below), we translate a formula $\psi \in \mathcal{F}$ into a CTL formula of the form $AG(p)$ and an automaton. We then verify the $AG(p)$ formula in a model slightly different from the original model.

$\mathcal{F}$ can be viewed as a generalization of the class of $AG(p)$ formulas. While disproving an $AG(p)$ formula is equivalent to finding a *single bad state*, disproving a formula $\psi \in \mathcal{F}$ is equivalent to finding a *single bad finite computation*.

Note that we do not include in $\mathcal{F}$ formulas such as $AX(\phi) \vee AX(\psi)$ since no single finite computation could demonstrate their failure.

Definition 6. $\mathcal{F}$ is the set of all formulas $\psi \in RCTL$ for which there exists a non empty regular expression R with $\mathcal{S}(R) = 0$ such that $\psi \equiv \{R\}(false)$

The statement $M \models \{R\}(false)$ simply states that the model M has no computations that belong to $\mathcal{L}(R)$.

Being in $RCTL$, formulas of the form $\{R\}(false)$ can be verified as described in Section 2. However, there is an alternative way to verify this type of formulas.

Theorem 7. *For every non-empty regular expression R with $\mathcal{S}(R) = 0$ and for every model M*

$$M \models \{R\}(false) \iff M \times \mathcal{A}(R) \models AG(\neg match_R)$$

This theorem reduces model checking of formulas from $\mathcal{F}$ to model checking of $AG(p)$ type formulas and hence allows one to check formulas from $\mathcal{F}$ on-the-fly with all the benefits that were described above. From theorem 7 it follows that for every erroneous finite computation, there is an $RCTL$ formula that detects it and can be verified on-the-fly.

The price one pays for running on-the-fly is that the model $M \times \mathcal{A}(R)$ is larger than M. However, the number of states in $\mathcal{A}(R)$ is linear in the length of R. In addition, $\mathcal{A}(R)$ has no influence on M (i.e. $\mathcal{A}(R)$ is a satellite). This makes the price of running on-the-fly negligible in light of the benefits one gets from this model checking technique.

In RuleBase, the user writes specifications in $RCTL$ and the tool tries to map into $\mathcal{F}$. If it succeeds, the run continues on-the-fly, otherwise it switches to normal CTL model checking as described in the previous section. The following definition describes a class of $RCTL$ formulas that can be mapped into $\mathcal{F}$.

Definition 8. $\mathcal{G}$, the subset of $RCTL$ that RuleBase verifies on-the-fly is defined recursively. Let $\varphi, \psi \in \mathcal{G}$, $p \in B$ and Q a non-empty regular expression with $\mathcal{S}(Q) = 0$.

1. $p \in \mathcal{G}$
2. $\varphi \wedge \psi \in \mathcal{G}$
3. $(p \to \varphi) \in \mathcal{G}$
4. $AX(\varphi) \in \mathcal{G}$
5. $AG(\varphi) \in \mathcal{G}$
6. $\{Q\}(\varphi) \in \mathcal{G}$

Many other useful Sugar operators, such as $until$ (weak until) and $next\_event$, can be translated into $\mathcal{G}$ (see Section 2). The following $RCTL$ formula belongs to $\mathcal{G}$ and hence, by the following theorem, can be verified on-the-fly.

$$AG(\{xy^*z\}(next\_event(x)(AX(next\_event(y)(\psi)))))$$

Theorem 9. $\mathcal{G} \subset \mathcal{F}$.

Proof. We translate every $\varphi \in \mathcal{G}$ into a regular expression $\mathcal{R}(\varphi)$ such that

$$\varphi \equiv \{\mathcal{R}(\varphi)\}(false) \qquad (*)$$

Let us define $\mathcal{R}$ recursively.

Definition 10. Let $\varphi, \psi \in \mathcal{G}, p \in B$ and Q a non-empty regular expression with $\mathcal{S}(Q) = 0$.

1. $\mathcal{R}(p) = \neg p$
2. $\mathcal{R}(\varphi \wedge \psi) = \mathcal{R}(\varphi) + \mathcal{R}(\psi)$
3. $\mathcal{R}(p \to \varphi) = p^{\sim}\mathcal{R}(\varphi)$
4. $\mathcal{R}(AX(\varphi)) = (true)\mathcal{R}(\varphi)$
5. $\mathcal{R}(AG(\varphi)) = (true)^*\mathcal{R}(\varphi)$
6. $\mathcal{R}(\{Q\}(\varphi)) = Q^{\sim}\mathcal{R}(\varphi)$

It is now straightforward to finish proving $(*)$, recursively on φ, going down the list of items in definition 8.

4 Experimental Results

As was mentioned before, according to our experience, a large portion (over 80%) of all practical formulas belong to the set $\mathcal{G}$ (see definition 8) and hence can be verified on-the-fly. In fact, RuleBase has two alternative modes for model checking formulas that belong to the set $\mathcal{G}$. That is, the original (normal) CTL model checking mode (presented in Section 2) on one hand, and the on-the-fly mode (presented in Section 3) on the other hand. In this section we present results comparing these two modes.

The results presented are of several blocks that belong to an IBM node bus adapter verified by RuleBase. Each of these blocks contains several thousands of state variables (5000 - 7000). After applying reductions techniques (both automatic and manual), the blocks were reduced to several hundreds of state variables each (see Table 1).

Table 1. The Models

Model Name	# of State Variables	# of Iterations	Reachable States
M1	244	202	1.69×10^9
M2	167	264	3.47×10^{11}
M3	419	281	3.33×10^{49}
M4	314	81	4.43×10^{15}

Table 2. Results M1

Specification	Mode	Status	Run Time Seconds	BDD Nodes
S1	normal	pass	7020	8.9×10^5
	on-the-fly	pass	4468	3.4×10^5
S2	normal	fail	2910	1.2×10^5
	on-the-fly	fail at iteration 51	911	4.7×10^4

On each of these examples (models) we ran several formulas. Each formula ran in both normal mode and on-the-fly mode, starting with the same initial BDD ordering. For the failures, we have indicated at which iteration the failure occurred in the on-the-fly mode. All examples were run on RS/6000 with up to 500 MB of memory.

Table 1 gives some information on these examples. The state variables include the variables of the environment. The number of iterations indicates the maximal number of cycles needed to reach to any given reachable state.

The rest of the tables (2 - 5) compare results of running formulas in both modes. Table 2 presents a slight advantage for the on-the-fly mode. In table 3, the results of formula T1 show that, in "pass" cases, the normal mode might be comparable to the on-the-fly mode though in most of the "pass" cases the advantage is still for the on-the-fly mode (see S1 and R1). It should not be surprising that in many "pass" cases the

Table 3. Results M2

Specification	Mode	Status	Run Time Seconds	BDD Nodes
T1	normal	pass	4590	2.1×10^5
	on-the-fly	pass	5408	2.4×10^5
T2	normal	fail	4695	2.6×10^5
	on-the-fly	fail at iteration 89	1136	1.7×10^5
T3	normal	fail	6325	2.5×10^5
	on-the-fly	fail at iteration 21	49	3.5×10^4

Table 4. Results M3

Specification	Mode	Status	Run Time Seconds	BDD Nodes
R1	normal	pass	17926	3.2×10^6
	on-the-fly	pass	7489	9.7×10^5
R2	normal	fail	18115	3.3×10^6
	on-the-fly	fail at iteration 46	208	8.6×10^4

Table 5. Results M4

Specification	Mode	Status	Run Time Seconds	BDD Nodes
Q1	normal	terminated	–	9.7×10^6
	on-the-fly	fail at iteration 25	770	3.2×10^5

on-the-fly mode requires less space. This happens because in the on-the-fly mode there is no need to compute the full transition relation on the entire reachable state space, only partial transition relations on the new states at every step of the reachability analysis are needed. In addition, the model checking algorithms to verify the specification are not applied in the on-the-fly mode which might save in space as well.

Formula T3 in table 3 shows the remarkable advantage of the on-the-fly mode in "fail" cases. A similar advantage is demonstrated by R2 (table 4).

The biggest advantage for the on-the-fly mode is sharply demonstrated in table 5. The formula Q1 could not run to completion in the normal mode. It successfully computed the reachable state space but it ran out of memory during the construction of the transition relation on the full reachable state space. On the other hand, in the on-the-fly mode it found an error at cycle 21 after less than 13 minutes.

5   Conclusion

We have introduced the specification language $RCTL$ with the motivation of narrowing the usability gap of CTL model checking. We identified a subset of $RCTL$ that can be verified on-the-fly, significantly reducing both space and time. The subset $\mathcal{F}$ of $RCTL$ that can be verified on-the-fly might look small from a theoretical point of view, but in practice consists of most of the formulas that are used in hardware specification (at least in our methodology). Verification of formulas that belong to this subset has been reduced to invariant checking, and model checking of these formulas has been reduced to reachability analysis.

Acknowledgements

We wish to thank Dana Fisman for her helpful feedback and for helping with the implementation, Gregory Ronin and Tali Yatzkar-Haham for their help with preparing the experimental results, and Yaron Wolfsthal for his insightful comments on the draft of the paper.

References

[BBEL]   I. Beer, S. Ben-David, C. Eisner, A. Landver, "RuleBase: an Industry-Oriented Formal Verification Tool", in Proc. 33rd Design Automation Conference 1996, pp. 655-660.

[CE81a]   E.M. Clarke and E.A. Emerson, "Design and synthesis of synchronization skeletons using Branching Time Temporal Logic", in Proc. Workshop on Logics of Programs, Lecture Notes in Computer Science, Vol. 131 (Springer, Berlin, 1981) pp. 52-71.

[CE81b]   E.M. Clark and E.A. Emerson, "Characterizing Properties of Parallel Programs as Fixed-point", in Seventh International Colloquium on Automata, Languages, and Programming, Volume 85 of LNCS, 1981.

[CGH97]   E. Clark, O. Grumberg and K. Hamaguchi, "Another Look at LTL Model Checking", Formal Methods in System Design, Volume 10, Number 1, Feb. 1997.

[CYF94]   B.Chen, M. Yamazaki, M. Fujita, "Bug Identification of a Real Chip Design by Symbolic Model Checking", Proc. European Design and Test Conference, 1994, pp. 132-136.

[EM95]   A. Th. Eiriksson and K.L. McMillan, "Using Formal Verification/ Analysis Methods on the Critical Path in System Design: A Case Study", 7th International Conference, CAV '95, pp. 367-380.

[GL94]   O. Grumberg and D.E. Long, "Model checking and modular verification", ACM Trans. on Programming Languages and Systems 16 (3), 1994.

[IN97]   H. Iwashita and T. Nakata, "Forward Model Checking Techniques Oriented to Buggy Designs", International Conference on Computer Aided Design, ICCAD '97.

[LP85]   O. Lichtenstein an A. Pnueli, "Checking that finite state concurrent programs satisfy their linear specification", Proceedings of the Twelfth Annual ACM Symposium on Principles of Programming Languages, Jan. 1985.

[Lon93]   D. Long, "Model Checking, Abstraction and Compositional Verification", Ph.D. Thesis, CMU, 1993.

[McM93]   K.L. McMillan, "Symbolic Model Checking", Kluwer Academic Publishers, 1993.

[VW86]   Y. Vardi and P. Wolper "An automatic theoretic approach to automatic program verification", Proceeding of the First Annual Symposium on Logic in Computer Science, IEEE Computer Society Press, June 1986.

[Wol81]   P. Wolper "Temporal Logic can be more expressive", 22nd Annual Symposium on Foundation of Computer Science, Oct. 1981.

From *Pre*-historic to *Post*-modern
Symbolic Model Checking*

Thomas A. Henzinger   Orna Kupferman   Shaz Qadeer

Department of EECS, University of California at Berkeley, CA 94720-1770, USA
Email:{tah,orna,shaz}@eecs.berkeley.edu

Abstract. Symbolic model checking, which enables the automatic verification of large systems, proceeds by calculating with expressions that represent state sets. Traditionally, symbolic model-checking tools are based on *backward* state traversal; their basic operation is the function *pre*, which given a set of states, returns the set of all predecessor states. This is because specifiers usually employ formalisms with future-time modalities, which are naturally evaluated by iterating applications of *pre*. It has been recently shown experimentally that symbolic model checking can perform significantly better if it is based, instead, on *forward* state traversal; in this case, the basic operation is the function *post*, which given a set of states, returns the set of all successor states. This is because forward state traversal can ensure that only those parts of the state space are explored which are reachable from an initial state and relevant for satisfaction or violation of the specification; that is, errors can be detected as soon as possible.

In this paper, we investigate which specifications can be checked by symbolic forward state traversal. We formulate the problems of symbolic backward and forward model checking by means of two μ-calculi. The *pre*-μ calculus is based on the *pre* operation; the *post*-μ calculus, on the *post* operation. These two μ-calculi induce query logics, which augment fixpoint expressions with a boolean emptiness query. Using query logics, we are able to relate and compare the symbolic backward and forward approaches. In particular, we prove that all ω-regular (linear-time) specifications can be expressed as *post*-μ queries, and therefore checked using symbolic forward state traversal. On the other hand, we show that there are simple branching-time specifications that cannot be checked in this way.

1 Introduction

Today's rapid development of complex and safety-critical systems requires verification methods such as model checking. In model checking [CE81,QS81], we ensure that a system exhibits a desired behavior by executing an algorithm that checks whether a mathematical model of the system satisfies a formal specification that describes the behavior. The algorithmic nature of model checking makes it fully automatic, and thus attractive to practitioners. At the same time, model checking is very sensitive to the size of the mathematical model of the system. Commercial model-checking tools need to cope with the exceedingly large state spaces that are present in real-life examples, making the so-called state-explosion problem perhaps the most challenging issue in computer-aided verification. One of the important developments in this area is the discovery of *symbolic* model-checking methods [BCM$^+$92]. In particular, use of BDDs [Bry86] for model representation has yielded model-checking tools that can handle very large state spaces [CGL93].

Traditional symbolic model-checking tools have been based on *backward* state traversal [McM93,BHSV$^+$96]. They compute with expressions that represent state sets using, in addition to positive boolean operations, the functions *pre* and $\widetilde{pre}$, which map a set of states to a subset

---

* This work is supported in part by ONR YIP award N00014-95-1-0520, by NSF CAREER award CCR-9501708, by NSF grant CCR-9504469, by ARO MURI grant DAAH-04-96-1-0341, and by the SRC contract 97-DC-324.041.

of its *predecessor* states. Formally, given a set U of states, the set $pre(U)$ contains the states for which there exists a successor state in U, and the set $\widetilde{pre}(U)$ contains the states all of whose successor states are in U. By evaluating fixpoint expressions over boolean and pre operations, complicated state sets can be calculated. For example, to find the set of states from which a state satisfying a predicate p is reachable, the model checker starts with the set U of states in which p holds, and repeatedly adds to U the set $pre(U)$, until no more states can be added. Formally, the model checker calculates the least fixpoint of the expression $U = p \vee pre(U)$. Symbolic model-checking techniques were first applied to branching-time specifications, and later extended to linear-time specifications, both via translations into fixpoint expressions [BCM+92,CGH94].

As an alternative to symbolic model checking, in *enumerative* model checking states are represented individually. Traditional enumerative model-checking tools check linear-time specifications by *forward* state traversal [Hol97,Dil96]. There, the basic operation is to compute, for a given state, the list of successor states. Forward state traversal has several obvious advantages over backward state traversal. First, for operational system models, successor states are often easier to compute than predecessor states. Second, only the reachable part of the state space is traversed. Third, optimizations such as *on-the-fly* [GPVW95] and *partial-order* [Pel94] methods can be incorporated naturally. For example, in on-the-fly model checking, only those parts of the state space are traversed which are relevant for satisfying (or violating) the given specification.

Some of the advantages of forward state traversal can be easily incorporated into symbolic methods. For example, we may first compute the set of reachable states by symbolic forward state traversal, and then restrict backward state traversal for model checking to the reachable states. This method, however, is unsatisfactory; for example, it cannot find even a short error trace if the set of reachable states cannot be computed. We present a tighter, and more advantageous, integration of forward state traversal with symbolic methods. In *symbolic forward* state traversal, we replace the functions pre and $\widetilde{pre}$ by the functions $post$ and $\widetilde{post}$, respectively, which map a set of states to a subset of its *successor* states. Formally, given a set U of states, the set $post(U)$ contains the states for which there exists a predecessor state in U, and the set $\widetilde{post}(U)$ contains the states all of whose predecessor states are in U. Then, we evaluate fixpoint expressions over boolean and post operations on state sets. It has recently been shown that certain branching-time as well as linear-time specifications, such as response (i.e., $\square(p \rightarrow \Diamond q)$), can be model checked by symbolic forward state traversal [INH96,IN97]. We attempt a more systematic study of what can and what cannot be model checked in this way. In particular, we show that all ω-regular (linear-time) specifications (which include all LTL specifications) are amenable to a symbolic forward approach, while some CTL (branching-time) specifications are not.

For this purpose, we define *post-μ*, a fixpoint calculus that is based on post operations in the same way in which the traditional μ-calculus, here called *pre-μ*, is based on pre operations [Koz83]. While *pre-μ* expressions refer to the future of a given state in a model, *post-μ* expressions refer to its past. Therefore, in stark contrast to the fact that every LTL and CTL specification has an equivalent expression in *pre-μ*, almost no LTL or CTL specification, including response, has an equivalent expression in *post-μ*. In order to compare pre and post logics, rather, we need to define *query logics*, whose formulas refer to a whole model, not an individual state. Query logics are based on the *emptiness predicate* $\mathcal{E}$. For a specification ϕ, which is true in some states of a model and false in others, the query $\mathcal{E}(\phi)$ is true in a model iff ϕ is false in all states of the model. The query logic *post-$\mu_\emptyset$* contains all queries of the form $\mathcal{E}(\phi)$ and $\neg\mathcal{E}(\phi)$, for *post-μ* expressions ϕ. On the positive side, we prove that every ω-regular (Büchi) specification has an equivalent query in *post-$\mu_\emptyset$*. As with the translation from Büchi automata to *pre-μ* expressions [EL86,BC96], the translation from Büchi automata to *post-$\mu_\emptyset$* queries is linear and involves only fixpoint expressions of alternation depth two. Moreover, we show that every co-Büchi specification has an equivalent query in alternation-free *post-$\mu_\emptyset$*, which can be checked efficiently (in linear time). On the negative side, we prove that there are CTL specifications that are not equivalent to any boolean combination of *post-$\mu_\emptyset$* queries.

Symbolic forward model checking combines the benefits of symbolic over enumerative state traversal with the benefits of forward over backward state traversal. In [INH96,IN97], the authors present experimental evidence that symbolic forward state traversal can be significantly more efficient than symbolic backward state traversal. Our preliminary experimental results confirm this observation. In addition, we give some theoretical justifications for the symbolic forward approach. We show that unlike enumerative forward model checking (which is traditionally based on depth-first state traversal) and unlike symbolic backward model checking, the symbolic forward approach guarantees *a.s.a.p. error detection*. Intuitively, if a model violates a safety specification, and the shortest error trace has length m, then the breadth-first nature of symbolic forward model checking ensures that the error will be found before any states at a distance greater than m from the initial states are explored.

The remainder of this paper is organized as follows. In Section 2 we define the logics *pre-μ* and *post-μ*, and the query logics they induce. In Section 3, we translate Büchi automata into equivalent *post-μ_θ* queries of alternation depth two, and co-Büchi automata into equivalent alternation-free *post-μ_θ* queries. We also show that the translation guarantees a.s.a.p. error detection for safety specifications. In Section 4, we compare the distinguishing and expressive powers of the various pre, post, and query logics. Finally, in Section 5 we put our results in perspective and report on some experimental evidence for the value of symbolic forward model checking.

2 Definition of Pre and Post Logics

2.1 Pre and post μ-calculi

The μ-calculus is a modal logic augmented with least and greatest fixpoint operators [Koz83]. In this paper, we use the equational form of the propositional μ-calculus, as in [BC96]. The modalities of the μ-calculus relate a set of states to a subset of its predecessor states. Therefore, we refer to the μ-calculus by *pre-μ*.

The formulas of *pre-μ* are defined with respect to a set P of propositions and a set V of variables. A *modal expression* is either p, $\neg p$, X, $\varphi \vee \psi$, $\varphi \wedge \psi$, $\exists\bigcirc\varphi$, or $\forall\bigcirc\varphi$, for propositions $p \in P$, variables $X \in V$, and modal expressions φ and ψ. Let I be a finite subset of the set of natural numbers. An *equational block* $B = \langle \lambda, \{X_i = \varphi_i \mid i \in I\}\rangle$ consists of a flag $\lambda \in \{\mu, \nu\}$ and a finite set of equations $X_i = \varphi_i$, where each X_i is a variable, each φ_i is a modal expression, and the variables X_i are pairwise distinct. If $\lambda = \mu$, then B is a *μ-block*; otherwise B is a *ν-block*. For the equational block B, let $vars(B) = \{X_i \mid i \in I\}$ be the set of variables on the left-hand sides of the equations of B. A *block tuple* $\mathcal{B} = \langle B_1, \ldots, B_n\rangle$ is a finite list of equational blocks such that the variable sets $vars(B_j)$, for $1 \leq j \leq n$, are pairwise disjoint. For the block tuple $\mathcal{B}$, let $vars(\mathcal{B}) = \bigcup_{1 \leq j \leq n} vars(B_j)$. For every variable $X \in vars(\mathcal{B})$, let $expand_\mathcal{B}(X)$ be the modal expression on the right-hand side of the unique equation in $\mathcal{B}$ whose left-hand side is X. A *pre-μ formula* $\phi = \langle \mathcal{B}, X_0\rangle$ is a pair that consists of a block tuple $\mathcal{B}$ and a variable $X_0 \in vars(\mathcal{B})$. The variable X_0 is called the *root variable* of ϕ. The formula ϕ is a *pre-μ sentence* if every variable that occurs in some modal expression of $\mathcal{B}$ is contained in $vars(\mathcal{B})$.

The semantics of a *pre-μ* formula is defined with respect to a Kripke structure and a valuation for the variables. A *Kripke structure* is a tuple $K = \langle P, W, R, L\rangle$ that consists of a finite set P of propositions, a finite set W of states, a binary transition relation $R \subseteq W \times W$ total in both the first and second arguments (i.e., for every state $w \in W$, there is a state w' such that $R(w, w')$ and there is a state w'' such that $R(w'', w)$), and a labeling function $L : W \to 2^P$ that assigns to each state a set of propositions. The set P of propositions contains the distinguished proposition *init*; a state $w \in W$ is *initial* if *init* $\in L(w)$. We define four functions *pre*, $\widetilde{pre}$, *post* and $\widetilde{post}$

from 2^W to 2^W as follows. For any set $U \subseteq W$ of states, let

$$pre(U) = \{w \in W \mid \text{there exists a state } w' \in U \text{ with } R(w, w')\},$$
$$\widetilde{pre}(U) = \{w \in W \mid \text{for all states } w' \text{ with } R(w, w'), \text{ we have } w' \in U\},$$
$$post(U) = \{w \in W \mid \text{there exists a state } w' \in U \text{ with } R(w', w)\},$$
$$\widetilde{post}(U) = \{w \in W \mid \text{for all states } w' \text{ with } R(w', w), \text{ we have } w' \in U\}.$$

A *K-valuation* for a set V of variables is a function $\Gamma : V \to 2^W$ that assigns to each variable a set of states. If Γ and Γ' are K-valuations for V, and $V' \subseteq V$ is a subset of the variables, we write $\Gamma[\Gamma'/V']$ for the K-valuation for V that assigns $\Gamma'(X)$ to each variable $X \in V'$, and $\Gamma(X)$ to each variable $X \in V \backslash V'$.

Given a Kripke structure $K = \langle P, W, R, L \rangle$ and a K-valuation Γ for a set V of variables, every modal expression φ over the propositions P and the variables V defines a set $\varphi^K(\Gamma) \subseteq W$ of states: inductively, $p^K(\Gamma) = \{w \in W \mid p \in L(w)\}$, $(\neg p)^K(\Gamma) = \{w \in W \mid p \notin L(w)\}$, $X^K(\Gamma) = \Gamma(X)$, $(\varphi \vee \psi)^K(\Gamma) = \varphi^K(\Gamma) \cup \psi^K(\Gamma)$, $(\varphi \wedge \psi)^K(\Gamma) = \varphi^K(\Gamma) \cap \psi^K(\Gamma)$, $(\exists \bigcirc \varphi)^K(\Gamma) = pre(\varphi^K(\Gamma))$, and $(\forall \bigcirc \varphi)^K(\Gamma) = \widetilde{pre}(\varphi^K(\Gamma))$. Given K, every block tuple $\mathcal{B} = \langle B_1, \ldots, B_n \rangle$ over P and V defines a function $\mathcal{B}^K$ from the K-valuations for V to the K-valuations for V: inductively, if $n = 0$, then $\mathcal{B}^K(\Gamma) = \Gamma$; if B_1 is a μ-block, then $\mathcal{B}^K(\Gamma)$ is the least fixpoint of the function $F_{\mathcal{B},\Gamma}^K$; if B_1 is a ν-block, then $\mathcal{B}^K(\Gamma)$ is the greatest fixpoint of $F_{\mathcal{B},\Gamma}^K$. The monotonic function $F_{\mathcal{B},\Gamma}^K$ from valuations to valuations is defined by

$$F_{\mathcal{B},\Gamma}^K(\Gamma')(X) = \begin{cases} expand(X)^K(\langle B_2, \ldots, B_n \rangle^K(\Gamma[\Gamma'/vars(B_1)])) & \text{if } X \in vars(B_1), \\ (\langle B_2, \ldots, B_n \rangle^K(\Gamma[\Gamma'/vars(B_1)]))(X) & \text{otherwise.} \end{cases}$$

Note that for a *pre-μ* sentence $\phi = \langle \mathcal{B}, X_0 \rangle$, the function $\mathcal{B}^K$ is a constant function. Given K, the sentence ϕ defines the set $\phi^K = \mathcal{B}^K(\Gamma)(X_0)$ of states (for any choice of Γ). For a state $w \in W$ and a *pre-μ* sentence ϕ, we write $w \models_K \phi$ if $w \in \phi^K$. For a Kripke structure K, we write $K \models \phi$, and say that K *satisfies* ϕ, if there is an initial state w of K such that $w \models_K \phi$.[1] The *model-checking problem for pre-μ* is to decide, given a Kripke structure K and a *pre-μ* sentence ϕ, whether $K \models \phi$.

Given a block tuple $\mathcal{B} = \langle B_1, \ldots, B_n \rangle$, the block B_i *depends* on the block B_j if $i \neq j$ and some variable that occurs in a modal expression of B_i is contained in $vars(B_j)$. The *pre-μ* sentence $\phi = \langle \mathcal{B}, X_0 \rangle$ is *alternation-free* if the dependency relation on the blocks of $\mathcal{B}$ is acyclic (i.e., its transitive closure is asymmetric). The model-checking problem for the alternation-free fragment of *pre-μ* can be solved in linear time [CS91].

The logic *post-μ* is obtained from the logic *pre-μ* by replacing the future modal operators $\exists \bigcirc$ and $\forall \bigcirc$ by the past modal operators $\exists \ominus$ and $\forall \ominus$, with the interpretations $(\exists \ominus \varphi)^K(\Gamma) = post(\varphi^K(\Gamma))$ and $(\forall \ominus \varphi)^K(\Gamma) = \widetilde{post}(\varphi^K(\Gamma))$. The semantics of *post-μ* can alternatively be defined as follows. For a Kripke structure $K = \langle P, W, R, L \rangle$, define the Kripke structure $K^{-1} = \langle P, W, R^{-1}, L \rangle$, where $R^{-1}(w, w')$ iff $R(w', w)$. For a *post-μ* sentence ϕ, define ϕ^{-1} to be the *pre-μ* sentence obtained from ϕ by replacing each occurrence of $\exists \ominus$ and $\forall \ominus$ by $\exists \bigcirc$ and $\forall \bigcirc$, respectively. Then, for every state w of K, we have $w \models_K \phi$ iff $w \models_{K^{-1}} \phi^{-1}$.

2.2 Query logics

We define query logics that are based on *pre-μ* and *post-μ*. The sentences of *pre-μ* refer to the future of a given state in a Kripke structure, and the sentences of *post-μ* refer to its past. By contrast, the sentences of query logics, called *queries*, refer to the whole structure and thus enable us to translate between pre and post logics. The query logics are obtained from *pre-μ* and

---

[1] Note that we work, for convenience, with the dual of the usual requirement that *all* initial states satisfy a *pre-μ* sentence.

post-μ by adding a predicate $\mathcal{E}$ on sentences, called the *emptiness predicate*. For a logic $\mathcal{L}$, the query logic $\mathcal{L}_\emptyset$ contains the two queries $\mathcal{E}(\phi)$ and $\neg\mathcal{E}(\phi)$ for each sentence ϕ of $\mathcal{L}$. The query logic $\mathcal{L}_\mathcal{E}$ is richer and its queries are constructed inductively as follows:

- $\mathcal{E}(\phi)$, where ϕ is a formula of $\mathcal{L}$,
- $\neg\theta_1$ and $\theta_1 \vee \theta_2$, where θ_1 and θ_2 are queries of $\mathcal{L}_\mathcal{E}$.

The satisfaction relation $\models$ for queries on a Kripke structure K is inductively defined as follows:

- $K \models \mathcal{E}(\phi)$ iff for all states s of K, we have $s \not\models \phi$,
- $K \models \neg\theta_1$ iff $K \not\models \theta_1$, and $K \models \theta_1 \vee \theta_2$ iff $K \models \theta_1$ or $K \models \theta_2$.

While our motivation for query logics is theoretical, for the purpose of comparing pre and post logics, query logics are also practical. This is because once the state set ϕ^K has been computed (either explicitly or implicitly, using BDDs), the evaluation of the query $\mathcal{E}(\phi)$ requires constant time. Therefore, checking a query in *pre-$\mu_\mathcal{E}$* or *post-$\mu_\mathcal{E}$* is no harder than model checking *pre-μ* or *post-μ*, respectively.

2.3 Equivalences on Kripke structures induced by pre and post logics

Let $K = \langle P, W, R, L \rangle$ and $K' = \langle P, W', R', L' \rangle$ be two Kripke structures with the same set of propositions. A relation $\beta \subseteq W \times W'$ is a *pre-bisimilarity relation* if for all states w and w', we have that $\beta(w, w')$ implies (1) $L(w) = L'(w')$, (2) for every state v with $R(w, v)$, there is a state v' with $R'(w', v')$ and $\beta(v, v')$, and (3) for every state v' with $R'(w', v')$, there is a state v with $R(w, v)$ and $\beta(v, v')$. Note that, in particular, $\beta(w, w')$ implies that either both w and w' are initial, or neither of them is initial. The pre-bisimilarity relation β is a *pre-bisimulation* between K and K' if for all states $w \in W$, there is a state $w' \in W'$ such that $\beta(w, w')$, and for all states $w' \in W'$, there is a state $w \in W$ such that $\beta(w, w')$. The pre-bisimilarity relation β is an *init-pre-bisimulation* between K and K' if for all initial states $w \in W$, there is an initial state $w' \in W'$ such that $\beta(w, w')$, and for all initial states $w' \in W'$, there is an initial state $w \in W$ such that $\beta(w, w')$. The relation $\beta \subseteq W \times W'$ is a *post-bisimulation* (resp. *init-post-bisimulation*) between K and K' if β is a pre-bisimulation (resp. init-pre-bisimulation) between K^{-1} and K'^{-1}. The following is an easy extension of a well-known result for *pre-μ* [BCG88].

Proposition 1. *Let K and K' be two Kripke structures.*

- *There is an init-pre-bisimulation (resp. init-post-bisimulation) between K and K' iff for all sentences ϕ of pre-μ (resp. post-μ), we have $K \models \phi$ iff $K' \models \phi$.*
- *The following three statements are equivalent:*
  - *(1) There is a pre-bisimulation (resp. post-bisimulation) between K and K'.*
  - *(2) For all queries θ of pre-$\mu_\emptyset$ (resp. post-$\mu_\emptyset$), we have $K \models \theta$ iff $K' \models \theta$.*
  - *(3) For all queries θ of pre-$\mu_\mathcal{E}$ (resp. post-$\mu_\mathcal{E}$), we have $K \models \theta$ iff $K' \models \theta$.*

3 Intersection of Pre and Post Logics

Of particular interest is the intersection of the query logics *pre-$\mu_\mathcal{E}$* and *post-$\mu_\mathcal{E}$*. It contains the queries that can be specified in both *pre-$\mu_\mathcal{E}$*, which often is more convenient for specifiers, and in *post-$\mu_\mathcal{E}$*, which often is more efficient for symbolic model checking. In this section we show that essentially all linear properties lie in this intersection. On the other hand, there are simple branching properties that do not lie in the intersection.

3.1 In

Consider a Kripke structure $K = \langle P, W, R, L \rangle$. An *observation* of K is a subset of the propositions P. An *error trace* of K is a finite or infinite sequence of observations. A *linear property* of K is a set of error traces.[2] Many useful linear properties, namely, the ω-regular linear properties, can be specified by finite automata. A *finite automaton* $A = \langle P, S, S_0, S_F, r, \ell \rangle$ consists of a finite set P of propositions, a finite set S of states, a set $S_0 \subseteq S$ of initial states, a set $S_F \subseteq S$ of accepting states, a binary transition relation $r \subseteq S \times S$, and a labeling function $\ell : S \to 2^P$ that assigns to each state a set of propositions. The following definitions regarding paths apply equally to Kripke structures and automata. A *path* $\pi = u_0, u_1, \ldots$ of K (resp. A) is a finite or infinite sequence of states such that for all $i \geq 0$, we have $R(u_i, u_{i+1})$ (resp. $r(u_i, u_{i+1})$). The path π is *initialized* if u_0 is an initial state. By $Inf(\pi)$ we denote the set of states that appear in π infinitely often. The labeling functions L and ℓ are lifted from states to paths in the obvious way.

With each finite automaton A we associate a sentence $\exists A$ that is interpreted over a Kripke structure K with the same propositions as A. The *model-checking problem for automata* is to decide, given K and A, whether $K \models \exists A$. We define $K \models \exists A$ if there exist an initialized path π_1 of K and an *accepting* initialized path π_2 of A such that $L(\pi_1) = \ell(\pi_2)$; such an observation sequence $L(\pi_1)$ is called an *error trace of K with respect to A*. Which paths of A are accepting depends on the interpretation we place on the automaton A. We consider here three different interpretations: safety automata, Büchi automata, and co-Büchi automata. For each interpretation we reduce the model-checking problem for automata to the model-checking problem for *post-$\mu_\emptyset$*, by translating automata into equivalent *post-$\mu_\emptyset$* queries. The *post-$\mu_\emptyset$* query θ is *equivalent* to the automaton A if for every Kripke structure K, we have $K \models \exists A$ iff $K \models \theta$.

In all translations, we will make use of the following. With each state s of the automaton A, we associate two variables, X_s and X_s'. In addition, we use the two variables X_F and X_F'. For each state s of A, let γ_s be a variable-free and modality-free expression that characterizes states locally, namely, $\gamma_s = \bigwedge_{p \in \ell(s)} p \wedge \bigwedge_{p \notin \ell(s)} \neg p$. Now, let B_A be the following μ-block, which consists of $|S| + 1$ equations, with $vars(B_A) = \{X_s \mid s \in S\} \cup \{X_F\}$:

$$X_s = \begin{cases} \gamma_s \wedge (init \vee \bigvee_{t \in pre(s)} \exists \odot X_t) & \text{if } s \in S_0, \\ \gamma_s \wedge \bigvee_{t \in pre(s)} \exists \odot X_t & \text{if } s \notin S_0, \end{cases}$$
$$X_F = \bigvee_{f \in S_F} X_f.$$

Note that the size of B_A is linear in the size of A.

Safety automata A *safety property* of a Kripke structure K is a set of *finite* error traces. The regular safety properties can be specified by safety automata. A *safety automaton* is a finite automaton A such that a path π of A is *accepting* if π is a finite path and its last state is an accepting state of A. It is not difficult to see that the safety automaton A is equivalent to the *post-$\mu_\emptyset$* query $\theta_A = \neg \mathcal{E}(\langle \langle B_A \rangle, X_F \rangle)$.

If a finite error trace exists, during model checking, we would like to find it as soon as possible. By evaluating the query θ_A as follows (in the standard way), this can indeed be guaranteed. The evaluation of the μ-block B_A over a Kripke structure K proceeds in iterations. Let $X^K(i) \subseteq W$ denote the value of variable $X \in vars(B_A)$ after the i-th iteration, and let $\Gamma^K(i)$ denote the K-valuation that assigns to each variable in $X \in vars(B_A)$ the value $X^K(i)$. Initially, $X^K(0) = \emptyset$ for all $X \in vars(B_A)$. In all subsequent iterations, the value of each variable $X \in vars(B_A)$ is updated according to the equation $X^K(i+1) = expand(X)^K(\Gamma^K(i))$. Since the modal expressions in B_A are monotonic, once $X_F^K(m) \neq \emptyset$ for some m, we know that

---

[2] Recall that we work, for convenience, in a setting that is dual to the one that considers linear properties to consist of all *non*-error traces.

$X_F^K(n) \neq \emptyset$ for all $n > m$. Hence, we can detect that $K \models \theta_A$ as soon as $X_F^K(m)$ is nonempty. The following theorem guarantees that if there is an error trace of length m, then we will find it in m iterations. In other words, using symbolic forward state traversal, we will explore only states up to distance m from initial states.

Theorem 1. *For every safety automaton A, an equivalent alternation-free post-$\mu_\emptyset$ query θ_A can be constructed in linear time. Further, for every Kripke structure K, if the shortest error trace in K with respect to A has length m, then $X_F^K(m) \neq \emptyset$, where X_F is the root variable of θ_A.*

Büchi automata Safety automata cannot specify infinite error traces. For that, we use Büchi automata. A *Büchi automaton A* is a finite automaton such that a path π of A is *accepting* if $Inf(\pi) \cap S_F \neq \emptyset$; that is, some accepting state of A occurs infinitely often in π. It is well-known [EL86,Dam94,BC96] that for every Büchi automaton A, there exists a *pre-$\mu_\emptyset$* query ϑ_A such that for every Kripke structure K, we have $K \models \exists A$ iff $K \models \vartheta_A$. We now show that there exists also a *post-$\mu_\emptyset$* query θ_A with the same property, thereby proving that the model-checking problem for Büchi automata lies in the intersection of *pre-$\mu_\emptyset$* and *post-$\mu_\emptyset$*. We define two equational blocks: a ν-block B_1 and a μ-block B_2. The block B_1 contains the following $|S_F| + 1$ equations, with $vars(B_1) = \{X'_f \mid f \in S_F\} \cup \{X'_F\}$:

$$X'_f = X_f \wedge \bigvee_{t \in pre(f)} \exists \odot X'_t,$$
$$X'_F = \bigvee_{f \in S_F} X'_f.$$

The block B_2 contains an equation for each state $s \in S \backslash S_F$, defined by

$$X'_s = \gamma_s \wedge \bigvee_{t \in pre(s)} \exists \odot X'_t.$$

Then, $\theta_A = \neg \mathcal{E}(\langle\langle B_1, B_2, B_A \rangle, X'_F\rangle)$. Notice that, as with *pre-$\mu_\emptyset$* [BC96], the translation is linear in the size of the Büchi automaton. Also, the equational blocks B_1 and B_2 depend on each other and the alternation depth of θ_A is two. Since Büchi automata are expressively equivalent to the ω-regular languages, the query logic *post-$\mu_\emptyset$* can specify all ω-regular properties.

Theorem 2. *For every Büchi automaton, an equivalent post-$\mu_\emptyset$ query of alternation depth two can be constructed in linear time.*

In particular, since all sentences of the linear temporal logic LTL can be translated to Büchi automata [VW94], Theorem 2, together with [EL86], implies that all LTL sentences lie in the intersection *pre-$\mu_\emptyset$* $\cap$ *post-$\mu_\emptyset$*. Hence, LTL model checking can proceed by symbolic forward state traversal. Since the translation from LTL to Büchi automata involves an exponential blow-up, the translation from LTL to *post-$\mu_\emptyset$* is also exponential.

Co-Büchi automata Recall that the translation from Theorem 2 results in formulas of alternation depth two. It has been recently argued [KV98] that a linear property given by a co-Büchi automaton can be translated into an *alternation-free pre-$\mu_\emptyset$* query.[3] Consequently, the model checking of linear properties that are specified by co-Büchi automata requires time that is only linear in the size of the Kripke structure. We now show that every co-Büchi automaton A can also be translated into an equivalent alternation-free *post-$\mu_\emptyset$* query θ_A, thereby proving that the model-checking problem for co-Büchi automata lies in the intersection of alternation-free *pre-$\mu_\emptyset$* and alternation-free *post-$\mu_\emptyset$*. A *co-Büchi automaton A* is a finite automaton such that a path π of

---

[3] The results in [KV98] refer to sentences of the form $\forall A$, for deterministic Büchi automata A. Since an ω-regular language can be specified by a deterministic Büchi automaton iff its complement can be specified by a co-Büchi automaton, the corresponding result for $\exists A$, for co-Büchi automata A, follows by duality.

A is *accepting* if $Inf(\pi) \subseteq S_F$; that is, all the non-accepting states of A occur in π only finitely often. We define an equational ν-block B_3 that contains the following $|S_F| + 1$ equations, with $vars(B_3) = \{X'_f \mid f \in S_F\} \cup \{X'_F\}$:

$$X'_f = X_f \wedge \bigvee_{t \in pre(f) \cap S_F} \exists \odot X'_t,$$
$$X'_F = \bigvee_{f \in S_F} X'_f.$$

Then, $\theta_A = \neg \mathcal{E}(\langle\langle B_3, B_A\rangle, X'_F\rangle)$. Notice that θ_A is alternation-free and linear in the size of A.

Theorem 3. *For every co-Büchi automaton, an equivalent alternation-free post-$\mu_\emptyset$ query can be constructed in linear time.*

3.2 Out

We now show that there exist branching temporal-logic specifications that cannot be model checked by evaluating *post-$\mu_\mathcal{E}$* queries. A *post-$\mu_\mathcal{E}$* query θ is *equivalent* to a *pre-μ* sentence ϕ if for every Kripke structure K, we have $K \models \phi$ iff $K \models \theta$. Consider the *pre-μ* sentence $\phi_1 = \langle\langle\langle\nu, \{X = \exists\odot p \wedge \exists\odot X\}\rangle\rangle, X\rangle$, which is equivalent to the CTL sentence $\exists\Box\exists\odot p$, and consider the Kripke structures K_1 and K'_1 appearing in Figure 1. It is easy to see that

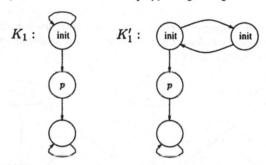

Fig. 1. K_1 and K'_1 are post-bisimilar but not pre-bisimilar.

there is a post-bisimulation between K_1 and K'_1. Hence, by Proposition 1, no *post-$\mu_\mathcal{E}$* query can distinguish between them. On the other hand, while the structure K_1 satisfies ϕ_1, the structure K'_1 does not satisfy ϕ_1. Using a similar argument, it can be shown that the *pre-μ* sentence that is equivalent to the CTL sentence $\exists\Diamond(r \wedge \exists\Diamond p \wedge \exists\Diamond q)$ can distinguish between two structures that have a post-bisimulation between them, implying there is no equivalent *post-$\mu_\mathcal{E}$* query. Interestingly, the *pre-μ* sentence $\langle\langle B_1, B_2\rangle, X_1\rangle$ with $B_1 = \langle\nu, \{X_1 = X_2 \wedge \exists\odot X_1\}\rangle$ and $B_2 = \langle\mu, \{X_2 = p \vee \exists\odot X_2\}\rangle$, which is equivalent to the CTL sentence $\exists\Box\exists\odot p$, and which is not equivalent to any LTL sentence [CD88], does have an equivalent query in *post-$\mu_\emptyset$*. The query is $\neg\mathcal{E}(\langle\langle B_3, B_4\rangle, X_1\rangle)$, with $B_3 = \langle\nu, \{X_1 = p \wedge X_2, X_2 = X_3 \wedge \exists\odot X_2\}\rangle$ and $B_4 = \langle\mu, \{X_3 = init \vee \exists\odot X_3\}\rangle$.

Proposition 2. *There exist pre-μ sentences (in fact, CTL sentences) that have no equivalent post-$\mu_\mathcal{E}$ queries.*

4 Hierarchy of Pre and Post Logics

Let $\mathcal{L}_1$ and $\mathcal{L}_2$ be two logics whose sentences are interpreted over Kripke structures. The logic $\mathcal{L}_2$ is *as expressive as* the logic $\mathcal{L}_1$ if for every sentence ϕ_1 of $\mathcal{L}_1$, there is a sentence $\phi_2 \in \mathcal{L}_2$

such that for every Kripke structure K, we have $K \models \phi_1$ iff $K \models \phi_2$. The logic $\mathcal{L}_2$ is *more expressive than* $\mathcal{L}_1$ if $\mathcal{L}_2$ is as expressive as $\mathcal{L}_1$ but $\mathcal{L}_1$ is not as expressive as $\mathcal{L}_2$. The logic $\mathcal{L}_2$ is *as distinguishing as* the logic $\mathcal{L}_1$ if for all Kripke structures K and K', if there is a sentence ϕ_1 of $\mathcal{L}_1$ such that $K \models \phi_1$ but $K' \not\models \phi_1$, then there is a sentence ϕ_2 of $\mathcal{L}_2$ such that $K \models \phi_2$ but $K' \not\models \phi_2$. Finally, the logic $\mathcal{L}_2$ is *more distinguishing than* $\mathcal{L}_1$ if $\mathcal{L}_2$ is as distinguishing as $\mathcal{L}_1$ but $\mathcal{L}_1$ is not as distinguishing as $\mathcal{L}_2$. In this section, we study the distinguishing and the expressive powers of *pre-μ* and *post-μ* and the query logics they induce. For this purpose, the sentences of query logics are the queries.

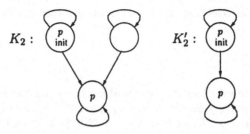

Fig. 2. K_2 and K_2' are init-post-bisimilar but not post-bisimilar

Proposition 3. *The distinguishing powers of pre and post logics are summarized in the figure below. An arrow from logic $\mathcal{L}_1$ to logic $\mathcal{L}_2$ indicates that $\mathcal{L}_1$ is as distinguishing as $\mathcal{L}_2$. A line without arrow indicates incomparability.*

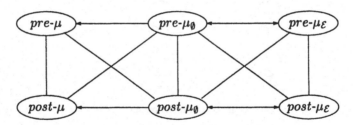

Proof. Proposition 1 implies that the distinguishing powers of *pre-$\mu_\emptyset$* and *pre-μ_ε* coincide, and similarly for *post-μ*. In order to prove the incomparability results, we show that the four relations init-pre-bisimulation, init-post-bisimulation, pre-bisimulation, and post-bisimulation are all distinct. Recall that there may be states in a Kripke structure that are not reachable from an initial state, as there may be states from which no initial state is reachable. Consider the Kripke structures K_2 and K_2' appearing in Figure 2. There is an init-pre-bisimulation and an init-post-bisimulation between K_2 and K_2', but no pre-bisimulation or post-bisimulation. Hence, (post) pre-bisimulation is more distinguishing than (init-post) init-pre-bisimulation. Now consider the Kripke structures K_1 and K_1' appearing in Figure 1. There is a post-bisimulation and an init-post-bisimulation between K_1 and K_1', but no pre-bisimulation or init-pre-bisimulation. Also, there is a pre-bisimulation and an init-pre-bisimulation between K_1^{-1} and $K_1'^{-1}$ but no post-bisimulation or init-post-bisimulation. Hence, pre-bisimulation and post-bisimulation as well as init-pre-bisimulation and init-post-bisimulation are incomparable. $\quad\square$

Proposition 4. *The expressive powers of pre and post logics are summarized in the figure below. An arrow from logic $\mathcal{L}_1$ to logic $\mathcal{L}_2$ indicates that $\mathcal{L}_1$ is as expressive as $\mathcal{L}_2$. A line without arrow indicates incomparability.*

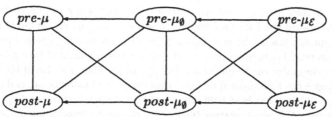

Proof. It is easy to see that if a logic $\mathcal{L}_2$ is not as distinguishing as a logic $\mathcal{L}_1$, then $\mathcal{L}_2$ is not as expressive as $\mathcal{L}_1$. Therefore, most of our expressiveness results follow from the corresponding results about distinguishability. In addition, as a Kripke structure K satisfies a sentence ϕ iff K satisfies the query $\neg\mathcal{E}(init \wedge \phi)$, the query logics $pre\text{-}\mu_{\emptyset}$ and $post\text{-}\mu_{\emptyset}$ are more expressive than $pre\text{-}\mu$ and $post\text{-}\mu$, respectively. In order to prove the advantage of the full query logics $pre\text{-}\mu_{\mathcal{E}}$ and $post\text{-}\mu_{\mathcal{E}}$ over its subsets $pre\text{-}\mu_{\emptyset}$ and $post\text{-}\mu_{\emptyset}$, it is easy to see that no query of the query logics $pre\text{-}\mu_{\emptyset}$ and $post\text{-}\mu_{\emptyset}$ is equivalent to the query $\mathcal{E}(p) \vee \mathcal{E}(q)$. $\qquad\square$

5 Discussion and Experimental Results

5.1 Intersection of pre and post logics

While previous works presented symbolic forward state-traversal procedures for model checking some isolated linear and branching properties [INH96,IN97], we attempted to study more systematically the class of properties that can be model checked using both symbolic forward and backward state traversal. In particular, we showed that all ω-regular linear properties (which includes all properties expressible in LTL) fall into this class, while some simple branching properties (expressible in CTL) do not. Furthermore, every query that can be specified in both $pre\text{-}\mu_{\emptyset}$ and $post\text{-}\mu_{\emptyset}$ cannot distinguish between structures that are both pre-bisimilar and post-bisimilar. Yet the exact characterization of the intersection $pre\text{-}\mu_{\emptyset} \cap post\text{-}\mu_{\emptyset}$ remains open. In [GK94], the authors identified a set of temporal-logic sentences called equi-linear. In particular, a $pre\text{-}\mu$ sentence is *equi-linear* if it cannot distinguish between two Kripke structures with the same language (i.e., observation sequences that correspond to initialized paths). Clearly, all LTL sentences are equi-linear. However, some CTL sentences that have no equivalent LTL sentence are also equi-linear. For example, it is shown in [GK94] that while the CTL sentence $\exists\Box\exists\Box Op$ is not equi-linear, the CTL sentence $\exists\Box\exists\Diamond p$ is equi-linear. Motivated by the examples from Section 3.2, we conjecture that equi-linearity precisely characterizes the properties that can be model checked using both symbolic forward and backward state traversal. Formally, we conjecture that a $pre\text{-}\mu$ sentence is equi-linear iff there is an equivalent $post\text{-}\mu_{\emptyset}$ query.

5.2 Union of pre and post logics

In this paper, we primarily think of $post\text{-}\mu_{\mathcal{E}}$ as a language for describing symbolic model-checking procedures for temporal-logic specifications. Furthermore, we have focused on specification languages that contain only future temporal operators. Since LTL with past temporal operators is no more expressive than LTL without past operators [LPZ85], every LTL+past sentence can also be translated into an equivalent $post\text{-}\mu_{\emptyset}$ query. In addition, $post\text{-}\mu$ also permits the easy evaluation of branching past temporal operators that cannot be evaluated using $pre\text{-}\mu$. For example, the sentence $\forall\Box(grant \rightarrow (\neg init)\forall\widetilde{W}req)$, where $\widetilde{W}$ is a past version of the "weak-until" operator [MP92], specifies that grants are given only upon request. Assuming a *branching* interpretation for past temporal operators [KP95], this sentence has an equivalent $post\text{-}\mu_{\emptyset}$ query, but no equivalent $pre\text{-}\mu_{\mathcal{E}}$ query; that is, it can be model checked by symbolic forward state traversal but not by symbolic backward state traversal.

While the intersection $pre\text{-}\mu_{\mathcal{E}} \cap post\text{-}\mu_{\mathcal{E}}$ identifies the queries that can be model checked by both symbolic forward and backward state traversal, it is the "union" $(pre\text{-}\mu \cup post\text{-}\mu)_{\mathcal{E}}$[4] that identifies the queries that can be model checked at all symbolically, by mixed forward and backward state traversal.[5] Furthermore, it is the alternation-free fragment of $(pre\text{-}\mu \cup post\text{-}\mu)_{\mathcal{E}}$ that identifies the queries that can be model checked *efficiently*. Thus it is also of interest to ask which temporal logics can be translated into the (alternation-free) union of pre and post query logics. Such temporal logics can have both future and past temporal operators. In particular, it is easy to see that every CTL+past sentence (under the branching interpretation for past) has an equivalent query in the alternation-free fragment of $(pre\text{-}\mu \cup post\text{-}\mu)_{\emptyset}$.

5.3 Experimental results

In our experiments, we performed BDD-based symbolic model checking on a parameterized sliding-window protocol for the reliable transmission of packets over an unreliable channel. The parameter to the protocol is *WINSIZE*, the number of outstanding unacknowledged messages at the sender end. In the protocol, the messages are modeled as boolean values. We checked whether all computations of the protocol satisfy the partial specification ϕ, which states that if the produced message $msgP$ toggles infinitely often at the sender end, then so does the consumed message $msgC$ at the receiver end. Formally, the specification ϕ is given by the LTL sentence $\square\lozenge(msgP \leftrightarrow \bigcirc\neg msgP) \rightarrow \square\lozenge(msgC \leftrightarrow \bigcirc\neg msgC)$. We note that this sentence cannot be handled by the methods presented in [INH96,IN97].

In the table below we list the running times (in seconds) for different values of *WINSIZE* for checking ϕ using VIS [BHSV+96] for both symbolic forward and backward state traversal. The quantity within the parentheses is the number of boolean variables used to encode the state space of the protocol. It is folk wisdom in symbolic model checking that using don't-care minimization based on unreachable states can dramatically improve the running times. So we also applied first symbolic forward state traversal to compute the set of reachable states and then symbolic backward state traversal for model checking, using the unreachable states as don't cares. These results are shown in the last column. A dash indicates an unsuccessful verification attempt. In the future, we hope to compare our approach also against *enumerative* forward state-traversal methods for LTL model checking.

WINSIZE	Forward	Backward	Reach-optimized backward
2 (30)	18	222	91
3 (45)	300	4584	-
4 (50)	5231	-	-

Acknowledgments

We thank Rajeev Alur, Bob Brayton, Ed Clarke, Allen Emerson, and Orna Grumberg for helpful discussions, and Carl Pixley for drawing the authors' attention to [INH96].

References

[BC96] G. Bhat and R. Cleavland. Efficient model checking via the equational μ-calculus. In *Proc. 11th IEEE Symposium on Logic in Computer Science*, pp. 304–312, 1996.

---

[4] By the *union* $pre\text{-}\mu \cup post\text{-}\mu$ we refer to the logic with all four modal operators $\exists\bigcirc$, $\forall\bigcirc$, $\exists\ominus$, and $\forall\ominus$. It has, of course, strictly more sentences than the union of the sets of $pre\text{-}\mu$ and $post\text{-}\mu$ sentences.

[5] In fact, not only can model checking algorithms be extended from $pre\text{-}\mu$ to $(pre\text{-}\mu \cup post\text{-}\mu)_{\mathcal{E}}$ without extra cost, the satisfiability problem for the union is also no harder than the satisfiability problem for either $pre\text{-}\mu$ or $post\text{-}\mu$ [Var98].

[BCG88] M.C. Browne, E.M. Clarke, and O. Grumberg. Characterizing finite Kripke structures in propositional temporal logic. *Theoretical Computer Science*, 59:115–131, 1988.

[BCM+92] J.R. Burch, E.M. Clarke, K.L. McMillan, D.L. Dill, and L.J. Hwang. Symbolic model checking: 10^{20} states and beyond. *Information and Computation*, 98(2):142–170, 1992.

[BHSV+96] R.K. Brayton, G.D. Hachtel, A. Sangiovanni-Vincentelli, F. Somenzi, A. Aziz, S.-T. Cheng, S. Edwards, S. Khatri, T. Kukimoto, A. Pardo, S. Qadeer, R.K. Ranjan, S. Sarwary, T.R. Shiple, G. Swamy, and T. Villa. VIS: a system for verification and synthesis. In *CAV 96: Computer Aided Verification*, LNCS 1102, pp. 428–432, Springer, 1996.

[Bry86] R.E. Bryant. Graph-based algorithms for boolean-function manipulation. *IEEE Trans. on Computers*, C-35(8), 1986.

[CD88] E.M. Clarke and I.A. Draghicescu. Expressivity results for linear-time and branching-time logics. In *Proc. Workshop on Linear Time, Branching Time, and Partial Order in Logics and Models for Concurrency*, LNCS 354, pp. 428–437, Springer, 1988.

[CE81] E.M. Clarke and E.A. Emerson. Design and synthesis of synchronization skeletons using branching time temporal logic. In *Proc. Workshop on Logic of Programs*, LNCS 131, pp. 52–71, Springer, 1981.

[CGH94] E.M. Clarke, O. Grumberg, and K. Hamaguchi. Another look at LTL model checking. In *CAV 94: Computer Aided Verification*, LNCS 818, pp. 415–427, Springer, 1994.

[CGL93] E.M. Clarke, O. Grumberg, and D. Long. Verification tools for finite-state concurrent systems. In *Decade of Concurrency – Reflections and Perspectives (Proc. REX School)*, LNCS 803, pp. 124–175, Springer, 1993.

[CS91] R. Cleaveland and B. Steffen. A linear-time model-checking algorithm for the alternation-free modal μ-calculus. In *CAV 91: Computer Aided Verification*, LNCS 575, pp. 48–58, Springer, 1991.

[Dam94] M. Dam. CTL* and ECTL* as fragments of the modal μ-calculus. *Theoretical Computer Science*, 126:77–96, 1994.

[Dil96] David L. Dill. The Murϕ Verification System. In *CAV 96: Computer Aided Verification*, LNCS 1102, pp. 390–393, Springer, 1996.

[EL86] E.A. Emerson and C.-L. Lei. Efficient model checking in fragments of the propositional μ-calculus. In *Proc. 1st Symposium on Logic in Computer Science*, pp. 267–278, 1986.

[GK94] O. Grumberg and R.P. Kurshan. How linear can branching-time be. In *Proc. 1st International Conference on Temporal Logic*, LNAI 827, pp. 180–194, Springer, 1994.

[GPVW95] R. Gerth, D. Peled, M.Y. Vardi, and P. Wolper. Simple on-the-fly automatic verification of linear temporal logic. In *Protocol Specification, Testing, and Verification*, pp. 3–18, Chapman, 1995.

[Hol97] G.J. Holzmann. The model checker SPIN. *IEEE Trans. on Software Engineering*, 23(5):279–295, 1997.

[IN97] H. Iwashita and T. Nakata. Forward model checking techniques oriented to buggy designs. In *Proc. IEEE/ACM International Conference on Computer Aided Design*, pp. 400–404, 1997.

[INH96] H. Iwashita, T. Nakata, and F. Hirose. CTL model checking based on forward state traversal. In *Proc. IEEE/ACM International Conference on Computer Aided Design*, pp. 82–87, 1996.

[Koz83] D. Kozen. Results on the propositional μ-calculus. *Theoretical Computer Science*, 27:333–354, 1983.

[KP95] O. Kupferman and A. Pnueli. Once and for all. In *Proc. 10th IEEE Symposium on Logic in Computer Science*, pp. 25–35, 1995.

[KV98] O. Kupferman and M.Y. Vardi. Freedom, weakness, and determinism: from linear-time to branching-time. In *Proc. 13th IEEE Symposium on Logic in Computer Science*, 1998.

[LPZ85] O. Lichtenstein, A. Pnueli, and L. Zuck. The glory of the past. In *Logics of Programs*, LNCS 193, pp. 196–218, Springer, 1985.

[McM93] K.L. McMillan. *Symbolic Model Checking*. Kluwer Academic Publishers, 1993.

[MP92] Z. Manna and A. Pnueli. *The Temporal Logic of Reactive and Concurrent Systems: Specification*. Springer, 1992.

[Pel94] D. Peled. Combining partial order reductions with on-the-fly model-checking. In *CAV 94: Computer Aided Verification*, LNCS 818, pp. 377–390, Springer, 1994.

[QS81] J.P. Queille and J. Sifakis. Specification and verification of concurrent systems in Cesar. In *Proc. 5th International Symp. on Programming*, LNCS 137, pp. 337–351, Springer, 1981.

[Var98] M.Y. Vardi. Reasoning about the past with two-way automata. In *Proc. 25th International Coll. on Automata, Languages, and Programming*, LNCS, Springer, 1998.

[VW94] M.Y. Vardi and P. Wolper. Reasoning about infinite computations. *Information and Computation*, 115(1):1–37, 1994.

Model Checking LTL Using Net Unforldings*

Frank Wallner

Institut für Informatik, Technische Universität München
Arcisstr.21, D-80290 München, Germany
email: wallnerf@in.tum.de

Abstract. Net unfoldings are a well-studied partial order semantics for Petri nets. In this paper, we show that the finite prefix of an unfolding, introduced by McMillan, is suited for model checking linear-time temporal properties. The method is based on the so-called automata-theoretic approach to model checking. We propose a technique to treat this approach within the framework of safe Petri nets, and give an efficient algorithm for detecting the system runs violating a given specification.

1 Introduction

Linear-time Temporal Logic (LTL) is an adequate formalism for specifying behavioural properties of distributed systems, including safety and liveness properties. Deciding whether a given system Σ satisfies a specification φ is called the *model checking problem*.

The *automata-theoretic approach* to model checking translates this problem into an automata-theoretic problem. This approach assumes that Σ can be represented as an automaton A with $L(A)$ being the set of its *runs*. The system satisfies φ iff $L(A)$ is a subset of the language L_φ of words satisfying φ.

Vardi, Wolper et al. [20,22] observed that for every formula φ it is possible to construct a Büchi automaton A_φ that accepts L_φ. Since negation of a formula φ is equivalent to complementing the corresponding language L_φ, the actual problem is to decide if there is a system run accepted by $A_{\neg\varphi}$. Defining an adequate product automaton A_p of A and $A_{\neg\varphi}$ that accepts the intersection of $L(A)$ and $L_{\neg\varphi}$, the problem is finally transformed to an emptiness-problem on automata: the system satisfies φ iff A_p is empty (accepts no word).

Checking emptiness of A_p requires the detection of *accepting cycles*, i.e., cycles containing an accepting state. There exist efficient algorithms for this issue [1,9] with time complexity linear in the size of the product automaton. However, this size is often enormous, due to the well-known state explosion problem: representing concurrency as interleaving may let A, and consequently A_p, grow exponentially in the size of the system. Several partial order methods [10,16–19] have been suggested to palliate this problem by reducing the state space according to the partial order semantics of the system, i.e., by discarding all the states and transitions not relevant for satisfying φ.

* This work was supported by the SFB 342 (subproject A3) of the DFG.

In contrast to these approaches, we will not reduce the state space, but rather directly use a partial-order representation of the behaviour of the distributed system under consideration. We assume Σ to be given as a safe Petri net, and explore its behaviour by unfolding the net to McMillan's *finite prefix* [14,7] of the branching process of Σ. This prefix contains every reachable state of the system. It was already observed by Esparza in [5] that the finite prefix can be used for model checking S4 (the modal logic based on the reachability relation of the global state space), which is strictly less expressive than LTL.

We show in this paper how to construct the product of a given Petri net and a Büchi automaton, yielding *Büchi nets*, i.e. nets with acceptance capabilities. We investigate, for which construction the prefix remains small, in some cases "exponentially compact" compared with the interleaving model. The main contribution, however, is a method for checking emptiness of a Büchi net using its finite prefix.

The paper is structured as follows. Section 2 briefly formalizes the automata-theoretic approach. In Section 3, Petri nets and unfoldings are introduced, and we show how the finite prefix of a Büchi net can be used to decide its emptiness. Section 4 describes an adequate product construction and the entire model checking procedure. Section 5 concludes the paper and refers to related work.

2   The automata-theoretic approach

Let us briefly recall the essential ideas and notions that underlie the automata-theoretic approach to model checking linear-time temporal properties.

Linear-time Temporal Logic. Let Π be a finite set of atomic propositions. The set of *LTL-formulae* over Π is defined inductively as follows: if $\varphi = \pi \in \Pi$ then φ is a formula; if φ and ψ are formulae then $\varphi \wedge \psi$, $\neg\varphi$, $\mathsf{X}\varphi$, and $\varphi\mathsf{U}\psi$ are formulae. The other operators of propositional logic are defined as usual, and we define $\Diamond\varphi := \mathsf{true}\mathsf{U}\varphi$, and $\Box\varphi := \neg\Diamond\neg\varphi$. The set of propositions appearing in φ is written as $\langle\varphi\rangle$.

A formula is interpreted on ω-words ξ over the alphabet 2^Π. An ω-*word* over 2^Π is an infinite sequence $\xi = x_0 x_1 \ldots$ with $x_i \in 2^\Pi$ for all $i \geq 0$. The elements of 2^Π are meant to assign truth values to Π in the obvious manner: the proposition π holds at x_i iff $\pi \in x_i$. We define $\xi(i) := x_i$, and $\xi^{(i)}$ is the suffix of ξ starting at x_i. We write $\xi \models \varphi$ to denote that ξ *satisfies* φ. By L_φ we denote the set of ω-words satisfying φ. The relation $\models$ is inductively defined as follows.

$$
\begin{aligned}
\xi &\models \pi & \text{iff} \quad & \pi \in \xi(0) \\
\xi &\models \neg\varphi & \text{iff} \quad & \xi \not\models \varphi \\
\xi &\models \varphi \wedge \psi & \text{iff} \quad & \xi \models \varphi \text{ and } \xi \models \psi \\
\xi &\models \mathsf{X}\varphi & \text{iff} \quad & \xi^{(1)} \models \varphi \\
\xi &\models \varphi\mathsf{U}\psi & \text{iff} \quad & \exists\, i \geq 0.\ \xi^{(i)} \models \psi \text{ and } \xi^{(j)} \models \varphi \text{ for all } j < i
\end{aligned}
$$

Büchi automata. A Büchi automaton over the alphabet 2^Π is a quadruple $A = (Q, q_0, \delta, \mathcal{F})$, where Q is a finite set of states, including the initial state q_0,

$\delta \subseteq Q \times 2^{\Pi} \times Q$ is the transition relation, and $\mathcal{F} \subseteq Q$ a set of *accepting states*. A *run* of A on an ω-word ξ over 2^{Π} is an infinite sequence $\sigma = q_0 q_1 \ldots$ such that $(q_i, \xi(i), q_{i+1}) \in \delta$ for all $i \geq 0$. A run σ is *accepting* if an accepting state occurs infinitely often in σ, and the automaton A *accepts* the word ξ iff there is an accepting run of A on ξ. $L(A)$ denotes the set of all ω-words accepted by A.

Theorem 1 ([20,22]). *Let φ be an LTL formula. There exists a Büchi automaton A_φ such that $L(A_\varphi) = L_\varphi$.*

Efficient methods for how to build the automaton A_φ from a given formula φ can be found in [21,8].

The automata-theoretic approach assumes the system to be given as an automaton A over an alphabet *Act* of actions, and a valuation v from the transitions of A to subsets of Π. In *action-based* semantics, v is determined by the action associated with the transition, in a *state-based* setting by the state that enables the transition. Given the system A and the automaton $A_{\neg\varphi}$ for the negation of φ, an adequate *product automaton* A_p is defined. The basic idea is that $(\langle s, q \rangle, \langle s', q' \rangle)$ becomes a transition of A_p if there is a transition (s, a, s') of the system evaluated to Π', and (q, Π', q') is a transition of $A_{\neg\varphi}$. The accepting states of A_p are the states $\langle s, q \rangle$ where q ia an accepting state of $A_{\neg\varphi}$. For this construction it holds that the product A_p is empty iff it contains no cycle including an accepting state iff the system automaton A satisfies the property φ.

3 Petri nets and unfoldings

Let us begin with a glance on Petri nets and their unfoldings. We will then show how to use McMillan's prefix for deciding the existence of accepting runs.

Petri nets. Let P and T be disjoint sets of *places* and *transitions*. The elements of $P \cup T$ are called *nodes*. A *net* is a triple $N = (P, T, F)$ with a *flow relation* F, given by its characteristic function $F : (P \times T) \cup (T \times P) \to \{0, 1\}$.

The *preset* of the node x is defined as ${}^\bullet x := \{y \in P \cup T \mid F(y, x) = 1\}$ and its *postset* as $x^\bullet := \{y \in P \cup T \mid F(x, y) = 1\}$. The preset (postset) of a set X of nodes is given by the union of the presets (postsets) of all nodes in X. By ${}^\circ x$ we denote the set ${}^\bullet x \setminus x^\bullet$, and analogously $x^\circ := x^\bullet \setminus {}^\bullet x$.

A *marking* of a net is a mapping $P \to \mathbb{N}_0$. We call $\Sigma = (N, M_0)$ a *net system* with initial marking M_0 if N is a net and M_0 a marking of N. A marking M *enables* the transition t if $M(p) \geq 1$ for each $p \in {}^\bullet t$. In this case the transition can *occur*, leading to the new marking M', given by $M'(p) = M(p) + F(t, p) - F(p, t)$ for every place p. We denote this occurrence by $M \xrightarrow{t} M'$. If there exists a chain $M_0 \xrightarrow{t_1} M_1 \xrightarrow{t_2} \ldots \xrightarrow{t_n} M_n$, the sequence $\gamma = M_0 t_1 M_1 t_2 \ldots t_n M_n$ is called a *computation*. A computation of infinite length is called a *run*. A marking M is *reachable* if there exists a computation γ such that M appears in γ. The reachable markings will also be called the *(reachable) states* of the system.

We will exclusively regard *safe systems*, in which all reachable states map each place to 0 or 1. So every state can be identified with the set of places it maps to 1, i.e., $M \subseteq P$ for every reachable state M. Note that this is no restriction. Often safe nets are used for modelling distributed systems because they can be seen as a composition of several components which are given as finite automata. Furthermore, so-called high-level net systems like coloured or algebraic nets can automatically be transformed into equivalent safe net systems.

Net system semantics for LTL. We define an adequate LTL semantics for safe net systems, distinguishing state and action oriented settings.

In a *state-based* interpretation, the atomic propositions Π are identified with the set P of places. A proposition p holds at state M iff $M(p) = 1$. Since every state can be expressed as a Boolean combination of marked and unmarked places, any set of propositions on states can be encoded using places as the only propositions. Formulae are interpreted on marking sequences: a run $\gamma = M_0 t_1 M_1 t_2 M_2 \ldots$ satisfies φ iff the ω-word $\xi(\gamma) = M_0 M_1 M_2 \ldots$ belongs to L_φ.

In an *action-based* interpretation, we assume a valuation $v : T \to 2^\Pi$, and we interpret formulae on sequences of transition occurrences: a run $\gamma = M_0 t_1 M_1 t_2 M_2 \ldots$ satisfies φ iff the ω-word $\sigma(\gamma) = v(t_1) v(t_2) \ldots$ belongs to L_φ.

We say that the system Σ satisfies φ iff every run of Σ satisfies φ.

Büchi nets. A *Büchi net* is a net with acceptance capabilities, i.e., a tuple $\Sigma_p = (\Sigma, \mathcal{F})$ where $\Sigma = (P, T, F, M_0)$ is a finite, safe net system and $\mathcal{F} \subseteq P$ a set of accepting places. A run γ of Σ_p is *accepting* if an *accepting transition* $t \in {}^\bullet\mathcal{F}$ appears infinitely often in γ, and Σ_p *is empty* if it has no accepting run. A Büchi net will be the product of a safe net system and a Büchi automaton, defined in the next section.

Net unfoldings. The partial-order representation of the behaviour of safe net systems is based on net unfoldings, also known as branching processes. We briefly recall the main definitions and results of [4].

Two nodes x, x' of the net $N = (P, T, F)$ are *in conflict*, denoted $x\#x'$, if there exist two distinct transitions t, t' with ${}^\bullet t \cap {}^\bullet t' \neq \emptyset$ such that (t, x) and (t', x') belong to the reflexive transitive closure of the flow relation F. If $x\#x$, we say x *is in self-conflict*.

An *occurrence net* [15] is a net $N' = (B, E, F)$ where the irreflexive transitive closure of F is well-founded and acyclic (and thus a strict partial order, written as $\prec$), where furtheron $|{}^\bullet b| \leq 1$ for every $b \in B$, and no element $e \in E$ is in self-conflict. The elements of B and E are called *conditions* and *events*, respectively. The reflexive closure $\preceq$ of $\prec$ is a partial order called *causality relation*. By $Min(N')$ we denote the minimal elements of N' w.r.t. $\preceq$.

Given two nets N_1 and N_2, the mapping $h : N_1 \to N_2$ is a *homomorphism* if $h(P_1) \subseteq P_2$, $h(T_1) \subseteq T_2$, and if for each $t \in T_1$ the restriction of h to ${}^\bullet t$ is a bijection between ${}^\bullet t$ and ${}^\bullet h(t)$, and similarly for $t^\bullet$ and $h(t)^\bullet$.

A *branching process* of a net system $\Sigma = (N, M_0)$ is a pair $\beta = (N', h)$ where $N' = (B, E, F)$ is an occurrence net and $h : N' \to N$ is a homomorphism that bijectively maps $Min(N')$ onto M_0, and that satisfies: if $h(e) = h(e')$ and ${}^\bullet e = {}^\bullet e'$ then $e = e'$, for all events $e, e' \in E$. In a word, we unfold the net N to an occurrence net N' such that each node x of N' refers to a node $h(x)$ of N.

The branching processes β_1 and β_2 are *isomorphic* if there exists a bijective homomorphism $h : N_1' \to N_2'$, such that the composition $h_2 \circ h$ equals h_1. If h is an injection that bijectively maps $Min(N_1')$ onto $Min(N_2')$, and $B_1 \subseteq B_2$ and $E_1 \subseteq E_2$, we call β_1 a *prefix* of β_2. Notice that a prefix is uniquely determined by its set of events. In [4] it is shown that each net system Σ has a unique maximal branching process up to isomorphism, called *unfolding of* Σ and denoted by $Unf_\Sigma = (N', h)$. Note that N' is infinite iff Σ has infinite computations.

Configurations and Cuts. For the remainder of the section, let $Unf_\Sigma = (N', h)$ and $N' = (B, E, F)$ be fixed. A *configuration* C of N' is a causally downward-closed, conflict-free set of events, i.e., for each $e \in C$: if $e' \preceq e$ then $e' \in C$, and for all $e, e' \in C$: $\neg(e \# e')$.

Two nodes of N' are *concurrent* if they are neither in conflict nor causally related. A set B' of conditions of N' is called a *co-set* if all elements of B' are pairwise concurrent. A co-set is called a *cut* if it is maximal w.r.t. set inclusion. For a finite configuration C, the set $Cut(C) := (Min(N') \cup C^\bullet) \setminus {}^\bullet C$ of conditions is a cut. The set $h(Cut(C))$ of places is a reachable marking of Σ, called the *marking* $Mark(C)$ *of* C. Conversely, for every reachable state M of Σ there exists a finite configuration C in Unf_Σ such that M is the marking of C. Often, a configuration C is identified with the state $Mark(C)$.

An essential observation on configurations is that their *continuations* are determined by their markings: let $\uparrow C \subseteq B \cup E$ be defined as the set of nodes x, such that $x \in \uparrow C$ iff $x \succeq b$ for some $b \in Cut(C)$ and $\neg(b \# x)$ for all $b \in Cut(C)$. By F_C (resp. h_C) we denote the restriction of the flow relation F (resp. of the homomorphism h) of Unf_Σ onto $\uparrow C$. We define the *continuation of* C as the branching process $\beta(C) := (N_C, h_C)$, where $N_C := (\uparrow C \cap B, \uparrow C \cap E, F_C)$. It is easy to see that for two finite configurations C, C' with equal marking it holds that $\beta(C)$ and $\beta(C')$ are isomorphic.

The set of predecessors of each event e is a configuration, called *local configuration of* e, given by $[e] := \{e' \in E \mid e' \preceq e\}$. We call two events e, e' *equivalent* if the markings of their local configurations coincide, i.e., $Mark([e]) = Mark([e'])$.

The finite prefix. In [14], K.L. McMillan defined a finite prefix of the unfolding of a finite-state net system, in which every state is represented by some cut. The idea is that if the prefix contains two equivalent events then the continuations of their local configurations are isomorphic and thus only one of them needs to be explored further, while the other one becomes a *cut-off* event. Formally, an event e is a cut-off event if there exists an event e' equivalent to e such that $|[e']| < |[e]|$. If there are several such events e' for the cut-off e, we fix one of them and refer to it as the *corresponding event* $cor(e)$ of e. By $off(e')$ we denote the set of cut-offs, such that e' is their corresponding event.

The *finite prefix* Fin_Σ is defined as the unique prefix of Unf_Σ with $E_{Fin} \subseteq E$ as set of events, where $e \in E_{Fin}$ iff no event $e' \prec e$ is a cut-off event. Let Off (Cor) denote the set of all cut-off (corresponding) events of Fin_Σ.

It is easy to prove that Fin_Σ is finite for net systems with finitely many states. Usually, Fin_Σ is much smaller than the state space of the system. However, sometimes it is larger. In [7] it is shown how to construct a *storage-optimal* prefix, essentially by determining cut-offs not by comparison of the size of their local configurations, but another well-founded, *strict* partial order instead. In the prefix constructed by the improved algorithm [7], it is always the case that two non-cut-off events have different markings. Therefore, the number of non-cut-off events never exceeds the number of reachable states of the system, and so Fin_Σ never is larger than the state space (up to a small constant).

Cycle-detection in the prefix. As indicated, the model checking problem requires the detection of a cycle containing an accepting transition. Let $T_a = {}^\bullet\mathcal{F}$ be the set of accepting transitions of the Büchi net $\Sigma_p = (\Sigma, \mathcal{F})$. The goal is to find a run γ such that infinitely often a transition $t \in T_a$ appears in γ.

The problem is solved in two steps: first we will construct a directed graph $G = (V, Edg)$ where $V = Off$ is the set of cut-off events of the prefix, and $Edg \subseteq V \times V$ a set of edges. An edge $e \to e'$ indicates that from state $[e]$ the state $[e']$ is reachable. Some of the edges will be labelled by a. Intuitively, $e \xrightarrow{a} e'$ means that on the partial computation leading from $[e]$ to $[e']$ an accepting transition occurs. Since every (local) configuration of the prefix is reachable, every node in G can be seen as being initial. The graph G is constructed by the algorithm given in Fig. 1, with T_a as the input parameter.

The second step is to apply a standard algorithm on G for detecting a strongly connected component [1] or a cycle [9] containing an a-labelled edge.

The key idea of the algorithm for constructing the graph G is as follows. Let e_1, e_1^0 be a cut-off and its corresponding event. Since $\beta([e_1])$ and $\beta([e_1^0])$ are isomorphic, every state that is reachable from $[e_1^0]$ is also reachable from $[e_1]$. Thus, if $e_1^0 \prec e_2$ for some other cut-off e_2, an edge $e_1 \to e_2$ is added to G. If $[e_2] \setminus [e_1^0]$ contains an accepting event then the edge is labelled by a.

The other case is a bit more involved. Let e_2^0 be the corresponding event of e_2, and assume $e_1^0 \preceq e_2^0$. This means that from state $[e_1^0]$ (equivalent to $[e_1]$) the state $[e_2^0]$ (equivalent to $[e_2]$) is reachable, and so an edge $e_1 \to e_2$ is added. But when and how has such an edge to be labelled? Clearly, if $[e_2^0] \setminus [e_1^0]$ contains an accepting event, the edge must be labelled. However, this is not the only case. Additionally, there may exist a state of the system (possibly not corresponding to a local configuration) where *concurrently* $[e_1^0]$ and $[e_2]$ are reachable. In this case, we have to consider the set $E_1^2 := [e_2] \setminus [e_1^0]$. If e_1^0 and e_2 are concurrent, and the set E_1^2 contains an accepting event, we label the edge $e_1 \to e_2$ with a. In the algorithm, let $\Gamma(e_1^0, e_2)$ denote the function computing the set of these events: $\Gamma(e_1^0, e_2) := E_1^2$, if e_1^0 and e_2 are concurrent, and the empty set else.

Proposition 2. $T_a \subseteq T$ *contains a transition that infinitely often can occur in* Σ *iff there exists a cycle in the graph* G, *containing an* a-*labelled edge.*

4 The automata-theoretic approach for Petri nets

We now want to lift the automata-theoretic approach to the framework of safe net systems. We show two different methods for constructing a product Büchi

BuildGraph(T_a)_____

```
1      V := Off;  Edg := ∅;  Ea := {e ∈ E_Fin | h(e) ∈ T_a};
2      forall e₁⁰ ∈ Cor  do
3          X := {e' ∈ Off | e' ⪰ e₁⁰};  Y := {e' ∈ Cor | e' ⪰ e₁⁰};
4          forall e₂ ∈ X  do
5              forall e₁ ∈ off(e₁⁰)  do
6                  if G contains no edge e₁ → e₂ then add e₁→ e₂ to Edg;
7                  if ([e₂] \ [e₁⁰]) ∩ E_a ≠ ∅ then label e₁→ e₂ with a;
8              enddo
9          enddo
10         forall e₂⁰ ∈ Y  do
11             forall (e₁, e₂) ∈ off(e₁⁰) × off(e₂⁰)  do
12                 if G contains no edge e₁→ e₂ then add e₁→ e₂ to Edg;
13                 if ( ([e₂⁰] \ [e₁⁰]) ∪ Γ(e₁⁰, e₂) ) ∩ E_a ≠ ∅ then label e₁→ e₂ with a;
14             enddo
15         enddo
16     enddo
```

Fig. 1. Algorithm for constructing the graph G.

net, corresponding to product automata of Section 2. This product is constructed as a *synchronization* or an *observation* on the net level.

In the entire section, we assume the system net under consideration to be *deadlock-free*, i.e., all of its computations are infinite.

Synchronization. We will first assume an action-based interpretation. In this case, the product net Σ_p of the automaton $A_{\neg\varphi}$ and of the system Σ under consideration is obtained by synchronizing the transitions according to the valuation v. Let $A_{\neg\varphi} = (Q, q_0, \delta, \mathcal{F})$ be fixed.

The product net Σ_p is an extension of Σ in the following sense: the states Q of the automaton are added to the set P of places of Σ, and initially $M_0 \cup \{q_0\}$ is marked. The accepting states $\mathcal{F}$ become the accepting places, and for each transition $(q, \Pi', q') \in \delta$, we add q to the preset and q' to the postset of every transition t of the system, with $v(t) = \Pi'$.

Proposition 3. *Let Σ_p be the synchronized product of Σ and $A_{\neg\varphi}$ as defined above. The system Σ satisfies φ in action-based semantics iff Σ_p is empty.*

Observation. In a state-based interpretation, the automaton $A_{\neg\varphi}$ can be seen as a process observing the marking sequences of Σ. Clearly, it suffices to observe only the places that appear as atomic propositions in φ as stated by Lemma 4 below.

Let $\xi = M_0 M_1 \ldots$ be the infinite marking sequence corresponding to a run γ, and $Q \subseteq P$ a set of places. By $M_i^Q := M_i \cap Q$ we denote the restriction of M_i onto the places in Q, and we define $\xi^Q := M_0^Q M_1^Q \ldots$.

Lemma 4. *If φ is an LTL formula and $Q \subseteq P$ a set of propositions such that $\langle\varphi\rangle \subseteq Q$, then $\xi \models \varphi$ iff $\xi^Q \models \varphi$ for every ω-word ξ over 2^P.*

We will construct Σ_p in such a way that the automaton and the system alternate their moves. Intuitively, if (q, P', q') is a transition of $A_{\neg\varphi}$, the automaton tests if the current marking is P'. In this case it moves from q to q' and enables Σ to make a move, which makes its move and again enables the automaton to observe the current marking. The mutual enabling is implemented using two "scheduler" places s_f, s_s. If s_f (s_s) is marked, then the automaton (the system) has to move next. The automaton must observe M_0, so initially s_f is marked.

The testing of a marking is done by connecting the relevant places with the transitions of the automaton. If $d = (q, P', q')$ is a transition of $A_{\neg\varphi}$, we add all the places in $P' \subseteq P$ to the preset and to the postset of d. Thus, d can occur if all places in P' are marked, and after d occurred, again P' is marked. In general, however, this is insufficient: the automaton changes from q to q' only if the current marking is *equal* to P', in particular, if no proposition in $P \setminus P'$ belongs to the marking. By simply adding P' to ${}^\bullet d$, the transition d can occur, no matter whether any place $p \notin P'$ is marked or not. Therefore, we have to presuppose some *complementary places* in Σ.

Let $p, \overline{p} \in P$. The place $\overline{p}$ is the complement of p, if $\overline{p}^\bullet = {}^\circ p$, ${}^\bullet\overline{p} = p^\circ$, and $M_0(\overline{p}) = 1 - M_0(p)$. Thus, $p \in M$ iff $\overline{p} \notin M$ for every reachable state M. Due to Lemma 4, only the propositions (places, here) that appear in φ are relevant. So, we have to extend Σ by a complementary place for every place in $\langle\varphi\rangle$. Note that this extension has no influence on the system's behaviour. Let us denote by $Obs(\varphi) := \{p, \overline{p} \mid p \in \langle\varphi\rangle\}$ the set of *observed* places.

The Büchi net Σ_p then is defined as follows: the places are $P \cup Q \cup \{s_s, s_f\}$, the transitions are $T \cup \delta$, the initial marking is $M_0 \cup \{q_0\} \cup \{s_f\}$, the accepting places are $\mathcal{F}$, and the flow relation is F, extended by

- $(s_s, t), (t, s_f)$ for all $t \in T$, and $(s_f, d), (d, s_s)$ for all $d \in \delta$;
- $(q, d), (d, q')$ for every $d = (q, P', q') \in \delta$, as well as $(p, d), (d, p)$ and $(\overline{r}, d), (d, \overline{r})$ for all $p \in P'$ and $r \in \langle\varphi\rangle \setminus P'$.

The construction is sketched in Fig. 2 for a transition $d = (q, \{p_1\}, q')$ of the automaton $A_{\neg\varphi}$ where $\langle\varphi\rangle = \{p_1, p_2\}$.

Proposition 5. *Let Σ_p be the observation product of Σ and $A_{\neg\varphi}$ as defined above. The system Σ satisfies φ in state-based semantics iff Σ_p is empty.*

Relaxing the observation. Since $A_{\neg\varphi}$ behaves strictly sequentially, each observation introduces causal dependency on observed transitions, which ruins the benefits of any partial-order representation. However, restricting ourselves to *stutter-invariant properties*, it is sufficient to observe only all the *visible* transitions [18]. A transition t is visible iff ${}^\circ t$ or t° contains some place of $Obs(\varphi)$.

In [13] it has been shown that stutter-invariant properties are expressed by the "next-free" fragment of LTL, i.e., LTL without the next step operator X. In this fragment one cannot distinguish between the ω-word $\xi = x_0 x_1 \ldots$ and an ω-word ξ' similar to ξ except that any of the x_is are repeated finitely often. Let $\mu(\xi)$ denote the ω-word where every maximal finite subsequence $xx \ldots x$ in ξ is substituted by x. Two ω-words ξ, ξ' are *stutter-equivalent* if $\mu(\xi) = \mu(\xi')$.

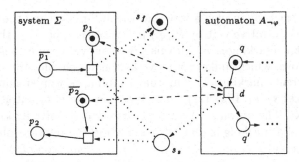

Fig. 2. The observation construction.

Lemma 6 ([13]). *If φ is a next-free LTL formula and ξ, ξ' are stutter-equivalent ω-words then $\xi \models \varphi$ iff $\xi' \models \varphi$.*

In the construction of the product this means, that *only the visible* system transitions and *all transitions of the automaton* are strictly alternating, while all concurrency among the non-visible transitions is preserved. The *reduced product* Σ_r thus is defined like Σ_p, except that for every non-visible transition t, the arcs (s_s, t) and (t, s_f) are discarded.

Unfortunately, with this construction it is possible that some run γ satisfies $\neg\varphi$, but it is *not* accepting. This is the case if only finitely many visible transitions occur in γ. Then the place s_s remains marked forever and thus no transition of the automaton will occur anymore. However, we have:

Proposition 7. *Let $\gamma = M_0 t_1 M_1 t_2 \ldots$ be a run of Σ_r, and t_{i_j} the jth occurrence of a transition of Σ in γ. For each state M_j of γ, let $P_j := M_j \cap P$ the restriction of M_j onto system places. The projection of γ onto system nodes then is defined as $Proj(\gamma) := P_0 t_{i_1} P_{i_1} t_{i_2} P_{i_2} \ldots$*
1. *If γ is a run of Σ_r then its projection $Proj(\gamma)$ onto system nodes is a run of Σ, and $\gamma \models \neg\varphi$ iff $Proj(\gamma) \models \neg\varphi$.*
2. *For every run γ' of Σ satisfying $\neg\varphi$, there exists a run γ of Σ_r, such that $\gamma' = Proj(\gamma)$ is the projection of γ onto system nodes, and $\gamma \models \neg\varphi$.*
3. *If γ is a run of Σ_r containing infinitely many visible transitions then the projection $Proj(\gamma)$ of γ satisfies $\neg\varphi$ iff γ is accepting.*

Model checking LTL. The fact that acceptance requires infinitely many visible transition occurrences may look like a drawback. To cope with this problem, we have to apply a *2-phase model checking* procedure ("mc_unf"):

Phase 1. We construct the reduced product Σ_r of Σ and $A_{\neg\varphi}$, and compute its finite prefix Fin_{Σ_r}. Now we build the graph G, applying BuildGraph(T_a) (Fig. 1), where T_a is the set of accepting transitions of $A_{\neg\varphi}$. *Additionally* we apply BuildGraph(T_b), where T_b is the set of *all* the automaton transitions, not only the accepting ones. The edges of the graph now may be labelled with a *and/or* b. Now, Tarjan's depthfirst search algorithm [1] determines the maximal strongly connected components (scc) of G. Each scc containing an a-labelled edge represents an accepting run. If such an scc is found then we reconstruct the corresponding violating run of the system and stop, else consider Phase 2.

Phase 2. We discard each scc containing an a- or b- or a,b-labelled edge. The *remaining* sccs correspond to infinite runs of Σ_r containing only finitely many occurrences of automaton (and, consequently, of *visible*) transitions. This means, that after finitely many steps, $M(p)$ remains unchanged for all observed places $p \in Obs(\varphi)$. Since each cut-off e in a remaining scc can be considered as being initial in G, each e in scc refers to a certain set of runs. All these e-runs have a unique, *last* reached automaton state q_e in common, determined by $q_e = Mark([e]) \cap Q$. That is, in all possible e-runs of Σ_r, the automaton get stuck in state q_e. Further note that the set $P_e := Mark([e]) \cap Obs(\varphi)$ of observed places is the last, forever-unchanged, "relevant" submarking in all these runs.

Thus, for each cut-off e in all the remaining sccs, we have to determine q_e and P_e, and have then to investigate if P_e allows an accepting cycle of the automaton starting at q_e. If so, the corresponding violating run of Σ can be reconstructed. Note that the Phase 2 needs only a fraction of the verification effort since $A_{\neg\varphi}$ is usually small compared with the size of the product.

Experimental results. A prototype implementation of the proposed method, using the very efficient unfolding procedure of [7], yielded promising results. Mainly, we observed that even large systems, synchronized with small automata, e.g. for (the negation of) the usual liveness property $\Box(p \Rightarrow \Diamond q)$, result in reasonably small prefixes. Liveness (resp. non-liveness) of Peterson's, Dekker's and Lamport's mutex-algorithms were checked within less than two seconds.

We also considered (the reactive version of) a leader election algorithm for a ring topology, described in [3]. The modelling is due to Stephan Melzer [6].

Essentially, the system consists of n processes, connected via a token ring. Each of the processes can be identified by its unique process number. The algorithm (in the reactive version) strives for repeated determination of a designated process, i.e., the one with the maximal number. We considered the liveness property $\Box\Diamond(elected = \text{true})$, expressing that infinitely often a designated process is found. The results are presented in Table 1. They are extremely positive, since for all n, the prefix contained only one cut-off event. The complementary property $\Diamond\Box(elected = \text{false})$ was shown to be not valid both by Spin [11] and our implementation in a second. All experiments were done within the PEP-tool [2].

n	Σ		Σ_r		Fin		time (sec.)	
	$|P|$	$|T|$	$|P|$	$|T|$	$|B|$	$|E|$	mc_unf	Spin
5	88	84	94	88	179	93	0.8	2.2
6	110	106	116	110	215	113	0.9	9.3
7	142	138	148	142	251	133	0.9	39.4
8	160	156	166	160	287	153	0.9	—[1]

Table 1. Results and comparison with SPIN for leader election.

[1] 64 MB main memory are exceeded.

5 Conclusion

Discussion. We have presented a method for model checking LTL in the framework of safe Petri nets, adopting the well-known automata-theoretic approach. We have shown how the finite prefix can be used for detecting the emptiness of a net with acceptance capabilities, and how to construct the product net of a given net system and a Büchi automaton, exhibiting enough concurrency to take profit from the partial order representation of behaviour.

How efficient is the proposed method? If one suppose a setting where only a small fraction of the behaviour influences the specification (i.e. there are few visible transitions), the "degree" of concurrency will remain high enough to exploit the advantages of net unfoldings, which are in some cases exponentially smaller than the global state space.

However, until now there is no better way to handle fairness constraints than including them into the formula, i.e., checking "$\varphi_{fair} \Rightarrow \varphi$". This may increase the number of visible transitions, and so possibly a larger part of the behaviour will be sequentialized. A more efficient method for treating fairness is desirable.

For a fast detection of violating runs when dealing with systems under development, we want to investigate an on-the-fly construction of the graph G: whenever a new cut-off event is detected during the unfolding procedure, the (partial) graph has to be "updated" and searched for an accepting cycle. If such a cycle is found, the unfolding needs not to be constructed further.

Related work. A closely related approach recently has been investigated in [6], also considering a product of a given safe net system and a Büchi automaton. There, a semidecision test is considered, that is a procedure which may answer "yes", in which case Σ satisfies the specification, or "don't know". The procedure works without ever constructing the state space, but uses structural net theory.

The common idea of the partial order methods proposed so far [10,16–19], bases on the observation that the order of execution of *concurrent* actions in many cases is irrelevant for the checked property φ. Intuitively, when several concurrent actions are enabled at a state, only some of them are selected, such that certain computation sequences and states may be discarded, yielding a *reduced system*. Since φ may be sensitive to certain interleavings of *visible* actions [18], all concurrent visible actions are considered to be causally dependent.

So-called *on-the-fly* methods are investigated in [10,17,19]. There, the Büchi automaton is incorporated in the construction of a *reduced product*. That is, instead of first reducing the system and then building the product, the Büchi automaton is used to guide the further exploration of concurrently enabled transition sets. In some cases, it is possible to detect accepting cycles during the construction, and thus not the entire product needs to be built.

In [12] it was shown that the visibility of actions (and thus the need to consider them dependent) may diminish during the construction of the reduced product, sometimes resulting in even better reduction.

Acknowledgments. I'd like to thank Stephan Melzer and Javier Esparza for many fruitful discussions. Special thanks to Stephan Melzer for the support with the implementation and the experiments.

References

1. A.V. Aho, J.E. Hopcroft, J.D. Ullman. *The Design and Analysis of Computer Algorithms.* Addison-Wesley, 1974.

2. E. Best, H. Fleischhack (eds.). PEP: Programming Environment based on Petri nets. Technical report, University of Hildesheim, 1995.

3. E. Chang, R. Roberts. An Inproved Algorithm for Decentralised Extrema-finding in Circular Distributed Systems. *Communication of the ACM*, 22(5):281–283, 1979.

4. J. Engelfriet. Branching processes of Petri nets. *Acta Informatica*, 28:575–591, 1991.

5. J. Esparza. Model checking using net unfoldings. *Science of Computer Programming*, 23:151–195, 1994.

6. J. Esparza, S. Melzer. Model Checking LTL Using Constraint Programming. In *Proc. of 18th Int. Conf. on Application and Theory of Petri Nets*, LNCS 1248, pp. 1–20, 1997.

7. J. Esparza, S. Römer, W. Vogler. An Improvement of McMillan's Unfolding Algorithm. In *Tools and Algorithms for the Construction and Analysis of Systems TACAS '96*, LNCS 1055, pp. 87–106, 1996.

8. R. Gerth, D. Peled, M. Vardi, P. Wolper. Simple On-the-fly Automatic Verification of Linear Temporal Logic. In *Protocol Specification, Testing, and Verification PSTV'95*, pp. 3–18, 1995.

9. P. Godefroid, G.J. Holzmann. On the Verification of Temporal Properties. In *Protocol Specification, Testing, and Verification PSTV'93*, 1993.

10. P. Godefroid, P. Wolper. A Partial Approach to Model Checking. In *Proc. of 6th IEEE Symp. on Logic in Computer Science*, pp. 406–415, 1991.

11. G.J. Holzmann. The model checker Spin. *IEEE Trans. on Software Engineering*, 23(5):279–295, 1997.

12. I. Kokkarinen, D. Peled, A. Valmari. Relaxed Visibility Enhances Partial Order Reduction. In *Proc. of 9th Computer-Aided Verification CAV'97*, LNCS 1254, pp. 328–339, 1997.

13. L. Lamport. What good is temporal logic? *Information Processing 83*, pp. 657–668, 1983.

14. K.L. McMillan. Using unfoldings to avoid the state explosion problem in the verification of asynchronous circuits. In *Proc. 4th Workshop on Computer-Aided Verification*, LNCS 663, pp. 164–174, 1992.

15. M. Nielsen, G. Plotkin, G. Winskel. Petri nets, event structures and domains. *Theoretical Computer Science*, 13(1):85–108, 1980.

16. D. Peled. All from one, one for all: on model checking using representatives. In *Proc. of 5th Computer-Aided Verification CAV'93*, LNCS 697, pp. 409–423, 1993.

17. D. Peled. Combining partial order reductions with on-the-fly model checking. In *Proc. of 6th Computer-Aided Verification CAV'94*, LNCS 818, pp. 377–390, 1994.

18. A. Valmari. A Stubborn Attack on State Explosion. *Formal Methods in System Design*, 1:297–322, 1992.

19. A. Valmari. On-the-fly Verification with Stubborn Sets. In *Proc. of 5th Computer-Aided Verification CAV'93*, LNCS 697, pp. 397–408, 1993.

20. M.Y. Vardi, P. Wolper. An automata-theoretic approach to automatic program verification. In *Proc. of 1st IEEE Symp. on Logic in Computer Science*, pp. 322–331, 1986.

21. P. Wolper. On the relations on programs and computations to models of temporal logic. In *Proc. of Temporal Logic in Specification*, LNCS 398, pp. 75–123, 1989.

22. P. Wolper, M.Y. Vardi, A.P. Sistla. Reasoning about infinite computation paths. In *Proc. of 24th IEEE Symp. on Foundations of Computer Science*, pp. 185–194, 1983.

Model Checking for a First-Order Temporal Logic Using Multiway Decision Graphs

Y. Xu[1], E. Cerny[1], X. Song[1], F. Corella[2], O. Aït Mohamed[1]

[1] D'IRO, Université de Montréal,
C.P. 6128, Succ. Centre-Ville, Montréal, H3C 3J7, Canada
[2] Hewlett-Packard Company, USA

Abstract. We study model checking for a first-order linear-time temporal logic. The computation model is based on *Abstract State Machines* (ASMs) in which data and data operations are described using abstract sorts and uninterpreted function symbols. ASMs are suitable for describing Register-Transfer level designs. We then define a first-order linear-time temporal logic called $\mathcal{L}_{MDG}$ which supports the abstract data representations. Both safety and liveness properties can be expressed in $\mathcal{L}_{MDG}$, however, only universal path quantification is possible. Fairness constraints can also be imposed. The property checking algorithms are based on implicit state enumeration of an ASM and implemented using Multiway Decision Graphs.

1   Introduction

Symbolic model checking has proven to be a very practical technique for the automatic verification of hardware designs [8, 9, 12]. However, these methods require the description of the design to be at the Boolean logic level, and thus they are in general not adequate for verifying circuits with large datapath because of the state-explosion problem.

Being motivated by a desire to combine the automation feature of model checking and the abstract representation of data in theorem proving, we developed model checking for a first-order linear-time temporal logic. Our approach is based on a computation model called an *abstract state machine* (ASM) where a data value can be represented by a single variable of abstract type, rather by a vector of Boolean variables, and a data operation is represented by an uninterpreted function symbol [5]. ASMs can be used to describe designs at the Register Transfer Level (RTL). We first define the first-order linear-time temporal logic $\mathcal{L}_{MDG}$ and then develop the corresponding property checking algorithms.

To check a property p in $\mathcal{L}_{MDG}$ on an ASM M, we first build additional ASMs M_j automatically for basic subformulas of p in which only the temporal operator X is allowed (called *Next_let_formulas*), then we compose the additional ASMs with M, and finally we check a simplified property on the composite machine. The property checking algorithms are based on implicit state enumeration as supported by Multiway Decision Graphs (MDGs) [5] whose complexity is independent of the width of the datapath. However the algorithms do not always terminate[1]. Decidability of model checking for

---

[1] Hence, strictly speaking, they should be called procedures rather than algorithms.

$\mathcal{L}_{MDG}$, just like decidability of reachability analysis for our ASMs, is left as an open question.

While our formalization of ASMs was introduced in [4], this is the first time that we address the model checking problem for ASMs.

To our knowledge, three previous developments reported in the literature are related to ours. Hungar, Grumberg and Damm [6] proposed a "true symbolic model checking" technique. They represented data and data operations by first-order formulas, and used FO-ACTL (first-order ACTL), a branching-time first-order temporal logic with universal path quantifier to specify properties. The method is based on the assumption that all data loops terminate, and on the separation of control and data path in typical circuits. If a property only contains control signals, then Boolean model checking is applied. When a property contains data, they replace all first-order components in the property formula with the Boolean constant true resulting in a propositional CTL formula. If this propositional CTL formula is not verified by a Boolean model checker, then the original property fails. Otherwise (the propositional CTL formula is verified), the tableau method is used to generate a pure first-order verification condition from the system and the property to be proven. They then verify the property by proving the validation of the verification condition using a theorem prover.

Cyrluk and Narendran defined a first-order temporal logic - Ground Temporal Logic (GTL) [1], which falls in between first-order and propositional temporal logics. The validity problem in GTL is the same as checking a linear time temporal logic formula for all computation paths. In [1], the authors showed that the full GTL is undecidable. They then identified a decidable fragment of GTL, consisting of ■p (always p) formulas where p is a GTL formula containing an arbitrary number of "Next" operators, but no other temporal operators. However, they did not show how to build the decision procedure for this decidable fragment.

Hojati, Brayton et al. [13, 14] proposed an integer combinational/sequential (ICS) concurrency model which uses finite relations, interpreted and uninterpreted integer functions and predicates, and interpreted memory functions to describe hardware systems with datapath abstraction. Verification of ICS models is performed using language containment. They showed that for a subclass of "control-intensive" ICS models, integer variables in the model can be replaced by enumerated variables (i.e., finite instantiations) and then the property verification can be carried out at the Boolean level without sacrificing accuracy. They gave a linear time algorithm for recognizing such a subset. For verifying properties of circuits containing data transformations modeled using interpreted and uninterpreted functions, finite instantiation cannot be used. In that case, they compute the set of states reachable in n steps using BDDs, and check that no error exists in these n steps.

Burch and Dill also used a subset of first-order logic, specifically, the quantifier-free logic of equality with uninterpreted functions for verifying microprocessor control circuitry [7]. Their logic is appropriate for verification of microprocessor control because it allows abstraction of datapath values and operations. However, their method, unlike ours, cannot verify properties involving temporal operators, especially, liveness properties.

Compared to [1], we shall see in the following sections that the decidable fragment of GTL is actually a subset of $\mathcal{L}_{MDG}$. Compared to ICS [13, 14], our ASM models are more general in the sense that the abstract sort variables in our system (corresponding to the integer variables in ICS models) can be assigned any value in their domain, rather a particular constant or function of constants as in the ICS model. For the class of ICS models where finite instantiations cannot be used, our verification system can still compute all the reachable states and check safety properties as well as certain liveness properties. For example, the abstract counter presented in Section 6 cannot be handled by the ICS model, but it can be described using the ASM model. Compared to [6], our first-order linear-time temporal logic is less expressive than FO-ACTL, since we only allow limited nesting of temporal operators. However, in our approach the property is checked on the whole model automatically, while in [6] a theorem prover is eventually needed to validate the pure first-order verification condition.

This paper is organized as follows: In Sections 2, we give a definition of abstract state machines (ASMs). In Section 3, we define the syntax and the semantics of $\mathcal{L}_{MDG}$. In Sections 4 and 5, we present the property checking algorithms, and show how to impose fairness constraints. In Section 6, we discuss implementation issues and present experimental results: property verification of an abstract counter. We conclude the paper in Section 7.

2 Abstract State Machines (ASMs)

Abstract State Machines (ASMs) are used in our approach to model the designs to be verified. We strongly recommend that interested readers refer to [5] for the definitions of a many-sorted first-order logic and Directed Formulas (DFs) before reading the definition of the ASMs. We cannot include them in this paper due to lack of space.

An abstract state machine M is described by a tuple $D = (X, Y, Z, F_I, F_T, F_O)$, where

1. X, Y and Z are sets of the input, state, and output variables, respectively. A variable in $X \cup Y \cup Z$ is called an *ASM_variable*. Let η be an one-to-one function that maps each state variable y to a distinct variable $\eta(y)$ obtained, for example, by adorning y with a prime. The variables in $Y' = \eta(Y)$ are used as the next-state variables disjoint from X, Y and Z. Given an interpretation ψ, an input vector is a ψ-compatible assignment to the set of input variables X; thus the set of input vectors (input alphabet) is Φ_X^ψ. Similarly, Φ_Z^ψ is the set of output vectors. A state is a ψ-compatible assignment to the set of state variables Y, hence, the state space is Φ_Y^ψ. A state ϕ can also be described by an assignment $\phi' = \phi \circ \eta^{-1} \in \Phi_{Y'}^\psi$, to Y'.
2. F_I is a DF of type $U \rightarrow Y$ representing the set of initial states where U is a set of abstract variables disjoint from $X \cup Y \cup Y' \cup Z$. Given an interpretation ψ, a state $\phi \in \Phi_Y^\psi$ is an initial state iff $\psi, \phi \models (\exists U) F_I$. Thus the set of initial states is $S_I = Set^\psi(F_I) = \{\phi \in \Phi_Y^\psi \mid \psi, \phi \models (\exists U) F_I\}$.
3. F_T is a DF of type $(X \cup Y) \rightarrow Y'$ representing the transition relation. Given an interpretation ψ, an input vector $\phi \in \Phi_X^\psi$ and a state $\phi' \in \Phi_Y^\psi$, a state $\phi'' \in \Phi_Y^\psi$ is a possible next state iff $\psi, \phi \cup \phi' \cup (\phi'' \circ \eta^{-1}) \models F_T$. Thus the transition relation is $R_T = \{(\phi, \phi', \phi'') \in \Phi_X^\psi \times \Phi_Y^\psi \times \Phi_Y^\psi \mid \psi, \phi \cup \phi' \cup (\phi'' \circ \eta^{-1}) \models F_T\}$.
4. F_O is a DF of type $(X \cup Y) \rightarrow Z$ representing the output relation. Given an interpretation ψ, the output relation is $R_O = \{(\phi, \phi', \phi'') \in \Phi_X^\psi \times \Phi_Y^\psi \times \Phi_Z^\psi \mid \psi, \phi \cup \phi' \cup \phi'' \models F_O\}$.

3 A First-Order Linear-Time Temporal Logic: $\mathcal{L}_{MDG}$

Given a description of an ASM, and a set of ordinary variables, the *atomic formulas* of $\mathcal{L}_{MDG}$ are Boolean constant T, F, or equations $t_1 = t_2$, where t_1 is an *ASM_variable*,

t_2 is an *ASM_variable* or a constant or an ordinary variable or a function of ordinary variables. The *Next_let_formulas* are defined as follows:

1. Each atomic formula is a *Next_let_formula*.
2. If p, q are *Next_let_formulas*, then so are:
   !p (*not p*), $p\&q$ (*p and q*), $p \mid q$ (*p or q*), $p \rightarrow q$ (*p implies q*), Xp, and
   LET $(v = t)$ IN p, where t is an *ASM_variable* and v an ordinary variable[2].

The properties allowed in $\mathcal{L}_{\mathcal{MDG}}$ can have the following forms:

$$Property ::= Next\_let\_formula$$
$$\mid \mathsf{G}(Next\_let\_formula)$$
$$\mid \mathsf{F}(Next\_let\_formula)$$
$$\mid Next\_let\_formula \mathsf{U} Next\_let\_formula$$
$$\mid \mathsf{G}(Next\_let\_formula \rightarrow \mathsf{F}Next\_let\_formula)$$
$$\mid \mathsf{G}(Next\_let\_formula \rightarrow (Next\_let\_formula \mathsf{U} Next\_let\_formula))$$

Semantics of $\mathcal{L}_{\mathcal{MDG}}$

A path π is a sequence of states. We use π^i to denote a path starting from π_i where π_i denote the ith state in π. All the formulas in $\mathcal{L}_{\mathcal{MDG}}$ are path formulas. We write $\pi, \sigma \models p$ to mean that a path formula p is true at path π under a ψ-compatible assignment σ to the ordinary variables. We use $Val_{s \cup \sigma}(t)$ to denote the value of term t under a ψ-compatible assignment s to state variables, input variables, and output variables and a ψ-compatible assignment σ to the ordinary variables. We define $\models$ inductively as follows:

$\pi, \sigma \models t_1 = t_2$ iff $Val_{\pi_0 \cup \sigma}(t_1) = Val_{\pi_0 \cup \sigma}(t_2)$.
$\pi, \sigma \models$ LET $(v=t)$IN p iff $\pi, \sigma' \models p$ where $\sigma' = \sigma \setminus \{(v, \sigma(v))\} \cup \{(v, Val_{\pi_0 \cup \sigma}(t))\}$
$\pi, \sigma \models$!p iff it is not the case that $\pi, \sigma \models p$.
$\pi, \sigma \models p\&q$ iff $\pi, \sigma \models p$ and $\pi, \sigma \models q$.
$\pi, \sigma \models p \mid q$ iff $\pi, \sigma \models p$ or $\pi, \sigma \models q$.
$\pi, \sigma \models p \rightarrow q$ iff $\pi, \sigma \models$!p or $\pi, \sigma \models q$.
$\pi, \sigma \models$ Xp iff $\pi^1, \sigma \models p$.
$\pi, \sigma \models$ Gp iff $\pi^j, \sigma \models p$ for all $j \geq 0$.
$\pi, \sigma \models$ Fp iff $\pi^j, \sigma \models p$ for some $j \geq 0$.
$\pi, \sigma \models p\mathsf{U}q$ iff for some $k \geq 0, \pi^k, \sigma \models q$, and $\pi^j, \sigma \models p$ for all $j(0 \leq j < k)$.

Given a property in $\mathcal{L}_{\mathcal{MDG}}$ regarding an ASM under a given interpretation ψ, the property holds on the ASM iff the property is true for every path π such that π_0 is an initial state and, for every i, there is a transition from π_i to π_{i+1} for some ψ-compatible assignment to the input variables.

4   Model Checking for Properties in $\mathcal{L}_{\mathcal{MDG}}$

Our approach to property checking consists of constructing additional ASMs that represent the *Next_let_formulas* appearing in the property, composing these additional

---

[2] We allow the formula LET $(v_1 = t_1)\&\ldots\&(v_n = t_n)$ INp as a shorthand for LET $(v_1 = t_1)$ IN (LET $(v_1 = t_1)$ IN $(\ldots$ LET $(v_n = t_n)$ INp $)\ldots)$; and we call $(v_1 = t_1)\&\ldots\&(v_n = t_n)$ a *Let_equation*.

ASMs with the original one, and then applying the appropriate algorithms to verify a simplified property on the composite machine. Given a *Next_let_formula* P regarding an ASM $D = (X, Y, Z, F_I, F_T, F_O)$, an ASM $D_P = (X_P, Y_P, Z_P, F_{IP}, F_{TP}, F_{OP})$ can be constructed to represent the *Next_let_formula*. The input variables of D_P are the *ASM_variables* of D which are referred to in the property, i.e., $X_P \subseteq X \cup Y \cup Z$. They represent the values at the "current" clock cycle. The set of the state variables Y_P and the transition relation F_{TP} are constructed so as to "remember" the values of the input variables of D_P or the results of comparisons of variables in the past n (or less than n) cycles, where n is the maximum nesting number of the X operators in the property. The set of state variables of D_P contains a special state variable *Flag* of boolean sort which indicates the truth of the *Next_let_formula* one cycle earlier. There is no output from D_P, i.e., Z_P is empty, hence there is no output relation either. The details of an algorithm for constructing an ASM representing a *Next_let_formula* are given in [16].

In the following subsections, we describe algorithms for verifying the various forms of the formulas in $\mathcal{L}_{MDG}$. When our property checking algorithms report success to a query, then the property holds for an ASM under any interpretation. It is possible that a property holds for the ASM under the intended interpretation of the abstract function symbols and constants, but not under every interpretation. In that case, we can obtain a false negative answer with respect to the original, non-abstracted problem. However, if all the data operations are viewed as black boxes, a property is expected to hold for every interpretation; it is in this sense that we say that our algorithms are applicable to designs where data operations are viewed as black boxes.

Recall that Disj computes disjunction and RelP computes relational product; both can be applied to any number of MDGs at once. Recall that PbyS(P, Q) removes from the MDG P any MDG paths (i.e. disjuncts) that are subsumed by the MDG Q.

4.1 Verification of G(Next_let_formula)

In this case we perform reachability analysis on the composite machine $M = (X_M, Y_M, Z_M, G_I, G_T, G_O)$, where:

- $X_M = X$ is the set of the input variables,
- $Y_M = Y \cup Y_P$ is the set of state variables, containing the variables in Y and in Y_P,
- $Z_M = Z$ is the set of output variables,
- G_I is a DF representing the set of initial states of M,
- G_T is a DF representing the transition relation of M,
- G_O is a DF representing the output relation of M.
  and in each state we check that $Flag = 1$.

The algorithm to verify G($Flag = 1$) is as follows:

1. Check_G(M, C)
   /* C is the DF $Flag = 1$ */
2. $R := G_I; S := G_I; K := 0;$
3. loop
4. $S_{notC} := $ PbyS(S, C);
5. if $S_{notC} \neq $ F then return failure;
   /* if the property is not satisfied in $Set(S)$, then report failure */
6. $K := K + 1;$
7. $I := $ Fresh$(X_M, K);$ /*generate input values */

8. $N := \mathsf{RelP}(\{I, S, G_T\}, X_M \cup Y_M, \eta');$/* compute next states*/
9. $S := \mathsf{PbyS}(N, R);$ /*compute frontier set of states*/
10. if $S = F$ then return success; /* if fixpoint reached, report success*/
11. $R := \mathsf{PbyS}(R, S);$ /* simplify R by removing states subsumed by S */
12. $R := \mathsf{Disj}(R, S);$ /* compute all states reached so far */
13. end loop;
14. end Check_G;

If the set of initial states represented by G_I does not satisfy the property we report failure. Otherwise, we compute the next new states and add them to those already visited until a fixpoint is reached. At each iteration, we verify the property on the newly generated states.

To check a property in the form of *Next_let_formula*, we construct a composite ASM in the same way as in the case of G(Next_let_formula), and then we verify that $Flag = 1$ on the states reached in $n + 1$ transitions from the initial states, where n is the maximum nesting depth of the X operators in the property, and the 1 cycle delay is caused by the register associated with Flag.

4.2   Verification of (Next_let_formula)∪(Next_let_formula)

We use additional ASMs to represent both *Next_let_formulas* and then transform the problem to the verification of $(FlagP = 1)\cup(FlagQ = 1)$ for all the initial states of the composite machine.

1.   check_U(M, C_p, C_q)
     /*M is the composite machine, G_I is the set of initial states
     /* G_T is the transition relation */
     /* C_p is the DF of $FlagP = 1$. C_q is the DF of $FlagQ = 1$ */
2. $\Sigma := \emptyset;$ /* Σ is a set of DFs, each DF represents a set of visited states */
3. $S := G_I;$
4. $K := 0;$
5.   loop
6. $S_{notq} := \mathsf{PbyS}(S, C_q);$ /*remove from S states with $FlagQ = 1$*/
7.   if $S_{notq} = F$ then return success;
8.   if $\exists T \in \Sigma, \mathsf{PbyS}(T, S_{notq}) = F$ then return failure;
         /*This step verifies if DF S_{notq} covers any DF in Σ, i.e.,
         for each DF T in $\Sigma, \mathsf{PbyS}(T, S_{notq}) = F$ is checked to
         detect a cycle. If there is a cycle, then failure is reported*/
9. $R = \mathsf{PbyS}(S_{notq}, C_p);$/* remove from S_{notq} states with $FlagP = 1$*/
10.   if $R \neq F$ then return failure;
11. $\Sigma := \Sigma \cup \{S_{notq}\};$ /* add DF S_{notq} as an element to Σ */
12. $K := K + 1;$
.13. $I := \mathsf{Fresh}(X_M, K);$ /* generate input values */
14. $S := \mathsf{RelP}(\{I, S_{notq}, G_T\}, X_M \cup Y_M, \eta');$/* compute next states */
15. end loop;
16. end Check_U

The algorithm removes from the set of reached states those states satisfying $FlagQ = 1$. If the leftover $Set(S_{notq})$ becomes empty, then the algorithm stops by reporting success. Otherwise, if there is at least one cycle along which all states satisfy $FlagP = 1$,

225

then there is at least one path starting from the initial state where pUq does not hold, the algorithm stops and reports failure. Otherwise, it checks whether all the states in $Set(S_{notq})$ satisfy $FlagP = 1$. If there are some states where $FlagP = 1$ does not hold, meaning that there is a path on which $FlagP = 1$ does not hold in every state before a state satisfying $FlagQ = 1$ is reached, then the algorithm also stops and reports failure. Otherwise, it computes the next states reachable from $Set(S_{notq})$ and repeats the process.

To verify $G(c \rightarrow pUq)$ on machine D, we build a composite machine M from D, an ASM representing c, an ASM representing p, and an ASM representing q, and then verify $G((FlagC = 1) \rightarrow ((FlagP = 1)U(FlagQ = 1)))$ on the composite machine. This is achieved by first computing all the reachable states of M (represented by W), by collecting from W those states that satisfy "$FlagC = 1$" ($V := \text{Conj}(W, C_c)$ where C_c is the DF of $FlagC = 1$), and finally by applying the Check_U algorithm with the set V as the initial set of states.

A property in the form of $F(Next\_let\_formula)$ can be verified by checking TU$Next\_let\_formula$ using the Check_U algorithm.

5 Verification of Liveness Properties with Fairness Constraints

5.1 Fairness constraints

When verifying liveness properties, one is usually interested only in the so-called fair infinite computation paths. A fair computation path is a path along which the states satisfy each fairness condition infinitely often.

In the literature, various methods for specifying fairness constraints have been developed for CTL model checking [2] and language containment using L-automata [15].

In our method, we impose fairness constraints using a subset of the criteria employed in the method based on language containment, namely, by specifying cycle sets. Let $H_i, i = 1, \ldots, n$, be n "exception" conditions, and S_ω the set of infinitely repeating states along a computation path. If at least one H_i holds on all s in S_ω, then the path is not fair and need not satisfy the property under investigation. That is, only those computation paths along which the states satisfy each $!H_i$ infinitely often are considered. We call the formula representing the exception condition H_i an $H\_formula$. The syntax of an $H\_formula$ is as follows:

1. The equation $t_1 = t_2$ is an $H\_formula$, where t_1 is an $ASM\_variable$ and t_2 is an $ASM\_variable$ or a constant.
2. If p, q are $H\_formulas$, then so are $!p, p\&q, p|q, p \rightarrow q, Xp$.

5.2 Verification of pUq with fairness constraints

To verify that pUq (where p and q are $Next\_let\_formulas$) holds for the initial states of an ASM D under fairness constraints $!H_1, !H_2, \ldots, !H_n$, we build additional ASMs to represent p, q, and H_i $(1 \leq i \leq n)$, and then transform the problem to checking $(FlagP = 1)U(FlagQ = 1)$ on the initial states of the composite machine derived from D and the additional ASMs with fairness constraints $!(FlagH_i = 1)$ $(1 \leq i \leq n)$.

Let (1) M be the composite machine, (2) G_I be the set of initial states, and G_T the transition relation, (3) C_p be the DF of $FlagP = 1$, and C_q be the DF of $FlagQ = 1$,

(4) H_i $(1 \leq i \leq n)$ be the DF of $FlagH_i = 1$. The algorithm for verifying $(FlagP = 1)\mathrm{U}(FlagQ = 1)$ under fairness constraints $!(FlagH_i = 1)$ $(1 \leq i \leq n)$ is as follows:

```
1.    Check_U_fair(M, C_p, C_q, H_1, ..., H_n)
2.    Σ := ∅;
3.    S := G_I; K := 0;
4.    loop1
5.      S_notq := PbyS(S, C_q);
6.      if S_notq = F then return success;
7.      if ∃T ∈ Σ, PbyS(T, S_notq) = F then return failure;
8.      R = PbyS(S_notq, C_p);
9.      if R ≠ F return failure;
10.     Σ := Σ ∪ {S_notq};
11.     S_1 := S_notq;
12.     for i = 1 to n do
13.       S_notH := PbyS(S_1, H_i);/*remove from S_1 the states with FlagH_i = 1 */
14.       S_2 := Conj(S_1, H_i); /*S_2 represents the states in S_1 with FlagH_i = 1 */
15.       if S_2 = F then S_4notq := F;
16.       if S_2 ≠ F then begin
17.         S_3 := S_2; S_f := S_2; L := 0;
18.         loop2 /* to compute all the states reachable from S_2 with FlagH_i = 1 */
19.           L := L + 1;
20.           I_2 := Fresh(X_M, L); /* generate new input values */
21.           N_1 := RelP({I_2, S_f, G_T}, X_M ∪ Y_M, η'); /* compute next states */
22.           N_2 := PbyS(N_1, C_q); /*remove from N_1 the states with FlagQ = 1 */
23.           N_3 := Conj(N_2, H_i); /*pick from N_2 the states with FlagH_i = 1 */
24.           if PbyS(N_3, C_p) ≠ F then return failure;
                /* if the states in N_3 do not satisfy FlagP = 1, report failure */
25.           S_f := PbyS(N_3, S_3); /* compute the frontier states */
26.           if S_f = F then exit loop2;
                /* if all the states reachable from S_2 have been visited, exit loop 2 */
27.           S_3 := PbyS(S_3, S_f);
28.           S_3 := Disj(S_3, S_f);/* add the states of S_f to S_3 */
29.         end loop2;
30.         S_41 := RelP({I_2, S_3, G_T}, X_M ∪ Y_M, η');
                /* compute the next states of S_3 */
31.         S_4 := PbyS(S_41, H_i); /* remove from S_41 the states with FlagH_i = 1 */
32.         S_4notq := PbyS(S_4, C_q);
33.         if PbyS(S_4notq, C_p) ≠ F then return failure;
34.       end_if
35.       S_1 = Disj(S_4notq, S_notH);
36.     end_for
37.     if S_1 ≠ F then begin
38.       K := K + 1;
39.       I_1 := Fresh(X_M, K);/* generate input values */
40.       S := RelP({I_1, S_1, G_T}, X_M ∪ Y_M, η'); /* compute the next states of S1 */
41.     end_if
42.   end loop1
43. end
```

In this algorithm, Σ is a set containing DFs representing each a set of states not satisfying $FlagQ = 1$ on the fair computation paths after a transition step, S represents the frontier set of states to be checked, and n is the number of fairness constraints.

In loop1, in steps $(5) - (10)$, S_{notq} represents the set of states in S not satisfying $FlagQ = 1$. If S_{notq} is empty, then the computation stops by reporting success. Otherwise, if S_{notq} covers any set in S, which means there is at least one cycle that is not one of the cycle sets, and the states in the cycle do not satisfy $(FlagQ = 1)$, then the algorithm stops and reports failure. If no cycle is detected, then we check whether the states in S_{notq} satisfy $FlagP = 1$. If not then report failure; if yes, then S_{notq} is added to Σ and the computation continues (lines $8 - 9 - 10$).

Lines (11) to (36) form a loop that is executed n times. This loop deals with each exception condition. At every i-th $(1 \le i \le n)$ iteration, S_2 represents the set of states in S_1 that satisfy the exception condition $FlagH_i = 1$, and S_{notH} represents the set of states in S_1 that does not satisfy $FlagH_i = 1$. If S_2 is not empty, the algorithm computes S_3 (loop $18 - 29$). This set represents all the states that are reachable from S_2 by any number of transition steps and each satisfies $FlagH_i = 1$ and $FlagP = 1$, but does not satisfy $FlagQ = 1$. In other words, S_3 could contain cycles which are formed by the states satisfying $FlagH_i = 1$ and $FlagP = 1$ but not $FlagQ = 1$. (The way to compute S_3 is the same as the reachability analysis, and it may not terminate). Then, one more transition is done to compute the set of states reachable by one transition step from the states of S_3, but not satisfying $FlagH_i = 1$, and these states are stored in S_4. S_{4notq} represents the set of states in S_4 that do not satisfy $FlagQ = 1$. If this set contains at least one state that does not satisfy $FlagP = 1$, then report failure (line 33). S_1 is the union of the set of states represented by S_{4notq} and S_{notH} at each iteration of the loop.

If S_1 is not empty, then S is computed to represent the states reachable in one transition step from the states in S_1. The computation continues in loop1 with S as the new frontier set of states to be checked.

In Fig. 1, we show an example that illustrates how this algorithm works. Suppose we wish to verify $(FlagP = 1)U(FlagQ = 1)$ under the fairness constraint $!(FlagH_1 = 1)$ on the state transition graph given in Fig. 1. We also indicate the values of $FlagP, FlagQ$ and $FlagH_1$ in each state. We shall see that the algorithm stops and reports success at the 3rd iteration in loop1. However, checking $(FlagP = 1)U(FlagQ = 1)$ without the fairness constraint would fail on the path $s_1 \to s_2 \to s_3 \to s_2 \to s_3 \to s_2 \to s_3 \ldots$.

To check $G(c \to pUq)$ where c, p, q are Next_let_formulas under the fairness constraints $!H_1, !H_2, \ldots, !H_n$ on an ASM D, we build a composite machine M from D, and ASMs representing c, p, q, H_i $(1 \le i \le n)$, and then transform the problem to checking $G((FlagC = 1) \to ((FlagP = 1)U(FlagQ = 1)))$ on M under the fairness constraints $!(FlagH_i = 1)$ $(1 \le i \le n)$. We then do reachability analysis to get all the reachable states of M (represented by W), collect from W the states satisfying "$FlagC = 1$" ($V := \text{Conj}(W, C_c)$ where C_c is a DF containing $FlagC = 1$), and finally apply the algorithm Check_U_fair with the set V as the set of initial states.

The Check_U_fair algorithm is conservative, i.e., it requires that for every path, $FlagP = 1$ is satisfied on all the states along the path before a state satisfying $FlagQ = 1$ is reached. Along some path, if the states repeating forever are covered by a cycle set and there is no other state reached from those states as shown in Fig. 2, Check_U_fair will report failure. However, it is not necessary that $FlagP = 1$ holds on those states, since this path should not be considered. Thus Check_U_fair may give a false negative answer. In real system, this situation happens rarely, however.

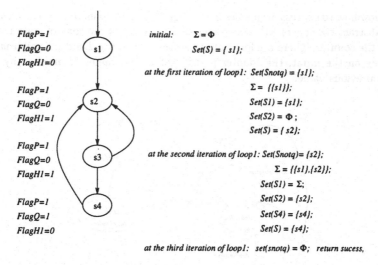

```
FlagP=1                       initial:      Σ = Φ
FlagQ=0      s1                           Set(S) = { s1};
FlagH1=0
                              at the first iteration of loop1: Set(Snotq) = {s1};
FlagP=1                                    Σ = {{s1}};
FlagQ=0      s2                            Set(S1) = {s1};
FlagH1=1                                   Set(S2) = Φ ;
                                           Set(S) = { s2};

FlagP=1
FlagQ=0      s3             at the second iteration of loop1: Set(Snotq)= {s2};
FlagH1=1                                    Σ = {{s1},{s2}};
                                           Set(S1) = Σ;
FlagP=1                                     Set(S2) = {s2};
FlagQ=1      s4                             Set(S4) = {s4};
FlagH1=0                                    Set(S) = {s4};

                           at the third iteration of loop1:  set(snotq) = Φ;  return sucess,
```

Fig. 1. An example of verifying $(FlagP = 1)U(FlagQ = 1)$ under the fairness constraint $!(FlagH_1 = 1)$

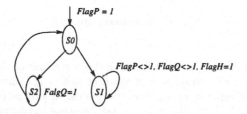

Fig. 2. Example of a false negative answer for verifying $(FlagP = 1)U(FlagQ = 1)$ under the fairness constraint $!(FlagH = 1)$

To verify that Fp (where p is a *Next_let_formula*) under fairness constraints, we verify (TUp). The method will not produce any false negatives answer since T is satisfied by any state in this case.

6 Implementation Issues and Experimental Results

To automatically verify properties expressed in $\mathcal{L}_{MDG}$, we developed programs to:

- check if the signals in a property are declared in the original circuit description;
- check the syntax of the property;
- build the additional circuits to represent the *Next_let_formulas* in the property and the exception conditions if fairness constraints are imposed;
- merge the description of the additional circuits with the description of the circuit to be verified;

The above programs are implemented in C with Yacc and Lex. The property checking algorithms are developed based on the current MDG package and they are implemented in Quintus Prolog V3.2.

229

To show how to express properties in our logic, and how to use our model checker, we use the abstract counter of [1] as an example. Fig. 3 shows the control state transition graph of the counter. There are four control states: $c\_Fetch, c\_Load, c\_Inc1, and c\_Inc2$. Depending on the input, the counter pc will get a new value, or increase by one, or keep the previous value.

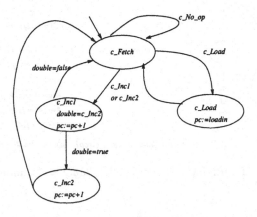

Fig. 3. An abstract counter

To use our model checker, we first describe the behaviour of the counter using the MDG-HDL language. The counter pc is of abstract sort. The control state is initialized to c_Fetch, the initial value of pc is a free variable called $init\_pc$ (i.e., the initial state is generalized to any value). It takes three transition steps to compute all the reachable states. We verified the following three properties:

Property 1: From state c_Fetch, if the input is c_Inc2, then the machine always reaches state c_Inc2 in two transition steps. This property can be expressed in $\mathcal{L}_{MDG}$ as follows:

$$G((state = c\_Fetch\&input = c\_Inc2) \rightarrow (XX(state = c\_Inc2)));$$

Property 2: From state c_Fetch, if the input is c_Inc2, then the machine reaches the state c_Fetch in three transition steps and the counter pc is increased by two. This property can be expressed in $\mathcal{L}_{MDG}$ as follows:

$$G((state = c\_Fetch\&input = c\_Inc2) \rightarrow$$
$$\text{LET } v_1 = pc \text{ IN } XXX(state = c\_Fetch \& pc = inc(inc(v_1))));$$

Property 3: From the state c_Fetch, the machine will eventually reach the state c_Load if the input is not c_No_op or c_Inc1 or c_Inc2 forever. The property can be expressed in $\mathcal{L}_{MDG}$ as:

$$G((state = c\_Fetch) \rightarrow (F(state = c\_Load)));$$

under the following fairness constraint:

$$!((state = c\_Fetch) \rightarrow ((input = c\_Inc1) \mid (input = c\_No\_op) \mid (input = c\_Inc2)));$$

These properties are verified by our model checker in less than one second. Table 1 shows the CPU time in seconds used in building the composite machine and checking the simplified property regarding Flag on the composite machine. The experiment is carried out on a SPARC Station 20 with 128 MB of memory.

	Building the composite machine		Checking the simplified property	
	CPU time (sec)	Memory (MB)	CPU time (sec)	Memory (MB)
Property 1	0.21	0.89	0.04	0.15
Property 2	0.31	0.90	0.12	1.75
property 3	0.37	1.65	0.06	0.51

Table 1. Experimental Results of Property Checking.

Using the decidable fragment of Ground Temporal Logic (GTL) [1], Properties 1 and 2 could be checked, but Property 3 could not be verified, since it is a liveness property. Using the "true symbolic model checking" [6], all the properties could be checked. But when verifying Property 2, as the abstract data pc appears in the property, we need to first strip the first-order parts in the formula to obtain a propositional formula $G((state = c\_Fetch \& input = c\_Inc2) \rightarrow (XXX(state = c\_Fetch)))$. When the propositional formula is verified, a first-order verification condition need to be generated and verified. Using the ICS model [14, 13], it happens that the abstract counter falls into the class of circuits where finite instantiation cannot be applied and thus it is not possible to compute all the reachable states; therefore, it seems that none of the above properties could be verified.

7 Concluding Remarks

We defined a first-order linear-time temporal logic $\mathcal{L}_{MDG}$ with only the universal path quantifier and developed property checking algorithms for $\mathcal{L}_{MDG}$. To check a property of $\mathcal{L}_{MDG}$ on an ASM M, we first build additional ASMs for the $Next\_let\_formulas$ (which contain the temporal operator X) that appear in the property, then compose the additional ASMs with M, and finally check a simplified property on the composite machine. We use MDGs to encode sets of states and the transition relation. The property checking procedures are based on implicit state enumeration and are carried out fully automatically. We illustrated the application of our property checker on an abstract counter. We have also proven the soundness of our verification procedures in [16].

Since we use first-order logic, the reachability analysis may not terminate [3], thus the property checking may not terminate either. We are currently exploring techniques that migrate this problem [11, 10].

References

1. Cyrluk D. and Narendran P. Ground temporal logic: A logic for hardware verification. In D. L. Dill, editor, *Computer Aided Verification*, volume 818 of *Lecture Notes in Computer Science*. Springer Verlag, 1994.

2. Emerson E. A. and Lei C. L. Modalities for Model Checking: Branching Time Logic Strikes Back. *Science of Computer Programming*, 8:275–306, 1987.
3. Clarke E. M. and Emerson E., A. Design and Synthesis of synchronization skeletons using branching time temporal logic. In *Workshop on Logics of Programs*, number 131 in Lecture Notes in Computer Science, pages 52–71, New York, 1981. Springer-Verlag.
4. Corella F., Langevin M., Cerny E., Zhou Z., and Song X. State enumeration with abstract descriptions of state machines. In *Proc. IFIP WG 10.5 Advanced Research Working Conference on Correct Hardware Design and Verification Methods (Charme'95)*, Frankfurt, Germany, October 1995.
5. Corella F., Zhou Z., Song X., Langevin M., and Cerny E. Multiway decision graphs for automated hardware verification. *Formal Methods in System Design*, 10(1):7–46, February 1997.
6. Hungar H., Grumberg O., and Damm W. What if Model Checking Must Be Truly Symbolic. In *Workshop on Tools and Algorithms for the Construction and Analysis of Systems (TACAS'95)*, Aarhus, Denmark, May 1995.
7. Burch J. R. and Dill D. L. Automatic verification of pipelined microprocessor control. In D. L. Dill, editor, *Proc. Work. on Computer-Aided Verification*, number 818 in Lecture Notes in Computer Science. Springer Verlag, 1994.
8. Burch J. R., Clarke E. M., and McMillan K. L. Symbolic model checking: 10^{20} States and Beyond. In *LICS*, 1990.
9. McMillan K. L. *Symbolic model checking: An approach to the state explosion problem*. PhD thesis, School of Computer Science, Carnegie Mellon University, Pittsburgh, 1992.
10. Aït Mohamed O., Cerny E., and Song X. MDG-based verification by retiming and combinational transformations. In Magdy A. Bayoumi and Graham Jullien, editors, *Proc. of the Great Lakes Symposium on VLSI (GLS-VLSI'98*, pages 356–361, Lafayette, Louisiana, USA, 1998. IEEE Computer Society Press.
11. Aït Mohamed O., Song X., and Cerny E. On the Non-termination of MDG-based Abstract State Enumeration. In *Proc. IFIP W 10.5 Advanced Research Working Conference on Correct Hardware Design and Verification Methods (Charme'97)*, Montréal, October 1997. IFIP, Chapmann & Hall.
12. Coudert O. and Madre J. C. A unified framework for the formal verification of sequential circuits. In *International Conference on Computer-Aided Design*, 1990.
13. Hojati R., Dill D. L., and Brayton R. K. Verifying linear temporal properties of data insensitive controllers using finite instantiations. In *Conference on Hardware Description Languages (CHDL'97)*, April 1997.
14. Hojati R. and Brayton R. K. Automatic datapath Abstraction In Hardware Systems. In *Conference on Computer-Aided Verification*, June 1995.
15. Kurshan R. P. Reducibility in Analysis of Coordination. volume 103 of *Lecture Notes in Computer Science*, pages 19–39. Springer-Verlag, 1987.
16. Xu Y. *Model checking for a first-order branching time temporal logic based on abstract description of state machines*. PhD thesis, D'IRO, University of Montréal, 1998. Draft.

On the Limitations of Ordered Representations of Functions

Jayram S. Thathachar*

Abstract. We demonstrate the limitations of various ordered representations that have been considered in the literature for symbolic model checking including BDDs [3], *-BMDs [6], HDDs [15], MTBDDs [13] and EVBDDs [25]. We introduce a lower bound technique that applies to a broad spectrum of such functional representations. Using an abstraction that encompasses all these representations, we apply this technique to show exponential size bounds for a wide range of integer and boolean functions that arise in symbolic model checking in the definition and implicit exploration of the state spaces. We give the first examples of integer functions including integer division, remainder, high/low-order words of multiplication, square root and reciprocal that require exponential size in all these representations. Finally, we show that there is a simple regular language that requires exponential size to be represented by any *-BMD, even though BDDs can represent any regular language in linear size.

1 Introduction

Model checking, proposed in [14], is a verification technique for determining whether a given property expressed as a temporal logic formula is satisfied by a system specification ([17] is an excellent source of references.) One of the major bottlenecks of model checking is the state explosion problem, i.e. the exponential growth in the number of states relative to the size of the system being verified.

Symbolic methods [9, 29, 8] have successfully combated this problem in many instances. Central to these methods is an underlying representation for various boolean and integer functions, and predicates combining such functions in arbitrary ways, in order to encode and implicitly explore state spaces. Ideally, these representations must satisfy certain important properties. First, they must be able to concisely represent the functions that occur in the definition of the components of the system being verified and arise in the implicit exploration of the state spaces. It is also necessary to combine these representations efficiently in order for composing boolean functions and integer functions using boolean and arithmetic operators, respectively. Finally, there should be efficient algorithms for testing various properties such as equivalence of representations and detecting satisfying assignments for boolean functions (more generally, finding roots of equations and inequalities involving boolean and integer functions).

BDDs (Ordered Binary Decision Diagrams) [3] are generalizations of decision trees to directed acyclic graphs, where the queries are made in some fixed order. Because they

---

* This work was supported by the National Science Foundation under Grant CCR-9303017. Mailing address: Department of Computer Science and Engineering, University of Washington, Box 352350, Seattle, Washington 98195 E-mail: jayram@cs.washington.edu

are canonical, easy to manipulate, and compactly represent many boolean functions that are natural components of circuit designs, they have been useful in many instances for equivalence testing of circuit designs against their specification. After their importance to symbolic model checking was realized, various optimizations and heuristics [8] have resulted in enormously successful BDD-based verification packages.

The main drawback of BDDs is in concisely representing some important functions, particularly integer functions such as multiplication which requires exponential size [4]. Therefore other extensions and alternatives, e.g [13, 29, 6, 15], have been proposed to overcome some of the limitations of BDDs (see [5] for references to the "alphabet soup" of various representation schemes). *-BMDs [6] and HDDs [15] are two notable examples that are able to efficiently represent multiplication and other integer functions. They have been used to verify and identify errors in SRT division circuits [7, 16] similar to the one used in the Intel Pentium chip. *-BMDs obtain some of their power by treating the outputs of integer functions as a whole rather than splitting them into bits and have been used for verifying many arithmetic circuit designs that were previously intractable [6]. HDDs combine many of the advantages of BDDs and *-BMDs and thus have been successfully incorporated into verification packages, e.g. [11].

However, none of these representations are satisfactory for verifying general systems. A common feature of all the verification approaches is that the system is evaluated in a bottom-up manner to represent its transition relation. Therefore, the complexity of the various components that arise in this bottom-up evaluation limits the success of a representation scheme. Such components typically include many other integer functions such as division, reciprocal etc. and predicates such as linear equalities, e.g. $xy = c$. Another issue, which arises in verifying arithmetic circuits, is that the outputs are truncated, e.g. certain multiplication circuits require that both the high-order and low-order words of the product be represented efficiently.[1] This research is aimed at understanding the effectiveness of these representations in dealing with these functions and predicates.

We show that none of the representations referred to above, including recently defined representations [12], can represent a variety of specific integer and boolean functions concisely. Our specific results include

- Exponential bounds in the *-BMD and HDD representation for natural integer functions such as division (*Div*), remainder (*Mod*), high-order word (*HiMult*) and low-order word (*LoMult*) of multiplication, integer square root (*Sqrt*), and reciprocal (*Inv*). These are the first theoretical results that show the limitations of *-BMDs and HDDs in representing integer functions. Some of the functions listed above are natural components of microprocessor instruction sets that need to be verified.
- Exponential bounds for many boolean predicates including factor verification, string matching, selection/equality, shifted equality, and undirected graph predicates such as connectivity, s-t connectivity and bipartiteness that hold in all the representations considered above.
- A simple regular language that requires *-BMDs of exponential size. In contrast, BDDs can represent any regular language in linear size.

Existing lower bounds for BDDs [4] or even read-once branching programs [32] do not extend to *-BMDs and HDDs. We derive our lower bounds by defining an abstrac-

---

[1] R. E. Bryant. Private Communication.

tion, called the *Binary Linear Diagram* (BLD), that encompasses all the representations referred to above. We then show that for any function f, the rank of a certain matrix associated with f is a lower bound on the size of any BLD for f. This matrix is (essentially) the one usually used for VLSI AT^2 bounds, and has been studied extensively in communication complexity by theoreticians. (An excellent source for results and references for this area is [24].) Our lower bound technique is analogous to previously known results in multiplicity automata theory which relate the size of a multiplicity automaton to the rank of the Hankel matrix computed by the automaton [20, 10].

Our technique provides insight into the contrast between boolean and integer representations. For example, consider multiplication. For the boolean function which computes the middle bit of the product, one of our results shows that the associated matrix has exponential rank, but it can be easily verified that the matrix of the integer function has constant rank. This gives us better intuition as to why the integer function has linear-sized *-BMDs but the middle-bit version requires exponential size in all the ordered representations.

For the boolean predicates listed above, the exponential bounds on the rank are a corollary of two of the approaches used for bounding the best-partition communication complexity of boolean functions. In the approach taken in [28, 31, 4], one constructs exponentially large fooling sets. By a theorem of [18], these results imply exponential bounds for the rank. The second approach involves directly bounding the rank, as in [22] for the graph predicates stated above, although there are fewer results that use this approach. On the other hand, the exponential bounds that we prove for the integer functions mentioned previously do not follow from standard communication complexity results but from directly analyzing the associated matrices and bounding their rank.

As mentioned earlier, *-BMDs represent many arithmetic functions that require exponential size BDDs. Enders [19] obtained the first separation result in the other direction: the graph predicate that checks whether a graph is a triangle has polynomial-sized BDDs but requires exponential size *-BMDs. A variety of separation results have been shown in [1], contrasting the representational power of bit-level and word-level ordered representations. Our result for regular languages is the first (as far as we know) that shows such a separation for some natural language class. It also validates the belief in [6] that the strengths and weaknesses of *-BMDs and BDDs are orthogonal.

The paper is organized as follows. In Section 2, we define the BLD representation and illustrate how it generalizes all the ordered representations. Section 3 describes the basic lower bound technique of relating the BLD size of a function to the rank of certain matrices associated with that function. Applying this technique, we prove in Section 4 that the integer functions *Div*, *Mod*, *HiMult*, *LoMult*, *Sqrt* and *Inv* require exponential-sized BLDs. In Section 5, we give exponential lower bounds for many boolean functions by either using fooling sets or directly bounding the rank. Finally, in Section 6, we demonstrate for a simple regular language that the *-BMD complexity is exponential.

2 Binary Linear Diagrams

Let $X = \{x_1, x_2, \ldots, x_n\}$ be a set of boolean variables. We consider functions that map boolean inputs (which assign 0-1 values to the variables) to elements of some fixed ground field $\mathcal{K}$. We also consider *subfunctions* of a function f obtained by setting some of the input variables to 0-1 values. If σ is a partial assignment of 0-1 values to $Y \subseteq X$, we denote the resulting subfunction by $f\lceil_\sigma$ (which is defined on $X\backslash Y$).

Definition 1. *An* (Ordered) Binary Linear Diagram (BLD) *is a labeled, directed acyclic graph with a designated node called the* source. *The nodes that have out-degree 0, called the* sinks, *are labeled with elements from* $\mathcal{K}$. *Every other node v has out-degree two and the two edges directed from v are distinguished as the 0-edge and 1-edge, respectively. The node that the 0-edge (respectively, 1-edge) is incident to is called the 0-child (respectively, 1-child). The node v is labeled with a variable from X and a 2×2 matrix with entries in $\mathcal{K}$.[2] For some order $O = x_{p_1}, x_{p_2}, \ldots, x_{p_n}$ on the variables, the BLD satisfies the constraint that the sequence of variables appearing in order along any path is a subsequence of O. The size of a BLD is defined as the number of nodes that it contains.*

We define the semantics of computation in a BLD by associating a node function g_v with each node v: if v is a sink, g_v is a constant function as given by its label; if v is a non-sink, labeled with a 2×2 matrix T_v and a variable x_{p_k} for some k, $1 \leq k \leq n$, g_v is defined on the variable set $\{x_{p_k}, x_{p_{k+1}}, \ldots, x_{p_n}\}$ in terms of its 0-child u, and 1-child w, by $\begin{bmatrix} (g_v)\lceil_{\overline{x_{p_k}}} \\ (g_v)\lceil_{x_{p_k}} \end{bmatrix} = T_v \begin{bmatrix} g_u \\ g_w \end{bmatrix}$. The function computed by the BLD is the node function associated with the source.

Note that unlike many of the ordered representations that have canonical representations of functions, it is possible to have different BLDs computing the same function. They are purely an abstraction of a large class of representations, used for proving lower bounds. For each representation, the corresponding BLD has the same underlying acyclic graph, variable and sink labels. The 2×2 matrix that labels any (non-sink) node is uniquely determined by the representation that the BLD corresponds to: for a BDD, the label is an identity matrix, for a *-BMD having no edge weights, it is $\begin{bmatrix} 1 & 0 \\ 1 & 1 \end{bmatrix}$, and for an HDD, it is the matrix that is assigned by the HDD to the variable label of that node. The following example illustrates how weights can be handled.

Example 1. Consider the integer multiplication function $f(x,y)$ for a pair of two-bit numbers $x = x_1 x_0$ and $y = y_1 y_0$. Figure 1 shows both the *-BMD representation and the corresponding BLD representation of f. Using our definition, the node function at node d is y_0 and at node c is $(1 - y_1) \cdot (1 \cdot y_0 + 0 \cdot 2) + y_1 \cdot (1 \cdot y_0 + 1 \cdot 2) = y_0 + 2 \cdot y_1$.

3 The Rank Bound for BLDs

We now describe our main result for getting lower bounds on the BLD complexity of a function, that is, lower bounds on the BLD size that hold independent of the order of the variables. A slightly weaker result can be inferred from standard results on *multiplicity*

---

[2] Alternatively, we could have defined BLDs using edge variables and weights for abstracting non-deterministic ordered representations such as Parity-OBDDs. Our bounds apply to this alternate definition as well.

automata which have been previously considered in stochastic automata [10], theory of formal series [23], and learning theory [2]. Informally, a multiplicity automaton is similar to a non-deterministic automaton with weights (in some field $\mathcal{K}$) on transitions and states. It computes a function $f : \{0,1\}^* \to \mathcal{K}$ such that for each input w, $f(w)$ equals the sum over all paths conforming to w of the product of weights of the transitions and the last state along each such path. Define the *Hankel matrix F* associated with f as an infinite matrix whose rows and columns are indexed by strings in $\{0,1\}^*$. The $(x,y)^{\text{th}}$ entry of F for strings x and y is $f(x \circ y)$. It is known that the size of a minimal automaton computing f equals $\mathrm{rank}(F)$ [10,20].

Given any BLD P computing a function f that uses the order $x_{p_1}, x_{p_2}, \ldots, x_{p_n}$, we transform it to a multiplicity automaton N via the following procedure. First, by adding dummy nodes, we transform P to a BLD P' of size at most $n \cdot \mathrm{size}(P)$ in which no variable is missed along any source-sink path. Next, we view P' as a multiplicity automaton N: nodes of P' become states of N, and the source of P' becomes the start state of N. For a node v in P' with the associated matrix $\begin{bmatrix} v_{00} & v_{01} \\ v_{10} & v_{11} \end{bmatrix}$, whose 0-child and 1-child are u_0 and u_1 respectively, we define the weight of the edge (v, u_b) in N corresponding to the symbol b' to be $v_{b'b}$, where $b, b' \in \{0,1\}$. The weight of a sink is equal to its label and equals 0 for non-sink nodes. If we identify any string $b = b_1 b_2 \ldots b_n \in \{0,1\}^n$ with the input that assigns b_i to x_{p_i} for all i, then it is not too difficult to show that N also computes f. Therefore, $\mathrm{size}(P) \geq \mathrm{rank}(F)/n$.

For our purposes, we consider certain special submatrices of F. Fix a k, $0 \leq k \leq n$. Let $L = \{x_{p_1}, x_{p_1}, \ldots, x_{p_k}\}$ and R be the remaining variables. Consider the submatrix $M_f = M_{f,k}^{p_1, p_2, \ldots, p_n}$ of F whose rows and columns correspond to all the 0-1 assignments to L and R, respectively. Using a proof similar to the one that relates the size of a multiplicity automaton to the rank of the associated Hankel matrix, we can show that the rank of M_f is also a lower bound on the BLD size. A brief sketch of this proof is as follows:[3] For each input $\sigma : L \to \{0,1\}$, we can associate a unique node in the BLD that can be reached from the source by tracing the path of 0-edges and 1-edges according to σ and stopping as soon as either a sink or a node labeled with a variable of R is reached. Let V_k denote the set of nodes associated, in the manner described above, with all the 0-1 input assignments to L. A proof by induction on k shows that the subfunction $f\lceil_\sigma$, for any input $\sigma : L \to \{0,1\}$, is linearly related to the node functions associated with the nodes in V_k. Therefore, the matrix M_f can be expressed as a product $T \cdot H$, where H is a matrix of $|V_k|$ rows corresponding to all the node functions. From elementary linear algebra, $\mathrm{rank}(M_f) \leq \mathrm{rank}(H) \leq |V_k|$. automata results.

Theorem 1. *For any k, $0 \leq k \leq n$, and for any order of the variables $x_{p_1}, x_{p_2}, \ldots, x_{p_n}$, let $M_{f,k}^{p_1, p_2, \ldots, p_n}$ denote the matrix where the $(\sigma, \pi)^{\text{th}}$ entry is $f(\sigma \cdot \pi)$, for each σ and π that assign 0-1 values to $\{x_{p_1}, x_{p_2}, \ldots, x_{p_k}\}$ and $\{x_{p_{k+1}}, x_{p_{k+2}}, \ldots, x_{p_n}\}$, respectively. Then, the size of any BLD that computes f, using an arbitrary order on the variables, is at least $\min_{p_1, p_2, \ldots, p_n} \max_k \mathrm{rank}(M_{f,k}^{p_1, p_2, \ldots, p_n})$.*

---

[3] We can extend this proof to the case where the BLD is defined using edge weights and labelings. Here, the rank bound does not follow from multiplicity automata results.

Corollary 1. *The statement in Theorem 1 holds when we substitute any of the ordered representations such as BDDs, *-BMDs, and HDDs in place of BLDs.*

We will use a form of Theorem 1 that is easier to apply for proving exponential bounds on the rank. Notice that the rank of the matrix $M_f = M_{f,k}^{p_1,p_2,\dots,p_n}$ depends only on L and R and not on the order of the variables in L or R. Therefore, denote this matrix by $M_f^{L,R}$. Let $\mathcal{P} \subseteq \{(L,R) | X = L \cup R\}$ be a family of partitions of X such that for every order $x_{p_1}, x_{p_2}, \dots, x_{p_n}$ of the variables, there is at least one k such that $(\{x_{p_1}, x_{p_2}, \dots, x_{p_k}\}, \{x_{p_{k+1}}, x_{p_{k+2}}, \dots, x_{p_n}\}) \in \mathcal{P}$. It follows that the *best-partition rank*, defined as the minimum rank of $M_f^{L,R}$ over all partitions in $\mathcal{P}$, is a lower bound on the BLD size.

Example 2. Consider the multiplication function $f(x,y)$ of Example 1. Let $g(x,y)$ denote the middle (second least significant) bit of xy. Setting $L = \{x_0, x_1\}$ and $R = \{y_0, y_1\}$,

$$
M_f = \begin{array}{c} \\ \overline{x_1}\overline{x_0} \\ \overline{x_1}x_0 \\ x_1\overline{x_0} \\ x_1x_0 \end{array}
\begin{array}{c} \overline{y_1}\overline{y_0} \ \ \overline{y_1}y_0 \ \ y_1\overline{y_0} \ \ y_1y_0 \\ \left[\begin{array}{cccc} 0 & 0 & 0 & 0 \\ 0 & 1 & 2 & 3 \\ 0 & 2 & 4 & 6 \\ 0 & 3 & 6 & 9 \end{array}\right] \end{array}
\qquad
M_g = \begin{array}{c} \\ \overline{x_1}\overline{x_0} \\ \overline{x_1}x_0 \\ x_1\overline{x_0} \\ x_1x_0 \end{array}
\begin{array}{c} \overline{y_1}\overline{y_0} \ \ \overline{y_1}y_0 \ \ y_1\overline{y_0} \ \ y_1y_0 \\ \left[\begin{array}{cccc} 0 & 0 & 0 & 0 \\ 0 & 0 & 1 & 1 \\ 0 & 1 & 0 & 1 \\ 0 & 1 & 1 & 0 \end{array}\right] \end{array}
$$

M_f has rank 1 (over reals or rationals), and remains constant at 1 for larger input sizes. In contrast, M_g has rank 2 over $GF[2]$. We will see shortly that this rank increases exponentially for larger input sizes (for any order of the variables).

4 Integer Functions with Exponential BLD Size

We consider integer functions of the form $f(x,y,\dots)$ where $x,y,\dots$ are n-bit integers encoded in binary. Define the division function $Div(x,y)$ as $\lfloor x/y \rfloor$ and the mod function $Mod(x,y)$ as $x \bmod y$. The functions $HiMult(x,y)$ and $LoMult(x,y)$ represent the high-order word and low-order word, respectively of the product xy, that is $HiMult(x,y) = \lfloor \frac{xy}{2^n} \rfloor$ and $LoMult(x,y) = xy \bmod (2^n)$. Finally, let the square root function $Sqrt(x)$ denote $\lfloor \sqrt{x} \rfloor$ and the reciprocal function $Inv(x)$ denote $\lfloor \frac{2^{2n}}{x} \rfloor$. The following theorem shows that the BLD complexity of each of these integer functions is exponential.

Theorem 2. *Let* BLD(f) *denote the minimum size of a BLD representing f over any field that includes the integers. Then,*

$$\mathrm{BLD}(Div) \geq 2^{n/16} - 1 \qquad \mathrm{BLD}(Mod) \geq 2^{n/16} - 3 \qquad \mathrm{BLD}(HiMult) \geq 2^{n/16}$$

$$\mathrm{BLD}(LoMult) \geq 2^{n/16} - 3 \qquad \mathrm{BLD}(Sqrt) \geq 2^{\Omega(n)} \qquad \mathrm{BLD}(Inv) \geq 2^{\Omega(n)}$$

Proof. Let the variable sets $X = x_{n-1}x_{n-2}\dots x_0$, $Y = y_{n-1}y_{n-2}\dots y_0$, etc., each represent n-bit integer inputs of a function f. For all the functions that we consider, we will choose a set $Z = U \cup V \subseteq X$ of $2m$ consecutive variables, where $U = \{x_{\ell+i} \mid 2m > i \geq m\}$, and $V = \{x_{\ell+i} \mid m > i \geq 0\}$, for some ℓ, m. Choose any (L,R) in the family of partitions $\{(L,R) \mid R = X \backslash L, |L \cap Z| = |Z|/2\}$. We refer to assignments to the variables of L (respectively, R) as *row* (respectively, *column*) assignments.

Proposition 1 ([4, Lemma 3]). *There exists an index set $I \subseteq \{1,2,\ldots,m\}$, with $|I| \geq m/8$, and integers p, $\ell+m \geq p \geq \ell+\max(I)$, and q, $\ell+2m \geq q \geq \ell+m+\max(I)$ such that the two sets $A = \{x_{q-k} \mid k \in I\} \subseteq U$ and $B = \{x_{p-k} \mid k \in I\} \subseteq V$, satisfy the property that either $A \subseteq L$ and $B \subseteq R$ or $A \subseteq R$ and $B \subseteq L$.*

Thus, the words U and V can be aligned in a such a way that the variables in A and B can be "matched" (see Figure 2). Without loss of generality, assume from the proposition above that $A \subseteq L$ and $B \subseteq R$. We will restrict all the variables that are *not* in $A \cup B$ (and only those variables) to certain fixed values that depend on f. We then show that the $2^{|I|} \times 2^{|I|}$ submatrix $N_f = N_f^{A,B}$ of M_f obtained by varying the row and column assignments in all possible ways but still conforming to the above restrictions has (almost) full rank. If $m = \Omega(n)$, then N_f and consequently M_f has exponential rank.

To simplify the presentation below, let $\hat{I}$ denote $\max(I)$. Each set of boolean values b_k, $k \in I$, can be thought of as assigning values to the variables of A or B and thus can be associated with a unique row or column of N_f. We identify the set b_k, $k \in I$, with the (unique) number $\sum_{k \in I} b_k 2^{-k}$. Let $0 \leq s_1 < s_2 < \ldots < s_{2^{|I|}} < 1$ be all the numbers arising in this way. (Although these are rational, $2^{\hat{I}} s_i$ is always an integer.) Permute the rows and columns of N_f so that the ith row and and i^{th} column are associated with s_i, for $1 \leq i \leq 2^{|I|}$. Let t be the integer which corresponds to the fixed assignment of values to the variables of $X \backslash (A \cup B)$.[4] Note that the input X which corresponds to the ith row and j^{th} column is $X_{ij} = 2^q s_i + 2^p s_j + t$. Our goal is to chose t in such a way that when computing $f(X_{ij}, \ldots)$, the integers $2^q s_i$ and $2^p s_j$ will be multiplied by suitable factors so as to obtain a term which "aligns" s_i and s_j. Since these numbers affect the same bit positions, we will use the alignment to affect the value of f for the various X_{ij}'s in a way that N_f has almost full rank.

Summarizing the paradigm, for each function f we choose U and V, and apply Proposition 1 to obtain I, p, q, A, and B. We then fix the values of all the variables not in $A \cup B$ and show that the resulting submatrix N_f has almost full rank. We omit the proof for *Inv*, which appears in the full version.

(a) Div: Let $n = 2m$. Choose $U = \{x_{2m-1}, \ldots, x_m\}$, and $V = \{x_{m-1}, \ldots, x_0\}$ and apply Proposition 1 to obtain I, p, q, A, and B. Set each of the variables in $X \backslash (A \cup B)$ to 0 so that $X_{ij} = 2^q s_i + 2^p s_j$. Fix Y to be the integer $2^{q-\hat{I}} + 2^{p-\hat{I}}$ by setting both $y_{p-\hat{I}}$ and $y_{q-\hat{I}}$ to 1 and each remaining variable in Y to 0.

Observe that for all i, j, $X_{ij} = (2^{\hat{I}} s_i) Y + 2^p(s_j - s_i)$. Since $|2^p(s_j - s_i)| < 2^p < Y$, it follows that (1) $Div(X_{ii}, Y) = 2^{\hat{I}} s_i$ and (2) for all $j < i$, $Div(X_{ij}, Y) = 2^{\hat{I}} s_i - 1$. Thus, from elementary linear algebra, $\operatorname{rank}(N_{Div}) \geq 2^{|I|} - 1 \geq 2^{n/16} - 1$.

(b) Mod: For the same parameters considered in part (a), note that $N_{Mod} = M - Y \cdot N_{Div}$, where the $(i,j)^{\text{th}}$ entry of M is $2^q s_i + 2^p s_j (= X_{ij})$. It can be verified that M has rank 2, implying that $\operatorname{rank}(N_{Mod}) \geq \operatorname{rank}(N_{Div}) - \operatorname{rank}(M) \geq 2^{n/16} - 3$.

(c) HiMult: Let $n = 2m$. Choose $U = \{x_{2m-1}, \ldots, x_m\}$, $V = \{x_{m-1}, \ldots, x_0\}$ and apply Proposition 1 to obtain I, p, q, A, and B. For each $k \in I' = \{1, 2, \ldots, \hat{I}\} \backslash I$, we set the

---

[4] In other words, if each $x_j \in X \backslash (A \cup B)$ is set to $c_j \in \{0,1\}$, then $\sum_{x_j \in X \backslash (A \cup B)} c_j 2^j = t$.

variable $x_{q-k} \in X \setminus (A \cup B)$ to 1, and all the remaining variables in $X \setminus (A \cup B)$ to 0; these variables form the integer $2^q r$, where $r = \sum_{k \in I'} 2^{-k}$. Therefore, $X_{ij} = 2^q(s_i + r) + 2^p s_j$. We also set both y_{2m-q} and y_{2m-p} to 1 and the remaining variables in Y to 0 so that the input Y corresponds to the integer $2^{2m-q} + 2^{2m-p}$. Now,

$$HiMult(X_{ij}, Y) = \left\lfloor \frac{X_{ij} \cdot Y}{2^{2m}} \right\rfloor = \left\lfloor \frac{(2^q(s_i + r) + 2^p s_j 2^{2m-p+q}) \cdot (2^{2m-q} + 2^{2m-p})}{2^{2m}} \right\rfloor$$

$$= 2^{q-p}(s_i + r) + \lfloor (s_i + s_j + r) + 2^{p-q} s_j \rfloor \quad (1)$$

Because $s_i + s_j + r = a_{ij} 2^{-\hat{I}}$, for some *integer* a_{ij}, and $2^{p-q} s_j < 2^{-\hat{I}}$, the expression in Line 1 simplifies to $2^{q-p}(s_i + r) + \lfloor s_i + s_j + r \rfloor$.

Suppose $s_i = \sum_{k \in I} b_k 2^{-k}$, for some $b_k, k \in I$. If $i^* = 2^{|I|} - i + 1$, then $s_{i^*} = \sum_{k \in I} \overline{b_k} 2^{-k}$, that is, s_{i^*} is the one's complement of s_i with respect to the bit positions in I. Therefore, $s_i + s_{i^*} = \sum_{k \in I} 2^{-k}$, implying that $s_i + s_{i^*} + r = \sum_{i=1}^{\hat{I}} 2^{-i} = 1 - 2^{-\hat{I}}$.

We have the following two cases. When $j \leq i^*$, $\lfloor s_i + s_j + r \rfloor \leq \lfloor s_i + s_{i^*} + r \rfloor = 0$. Thus, $HiMult(X_{ij}, Y) = 2^{q-p}(s_i + r)$. On the other hand, $s_i + s_{i^*+1} + r \geq s_i + s_{i^*} + 2^{-\hat{I}} + r = 1$, so $\lfloor s_i + s_{i^*+1} + r \rfloor \geq 1$. Therefore, $HiMult(X_{i^*+1,j}, Y) \geq 2^{q-p}(s_i + r) + 1$. It follows that $rank(N_{HiMult}) \geq 2^{|I|} - 1 \geq 2^{n/16} - 1$.

(d) LoMult: With the same parameters as in part (c), $N_{LoMult} = M - 2^m N_{HiMult}$, where the $(i, j)^{th}$ entry of M is $X_{ij} \cdot Y = (2^{2m-q} + 2^{2m-p}) X_{ij}$. Therefore,

$$rank(N_{LoMult}) \geq rank(N_{HiMult}) - rank(M) \geq rank(N_{HiMult}) - 2 \geq 2^{n/16} - 3.$$

(e) Sqrt: Let $n = 10m$, $U = \{x_{5m-1}, x_{5m-2}, \ldots, x_{4m}\}$, $V = \{x_{4m-1}, x_{4m-2}, \ldots, x_{3m}\}$, for large enough m, and apply Proposition 1 to obtain I, p, q, A, and B. Fix each of the variables $x_{2q-2\hat{I}-2}, x_{2p-2\hat{I}-2}, x_{p+q-2\hat{I}-1}$ to 1 (which are in $X \setminus (A \cup B)$ because $2p - 2\hat{I} - 2 > 5m$) and all the remaining variables in $X \setminus (A \cup B)$ to 0. Therefore, $X_{ij} = r^2 + 2^q s_i + 2^p s_j$, where $r = 2^{q-\hat{I}-1} + 2^{p-\hat{I}-1}$.

We claim that for $i \geq 2$, (a) $X_{ii} < (r + 2^{\hat{I}} s_i)^2 < X_{i,i+1}$ and (b) for all $j \leq i$, $X_{ij} \geq (r + 2^{\hat{I}} s_i - 1)^2$, which would imply the desired inequality, $rank(N_{Sqrt}) \geq 2^{|I|} - 2 = 2^{\Omega(n)}$. Observe that $(r + 2^{\hat{I}} s_i)^2 = r^2 + 2^q s_i + 2^p s_i + (2^{\hat{I}} s_i)^2$. Since $3\hat{I} \leq 3m \leq p$, it follows that $(2^{\hat{I}} s_i)^2 < 2^{2\hat{I}} \leq 2^{p-\hat{I}} \leq 2^p(s_{i+1} - s_i)$, proving part(a) of the claim. Since $p \geq 3\hat{I}$ and $q - p \geq \hat{I}$, part(b) of the claim follows by verifying for each j that

$$(r + 2^{\hat{I}} s_i - 1)^2 = r^2 + 2^q s_i - (2^{q-\hat{I}} - 2^p s_i) - (2^{p-\hat{I}} - (2^{\hat{I}} s_i - 1)^2) \leq r^2 + 2^q s_i \leq X_{ij}.$$

5 Boolean Functions with Exponential BLD Size

For a fixed partition of X into L and R, the matrix $M_f^{L,R}$ has been used to study communication complexity of f ([33]). Among the approaches that give lower bounds on this measure are (i) constructing large *boolean fooling sets* and (ii) computing the rank of $M_f^{L,R}$ [30]. A fooling set consists of pairs of input assignments to L and R such that for any two distinct pairs (σ, π) and (σ', π'), $f(\sigma \cdot \pi) = f(\sigma' \cdot \pi')$, but $f(\sigma \cdot \pi') \neq f(\sigma' \cdot \pi)$. The following proposition [18], which extends to unequal-sized partitions, shows that exponentially large fooling sets imply exponential rank.

Proposition 2 ([18]). *For any boolean function f, and any equipartition of its variable set into L and R, let $M_f^{L,R}$ be the associated matrix of f with respect to this partition. Let $r = \operatorname{rank}(M_f^{L,R})$ over any field. If s is the size of a fooling set, then $r \geq \sqrt{s} - 1$.*

For the best-partition rank, the more relevant measure is the best-partition communication complexity [31] in which one computes the communication complexity for the best choice of a partition into L and R in some appropriate family of partitions. By Proposition 2 and the discussion following the statement of Theorem 1, any function for which lower bounds on the best-partition communication complexity have been proved either by constructing exponential size fooling sets or by proving exponential rank bounds for all partitions imply exponential bounds on the BLD complexity. Examples of such functions are in [28], [31], [4], [27] and [22], of which we list some below.

Corollary 2. *The following predicates require BLDs of exponential size:*

PATTERN MATCHING: *Verify if the binary pattern string of αn bits occurs in the binary text string of $(1 - \alpha)n$ bits, where $0 < \alpha < 1$.*

FACTOR VERIFICATION: *Verify if two n-bit numbers multiply to a 2n-bit number.*

MIDDLE BIT OF PRODUCT: *Does the middle bit of the product of two n bit numbers equal 1?*

SELECTION/EQUALITY TESTING: *For two n bit numbers, x and y such that x has $n/2$ bits set to 1, check if the $n/2$-bit number obtained by selecting the bits in y at positions corresponding to 1s in x equals the remaining $n/2$-bit number in y.*

SHIFTED EQUALITY: *Given two input strings and a number i, does the first string equal the second shifted circularly to the right i times? (Lam and Ruzzo [26] generalized this to show that any function f that has a large fooling set under some fixed partition has a shifting version that has large fooling sets under all partitions. However, these shifted versions may not be natural.)*

GRAPH PROPERTIES: *Verifying any of the following predicates on undirected graphs: Connectivity, Bipartiteness, and s-t-Connectivity.*

6 *-BMDs and Regular Languages

We saw earlier that the rank approach is useful for proving bounds that apply uniformly to all the ordered representations. A related and important problem is to contrast specific representations in order to understand what representations are best suited for a class of functions or languages. For *regular* languages, we know that BDDs can represent any regular language in *linear* size by keeping track of the state in the automaton that represents it. The following theorem shows that there is a simple regular language that has exponential complexity in the *-BMD representation. The proof is omitted and appears in the full paper.

Theorem 3. *For $i = 0, 2, 3, 4$, let $A_i = \{w \in \{0,1\}^7 : w$ has i 1s $\}$. Any *-BMD representing the regular language $S = A_0^* A_3 (A_0 \cup A_2)^* \cup A_0^* A_4 A_0^*$ requires size $2^{\Omega(n)}$.*

241

7 Conclusions

We have shown that a variety of integer functions such as integer division, remainder, high/low-order words of multiplication, square root, and reciprocal require exponential-sized BLDs. We then showed similar results for a variety of boolean functions by relating its complexity to two measures, the fooling set size and the rank. The generality in the BLD definition implies that minor variations in the known ordered representations will not be sufficient and we may have to consider non-linear definitions to be able to handle the hard functions. Another approach is to consider read-once representations that relax the notion of an implicit order on the variables, e.g. Free Binary Decision Diagrams [21] and their generalizations similar to BLDs.

References

1. B. Becker, R. Drechsler, and R. Enders. On the computational power of bit-level and word-level decision diagrams. In *4. GI/ITG/GME Workshop zur Methoden des Entwurfs und der Verifikation Digitaler Systeme*, Berichte aus der Informatik, pages 71–80, Kreischa, March 1996. Shaker Verlag, Aachen.
2. Amos Beimel, Francesco Bergadano, Nader H. Bshouty, Eyal Kushilevitz, and Stefano Varricchio. On the applications of multiplicity automata in learning. In *37th Annual Symposium on Foundations of Computer Science*, Burlington, Vermont, 14–16 October 1996. IEEE.
3. R. E. Bryant. Graph-based algorithms for boolean function manipulation. *IEEE Transactions on Computers*, C-35(8):677–691, August 1986.
4. R. E. Bryant. On the complexity of VLSI implementations and graph representations of boolean functions with application to integer multiplication. *IEEE Transactions on Computers*, 40(2):205–213, February 1991.
5. R. E. Bryant. Binary decision diagrams and beyond: Enabling technologies for formal verification. In *International Conference on Computer Aided Design*, pages 236–245, Los Alamitos, Ca., USA, November 1995. IEEE Computer Society Press.
6. R.E. Bryant and Y.-A. Chen. Verification of arithmetic circuits with binary moment diagrams. In *32nd ACM/IEEE Design Automation Conference*, Pittsburgh, June 1995.
7. R.E. Bryant and Y.-A. Chen. Bit-level analysis of an SRT divider circuit. In *33rd ACM/IEEE Design Automation Conference*, 1996.
8. J.R. Burch, E.M. Clarke, D.E. Long, K.L. MacMillan, and D.L. Dill. Symbolic model checking for sequential circuit verification. *IEEE Transactions on Computer-Aided Design of Integrated Circuits and Systems*, 13(4):401–424, April 1994.
9. J.R. Burch, E.M. Clarke, K.L. McMillan, D.L. Dill, and L.J. Hwang. Symbolic model checking: 10^{20} states and beyond. In *Proceedings of the Fifth Annual IEEE Symposium on Logic in Computer Science*, pages 1–33, Washington, D.C., June 1990. IEEE CS Press.
10. J. W. Carlyle and A. Paz. Realizations by stochastic finite automata. *Journal of Computer and System Sciences*, 5(1):26–40, February 1971.
11. Y.-A. Chen, E. Clarke, P. H. Ho, Y. Hoskote, T. Kam, M. Khaira, J. O'Leary, and X. Zhao. Verification of all circuits in a foating-pont unit using word-level model checking. In *First International Conference on Formal Methods in Computer-Aided Design*, volume 1166 of *Lecture Notes Comp. Sci.*, pages 19–33, Palo Alto, CA, November 1996. Springer Verlag.
12. Ying-An Chen and R.E. Bryant. *PHDD: an efficient graph representation for floating point circuit verification. In *International Conference on Computer Aided Design*, pages 2–7, Los Alamitos, Ca., USA, November 1997. IEEE Computer Society Press.

13. E. Clarke, K.L. McMillian, X. Zhao, M. Fujita, and J.C.-Y. Yang. Spectral transforms for large boolean functions with application to technologie mapping. In *30th ACM/IEEE Design Automation Conference*, pages 54–60, Dallas, TX, June 1993.

14. E. M. Clarke and E. A. Emerson. Synthesis of synchronization skeletons from branching time temporal logic. *Lecture Notes Comp. Sci.*, 131:52–71, 1982.

15. E. M. Clarke, M. Fujita, and X. Zhao. Hybrid decision diagrams — overcoming limitations of MTBDDs and BMDs. In *International Conference on Computer Aided Design*, pages 159–163, Los Alamitos, CA, November 1995. IEEE Computer Society Press.

16. E. M. Clarke, S. M. German, and X. Zhao. Verifying the SRT division algorithm using theorem proving techniques. *Lecture Notes in Computer Science*, 1102, 1996.

17. Edmund M. Clarke and Jeanette M. Wing. Formal methods: State of the art and future directions. *ACM Computing Surveys*, 28(4):626–643, December 1996.

18. M. Dietzfelbinger, J. Hromkovic, and G. Schnitger. A comparison of two lower bound methods for communication complexity. In *Symposium on Mathematical Foundations of Computer Science*, pages 326–335, 1994.

19. R. Enders. Note on the complexity of binary moment diagram representations. In *IFIP WG 10.5 Workshop on Applications of Reed-Muller Expansion in Circuit Design*, pages 191–197, 1995.

20. M. Fliess. Matrices de Hankel. *J. Math. Pures et Appl.*, 53:197–224, 1974.

21. J. Gergov and Ch. Meinel. Efficient boolean manipulation with OBDD's can be extended to read-once only branching programs. *IEEE Transactions on Computers*, 43(10):1197–1209, October 1994.

22. András Hajnal, Wolfgang Maass, and György Turán. On the communication complexity of graph properties. In *Proceedings of the Twentieth Annual ACM Symposium on Theory of Computing*, pages 186–191, Chicago, Illinois, 2–4 May 1988.

23. Harju and Karhumaki. The equivalence problem of multitape finite automata. *Theoretical Computer Science*, 78, 1991.

24. Eyal Kushilevitz and Noam Nisan. *Communication complexity*. Cambridge University Press, Cambridge [England] ; New York, 1997.

25. Y.-T. Lai and S. Sastry. Edge-valued binary decision diagrams for multi-level hierarchical verification. In *29th ACM/IEEE Design Automation Conference*, pages 608–613, 1992.

26. Tak Wah Lam and Larry Ruzzo. Results on communication complexity classes. *Journal of Computer and System Sciences*, 44, 1992.

27. Thomas Lengauer. VLSI theory. In *Handbook of Theoretical Computer Science*, volume 1. The MIT Press/Elsevier, 1990.

28. Richard J. Lipton and Robert Sedgewick. Lower bounds for VLSI. In *Conference Proceedings of the Thirteenth Annual ACM Symposium on Theory of Computation*, pages 300–307, Milwaukee, Wisconsin, 11–13 May 1981.

29. K.L. McMillan. *Symbolic Model Checking*. Kluwer Academic Publishers, 1993.

30. Kurt Mehlhorn and Erik M. Schmidt. Las Vegas is better than determinism in VLSI and distributed computing (extended abstract). In *Proceedings of the Fourteenth Annual ACM Symposium on Theory of Computing*, pages 330–337, San Francisco, California, May 1982.

31. C. Papadimitriou and M. Sipser. Communication complexity. *Journal of Computer and System Sciences*, 28, 1984.

32. Stephen Ponzio. A lower bound for integer multiplication with read-once branching programs. In *Proceedings of the Twenty-Seventh Annual ACM Symposium on Theory of Computing*, pages 130–139, Las Vegas, Nevada, 29 May–1 June 1995.

33. Andrew Chi-Chih Yao. Some complexity questions related to distributive computing (preliminary report). In *Conference Record of the Eleventh Annual ACM Symposium on Theory of Computing*, pages 209–213, Atlanta, Georgia, 30 April–2 May 1979.

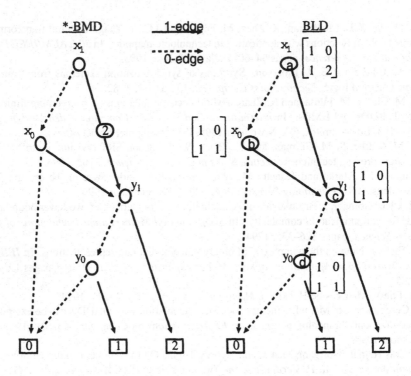

Fig. 1. *The *-BMD (left) and BLD(right) for multiplication using the order x_1, x_0, y_1, y_0.*

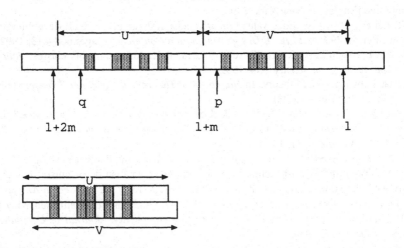

Fig. 2. *This figure illustrates Proposition 1. The sets $A \subseteq U$ and $B \subseteq V$ (shown shaded in the figure) can be matched by suitably aligning the words U and V.*

BDD Based Procedures for a Theory of Equality with Uninterpreted Functions

Anuj Goel[1], Khurram Sajid[2], Hai Zhou[1], Adnan Aziz[1], and Vigyan Singhal[3]

[1] The University of Texas at Austin
[2] Intel Corporation
[3] Cadence Berkeley Labs

Abstract. The logic of equality with uninterpreted functions has been proposed for verifying abstract hardware designs. The ability to perform fast satisfiability checking over this logic is imperative for this verification paradigm to be successful. We present symbolic methods for satisfiability checking for this logic. The first procedure is based on restricting analysis to finite instantiations of the design. The second procedure directly reasons about equality by introducing Boolean-valued indicator variables for equality. Theoretical and experimental evidence shows the superiority of the second approach.

1 Verifying High-Level Designs Using the Theory of Equality

A common problem with automatic formal verification is that the computational resources required for verification increase rapidly with the size of the design. State-of-the art tools for verification of gate-level designs are not capable of routinely verifying designs possessing more than a hundred to two hundred binary-valued latches.

This observation motivates the development of tools which can operate on designs at a higher level of abstraction. Loosely speaking, the basic premise is that abstract designs, being less specified, are simpler and consequently easier to verify. Another benefit of this approach is that bugs are caught at earlier stages of the design process.

We are interested in the verification of designs at the high-level. This necessitates reasoning about designs where a lot of complexity has been abstracted away. The use of uninterpreted functions (UIFs) has been proposed as a powerful abstraction mechanism for hardware verification [10, 14]. Essentially, UIFs allow the verification tool to avoid getting bogged down by complex details which are irrelevant to the property being proved. In our work, we will use abstractions where datapath is abstracted away by using unbounded integers, complex combinational functions such as multipliers can be abstracted as uninterpreted functions, complex bypass circuitry required in pipeline designs can be captured by the compare operator, and propositional logic can be used to derive control signals. Moreover, memories can also be incorporated in this framework as partially interpreted functions by adding constraints which relate reads and writes [13].

In this context, the primary verification problem we solve is design equivalence; this includes such applications as verifying equivalence of pipelined and nonpipelined processors. This can be posed as a problem in satisfiability checking for quantifier-free formulas involving both equality and UIFs. As shown by Ackermann [1], this problem can be reduced to satisfiability checking of quantifier-free formulas involving only equality through a suitable generalization of the following: given a formula ϕ containing terms $f(x_1)$ and $f(x_2)$, replace $f(x_1)$ and $f(x_2)$ and by fresh variables y_1 and y_2 to obtain a formula ψ; then ϕ is satisfiable iff $(x_1 = x_2 \rightarrow y_1 = y_2) \wedge \psi$ is satisfiable. The additional complexity of validity checking for the theory of equality over propositional logic arises from the fact that the properties of equality need to be taken into account. For example, the formula $(x_1 = x_2) \wedge (x_2 = x_3) \wedge \neg(x_1 = x_3)$ is not satisfiable, since it violates the transitivity of equality.

A number of decision procedures exist for the theory of equality with UIFs and its extensions. Pioneering work was done by Shostak [13], who considered linear arithmetic in conjunction with UIFs. His procedure replaces terms generated from UIFs by new variables as previously described; the formula is then converted to a conjunctive normal form, and each conjunct is checked for satisfiability using Integer Linear Programming. In this way, formula satisfiability (and, by duality, validity) can be checked.

Extensions to the basic algorithm of Shostak have been made in many recent papers on processor verification [3, 10, 2]. Essentially, their approach is a variant of the Davis-Putnam procedure for validity checking over propositional logic, with suitable extensions for handling the properties of equality. One source of their efficiency is the ability to split on subformulas; they also use heuristic rewrite rules for formula simplification. Their target application was the verification of pipelined processors. Their notion of correctness is based on the equivalence of the machine state of the nonpipelined machine after processing an instruction and the state resulting in the pipelined machine after executing the same instruction and flushing it out. (This is the standard "commutative diagram" approach to verification [3].) Equivalence is formulated as in terms of the validity of a quantifier free formula involving both equality and UIFs.

One difference of our work with the work of [2] is that while they use formulas to encode the designs, we use BDDs which also incorporate the constraints that are required of the UIFs. If these BDDs can be built and manipulated, the validity checking problem is considerably simplified, and should work more robustly than a rewrite-based approach. However, a naive method for building these BDDs does not work; BDDs become too big. We present a novel encoding technique so that the validity checking problem can be efficiently represented using BDDs.

Hojati et al [8, 9] use finite instantiations to handle UIFs (we also discuss a finite instantiation based method in Section 3.1). In [8], they require an explicit invocation of Shostak's method to decide equality between two terms containing UIFs; it is not described if Shostak's algorithm is used directly or another approach is used. Their results were negative from a computational point of view, and they conjectured this was because of the absence of a good variable ordering; our experiments corroborate this. We have developed a new approach for encoding the UIF verification problem with BDDs which results in significantly improved runtime, and enjoys nice theoretical properties — this is the approach presented in this paper (Section 3.2). In our preferred method, constraints due to UIFs (based on Ackermann's reduction) are directly represented by BDDs. We provide experimental evidence that this method performs much better than a finite instantiation based method.

1.1 Symbolic Procedures for the Theory of Equality

We motivate the use of symbolic procedures for the theory of equality by drawing analogies to the problem of verifying the equivalence of gate-level combinational netlists. One approach to the equivalence problem is to form a single "product netlist" wherein corresponding inputs are tied together, and corresponding outputs are XOR-ed. Inequivalence can then be checked by forming a large conjunction of propositional formulas corresponding to the "characteristic functions" of the gates, and a formula asserting that a pair of outputs differ; the designs differ iff the conjunction is satisfiable.

Today, state-of-the-art tools for Boolean verification use BDDs and heavily exploit the structure of the design; the original tools were based on case splitting (e.g., ATPG-based methods) [11]. Currently, all approaches for verification in the theory of equality with UIFs proceed by case splitting on terms occurring in the formula; heuristic rewriting of subformulas is also performed. Based on experiences with analogous approaches for Boolean verification, we predict that these techniques may not be viable as the examples get larger or more complex, especially when the examples are not hand designs but are outputs of automatic CAD tools, e.g., high-level synthesis tools.

2 Definitions

Designs will be specified as *netlists*. Before entering into a formal discussion of syntax and semantics for designs, we provide some illustrative examples. The design of Figure 1(a) takes 4 integer-valued inputs — x_1, x_2, x_3, x_4. The signal t_1 is Boolean-valued, and takes the value 1 exactly when x_1 and x_2 are equal. Intuitively, the structure labeled with "=" returns 1 when its inputs are equal, and 0 otherwise. The signal u_1 is integer-valued; it is equal to x_1 when t_1 is 1, and x_2 when t_1 is 0. The structure labeled with MUX operates as a multiplexer. The signal t_2 is Boolean-valued; it takes the value 1 exactly when x_4 is equal to u_1.

The design of Figure 1(b) is identical to the example presented in Figure 1(a), except that the 1-input to the multiplexer has been replaced by x_2. Observe however, that the signals t_2 and s_2 take the same value for any input, since the 0-inputs to the corresponding multiplexers are the same, and the 1-input is selected exactly when $x_1 = x_2$. Figure 1(c) is a more complex design containing complex Boolean gates.

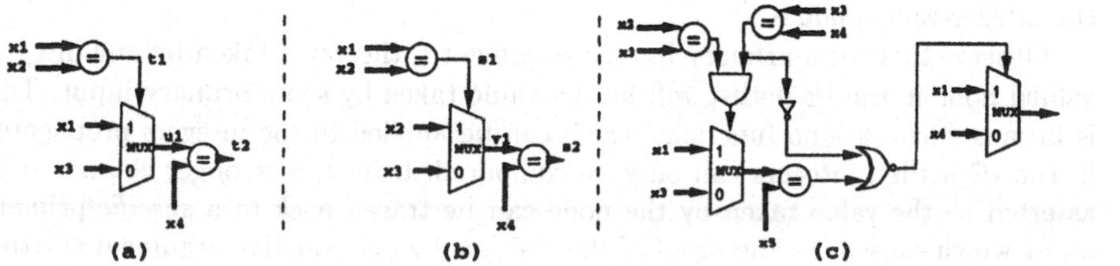

Fig. 1. Design examples.

Definition 1. An *IE netlist* is a directed acyclic graph, where the nodes correspond to *primitive circuit elements*, and the edges correspond to connections between these elements. Each node is labeled with a distinct variable w_i. The four basic primitive circuit elements are *primary inputs, multiplexers, equality checkers,* and *2-input NAND gates*. Some nodes are also labeled as being *primary outputs*. If an edge (u, v) exists in the IE netlist, u is said to be a *fanin* of v.

Nodes will be of two *types* — Boolean-valued and integer-valued. Nodes corresponding to primary inputs and multiplexers are integer typed, and nodes corresponding to equality checkers and 2-input NAND gates are Boolean. Multiplexers are required to have a single Boolean-valued input, and two integer-valued inputs; equality checkers should have two integer-valued inputs. A 2-input NAND gate has two Boolean-valued inputs.

Note that the restriction to 2-input NAND gates is not serious, since they are functionally complete. Constant-valued nodes and Boolean-valued inputs can also be handled in the framework presented above. The technical issues they bring up are minor, but impinge on the clarity of presentation; for simplicity we ignore them.

For an IE netlist, given an *input* (i.e., a function mapping primary input nodes to integer values), one can uniquely compute the values of each node in the IE netlist by evaluating the functions at gates in topological order, starting at the primary inputs. More precisely, let ι be an input; then ι uniquely defines a value $\nu_\iota(s)$ to the signal s in the IE netlist through the following recursive rules:

Definition 2. IE Netlist Semantics

1. If s is a primary input then $\nu_\iota(s) = \iota(s)$.
2. If s is the output of an equality node with fanins $\langle v, w \rangle$ then $\nu_\iota(s) = 1$ if $\nu_\iota(v) = \nu_\iota(u)$, and 0 otherwise.
3. If s is the output of a multiplexer node with fanins $\langle c, v, w \rangle$ then $\nu_\iota(s) = \nu_\iota(v)$ if $\nu_\iota(c) = 1$, and $\nu_\iota(w)$ otherwise.
4. If s is the output of a 2-input NAND with fanins $\langle v, w \rangle$ then $\nu_\iota(s) = 1$ if $\nu_\iota(v) = 0$ or $\nu_\iota(u) = 0$, and 0 otherwise.

In this way, a IE netlist D on inputs $a_1, a_2, \ldots, a_n$ and outputs $b_1, b_2, \ldots, b_m$ *defines* a function $f_D : \omega^n \to \omega^m$ (here $\omega = \{0, 1, 2, \ldots\}$ is the set of natural numbers). Intuitively, two designs are functionally equivalent if in any environment they can be used interchangeably; a necessary and sufficient condition for this is for them to have identical defined functions. Note that an IE netlist can operate on arbitrary inputs and not just integers, since no operation other than equality is applied to the integer-valued nodes.

Observe that for a primary input assignment ι, the value taken by any integer-valued node in the IE netlist will be the value taken by some primary input. This is because there are no functions which can be applied to the integers propagated in the IE netlist; integers can only be compared. Indeed, a stronger claim can be asserted — the value taken by the node can be traced back to a *specific* primary input which caused it. The proof of the claim is by an inductive argument starting at the PIs, where it vacuously holds. Any other integer-valued node must be the output of a multiplexer; the result follows by applying induction to the mux inputs.

We'll define the input x_i to *flow* to s under the input assignment ι when the value taken by s under ι is traced back to x_i. For example, the input x_1 flows to

u_1 for the design in Figure 1(a) under the input $x_1 = 2, x_2 = 2, x_3 = 3, x_4 = 4$; x_2 does not flow to u_1 under this assignment, even though the value taken at u_1 is the same as that at x_2.

2.1 Relating Designs, Equality with UIFs, and IE Netlists

As stated in the introduction, we are concerned with designs which operate on unbounded integers, wherein the datapath has been abstracted away using UIFs, and equality is the only operation which is applied to integer variables; design inequivalence can then be cast as the satisfiability of a quantifier-free formula involving equality and UIFs. IE netlists can not directly represent UIFs; however, the outputs of the UIF blocks can be replaced by new primary inputs. When comparing the resulting IE netlists, these new inputs must satisfy the constraint that if the inputs to two instances of the same UIF are equal, then the outputs of the two instances are equal; this constraint can be added to the IE circuit using simple circuitry (an equality checker and a gate). As is the case for Shostak's procedure [13], the soundness and completeness of this construction follows from [1].

3 IE Netlist Satisfiability Checking

IE Netlist Satisfiability Checking consists of taking an IE-netlist and determining if an input assignment exists for which a specified Boolean-valued output can take the value 1.

Note that the usual "product construction" for checking the equivalence of gate-level netlists can be applied to the problem of equivalence checking for IE netlists; this is illustrated in Figure 2. Observe that the construction results in exactly one Boolean-valued primary output, and so the equivalence problem for IE netlists can be easily reduced to the IE netlist satisfiability checking.

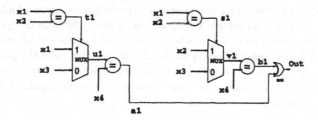

Fig. 2. Product construction for equivalence checking.

It is natural to ask at this point if there is a decision procedure for IE netlist satisfiability checking, and if so, what the computational complexity of the problem is.

3.1 Finite Model Approach

The existence of a decision procedure follows immediately from the fact that a "finite model" folk-theorem holds for holds for the existential fragment of the theory of equality: an existential formula in the language of equality is satisfiable iff it is satisfiable in some model whose universe has cardinality equal to the number of variables occurring in the formula.

Reduction to Combinational Satisfiability The problem of determining if there is an input to an IE netlist which sets a designated Boolean-valued output to 1 can be reduced to checking the satisfiability of an existential sentence in the first order logic of pure equality; the encoding is very similar to that used to convert the procedure for reducing Boolean-valued netlist satisfiability to satisfiability of a CNF formula from propositional logic. Hence the integer valued variables can be replaced by n-valued variables, which in turn can be encoded in $\lceil \log(n) \rceil$ Boolean-valued variables. Thus the satisfiability problem can be efficiently (polytime) transformed to a problem of checking the satisfiability of Boolean-valued netlists.

3.2 A Better Encoding

In this section we develop a superior encoding of IE netlist satisfiability instances into Boolean netlist satisfiability. We introduce a minimal set of Boolean variables — one for each distinct comparison which is made between primary inputs. We will show that the design functionality can be characterized by Boolean-valued functions of these Boolean variables.

Specifically, for an IE netlist D on inputs $x_1, \ldots, x_n$ introduce Boolean variables e_{ij} for $1 \leq i < j \leq n$. For a Boolean-valued node s in D, we will construct a Boolean function f^s over the set of variables $\{e_{12}, e_{13}, \ldots, e_{23}, e_{24}, \ldots, e_{1(n-1)}, e_{(n-1)n}\}$; for an integer-valued node t, we will construct a vector of n Boolean-valued functions $[f_1^t\, f_2^t \, \ldots \, f_n^t]$ over the same set of variables.

Intuitively, the variables e_{ij}'s indicate whether the i-th and j-th integer inputs are equal or not. For a Boolean node, the function f at the node is a Boolean function of these indicator variables, and it represents the condition under which the circuit node evaluates to 1. For an integer node, such as a mux, the k-th component of the n-tuple function f represents the condition under which the circuit node assumes the value of the k-th integer input. Note the distinction between the primary input that flows to s under ι, and the value $\nu_\iota(s)$; for the input ι, it may be the case that $\nu_\iota(s)$ is equal to the value taken by more than one primary inputs, but there will still be a unique input x_k which flows.

Definition 3. e_{ij} **Encoded Functions**

1. If s is a primary input, say x_k, then $f_k^s = 1$ and for $j \neq k$, $f_j^s = 0$.
2. If s is a 2-input NAND gate with inputs u and v, then $f^s = (f^u \cdot f^v)'$.
3. If s is the output of a mux with control c, and data inputs u, v, then $f_k^s = f^c \cdot f_k^u + (f^c)' \cdot f_k^v$.
4. If s is the output of an equality node with inputs u, and v then

$$f^s = \sum_{i=1}^n [f_i^u \cdot f_i^v] + \sum_{i=1}^n \sum_{i \neq j} [f_i^u \cdot f_j^v \cdot e_{\min(i,j)\,\max(i,j)}]$$

Example: Consider the IE netlist shown in Figure 2. The functions at the nodes are as follows:

$$\langle f_1^{x_1}, f_2^{x_1}, f_3^{x_1}, f_4^{x_1} \rangle = \langle 1,0,0,0 \rangle \qquad \langle f_1^{x_2}, f_2^{x_2}, f_3^{x_2}, f_4^{x_2} \rangle = \langle 0,1,0,0 \rangle$$

$$\langle f_1^{x_3}, f_2^{x_3}, f_3^{x_3}, f_4^{x_3} \rangle = \langle 0,0,1,0 \rangle \qquad \langle f_1^{x_4}, f_2^{x_4}, f_3^{x_4}, f_4^{x_4} \rangle = \langle 0,0,0,1 \rangle$$

$$f^{t_1} = e_{12}$$

$$\langle f_1^{u_1}, f_2^{u_1}, f_3^{u_1}, f_4^{u_1} \rangle = \langle e_{12}, 0, e_{12}', 0 \rangle \qquad \langle f_1^{v_1}, f_2^{v_1}, f_3^{v_1}, f_4^{v_1} \rangle = \langle 0, e_{12}, e_{12}', 0 \rangle$$

$$f^{a_1} = e_{12} \cdot e_{14} + e_{12}' \cdot e_{34} \qquad f^{b_1} = e_{12} \cdot e_{24} + e_{12}' \cdot e_{34}$$

$$f^{Out} = e_{12} \cdot (e_{14} \cdot e_{24}' + e_{14}' \cdot e_{24})$$

Note that f^{Out} does not depend on e_{34}.

Encoding the network using these e_{ij}'s allows us to directly store the relationship between the function nodes and the equality of pairs of inputs. For many validity checking applications, it is the equality of intermediate circuit functions which is exploited in simplifying or complicating (by pipeline bypass logic, for example, in a pipelined implementation) logic circuitry. Encoding the equality by pairwise variables allows us to represent relationship between equalities directly by having single BDD variables for each of these e_{ij} variables. Of course, as we see later in this section, to prevent false negatives, we will need to introduce procedures that ensure the transitivity of equality.

The claim that the functions defined above characterize the IE netlist is formalized by the following two lemmas:

Lemma 1 (Completeness). Let ι be an input and s a node in the design. Let ϵ be the extension of ι to the e_{ij} variables, i.e., $\epsilon(e_{ij}) = 1$ exactly when $\iota(x_i) = \iota(x_j)$. Then if s is Boolean-valued, $f^s(\epsilon) = \nu^\iota(s)$; if s is integer-valued, then $f_k^s(\epsilon) = 1$ exactly when x_k flows to s under ι.

The proof follows by an easy induction on the depth of the node from the primary inputs.

The functions computed above are not "sound"; values taken by them may not be achievable in the design. This is because the there is no guarantee that the basic axioms of equality are satisfied; Figure 2 provides an example. As shown previously, the output of the product network is assigned the function $e_{12} \cdot (e_{14} \cdot e_{24}' + e_{14}' \cdot e_{24})$. However, closer inspection shows that it is not possible to find an input ι so that the ϵ extension results in ι e_{12} and e_{14} to be 1 and e_{24} to be 0 or e_{12} and e_{24} to be 1 and e_{14} to be 0 simultaneously; the transitivity of equality would be violated.

Definition 4. An assignment ϵ to the e_{ij} variables is said to be *consistent* if it satisfies $\bigwedge_{1 \le i < j < k \le n} [\epsilon(e_{ij}) \cdot \epsilon(e_{jk}) \rightarrow \epsilon(e_{ik})]$.

Intuitively, a consistent assignment is one which satisfies the transitivity of equality; for consistent assignments, the converse of Lemma 1 holds:

Lemma 2 (Soundness). Let ϵ be a consistent assignment to the e_{ij} variables. Let s be a node in the design. If s is Boolean-valued, there is an input ι so that $f^s(\epsilon) = \nu^\iota(s)$; if s is integer-valued and $f_k^s(\epsilon) = 1$ then there is an input ι so that the input x_k flows to s under ι.

The proof is based on the fact that ϵ yields an equivalence relation on the primary inputs, from which the desired input can be constructed.

3.3   Satisfiability using the e_{ij} encoding

It follows from these two lemmas that the functions in Definition 3 characterize the IE netlist. In particular, they suggest the following approach to satisfiability checking for IE netlists: build BDDs for the e_{ij}-encoded Boolean functions, and then check if there is a consistent assignment under which the output BDD evaluates to 1.

Unfortunately, finding a consistent satisfying assignment for a BDD over the e_{ij} variables will not be easy. The problem we are concerned about can be formulated as follows.

BDD Satisfiability under Consistency (BDD ConSAT)
INSTANCE: A BDD on variables $e_{ij}, 1 \leq i < j \leq n$
QUESTION: Is the BDD satisfiable under some minterm ϵ satisfying the consistency requirement: $\bigwedge_{1 \leq i < j < k \leq n} [\epsilon(e_{ij}) \cdot \epsilon(e_{jk}) \rightarrow \epsilon(e_{ik})]$

Theorem 1. *BDD ConSAT is NP-Complete.*

Proof. Given an assignment for the e_{ij} variable, both the BDD and the consistency requirement can be evaluated in polynomial time. This tells us the simple fact that BDD SAT is in NP.

We now show BDD ConSAT to be NP-hard by transforming the problem of PATH WITH FORBIDDEN PAIRS [7] to it.

INSTANCE: Directed graph $G = (V, A)$, specified vertices $s, t \in V$, collection $C = \{(a_1, b_1), \ldots, (a_n, b_n)\}$ of pairs of vertices from V.
QUESTION: Is there a directed path from s to t in G that contains at most one vertex from each pair in C?

This problem remains NP-complete even under the restriction that G is acyclic with no in- and out-degree exceeding 2 and all the given pairs are disjoint. Our transformation will use a version with this restriction.

Given such an instance of PATH WITH FORBIDDEN PAIRS, we can construct an instance of BDD ConSAT as follows.

First, we will modify the instance of PATH WITH FORBIDDEN PAIRS such that each vertex appearing in the pairs has exactly one out-edge. This can be done as follows. For each vertex v, which appears in the pairs and whose out-degree is not 1, we will split it into two vertices v_1 and v_2. All in-edges now end on v_1 and all out-edges now start from v_2 and there is one edge goes from v_1 to v_2. We also substitute v by v_1 in the pairs. It is obvious that the new instance still obeys the restriction and it has a "yes" answer if and only if the original one has one.

Now we will transform the modified DAG into a BDD by labeling and adding vertices and edges. First we will add one vertex labeled $e_{n+1,n+2}$ and an out-edge labeled 0 going to s. We also label vertex t as constant 1. For each pair (a_i, b_i), we will label them as $e_{i,n+1}, e_{i,n+2}$, respectively, and their out-edges as 1. For any vertex which is still not labeled, we will label it as $e_{1,k}$, where k is an index different with any previously used one. We will also add a new vertex and label it as constant 0, and let each vertex whose out-degree is 1 have another edge entering it. The unlabeled edges will be labeled 1 or 0 arbitrarily but under the condition that the out-edges of any vertex are labeled one 1 and one 0. Because of the restriction we added on the instance of PATH WITH FORBIDDEN PAIRS, it is easy to check that what we have constructed is actually a BDD. However, it might have redundancy and can be reduced. But based on the fact that each vertex appearing in the pairs has exactly one out-edge, these vertices will not be inferenced.

Based on our construction, we can now prove that the instance of PATH WITH FORBIDDEN PAIRS has yes answer if and only if the constructed BDD is satisfiable under the consistent requirement.

($\Rightarrow$) If there is a path from s to t in G that contains at most one vertex from each pair in C, then corresponding vertices will form a path in BDD, which, when adding $e_{n+1,n+2}$ at the head, forms a path from $e_{n+1,n+2}$ to 1. This path gives an assignment which satisfies the BDD. We need only prove it obeys the consistent requirement. This is trivial because only those vertices appearing in a pair can give trouble but the path contains at most one of them.

($\Leftarrow$) If the BDD is satisfiable under the consistent requirement, then there is a path goes from $e_{n+1,n+2}$ to 1. It corresponds to a path in G from s to t. This path can only contains at most one vertex from each pair. Otherwise, the assignment will make $e_{i,n+1} = 1, e_{i,n+2} = 1$ but $e_{n+1,n+2} = 0$, which is contradictory with the fact that the assignment obeys the consistent requirement.

3.4 Heuristically finding a consistent minterm

We now develop a heuristic for solving the BDD ConSAT problem. First, observe that a cube c whose literals are drawn from the set of variables $e_{12}, e_{13}, \ldots, e_{(n-1)n}$ naturally gives rise to a partial assignment ϵ_c to the variables. For example, the cube $\kappa = e_{12} \cdot e'_{14} \cdot e_{23}$ corresponds to the partial assignment ϵ_κ where $\epsilon_\kappa(e_{12}) = 1, \epsilon_\kappa(e_{14}) = 0, \epsilon_\kappa(e_{23}) = 1$.

Lemma 3. For any cube c, if the resulting partial variable assignment ϵ_c is consistent, then there is a minterm in the cube which is consistent.

Proof. The result follows from the following construction: start with the partition of the set $\{1, 2, \ldots, n\}$ into n distinct equivalence classes; recursively merge equivalence classes to which i and j belong if $\epsilon_c(e_{ij}) = 1$. Call the resulting partition P_ϵ. Since ϵ_c is consistent, there can not be a and b so that a and b lie in the same equivalence class of P_ϵ but $\epsilon_c(e_{ab}) = 0$. Hence the minterm $\hat{\epsilon}$ given by $\hat{\epsilon}(e_{ij}) = 1$ iff i and j lie in the same equivalence class of P_ϵ is consistent; furthermore, it lies in c.

The proof is constructive, and yields an algorithm for checking cube satisfiability; efficient querying and updating of the partition can be performed by a variant of the union-find algorithm [5]. Thus, a procedure for finding a consistent minterm in a BDD is to iterate over a set of cubes (a "cover") which contains all the minterms in the BDD. Such a cover can be derived from the BDD by recursive application of the Shannon decomposition, starting from the top variable.

The iteration time is potentially exponential in the size of the BDD; the search can be made far more efficient by bounding the search. If cube c_1 contains cube c_2, and c_1 has no consistent assignments, then c_2 has no consistent assignments. When iteratively generating cubes, we prune the search by finding early contradictions; this is the source of a major speedup. This is similar to the procedure of Chan et al [4] for pruning BDDs over variables corresponding to complex arithmetical constraints. One source of relative efficiency for us is that because we are dealing purely with equality, we can incrementally check inconsistency as we explore the BDD.

Another potential way to prune the search is to identify nodes appearing in the BDD for which the corresponding subfunction rooted at that node has no satisfying assignments; we have not experimented with this.

4 Experiments

We implemented the procedure for constructing the e_{ij}-encoded functions from an IE netlist on top of VIS [6], which is a popular gate-level BDD-based verification tool. (For the finite instantiation approach, there was no code to write, since VIS has the capability of building BDDs for binary netlists.)

In order to perform a comparison of the two symbolic methods for IE netlist satisfiability checking we first created a series of examples. These correspond to verifying processors using commutative diagrams [10]. Specifically, they arise in the verification of a pipelined processor; the approach taken is that of Burch and Dill, wherein a pipelined processor is flushed after executing one instruction; the resulting state is compared with the state resulting from execution of the same instruction on a nonpipelined implementation. Our examples are derived from the comparison of the pipelined and non-pipelined version of the 3-stage pipelined ALU used in [3]; this design has uninterpreted functions which correspond to the ALU and Reads/Writes to the register file.

Constraints corresponding to the UIFs are added to the designs: for ALU, each constraint ensures that if the inputs to a pair of ALUs is the same, the outputs with be the same; for Reads/Writes, each constraint ensures that if we read a memory address that has been written to, we will read the same data was written. The five examples correspond to different number of constraints. The entire set of constraints is not necessary to show that the designs are equivalent; PIPE1, PIPE2, PIPE3 all contain enough constraints to prove equivalence. (We were able to find a minimal set of constraints by starting with no constraints, and iteratively adding constraints to eliminate false negatives.) PIPE3 has more constraints than PIPE2, which in turn has more than PIPE1; this is reflected in the increased computational effort to perform verification. The constraints used in PIPE4, PIPE5 are not enough to to prove equivalence, but they do have some superfluous constraints, resulting in higher verification times. A feel for complexity of the designs can be had from the fact that they had approximately 28 inputs, 60 equality blocks, 200 2-input NAND gates, and 40 Mux elements.

Table 1 shows the results we obtained. For both approaches, we report the computational resources expended in verification — memory in the form of peak and final BDD size, and total computation time. These experiments were performed on a Pentium-200 with 64 Mbytes running Linux. The column headed *Satisfiable* indicates whether the netlist output was satisfiable. Note that for the finite instantiation approach, the resulting BDD has only one node (the 0 node) when the output is not satisfiable; the e_{ij}-encoded function for the output is nonempty, but has no consistent minterms.

It is noteworthy that for the finite instantiation approach, the default BDD variable ordering would always result in memory overflows; dynamic variable reordering [12] had to be enabled for the process to complete. Even so, the example PIPE5.V would exhaust available memory. For the equality based approach, variables are allocated dynamically, and added to the end of the order; no variable re-ordering was needed.

We observed that the number of BDD variables needed for the e_{ij} encoded function approach was never more than twice the number of inputs and hence substantially smaller than for the finite instantiation approach, which always requires $n \cdot \lceil \log(n) \rceil$ Boolean variables (where n is the number of inputs). This is surprising, since the e_{ij} encoded approach may need as many as $n \cdot (n-1)/2$ Boolean variables. However, not all inputs are compared in the design; input comparisons are "sparse". We create variables on demand, resulting in the saving.

The running time for the e_{ij}—encoded approach includes both the time to build the functions, and to search the output BDD for a consistent minterm; the latter was very fast, taking of the order of tens of milliseconds. The results clearly are in favor of the e_{ij} encoding; hence, we propose it as the method of choice for BDD-based satisfiability checking.

The runtimes are higher than those reported in [3]; this is not surprising given the large overheads associated with initialization of the data structures we use for design representation. The results demonstrate that BDD methods are feasible, contradicting prevailing beliefs. In the next section, we point out an enhancement which we believe should make the BDD based approach highly competitive with the existing formula-based approaches.

Benchmark	Finite Instantiations			e_{ij} Encoding			Satisfiable
	Max BDD	Final BDD	Time	Max BDD	Final BDD	Time	
PIPE1.V	3,932	1	12.5	62	36	0.3	No
PIPE2.V	42,875	1	137.2	218	146	0.3	No
PIPE3.V	131,889	1	447.0	536	355	0.4	No
PIPE4.V	141,016	79,336	590.7	413	376	0.5	Yes
PIPE5.V	∞	?	∞	1523	1335	0.5	Yes

Table 1. Comparing Symbolic Procedures for Equality.

5 Conclusion

In summary, our major contribution is the extension of BDD techniques to the existential fragment of the theory of equality. On the theoretical side, we have developed semantic foundations and addressed complexity issues. Our experiments justify the use of symbolic procedures; encoding each comparison of inputs by a Boolean variable is superior to the direct mapping of inputs to an appropriately sized vector of Boolean-valued variables.

There are many ways in which this work can be extended. Perhaps the most important is the incorporation of the "miter" concept for identifying equivalent nodes; this has been extremely successful in the Boolean verification world [11], enabling the verification of million gate circuits. We are developing a specification language for designs with UIFs, a data structure for representing the same, and a set of routines for restructuring and verifying the design; this will be made available to the general public.

We are currently working on incorporating other interpreted functions and relations, such as addition and inequality; this is motivated by the observation that the abstraction of designs to UIFs with equality is too "coarse" for certain applications (e.g., replacing increment circuitry for a program counter, by a UIF may result in false negatives). It may be possible to get by with a simple approximation; for example, certain properties may depend only on the associative and commutative properties of plus.

References

1. Wilhelm Ackermann. *Solvable Cases of the Decision Problem*. Studies in Logic and the Foundations of Mathematics. North-Holland, Amsterdam, 1954.
2. C. Barrett, D. Dill, and Jeremy Levitt. Validity Checking for Combinations of Theories with Equality. In *Proc. of the Formal Methods in CAD Conf.*, November 1996.
3. J. Burch and D. Dill. Automatic Verification of Microprocessor Control. In *Proc. of the Computer Aided Verification Conf.*, July 1994.
4. W. Chan, R. Anderson, P. Deame, and D. Notkin. Combining Constraint Solving and Symbolic Model Checking for a Class of Systems with Non-linear Constraints. In *Proc. of the Computer Aided Verification Conf.*, July 1997.
5. T. H. Cormen, C. E. Leiserson, and R. H. Rivest. *Introduction to Algorithms*. MIT Press, 1989.
6. R. K. Brayton et al. VIS: A system for Verification and Synthesis. In *Proc. of the Computer Aided Verification Conf.*, July 1996.
7. M. R. Garey and D. S. Johnson. *Computers and Intractability*. W. H. Freeman and Co., 1979.
8. R. Hojati, A. Isles, D. Kirkpatrick, and R. Brayton. Verification Using Finite Instantiations and Uninterpreted Functions. In *Proc. of the Formal Methods in CAD Conf.*, November 1996.
9. R. Hojati, A. Kuchlmann, S. German, and R. Brayton. Validity Checking in the Theory of Equality Using Finite Instantiations. In *Proc. Intl. Workshop on Logic Synthesis*, May 1997.
10. Robert B. Jones, David Dill, and Jerry R. Burch. Efficient Validity Checking for Processor Validation. In *Proc. Intl. Conf. on Computer-Aided Design*, pages 2–6, 1995.
11. Andreas Kuchlmann and Florian Krohm. Equivalence Checking Using Cuts and Heaps. In *Proc. of the Design Automation Conf.*, June 1997.
12. R. Rudell. Dynamic Variable Ordering for Binary Decision Diagrams. In *Proc. Intl. Conf. on Computer-Aided Design*, pages 42–47, November 1993.
13. R. E. Shostak. A practical decision procedure for arithmetic with function symbols. *Journal of the ACM*, 26(2):351–360, 1979.
14. Mandayam Srivas and Mark Bickford. Formal verification of a pipelined microprocessor. *IEEE Software*, 7(5):52–64, September 1990.

Computing Reachable Control States of Systems Modeled with Uninterpreted Functions and Infinite Memory

Adrian J. Isles, Ramin Hojati and Robert K. Brayton
{aji, hojati, brayton}@eecs.berkeley.edu

Department of Electrical Engineering and Computer Sciences,
University of California, Berkeley, CA 94720

Abstract. We present an approach for automatically computing the set of control states reachable in systems modeled with uninterpreted functions, predicates and infinite memory. In general, the abstract state spaces of systems modeled in this fashion are infinite and exact state enumeration based procedures may not terminate. Using the Integer Combinational Sequential (ICS) concurrency model *[HB95]* as our underlying formalism, we show how 'on-the-fly' state reduction techniques, which preserve control invariance properties, can be used to significantly speed-up reachability computations on such abstract hardware representations, collapsing infinite state spaces to finite ones in some cases. The approach presented in this paper is automatic and if it terminates, will produce the exact set of reachable control states of abstract hardware models. Our techniques have been implemented in an ICS state reachability tool and experimental results are given on several examples.

1 Introduction

The use of interpreted and uninterpreted integer functions, interpreted equality, and interpreted memory operations has been shown to be very useful for abstracting away the complexity of datapath found in hardware. In general, the abstract state space of a system modeled in this fashion is infinite and exact state enumeration based procedures may not terminate. However, many important properties that one would like to verify of such systems can be expressed in terms of determining if a set of control states of the system is reachable. In some cases, the infinite state spaces of such systems can be reduced to a finite set which preserve all behaviors with respect to such properties. In this paper, we address the problem of automatically computing the set of reachable control states of systems described with abstract datapath representations utilizing state reduction techniques to reduce the number of reached states.

The Integer Combinational/Sequential (ICS) concurrency model, presented in *[HB95]*, can be used to model abstract hardware representations. Here, control is represented using finite relations and latches ranging over finite domains. Control can move data around in the datapath and can get information about their values by applying uninterpreted or interpreted predicates to them. The datapath component consists of variables and latches that are assigned (ICS) terms, which are abstract representations of integer values of unbounded width. Uninterpreted functions are provided in the datapath for performing computations. Finally, interpreted memory operations model memory with an unbounded number of locations. An ICS state consists of assignments of finite values to the finite latches, terms to the integer latches, and predicates on terms. In addition, a memory is represented as a table of address/data-value pairs, both of which are also ICS terms.

1.1 Our Approach

We show how automatic state reductions can be used during state enumeration when computing the set of reachable control states of a model. Note that the set of reachable control states is obtained by projecting the state space on to its finite latch assignments. We also propose a new state data structure, called *ICS State Pairs (ISPs)*, that can be used to efficiently compute the set of reachable control states of systems modeled with ICS. Intuitively, an ISP is a pair $(c(x), d)$ representing a set of ICS states all of which have the same terms assigned to integer latches, memory, and predicates, but different assignments to the finite state variables. $c(x)$ is an ROBDD *[Bry86]* representing a set of assignments to the finite latch variables x appearing in the model, and d a directed acyclic graph (DAG) that is a syntactical representation of terms assigned to integer latches, memory, and predicates. During state enumeration, the set of reachable states is stored as a set of ISPs. Transitions between states are performed using standard image computation for the finite part, and a special form of symbolic simulation for the integer part. State reductions *[HIB97]* are also performed during symbolic simulation to minimize the number of states that need to be explored. Using the distinction given in *[CZXLC94]*, our approach can be considered a combination of *abstract explicit* and *abstract implicit state enumeration*. It is an abstract explicit technique in the sense that we do not build formulas for alternate datapath assignments that may occur due to case splitting. Thus, an assignment of $z := mux(b, g(a,b), f(x))$ could result in two ISPs $(b = 0, z = g(a,b))$ and $(b = 1, z = f(x))$. An alternative would be to represent this behavior implicitly using a single formula, $(z = g(a,b) \wedge b = 0) \vee (z = f(x) \wedge b = 1)$, as could be done using the approach in *[CZXLC94]*. Of course, our approach is implicit in the sense that we represent the finite part using BDDs and our algorithm reduces to implicit state enumeration in the absence of datapath. By treating datapath and control separately, we can exploit well-known techniques for manipulating each. During state enumeration, the number of ISPs grows only in the number of different assignments to integer assignments that have been seen.

Our approach is automatic and if it terminates will produce the exact set of reachable control states of the system. Note that it was shown in *[HIKB67]* that, in general, computing this set is undecidable. Hence, no algorithm can guarantee that it can always compute the set of control states of every ICS model. If our procedure does not terminate, it can still be used for partial verification, by performing reachability for a finite number of steps (no false negatives are produced). In addition, not only can our approach be used as a standalone verification technique, but maybe useful in conjunction with other verification procedures that require an approximation to the set of reachable states as input, such as the ones reported in *[BD94, JDB95]*.

1.2 Previous Work

The modeling of hardware using uninterpreted functions has been a traditional approach used in the theorem proving community for abstracting away datapath found in hardware such as microprocessors *[Hunt85, SB90]*. Many of these techniques are not automatic and require a great deal of user guidance. *[BD94]* presented an automatic approach for verifying that a pipeline microprocessor, modeled with uninterpreted functions, implements its instruction set architecture (ISA). Their technique requires an approximation to the set of reachable states as input. One of the primary advantages of ICS is that this ISA verification can be performed without requiring any such state invariant from the user. However, it may be possible for our technique to be used to compute state invariants needed as input to their approach. As will be shown in Section 5, this is a computationally simpler task in our framework than performing full ISA verification. Another technique that is similar in flavor to ICS is a data structure called Multiway Decision Graphs (MDGs) *[CZXLC94]*. An MDG is a decision diagram that is similar to a BDD except that it allows for uninterpreted function symbols to be represented in the graph. Their technique is implicit, but they do not fully model interpreted equality or interpreted memory operations. The approaches in *[Cor94, LC91]* also seem similar to ours, except they represent control states explicitly. *[IHB96]* implemented an algorithm for ICS reachability as proposed in *[HB95]* and presented experimental results on verifying systems modeled using ICS. The results where poor, however, due to an explosion in the number of states on even simple designs. *[HIB97]* presented a set of state reduction techniques, some of which are used in this paper, but no algorithm was given for using them when performing reachability computations.

The flow of the rest of this paper is as follows. In Section 2, an overview of ICS is given. The reader is encouraged to read *[HB95]* for a more detailed presentation. In Section 3, we review state reduction techniques that can be used with perform state enumeration. In Section 4, we present ISPs and show how they can be used for reachability. In Section 5, experimental results are given.

2 An Overview of ICS Models

In this section, an overview of a subset of the ICS syntax and semantics is given. ICS models hardware are similar to conventional models representing hardware, with additional constructs that can be used to model non-deterministic gates, integer functions, integer predicates and infinite memory.

2.1 Syntax

The primitives consist of variables and *generalized gates* that can include tables, interpreted functions and predicates, uninterpreted functions and predicates, constant creators, latches, and memory functions.

Variables. Variables are of two types: finite and integer. Finite variables take values from some finite domain and integer variables are assigned symbolic expressions called *ICS terms*. These terms are built recursively from numerals, constants, and interpreted and uninterpreted functions. Therefore, numerals and constants are ICS terms, and if f is an n-ary function and $t_1,\ldots,t_n$ are ICS terms, then $f(t_1,\ldots,t_n)$ is also an ICS term.

Tables. A table is a relation defined over a set of finite variables, divided into inputs and outputs.

Interpreted Functions and Predicates. A predefined set of functions and relations over integers are built in. The interpreted functions are $x := y$ and $z := mux(b, x, y)$, where x, y are integer variables and b is binary. The interpreted predicates $x = y$ and $x = c$ are also allowed where c is a non-negative integer.

Uninterpreted Functions and Predicates. These are a set of function and predicate symbols where only their arities and domain variables are given. Predicates of the form $x = term$, where x is an integer variable, and $term$ is an ICS term are also allowed.

Constant Creators. A constant creator is a special element with no inputs which creates a new *fresh constant* (i.e. a function with no argument) each time called. A constant creator can be used to model unconstrained integer input.

Latches. A latch is defined on two variables over the same domain: input (or next state) and output (or present state). Latches can either be finite or integer-valued.

Memory Functions. Two functions *read* and *write* are provided with their usual interpretation; *read* is a binary function of a memory element and a location; *write* is a ternary function, whose arguments are a memory element, a location, and a value.

Definition 2.1.1 A *state* is a triple (*latches*, *memories*, *predicates*), where,
a. *latches* is a set of assignments to the latches.
b. *memories* is a set of memory elements, where a memory element is a set of pairs of ICS terms, where the first denotes a location and the second a value.
c. *predicates* is a set of atomic formulas, where an atomic formula is any interpreted or uninterpreted predicate applied to ICS terms.

Definition 2.1.2 The set *Terms(s)* of a state s denotes the set of all ICS terms, closed under subterms, assigned to the integer latches, memories and predicates of s.

Definition 2.1.3 Given two ICS terms t_1 and t_2, and two sets of atomic formulas $P = \{p_1, \ldots p_n\}$ and $Q = \{q_1, \ldots q_n\}$, t_1 is equal to t_2 subject to P and Q, iff the formula $p_1 \wedge \ldots \wedge p_n \wedge q_1 \wedge \ldots \wedge q_m \to t_1 = t_2$ is valid (i.e. true under any interpretation, given to all constants, uninterpreted function symbols, and uninterpreted predicates appearing in P, Q, t_1, and t_2). The equality of two ICS terms can be decided using the algorithm given in *[Sho79]*.

2.2 Operational Semantics

Given a state $s = (L, M, P)$, a transition to a state $s' = (L', M', P')$ of s is obtained by starting from inputs and present state latch variables and assigning a value to each variable $o = g(i_1, \ldots, i_n)$ that is consistent with its inputs $i_1, \ldots, i_n$ and generalized gate g. We denote the *partial state* $s(g)$ as the values assigned to all variables, predicates and memory before the gate g has been processed. Once all gates are processed, we assign to L' the values given to the next state latch variables of the partial state. Similarly, we give M' and P' the new assignments to M and P that are assigned in the partial state obtained at the end of the procedure. In the following, if i_k is an integer variable, then it is assigned a term t_k by $s(g)$. Otherwise, it is assigned a finite value z_k by $s(g)$.

1. If g represents a constant creator, then introduce a new fresh constant c_l and let $o = c_l$.
2. If g represents an uninterpreted function f_i, then assign o the term $f_i(t_1,...,t_n)$.
3. If g represents the function $mux(i_b, i_1, i_2)$, where i_b is a binary value, and i_1, i_2 are integer variables, assign o the term t_1 if $z_b = 0$ and t_2 if $z_b = 1$.
4. If g represents a finite relation R_g, assign o a value z_o such that $(z_1,...,z_n,z_o) \in R_g$
5. If g represents an integer predicate $p(i_1,...,i_n)$ and if $P \rightarrow p(t_1,...,t_n)$ is valid, then assign $o = 1$. If $P \rightarrow \neg p(t_1,...,t_n)$ is valid, then let $o = 0$. Otherwise, create two partial states, one with $o = 1$ and $P = P \cup \{p(t_1,...,t_n)\}$, and the other with $o = 0$ and $P = P \cup \{\neg p(t_1,...,t_n)\}$.
6. If g represents $read(M_k, i_1)$ where t_1 is a term representing an address, if there exists an address/value pair $(a, d) \in M_k$ where $P \rightarrow t_1 = a$ is valid, the assign $o = d$. Otherwise, perform all of the following, which may result in multiple partial states. 1) For each memory addresses $(a_l, d_l) \in M_k$ where $P \rightarrow t_1 = a_l$ is satisfiable, create a new partial state with $P = P \cup \{(t_1 = a_l)\}$ and $o = d_l$. 2) Create a new partial state with $P = P \cup \{(t_1 \neq a_l)\}$ for each $(a_l, d_l) \in M_k$, where $P \rightarrow t_1 \neq a_l$ is satisfiable. Introduce a new fresh constant d' and let $M_k = M_k \cup \{(t_1, d')\}$ and $o = d'$. Case (1) corresponds to reading an address that has previously been written. Case (2) corresponds to reading a memory location that has never been written to before, in which case, a new constant d' is returned.
7. If g represents $write(M_k, i_1, i_2)$, then proceed similarly to a read.

Note that case splitting can result in (4), (5), (6), and (7). However, the resulting state graph is finite branching, i.e. for every state, there are a finite number of successor states.

State enumeration can be performed by computing a fixed point starting from the initial state of the model using the operational semantics described above. Note that two states of a model are the same if and only if they are assigned the same values to all latches, predicates, and memory for all interpretations given to the uninterpreted functions, predicates and constants appearing in both states.

2.3 State Reductions for Property Verification
Verification of systems modeled with ICS can be performed via language containment. Here properties and fairness constraints are placed only on the finite latches in the model. Thus, any state reduction technique that preserves the sequential behavior of all the finite variables will not cause any loss in verification accuracy. This is notion is formally defined below.

Definition 2.3.1 Given a state s of an ICS model M, we denote by $F(s)$ the set of traces (strings in the language) starting from s projected onto the set of finite variables in M. s is said to be *trace equivalent* to a state t iff $F(s) = F(t)$. s is said to be *trace contained* in another state t iff $F(s) \subseteq F(t)$.

In *[HIB97]*, a set of sufficient conditions was given for detecting trace equivalent ICS states. These techniques are able to detect trace equivalent states in certain situations where the same values are assigned to the finite variables and assignments of terms in the integer part are different. An example of such a condition is *isomorphic states*. Here we say that two states are isomorphic if renaming the set of symbolic constants in the first state results in the second. In *[HIB97]*, it was shown that if two states are isomorphic, then they are trace equivalent. An example of two isomorphic states is given in Figure 2.1.

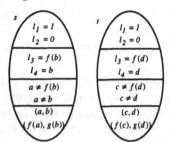

State s is isomorphic to state t since they are assigned the same values to the finite latches and renaming the constants a and b appearing in s to c and d results in a state that is syntactically equivalent to t.

Figure 2.1

3 Detecting Trace Containment

It is easy to show that if a state t is trace contained in a state s, then the set of control state assignments that are reachable from t are also reachable from s. Thus, if computing the set of reachable control states is the objective, it suffices to explore transitions from new states that are not trace contained in previously seen states. This optimization can not only reduce the time and space requirements during state enumeration, but also greatly increases the chances of reaching a fixed point. In this section, we introduce a sufficient condition, called *sub-isomorphic ICS states*, for [-pdetecting trace containment between ICS states. Intuitively, a state s is sub-isomorphic to a state t if s can be obtained from t by replacing terms with constants and deleting extra memory locations and predicates. The formal definition is given below.

Definition 3.2 A state s is *sub-isomorphic* to a state t if they both assign the same values to the finite state variables in the model and there exists a function $\pi : Terms(s) \rightarrow Terms(t)$ where any constant in $Terms(s)$ can map to any term in $Terms(t)$ and the following condition holds. 1) For each numeral $i \in Terms(s)$, there exist $i \in Terms(t)$, and $\pi(i) = i$. 2) For each term $g(u_1,...,u_n) \in Terms(s)$ with an outermost function symbol g, $\pi(g(u_1,...,u_n)) = g(\pi(u_1),...,\pi(u_n))$. 3) π agrees with all assignments of latches, memory and predicates in the state. Thus, if a term u has been assigned to the i-th latch in s, $\pi(u)$ is assigned to the i-th latch in t. For memory, each address/value pair $(a,d) \in M_k$ in s maps to a location $(\pi(a),\pi(d)) \in M_k$ appearing in t. Similarly, each predicate $p(u_1,...,u_n)$ appearing in s, maps to a predicate $p(\pi(u_1),...,\pi(u_n))$ appearing in t.

In *[HIB97]* it was shown that deleting predicates, memory locations or replacing terms with fresh constants results in a state with more behaviors. Theorem 3.2 uses this to prove that sub-isomorphic checking is a sufficient condition for detecting trace containment.

Theorem 3.2 If s is a *sub-isomorphic* state of t, then $F(t) \subseteq F(s)$.

Proof. Let $\pi : Terms(s) \rightarrow Terms(t)$ be a function inducing a sub-isomorphism between s and t. Construct a state t' from t by first deleting all memory locations and predicates which according to π does not correspond to any memory location or predicate in s. In addition, for each constant $c \in Terms(s)$, replace occurrences of $\pi(c) \in Terms(t)$ with a constant $\hat{c}$. Then $F(t) \subseteq F(t')$, by *[HIB97]*. Note t' and s are isomorphic, i.e. one can be obtained from the other by renaming the constants of one with the other, and thus $F(t') \subseteq F(s)$.

4 ICS State Enumeration: Data Structures and Algorithms

Function *ISP_Reach*
$R = (c_0(x), d_0)$; $N = R$
while $N \neq 0$ {
    foreach $(c(x), d) \in N$ {
        foreach $(c'(x), d') \in Next((c(x), d))$ {
        $(\tilde{c}(x), \tilde{d}) = Membership(R, (c'(x), d'))$
        if $\tilde{c}(x) \neq 0$ $N' = N' \cup (\tilde{c}(x), d')$
        }
    }
    $N - N'$; $N' - 0$
}

Function *Membership*
$\tilde{c}(x) = c'(x), \tilde{d} = d'$
foreach $(c_i(x), d_i) \in R$ {
    if *isSubIsomorphic*(d_i, d') {
        $\tilde{c}(x) = \tilde{c}(x) \wedge \bar{c}_i(x)$
        if $\tilde{c}(x) = 0$ **return**
        if *found* = FALSE **and**
            isIsomorphic(d_i, d')
        $\tilde{d} = d_i$; *found* = TRUE
    }
}
if *found* = FALSE $R = R \cup \{(\tilde{c}(x), \tilde{d})\}$

Figure 4.1 *State Enumeration Using ISPs*

In this section, we present new data structure, called *ICS State Pairs* (ISPs), for performing state enumeration using ICS models. ISPs allow for sets of states that have the same assignment to datapath values to be represented efficiently. Intuitively, an ISP is a pair $(c(x), d)$, where $c(x)$ is an ROBDD representing a set of assignments to the finite latch variables x, and d is a directed acyclic graph (DAG) representing terms assigned to integer latches, memory, and predicates. Thus, $(c(x), d)$ represents a set of ICS states that all have the same set of ICS terms assigned to the integer variables but may have different assignments to the finite state variables. The state enumeration algorithm using ISPs, *ISP_Reach*, is presented in Figure 4.1. Here, R is a set of ISPs representing the set of reachable states of the system and N the frontier set. Starting from the initial state(s) of the model, represented by $(c_0(x), d_0)$, the algorithm computes transitions to states for which there are no states in R that are sub-isomorphic to it. $Next((c(x), d))$ returns a set of ISPs representing the set of states that have one step transitions from the states in $(c(x), d)$. Next states of the finite part can be computed using BDDs. A special form of symbolic simulation is be used for computing the next states of the integer part. The function *Membership* searches the set of ISPs in R and removes finite states, which have sub-isomorphic integer assignments. Therefore, if $(c_1(x), d_1)$ is in R and a new state $(c_2(x), d_2)$ is found, then the states $c_2(x) \wedge c_1(x)$ can be removed from $c_2(x)$ if d_1 is sub-isomorphic to d_2. The rest of this section presents the details of the algorithm. In Section 4.1, we formally define ICS State Pairs and isomorphic checking using ISPs. In Section 4.2, we discuses how transitions between states represented as ISPs are computed.

4.1 ICS State Pairs

Consider a set of ICS states S of a model M with different assignments to the finite latch variables $x = (x_1, \ldots, x_l)$ but with isomorphic assignments to the datapath state variables (consisting of integer latches, predicates, and memory). We can represent S by an *ISP* $(c(x), d)$. Here $c(x)$ is an ROBDD representing the characteristic function $X_c : 2^l \rightarrow \{0,1\}$ of the set of all assignments to x by the states in S. $d = (V_d, E_d)$ is a labeled directed acyclic graph that is a syntactical representation of the set of assignments to integer latches, memory, and predicates, and is isomorphic to all datapath assignments of states in S. This representation is an extension of a congruence closure graph presented in *[NO80]* and we use their notation here. For each vertex $v \in V_d$, $\lambda(v)$ represents its label, $\delta(v)$ its out degree. The edges leaving each vertex are ordered, such that $v[i]$ is the i-th successor of v. Each term t is represented by a vertex v_t. For a constant term $t = c_i$ (or numeral), $\lambda(v_t) = c_i$ and $\delta(v_t) = 0$. If $t = f_i(t_1, \ldots t_n)$, then $\lambda(v_t) = f_i$, $\delta(v_t) = n$ and $v_t[1], \ldots, v_t[n]$ represent the terms $t_1, \ldots, t_n$. The root vertices in d represent assignments of terms to integer latches, memory and predicates. Thus, if v represents an assignment of t to the integer latch l_i, then $\lambda(v) = l_i$, $\delta(v) = 1$ and $v[1]$ represents t. If v represents an assignment of (a_i, d_i) to the memory element M_i, then $\lambda(v) = M_i$, $\delta(v) = 2$ and $v[1]$ and $v[2]$ respectively represent terms a_i and d_i. If v represents an n-ary predicate $p_i(t_1, \ldots, t_n)$, then it is defined similarly, except that if the predicate is false in a state, then $\lambda(v) = \neg p_i$.

Given two ISPs $(c_1(x), d_1)$, $(c_2(x), d_2)$, we say that d_1 is *sub-isomorphic* to d_2 if there exists a function $\sigma : V_1 \rightarrow V_2$ such that if $\sigma(v_1) = v_2$ and $\lambda(v_1) \neq c_i$ then $\lambda(v_1) = \lambda(v_2)$ and $\sigma(v_1[i]) = v_2[i]$. If d_1 is isomorphic to d_2, then σ is one-to-one and such that if $\sigma(v_1) = v_2$, and $\lambda(v_1) = c_i$ then $\lambda(v_2) = c_j$, otherwise $\lambda(v_1) = \lambda(v_2)$, and $\sigma(v_1[i]) = v_2[i]$. Note that for the root vertex corresponding to a latch assignment, there is only one vertex that is can map to. However, for root vertices corresponding to memories, there may be multiple cases, since all address/value pairs assigned in the same memory element will have the same label. This is also the case for root vertices corresponding to predicates, since each such vertex is only labeled by the operation that it represents. It is straightforward to prove that two states are sub-isomorphic if and only if their ISP representations are sub-isomorphic.

Currently, we check for isomorphism (and sub-isomorphism) by choosing a mapping between root vertices in d_1 and d_2, and then recursively mapping each successor vertex down to the leaves. In the worst case, however, all possible cases may have to be explored.

4.2 Computing ISP State Transitions

Given $(c(x), d)$ corresponding to a set of states of M, $Next(c(x), d)$ computes the set $\{(c_1'(x), d_1'), (c_2'(x), d_2'), ...\}$ representing successor states in $(c(x), d)$. This next state computation is performed using a combination of an implicit technique to represent transitions between state variables in the finite part and explicit techniques for the integer datapath and memory. In the following, we denote by $b = (b_1, ..., b_m)$ a set of variables corresponding to predicate gates, which are 'inputs' to the finite part from the integer part. $w = (w_1, ..., w_n)$ denotes the set of variables corresponding to 'outputs' of the finite part going to the integer part, and $y = (y_1, ..., y_l)$ denotes the set of next state variables of the finite latches. To compute transitions between finite states, we first create a BDD representing the transition relation, $T_F(x, w, b, y)$, of the finite part. This can be obtained by taking the intersection of all the finite relations in M. Computing next states is then performed in two steps. First, we compute the function $U(w, b, y) = \exists x (T_F(x, w, b, y) \wedge c(x))$, which represents the set of possible transitions of the finite part. $T_F(x, w, b, y)$ assumes that b and w are free inputs and outputs of the finite part, therefore, some transitions in $U(w, b, y)$ may not be possible. Next, for each possible set of assignments of b, w, and y given in $U(w, b, y)$, we compute the set of next states $\{d_i'\}$ of the integer part by starting with w and d and performing a special form of symbolic simulation. If the outputs of the integer part are not consistent with b, then the transition is invalid and thrown out. Otherwise, we create a set of pairs $\{(c'(x), d_i')\}$, where $c'(x)$ corresponds to assignments given by y. In general, since we attempt to compute d_i' for each possible assignment of b, w, and y, the number of cases that need to be considered is equivalent to the number of minterms in $U(w, b, y)$. In the next section, we show that we can consider assignments of b, w, y corresponding to a cube in $U(w, b, y)$ simultaneously. Since the number of cubes representing $U(w, b, y)$ can be exponentially smaller than the number of minterms, this optimization allows us to significantly speed up next state computation. In section 4.2.2, we discuss performing symbolic simulation of the integer part.

4.2.1 Cube Enumeration

In the following, we denote by 2 an absent literal in a cube, i.e. a *don't care*. Intuitively, the absence of a literal in a cube of $U(w, b, y)$ represents a set of assignments that are independent of case splitting (or case removal) that may occur in the integer part. Thus, $b_i = 2$ implies that the set of all other assignments to b, w, and y in the cube are the same for both $b_i = 0$ and $b_i = 1$. Even if $b_i = 0$ is inconsistent with the datapath, the choice of $b_i = 1$ does not require the other assignments to b, w, and y, to be reconsidered. Below we give the procedure for performing symbolic simulation with cubes, depending on whether the absent literal corresponds to a mux input (w_i), predicate output (b_i), or next state assignment (y_i) during symbolic execution of gates in M.

Mux Input. Assume $g = mux(w_i, i_1, i_2)$ and let t_1 and t_2 be the terms assigned to i_1 and i_2 by the partial state $s(g)$. If $P \rightarrow t_0 = t_1$ is valid, then assign the output t_1.

Here both cases do not need to be considered, since they will result in the same output assignment. If $t_1 = c$ (or t_2) is an unconstrained constant (is not assign to any other variable state), then assign $o = c$. Here, the case where $w_i = 1$ is contained in the case where $w_i = 0$. Otherwise, create two new partial states and consider both cases $w_i = 0$ and $w_i = 1$ separately.

Predicate Output. Simply continue value propagation. Note that there is an additional advantage here, since a validity check to determine the gate output value does not need to be performed. The correctness of this procedure can be argued by the operational semantics and the fact that it can be shown $F(s) = F(s_p) \cup F(s_{\bar{p}})$ (s_p denotes a state where a predicate p is true).

Finite Next State. If $y_i = 2$, then the next state integer assignment are the same for both $y_i = 0$ and $y_i = 1$ and thus both cases can be considered simultaneously.

4.2.2 Symbolic Simulation of the Datapath

Symbolic simulation is performed directly from the operational semantics. Terms are propagated through the gates in topological order. As reflected in the operation semantics, processing predicate gates and memory operation requires a validity check to be performed. We use the algorithm given in *[NO80]* to perform this check (it can be performed directly on the DAG). If case splitting results, case splitting results in a new DAG being created. Note that state reductions that can be performed by deleting extra information are also performed on-the-fly during execution of the gates of M .

5 Experimental Results

We have implemented the techniques presented in this paper in our second-generation ICS state reachability tool. In this section, we present experimental results on using our tool for performing both pipeline microprocessor verification and computing state invariants. All the experiments below were performed on a DEC-Alpha server running at 250Mhz with 1GB of main memory. Our ICS reachability tool uses the VIS *[VIS96]* verification system as a front end and the Cudd BDD package *[Som97]*. The results of all our experiments are shown in Table 5.1. The columns consist of the number of ICS states reached, the number of ISPs, the number of control states, and the number of CPU seconds. In the following, a detail description is given of the experiments that were run. For the two example that did not terminate (ITC and DLX ISA), the results are reported until memory out occurred.

Architectural Verification. ICS can be used to perform architectural verification for pipeline microprocessors, in which one verifies that a pipelined implementation of a microprocessor satisfies its unpipelined specification. The unpipelined version, called the spec, represents the instruction set architecture, which consists of the programmer visible state and instructions. Programmer visible states include logical registers, the program counter and memory. Intuitively, one would like to verify that for any sequence of instructions given to both machines, when the pipeline completes, its programmer visible state will equal the programmer visible state given in the spec. ICS allows the pipeline processor specification and correctness criteria to be expressed very naturally as a safety property. Starting from the initial state, we run the two machines in parallel under the same set of instructions. A non-deterministic stall is then asserted after an arbitrary number of instructions have been executed. Once the pipeline becomes empty, a comparison is made between the architectural states of the pipeline and the spec. One may also want to check that if a stall is asserted then the pipeline will eventually become empty. This check, which is naturally a liveness property, can be expressed as a safety property by showing that the number of cycles to flush the pipeline is bounded by a constant as determined by the user. We have applied this correctness criterion for verifying a 3-stage presented in *[BCMD90, BD94]* and our tool was able to reach a fixed point (CMU ISA in Table 5.1). In addition, we introduced two bugs into our design and our tool was able to capture both.

We also attempted to verify the 5-stage DLX pipeline presented in *[HP90]*. Unlike the 3-stage pipeline, the rates at which the DLX pipeline and its spec execute instructions are different. We solved this problem by using an instruction memory to model the program input and an *(arbitrary)* program location to denote the end of the program (instead of a stall signal). This approach requires no synchronization between the two machines. Our tool ran out of memory on this experiment (DLX ISA in Table 5.1), but we were able to find a bug that occurred in the branching logic of the machine.

It is clear that our method is computationally more expensive that the techniques presented in *[BD94, JDB95]*. The theoretical advantage here is in the generality and simplicity of the specification. The practical advantage is that we do not produce false negatives (or false positives), thus every bug that is found is a true error. Moreover, the user doesn't need to specify a state invariant.

Computing Reachable States for Invariance Properties. We computed the set of reachable control states for both the CMU and DLX pipeline (without the specification machine) and our tool was able to reach a fixed point for both examples (CMU Invariant and DLX Invariant in Table 5.1). We also ran our tool on the Island Tunnel Controller design presented in *[FJ95]* (ITC in Table 5.1). However, our procedure did not terminate for similar reasons as those given in *[ZSTCCL96]*.

Example	ICS States	ISPs	Control States	Time (sec)
CMU ISA	9	6	7	0.2
DLX ISA	4810	4753	33	2529.2
CMU Invariant	7	4	3	0.1
DLX Invariant	397	44	118	13.8
ITC	2996	746	18	2953.3

Table 5.1 *Experimental Results*

6 Conclusions

We have presented a new approach for automatically computing the set of reachable control states of systems modeled using ICS which allows datapath to be represented abstractly, hence enabling property verification on larger systems than what is possible with standard BDD-based techniques. Our approach is automatic and if it terminates will produce the exact set of reachable control states of the system. It can also be used for partial verification, by performing reachability for a finite number of steps. Our experimental results show that our approach maybe useful not only as a standalone verification technique, but in conjunction with other verification procedures that may require an approximation to the set of reachable control states as input.

References

[Bry86] R. E. Bryant, *"Graph Based Algorithms for Boolean Function Manipulation"*, IEEE Trans. on Computers, C-35(8):677-691, August 1986.

[BCMD90] Jerry R. Burch, E. M. Clarke, K. L. McMillan, David L. Dill, *"Sequential Circuit Verification Using Symbolic Model Checking"*, Proc. Of the Design Automation Conf., 1990.

[BD94] Jerry R. Burch, David L. Dill, *"Automatic Verification of Pipelined Microprocessor Control"*, Computer Aided Verification, Stanford, CA, June 1994.

[Cor94] F. Corella, *"Automatic Verification of Behavioral Equivalence for Microprocessors"*, IEEE Transactions on Computers, 43(1):115-117, January 1994.

[CZXLC94] F. Corella, Z. Zhou, X. Song, M. Langevin, E. Cerny, *"Multiway Decision Graphs for Automated Hardware Verification"*, IBM technical report RC19676, July 1994.

[FJ95] K. Fisler and S. Johnson, *"Integrating Design and Verification Environments through a Logic Supporting Hardware Designs"*, Proc. IFIP Conference on Hardware Description Languages and their Applications, Chiba, Japan, Aug. 1995.

[HP90] John L. Hennessy, David A. Patterson, *"Computer Architecture A Quantitative Approach"*, Morgan Kaufmann Publishers, 1990.

[HB95] Ramin Hojati, Robert K. Brayton, *"Automatic Datapath Abstraction of Hardware Systems"*, Conference on Computer-Aided Verification, June 1995.

[HIB97] Ramin Hojati, Adrian J. Isles, and Robert K. Brayton, *"Automatic State Reduction Techniques for Hardware Systems Modeled Using Uninterpreted Functions and Infinite Memory"*, IEEE International High Level Design Validation and Test Workshop, Nov 1997.

[HIKB97] Ramin Hojati, Adrian J. Isles, Desmond Kirkpatrick, and Robert K. Brayton, *"Verification Using Uninterpreted Functions and Finite Instantiations"*, Formal Methods in CAD, November 1996.

[Hunt85] W. A. Hunt, Jr. *"FM8501: A verified microprocessor"*, Technical Report 47, University of Texas at Austin, Institute for Computer Science, Dec. 1985.

[IHB96] Adrian J. Isles, Ramin Hojati, and Robert K. Brayton, *"Reachability Analysis of ICS Models"*, SRC Techcon, September 1996.

[JDB95] R.B Jones, D. L. Dill and J. R. Burch, *"Efficient Validity Checking for Processor Verification"*, IEEE/ACM International Conference of Computer Aided Design, 1995

[LC91] M. Langevin, E. Cerny, *"Comparing Generic State Machines"*, Computer Aided Verification, July, 1991.

[NO80] Greg Nelson, Derek C. Oppen, *"Fast Decision Procedures Based on Congruence Closure"*, Journal of the ACM, 27(2):356-364, April 1980, June 1995.

[Sho79] R. E. Shostak, *"A Practical Decision Procedure for Arithmetic With Function Symbols"*, JACM Volume 26, No. 2, April 1979, pp. 351-360.

[Som97] F. Somenzi, *"CUDD: CU Decision Diagram Package, Release 2.1.1"*, Department of ECE, University of Colorado at Boulder, February 1997.

[SB90] M. Srivas and M. Bickford. *"Formal Verification of a Pipelined Microprocessor"*. IEEE Software, 7(5):52-64, Sept 1990.

[VIS96] The VIS Group, *"VIS: A system for Verification and Synthesis"*, Conference on Computer Aided Verification, July 1996.

[ZSTCCL96] Z. Zhou, X. Song, S. Tahar, E. Cerny, F. Corella, M. Langevin, *"Formal Verification of the Island Tunnel Controller Using Multiway Decision Graphs"*, Formal Methods in Computer-Aided Design, November 1996.

Multiple Counters Automata, Safety Analysis and Presburger Arithmetic

Hubert Comon and Yan Jurski

LSV, ENS Cachan
61 av. président Wilson
94235 Cachan cedex
France
E-mail {comon,jurski}@lsv.ens-cachan.fr

Abstract. We consider automata with counters whose values are updated according to signals sent by the environment. A transition can be fired only if the values of the counters satisfy some guards (the guards of the transition). We consider guards of the form $y_i \# y_j + c_{i,j}$ where y_i is either x'_i or x_i, the values of the counter i respectively after and before the transition, and $\#$ is any relational symbol in $\{=, \leq, \geq, >, <\}$. We show that the set of possible counter values which can be reached after any number of iterations of a loop is definable in the additive theory of $\mathbb{N}$ (or $\mathbb{Z}$ or $\mathbb{R}$ depending on the type of the counters). This result can be used for the safety analysis of multiple counters automata.

1 Introduction

Finite state automata provide a nice framework for the verification of reactive systems. Their main advantage is the equivalence between recognizability and definability in some decidable logic (e.g. Monadic Second Order Logic or some of its fragments such as temporal logics). This allows to verify fully automatically that some structure defined by an automaton satisfies a given formula. Automata techniques are even optimal for the model checking of temporal formulas (see [2]). The counterpart of these nice properties is the relatively weak expressiveness of the finite state automata models. Many actual reactive systems require additional data structures in order to be described in an accurate way. Many models extending finite automata have been introduced in the literature. The most well-known one is probably timed automata [1] which allow to consider some "real time" constraints while keeping the nice decidability properties (with a higher complexity).

One of the most important purpose of verification is the so-called *safety analysis* which reduces most of the time to the following question: "is a bad state reachable from the initial configuration ?" For finite state automata, it is not difficult to compute all reachable states. This is however a more delicate question with infinite states systems: the computability of reachable configurations depends on the model under consideration. Here, we aim at contributing to this question by giving some decidability results. The model we consider is a "multiple counters automaton". A configuration is not only described by a state of the system, but also by the values of finitely many *counters* which may take arbitrary (integer or real) values. Such counters (also called *clocks* in other contexts) do not necessary measure the elapsed time (as in timed automata), but they may as well count some other data such as the distance covered by a car or the speed of a train. Transitions from a state to another depend also on the satisfaction of formulas by the actual counter values. Such a model is used in several papers, such as in [12]. For instance, Minsky machines [13] can be viewed as such multiple counter automata, which means that reachability is undecidable in general.

There are two ways to overcome this problem: either we restrict the class of models we consider or else we consider (lower or upper depending on the problem) approximations of the model. Essentially, these two points of view are not different: if we find some appropriate restriction of the models, then this corresponds to an appropriate class of approximations. The question then is to find a class which is as expressive as possible and for which reachability is still decidable. Assume for instance that counters may take integer values. Then we would like to describe sets of (reachable) configurations by Presburger formulas, assuming that the guards of the transitions are also expressed in Presburger arithmetic. This is not always possible because loops in the automaton yield fixed points which correspond to infinite disjunctions of Presburger formulas and actually, even with a single state, the set of reachable counters values can be a non-recursive set of integers (or reals if we consider real-valued counters).

In this paper, we consider a fragment (or an approximation) yielding a decidable class. Our main result is the following: assume that the counters values before (unprimed names) and after a transition (primed names) are solutions of conjunctions of atomic formulas of the form $x \# y' + c$ or $x \# y + c$ or $x' \# y' + c$ or $x \# c$ or $x' \# c$ where $c \in \mathbb{Z}$ (resp $c \in \mathbb{R}$) and $\# \in \{\leq, \geq, =, >, <\}$. Then we show that the fixed point of iterating a composition of such transitions is expressible in Presburger arithmetic. For automata with multiple nested iterations, then the same result holds provided that intermediate fixed points are expressible in the adequate fragment.

Related works

There are several authors who considered other fragments and other approximations. Let us briefly mention them and compare with our result. N. Halbwachs in [12] considers a similar model. A priori, the fixed point of a loop whose guard is $g(\mathbf{x}, \mathbf{x}')$ is the set of counters values which satisfy the infinite disjunction (n is the number of iterations) $\bigvee_{n=0}^{+\infty} (\exists \mathbf{x_1} \dots \exists \mathbf{x_n}.g(\mathbf{x}, \mathbf{x_1}) \wedge \dots g(\mathbf{x_n}, \mathbf{x}'))$. N. Halbwachs, following [7], considers a *widening* operation ∇ and he computes an upper approximation of the above infinite disjunction $\bigvee_{n=0}^{+\infty} P_i$ by considering the limit of $P_0, P_0 \nabla P_1, P_0 \nabla P_1 \nabla P_2 \dots$ which is always reached after finitely many steps. Basically, the widening construction removes some of the constraints of either argument, until one of the constraint subsumes the other. Several strategies for computing the polyhedron are given in [12]. [1] Consider however the following example:

Example 1. There is only one state, one loop and two counters: initially the counters values satisfy $1 \leq x \leq 2, 1 \leq y \leq 2$. The guard of the transition is given by $x + 1 \leq x' \leq x + 2, y + 1 \leq y' \leq y + 2$. Successive values of the counters after each iteration are represented in figure 1. Following [12], we would get the

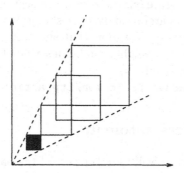

Fig. 1. Successive values of the counters

whole quarter of plan as an upper approximation. The exact computation is however possible, yielding $2y \geq x \wedge 2x \geq y$ (which is depicted on the figure using dashed lines). The guards satisfy our conditions, hence we will get this exact computation using our result.

P. Revesz in [15] also considers similar fixed point computation. The guards are of the form $x'_i \geq x_j + k$ with $k \geq 0$, which disallows for instance equalities: it is not possible to express e.g. $x' = x + 1$. On the other hand, he is able to handle several loops. The application of this result to verification is investigated in [11]. It is also extended, allowing periodicity conditions in [17].

B. Boigelot and P. Wolper consider in [4] guards of the form $x'_i = x_i + b$ plus additional guards involving only unprimed variables. They also get an exact fixed point computation in Presburger's arithmetic. Our result is more general in the sense that we may also have relations $x'_i \# x_j + b$ (i.e. relations between different counters) and inequalities as well. On the other hand, the precondition on unprimed variables is more general in [4] than in our result.

L. Fribourg and H. Olsen [10] consider a similar situation as in [4], except that their preconditions are less general. On the other hand, they consider the case of several loops, which is not the case in [4].

B. Boigelot in [3] characterizes precisely the functions from $\mathbb{Z}^n$ to $\mathbb{Z}^n$ of the form $f(x) = Ax + b$ such that the set of iterations of f is definable in weak monadic second order logic. This result is the most accurate one for the guards $x' = Ax + b$. However, there is no inequality here and no guard relating unprimed variables.

---

[1] even if the guards in [12] are only linear substitutions, it can be extended to certain kind of linear inequality, and for instance to our example.

In [5], the authors consider guards which can be arbitrary Presburger formulas. This model is more general than ours. However, they do not have any decidability result (the model is too expressive). They provide with approximations computations which yield semi-decision algorithms.

The paper is organized as follows. We start in section 2 with our model of multiple counters automata together with some examples of systems which are naturally expressed in this framework. We also explain the relationship with timed automata. Then we state our main result in section 3. Its proof is sketched in section 4. It relies on a careful analysis of shortest paths in a graph with an unbounded number of vertices. We show that shortest paths always lay in some particular sets of paths whose weights can be described by a Presburger formula. The full paper can be retrieved on
`http://www.lsv.ens-cachan.fr/~comon/ftp.articles/mca.ps`.

2 Multiple counters automata

In the following definition as well as in the rest of the paper, we consider integer valued counters. However, they can be real-valued as well without changing our results.

Definition 1. A *multiple counters automata* is a tuple $(Q, q_i, C, \delta \subseteq Q \times G(C, C') \times Q)$ where

- Q is a finite set of *states*
- $q_i \in Q$ is an *initial state*
- C is a finite set of *counter names*; C' is the set of primed counter names.
- $G(C, C')$ is the set of *guards* built on the alphabets C, C'. A member of $G(C, C')$ is a conjunction of atomic formulas of one of the forms $x \# y + c$, $x \# c$ where $x, y \in C \cup C'$, $\# \in \{\geq, \leq, =, >, <\}$. and $c \in \mathbb{Z}$. (or in $\mathbb{R}$)

A *configuration of the automaton* is a pair (q, v) where $q \in Q$ and v is a mapping from C into $\mathbb{N}$ (or $\mathbb{Z}$ or $\mathbb{R}$ or $\mathbb{R}_+$; as it is easy to see, this will not make any difference).

The automaton may *move* from a configuration (q, v) to a configuration (q', v'), which we write $(q, v) \rightarrow (q', v')$ if there is a triple $(q, g, q') \in \delta$ such that $v(C), v'(C') \models g$, with the standard interpretation of relational symbols.

Example 2. We consider a fragment[2] of the train example of [12]. On this example b is the number of beacons which have been encountered. It is given by the environment and measures the covered distance. s is the number of ticks which are sent by a global counter. Figure 2 shows transitions for which the train is on time an remains on time. g is the guard $b' = b, s' = s + 1, s \leq b + 8$ and h is the guard $b \leq s + 8, b' = b + 1, s' = s$. For instance, $(1,(2,7))$ and $(1,(2,8))$ are two possible consecutive configurations since $(2, 7), (2, 8) \models g$.

---

[2] This is because of size constraints of this paper. We consider the whole example, as well as some other examples in detail in the extended version of this paper.

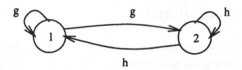

Fig. 2. A fragment of the train example

Safety analysis reduces to the computation of reachable configurations (or a superset of the reachable configurations). It is possible to compute this set, starting with inner loops and trying to compute meta-transitions. The concept of meta-transition, is presented in [4]. It amounts to consider a (possibly infinite) succession of elementary transitions of the automaton as a single transition, the guard being the conjunction of the guards of individual transitions (intermediate counter values being existentially quantified).

Example 3. Consider example 2. The sequence of transitions g^*g (from state 1 to state 2) can be replaced with a meta-transition g^+ whose guard is $s \le b+8, b' = b, s' \le b + 9, s \le s' - 1$ and h^*h can be replaced with a meta-transition h^+ whose guard is $b \le s + 8, b \le b' - 1, b' \le s + 9, s' = s.$[3] g^+h^+ itself (which goes from 1 to itself) can be replaced with the meta transition whose guard is $s \le s' - 1, s' \le b + 9, b' \le s' + 9, b \le b' - 1$. Now, computing reachable configurations in state 1 reduces to compute the reachable configurations of a single state automaton with a single loop containing the computed guard.

Relationship with timed automata

At a first sight, timed automata are different from counter automata because the clocks always run at the same speed in the latter model whereas updates of the clocks seem to be possible only during a transition in the former model.

However, using a trick proposed recently by L. Fribourg [9], it is not difficult to translate timed automata into (real-valued) counter automata, at the price of adding a new clock, which is never reset. This translation does not change the structure of the automaton (transition and states are the same; the invariants and guards of the timed automata are used to compute the corresponding guard of the multiple counters automaton). Therefore, timed automata are a particular case of multiple clocks automata.

Further on, if we allow drifting clocks, then the simple above translation does not work any more, as it would yield guards of the form $\alpha \times x \le y \le \beta \times x$, which are not allowed in our model.

---

[3] The computation of meta-transitions can be performed using the result of the present paper.

3 Fixed point computations

Computing a meta transition for the composition of two transitions is an easy task. The main problem is to compute the fixed point of an iteration of a transition. Our main result, is that this is possible for a single loop, keeping the decidability of the computed guard:

Theorem 2. *Given a transition (q, g, q), there is an (effectively computable) Presburger arithmetic formula $\phi(C, C')$ such that $v, v' \models \phi(C, C')$ iff there exists an $n \in \mathbf{N}$ such that*

$$v, v' \models \exists C_1, \ldots, \exists C_n . g(C, C_1) \wedge \ldots \wedge g(C_n, C')$$

This result is not obvious as the formula $\exists n, \exists C_1, \ldots, \exists C_n . g(C, C_1) \wedge \ldots \wedge g(C_n, C')$ does not belong to Presburger arithmetic. It cannot be translated either (at least in an obvious way) into monadic second order logic: the counters vectors $C_1, \ldots, C_n$ are ordered (and their ordering is relevant), hence we cannot simply associate with each sequence of components a set of integers.

As usual in constraint solving we may represent inequalities $x \leq y + d$ using a graph whose vertices are the variables and edges are labeled with the delay d. (This is used for instance in many scheduling applications, see e.g. [6]). Here we have an unbounded number of variables: m variables for each of $C_1, \ldots, C_n$. m is known in advance. However, n is unbounded (and actually existentially quantified). Hence we consider a graph $G(g, n)$ whose number of vertices is unbounded $(n \times m)$. The purpose then is to compute a Presburger formula, which depends on n, and which expresses minimal paths in such a graph. As the number of vertices is unbounded, it is not possible to apply classical graph algorithms (such as Bellman-Ford [6]).

In the next section, which is devoted to the proof of this theorem, we develop a machinery to express these shortest paths; we first define the graph representation of the problem. Then we fold the unbounded graph into a finite (fixed) graph and investigate the relations between the graph and its folded version, showing to which extent paths in one graph are related with paths in the other graph.

Applications

Let us first state some consequences of the theorem. We say that a multiple counters automaton (or a part of an automaton) is *flat* if there is no nested loop in the transition graph.

Corollary 3. *Let $\mathcal{A}$ be a flat automaton and q, q' be two states of $\mathcal{A}$. Then there is a (effectively computable) Presburger formula $\phi_{q,q'}(\mathbf{x}, \mathbf{x}')$ such that $\mathbf{v}, \mathbf{v}' \models \phi_{q,q'}(\mathbf{x}, \mathbf{x}')$ iff $(q', \mathbf{v}')$ is accessible from $(q, \mathbf{v})$.*

In other words, the *binary* accessibility relation is definable in Presburger arithmetic, which yields, thanks to [8]:

Corollary 4. *The Model checking of* EF *formulas is decidable for (infinite) transitions systems that are defined by flat automata.*

The same results hold for real-valued counters. We only have to replace Presburger arithmetic with another theory; let $\mathcal{R}$ be the additive theory of real numbers with a predicate $\mathsf{Int}(x)$ which is satisfied by all integer values. This first-order theory is decidable, as it can be expressed in S1S (the monadic second-order logic), where real numbers are identified with infinite words (see e.g. [16]).

Corollary 5. *The binary accessibility relation for flat real-valued multiple counter automata is definable in* $\mathcal{R}$.

Then, for flat timed automata, the same result holds, thanks to Fribourg's trick [9].

4 Proof of theorem 2

4.1 Weighted graphs of unbounded size

First, for any guard, it is possible to assume without loss of generality that g is a conjunction of inequalities $x \leq y' + d$, $x' \leq y + d$, $x \leq y + d$, $x' \leq y' + d$. Indeed, strict inequalities can be replaced with non-strict inequalities, adding or removing 1 from the constant[4]. Equalities are replaced with two inequalities. Finally, we can take care of $x \leq c$, where c is a constant by adding a dummy counter whose value is always 0.

We consider weighted (directed) graphs $G(g, n)$ whose vertices are pairs (i, t) with $i \in [1..m]$ and $t \in [0..n]$ are integers, n being a parameter $n \geq 1$ and $m = |C|$. Given a guard g, the set of edges of $G(g, n)$ consists of the following pairs:

- for $i, j \in [1..m]$ and $t \in [0..n-1]$, $(i, t) \xrightarrow{d} (j, t+1)$ iff g contains an inequality $x_i \leq x'_j + d$.
- for $i, j \in [1..m]$ and $j \in [1..n]$, $(i, t) \xrightarrow{d} (j, t-1)$ iff g contains an inequality $x'_i \leq x_j + d$
- for $i, j \in [1..m]$ and $t \in [1.., n]$, $(i, t) \xrightarrow{d} (j, t)$ iff g contains an inequality $x'_i \leq x'_j + d$
- for $i, j \in [1..m]$ and $t \in [0..n-1]$, $(i, t) \xrightarrow{d} (j, t)$ iff g contains an inequality $x_i \leq x_j + d$.

Example 4. Consider again example 2 and the meta-transition of example 3. The graph corresponding to the new guard $s \leq s' - 1, s' \leq b + 9, b' \leq s' + 9, b \leq b' - 1$ is depicted on figure 3.

---

[4] For real-valued interpretations, strict inequalities cannot be removed and we have to consider in the graph both strict and non-strict inequalities. This complicates a little bit the picture, however nothing essential is changed.

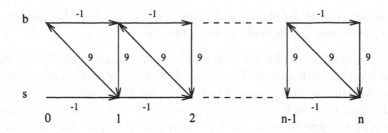

Fig. 3. The graph corresponding to a meta-transition of example 3

A *path* from a to b in a graph G is a finite sequence $e_1, \ldots, e_{N-1}$ of edges $a_i \xrightarrow{d_i} a_{i+1}$ such that $a_1 = a$ and $a_N = b$. A path is sometimes identified with the sequence of vertices $a_1, \ldots, a_N$ when there is no ambiguity.

Let $\psi_n(C, C')$ be the formula $\exists C_1, \ldots, \exists C_n . g(C, C_1) \wedge \ldots \wedge g(C_{n-1}, C')$. Then proving the theorem amounts to show how to compute a formula which is equivalent to $\exists n.\psi_n(C, C')$.

Let $\Gamma(i, t, i', t')$ be the set of all paths from (i, t) to (i', t') in $G(g, n)$. (This set can be infinite). The *weight* $w(\gamma)$ of a path γ is the sum of weights of all edges along the path.

The following lemma shows that we can eliminate intermediate steps, sticking to paths from a fixed number of vertices to a fixed number of vertices. However, the set of paths is still potentially infinite.

Lemma 6. $v, v' \models \psi_n(C, C')$ *iff for every indices* $i, j \in [1..m]$

- *for all paths* $\gamma \in \Gamma(i, 0, j, n)$, $v, v' \models x_i \le x'_j + w(\gamma)$
- *for all paths* $\gamma \in \Gamma(i, n, j, 0)$, $v, v' \models x'_i \le x_j + w(\gamma)$
- *for all paths* $\gamma \in \Gamma(i, 0, j, 0)$, $v, v' \models x_i \le x_j + w(\gamma)$
- *for all paths* $\gamma \in \Gamma(i, n, j, n)$, $v, v' \models x'_i \le x'_j + w(\gamma)$
- *for all paths* $\gamma \in \Gamma(i, n-1, i, n-1)$, $w(\gamma) \ge 0$, *if* $n \ge 2$.

4.2 The folded graph

In this section, we consider the "untimed" version of $G(g, n)$, which corresponds to identify vertices which only differ in their second components. Basically, we can compute on this "folded version" H of $G(g, n)$ a formula $\Phi_{i,j}$ which defines the set of all weights of paths from i to j.

Let H be the three-coloured weighted graph whose vertices are $[1..m]$ and whose edges are given by g:

- $i \xrightarrow[1]{d} j$ if $x_i \le x_j + d$ or $x'_i \le x'_j + d$ is in g
- $i \xrightarrow[2]{d} j$ if $x'_i \le x_j + d$ is in g
- $i \xrightarrow[3]{d} j$ if $x_i \le x'_j + d$ is in g

For each edge e in G we associate in an obvious way an edge in H: $\pi((i,t) \overset{d}{\to} (j,t')) = i \overset{d}{\underset{k}{\to}} j$ with $k = 1$ if $t = t'$, $k = 2$ if $t' < t$ and $k = 3$ if $t' > t$. π is extended to paths of $G(g,n)$.

Example 5. Figure 4 shows the folded version of the graph given on figure 3.

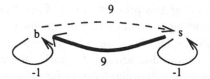

Fig. 4. The folded graph

Now, we need not to consider all paths in $\Gamma(i,t,j,t')$: according to lemma 6, we may only consider one path of H for each possible weight. Formally, if $\gamma \in \Gamma(i,t,j,t')$ and $\alpha(\gamma,e)$ is the multiplicity of e in $\pi(\gamma)$,

$$w(\gamma) = w(\pi(\gamma)) = \sum_{e \in H} \alpha(\gamma,e) \times w(e)$$

Conversely, if we give the multiplicities α_e of each edge e, there is a path corresponding to these multiplicities, iff they statisfy a given formula. Basically, such formula can be derived from Parikh's theorem [14]. That is what is stated in the next lemma. In what follows, α (resp. z) is a vector indexed by the set of edges of H: $\alpha = (\alpha_{e_1}, ..., \alpha_{e_n})$.

Lemma 7. *For every i,j, there is a Presburger formula $\rho^{i,j}$ such that $\alpha \models \rho^{i,j}$ iff there is a path γ from i to j in H such that $w(\gamma) = \sum_{e \in H} \alpha_e \times w(e)$.*

Remark: If H does not involve colour 1 and either does not involve colour 2 or colour 3, then we can already conclude the proof of theorem 2: from lemma 6, and since there is no (non-empty) path in $\Gamma(i,0,j,0) \cup \Gamma(i,n,j,n) \cup \Gamma(i,n-1,i,n-1)$ and either no path in $\Gamma(i,0,j,n)$ or no path in $\Gamma(i,n,j,0)$, we only have to find an equivalent Presburger formula for $\exists n. \bigwedge_{\gamma \in \Gamma(i,0,j,n)} x_i \leq x'_j + w(\gamma)$ (resp. $\exists n. \bigwedge_{\gamma \in \Gamma(i,n,j,0)} x'_i \leq x_j + w(\gamma)$). Such a formula would be

$$\exists n. \bigwedge_{i=1}^{m} \bigwedge_{j=1}^{m} \forall z. (n = \sum_{e \in H} z_e \wedge \rho^{i,j}) \Rightarrow x_i \leq x'_j + \sum_{e \in H} z_e \times w(e)$$

However, in general, a path in H does not necessary correspond to a path in G. Relationships between paths of H and paths of $G(g,n)$ can be described more accurately. If γ is a path of H, we let $N_i(\gamma)$ be the number of edges of γ whose colour is i and $\delta_t(\gamma) = N_3(\gamma) - N_2(\gamma)$.

Lemma 8. *A path γ in H is the projection of some path in $G(g,n)$ only if there are $\delta_1, \delta_2 \in \mathbb{Z}$ such that $0 \leq \delta_2 - \delta_1 \leq n$ and for every prefix γ' of γ, $\delta_t(\gamma') \in [\delta_1 .. \delta_2]$.*

Conversely, if there are $\delta_1, \delta_2 \in \mathbb{Z}$ such that $0 \leq \delta_2 - \delta_1 \leq n$ and for every prefix γ' of γ, $\delta_t(\gamma') \in [\delta_1 + 1 .. \delta_2 - 1]$, then γ is the projection of a path in $G(g,n)$.

Now, the problem is that the property of prefixes given in lemma 8 cannot be characterized by counting the number of occurrences of each edge in a path only; we have to exploit the fact that we are only interested in minimal weight paths. Moreover, we will show that among the paths of minimal weight (relating two given vertices) there are "regular" ones, for which we can compute the boundedness condition of lemma 8.

4.3 Exploiting the quasi-ordering on paths

Now, we come to the hard part of the proof which cannot be detailed in this short paper. Let us only give the milestones. First, we rule out the case of cycles; if there is a cycle γ in H such that $w(\gamma) \geq 0$, it is not a minimal weighted path and if $w(\gamma) < 0$, the fixed point of the iteration is reached after a computable bounded number of steps :

Lemma 9. *If there is a cycle γ in H of length k such that $w(\gamma) < 0$ and $\delta_t(\gamma) = 0$, then $\psi_n(C, C')$ is unsatisfiable for $n \geq 1 + \frac{k}{2}$.*

Now, we give some transformation rules on paths, which preserve the weight of minimal weight paths, and whose termination is guaranteed by the cycle-freeness of G. One transformation consists in locally gathering together elementary cycles:

Lemma 10. $\forall \alpha, \exists B, \forall k \in [0..n - B], \forall i, j \in [0, m], \forall \gamma \in \Gamma(i, k, j, B + k), \exists \gamma' \in \Gamma(i, k, j, B + k), w(\gamma) = w(\gamma') \land \pi(\gamma') = c_1.(\sigma)^{\alpha}.c_2$ *with σ an elementary cycle of H.*

Next, we apply two rules which duplicate or remove elementary cycles, yielding paths of smaller (or equal) weight and which are more "regular" (see fig 5).

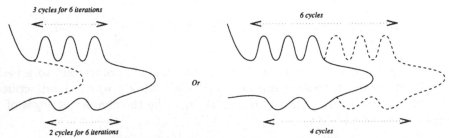

Fig. 5. how to construct the regular path

If the path is long enough, then we get a normal form which is depicted on figure 6 : the paths η_k and η'_k have a width bounded by a constant B (independent from n) and θ_k, θ'_k go from one extremity to the other. They consist themselves of a path of length bounded by B followed by an iteration of a particular cycle of H, followed by a bounded length path. Moreover, the number of such paths η_k is smaller than the number of counters.

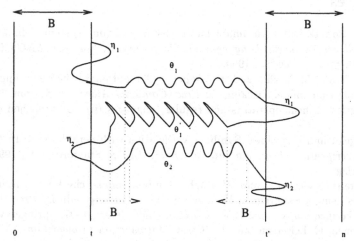

Fig. 6. Only paths going "back and forth" have to be considered

Then when n is large enough $(n \geq 2B)$, $\psi_n(C, C')$ is logically equivalent to a formula

$$\exists \mathbf{x}^B, \exists \mathbf{x}^{n-B}, \Phi_1(\mathbf{x}, \mathbf{x}^B) \wedge \Phi_2(\mathbf{x}^B) \wedge \Phi_3(\mathbf{x}^B, \mathbf{x}^{n-B}) \wedge \Phi_2(\mathbf{x}^{n-B}) \wedge \Phi_1(\mathbf{x}^{n-B}, \mathbf{x}')$$

Φ_1 expresses the constraints generated by B iterations of the loop Φ_2 expresses the constraints between counters values after B iterations and which correspond in the graph to paths η, whose width is bounded by K. Φ_3 expresses paths that are the iteration of elementary cycles of H, and which brings from the $(B+i)$ths values of the counters to the $n - B - j$ths values of the counters, for $i, j \in [0, B]$.

5 Conclusion

We have shown that the fixed point of a single loop of multiple counters automata is definable in the additive theory of $\mathbb{N}$ (resp. $\mathbb{R}$, resp. $\mathbb{Z}$). Thanks to this result, it is possible to compute the exact set of reachable configurations in a number of situations for which such a computation was unknown. This also provides better approximations for the general case. The complexity of the resulting reachability analysis is high (a double exponential in the number of counters since the length of the formula is exponential in the number of counters in the worst case). It seems however to be manageable on the examples: the upper bound needs not to be met on all examples.

Acknowledgements

We acknowledge L. Fribourg for many discussions on multiple counters automata.

References

1. R. Alur and D. Dill. Automata for modeling real-time systems. In *Proc. 17th Int. Coll. on Automata, Languages and Programming, Warwick, LNCS 443*, pages 322–335. Springer-Verlag, 1990.
2. O. Bernholtz, M. Vardi, and P. Wolper. An automata-theoretic approach to branching time model checking. In *Proc. Computer Aided Verification*, 1994.
3. B. Boigelot. Linear operators and regular languages (ii). Unpublished draft, jan 1997.
4. B. Boigelot and P. Wolper. Symbolic verification with periodic sets. In *Computer Aided Verification, Proc. 6th Int. Conerence*, LNCS, Stanford, June 1994. Springer-Verlag.
5. T. Bultan, R. Gerber, , and W. Pugh. Symbolic model checking of infinite state systems using presburger arithmetic. In O. Grumberg, editor, *Proc. Computer Aided Verification*, volume 1254 of *LNCS*, Haifa, Israel, 1997. Springer-Verlag.
6. T. Cormen, C. Leiserson, and R. Rivest. *Introduction to algorithms*. MIT Press, 1990.
7. P. Cousot and N. Halbwachs. Automatic discovery of linear restraints among variables of a program. In *Proc. Int. Conf. on Princinples Of Programming Languages (POPL)*, 1978.
8. J. Esparza. Decidability of model checking for infinite-state concurrent systems. *Acta Informatica*, 34:85–107, 1997.
9. L. Fribourg. A closed form evaluation for extending timed automata. Technical Report 1998-02, Laboratoire Spécification et Vérification, ENS Cachan, Mar. 1998.
10. L. Fribourg and H. Olsen. A decompositional approach for computing least fixedpoint of datalog programs with z-counters. *J. Constraints*, 1997.
11. L. Fribourg and J. Richardson. Symbolic verification with gap-order constraints. Research Report LIENS-96-3, Ecole Normale Supérieure, Paris, Feb. 1996.
12. N. Halbwachs. Delay analysis in synchronous programs. In *Proc. Computer Aided Verification*, LNCS 697, pages 333–346. Springer-Verlag, 1993.
13. M. Minsky. *Computation, Finite and Infinite Machines*. Prentice Hall, 1967.
14. R. Parikh. On context-free languages. *J. ACM*, 13, 1966.
15. P. Revesz. A closed form for datalog queries with integer order. In *Proc 3rd International Conference on Database Theory*, pages 187–201, Paris, 1990.
16. W. Thomas. Automata on infinite objects. In J. van Leeuwen, editor, *Handbook of Theoretical Computer Science*, pages 134–191. Elsevier, 1990.
17. D. Toman, J. Chomicki, and D. S. Rogers. Datalog with integer periodicity constraints. In *Int. Symp. on Logic Programming*, 1994.

A Comparison of Presburger Engines for EFSM Reachability

Thomas R. Shiple[1]   James H. Kukula[2]   Rajeev K. Ranjan[1]

[1] Synopsys, Inc., Mountain View, CA. {shiple,rajeevr}@synopsys.com
[2] Synopsys, Inc., Beaverton, OR. kukula@synopsys.com

Abstract. Implicit state enumeration for extended finite state machines relies on a decision procedure for Presburger arithmetic. We compare the performance of two Presburger packages, the automata-based Shasta package and the polyhedra-based Omega package. While the raw speed of each of these two packages can be superior to the other by a factor of 50 or more, we found the asymptotic performance of Shasta to be equal or superior to that of Omega for the experiments we performed.

1 Introduction

Peano arithmetic, the theory of arithmetic with multiplication and addition, is undecidable. However, decision procedures do exist for the subset of arithmetic, known as Presburger arithmetic, that excludes multiplication [13]. Presburger formulas are built up from natural number constants, natural number variables, addition, equality, inequality, and the first order logical connectives. An example of such a formula is[1]

$$\exists x(y = 2x + 1).$$

Even though the best known procedure for deciding Presburger arithmetic is triply exponential in the length of the formula [16], several practical applications for Presburger arithmetic have been found. Pugh [17] uses Presburger arithmetic for data dependence analysis in optimizing compilers. Amon *et al.* [1] use Presburger arithmetic to perform symbolic verification of timing diagrams. Another application, and the one on which we will be focusing, is reachability analysis of extended finite state machines (EFSMs) [3, 8, 9, 12].

An EFSM is a system with a finite state controller interacting with an integer datapath of unbounded width [9]. Each transition of the controller has a gating predicate over the integer variables, and an update function specifying the new values of the integer variables when the transition is taken. Figure 1 depicts a simple EFSM with five control states, seven input variables ($r, i_{a_x}, i_{a_y}, i_{b_x}, i_{b_y}, i_{d_x}, i_{d_y}$), seven data variables ($a_x, a_y, b_x, b_y, d_x, d_y, i$), and ten transitions. This machine reads data and then checks a series of inequalities that determines whether the variable i should be assigned a 0 or 1 value.

---
[1] $2x$ is an abbreviation for $x + x$.

If the gating predicates and update functions of an EFSM are definable in Presburger arithmetic, then the entire transition relation of the EFSM can be represented as a single Presburger formula. If the set of initial states is also Presburger definable, then BFS-based implicit state enumeration can be performed completely within Presburger arithmetic. Thus, Presburger arithmetic provides an elegant framework for performing state reachability of EFSMs.

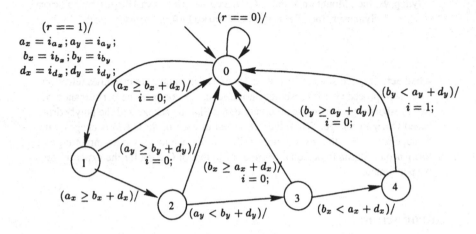

Fig. 1. An EFSM.

Two basic approaches have emerged for representing, manipulating, and checking the satisfiability of Presburger formulas: automata-based and polyhedra-based. In the automata-based approach, the naturals are encoded as bit strings using base 2 encoding [4, 6, 19]. For a Presburger formula defined over k variables, a technique has been developed to directly translate the formula into a deterministic, finite state automaton (DFA) that accepts a k-tuple of bit strings if and only if the k-tuple is a solution to the given formula [4]. Since minimum state DFAs are unique, automata provide a canonical form for Presburger formulas. In the polyhedra-based approach, Fourier-Motzkin variable elimination is used to eliminate the quantifiers from a Presburger formula [13, 17]. The result is a union of convex polyhedra that is typically represented by a set of matrices; this representation is not canonical. A useful analogy can be made to data representations in the Boolean domain: automata are like binary decision diagrams (BDDs), and polyhedra are like sums of products (SOPs).

To the best of our knowledge, a direct experimental comparison of the performance of these two basic approaches has never been made. The contribution of this work is to perform such a comparison. For the polyhedra approach, we use the Omega package of Pugh et al. [15, 17]. For the automata approach, we developed the Shasta package, which incorporates the procedure of Boudet and Comon [4] for translating linear equalities and inequalities to automata, and also uses the automaton data structure of Henriksen et al. [14].

The context for our comparison is state reachability for EFSMs. It is not clear a priori which approach would be better. In the Boolean domain, experience shows that BDDs are generally superior to SOPs, but there are cases where SOPs are exponentially more compact than BDDs [11]. In the final analysis, our experiments show that while the raw speed of each Presburger engine can be superior to the other by a factor of 50 or more, the asymptotic performance of Shasta is equal or superior to that of Omega.

The remainder of the paper is organized as follows. Section 2 presents more detail on the automata approach for solving Presburger arithmetic, and Section 3 does the same for the polyhedra approach. Section 4 describes the experimental setup and analyzes the experimental results.

2 Automata Approach for Solving Presburger Arithmetic

Automata can be used as a data structure to represent Presburger formulas, or more precisely, the set of solutions to Presburger formulas. In this section, we review the general ideas behind this concept, and discuss some specifics of the Shasta automata package used in the experiments.

The first step to consider in representing Presburger formulas by automata is the encoding of natural numbers. For this, a base 2 encoding is used, with least significant bit first, and arbitrary padding with zeroes on the end. Thus, both 011 and 01100 represent the number 6. A tuple of naturals is represented by simply stacking equal length representations of the elements. Thus, the tuple $(x_1, x_2, x_3) = (4, 7, 11)$ can be represented by a string of bit vectors:

$$
\begin{array}{ll}
\text{string} \longrightarrow & \\
x_1 : 0\ 0\ 1\ 0 & \text{bit} \\
x_2 : 1\ 1\ 1\ 0 & \text{vector} \\
x_3 : 1\ 1\ 0\ 1 & \downarrow
\end{array}
$$

An automaton representing a Presburger formula over k variables reads a bit vector of height k at each step, consuming the least significant bit of each variable in the first step, the next least significant bit in the second step, and so on.

The atomic formulas of Presburger arithmetic are linear equalities and inequalities. Büchi indirectly showed how these formulas can be represented by automata by demonstrating how they can be embedded in the logic WS1S [6]. Recently, Boudet and Comon developed a direct method for translating an atomic formula into an automaton; the Shasta package uses this algorithm. Figure 2 shows the automaton that recognizes the natural number tuples satisfying the linear equality $x_1 + x_2 = x_3$. To illustrate its operation, for the input tuple (4,7,11), the automaton starts at the initial state and reads the first bit vector, 011, which leads the automaton back to the initial state. After reading all the bit vectors, the automaton will be in the accepting state, reflecting that $4 + 7 = 11$.

Presburger formulas are constructed by combining atomic formulas using the first order logical connectives. These connectives are handled by standard automata operations: logical conjunction translates to automata intersection, logical negation to automata complementation, and existential quantification to automata projection. Quantification deserves a closer look. Consider the formula $\exists x_2(x_1 + x_2 = x_3)$; this defines the relation $x_1 \leq x_3$. The automaton for this formula can be derived by simply "erasing" the second component of each transition label of the automaton in Figure 2, yielding a nondeterministic automaton. To return to a canonical form, this automaton would

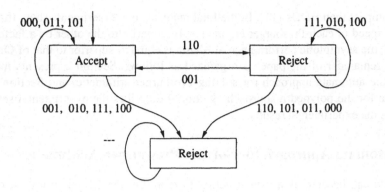

Fig. 2. The automaton representing $x_1 + x_2 = x_3$.

need to be determinized and minimized (Shasta automatically applies state minimization after every operation). Given a minimized automaton, satisfiability can be checked in constant time.

The Shasta package incorporates the automaton data structure of Henriksen *et al.* [14]. Rather then having 2^k labels annotating the outgoing transitions of each state, a BDD with multiple terminals is used. Specifically, each state of an automaton points to a BDD that determines the next state as a function of the incoming bit vector. The terminal nodes of the BDD are the possible next states, and the BDDs for different states can share common subgraphs. Figure 3 shows the same automaton as Figure 2, with its transitions represented by BDDs.

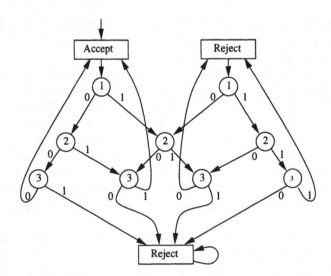

Fig. 3. The automaton representing $x_1 + x_2 = x_3$, with transitions represented by BDDs.

Shasta actually goes slightly beyond Presburger arithmetic by treating Boolean variables specially, rather than just as natural number variables that only take the values 0 and 1. This is done simply by ordering all the Boolean variables first, and reading their values just once. The effect at the data structure level is an automaton rooted by a "pure" BDD, whose terminals are states of the automaton.

Presburger arithmetic is strictly defined over just the naturals, not all the integers. The Shasta package follows this definition. However, it is possible to extend Presburger arithmetic to the integers by encoding each integer as a pair of natural numbers [18].

3 Polyhedra Approach for Solving Presburger Arithmetic

The set of solutions to a Presburger formula can be represented in a sum of products form, whose primitive formulas are linear equalities, inequalities, and congruences:

$$
\bigvee_k \left[\bigwedge_j (0 = a_{0jk} + \sum_i a_{ijk} x_i) \wedge \bigwedge_j (0 < b_{0jk} + \sum_i b_{ijk} x_i) \right.
$$

$$
\left. \wedge \bigwedge_j (0 \equiv_{d_{jk}} c_{0jk} + \sum_i c_{ijk} x_i) \right] \tag{1}
$$

Here $\equiv_d$ means equivalent modulo d, a_{ijk}, b_{ijk}, c_{ijk}, and d_{jk} are all integer constants, and x_i are integer variables. This formula can be given a geometric interpretation: the conjunction of equalities defines a linear subspace, the conjunction of inequalities defines a convex polyhedron, and the congruences pick out periodic sets.

The essential function required of a Presburger engine is to check the satisfiability of a formula. To check satisfiability in a polyhedra-based approach, a Presburger formula must first be converted to a sum of products, as in Equation 1. The next step is to existentially quantify any free variables. If the resulting formula, involving only constants, is true, then the original formula is satisfiable. Thus, we need to construct, for any Presburger formula, a representation in the form of Equation 1 [13]. As mentioned in Section 2, Presburger formulas are built up from linear equalities and inequalities using conjunction, complementation, and quantification. Linear equalities and inequalities are just trivial instances of the representation in Equation 1. Any conjunction can be simply distributed over the disjunctions to produce a new disjunctive form. Complementation of an entire SOP formula can be converted by De Morgan's rule into combinations of complementations of primitive formulas. The complements of the primitive formulas can be expressed in terms of uncomplemented primitive formulas.

Lastly, we need to see how to existentially quantify a variable in this representation and express the result in the same form. The details of this operation are too complex to provide in this brief treatment, but the main steps can be outlined. First, to quantify a variable x, all the primitive formulas need to be scaled so that x appears with the same coefficient, a, which will be the least common multiple of the coefficients of x in the original primitive formulas. Then ax can be replaced by a new variable y, adding the new term $0 \equiv_a y$ to our formula.

Finally, to eliminate y, if there any equalities that include y then one can just use Gaussian elimination, picking one equality to provide a formula to substitute for y in all its other occurrences. If y does not occur in any equality, then Fourier-Motzkin elimination can be used to check the various inequalities for the existence of a solution. The basic idea is that for every pair of inequalities $f < y$ and $y < g$, the inequality $f < g$ must be satisfied. One also needs to guarantee that the gap between f and g includes some integer that satisfies the various congruence equations. There are a finite number of congruence classes, so the possible solutions can be enumerated. Enumerating the pairs of inequalities and the congruence classes can generate a large number of new inequalities. This potential for combinatorial explosion is what makes Presburger arithmetic complex.

The main challenge in using this polyhedra-based representation is efficiency. The representation is not canonical. Given one representation for the set of solutions to a formula, one can apply various minimization tactics to search for a smaller equivalent representation. These tactics can get very expensive and one cannot tell in advance whether they will succeed in reducing the size of the representation. At the same time very simple tactics can be quite effective.

The Omega package [15, 17] uses sophisticated versions of these techniques to provide a complete set of Presburger arithmetic operations. It offers user control over when, and to what degree, minimization of formulas should be applied. With such polyhedra-based techniques, it is most natural to support positive and negative numbers on an equal footing. Note that the Omega package does not provide any direct support for Boolean variables, unlike the Shasta package.

4 Experimental Results

The purpose of the experiments is to compare the relative performance of the automata-based Shasta engine to the polyhedra-based Omega engine. In this section, we first discuss in more detail the context of the experiments, namely EFSM reachability, then describe the experimental framework and examples used, present the experimental data, and finally draw some conclusions.

4.1 EFSM Reachability

EFSMs differ from FSMs in that some of the input and state variables of an EFSM can be unbounded natural numbers. Nonetheless, the BFS-based implicit state enumeration technique used for FSMs [10] can be carried directly over to the EFSM domain. Let x_i, x_s, x'_s, and x_o represent the sets of natural number variables[2] for the inputs, present states, next states, and outputs, respectively, of an EFSM, and let I and T represent the set of initial states and the monolithic transition relation, respectively. Then the set of states reachable in j or fewer steps is given by:

$$R_0(x_s) = I(x_s)$$
$$R_j(x'_s) = R_{j-1}(x'_s) \lor \exists x_s, x_i, x_o(R_{j-1}(x_s) \land T(x_i, x_s, x'_s, x_o))$$

---

[2] For this explanation, we do not distinguish Boolean variables.

If I and T are Presburger definable, then R_j is a Presburger formula, and hence the entire calculation can be carried out using a Presburger engine. One major difference between FSM state enumeration and EFSM state enumeration is that the latter is not guaranteed to converge, because EFSMs are infinite state systems. Our reachability algorithm tests for convergence after each step; some of our examples converge, others do not.

4.2 Experimental Framework and Examples

The examples are described in a dialect of Verilog that includes wires carrying unbounded integer values, and arithmetic modules that operate on them. In particular, each example is specified as a multi-level circuit, where the components can be adders, subtractors, multiplexors, comparators, Boolean logic gates, and Boolean and integer valued flip-flops. There is a single clock that drives all the flip-flops.

We incorporated EFSM reachability into the VIS program [5] by making several modifications and additions to VIS. First, we added a generic Presburger engine interface which, at the flip of a runtime switch, can use either the Shasta or Omega engines. This way we perform the same sequence of elementary operations with both engines, ensuring a fair comparison. Second, we modified the front end of VIS to accept the Verilog dialect mentioned above. Third, we wrote a new routine to build the transition relation using a series of generic Presburger engine calls. Specifically, a monolithic transition relation is built by introducing a variable for each internal circuit net, constructing the input/output relation of each circuit component, forming the conjunction of all the component relations, and then existentially quantifying all the internal variables. Finally, we added a new reachability routine that also makes use of generic Presburger calls. Customary BDD techniques, such as early variable quantification and the use of don't cares for minimization, could be applied in the Presburger framework also, but this has not been done.

We developed several small EFSM examples; these are either typical circuits found in DSP, communication protocol, and computer applications, or they are intended to test hypotheses regarding the relative strengths of the two engines. The circuits are briefly characterized in Table 1; *sequential depth* refers to the greatest lower bound on the path length from an initial state to any reachable state. A brief description of each example follows.

- "ticket" is the ticket mutual-exclusion algorithm from [8], with 2 clients. A client can enter the critical section when its local ticket number becomes equal to the last used ticket number, plus one. An extra Boolean input is used to model the interleaving semantics used in [8].
- "perfect" reads a number a and then computes the sum of all the divisors of a (excluding a itself). If the sum equals a, then a is called "perfect".
- "sdiv" is a serial divider. A numerator and denominator are read and saved, and then the denominator is repeatedly subtracted from the numerator until the remainder is less than the denominator.
- "euclid" implements Euclid's greatest common divisor algorithm. Two numbers are read and saved. At each cycle the smaller number is subtracted from the larger number until they become equal.

Example	State Variables		Input Variables		Internal Variables		Sequential Depth
	Boolean	Integer	Boolean	Integer	Boolean	Integer	
ticket	6	4	1	0	43	6	∞
perfect	0	4	1	1	3	13	∞
sdiv	0	4	1	2	1	8	∞
euclid	0	4	1	2	2	8	∞
bound	6	6	1	6	25	10	5
movavg$n$	n	$n+1$	0	1	1	$2n+2$	$2n$
shiftbool$n$	n	0	0	0	0	0	n
shiftint$n$	0	n	0	0	0	0	n
shifteq$n$	0	n	0	0	n	0	n

Table 1. Characteristics of circuits.

- "bound" is the EFSM shown in Figure 1. It reads the x, y coordinates of two points and a difference vector, and checks whether the two points are closer than that difference. The control states are one-hot encoded.
- "movavg$n$" reads in a stream of numbers and keeps the sum of the last n numbers read. It has n registers to store the stream of inputs, and uses a one-hot control word to keep track of which register to update next.
- "shiftint$n$" is an integer circular shift register of length n. It has no inputs, and its initial state is $1, 0, \ldots, 0$.
- "shiftbool$n$" is exactly like shiftint$n$, except that its variables are Boolean, rather than integer. Its initial state is TRUE, FALSE, ... , FALSE.
- "shifteq$n$" is an integer circular shift register where, for a given register, if it holds a 0, then a 0 is passed, else a 1 is passed. Thus, for any initial state, after one step, all registers will contain either 0 or 1, and the behavior thereafter is like a pure circular shift register. The initial state is $1, 0, \ldots, 0$.

We had to address the treatment of negative integers, since Shasta and Omega differ on this point. Rather than encumbering Shasta by extending it to negatives, or burdening Omega by adding "≥ 0" constraints on each variable, we decided to let each run in its "natural" mode. All of the examples were originally conceived as operating on the naturals; when presented with negative input values, some of the examples (e.g., sdiv) do not compute meaningful results, but we feel that Omega does not have to work "harder" because of this.

As mentioned in Section 3, Omega does not support Boolean variables as a special type. We experimented with two different encodings for Boolean variables for Omega: 1) FALSE is 0 and TRUE is $\neq 0$, and 2) FALSE is ≤ 0 and TRUE is > 0. We found that the second gives better results. Also, for the Omega experiments, formula minimization was applied after every Presburger operation, except for building atomic formulas, by calling the Omega function "simplify" with arguments (2, 2).

4.3 Results and Discussion

Computation of reachable states for any particular EFSM design proceeds in two phases. First we build, starting from the netlist representation of the EFSM, a single Presburger formula that defines its transition relation. Columns 3–6 in Table 2 show the CPU time (in seconds) and memory costs (in kilobytes) for this phase of the computation for each example, for both Shasta and Omega. The second phase of the computation is the iterative accumulation of reachable states, starting with an initial state, computing images, and checking for a fixed point. In those designs where a fixed point exists we let the computation proceed to that fixed point. In those designs where a fixed point does not exist, we run the computation out to where computational costs have grown significantly. Columns 7–10 in Table 2 show the costs for this phase of the computation.

Example	Depth	Build Transition Relation				Reachability			
		Shasta		Omega		Shasta		Omega	
		Time	Mem.	Time	Mem.	Time	Mem.	Time	Mem.
ticket	10	17.5	721	1061.5	16335	10.6	0	308.2	0
perfect	20	6.8	582	2.3	1507	36.3	1483	2636.9	11043
sdiv	40	1.8	25	0.4	672	2953.8	65872	414.6	3891
euclid	6	2.3	90	0.5	762	275.8	60834	83.4	2908
bound	5	196.0	46596	34961.6	29516	241.4	0	253.8	8602
movavg2	4	1.9	197	0.9	745	0.7	0	0.4	0
movavg3	6	3.6	950	3.9	1221	3.2	0	1.8	0
movavg4	8	6.7	2417	16.7	1909	13.3	16	6.0	0
movavg5	10	13.9	5956	74.5	3408	49.5	25	18.6	0
movavg6	12	43.5	16253	470.4	7160	208.8	0	51.3	0
shiftbool6	6	0.5	66	4.0	1376	0.8	8	1.7	434
shiftbool7	7	0.6	74	17.6	2630	1.2	8	3.5	1360
shiftbool8	8	0.8	74	80.1	5186	1.7	25	8.0	2777
shiftbool9	9	0.9	90	377.7	10420	2.3	25	17.6	5603
shiftbool10	10	1.0	98	1751.2	21266	3.0	41	41.6	11248
shiftint12	12	0.9	123	0.2	541	4.8	57	146.5	2048
shiftint13	13	1.1	147	0.2	590	6.0	66	238.2	2531
shiftint14	14	1.2	147	0.2	623	7.2	74	372.3	3097
shiftint15	15	1.3	180	0.2	655	8.8	74	550.7	3711
shiftint16	16	1.4	205	0.2	696	10.7	74	785.5	4391
shifteq4	4	1.2	295	6.1	1204	0.8	41	0.9	303
shifteq5	5	2.5	786	66.5	3039	4.8	106	3.0	1622
shifteq6	6	8.7	3195	742.4	9126	33.7	254	11.6	5292

Table 2. Results on building transition relations and performing reachability.

All experiments were run on a Sun Ultrasparc 3000 with a 168 MHz clock and 512 MB of main memory. The CPU times shown are as reported by the standard UNIX function "time". Transition relation build times do not include the time to read the input files. The memory costs shown are not very accurate, especially for reachability. We use the UNIX "sbrk(0)" function to determine the highest address of allocated memory before and after a function, and report the difference. This fails to account for the use of recycled free memory (this explains the 0KB figures in the table), and may also include memory speculatively allocated but not actually used.

Neither Shasta nor Omega emerge as consistently superior. In building transition relations, we never observed Omega running significantly[3] faster than Shasta. On the other hand, there are examples where Shasta runs much faster than Omega (ticket, bound, movavg$n$, shiftbool$n$, and shifteq$n$).

For the reachability computation itself the results are more mixed. There are examples where Shasta runs much faster than Omega; for other examples, Omega runs much faster than Shasta. In particular for the euclid design, Shasta could complete only 6 steps (due to memory use), while Omega could complete eight steps (we show the costs through step six for both tools). Considering both the model build and reachability phases together, Shasta is significantly faster on shiftbool$n$ and ticket, while there are no examples where Omega is significantly faster for both phases.

The above analysis compares the absolute runtimes of the two engines. By varying the reachability depth on the fixed-sized examples, and by varying the circuit size on the parameterized examples, we are able to empirically estimate the asymptotic performance of the two tools (Table 3). Overall, Shasta has the same or better (perfect, shiftbool$n$ and shiftint$n$) asymptotic performance in all cases analyzed.

Example	Phase	Shasta	Omega	Function of	see Figure
euclid	reach.	exponential	exponential	reachability	4a
sdiv	reach.	cubic	cubic	depth	4b
perfect	reach.	quadratic	quintic		4c
movavg$n$	build	exponential	exponential		
	reach.	exponential	exponential		4d
shiftbool$n$	build	exponential	exponential		
	reach.	exponential	exponential	circuit	
shiftint$n$	build	linear	linear	size	
	reach.	quadratic	exponential		
shifteq$n$	build	linear	exponential		
	reach.	quadratic	exponential		

Table 3. Asymptotic performance.

One conceivable factor that could give Shasta an advantage is its special treatment of Boolean variables. If we focus on the build phase, the presence of a significant number of Boolean state or internal variables (examples ticket, bound, movavg$n$, shiftbool$n$, shifteq$n$) is a perfect predictor of when Shasta outperforms Omega. However, for reachability, the presence of Boolean state variables does not assure Shasta is better: Shasta is faster for ticket and shiftbool$n$, but is the same or slower for bound and movavg$n$. Furthermore, Shasta's superiority in reachability on shiftbool$n$ cannot be explained simply by the presence of Boolean variables, since it similarly outperforms Omega on shiftint$n$, which has no Boolean variables. Recently, Bultan et al. [7] proposed a variant of Omega, where a Presburger formula with integer and Boolean variables is represented by a set of Omega and BDD pairs. They observed a drastic improvement over

---

[3] For runtimes of more than 7 seconds, "significantly" means, here and throughout, more than a factor of 3.

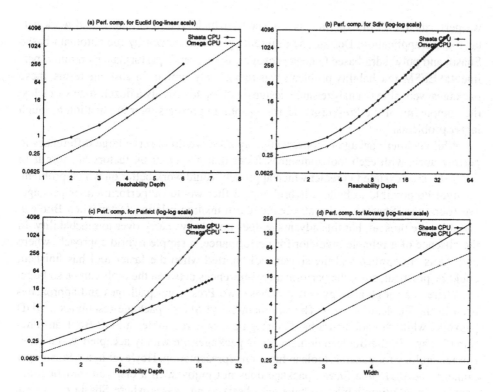

Fig. 4. Various plots comparing the performance of Omega vs. Shasta. The vertical axis is CPU time in seconds. Note that graphs a and d are log-linear, and b and c are log-log.

the standard Omega tool on the one example they studied; it would be instructive to perform a direct comparison within our framework.

Does the implementation of Shasta reflect the true potential of the automata-based approach? Fortunately, we were able to answer this question to some degree by comparing Shasta directly to Mona, a second-generation automata package that supports the logic WS1S [2, 14]. Rather than trying to integrate Mona into VIS, we just manually coded two examples (sdiv and euclid) in Mona's WS1S language, using the embedding suggested by Büchi. We also hardcoded the reachability computation out to a fixed number of steps for each example. By ensuring the same variable ordering, we were able to exactly match the automata (with BDD transitions) built by both Shasta and Mona. A performance comparison between Shasta and Mona on these two examples revealed that Mona consistently outperforms Shasta by almost a factor of 2 in runtime. In conclusion, even though the runtimes of Shasta could be reasonably halved, this does not fundamentally alter the observations made above in comparing Shasta to Omega.

5 Conclusions

Our research is focused on performing implicit state enumeration of EFSMs. The heart of such an approach is a computational engine for deciding the validity of Presburger formulas. Having found two very different types of engines discussed in the literature, we performed a set of experiments to discover which type of engine would work better for our application. Despite the different approaches taken by the automata-based Shasta and polyhedra-based Omega packages, their overall performance on our experimental EFSM reachability problems was remarkably similar. In absolute terms, these packages were able to analyze small designs with up to roughly a dozen state variables; the complexity of the Presburger decision problem prevents their application to much larger problems.

While neither package is consistently superior, we do observe large differences in performance, with each tool sometimes faster than the other by factors of more than 50. If it were possible to predict which approach would work better on which problem, it might be possible to build a hybrid engine that would outperform either package. We found that Shasta consistently builds the transition relation faster when Boolean variables are present, but this advantage does not always carry over to reachability. In the absence of a reliable predictor for performance, a simple hybrid approach, where both tools are applied and the slower tool aborted when the faster tool has finished, could be practical, since the performance differences between the tools can be so large.

There is a rough analogy between these two Presburger packages and approaches used in the Boolean domain. The automata-based Shasta package resembles a BDD package, while the polyhedra-based Omega package resembles a SOP Boolean function package. In the Boolean domain, BDD packages are widely accepted as the superior technology for general Boolean function representation. However in the Presburger domain, the BDD-like Shasta package does not enjoy such a clear cut practical advantage. In addition, while we have not observed any cases where Shasta has worse asymptotic performance, in the Boolean domain cases are known to exist where a SOP representation is superior to BDDs [11]. Thus, we expect that similar situations exist in the Presburger domain where Omega will outperform Shasta not only in raw terms, but also in asymptotic performance.

Acknowledgments We thank Kurt Keutzer for suggesting to us the use of Presburger arithmetic for analyzing EFSMs, and Adnan Aziz for modifying VIS to support EFSMs.

References

1. T. Amon, G. Borriello, T. Hu, and J. Liu. Symbolic timing verification of timing diagrams using Presburger formulas. In *Proc. 34th Design Automat. Conf.*, pages 226–237, June 1997.
2. M. Biehl, N. Klarlund, and T. Rauhe. Mona: Decidable arithmetic in practice. In B. Jonsson and J. Parrow, editors, *Fourth International Symposium Formal Techniques in Real-Time and Fault-Tolerant Systems*, volume 1135 of *LNCS*, Uppsala, Sweden, 1996. Springer-Verlag.
3. B. Boigelot and P. Wolper. Symbolic verification with periodic sets. In D. L. Dill, editor, *Proc. Computer Aided Verification*, volume 818 of *LNCS*, pages 55–67, Stanford, CA, June 1994. Springer-Verlag.
4. A. Boudet and H. Comon. Diophantine equations, Presburger arithmetic and finite automata. In H. Kirchner, editor, *Trees and Algebra in Programming - CAAP*, volume 1059 of *LNCS*, pages 30–43. Springer-Verlag, 1996.
5. R. K. Brayton, G. D. Hachtel, A. Sangiovanni-Vincentelli, F. Somenzi, A. Aziz, S.-T. Cheng, S. Edwards, S. Khatri, Y. Kukimoto, A. Pardo, S. Qadeer, R. K. Ranjan, S. Sarwary, T. R. Shiple, G. Swamy, and T. Villa. VIS: A system for verification and synthesis. In R. Alur and

T. A. Henzinger, editors, *Proceedings of the Conference on Computer-Aided Verification*, volume 1102 of *LNCS*, pages 428–432, New Brunswick, NJ, July 1996. Springer-Verlag.

6. J. R. Büchi. On a decision method in restricted second order arithmetic. In *Proc. Int. Congress Logic, Methodology, and Philosophy of Science*, pages 1–11, Berkeley, CA, 1960. Stanford University Press.

7. T. Bultan, R. Gerber, and C. League. Verifying systems with integer constraints and boolean predicates: A composite approach. In *Proceedings of the 1998 International Symposium on Software Testing and Analysis (ISSTA '98)*, 1998.

8. T. Bultan, R. Gerber, and W. Pugh. Symbolic model checking of infinite state programs using Presburger arithmetic. In O. Grumberg, editor, *Proc. Computer Aided Verification*, volume 1254 of *LNCS*, pages 400–411, Haifa, June 1997. Springer-Verlag.

9. K.-T. Cheng and A. Krishnakumar. Automatic functional test generation using the extended finite state machine model. In *Proc. 30th Design Automat. Conf.*, pages 86–91, June 1993.

10. O. Coudert, C. Berthet, and J. C. Madre. Verification of synchronous sequential machines based on symbolic execution. In J. Sifakis, editor, *Proceedings of the Workshop on Automatic Verification Methods for Finite State Systems*, volume 407 of *LNCS*, pages 365–373. Springer-Verlag, June 1989.

11. S. Devadas. Comparing two-level and ordered binary decision diagram representations of logic functions. *IEEE Trans. Computer-Aided Design*, 12(5):722–723, May 1993.

12. S. Devadas, K. Keutzer, and A. Krishnakumar. Design verification and reachability analysis using algebraic manipulation. In *Proc. Int'l Conf. on Computer Design*, pages 250–258, Oct. 1991.

13. H. B. Enderton. *A Mathematical Introduction to Logic*. Academic Press, New York, 1972.

14. J. G. Henriksen, J. Jensen, M. Jørgensen, N. Klarlund, R. Paige, T. Rauhe, and A. Sandholm. Mona: Monadic second-order logic in practice. In *Tools and Algorithms for the Construction and Analysis of Systems, First International Workshop, TACAS '95*, volume 1019 of *LNCS*, pages 89–110. Springer-Verlag, May 1995.

15. W. Kelly, V. Maslov, W. Pugh, E. Rosser, T. Shpeisman, and D. Wonnacott. The Omega library (Version 1.1.0) interface guide. http://www.cs.umd.edu/ projects/omega, Nov. 1996.

16. D. Oppen. A $2^{2^{2^{pn}}}$ upper bound on the complexity of Presburger arithmetic. *Journal of Computer and System Sciences*, 16(3):323–332, July 1978.

17. W. Pugh. A practical algorithm for exact array dependence analysis. *Communications of the ACM*, 35(8):102–114, Aug. 1992.

18. B. L. van der Waerden. *Modern Algebra*, volume 1. Ungar, 1953.

19. P. Wolper and B. Boigelot. An automata-theoretic approach to Presburger arithmetic constraints. In *Proc. of Static Analysis Symposium*, volume 983 of *LNCS*, pages 21–32. Springer-Verlag, Sept. 1995.

Generating Finite-State Abstractions of Reactive Systems Using Decision Procedures*

Michael A. Colón and Tomás E. Uribe

Computer Science Department, Stanford University
Stanford, CA 94305
colon|uribe@cs.stanford.edu

Abstract. We present an algorithm that uses decision procedures to generate finite-state abstractions of possibly infinite-state systems. The algorithm compositionally abstracts the transitions of the system, relative to a given, fixed set of assertions. Thus, the number of validity checks is proportional to the size of the system description, rather than the size of the abstract state-space. The generated abstractions are weakly preserving for ∀CTL* temporal properties. We describe several applications of the algorithm, implemented using the decision procedures of the Stanford Temporal Prover (STeP).

1 Introduction

An attractive method for proving a temporal property φ for a reactive system S is to find a simpler *abstract system* A such that if A satisfies φ, then S satisfies φ as well. In particular, if A is finite-state, the validity of φ for A can be established automatically using a model checker, which may not have been possible for S due to an infinite or overly large state-space.

There are two obstacles to this approach. First, the construction of A is often manual and has to be proved correct at a later stage. This process can be error-prone if the proof is not formal, and tedious otherwise. Second, abstractions may not be *fine* enough: if A is too abstract, A may not satisfy φ, even if S does. We address the first problem by automatically constructing an A that is guaranteed to be a correct abstraction, based on limited user input. We begin to address the second by constructing abstractions quickly: abstractions that are found to be too coarse can be *refined* with little effort and tested again. Thus, finding the right abstraction is an iterative process where the user tests a number of candidate abstractions, possibly guided by feedback from a model checker. The procedure we present can be the basic building block in this process.

As in the procedure of Graf and Saidi [GS97], we use validity checking to generate a finite-state abstraction based on a set of formulas $B = \{b_1, \ldots, b_n\}$.

---

* This research was supported in part by the National Science Foundation under grant CCR-95-27927, the Defense Advanced Research Projects Agency under NASA grant NAG2-892, ARO under grant DAAH04-95-1-0317, ARO under MURI grant DAAH04-96-1-0341, and by Army contract DABT63-96-C-0096 (DARPA).

However, rather than performing an exhaustive search of the reachable abstract states while constructing $\mathcal{A}$, our algorithm transforms $\mathcal{S}$ to $\mathcal{A}$ directly, leaving the exploration of the abstract state-space to a model checker. Thus, the number of validity checks performed by our algorithm is proportional to the number of formulas in B and the size of the representation of $\mathcal{S}$, rather than the size of the abstract state-space. Furthermore, our procedure is applicable to systems whose abstract state-space is too large to enumerate explicitly, but can still be handled by a symbolic model checker [McM93].

The price paid by our approach, compared to [GS97], is that a coarser abstraction may be obtained. However, we offset this by using a richer abstract state-space: the complete boolean algebra of expressions over $B = \{b_1, \ldots, b_n\}$, rather than only the monomials over this set. Our procedure can be seen as a form of abstract interpretation [CC77], with this algebra as the abstract domain.

1.1   Related Work

Our abstraction procedure is related to the work of [GS97] and [SUM96]. The procedure of [GS97] is the closest to ours, as discussed above. In deductive model checking [SUM96], the abstract system and its state-space are generated interactively, using theorem proving, based on the refinement of an initial, maximally abstract system. The refinement proceeds until the property in question can be proved or disproved. That procedure is thus *top-down*, as opposed to the more *bottom-up*, property-independent approaches that this paper and [GS97] propose.[1] In contrast to both [GS97] and [SUM96], we perform validity checking at "compile time," rather than at model check time.

Abstraction frameworks: Theoretical foundations of property-preserving abstraction are presented in [Dam96,LGS$^+$95,CGL94]. We present the necessary results on abstraction in Section 3. Deductive rules for proving simulation and abstraction are presented in [KMP94]. In contrast, our approach is to transform a concrete system into a property-preserving abstract system automatically, obviating the need to prove property preservation for an abstraction given *a priori*.

Approaches based on abstract interpretation [CC77] are presented in, e.g., [CGL94,Dam96,DGG97]. Much of this work is specialized to the case of finite-state systems. We include some simple fairness considerations, a special case of those in the verification rules of [KMP94], which do not appear in most work on abstract interpretation.

Other work uses abstractions that are more explicitly given by the user. For instance, [DF95] applies abstraction and error trace analysis to infinite state systems. The abstraction is generated automatically, given a *data abstraction* that maps concrete variables and operators to abstract ones. [BBM97] uses abstract interpretation to generate invariants and intermediate assertions for fair transition systems. Like ours, their procedure is compositional and automatic,

---

[1] These procedures can be given a top-down flavor by including in the set B atoms from the temporal formula being verified.

given a suitable abstract domain. Their emphasis is on finding abstraction domains where the reachable state-space can be approximated to produce useful invariants. We, however, are motivated by the need to prove general temporal properties over the abstract system. Nonetheless, our abstractions can be used to generate invariants as well. These invariants can, in turn, be used to generate more precise abstractions.

Over- and under-approximations: Pardo and Hachtel [PH97] present an automatic BDD-based method for symbolic model checking, where the size of BDD's is reduced using over- and under-approximations of subformulas, depending on their polarity. We use polarity in an analogous way. Another approximated BDD-based symbolic model checking procedure is presented in [KDG95], based on the abstract interpretation framework of [Dam96]. These procedures do not change the state-space of the system, but instead approximate the transition relation to produce smaller BDDs.

Dill and Wong-Toi [DW95,Won95] use abstract-interpretation to verify timed safety automata, over- and under-approximating sets of states and next-state relations. This work approximates set operations during model checking, as well as statically approximating the transitions themselves, using methods specialized to real-time systems. The algorithm we propose for over- and under-approximating transitions could be used in similar settings as well.

2 Preliminaries

2.1 Fair and Clocked Transition Systems

Fair transition systems [MP95] are a convenient formalism for specifying finite- and infinite-state reactive systems, using an assertion language based on first-order logic. A fair transition system (FTS) $S = \langle \Sigma, \Theta, \mathcal{T} \rangle$ is given by a set of *system states* Σ, an *initial condition* Θ, and a set of *transitions* $\mathcal{T}$. Each state in Σ is a valuation of a finite set of typed *system variables* $\mathcal{V}$. If Σ is finite, S is said to be *finite-state*.

Definition 1 (Assertion). *A first-order formula whose free variables are a subset of $\mathcal{V}$ is an* assertion, *or* state-formula, *and represents the set of states that satisfy it. For an assertion φ, we say that $s \in \Sigma$ is a φ-state iff $s \models \varphi$, that is, φ holds given the values of $\mathcal{V}$ at s.*

The initial condition Θ is an assertion that characterizes the set of initial states. With each transition $\tau \in \mathcal{T}$ we associate its *transition relation* $\rho_\tau(\mathcal{V}, \mathcal{V}')$, a first-order formula over the system variables $\mathcal{V}$ and a primed set $\mathcal{V}'$, indicating their values at the next state. A transition is *enabled* if it can be taken at a given state. We define $enabled(\tau) \stackrel{\text{def}}{=} \exists \mathcal{V}'.\rho_\tau(\mathcal{V}, \mathcal{V}')$. We define $post(\tau, \varphi)$ as the assertion $\exists \mathcal{V}_0. (\rho_\tau(\mathcal{V}_0, \mathcal{V}) \wedge \varphi(\mathcal{V}_0))$, which characterizes the states reachable from φ-states by taking transition τ. As usual, we define φ' to be the result of replacing each free variable x of φ with x'. For a set of expressions E, let $E' \stackrel{\text{def}}{=} \{\varphi' \mid \varphi \in E\}$.

A *run* of S is an infinite sequence of states $s_0, s_1, \ldots$, such that $s_0 \models \Theta$ and for all $i \geq 0$, $\rho_\tau(s_i, s_{i+1})$ for some $\tau \in \mathcal{T}$. In this case, we say that τ is *taken* at s_i. Transitions can be labeled as *just* or *compassionate*. A just (or *weakly fair*) transition cannot be continuously enabled without being taken; a compassionate (or *strongly fair*) transition cannot be enabled infinitely often but taken only finitely many times. A *computation* is a run that satisfies all fairness requirements. To ensure that run prefixes can always be extended to an infinite sequence, we assume an *idling transition*, with transition relation $V = V'$.

Clocked transition systems [MP96] are an extension of fair transition systems that is intended to model reactive systems with real-time constraints. A clocked transition system (CTS) is a fair transition system $S = \langle \Sigma, \Theta, \mathcal{T} \rangle$, whose system variables are partitioned into a set of *discrete variables* D and a set of real-valued *clock variables* C. Instead of an idling transition, $\mathcal{T}$ includes a *tick transition*, which is the only transition that can advance time. The progress of time is restricted by a *time-progress condition* Π, an assertion over D and C. The transition relation for *tick* is:

$$\rho_{tick} : \exists \Delta > 0. \begin{pmatrix} (D' = D) \wedge (C' = C + \Delta) \\ \wedge \\ \forall t \in [0, \Delta].\Pi(D, C + t) \end{pmatrix},$$

where $C' = C + \Delta$ stands for $c_1' = c_1 + \Delta \wedge \ldots \wedge c_k' = c_k + \Delta$, and $\Pi(D, C + t)$ stands for $\Pi(d_1, \ldots, d_j, c_1 + t, \ldots, c_k + t)$, where $D = \{d_1, \ldots, d_j\}$.[2]

We do not impose fairness conditions on the transitions of a clocked transition system. Instead, upper bounds on the time that can pass before an enabled transition is taken can be specified using the time-progress condition. The computations of a CTS are the runs where time grows beyond any bound.

2.2 Temporal Logic

We use linear-time temporal logic (LTL) to express properties of reactive systems. Temporal formulas are built from assertions, boolean operators $(\wedge, \vee, \neg, \rightarrow)$, and temporal operators $(\Box, \Diamond, \mathcal{U}, \mathcal{W})$, as usual. (See [MP95] for details.) LTL properties are part of the universal fragment of CTL*, that is, a subset of $\forall$CTL* [Eme90]. Our procedure applies to the verification of $\forall$CTL* properties, and hence also to LTL.

2.3 Example

Figure 1 presents a fragment of Fischer's real-time mutual exclusion algorithm, as described in [MP96], using the simple programming language of [MP95]. The algorithm assumes uniform positive bounds L and U on the time each process can wait before executing its next statement: an enabled transition must wait at least L and at most U before being taken. If $2L > U$, the algorithm guarantees that both processes are never in their critical sections simultaneously.

---

[2] Clocked transition systems also contain a *master clock* T, which can only be changed by the *tick* transition; Θ should imply $T = 0$. We will not need T for our example.

$$\begin{array}{c}\textbf{local } x : \{0,1,2\} \textbf{ where } x = 0\end{array}$$

$$P_1 :: \begin{bmatrix} \ell_0: \textbf{await } x = 0 \\ \ell_1: \ x := 1 \\ \ell_2: \textbf{skip} \\ \ell_3: \textbf{await } x = 1 \\ \ell_4: \textbf{critical} \end{bmatrix} \quad \| \quad P_2 :: \begin{bmatrix} m_0: \textbf{await } x = 0 \\ m_1: \ x := 2 \\ m_2: \textbf{skip} \\ m_3: \textbf{await } x = 2 \\ m_4: \textbf{critical} \end{bmatrix}$$

Fig. 1. Fischer's mutual exclusion algorithm.

To model the program as a clocked transition system, we introduce two control variables π_1 and π_2, ranging over $\{\ell_0,\dots,\ell_4\}$ and $\{m_0,\dots,m_4\}$ respectively, and two clock variables c_1 and c_2. As Θ, we take the assertion $\pi_1 = \ell_0 \wedge \pi_2 = m_0 \wedge c_1 = 0 \wedge c_2 = 0 \wedge x = 0$. We then introduce a transition for each statement, e.g., statement ℓ_1 yields transition τ_{ℓ_1}, with relation

$$\rho_{\ell_1} : \begin{pmatrix} \pi_1 = \ell_1 \ \wedge \ c_1 \geq L \ \wedge \\ \pi'_1 = \ell_2 \ \wedge \ c'_1 = 0 \ \wedge \ x' = 1 \end{pmatrix} \wedge \ \pi'_2 = \pi_2 \ \wedge \ c'_2 = c_2 \ .$$

Finally, we take as the time-progress condition $\Pi : c_1 \leq U \wedge c_2 \leq U$, and add the transition *tick*.

Mutual exclusion is expressed by the LTL formula $\Box \neg (\pi_1 = \ell_4 \wedge \pi_2 = m_4)$.

3 Abstraction

Abstraction reduces the verification of a temporal property φ over a *concrete system* S, to checking a related property over a simpler, *abstract system* A. For simplicity, we write $A \models \varphi$ to indicate that the corresponding property holds for the abstract system.

In the following, we use the notation of [Dam96] whenever possible. Given a set of temporal properties T and two systems S and A, we say that A is a *weakly preserving* abstraction of S for T iff for any $\varphi \in T$, if $A \models \varphi$ then $S \models \varphi$. (A is said to be a *strongly preserving* abstraction if the converse is also true, but we will only use weakly preserving abstractions in this paper.)

Based on the ideas of *abstract interpretation* [CC77], the abstract system can be constructed from an abstract set of states Σ^A and a partial order $\preceq$, where $a_1 \preceq a_2$ if a_1 is a "more precise" abstract state than a_2. Such abstractions are often presented in terms of *Galois connections*, where the two posets connected are $(2^\Sigma, \subseteq)$ and $(\Sigma^A, \preceq)$, where Σ is the concrete state-space. (see, e.g., [LGS+95,Dam96]). A *concretization function* $\gamma : \Sigma^A \mapsto 2^\Sigma$ maps each abstract state to the set of concrete states it represents, and an *abstraction function* $\alpha : 2^\Sigma \mapsto \Sigma^A$ maps each set of concrete states to the most precise abstract state that represents it. The pair (α, γ) is a Galois connection iff for all $x \in 2^\Sigma$ and all $y \in \Sigma^A$, $\alpha(x) \preceq y$ if and only if $x \subseteq \gamma(y)$. We extend γ to sets of abstract states $S \in 2^{\Sigma^A}$ with $\gamma(S) \stackrel{\text{def}}{=} \bigcup_{a \in S} \gamma(a)$.

The following abstract domain is often (implicitly) used in deductive verification:

Definition 2 (Assertion-based abstraction). *As the abstract domain $\Sigma^{\mathcal{A}}$, choose the complete boolean algebra $\mathcal{BA}(B)$ (using $\wedge^{\mathcal{A}}, \vee^{\mathcal{A}}, \neg^{\mathcal{A}}$) over a finite set of assertions B, where $s_1^{\mathcal{A}} \preceq s_2^{\mathcal{A}}$ iff $s_1^{\mathcal{A}}$ implies $s_2^{\mathcal{A}}$. Then let $\gamma(f) = \{s \in \Sigma \mid s \models f\}$ and $\alpha(S) = \bigwedge^{\mathcal{A}} \{s^{\mathcal{A}} \in \mathcal{BA}(B) \mid S \subseteq \gamma(s^{\mathcal{A}})\}$. We call this the assertion-based abstract domain with basis B.*

We now have a *Galois insertion* from $(2^{\Sigma}, \subseteq)$ to $(\Sigma^{\mathcal{A}}, \preceq)$, since $\alpha(\gamma(f)) = f$ for all $f \in \mathcal{BA}(B)$.

Notation: Note that we use $\wedge^{\mathcal{A}}, \vee^{\mathcal{A}}, \neg^{\mathcal{A}}$ for operations in the abstract domain, while $\wedge, \vee, \neg, \rightarrow$ are the usual connectives in the general assertion language.

We will continue to characterize sets of concrete states using assertions, which need not be points in the abstract state-space. For a formula $s^{\mathcal{A}} \in \mathcal{BA}(B)$, we will write $\gamma(s^{\mathcal{A}})$ to characterize the set of states it represents, rather than simply $s^{\mathcal{A}}$, to highlight the fact that $s^{\mathcal{A}}$ is an abstract state, while $\gamma(s^{\mathcal{A}})$ is an assertion (representing a set of concrete states). More formally, $\gamma(s^{\mathcal{A}})$ is obtained from $s^{\mathcal{A}}$ by replacing $\wedge^{\mathcal{A}}$, $\vee^{\mathcal{A}}$ and $\neg^{\mathcal{A}}$ by $\wedge$, $\vee$ and $\neg$; the boolean variables in $s^{\mathcal{A}}$, which are elements of B, appear as corresponding subformulas in $\gamma(s^{\mathcal{A}})$. In this way, the extension of γ to sets can be characterized as $\gamma(S) = \bigvee_{a \in S} \gamma(a)$. For assertions f_1 and f_2, we sometimes write $f_1 \subseteq f_2$ when $f_1 \rightarrow f_2$ is valid.

The correctness of our abstractions is based on the following lemma.

Lemma 1 (Weak Preservation of ∀CTL*—a sufficient condition). *Let B be a finite set of assertions, $S = \langle \Sigma, \Theta, \mathcal{T} \rangle$, and $\mathcal{A} = \langle \Sigma^{\mathcal{A}}, \Theta^{\mathcal{A}}, \mathcal{T}^{\mathcal{A}} \rangle$. If*

1. *Initial condition: $\Theta \subseteq \gamma(\Theta^{\mathcal{A}})$ (that is, Θ is over-approximated by $\Theta^{\mathcal{A}}$),*
2. *For each transition $\tau \in \mathcal{T}$ there is a transition $\tau^{\mathcal{A}} \in \mathcal{T}^{\mathcal{A}}$ such that $\rho_{\tau} \subseteq \gamma(\rho_{\tau^{\mathcal{A}}})$ (that is, τ is over-approximated by $\tau^{\mathcal{A}}$), and*
3. *Fairness: If $\tau^{\mathcal{A}} \in \mathcal{T}^{\mathcal{A}}$ is just (resp. compassionate), then there is a just (resp. compassionate) $\tau \in \mathcal{T}$ such that: (a) $\gamma(enabled(\tau^{\mathcal{A}})) \subseteq enabled(\tau)$, and (b) $post(\tau, enabled(\tau)) \subseteq \gamma(post(\tau^{\mathcal{A}}, enabled(\tau^{\mathcal{A}})))$,*

then the abstract system $\mathcal{A}$ is a weakly preserving abstraction of S for ∀CTL*.

The third requirement limits the fairness constraints that can be imposed on transitions in $\mathcal{A}$. Note that the more fairness constraints $\mathcal{A}$ has, the more ∀CTL* properties it will satisfy. If *(3)* does not hold, only safety properties will be preserved. Note that *(b)* is guaranteed if $\rho_{\tau} \subseteq \gamma(\rho_{\tau^{\mathcal{A}}})$, in which case *(a)* implies $\gamma(enabled(\tau^{\mathcal{A}})) \leftrightarrow enabled(\tau)$.

This lemma still holds if the inclusions are valid only for the reachable states of S, i.e., invariants of S can be used to establish them. More general conditions for simulation and refinement between fair transition systems are presented in [KMP94] as deductive verification rules.

4 Generating Finite-State Abstractions

In the following, let $B = \{b_1, \ldots, b_n\}$ be a fixed assertion basis. We assume we have at our disposal a procedure *checkValid*, which can sometimes decide the validity of assertions: if *checkValid(p)* returns *true*, then p is valid. That is, this validity checker is assumed to be sound, but is not required to be complete.

The workhorse of our abstraction algorithm is a procedure that approximates assertions over $\mathcal{V}$ and $\mathcal{V}'$ as assertions over B and B'. The procedure descends through the boolean structure of the formula, building an assertion to serve as a *context* and keeping track of the polarity of subexpressions until it reaches the atoms. The procedure then over- or under-approximates each atom using an element of $\mathcal{BA}(B \cup B')$.

4.1 Abstracting Atoms

Atoms are abstracted by testing them, in context, against a set of *points* $P \subseteq \mathcal{BA}(B \cup B')$:

$$\alpha_{atom}(+, C, a) = \bigwedge {}^{\mathcal{A}} \{p \in P \mid checkValid((C \wedge a) \to \gamma(p))\} \quad \text{(over-approximation)}$$

$$\alpha_{atom}(-, C, a) = \bigvee {}^{\mathcal{A}} \{p \in P \mid checkValid((C \wedge \gamma(p)) \to a)\} \quad \text{(under-approximation)}$$

Intuitively, the context C indicates that we are only concerned with results that lie within C. Thus, when over-approximating a in context C, we can consider $a \wedge C$ instead, a smaller set. This yields a smaller result, and hence a more precise over-approximation. Similarly, when under-approximating a in context C, we can under-approximate $a \vee \neg C$ instead. This will give a larger result, and hence a better overall under-approximation.

4.2 Abstracting Assertions

We extend α_{atom} to a function α that abstracts assertions as follows:

$$\alpha(\pi, C, a) = \alpha_{atom}(\pi, C, a), \text{ if } a \text{ is an atom}$$

$$\alpha(\pi, C, \neg q) = \neg^{\mathcal{A}} \alpha(\pi^{-1}, C, q), \text{ where } +^{-1} \stackrel{\text{def}}{=} - \text{ and } -^{-1} \stackrel{\text{def}}{=} +$$

$$\alpha(+, C, q \wedge r) = \text{let } \hat{q} = \alpha(+, C, q) \text{ in } \hat{q} \wedge^{\mathcal{A}} \alpha(+, C \wedge \gamma(\hat{q}), r)$$

$$\alpha(+, C, q \vee r) = \text{let } \hat{q} = \alpha(+, C, q) \text{ in } \hat{q} \vee^{\mathcal{A}} \alpha(+, C \wedge \neg\gamma(\hat{q}), r)$$

$$\alpha(-, C, q \wedge r) = \text{let } \hat{q} = \alpha(-, C, q) \text{ in } \hat{q} \wedge^{\mathcal{A}} \alpha(-, C \wedge \neg\gamma(\hat{q}), r)$$

$$\alpha(-, C, q \vee r) = \text{let } \hat{q} = \alpha(-, C, q) \text{ in } \hat{q} \vee^{\mathcal{A}} \alpha(-, C \wedge \gamma(\hat{q}), r)$$

An assertion f is thus abstracted using $O(|P| \cdot |f|)$ validity checks. The main claim that justifies the correctness of the algorithm is:

Proposition 1. *For assertions C and f,*
$C \to (\gamma(\alpha(-, C, f)) \to f)$ *and* $C \to (f \to \gamma(\alpha(+, C, f)))$ *are valid.*

Notice that this algorithm applies to any abstract domain that is a boolean algebra, provided the operations for $\wedge^{\mathcal{A}}$, $\vee^{\mathcal{A}}$, $\neg^{\mathcal{A}}$ and γ are available. Similarly, it applies to any assertion language for which a validity checker is available.

4.3 Abstracting Systems and Properties

Given a concrete transition system $S = \langle \Sigma, \Theta, T \rangle$, its abstraction is $A = \langle \mathcal{BA}(B), \Theta^A, T^A \rangle$, where Θ^A is the result of over-approximating Θ, and T^A is the result of over-approximating each transition relation in T.

The initial context can contain known invariants of S. When abstracting the atoms of an initial condition or the assertions of a temporal property (see below), we test against the set of unprimed points

$$P_U \overset{\text{def}}{=} B \cup \{\neg b_i \mid b_i \in B\} \ .$$

For transition relations, we test against the set of mixed points

$$P_M \overset{\text{def}}{=} P_U \cup P'_U \cup \{p_1 \to p_2 \mid p_1 \in P_U \land p_2 \in P'_U\} \ .$$

Thus, the algorithm abstracts a transition relation ρ_τ using $O(n^2|\rho_\tau|)$ validity checks, where $n = |B|$. For an assertion f with no primed variables, $O(n|f|)$ validity checks are needed. Enlarging these point sets can increase the quality of the abstraction, as discussed in Section 4.4; however, these relatively small sets sufficed to verify most of the examples in Section 5.

System A is an n-bit finite-state system. Since $\Theta \subseteq \gamma(\Theta^A)$ and $\rho_\tau \subseteq \gamma(\rho_{\tau^A})$ for all $\tau \in T$, conditions *(1)* and *(2)* of Lemma 1 are satisfied. We satisfy condition *(3)* by propagating the fairness of τ to τ^A only if we can establish the validity of $\gamma(enabled(\tau^A)) \to enabled(\tau)$. In this case, the two enabling conditions are equivalent.[3] If the basis includes the atoms in the guard of τ, this is guaranteed to be the case. (If an assertion f contains only atoms in B, then its abstraction is equivalent to f, modulo invariants.) In the worst case no fairness carries over and only safety properties of A (and hence S) can be proved.

A temporal property φ is abstracted by under-approximating the assertions it contains (over-approximating those with negative polarity). This method guarantees that every model of the abstract property corresponds to a model of the concrete one. Thus, if all computations of the abstract system satisfy φ^A, all computations of the concrete system will satisfy φ. If the basis includes all of the assertions appearing in the property, the property approximation is exact.

4.4 Optimizations

Preserving concrete variables: We allow finite-domain variables of S to be propagated through to A, leaving it to the model checker to represent them explicitly or encode them as bits. We implement this by having α be the identity on finite-domain subexpressions whose free variables do not appear in the basis. (Note, however, that the algorithm can always be used to abstract finite-state systems to smaller abstract ones.)

---

[3] In general, the known invariants of S can be used to establish the conditions of Lemma 1, so the two could differ on unreachable states.

Reducing the test point set: Our implementation includes a few simple strategies for eliminating trivial or redundant test points. For example, if an atom implies b_i, it is unnecessary to test the point $\neg b_i \to b'_j$. Also, if τ does not modify the free variables of b_i, we eliminate the points $\{p \to b'_i \mid p \in P_U\}$.

Enlarging the test point set: There are occasions when additional points must be tested to obtain a sufficiently precise abstraction. For example, ρ_τ may imply $(b_i \wedge b_j) \to b'_k$, but imply neither $b_i \to b'_k$ nor $b_j \to b'_k$. However, we are unwilling to incur the potentially exponential cost of a naive enumeration of such points. Instead, we allow the user to specify additional points to test when specifying the basis. Alternatively, the user may enlarge the basis, but this will in general also increase the time and space used at model-check time.

Conjunctions of literals: When a subexpression consists solely of conjunctions of literals, we eliminate redundant validity checks by testing each point once for the entire subexpression. That is, we terminate the recursion early, since testing the points for each atom will not improve the quality of the abstraction.

4.5 Example

We used the following basis to abstract Fischer's algorithm:

$$
\begin{array}{ll}
b_1\colon c_1 \geq L & \qquad b_4\colon c_2 \geq c_1 \\
b_2\colon c_2 \geq L & \qquad b_5\colon c_1 \geq c_2 + L \\
b_3\colon c_1 \geq c_2 & \qquad b_6\colon c_2 \geq c_1 + L
\end{array}
$$

The starting context consisted of assumptions $L > 0$, $U > 0$, $U \geq L$ and $2L > U$, and invariants $c_1 \geq 0$ and $c_2 \geq 0$. The initial condition was abstracted to

$$
\pi_1 = \ell_0 \wedge \pi_2 = m_0 \wedge x = 0 \wedge \neg b_1 \wedge \neg b_2 \wedge b_3 \wedge b_4 \wedge \neg b_5 \wedge \neg b_6
$$

(where we now write $\wedge, \vee, \neg$ rather than $\wedge^A, \vee^A, \neg^A$). Transition ℓ_1 was abstracted to

$$
\rho^A_{\ell_1} : \left(
\begin{array}{c}
\pi_1 = \ell_1 \wedge \pi'_1 = \ell_2 \wedge x' = 1 \wedge \pi'_2 = \pi_2 \wedge \\
b_1 \wedge \neg b'_1 \wedge b'_4 \wedge \neg b'_5 \wedge (b_2 \to \neg b'_3) \wedge (b_2 \to b'_6) \wedge \\
(\neg b_3 \to \neg b'_3) \wedge (\neg b_3 \to b'_6) \wedge (b_4 \to \neg b'_3) \wedge (b_4 \to b'_6) \wedge \\
(\neg b_5 \to \neg b'_3) \wedge (b_6 \to \neg b'_3) \wedge (b_6 \to b'_6)
\end{array}
\right) .
$$

The other transitions were similarly abstracted. (The *tick* transition, which contains quantifiers, was treated as a single literal when abstracted.) With our implementation (see Section 5), the abstract system was generated in 28 seconds, and mutual exclusion was automatically model checked in one second.

5 Experimental Results

We implemented our abstraction procedure using the deductive and algorithmic support found in the Stanford Temporal Prover, STeP [BBC+96]. STeP includes

System	# transitions	Basis size	Abstraction time	Model check time
Bakery	14	3	3s	<1s
Fischer	11	6	28s	1s
Alternating-bit	7	4	14s	<1s
Bounded Retransmission	13	7	70s	4s

Table 1. Abstraction and model check times.

decision procedures for datatypes, partial orders, linear arithmetic, congruence closure and bit-vectors. They are integrated into a general validity checker that is complete for ground formulas, relative to the power of the decision procedures, and can be applied to first-order formulas as well [BSU97]. STeP also includes explicit-state and symbolic LTL model checking for fair transition systems.

We have tested our implementation on a few examples, including two mutual exclusion algorithms and two data-communication protocols. All of these examples are infinite-state: they contain variables whose range is unbounded (integers, lists, and real-valued clocks). For each example, Table 1 gives the size of the basis, the time to generate the abstract system, and the time to model check the properties of interest against the generated abstraction, using STeP's explicit-state model checker.[4] (The concrete systems, properties, bases and abstract systems are available on the web at http://rodin.stanford.edu/abstraction.)

The Bakery algorithm is a two-process mutual exclusion algorithm (see, e.g., [MP95]). The property we verify is mutual exclusion, which proves to be particularly easy to establish since it is sufficient to take as a basis the set of assertions that guard transitions.

In the alternating-bit protocol, a sender and a receiver communicate over two lossy channels. The property we verify is that the receiver's list is always a prefix of the list that the sender is transmitting. The basis for this example was found by *trace-based refinement*: starting with the guards of the transitions, we added assertions to the basis in response to abstract counter-examples found by the model checker. We also found it necessary to add a test point so that the validity checker could derive the necessary inductive properties of lists.

The bounded retransmission protocol in, e.g., [HS96,GS97,DKRT97] is an extension of the alternating-bit protocol where a limit is placed on the number of transmissions of a particular item. As with the alternating-bit protocol, we verify the prefix property of the receiver's list. In addition, we verify that the sender and receiver report their status consistently: either they both report OK, they both report NOT_OK, or the sender reports DONT_KNOW and the receiver reports OK or NOT_OK. To generate the basis, we started with the basis used for the alternating-bit protocol and added the guards of the transitions.

---

[4] While we recognize that the abstraction times are highly dependent on the speed of the validity checker, we present them to give a feel for how quickly the abstractions can be generated in practice.

While verifying the consistency of the status reports, STeP's model checker discovered an abstract counter-example that uncovered an oversight in our original implementation. If the list to be transmitted is empty, the sender finishes immediately, reporting OK. The receiver, not having received a frame whose last bit was set, assumes the sender aborted transmission and reports NOT_OK. To correct this problem, we require that the list be non-empty, since the bounded retransmission protocol is not designed to transmit empty lists.

6 Conclusions

We have presented a procedure for abstracting transition systems in a compositional manner, using a finite-state abstraction domain. Instead of using theorem-proving to explore the abstract state-space, we use it to abstract the transition relations that describe the system. The abstract state-space can then be explored, explicitly or symbolically, by a model checker.

The procedure provides an alternative method for combining deductive and algorithmic verification. The use of deductive tools makes our procedure applicable to infinite-state systems. The efficiency of the abstraction procedure, and the use of finite-state model checking at the abstract level, gives the procedure a level of automation comparable to that of finite-state algorithmic methods. As with deductive methods, the availability of new decision procedures for particular theories increases the power of the algorithm.

The choice of the abstraction basis B can be based on the user's understanding of the system, analogous to the use of intermediate assertions in deductive verification. The procedure is completely automatic once this basis is chosen, and its efficiency allows for various alternatives to be quickly tested. However, techniques for the generation (manual and automatic) of the abstraction basis remain to be tested and explored.

Acknowledgements: We thank Nikolaj Bjørner, Zohar Manna, Hassen Saidi and Henny Sipma for their feedback and comments.

References

[AH96] R. Alur and T.A. Henzinger, editors. *Proc. 8th Intl. Conference on Computer Aided Verification*, vol. 1102 of *LNCS*. Springer-Verlag, July 1996.

[BBC+96] N.S. Bjørner, A. Browne, E.S. Chang, M. Colón, A. Kapur, Z. Manna, H.B. Sipma, and T.E. Uribe. STeP: Deductive-algorithmic verification of reactive and real-time systems. In Alur and Henzinger [AH96], pages 415–418.

[BBM97] N.S. Bjørner, A. Browne, and Z. Manna. Automatic generation of invariants and intermediate assertions. *Theoretical Computer Science*, 173(1):49–87, February 1997. Preliminary version appeared in 1st *Intl. Conf. on Principles and Practice of Constraint Programming*, vol. 976 of LNCS, pp. 589–623, Springer-Verlag, 1995.

[BSU97] N.S. Bjørner, M.E. Stickel, and T.E. Uribe. A practical integration of first-order reasoning and decision procedures. In 14th *Intl. Conf. on Automated Deduction*, vol. 1249 of *LNCS*, pages 101–115. Springer-Verlag, July 1997.

[CC77] P. Cousot and R. Cousot. Abstract interpretation: A unified lattice model for static analysis of programs by construction or approximation of fixpoints. In 4th ACM Symp. Princ. of Prog. Lang., pages 238–252. ACM Press, 1977.

[CGL94] E.M. Clarke, O. Grumberg, and D.E. Long. Model checking and abstraction. ACM Trans. on Prog. Lang. and Systems, 16(5):1512–1542, September 1994.

[Dam96] D.R. Dams. Abstract Interpretation and Partition Refinement for Model Checking. PhD thesis, Eindhoven University of Technology, July 1996.

[DF95] J. Dingel and T. Filkorn. Model checking of infinite-state systems using data abstraction, assumption-commitment style reasoning and theorem proving. In Wolper [Wol95], pages 54–69.

[DGG97] D.R. Dams, R. Gerth, and O. Grümberg. Abstract interpretation of reactive systems. ACM Transactions on Prog. Lang. and Systems, 19(2):253–291, 1997.

[DKRT97] P.R. D'Argenio, J.P. Katoen, T. Ruys, and G.T. Tretmans. The bounded retransmission protocol must be on time! In 3rd TACAS Workshop, vol. 1217 of LNCS, pages 416–432. Springer-Verlag, 1997.

[DW95] D.L. Dill and H. Wong-Toi. Verification of real-time systems by successive over and under approximation. In Wolper [Wol95], pages 409–422.

[Eme90] E.A. Emerson. Temporal and modal logic. In J. van Leeuwen, editor, Handbook of Theoretical Computer Science, vol. B, pages 995–1072. Elsevier Science Publishers (North-Holland), 1990.

[Gru97] O. Grumberg, editor. Proc. 9th Intl. Conference on Computer Aided Verification, vol. 1254 of LNCS. Springer-Verlag, June 1997.

[GS97] S. Graf and H. Saidi. Construction of abstract state graphs with PVS. In Grumberg [Gru97], pages 72–83.

[HS96] K. Havelund and N. Shankar. Experiments in theorem proving and model checking for protocol verification. In Formal Methods Europe, pages 662–681, March 1996.

[KDG95] P. Kelb, D. Dams, and R. Gerth. Practical symbolic model checking of the full μ-calculus using compositional abstractions. Technical Report 95/31, Eindhoven University of Technology, The Netherlands, October 1995.

[KMP94] Y. Kesten, Z. Manna, and A. Pnueli. Temporal verification of simulation and refinement. In A Decade of Concurrency, vol. 803 of LNCS, pages 273–346. Springer-Verlag, 1994.

[LGS+95] C. Loiseaux, S. Graf, J. Sifakis, A. Bouajjani, and S. Bensalem. Property preserving abstractions for the verification of concurrent systems. Formal Methods in System Design, 6:1–35, 1995.

[McM93] K.L. McMillan. Symbolic Model Checking. Kluwer Academic Pub., 1993.

[MP95] Z. Manna and A. Pnueli. Temporal Verification of Reactive Systems: Safety. Springer-Verlag, New York, 1995.

[MP96] Z. Manna and A. Pnueli. Clocked transition systems. Tech. Report STAN-CS-TR-96-1566, Computer Science Department, Stanford University, April 1996.

[PH97] A. Pardo and G. Hachtel. Automatic abstraction techniques for propositional μ-calculus model checking. In Grumberg [Gru97], pages 12–23.

[SUM96] H.B. Sipma, T.E. Uribe, and Z. Manna. Deductive model checking. In Alur and Henzinger [AH96], pages 208–219.

[Wol95] P. Wolper, editor. Proc. 7th Intl. Conference on Computer Aided Verification, vol. 939 of LNCS. Springer-Verlag, July 1995.

[Won95] H. Wong-Toi. Symbolic Approximations for Verifying Real-Time Systems. PhD thesis, Computer Science Department, Stanford University, March 1995. Tech. Report CS-TR-95-1546.

On-the-Fly Analysis of Systems with Unbounded, Lossy FIFO Channels

Parosh Aziz Abdulla[1], Ahmed Bouajjani[2], and Bengt Jonsson[1]

[1] Dept. of Computer Systems, P.O. Box 325, S-751 05 Uppsala, Sweden,
{parosh,bengt}@docs.uu.se
[2] VERIMAG, Centre Equation, 2 av. de Vignate 38610 Gieres, France,
Ahmed.Bouajjani@imag.fr

Abstract. We consider symbolic on-the-fly verification methods for systems of finite-state machines that communicate by exchanging messages via unbounded and lossy FIFO queues. We propose a novel representation formalism, called *simple regular expressions* (SREs), for representing sets of states of protocols with lossy FIFO channels. We show that the class of languages representable by SREs is exactly the class of downward closed languages that arise in the analysis of such protocols. We give methods for (i) computing inclusion between SREs, (ii) an SRE representing the set of states reachable by executing a single transition in a system, and (iii) an SRE representing the set of states reachable by an arbitrary number of executions of a control loop of a program. All these operations are rather simple and can be carried out in polynomial time. With these techniques, one can construct a semi-algorithm which explores the set of reachable states of a protocol, in order to check various safety properties.

1 Introduction

One of the most popular models for specifying and verifying communication protocols is that of *Communicating Finite State Machines (CFSM)* [10,8]. This model consists of finite-state processes that exchange messages via unbounded FIFO queues. Several verification methods have been developed for CFSMs [10, 11,15,18–20]. However, since all interesting verification problems are undecidable [10], there is in general no completely automatic verification method for this class of systems.

A way to obtain a decidable verification problem is to consider *lossy channel systems*, where the unbounded FIFO channels are assumed to be *lossy*, in the sense that they can at any time lose messages. This restricted model covers a large class of communication protocols, e.g., link protocols. In our earlier work [2], we showed the decidability and provided algorithms for verification of safety properties and some forms of liveness properties for lossy channel systems. Our algorithm for verifying safety properties is *global*, in the sense that it performs a backward search, starting from a set of "bad" states and trying to reach some initial state. In contrast, many efficient verification methods are so-called on-the-fly algorithms [17,13], in which the state-space is explored in a forward search, starting from the initial states. In this paper, we therefore consider how forward verification can be carried out for lossy channel systems.

For that we adopt a symbolic verification approach. One of the main challenges in developing verification methods for a class of systems is to choose a symbolic representation of (possibly infinite) sets of states of a system. The symbolic representation should be expressive, yet allow efficient performance of certain operations which are often used in symbolic verification algorithms. Examples of such operations include checking for inclusion, and computing the states that can be reached by executing a transition of the system. In order to speed up the search through the state space, it is also desirable to be able to calculate, in one step, the set of states that can be reached by executing *sequences* of transitions. For instance, we can consider the set of sequences corresponding to an arbitrary number of executions of a control loop. This technique to speed up the reachability search has been applied e.g. for systems with counters[9] and *perfect* channel systems [3, 5]. Once a symbolic representations has been obtained it can used for many types of verification and model checking problems.

In this paper, we propose a novel representation formalism, called *simple regular expressions* (SREs), for use in verifying protocols modelled as lossy channel systems. SREs constitute a simple subclass of regular expressions. To our knowledge, this class has not been studied before. Because of the lossiness, we need only to represent sets of channel contents that are closed with respect to the subsequence relation. For example, if a channel can contain the sequence abc, then it can also contain the sequences ab, ac, bc, a, b, c, and ϵ. It is well-known that downward closed languages are always regular. We strengthen this result and show that in fact the class of downward closed languages corresponds exactly to those recognized by SREs. This implies that for any lossy channel system we represent the set of reachable states as an SRE. We suggest methods for computing:

- inclusion between SREs, which can be done in quadratic time,
- an SRE obtained by executing a single transition, and
- an SRE obtained by an arbitrary number of executions of a control loop of a program. It turns out that this operation is not very complicated and can be carried out in polynomial time.

With these techniques, one can straightforwardly construct an algorithm which explores the set of reachable states of a protocol, in order to check various properties. This algorithm is parametrized by the set of control loops that are used to speed up the reachability set computation. We also show how one can perform model-checking of LTL properties, using a standard construction of taking the cross-product of the protocol and a Büchi automaton that recognizes the complement of the LTL property in question. It should be noted that all these methods are incomplete, i.e., they may sometimes not terminate. The incompleteness of our methods is unavoidable despite the facts that reachability is decidable for lossy channel systems, and that the set of reachable states is representable by an SRE. This is due to a basic result [12] saying that there is no general algorithm for generating the set of reachable states.

As an illustration of the applicability of our methods and the SRE representation, we look at a few communication protocols that have been verified earlier in the literature. It turns out that the sets of reachable states of these protocols can be conveniently represented as SREs.

Related Work There are several other results on symbolic verification of perfect channel systems. Pachl [18] proposed to represent the set of reachable states of a protocol as a recognizable set. A recognizable set is a finite union of Cartesian products of regular sets. Pachl gave no efficient algorithms for computing such a representation. In [14] a symbolic analysis procedure is proposed using a class of regular expressions which is not comparable with SRE's. However, the computed reachability set by this procedure is not always exact.

Boigelot and Godefroid [3, 5] use finite automata (under the name QDDs) to represent recognizable sets of channel contents. In [5] it has been shown that the effect of every loop is recognizable for a system with a *single* fifo-channel. As soon as two channels are considered, the effect of a loop may be non-recognizable (i.e., not QDD representable). This is due to the fact that the repeated execution of a loop may create constraints between the number of occurrences of symbols in different channels. For instance, the iteration of a loop where a message is sent to two different channels generates pairs of sequences with the *same* length (assuming the channel is initially empty). In [5] a complete characterization is given of the types of loops which preserve recognizability. To compute and represent the effect of any loop in a perfect fifo-channel, a representation structure, called CQDDs (constrained QDDs), combining finite automata with linear arithmetical constraints is needed [7]. In the case of lossy channels, the links between the number of occurrences in different channels are broken due to lossiness, and this simplifies the computation of the effect of loops, conceptually and practically (i.e., from the complexity point of view).

We argue that SREs offer several advantages when used as a symbolic representation in the context of lossy channel systems. First, the operations on QDD's and CQDD's are of exponential complexity and are performed by quite non-trivial algorithms (see e.g. [4, 6]), whereas all operations on SRE's can be performed by much simpler algorithms and in polynomial time. Moreover, we describe a normal form for SREs, and provide a polynomial procedure to transform an SRE to an equivalent normal SRE. While QDD's admit a canonical form via minimization, a corresponding result is not known for CQDD's. Also, SREs are closed under the performance of any loop, while QDDs are closed only under certain restricted types of loops.

Finally, although the data structures (QDDs and CQDDs) used in [3, 5, 7] are more general than SREs, the algorithms in [3, 5, 7] are not able to simulate the ones we present in this paper. The reason is that the lossy transitions are implicit in our model, whereas all transitions are explicitly represented in the algorithms in [3, 5, 7]. Thus to simulate in [3, 5, 7] the effect of iteration of a loop in the lossy channel model, we have to add transitions explicitly to model the losses. These transitions add in general new loops to the system, implying that a loop in the lossy channel system is simulated by a *nested* loop in the perfect channel system. However analysis of nested loops is not feasible in the approaches of [3, 5, 7].

Outline In the next section we give some preliminaries. In Section 3 we introduce the class Simple Regular Expressions (SREs). In Section 4 we describe how to check entailment among SREs. In Section 5 we give a normal form for SREs. In Section 6 we define operations for computing post-images of sets of configurations, represented as SREs. In Section 7 we show how to use SREs to perform on-the-fly verification algorithms for lossy channel systems. In Section 8 we illustrate our method with an example. Finally, in Section 9 we present conclusions and directions for future work.

2 Preliminaries

Assume a finite alphabet M. For $x, y \in M^*$ we let $x \bullet y$ denote the concatenation of x and y. We use x^n to denote the concatenation of n copies of x. The empty string is denoted by ϵ. We use $x \preceq y$ to denote that x is a (not necessarily contiguous) substring of y.

Consider a system modeled by a finite set of finite-state machines, that communicate through sending and receiving message via a finite set of unbounded FIFO channels. The channels are assumed to be *lossy* in the sense that they can nondeterministically lose messages. We model such a system as a lossy channel system.

Definition 1. *A* Lossy Channel System $\mathcal{L}$ *is a tuple* $\langle S, s_{init}, C, M, \delta \rangle$, *where*

   S *is a finite set of* (control) *states. The control states of a system with n finite-state machines is formed as the Cartesian product* $S = S_1 \times \cdots \times S_n$ *of the control states of each finite-state machine.*
s_{init} $\in S$ *is an* initial *state, The initial state of a system with n finite-state machines is a tuple* $\langle s_{init1}, \ldots, s_{initn} \rangle$ *of initial states of the components.*
   C *is a finite set of* channels,
   M *is a finite set of* messages,
   δ *is a finite set of* transitions, *each of which is a triple of the form* $\langle s_1, Op, s_2 \rangle$, *where* s_1 *and* s_2 *are states, and* Op *is a mapping from* C *to* (channel) *operations. An operation is either a* send *operation* $!a$, *a* receive *operation* $?a$, *or an empty operation* nop, *where* $a \in M$. □

A transition of form $\langle s_1, Op, s_2 \rangle$ represents a change of the control state from s_1 to s_2 while performing all the operations in Op. The operations $!a$, $?a$, nop represent sending a to the channel, receiving a from the channel, and not changing the content of the channel, respectively.

Global states of a lossy channel system are represented by configurations. A *configuration* γ of $\mathcal{L}$ is a pair $\langle s, w \rangle$, where $s \in S$ is a control state and w is a mapping from C to M^*. For two mappings w and w' from C to M^*, we use $w \preceq w'$ to denote that $w(c) \preceq w'(c)$ for each $c \in C$. We use ϵ to denote the mapping where each channel is assigned ϵ. The *initial configuration* γ_{init} of $\mathcal{L}$ is the pair $\langle s_{init}, \epsilon \rangle$. For each transition $\langle s_1, Op, s_2 \rangle \in \delta$, we define a *transition* *relation* $\xrightarrow{\langle s_1, Op, s_2 \rangle}$ on configurations, such that $\langle s_1, w_1 \rangle \xrightarrow{\langle s_1, Op, s_2 \rangle} \langle s_2, w_2 \rangle$ if and only if for each channel $c \in C$ we have

- if $Op(c) = !a$, then $w_2(c) = w_1(c) \bullet a$.
- if $Op(c) = ?a$, then $a \bullet w_2(c) = w_1(c)$.
- if $Op(c) = nop$, then $w_2(c) = w_1(c)$.

We define a *weak* transition relation on configurations: $\langle s_1, w_1 \rangle \xRightarrow{\langle s_1, Op, s_2 \rangle} \langle s_2, w_2 \rangle$ if and only if there are w_1' and w_2' such that $w_1' \preceq w_1$ and $w_2 \preceq w_2'$ and $\langle s_1, w_1' \rangle \xrightarrow{\langle s_1, Op, s_2 \rangle} \langle s_2, w_2' \rangle$. Intuitively, $\langle s_1, w_1 \rangle \xRightarrow{\langle s_1, Op, s_2 \rangle} \langle s_2, w_2 \rangle$ denotes that $\langle s_2, w_2 \rangle$ can be obtained from $\langle s_1, w_1 \rangle$ by first losing messages from the channels, then performing the transition $\langle s_1, Op, s_2 \rangle$ and thereafter losing messages from channels. We let $\langle s_1, w_1 \rangle \Longrightarrow \langle s_2, w_2 \rangle$ denote that there is a transition $\langle s_1, Op, s_2 \rangle$ such that $\langle s_1, w_1 \rangle \xRightarrow{\langle s_1, Op, s_2 \rangle} \langle s_2, w_2 \rangle$. We let $\xRightarrow{*}$ denote the reflexive transitive closure of $\Longrightarrow$. A configuration γ' is said to be *reachable* from a configuration γ if $\gamma \xRightarrow{*} \gamma'$. A configuration γ is said to be *reachable* if γ is reachable from the initial configuration γ_{init}. For a state s, we define $\mathcal{R}(s) = \left\{ w \mid \gamma_{init} \xRightarrow{*} \langle s, w \rangle \right\}$.

In symbolic verification, we are interested in manipulating sets of configurations, e.g., in order to compute $\mathcal{R}(s)$. Let Γ be a set of configurations. We use $\Gamma(s)$ to denote the set $\{w \mid \langle s, w \rangle \in \Gamma\}$. and $post(\langle s_1, Op, s_2 \rangle, \Gamma)$ to denote the set $\left\{ \gamma' \mid \exists \gamma \in [\![\Gamma]\!]. \ \gamma \xRightarrow{\langle s_1, Op, s_2 \rangle} \gamma' \right\}$.

3 Simple Regular Expressions (SREs)

We define a class of languages which can be used to describe the set of reachable configurations of a lossy channel system. Let M be a finite alphabet. We define the set of *regular expressions (REs)*, and the languages generated by them in the standard manner. For a regular expression r, we use $[\![r]\!]$ to denote the language defined by r. For regular expressions r_1 and r_2, we use $r_1 \equiv r_2$ ($r_1 \sqsubseteq r_2$) to denote that $[\![r_1]\!] = [\![r_2]\!]$ ($[\![r_1]\!] \subseteq [\![r_2]\!]$). By $r_1 \sqsubset r_2$ we mean that $r_1 \sqsubseteq r_2$ and $r_1 \not\equiv r_2$. In case $r_1 \sqsubseteq r_2$ we say that r_1 *entails* r_2. We use $\lambda(r)$ to denote the set of elements of M appearing in r.

We define a subset of the set of regular expressions, which we call the set of *simple regular expressions*, as follows.

Definition 2. *Let M be a finite alphabet. An atomic expression over M is a regular expression of the form*

- $(a + \epsilon)$, *where $a \in M$, or of the form*
- $(a_1 + \ldots + a_m)^*$, *where $a_1, \ldots, a_m \in M$.*

A product p over M is a (possibly empty) concatenation $e_1 \bullet e_2 \bullet \cdots \bullet e_n$ of atomic expressions $e_1, \ldots, e_n$ over M. We use ϵ to denote the empty product, and assume that $[\![\epsilon]\!] = \{\epsilon\}$.

A simple regular expression (SRE) r over M is of the form $p_1 + \ldots + p_n$, where $p_1, \ldots, p_n$ are products over M. We use $\emptyset$ to denote the empty SRE, and assume that $[\![\emptyset]\!]$ is the empty language $\emptyset$. A language L is said to be simply regular if it is representable by an SRE.

Let C and M be finite alphabets. A C-indexed language over M is a mapping from C to languages over M. A C-indexed RE (SRE) R over M is a mapping from C to the set of REs (SREs) over M. The expression R defines a C-indexed language K over M where $w \in K$ if and only if $w(c) \in [\![R(c)]\!]$ for each $c \in C$. The entailment relation is extended to indexed REs in the obvious manner. An indexed language is said to be simply recognizable if it is a finite union of languages recognized by indexed SREs. $\square$

Definition 3. Let M and C be finite alphabets. For a language $L \subseteq M^*$, we say that L is downward closed if $x \in L$ and $y \preceq x$ imply $y \in L$. The definition is generalized in the natural way to C-indexed languages over M. $\square$

Theorem 1. For a finite alphabets M and C and a C-indexed language L over M, if L is downward-closed then L is simply recognizable.

Proof. It is well-known that each downward-closed language is regular. The result follows from Higman's theorem [16] which states the following: for any finite alphabet M, and for any infinite sequence $x_1, x_2, \ldots$ of strings over M, there are $i < j$ such that $x_i \preceq x_j$.

Using induction on the set of REs, we can show that for each RE r, if $[\![r]\!]$ is downward-closed, then there is an SRE r' such that $r' \equiv r$. The result follows immediately. $\square$

Since the set of reachable configurations of a lossy channel system is downward-closed, we get the following.

Corollary 1. For a lossy channel system $\mathcal{L}$ and a state s in $\mathcal{L}$, the set $\mathcal{R}(s)$ is simply recognizable.

However, it is shown in [12] that we cannot in general compute a representation of $\mathcal{R}(s)$. The uncomputability of $\mathcal{R}(s)$ is shown through a reduction to an undecidable problem reported in [1]. More precisely, in [1] we show the undecidability of the *recurrent state problem*: given a lossy channel system $\mathcal{L}$ and a state s in $\mathcal{L}$, is there a computation of $\mathcal{L}$ visiting s infinitely often? In [12] the uncomputability of a representation of $\mathcal{R}(s)$ is reduced to the recurrent state problem as follows. We add a new channel c to the lossy channel system. Whenever a computation reaches s, an arbitrary message is sent to c. Suppose that we can compute an indexed SRE R such that $[\![R]\!] = \mathcal{R}(s)$. It is clear that the existence of a computation visiting s infinitely often is equivalent to the finiteness of $[\![R(c)]\!]$.

Theorem 2. [12] For a lossy channel system $\mathcal{L}$ and a state s in $\mathcal{L}$, there is, in general, no algorithm for computing a representation of $\mathcal{R}(s)$.

Although we can compute a representation of the set of configurations from which a given configuration is reachable ([2]), we cannot in general compute a representation of the set of configuration which are reachable from a given configuration (Theorem 2). This means that we can have a complete algorithm for performing backward reachability analysis in lossy channel systems, while any procedure for performing forward reachability analysis will necessarily be incomplete.

4 Entailment among SREs

In this section, we consider how to check entailment between SREs. First, we show a preliminary lemma about entailment.

Lemma 1. *For products $p, p_1, \ldots, p_n$, if $p \sqsubseteq p_1 + \ldots + p_n$ then $p \sqsubseteq p_i$ for some $i \in \{1 \ldots n\}$.*

Proof. Given any natural number k, we define a sequence x such that $x \in [\![p]\!]$ and $x \notin [\![p']\!]$, for any product p', where $p \not\sqsubseteq p'$ and where p' contains at most k atomic expressions. The result follows immediately. Let $p = e_1 \bullet \cdots \bullet e_m$. We define $x = y_1 \bullet \cdots \bullet y_m$, where y_i is defined as follows. If $e_i = (a + \epsilon)$ then $y_i = a$. If $e_i = (a_1 + \ldots + a_\ell)^*$ then $y_i = (a_1 \bullet \cdots \bullet a_\ell)^{k+1}$. $\square$

Let us identify atomic expressions of form $(a_1 + \ldots + a_m)^*$ which have the same set $a_1, \ldots, a_m$ of symbols. Then $\sqsubseteq$ is a partial order on atomic expressions. It is the least partial order which satisfies

$$(a + \epsilon) \sqsubseteq (a_1 + \ldots + a_m)^* \qquad \text{if } a \in \{a_1, \ldots, a_m\}$$
$$(a_1 + \ldots + a_m)^* \sqsubseteq (b_1 + \ldots + b_n)^* \text{ if } \{a_1, \ldots, a_m\} \subseteq \{b_1, \ldots, b_n\}$$

Lemma 2. *Entailment among products can be checked in linear time.*

Proof. The result follows from the fact that $\epsilon \sqsubseteq p$, $p \not\sqsubseteq \epsilon$ if $p \neq \epsilon$, and $e_1 \bullet p_1 \sqsubseteq e_2 \bullet p_2$ if and only if one of the following holds:

- $e_1 \not\sqsubseteq e_2$ and $e_1 \bullet p_1 \sqsubseteq p_2$.
- $e_1 = e_2 = (a + \epsilon)$ and $p_1 \sqsubseteq p_2$.
- $e_2 = (a_1 + \cdots + a_n)^*$, $e_1 \sqsubseteq e_2$, and $p_1 \sqsubseteq e_2 \bullet p_2$. $\square$

Lemma 3. *Entailment among SREs can be checked in quadratic time.*

Proof. The proof follows from Lemma 1 and Lemma 2. $\square$

Corollary 2. *Entailment among indexed SREs can be checked in quadratic time.*

5 Normal Forms for SREs

In this section, we show how to compute normal forms for SREs. First we define a normal form for products.

Definition 4. *A product $e_1 \bullet \cdots \bullet e_n$ is said to be* normal *if for each $i : 1 \leq i < n$ we have $e_i \bullet e_{i+1} \not\sqsubseteq e_{i+1}$ and $e_i \bullet e_{i+1} \not\sqsubseteq e_i$.* $\square$

Lemma 4. *For each product p, there is a unique normal product, which we denote $\bar{p}$, such that $\bar{p} \equiv p$. Furthermore, $\bar{p}$ can be derived from p in linear time.*

Proof. We can define $\bar{p}$ from p by simply deleting atomic expressions which are redundant according to Definition 4. $\square$

Similarly, we can define a normal form for SREs.

Definition 5. *An SRE $r = p_1 + \ldots + p_n$ is said to be normal if each p_i is normal for $i : 1 \le i \le n$, and $p_i \not\sqsubseteq p_j$, for $i, j : 1 \le i \ne j \le n$. $\square$*

In the following, we shall identify SREs if they have the same sets of products.

Lemma 5. *For each SRE r, there is a unique (up to commutativity of products) normal SRE, which we denote by $\bar{r}$, such that $\bar{r} \equiv r$. Furthermore, $\bar{r}$ can be derived from r in quadratic time.*

Proof. The proof follows from Lemma 2, Lemma 1 and Lemma 4. $\square$

6 Operations on SREs

In this section, we will define operations for computing post-images of sets of configurations, represented as SREs, with respect to transitions of a lossy channel system. We will also define operations for computing post-images of sets of configurations with respect to an arbitrary number of repetitions of an arbitrary control loop in a lossy channel system.

Throughout this section, we assume a fixed finite set C of channels and a finite alphabet M. We will first consider operations on SREs corresponding to single transitions, and thereafter consider loops.

6.1 Computing the Effect of Single Transitions

Consider a language L and an operation $op \in \{!a, ?a, nop\}$. We define $L \otimes op$ to be the smallest downward closed language such that $y \in (L \otimes op)$ if there is an $x \in L$ satisfying one of the following three conditions: (i) $op = !a$, and $y = x \bullet a$; or (ii) $op = ?a$, and $a \bullet y = x$; or (iii) $op = nop$, and $y = x$.

For an indexed language K, and a mapping Op from C to operations, we define $K \otimes Op$ to be the indexed language where $(K \otimes Op)(c) = K(c) \otimes Op(c)$, for each $c \in C$. Notice that, for a lossy channel system $\mathcal{L}$, a transition $\langle s_1, Op, s_2 \rangle$, and a set Γ of configurations in $\mathcal{L}$, the set $post(\langle s_1, Op, s_2 \rangle, \Gamma)$ is given by $\{\langle s_2, w \rangle \mid w \in (\Gamma(s_1) \otimes Op)\}$.

The following propositions show how to compute the effect of single operations on SREs.

Lemma 6. *For an SRE r and an operation op, there is an SRE, which we denote $r \otimes op$, such that $\llbracket r \otimes op \rrbracket = \llbracket r \rrbracket \otimes op$. Furthermore, $r \otimes op$ can be computed in linear time.*

313

Proof. For a product p and an operation op, we have $p \otimes (!a) = p \bullet (a + \epsilon)$, and $p \otimes (nop) = p$. Furthermore, $\epsilon \otimes (?a) = \emptyset$. and if $p = e \bullet p_1$, then

$$p \otimes (?a) = \begin{cases} p & \text{if } e = (a_1 + \ldots + a_n)^* \text{ and } a \in \{a_1 + \ldots + a_n\} \\ p_1 & \text{if } e = (a + \epsilon) \\ p_1 \otimes (?a) & \text{otherwise} \end{cases}$$

For an SRE $p_1 + \ldots + p_m$ we have

$$(p_1 + \ldots + p_m) \otimes op = (p_1 \otimes op) + \ldots + (p_m \otimes op)$$

Lemma 6 can be generalized in the obvious manner to indexed SREs.

6.2 Computing the Effect of Loops

We study methods to accelerate reachability analysis of lossy channels systems. The basic idea is that, rather than generating successor configurations with respect to single $\Longrightarrow$-transitions, we shall consider the effect of performing sets of *sequences* of transitions in each step. We consider *control loops*, i.e., sequences of transitions starting and ending in the same control state. If ops is the sequence of channel operations associated with a control loop, then we shall calculate the effect on an SRE of performing an arbitrary number of iterations of ops. In Lemma 7, we show that for each SRE and sequence ops, there is an n such that the set of all strings which can be obtained through performing n or more iterations of ops on the SRE can be characterized by a (rather simple) SRE. In other words, the effect of the loop "stabilizes" after at most n iterations, in the sense it only generates strings belonging to a single SRE. This implies that the effect of performing an arbitrary number of iterations of the loop can be represented as the union of n SREs: one of them represents all iterations after n, while the remaining SREs each represents the effect of iterating the loop exactly j times for $j : 1 \leq j \leq n - 1$. In Corollary 3 we generalize the result to indexed SREs.

For strings x and y, we use $x \preceq_c y$ to denote that there are x_1 and x_2 such that $x = x_1 \bullet x_2$ and $x_2 \bullet x_1 \preceq y$. The relation $\preceq_c$ can be decided in quadratic time. We use $x \preceq^+ y$ to denote that there is a natural number $m \geq 1$ such that $x^{m+1} \preceq y^m$. It can be shown that if m exists then m can be found in the interval $1 \leq m \leq |y|$. It follows that the relation $\preceq^+$ can be checked in quadratic time. For a sequence $ops = op_1 op_2 \cdots op_n$ of operations, we define $L \otimes ops$ to be $L \otimes op_1 \otimes op_2 \otimes \cdots \otimes op_n$. We use ops^m (Ops^m) to denote the concatenation of m copies of ops (Ops). By $ops!$ ($ops?$) we mean the subsequence of ops which contains only send (receive) operations. For a product p, let $|p|$ denote the number of atomic expressions in p.

Lemma 7. *For a product p and a sequence ops of operations, the following holds. There is a natural number n and a product p' such that either $p \otimes ops^n = \emptyset$ or $p' = \cup_{j \geq n}[p \otimes ops^j]$. Furthermore, the value of n is linear in the size of p, and p' can be computed in quadratic time.*

Proof. Let $\lambda(ops!) = \{b_1, \ldots, b_k\}$. There are four cases. In the first two cases the loop can be iterated an infinite number of times and the channel contents will be unbounded. In case 3 the loop can be iterated an infinite number of times but the channel contents will be bounded. In case 4 deadlock occurs after at most n iterations.

1. If $(ops?)^* \subseteq [\![p]\!]$. This means that either $ops?$ is empty or there is an atomic expression in p of the form $(a_1 + \ldots + a_m)^*$ where $\lambda(ops?) \subseteq \{a_1, \ldots, a_m\}$. In case $ops?$ is empty, we let $n = 0$ and $p' = p \bullet (b_1 + \cdots + b_k)^*$. Otherwise, let e be the first expression in p (starting from the left) which satisfies the above property, and let $p = p_1 \bullet e \bullet p_2$. We define $n = |p_1|$ and $p' = e \bullet p_2 \bullet (b_1 + \cdots + b_k)^*$.

   Intuitively, after consuming the words in p_1, the loop can be iterated an arbitrary number of times producing and adding to the right a corresponding number of $ops!$. Hence, due to lossiness, the global effect is obtained by concatenating to the right of $e \bullet p_2$ the downward closure of $(ops!)^*$, which is precisely $(b_1 + \cdots + b_k)^*$.

2. If $(ops?)^* \not\subseteq [\![p]\!]$, $ops? \preceq^+ ops!$, and $p \otimes ops \neq \emptyset$, then we define $n = |p|$ and $p' = (b_1 + \cdots + b_k)^*$.

   Intuitively, since $(ops?)^* \not\subseteq [\![p]\!]$, the original contents of the channel will be consumed after at most n iterations. Furthermore, $ops? \preceq^+ ops!$ implies that there is an m such that $(ops?)^{m+1} \preceq (ops!)^m$. Hence that contents of the channel will grow by at least $ops!$ after each $m + 1$ iterations. By iterating the loop sufficiently many times we can concatenate any number of copies of $ops!$ to the end of the channel. Again, by lossiness, the total effect amounts to $(b_1 + \cdots + b_k)^*$. The condition $p \otimes ops \neq \emptyset$ guarantees that the first iteration of the loop can be performed. This is to cover cases where e.g. the channel is initially empty and the receive operations are performed first in the loop.

3. If $(ops?)^* \not\subseteq [\![p]\!]$, $ops? \not\preceq^+ ops!$, $ops? \preceq_c ops!$, and $p \otimes ops^2 \neq \emptyset$, then $n = |p| + 1$ $p' = p \otimes ops^{n+1}$.

   Although the loop can be iterated any number of times, the contents of the channel will not grow after the nth iteration. Observe that we demand $p \otimes ops^2 \neq \emptyset$. The condition $p \otimes ops \neq \emptyset$ (in case 2) is not sufficient here. A counter-example is $p = ba$ and $ops = (?b)(?a)(!a)(!b)$. We get $p \otimes ops = ab$ and $p \otimes ops^2 = \emptyset$. An explanation is that, for strings x and y, the relation $x \preceq^+ y$ (a condition of case 2) implies $x \preceq y$, while $x \preceq_c y$ (the corresponding condition in case 3) implies $x \preceq y^2$ but not $x \preceq y$.

4. If conditions 1, 2, or 3 are not satisfied, then $n = |p| + 1$. We have $p \otimes ops^n = \emptyset$. In this case the loop can be executed at most n times, after which the channel becomes empty, and we deadlock due to inability to perform receive operations.

Notice that the proof of Lemma 7 gives us a complete characterization of whether a loop can be executed infinitely often from a certain configuration (i.e., in cases 1. - 3.), and whether in such a case the contents of channel grows unboundedly or stays finite.

Also, observe that in case we have an SRE (instead of a product) then we can apply the lemma to each product separately.

The result of Lemma 7 can be generalized to indexed SREs in a straightforward manner: The loop can be executed infinitely often if and only if the loop can be executed infinitely often with respect to each channel. If the loop can be executed infinitely often, then we take the Cartesian products of the expressions computed according to Lemma 7. This gives us the following.

Corollary 3. *For an indexed SRE R and a sequence Ops of indexed operations, there is an indexed SRE, which we denote by $R \otimes Ops^*$, such that $[\![R \otimes Ops^*]\!] = \cup_{0 \leq j}[\![R \otimes Ops^j]\!]$. Furthermore, $R \otimes Ops^*$ can be computed in quadratic time.*

7 Use in Verification Algorithms

The SRE representation and the operations presented in this paper can be used in on-the-fly verification algorithms for lossy channel systems. The techniques are rather standard, so here we only provide a sketch.

Suppose we want to check whether some set Γ_F of configurations is reachable. We then search through the (potentially infinite) set of reachable configurations, as follows.

We use *symbolic states* to represent sets of configurations. A *symbolic state* ϕ is a pair $\langle s, R \rangle$, where s is a control state , and R is an indexed SRE describing the contents of the channels. The language $[\![\phi]\!]$ defined by ϕ is the set of configurations $\{\langle s, w \rangle \; ; \; w \in [\![R]\!]\}$. We extend the entailment relation in the obvious way so that $\langle s, R \rangle \sqsubseteq \langle s', R' \rangle$ if and only if $s = s'$ and $R \sqsubseteq R'$.

We maintain a set V which we use to store symbolic states which are generated during the search. At the start, the set V contains one unexplored symbolic state representing the initial configuration. From each unexplored element in V, we compute two sets of new elements: one which corresponds to performing single transitions (Lemma 6), and another which describes the effect of a selected set of control loops. When a new element ϕ is generated, it is compared with those which are already in V. If $\phi \sqsubseteq \phi'$ for some $\phi' \in V$, then ϕ is discarded (it will not add new configurations to the searched state space). It is also checked whether ϕ has a non-empty intersection with Γ_F. This is easy if e.g., Γ_F is a recognizable set. If the intersection is non-empty, the algorithm terminates. Otherwise, the algorithm is terminated when no new symbolic states can be generated.

When performing control loops during the analysis, there is a choice in how many loops to explore. A reasonable strategy seems to be to investigate the sequences of transitions which correspond to *simple control loops* in the program. A simple control loop is a loop which enters each control state at most once. By applying these control loops we get new symbolic states which can be computed according to Corollary 3.

During our search, it can happen that a new element ϕ is added to V, although ϕ will not add any new configurations to the explored state space. This is due to the fact that even if $\phi \not\sqsubseteq \phi'$ for all $\phi' \in V$, the relation $[\![\phi]\!] \subseteq \bigcup_{\phi' \in V}[\![\phi']\!]$ may still hold. The test for discarding new SREs can therefore be modified so that ϕ is discarded if and only if $[\phi] \subseteq \bigcup_{\phi' \in V}[\phi']$. This would make the algorithm terminate more often (fewer elements need to be added to V). However, for indexed SREs (and hence for symbolic states), the above test has an exponential complexity in the number of channels.

From Theorem 2, we know that our algorithm is incomplete. The algorithm will always find reachable configurations in Γ_F, but it will not necessarily terminate if all configurations in Γ_F are unreachable.

In fact, we can use a slight extension of this procedure to check whether a lossy channel system satisfies a linear temporal logic formula over the control states of the system. By standard techniques [21], we can transform this problem into checking whether a lossy channel system, in which some control states are designated as "accepting", has an infinite computation which visits some accepting control state infinitely often. In our earlier work [1], we showed that this problem is undecidable. However, an incomplete check can be performed as part of the state-space generation in the previous paragraph. More precisely, when exploring a set of configurations with an accepting control state we can, as part of exploring the loops, check whether there is a control loop that can be executed an infinite number of times. We only need to check whether one of the three first conditions in the proof of Lemma 7 holds.

8 Example

In this section we apply our algorithm (Table 1) to a sliding window protocol (shown in Figure 1). We use a symbolic representation of the form $\langle s_i, q_j, r_1, r_2 \rangle$, where s_i and q_j are the control states of the sender and the receiver, respectively, and r_1 and r_2 are SREs which describe the contents of the message and acknowledgement channels. We explore the state space as described in the preceding section, investigating the effect of simple control loops in the program.

In Figure 1, we start from $\langle s_1, q_1, \epsilon, \epsilon \rangle$ and apply the speed-up operation obtaining ϕ_0. From ϕ_0 we perform a single transition moving from q_1 to q_2, and then perform the speed-up operation obtaining ϕ_1. In a similar manner we obtain ϕ_2 and ϕ_3 from ϕ_1, etc. Observe that, e.g. ϕ_5 entails ϕ_7, so ϕ_5 is discarded.

9 Conclusions

We present a method for performing symbolic forward reachability analysis of *unbounded lossy channel systems*. In spite of the restriction of lossiness, we can model the behaviour of many interesting systems such as link protocols which are designed to operate correctly even in the case where the channels are lossy and can lose messages. Also lossy channel systems offer conservative approximations when checking linear time properties of systems with *perfect* channels. This is because the set of computations of a lossy channel system is a superset of the set of computations of the corresponding system with perfect channels, and hence if a linear time property holds in the first it will also hold in the second.

In this paper, we accelerate the forward search of the state space, by considering (besides single transitions) the effect of "meta-transitions" which are simple loops entering each control state at most once. We intend to investigate more

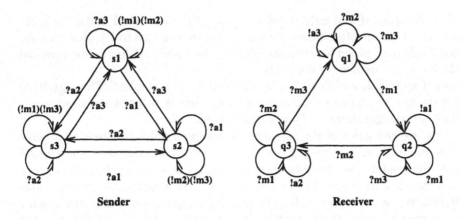

Fig. 1. Example: A Sliding Window Protocol

general types of meta-transitions. For example consider the case where we have two loops sending two different messages (say a_1 and a_2) to the same channel. In the algorithm we propose we cannot cover the fact that the combination of the two loops would give the expression $(a_1 + a_2)^*$ in the channel. We are currently carrying out experiments to evaluate the performance of our algorithm. It would be particularly interesting to compare the forward reachability algorithm we present here with the performance of the backward reachability algorithm reported in [2].

References

[1] Parosh Aziz Abdulla and Bengt Jonsson. Undecidable verification problems for programs with unreliable channels. *Inform. and Comput.*, 130(1):71–90, 1996.

[2] Parosh Aziz Abdulla and Bengt Jonsson. Verifying programs with unreliable channels. *Inform. and Comput.*, 127(2):91–101, 1996.

[3] B. Boigelot and P. Godefroid. Symbolic verification of communication protocols with infinite state spaces using QDDs. In *CAV'96*, LNCS 1102.

[4] B. Boigelot, P. Godefroid, B. Willems, and P. Wolper. The power of QDDs. Available at http://www.montefiore.ulg.ac.be/~biogelot/research/BGWW97.ps.

[5] B. Boigelot, P. Godefroid, B. Willems, and P. Wolper. The power of QDDs. In *SAS'97*, LNCS. 1997.

[6] A. Bouajjani and P. Habermehl. Symbolic reachability analysis of fifo-channel systems with nonregular sets of configurations. http://www.imag.fr/VERIMAG/PEOPLE/Peter.Habermehl.

[7] A. Bouajjani and P. Habermehl. Symbolic reachability analysis of fifo-channel systems with nonregular sets of configurations. In *ICALP '97*, LNCS 1256. 1997.

[8] G. V. Bochman. Finite state description of communicating protocols. *Computer Networks*, 2:361–371, 1978.

[9] B. Boigelot and P. Wolper. Symbolic verification with periodic sets. In *CAV'94*, LNCS 818. 1994.

ϕ_0	$\langle s_1, q_1, (m_1 + m_2)^*, (a_3)^* \rangle$	ϕ_1
ϕ_1	$\langle s_1, q_2, (m_1 + m_2)^*, (a_3)^* \bullet (a_1)^* \rangle$	ϕ_2, ϕ_3
ϕ_2	$\langle s_2, q_2, (m_1 + m_2)^* \bullet (m_2 + m_3)^*, (a_1)^* \rangle$	ϕ_4
ϕ_3	$\langle s_1, q_3, (m_1 + m_2)^*, (a_3)^* \bullet (a_1)^* \bullet (a_2)^* \rangle$	ϕ_4, ϕ_5
ϕ_4	$\langle s_2, q_3, (m_1 + m_2)^* \bullet (m_2 + m_3)^*, (a_1)^* \bullet (a_2)^* \rangle$	ϕ_6, ϕ_7
ϕ_5	$\langle s_3, q_3, (m_1 + m_2)^* \bullet (m_1 + m_3)^*, (a_2)^* \rangle$	Ent ϕ_7
ϕ_6	$\langle s_2, q_1, (m_2 + m_3)^*, (a_1)^* \bullet (a_2)^* \bullet (a_3)^* \rangle$	ϕ_8, ϕ_9
ϕ_7	$\langle s_3, q_3, (m_1 + m_2)^* \bullet (m_2 + m_3)^* \bullet (m_1 + m_3)^*, (a_2)^* \rangle$	ϕ_8
ϕ_8	$\langle s_3, q_1, (m_2 + m_3)^* \bullet (m_1 + m_3)^*, (a_2)^* \bullet (a_3)^* \rangle$	ϕ_{10}, ϕ_{11}
ϕ_9	$\langle s_1, q_1, (m_2 + m_3)^* \bullet (m_1 + m_2)^*, (a_3)^* \rangle$	Ent ϕ_{11}
ϕ_{10}	$\langle s_3, q_2, (m_1 + m_3)^*, (a_2)^* \bullet (a_3)^* \bullet (a_1)^* \rangle$	ϕ_{12}, ϕ_{13}
ϕ_{11}	$\langle s_1, q_1, (m_2 + m_3)^* \bullet (m_1 + m_3)^* \bullet (m_1 + m_2)^*, (a_3)^* \rangle$	ϕ_{12}
ϕ_{12}	$\langle s_1, q_2, (m_1 + m_3)^* \bullet (m_1 + m_2)^*, (a_3)^* \bullet (a_1)^* \rangle$	ϕ_3, ϕ_{14}
ϕ_{13}	$\langle s_2, q_2, (m_1 + m_3)^* \bullet (m_2 + m_3)^*, (a_1)^* \rangle$	Ent ϕ_{14}
ϕ_{14}	$\langle s_2, q_2, (m_1 + m_3)^* \bullet (m_1 + m_2)^* \bullet (m_2 + m_3)^*, (a_1)^* \rangle$	ϕ_4

Table 1. Reachability Analysis of the Sliding Window Protocol

[10]   D. Brand and P. Zafiropulo. On communicating finite-state machines. *Journal of the ACM*, 2(5):323–342, April 1983.

[11]   A. Choquet and A. Finkel. Simulation of linear FIFO nets having a structured set of terminal markings. In *Proc. 8th European Workshop on Applications and Theory of Petri Nets*, 1987.

[12]   Gérard Cécé, Alain Finkel, and S. Purushothaman Iyer. Unreliable channels are easier to verify than perfect channels. *Inform. and Comput.*, 124(1):20–31, 10 January 1996.

[13]   C. Courcoubetis, M. Vardi, P. Wolper, and M. Yannakakis. Memory efficient algorithms for the verification of temporal properties. In *CAV'90*.

[14]   A. Finkel and O. Marcé. Verification of infinite regular communicating automata. Technical report, LIFAC, ENS de Cachan, 1996. Tech. Rep.

[15]   M.G. Gouda, E.M. Gurari, T.-H. Lai, and L.E. Rosier. On deadlock detection in systems of communicating finite state machines. *Computers and Artificial Intelligence*, 6(3):209–228, 1987.

[16]   G. Higman. Ordering by divisibility in abstract algebras. *Proc. London Math. Soc.*, 2:326–336, 1952.

[17]   G.J. Holzmann. *Design and Validation of Computer Protocols*. Prentice Hall, 1991.

[18]   J.K. Pachl. Protocol description and analysis based on a state transition model with channel expressions. In *Protocol Specification, Testing, and Verification VII*, May 1987.

[19]   W. Peng and S. Purushothaman. Data flow analysis of communicating finite state machines. *ACM Trans. on Programming Languages and Systems*, 13(3):399–442, July 1991.

[20]   A.P. Sistla and L.D. Zuck. Automatic temporal verification of buffer systems. In Larsen and Skou, editors, *CAV'91*, LNCS 575. 1991.

[21]   M. Y. Vardi and P. Wolper. An automata-theoretic approach to automatic program verification. In *LICS'86*, IEEE, 1986.

Computing Abstractions of Infinite State Systems Compositionally and Automatically *

S. Bensalem[1], Y. Lakhnech[2] and S. Owre[3]

[1] VERIMAG, Centre Equation – 2, avenue de Vignate,
F-38610 Giéres, France. Email: Bensalem@imag.fr
[2] Institut für Informatik und Praktische Mathematik, Preußerstr. 1-9,
D-24105 Kiel, Germany. Email: yl@informatik.uni-kiel.de
[3] Computer Science Laboratory, SRI International,
Menlo Park, CA 94025, USA. Email : owre@csl.sri.com

Abstract. We present a method for computing abstractions of infinite state systems *compositionally* and *automatically.* Given a concrete system $S = S_1 \parallel \cdots \parallel S_n$ of programs and given an abstraction function α, using our method one can compute an abstract system $S^a = S_1^a \parallel \cdots \parallel S_n^a$ such that S simulates S^a. A distinguishing feature of our method is that it does not produce a single abstract state graph but rather preserves the structure of the concrete system. This feature is a prerequisite to benefit from the techniques developed in the context of model-checking for mitigating the state explosion. Moreover, our method has the advantage that the process of constructing the abstract system does *not* depend on whether the computation model is synchronous or asynchronous.

1 Introduction

A major task in proving correctness of protocols consists in proving invariance properties. Indeed, every safety property can be reduced to an invariance property and to prove progress properties one needs to establish invariance properties [21]. Proving invariance properties is especially crucial for infinite and large finite state systems which escape algorithmic methods.

The standard way to prove invariance properties of infinite state systems is by induction. To prove that φ is an invariant of S one has to come up with a stronger invariant ψ that is preserved by every transition of S. The invariant ψ is usually called an auxiliary invariant. This deductive method has three drawbacks: 1) it is often hard to find suitable auxiliary invariants, 2) when a choice for an auxiliary invariant fails, one has little hint how to strengthen the invariant and 3) one obtains no counterexample in the form of a trace when the considered program does not satisfy the invariance property. Techniques for generating and strengthening invariants (cf. [22, 2, 1, 27]) seem to give limited results when

---

* This work has been partly performed while the first two authors were visiting the Computer Science Laboratory, SRI International. Their visits were funded by NSF Grants No. CCR-9712383 and CCR-9509931.

applied to protocols where the control is partly encoded within the data part, in particular when shared variables are extensively used for synchronization.

On the other hand, verification by abstraction appears to be promising for reasoning about control intensive protocols in which control is finite but the data part is infinite or very large. The use of abstraction techniques to model-check finite state reactive systems is by now a well-established approach [3, 20, 8, 18, 19, 5, 17]. There are methods/tools that compute an abstract system from the text of a finite state program and an abstraction relation [3, 7, 12, 6, 9]. It should be realized that it is important to avoid the construction of the concrete model which represents the semantics of the considered program before generating the abstract system. Otherwise, one would have to store the concrete system which might be too large. The produced abstract system is usually smaller than the concrete one, and hence is much simpler to model-check.

Verification by abstraction can also be applied to infinite state systems as shown in [10, 11, 25, 15]. However, in all these approaches the verifier has to provide the abstract system and an important amount of user intervention is required to prove that the concrete system simulates the abstract one. What is needed is a method to automatically compute an abstract system for a given infinite state system and an abstraction relation. A method that achieves this for a restricted form of abstraction functions, namely those induced by a set of predicates on the concrete states, is given in [13]. This method has, however, the drawback that it generates an abstract graph rather than the text of an abstract program with the consequence that one can neither apply further abstractions nor techniques for avoiding the state explosion problem as, for example, partial-order techniques.

We present a method that computes an abstract system $S^a = S_1^a \parallel \cdots \parallel S_n^a$, for a given system $S = S_1 \parallel \cdots \parallel S_n$ and abstraction function α, such that S simulates S^a is guaranteed by the construction. Hence, by known preservation results, if S^a satisfies an invariant φ then S satisfies the invariant $\alpha^{-1}(\varphi)$. Since the produced abstract system is not given by a graph but in a programming language, one still can apply all the known methods for avoiding the state explosion problem, while analyzing S^a. Moreover, there is a clear correspondence between concrete and abstract transitions. This allows for debugging the concrete system, since it can be checked whether a given trace of the abstract system corresponds to a concrete trace. Furthermore, since the process of generation of the abstract system does not depend on the assumed semantics of the parallel operator, our method works for both the synchronous and the asynchronous computation model.

The basic idea behind our method is simple. In order to construct an abstraction of S, we construct for each concrete transition τ_c an abstract transition τ_a. To construct τ_a we proceed by elimination starting from the universal relation, which relates every abstract state to every abstract state, and eliminate pairs of abstract states in a conservative way, i.e. it is guaranteed that after elimination of a pair the obtained transition is still an abstraction of τ_c. To check whether a pair (a, a') of abstract states can be eliminated we have to check that the concrete transition τ_c does not lead from any state c with $\alpha(c) = a$ to any state c' with $\alpha(c') = a'$. This amounts to proving a Hoare triple. The elimination method is in general too complex. Therefore, we combine it with three techniques that allow to check many fewer Hoare triples. These techniques are based on partitioning the set of abstract variables, using substitutions, and a new preservation result which allows to use the invariant to be proved during the construction process of the abstract system. A partitioning of the set of abstract variables allows to consider a small group of abstract variables at a time. This reduces the number of Hoare triples to check, as the number of transitions of the universal relation is exponential in the number of variables. However, in general, such a partitioning leads to a more non-deterministic abstract system. We give sufficient conditions under which a partitioning of the abstract variables does not increase the non-determinism of the abstract system. We also identify cases in which an abstraction of a transition can be computed solely by applying syntactic substitutions without using the elimination method. In many examples, a major part of the transitions can be handled by syntactic substitutions or by a combination of the elimination method with syntactic substitutions. Finally, our new preservation result allows us to consider only Hoare triples whose precondition implies the invariant to prove. Obviously, this reduces the number of Hoare triples to check.

We implemented our method using the theorem prover PVS [26] to check the Hoare triples generated by the elimination method. The first-order formulas corresponding to these Hoare triples are constructed automatically and a strategy that is given by the user is applied. The produced abstract system is optionally represented in the specification language of PVS or in that of SMV [24]. Thus, our implementation provides a bridge between PVS and SMV. We applied our method and its implementation on a number of examples. In this paper, we report on the verification of the Bounded Retransmission protocol. The Bounded Retransmission protocol has been verified using theorem proving in [14, 16, 15]. An automatic verification of some of the correctness aspects of the protocol is reported in [13]. We achieved an automatic verification of all correctness aspects of the protocol.

Related Work As mentioned above a method for computing abstractions of infinite state systems is presented in [13]. In contrast to [13], our method produces an abstract system which has the same structure as the concrete one. This allows for further application of abstractions and other techniques for avoiding the state explosion problem. Moreover, this gives a clear correspondence between concrete and abstract transitions, which is useful for debugging the concrete system. Our method can also deal with abstraction functions that only abstract some of the variables which range over infinite domains. This is not the case for the method in [13], since it generates a global control graph. One other advantage of our method is that it does not depend on the computation model, whether it is synchronous or asynchronous.

The basic idea behind our method for constructing an abstract system is related to the splitting algorithm of [7, 5, 6]. The purpose of the splitting algorithm is to refine an abstract structure in order to preserve properties in two directions, i.e., such that the concrete and the abstract system satisfy the same properties. We are, however, only interested in preservation of invariance properties in one direction, since this allows for more efficient methods for computing abstractions. Moreover, the splitting algorithm is based on splitting abstract states while our method is based on elimination of transitions.

The basic idea underlying the methods of [3, 7, 9] for computing abstractions of finite state systems is that of abstract interpretation [4]. Here, the abstract system is completely determined by abstract versions of the primitive operators. This is not the case in our method, since we do not consider the abstraction of the primitive operators in separation but we compute the abstraction of a complete transition. In general, the methods based on abstract interpretation are efficient but yield abstract systems which are more non-deterministic than the abstract systems computed by our method.

2 Preliminaries

Given a set X of typed variables, a *state over* X is a type-consistent mapping that associates with each variable $x \in X$ a value. We denote by Σ the set consisting of all states. A *syntactic* transition system is given by a triple $(X, \theta(X), \rho(X, X'))$, where X is a set of typed variables, $\theta(X)$ is a predicate describing the set of initial states and $\rho(X, X')$ is a predicate describing the transition relation. We associate in the usual way a transition system with every syntactic transition system. Given relations $R_i \subseteq \Sigma_i \times \Sigma_i'$, for $i = 1, 2$, we define their *synchronous product* $R_1 \otimes R_2 \subseteq (\Sigma_1 \cup \Sigma_2) \times (\Sigma_1' \cup \Sigma_2')$, by $(s, s') \in R_1 \otimes R_2$ iff $(s_{|\Sigma_i}, s'_{|\Sigma_i'}) \in R_i$, for $i = 1, 2$, where $s_{|\Sigma_i}$ denotes the restriction of the mapping s to Σ_i. Thus, if $\Sigma_1 = \Sigma_2$ and $\Sigma_1' = \Sigma_2'$ then $R_1 \otimes R_2 = R_1 \cap R_2$. The *synchronous composition* of transition systems $S_i = (\Sigma_i, I_i, R_i)$, $i = 1, 2$, denoted $S_1 \otimes S_2$, is given by the system $(\Sigma_1 \cup \Sigma_2, \{s \mid s_{|\Sigma_i} \in I_i\}, R_1 \otimes R_2)$. A *computation* of a transition system $S = (\Sigma, I, R)$ is a sequence $s_0, \cdots, s_n$ such that $s_0 \in I$ and $(s_i, s_{i+1}) \in R$, for $i \leq n - 1$. A state $s \in \Sigma$ is called *reachable* in S, if there is a computation $s_0, \cdots, s_n$ of S with $s_n = s$. A set $P \subseteq \Sigma$ is called an *invariant* of S, denoted by $S \models \Box P$, if every state that is reachable in S is in P. Given a set $P \subseteq \Sigma$ of states and a relation $R \subseteq \Sigma^2$ the *weakest liberal precondition* of R with respect to P, denoted by $\mathrm{WP}(R, P)$, is the set consisting of states s such that for every state s', if $(s, s') \in R$ then $s' \in P$. All the semantic notions introduced so far have their syntactic counterparts which we assume as known. Moreover, we will tacitly interchange syntax and semantics, e.g., predicates and sets of states etc., unless there is a necessity to make a distinction.

3 Proving Invariants by Abstraction

In this section we present a simulation notion that depends on the invariance property to be proved and also present a preservation result for this new notion.

Definition 1. Let $S^c = (\Sigma^c, I^c, R^c)$ and $S^a = (\Sigma^a, I^a, R^a)$ be two transition systems. We say that S^a is an abstraction of S^c w.r.t. $\alpha \subseteq \Sigma^c \times \Sigma^a$ and $\varphi^c \subseteq \Sigma^c$, denoted by $S^c \sqsubseteq_\alpha^{\varphi^c} S^a$, if the following conditions are satisfied: 1) α is a total relation, 2) for every state $s_0^c, s_1^c \in \Sigma^c$ and $s_0^a \in \Sigma^a$ with $s_0^c \in \varphi^c$ and $(s_0^c, s_0^a) \in \alpha$, if $(s_0^c, s_1^c) \in R^c$ then there exists a state $s_1^a \in \Sigma^a$ such that $(s_0^a, s_1^a) \in R^a$ and $(s_1^c, s_1^a) \in \alpha$, and 3) for every state s^c in I^c there exists a state s^a in I^a such that $(s^c, s^a) \in \alpha$. □

It can be proved by induction on n that if $S^c \sqsubseteq_\alpha^{\varphi^c} S^a$ then for every computation $s_0^c, \cdots, s_n^c$ of S^c such that $s_i^c \in \varphi^c$, for every $i < n$, there exists a computation $s_0^a, \cdots, s_n^a$ of S^a such that $(s_i^c, s_i^a) \in \alpha$, for every $i \leq n$. Therefore, we have:

Theorem 2. *Let S^c and S^a be transition systems such that $S^c \sqsubseteq_\alpha^{\varphi^c} S^a$. Let $\varphi^a \subseteq \Sigma^a$ and $\varphi \subseteq \Sigma^c$. If $\alpha^{-1}(\varphi^a) \subseteq \varphi^c \cap \varphi$, $S^a \models \Box \varphi^a$, and $I^c \subseteq \varphi^c$, then $S^c \models \Box(\varphi^c \cap \varphi)$.* □

Notice that the usual notion of simulation and its corresponding preservation result (cf. [3, 19]) can be obtained from Definition 1 and Theorem 2 by taking $\varphi^c = \Sigma^c$. The advantage of Definition 1 is that it allows abstractions with fewer transitions and less reachable states. This is particularly important when we are seeking a method that automatically computes finite abstractions for analysis by model-checking techniques. In the sequel, in case $\varphi^c = \Sigma^c$, we write $S^c \sqsubseteq_\alpha S^a$ instead of $S^c \sqsubseteq_\alpha^{\varphi^c} S^a$ and say that S^a is an abstraction of S^c with respect to α.

Thus, to prove that a transition system S^c satisfies an invariance property φ^c it suffices to find a *finite* abstraction S^a of S^c w.r.t. some relation α such that $S^a \models \Box \varphi^a$ for some $\varphi^a \subseteq \Sigma^a$ with $\alpha^{-1}(\varphi^a) \subseteq \varphi^c$. This method is complete. Indeed, it suffices to take an abstract system with two states s_0^a and s_1^a and a relation α such that $(s^c, s_0^a) \in \alpha$ iff s^c is reachable in S^c; and $(s^c, s_1^a) \in \alpha$ iff s^c is not reachable in S^c. The abstract system S^a has s_0^a as unique initial state. Obviously, $S^c \sqsubseteq_\alpha S^a$ and $S^a \models \Box\{s_0^a\}$. Moreover, since $S^c \models \Box \varphi^c$, we have $\alpha^{-1}(s_0^a) \subseteq \varphi^c$. On the other hand, if $S^c \models \Box \varphi^c$ can be proved using an abstraction S^a of S^c w.r.t. α, then it can also be proved using the auxiliary invariant $\alpha^{-1}(\mathcal{R}(S^a))$, where $\mathcal{R}(S^a)$ is the set of the reachable states of S^a. Thus, from a theoretical point of view proving invariance properties using abstractions is as difficult as using auxiliary invariants. Still in practice it is often the case that the method based on abstractions is easier.

4 Computing Abstractions

In this section we consider the problem of computing an abstraction of a transition system S^c w.r.t. a relation α. Thus, consider a syntactic transition system $S^c = (C, \theta^c, \rho^c)$. Let α be a predicate whose set of free variables is $C \cup A$. Let $\alpha[S^c] = (A, \alpha[\theta^c], \alpha[\rho^c])$ where $\alpha[\theta^c]$ is given by $\exists C \cdot (\theta^c \wedge \alpha)$ and $\alpha[\rho^c]$ by $\exists C \exists C' \cdot (\alpha \wedge \alpha' \wedge \rho^c)$ and α' is obtained from α by substituting every variable $c \in C$ by c' and every variable $a \in A$ by a'. It can then be easily proved that $\alpha[S^c]$ is an abstraction of S^c. In case α is a function, $\alpha[S^c]$ is the smallest abstraction of S^c w.r.t. α. Unfortunately, it is not possible in general to analyze $\alpha[S^c]$ by model-checking even when all the variables in A range over finite domains. The reason is that the description of $\alpha[S^c]$ involves quantification over the variables in C which may range over infinite domains. In the sequel of this section we present a method for computing abstractions which avoids the quantification problem described above.

The elimination method Consider a transition relation given by a predicate $\rho(C, C')$ and consider an abstraction relation given by a predicate $\alpha(C, A)$, where A is a set of abstract variables. There is an obvious abstraction of ρ w.r.t. α which is the universal relation on Σ^a given by the everywhere true predicate. Let us denote it by $\mathcal{U}_A$. Of course one cannot use the abstract relation $\mathcal{U}_A$ to prove any interesting invariant, i.e., one which is not a tautology. One can, however, obtain a more interesting abstraction of $\rho(C, C')$ by eliminating transitions from $\mathcal{U}_A$. The following lemma states which transitions can be safely eliminated:

Lemma 3. *Let S^c, S^a be transition systems such that $S^c \sqsubseteq_\alpha^{\varphi^c} S^a$. Let s_0^a, s_1^a be abstract states. If $\alpha^{-1}(s_0^a) \Rightarrow \mathrm{WP}(R^c, \Sigma^c \setminus \alpha^{-1}(s_1^a))$ then $S^c \sqsubseteq_\alpha^{\varphi^c} S'^a$, where S'^a consists of the same components as S^a except that its transition relation is $R^a \setminus \{(s_0^a, s_1^a)\}$.* □

In other words, if the concrete transition does not lead from a concrete state s_0^c with $(s_0^c, s_0^a) \in \alpha$ to a concrete state s_1^c with $(s_1^c, s_1^a) \in \alpha$, then we can safely eliminate the transition (s_0^a, s_1^a) from S^a. Notice that since the concrete system in general is infinite state the condition $\alpha^{-1}(s_0^a) \Rightarrow \mathrm{WP}(R^c, \Sigma^c \setminus \alpha^{-1}(s_1^a))$ has to be checked by means of a theorem prover. Notice also that if we eliminate all the pairs (s_0^a, s_1^a) for which this condition is satisfied, we get as result the abstract system $\alpha[S^c]$.

The elimination method in its rough form is not feasible since it requires too many formulas to be checked for validity. Indeed, if there are n boolean abstract variables then there are 2^{2n} such conditions to be checked. Therefore, we present techniques which make the elimination method feasible as shown in section 6.

Partitioning the abstract variables A simple and practical way to enhance the elimination method consists of partitioning the set A of abstract variables into subsets $A_1, \cdots, A_m$ and considering the effect of the abstraction of a concrete transition ρ on each set A_i separately. Let us consider this in more detail. We assume that the considered abstraction relation α is a function and we denote by α_i the projection of α onto A_i, i.e. $\alpha_i(s) = \alpha(s)_{|A_i}$, for every concrete state s and $i \leq m$. Then, we have the following lemma:

Lemma 4. *Let $\varphi^c \subseteq \Sigma^c$. For $i \leq m$, let $S_i^a = (A_i, I_i^a, R_i^a)$ and let $S^a = \bigotimes_{i \leq m} S_i^a$. Then, $S^c \sqsubseteq_{\alpha_i}^{\varphi^c} S_i^a$, for $i \leq m$ iff $S^c \sqsubseteq_\alpha^{\varphi^c} S^a$.* □

For the truth of this statement it suffices to have one of the assumptions that α is a function or $A_1, \cdots, A_m$ is a partition of A. It is, however, in general unsound if we do not have either of these assumptions. The lemma suggests to partition the set of abstract variables and consider each element of the partitioning in isolation. If we have n boolean abstract variables and partition them into two sets of n_1 and n_2 elements then, when applying the elimination method, we have to check for $2^{2n_1} + 2^{2n_2}$ validities instead of for $2^{2(n_1+n_2)}$ validities.

Now, the question arises whether an abstract system that is computed using a partitioning is at most non-deterministic as the system computed without using the partitioning, i.e. whether $\alpha[S^c] = \bigotimes_{i \leq m} \alpha_i[S^c]$ holds. The answer is that in general $\bigotimes_{i \leq m} \alpha_i[S^c]$ has more transitions than $\alpha[S^c]$, because there might be dependencies between the α_i's which are not taken into account during the process of computing $\alpha_i[S^c]$. We can, however, state the following lemma:

Lemma 5. *Assume that the set C of concrete variables can be partitioned into sets $C_1, \cdots C_m$ such that R^c can be written in the form $R_1^c \otimes \cdots \otimes R_m^c$, where each R_i^c is a relation on states over C_i. Assume also that each α_i can be considered as a function of C_i. Then, $\alpha[S^c] = \bigotimes_{i \leq m} \alpha_i[S^c]$.* $\qquad\square$

In fact, it is often the case that most of the dependencies between the α_i's are captured as an invariant of S^c, which can then be used during the computation of the abstract system.

Given two partitions $P = \{A_1, \cdots, A_m\}$ and $P' = \{A_1', \cdots, A_{m'}'\}$ of A, we say that P is finer than P', if for every $i \leq m$ there is $j \leq m'$ such that $A_i \subseteq A_{j'}$. In this case, we write $P \leq P'$. The following lemma states that, in general, finer partitions lead to more transitions in the abstract system.

Lemma 6. *Let P and P' be partitions of A such that $P \leq P'$. Moreover, for every $j \leq m'$, let α_j' denote the projection of α on A_j', i.e., $\alpha_j'(s) = \alpha(s)_{|A_j'}$, for every concrete state s. Then, $\bigotimes_{j \leq m'} \alpha_j'[S^c] \sqsubseteq_{Id_A} \bigotimes_{i \leq m} \alpha_i[S^c]$, where Id_A is the identity on the abstract states.* $\qquad\square$

Using substitutions In many cases we do not need to apply the elimination method to compute the abstraction of a transition τ; instead we can achieve this using syntactic substitutions. To explain how this goes we assume in this section that transitions are given as guarded simultaneous assignments of the form $g(\mathbf{c}) \rightarrow \mathbf{c} := \mathbf{e}$. Thus, consider a transition τ and an abstraction function α given by $\bigwedge_{a \in A} a \equiv e_a$, i.e., $\alpha(s)(a) = s(e_a)$, for every concrete state s, where $s(e_a)$ denotes the evaluation of e_a in s. To compute the abstraction of τ one can proceed as follows:

1) Determine a list $c_1 = v_1, \cdots, c_n = v_n$ of equations, where $c_i \in C$ and v_i is a constant, such that $c_i = v_i$ follows from the guard g.
2) Substitute each variable c_i with v_i in $\mathbf{e}$ obtaining a new concrete transition τ' with $\tau' \equiv g(\mathbf{c}) \rightarrow \mathbf{c} := \mathbf{e}'$ and $\mathbf{e}' = \mathbf{e}\,[v_1/c_1, \cdots, v_n/c_n]$.
3) Let $\beta(a)$ be $e_a[\mathbf{e}'/\mathbf{c}]$, for each $a \in A$.
4) We say that an abstract variable a is determined by β, if one of the following conditions is satisfied:
   (a) there is a variable-free expression e such that for every concrete state s, $s(\beta(a)) = s(e)$ holds, or
   (b) there is an abstract variable $\bar{a}$ such that $\beta(a)$ and $e_{\bar{a}}$ are syntactically equal.
   Let $\gamma(a)$ be e in the first case and $\bar{a}$ in the second.

5) If all variables in A are determined by β then the transition with guard $\alpha(g)$ and which assigns $\gamma(a)$ to every abstract variable a is an abstraction of τ w.r.t. α.

To see that 5) is true notice that transitions τ and τ' are semantically equivalent and that for all concrete states s and s' if $(s, s') \in \tau'$ then $\alpha(s')(a) = \alpha(s)(\gamma(a))$, for every $a \in A$.

Thus, in case all abstract variables are determined by β the complete abstraction of τ is determined by substitutions without need for the elimination method. However, in general we can apply the procedure described above followed by the elimination method to determine the assignments to the abstract variables which are not determined by β.

Example 1. To illustrate how we can use syntactic substitution to compute the abstraction of a concrete transition, we consider the Bakery mutual exclusion algorithm, which has an infinite state space.

Transition system S_1:

$$\tau_1 : pc_1 = l_{11} \qquad\qquad\qquad\qquad \longrightarrow \quad y_1 := y_2 + 1, pc_1 := l_{12}$$
$$\tau_2 : pc_1 = l_{12} \wedge (y_2 = 0 \vee y_1 \leq y_2) \longrightarrow \quad pc_1 := l_{13}$$
$$\tau_3 : pc_1 = l_{13} \qquad\qquad\qquad\qquad \longrightarrow \quad y_1 := 0, pc_1 := l_{11}$$

Transition system S_2:

$$\tau_4 : pc_2 = l_{21} \qquad\qquad\qquad\qquad \longrightarrow \quad y_2 := y_1 + 1, pc_2 := l_{22}$$
$$\tau_5 : pc_2 = l_{22} \wedge (y_1 = 0 \vee y_2 < y_1) \longrightarrow \quad pc_2 := l_{23}$$
$$\tau_6 : pc_2 = l_{23} \qquad\qquad\qquad\qquad \longrightarrow \quad y_2 := 0, pc_2 := l_{21}$$

Here pc_i ranges over $\{l_{i1}, l_{i2}, l_{i3}\}$ and y_i ranges over the set of natural numbers. As abstract variables we use the boolean variables a_1, a_2, a_3 and the variables pc_1^a and pc_2^a. The abstraction function α is given by the predicate $\bigwedge_{i=1,2} a_i \equiv (y_i = 0) \wedge a_3 \equiv (y_1 \leq y_2) \wedge \bigwedge_{i=1,2} pc_i^a \equiv pc_i$.

Let us consider transition τ_1 of S_1 and apply step 1) to 5) to it. It can be easily seen that we obtain $\beta(pc_1^a) \equiv l_{12}$, $\beta(a_1) \equiv 1 + y_2 = 0$, $\beta(a_3) \equiv 1 + y_2 \leq y_2$, $\beta(pc_2^a) \equiv pc_2$, and $\beta(a_2) \equiv y_2 = 0$. Moreover, $\alpha(pc_1 = l_{11}) \equiv pc_1^a = l_{11}$. Since $1 + y_2 = 0$ and $1 + y_2 \leq y_2$ are equivalent to false, we obtain as abstract transition $pc_1^a = l_{11} \to a_1 := \text{false}, a_3 := \text{false}, pc_1^a := l_{11}$. Also the abstraction of transitions τ_2 to τ_5 are computed by substitutions. For transition τ_6, the assignment to variables a_2 and pc_2^a are determined by substitutions, while we need the elimination method to determine the effect on a_3.

5 A PVS-based Implementation

We have implemented a tool that computes an abstraction of a network $S_1 \parallel \cdots \parallel S_n$, where $\parallel$ is the synchronous or asynchronous composition of transition systems. As a specification language for concrete systems we use a subset of the specification language of PVS. The produced abstract system is optionally described in PVS or SMV. The PVS theorem-prover is used to check the formulas generated by the elimination method. The user supplies a list of proof strategies which are used to check these formulas. Besides the proof strategies the user provides the following components:

1) A PVS theory describing the concrete system. The user can choose whether to use the invariant to be checked during generation of the abstract system as given by definition 1. The user can also give a list of already proved invariants of the concrete system which are then used while constructing the abstract system.

2) A PVS-theory describing the abstract state space and defining the abstraction function. We implemented a procedure that computes a first abstraction function which associates a boolean variable with every atomic formula of the form $r(x_1, \cdots, x_n)$ which appears in a guard, if there is at least one concrete variable among $x_1, \cdots, x_n$ that ranges over an infinite data domain, and which associates a boolean variable with every expression of the form $x' = \exp$ which appears in a concrete transition, if x ranges over an infinite data type and does not occur in exp.[4]

The user can optionally provide a set of concrete variables for which our tool computes for each atomic operation on these variables an abstract operation. The computed abstract operations are then stored and reused each time an abstraction of the concrete system is computed unless the abstraction function has been modified.

The generation of the abstract system is *completely automatic* and compositional as we consider transition by transition. Thus, for each concrete transition we obtain an abstract transition (which might be non-deterministic). This is a very important property of our method, since it enables the debugging of the concrete system or alternatively enhancing the abstraction function. Indeed, the constructed abstract system may not satisfy the desired property, for three possible reasons: 1) the concrete system does not satisfy the invariant, 2) the abstraction function is not suitable for proving the invariant, or 3) the provided proof strategies are too weak. Now, a model-checker such as SMV provides a trace as a counterexample, if the abstract system does not satisfy the abstract invariant. Since we have a clear correspondence between abstract and concrete transitions, we can examine the trace and find out which of the three reasons listed above is the case. In particular if the concrete system does not satisfy the invariant then we can transform the trace given by SMV to a concrete trace, and verify whether it is a concrete counterexample.

6 A Case Study

We consider the verification of the Bounded Retransmission protocol [23], BRP for short. The BRP protocol is an extension of the alternating bit protocol, where

---

[4] In [13] it is proposed to take as abstraction the partition of the concrete state space which is induced by the literals appearing in the guards. This abstraction is, however, generally too coarse.

files of individual data are transmitted and the number of retransmissions per datum is bounded by a parameter. The protocol has been verified using theorem proving [14, 16, 15], where a large number of auxiliary invariants were needed. In the original formulation of the case study the requirements on the protocol are given by an abstract protocol, BRP-spec, and the task is to prove that the concrete protocol BRP simulates (is a refinement of) BRP-spec. In [13] it has been shown by computing an abstraction of BRP that the concrete protocol satisfies a set of temporal properties which have been extracted from the specification BRP-spec. There is, however, no guarantee that the checked temporal properties exclude all the behaviors excluded by BRP-spec: They do not exclude, for instance, that the protocol cheats both the sending and receiving clients by telling them that the transmission was successful while this is not the case. Using our method and its implementation we have been able to automatically prove that BRP implements BRP-spec.

Description of the protocol The BRP protocol accepts requirements REQ(f) from a producer to transmit a file f of data to a consumer (See Fig 1). The protocol consists of a sender at the producer side and a receiver at the consumer side. The sender transmits data frames to the receiver via channel **K** and

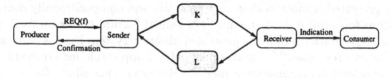

Fig. 1. The Bounded Retransmission Protocol.

waits for acknowledgment via channel **L**. Since these channels may lose messages timeouts are used to identify a loss of messages. After sending a message, the sender waits for an acknowledgment. When the acknowledgment arrives, the sender either proceeds with the next message in the file, if there is one, or sends a confirmation message to the producer. If a timeout occurs before reception of an acknowledgment, the sender retransmits the same message. This procedure is repeated as often as specified by a parameter *max*. On its side, the receiver after acknowledging a message that is not the last one waits for further messages. If no new message arrives before a timeout, it concludes that there is a loss of contact to the sender and reports this to the consumer. The protocol is responsible for informing the producer whether the file has been transmitted correctly, whether transmission failed, or whether the last message is possibly lost. On the consumer side, the protocol passes data frames indicating whether the datum is the first one in a file, the last one, or whether it is an intermediate one.

Correctness criterion To reduce the problem of proving that BRP simulates BRP-spec to an invariance problem, we follow the same approach as in [16]. Thus, we consider a superposition of BRP and BRP-spec and prove that the superposed protocol, BRP$^+$, satisfies the invariance property $\Box$*Safe*, where *Safe* is a variable that is set to false as soon as BRP makes a transition that is not allowed by BRP-spec. It should be realized that BRP$^+$ contains for many variables of the protocol two different copies corresponding to the variable in BRP and BRP-spec, respectively. So, for instance there are two variables *file* and *afile* which correspond to the file to be sent and two variables *head* and *ahead* which correspond to the position of the data being processed in *file* and *afile*, respectively.

Verification of the protocol The BRP protocol represents a family of parameterized protocols. The parameters are the number of allowed retransmissions *max*, the length of a file *Last*, and finally, the data type *Data*. To obtain a finite abstraction of the protocol it is natural to eliminate these parameters by introducing additional nondeterminism. The abstraction we used is essentially obtained by the procedure we proposed in section 5. The only exception concerns an abstract variable that encodes the distance between the position variables *head* and *ahead*. A finite abstract system has been fully automatically produced within one hour and 20 minutes on an Ultra Sparc[5] and has been successfully model-checked by SMV within 2.11 seconds.

7 Conclusion

We have presented a method that automatically and compositionally computes abstractions for infinite state systems. The salient feature of our method, apart from being automatic, is that the generated abstract system has the same structure as the concrete one. This makes our method applicable for synchronous as well as asynchronous computation models. Moreover, this allows for the application of other techniques for reducing the state explosion problem as well as for debugging the concrete system. An other important feature of our method is that it is incremental, in the following sense. Assume that we computed an abstraction S^a of a system S with respect to an abstraction function α. Assume that we want to add new abstract variables to those in α, that is, we consider a new abstraction function α' which agrees with α on the old abstract variables. Then, all transitions which have been eliminated during the generation of S^a need not be considered for the construction of an abstraction of S with respect to α'. Furthermore, it is worth mentioning that, by the preservation results of [8, 19], one can use our method to compute a finite abstract system that can be used to verify every temporal property that does not include an existential quantification over computation paths.

Though our method is based on a rather simple mathematical background, we view it as practically important. We implemented the method using PVS to check the conditions generated by the elimination method. The generated abstract system is optionally described in the specification language of PVS or of SMV. Thus, our implementation presents a bridge between the PVS theorem prover and the SMV model-checker.

We applied our method on several examples. In addition to the BRP described in this paper we computed a finite abstraction of the Alternating bit

---

[5] The implementation of [13] takes five hours for a version of the BRP with fewer variables.

protocol following the example in [25] and verified the Bakery and Peterson's mutual exclusion algorithms, the reader-writer example, and a simplified version of the Futurebus+ cache coherence protocol. For all of these examples an abstract system has been fully automatically and efficiently generated.

Currently, we are integrating our implementation with our techniques for generating auxiliary invariants [1]. We are also planning to investigate methods to automate the debugging process of the concrete system. What is needed is a module that transforms a trace of the abstract system into a concrete one and then checks whether this trace corresponds to a computation of the concrete system.

References

1. S. Bensalem and Y. Lakhnech. Automatic generation of invariants. Accepted in Formal Methods in System Design. To appear.
2. N. Bjørner, A. Browne, and Z. Manna. Automatic generation of invariants and intermediate assertions. *Theoretical Computer Science*, 173(1), 1997.
3. E.M. Clarke, O. Grumberg, and D.E. Long. Model checking and abstraction. *ACM Transactions on Programming Languages and Systems*, 16(5), 1994.
4. P. Cousot and R. Cousot. Abstract interpretation: A unified lattice model for static analysis of programs by construction or approximation of fixpoints. In *4th ACM symp. of Prog. Lang.*, pages 238–252. ACM Press, 1977.
5. D. Dams. *Abstract interpretation and partition refinement for model checking.* PhD thesis, Technical University of Eindhoven, 1996.
6. D. Dams, R. Gerth, G. Döhmen, R. Herrmann, P. Kelb, and H. Pargmann. Model checking using adaptive state and data abstraction. In *CAV'94*, volume 818 of *LNCS*. Springer-Verlag, 1994.
7. D. Dams, R. Gerth, and O. Grumberg. Generation of reduced models for checking fragments of CTL. In *CAV'93*, volume 697 of *LNCS*. Springer-Verlag, 1993.
8. D. Dams, R. Gerth, and O. Grumberg. Abstract interpretation of reactive systems: Abstractions preserving ACTL*, ECTL* and CTL*. In *ROCOMET'94*. IFIP Transactions, North-Holland/Elsevier, 1994.
9. D. Dams, R. Gerth, and O. Grumberg. Abstract interpretation of reactive systems. *ACM Transactions in Programming Languages and Systems*, 19(2), 1997.
10. J. Dingel and Th. Filkorn. Model checking for infinite state systems using data abstraction. In *CAV'95*, volume 939 of *LNCS*, pages 54–69. Springer-Verlag, 1995.
11. S. Graf. Characterization of a sequentially consistent memory and verification of a cache memory by abstraction. Accepted to Distributed Computing, 1995.
12. S. Graf and C. Loiseaux. A tool for symbolic program verification and abstraction. In *CAV'93*, volume 697 of *LNCS*. Springer-Verlag, 1993.
13. S. Graf and H. Saidi. Construction of abstract state graphs with PVS. In *CAV'97*, volume 1254 of *LNCS*, 1997.
14. F.F. Groote and J.C. van de Pol. A bounded retransmission protocol for large packets. In *A case study in computer checked verification*, Logic Group Preprint Series 100. Utrecht University, 1993.
15. K. Havelund and N. Shankar. Experiments in theorem proving and model checking for protocol verification. In *FME'96*, volume 1051 of *LNCS*. Springer-verlag, 1996.

16. L. Helmink, M.P.A. Sellink, and F.W. Vaandrager. Proof-checking a data link protocol. Technical Report CS-R9420, CWI, March 1994.
17. P. Kelb. *Abstraktionstechniken für Automatische Verifikationsmethoden.* PhD thesis, University of Oldenburg, 1995.
18. R.P. Kurshan. *Computer-Aided Verification of Coordinating Processes, the automata theoretic approach.* Princeton Series in Computer Science. 1994.
19. C. Loiseaux, S. Graf, J. Sifakis, A. Bouajjani, and S. Bensalem. Property preserving abstractions for the verification of concurrent systems. *Formal Methods in System Design,* 6(1), 1995.
20. D. E. Long. *Model Checking, Abstraction, and Compositional Reasoning.* PhD thesis, Carnegie Mellon, 1993.
21. Z. Manna and A. Pnueli. Completing the temporal picture. *Theoretical Computer Science,* 83(1):97–130, 1991.
22. Z. Manna and A. Pnueli. *Temporal Verification of Reactive Systems: Safety.* Springer-Verlag, 1995.
23. S. Mauw and G.J. Veltink editors. *Algebraic Specification of Communication Protocols.* Number 36 in Cambridge Tracts in Theoretical Computer Science. 1993.
24. K.L. McMillan. *Symbolic model checking.* Kluwer Academic Publ., Boston, 1993.
25. O. Müller and T. Nipkow. Combining model checking and deduction for I/O-automata. In *TACAS'95,* volume 1019 of *LNCS,* 1995.
26. S. Owre, J. Rushby, N. Shankar, and F. von Henke. Formal verification for fault-tolerant architectures: Prolegomena to the design of PVS. *IEEE Transactions on Software Engineering,* 1995.
27. J. X. Su, D. L. Dill, and C. Barrett. Automatic generation of invariants in processor verification. In *FMCAD '96,* volume 1166 of *LNCS,* 1996.

Normed Simulations

David Griffioen[1,2]* Frits Vaandrager[2]

[1] CWI
P.O. Box 94079, 1090 GB Amsterdam, The Netherlands

[2] Computing Science Institute, University of Nijmegen
P.O. Box 9010, 6500 GL Nijmegen, The Netherlands
{davidg,fvaan}@cs.kun.nl

Abstract. In existing simulation proof techniques, a single step in a low-level system may be simulated by an extended execution fragment in a high-level system. As a result, it is undecidable whether a given relation is a simulation, even if tautology checking is decidable for the underlying specification logic. This paper introduces various types of *normed simulations*. In a normed simulation, each step in a low-level system can be simulated by at most one step in the high level system, for any related pair of states. We show that it is decidable whether a given relation is a normed simulation relation, given that tautology checking is decidable. We also prove that, at the semantic level, normed simulations form a complete proof method for establishing behavior inclusion, provided that the high-level system has finite invisible nondeterminism. As an illustration of our method we discuss the verification in PVS of a leader election algorithm that is used within the IEEE 1394 protocol.

1 Introduction

Simulation relations and refinement functions are widely used to prove that a low-level specification of a reactive system correctly implements a higher-level one [1, 13]. Technically, a *simulation* (or *refinement*) is a relation (or function) R between the states of a low-level system A and a high-level system B, that satisfies conditions such as

$$(s, u) \in R \land s \xrightarrow{a}_A s' \Rightarrow \exists u' : u \xrightarrow{a}_B u' \land (s', u') \in R \tag{1}$$

(If a low-level state s and a high-level state u are related, and A can make a transition from s to s', then there exists a matching transition in B from u to a state u' that is related to s'.) The existence of a simulation implies that any behavior that can be exhibited by A can also be exhibited by B.

The main reason why simulations are useful is that they reduce *global* reasoning about behaviors and executions to *local* reasoning about states and transitions. However, to the best of our knowledge, all complete simulation proof methods that appear in the literature fall back on some form of global reasoning

---

* Supported by the Netherlands Organization for Scientific Research (NWO) under contract SION 612-316-125.

in the case of systems that perform internal (or stuttering) steps. The usual transfer condition for *forward simulations* [13], for instance, says

$$(s, u) \in R \land s \xrightarrow{a}_A s' \Rightarrow \exists \text{ execution fragment } \alpha : first(\alpha) = u \qquad (2)$$
$$\land \ trace(\alpha) = trace(a) \land (s', last(\alpha)) \in R$$

(Each low-level transition can be simulated by a sequence of transitions which, apart from the action that has to be matched, may also contain an arbitrary number of internal steps.) Thus the research program to reduce global reasoning to local reasoning has not been carried out to its completion.

In manual proofs of simulation relations, the occurrence of executions in transfer condition (2) usually does not pose a real problem: often the matching execution fragments that have to be constructed are short since internal steps are rare in high-level specifications; moreover humans tend to be quite good in reasoning about sequences, and move effortlessly from transitions to executions and back. In contrast, it turns out to be rather cumbersome to formalize arguments involving sequences using existing theorem provers (see [5] for a comparative study). In fact, in several papers in which formalizations of simulation proofs are described, the authors only define a restricted type of simulation or refinement in which each transition of the low-level system is formalized by one or zero transitions of the high-level system [11, 15, 6]. In approaches such as [18], in which the full transfer condition (2) is formalized, the user has to supply the simulating execution fragment α to the prover explicitly in each case of the proof, which makes the verification process highly interactive.

In this paper, we introduce a simulation proof method which remedies the above problems. The key idea is to define a function n that assigns a norm $n(s \xrightarrow{a} s', u)$, in some well-founded domain, to each pair of a transition in A and a state of B. If u has to simulate step $s \xrightarrow{a} s'$ then it may either do nothing (if a is internal and s' is related to u), or it may do a corresponding a-step, or it may perform an internal action leading to a state u' such that the norm $n(s \xrightarrow{a} s', u')$ decreases. We establish that the *normed forward simulations* and *normed backward simulations* together constitute a complete proof method for establishing trace inclusion. In addition we show how *history* and *prophecy relations* (which are closely related to the history and prophecy variables of [1]) can be enriched with a norm function, to obtain another complete proof method in combination with a simple notion of refinement mapping.

When proving invariance properties of programs, one is faced with two problems. The first problem is related to the necessity of proving tautologies of the assertion logic, whereas the second manifests in the need of finding sufficiently strong invariants. In order to address the first problem, powerful decision procedures have been incorporated in theorem provers such as PVS [16]. If tautology checking is decidable then it is decidable whether a given state predicate is valid for the initial states and preserved by all transitions. The task of finding such a predicate, i.e. solving the second problem, is the responsibility of the user, even though some very powerful heuristics have been devised to automate this search [2]. Analogously, if systems A and B, and a conjectured simulation relation R

and norm function n can all be expressed within a decidable assertion logic, and if the transition relations of A and B can be specified using a finite number of deterministic transition predicates, then it is decidable whether the pair (R, n) is a normed simulation. This result, which does not hold for other methods such as [1, 13], is a distinct advantage of normed simulations.

The preorders generated by normed forward simulations are strictly finer than the preorders induced by the simulations of [13]. In fact, it is easy to characterize normed forward simulations in terms of *branching simulations* [9]. We believe it will be possible to come up with a notion of normed simulation that induces the same preorder as forward simulations, but technically this will be much more involved. In [9] it is argued that branching bisimulations have much nicer mathematical properties than Milner's weak bisimulations. Similarly, the mathematical theory of normed simulations appears to be nicer and more tractable than the theory of simulations developed in [13].

The idea of using norm functions to prove simulation relations also occurs in [10], where it is used to prove branching bisimilarity in the context of the process algebra μCRL. However, in [10] the norm function is defined on the states of B only, and does not involve the transitions of A. Furthermore the method of [10] only applies to divergence free processes. Norm functions very similar to ours were also studied by Namjoshi [14]. He uses them to obtain a characterization of the stuttering bisimulation of [3], which is the equivalent of branching bisimulation in a setting where states rather than actions are labelled (see [4]). Both [10] and [14] do not address effectiveness issues. Although we present normed simulations in a setting of labeled transition systems, it should not be difficult to transfer our results to a process algebraic setting such as [10] or a state based setting such as [14].

As a substantial example of the use of normed simulations, we discuss the formalization in PVS of the verification of a leader election algorithm that plays a role in the tree identify phase of the physical layer of the IEEE 1394 protocol [12, 6]. We establish a normed prophecy relation from a high-level specification of the protocol to an intermediate specification, and a normed history relation from the intermediate specification to a low-level specification.

2 A Theory of Normed Simulations

In this section we build on some (standard) definitions and notations presented in [13]. In fact, our aim is to derive the same results as in [13], only for different types of simulations.

2.1 Step Refinements

The simplest type of simulation we consider is a *step refinement*. A *step refinement* from automaton A to automaton B is a partial function r from *states*(A) to *states*(B) that satisfies the following two conditions:

1. If $s \in start(A)$ then $s \in domain(r)$ and $r(s) \in start(B)$.

2. If $s \xrightarrow{a}_A s' \wedge s \in domain(r)$ then $s' \in domain(r)$ and
   - $r(s) = r(s') \wedge a = \tau$, or
   - $r(s) \xrightarrow{a}_B r(s')$.

Write $A \leq_R B$ if there exists a step refinement from A to B. It is easy to check that $\leq_R$ is a preorder (i.e., is transitive and reflexive). If $A \leq_R B$ then we can construct, for each execution α of A, a corresponding execution of B with the same trace. This idea is formalized below.

Suppose A and B are automata, $R \subseteq states(A) \times states(B)$, and $\alpha = s_0 a_1 s_1 a_2 s_2 \cdots$ and $\alpha' = u_0 b_1 u_1 b_2 u_2 \cdots$ are executions of A and B, respectively. Let $index(\alpha)$ and $index(\alpha')$ denote the index sets of α and α'. We say that α and α' are R-related, written $(\alpha, \alpha') \in R$, if there exists an $index$ $mapping$, i.e., a total, nondecreasing function $m : index(\alpha) \to index(\alpha')$ such that, for all $i \in index(\alpha)$ and $j \in index(\alpha')$,

1. $m(0) = 0$,
2. $(s_i, u_{m(i)}) \in R$,
3. $i > 0 \;\Rightarrow\; a_i = b_{m(i)} \vee (a_i = \tau \wedge m(i) = m(i-1))$,
4. $m(i) < j \wedge (i+1 \in index(\alpha) \Rightarrow j < m(i+1)) \;\Rightarrow\; (s_i, u_j) \in R \wedge b_j = \tau$.

Write $(A, B) \in R$ if for every execution α of A there is an execution α' of B such that $(\alpha, \alpha') \in R$, and write $[A, B] \in R$ if for every finite execution α of A there is a finite execution α' of B such that $(\alpha, \alpha') \in R$.

An index mapping maps low-level states to corresponding high-level states such that the start states correspond (Condition 1), corresponding states are related by R (Condition 2), each non-τ action in the low-level execution corresponds to an action in the high-level execution (Condition 3), and each non-τ action in the high-level execution corresponds to an action in the low-level execution (Condition 4). Our notion of correspondence is similar to the one presented in [8, 19]. Within the theory of I/O automata, execution correspondence plays a crucial role in proofs of preservation of both safety and liveness properties. Our notion is more restrictive than the one of [8, 19], but has the advantage that it also preserves until properties.

Theorem 1. *(Execution correspondence) (1) If $(\alpha, \alpha') \in R$ then $trace(\alpha) = trace(\alpha')$. (2) If $(A, B) \in R$ then $A \leq_T B$. (3) If $[A, B] \in R$ then $A \leq_{*T} B$.*

Theorem 2. *(Soundness of refinements) If r is a step refinement from A to B then $(A, B) \in r$.*

Combining Theorems 1 and 2 gives that $A \leq_R B$ implies $A \leq_T B$. In addition, Theorem 2 allows us to use refinement relations as a sound technique for proving implementation relations between live automata, as in [8, 19].

2.2   Normed Forward Simulations

A *normed forward simulation* from A to B consists of a relation f over $states(A) \times states(B)$ and a function $n : steps(A) \times states(B) \to S$, for some well-founded set S, such that (here $f[s]$ denotes the set $\{u \mid (s, u) \in f\}$):

1. If $s \in start(A)$ then $f[s] \cap start(B) \neq \emptyset$.
2. If $s \xrightarrow{a}_A s' \wedge u \in f[s]$ then
   - $u \in f[s'] \wedge a = \tau$, or
   - $\exists u' \in f[s'] : u \xrightarrow{a}_B u'$, or
   - $\exists u' \in f[s] : u \xrightarrow{\tau}_B u' \wedge n(s \xrightarrow{a}_A s', u') < n(s \xrightarrow{a}_A s', u)$.

Write $A \leq_F B$ if there exists a normed forward simulation from A to B.

The intuition behind this definition is that when $s \xrightarrow{a}_A s'$ and $(s, u) \in f$, either the transition in A is a stuttering step (first clause), or there is a matching step in B (second clause), or B can do a stuttering step which decreases the norm (third clause). Since the norm decreases at each application of the third clause, it can only be applied a finite number of times. In general, the norm function may depend both on the transitions in A and on the states of B. However, if B is *convergent*, i.e., there are no infinite τ-paths, then one can simplify the type of the norm function (though not necessarily the definition of the norm function itself!) to $n : states(B) \to S$. In fact, in the approach of [10], which only applies to convergent processes, the norm function is required to be of this restricted type. It is not hard to see that in the example of Figure 1, where B is divergent, the norm necessarily depends on the selected step in A.

As each step refinement is a normed forward simulation (for an arbitrary norm function) $A \leq_R B$ implies $A \leq_F B$. It is also not so difficult to prove that $\leq_F$ is a preorder. The following theorem states that normed forward simulations induce the same preorder on automata as "branching forward sim-

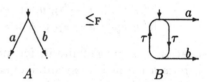

Fig. 1. Norm function must take steps of A into account.

ulations". Basically the same result has been obtained by Namjoshi [14] in the setting of stuttering bisimulations.

Theorem 3. $A \leq_F B$ *iff there is a branching forward simulation from A to B, i.e., a relation f over $states(A) \times states(B)$ such that*

1. *If $s \in start(A)$ then $f[s] \cap start(B) \neq \emptyset$.*
2. *If $s \xrightarrow{a}_A s' \wedge u \in f[s]$ then*
   - *$u \in f[s'] \wedge a = \tau$, or*
   - *$\exists u_0, .., u_n \in f[s] \exists u' \in f[s'] : u_0 = u \wedge (\forall i < n : u_i \xrightarrow{\tau}_B u_{i+1}) \wedge u_n \xrightarrow{a}_B u'$.*

An interesting implication of our proof of Theorem 3 is that if there is a normed forward simulation from A to B, there is in fact a normed forward simulation with a norm function that has the set of natural numbers as its range.

The proofs of the following Theorems 4 and 5 are standard and similar to the proofs of the corresponding results in [13] and elsewhere.

Theorem 4. *(Soundness of forward simulations) If f is a normed forward simulation from A to B then $(A, B) \in f$.*

Theorem 5. *(Partial completeness of forward simulations) If B is deterministic and $A \leq_{*T} B$, then $A \leq_F B$.*

It is interesting to note that there is only one result from [13] that does not carry over to the setting of this paper. This result says that if A is a forest, i.e., each state can be reached via exactly one execution, and $A \leq_F B$ then $A \leq_R B$. The automata A and B of Figure 1 constitute a counterexample.

2.3 Normed Backward Simulations

A *normed backward simulation* from A to B consists of a total relation b over $states(A) \times states(B)$ and a function $n : (steps(A) \cup start(A)) \times states(B) \to S$, for some well-founded set S, such that

1. If $s \in start(A) \land u \in b[s]$ then
   - $u \in start(B)$, or
   - $\exists u' \in b[s] : u' \xrightarrow{\tau}_B u \land n(s, u') < n(s, u)$.
2. If $s' \xrightarrow{a}_A s \land u \in b[s]$ then
   - $u \in b[s'] \land a = \tau$, or
   - $\exists u' \in b[s'] : u' \xrightarrow{a}_B u$, or
   - $\exists u' \in b[s] : u' \xrightarrow{\tau}_B u \land n(s' \xrightarrow{a}_A s, u') < n(s' \xrightarrow{a}_A s, u)$.

Relation b is image-finite if, for all s, the set $b[s]$ is finite. Write $A \leq_B B$ if there is a normed backward simulation from A to B, and $A \leq_{iB} B$ if there is an image-finite normed backward simulation from A to B. It is routine to prove that $\leq_B$ and $\leq_{iB}$ are preorders, and to characterize these relations in terms of "branching backward simulations" as in Theorem 3.

The proofs of the following Proposition 1, Theorem 6 and Theorem 7 again closely follow the proofs of the corresponding results in [13].

Proposition 1. *(1) $A \leq_R B \Rightarrow A \leq_{iB} B$. (2) If all states of A are reachable, B is deterministic and $A \leq_B B$, then $A \leq_R B$. (3) $A \leq_{iB} B \Rightarrow A \leq_B B$. (4) If all states of A are reachable, B has finite invisible nondeterminism and $A \leq_B B$, then $A \leq_{iB} B$.*

Theorem 6. *(Soundness of backward simulations) If b is a normed backward simulation from A to B then $[A, B] \in b$. If, moreover, b is image-finite then $(A, B) \in b$.*

Theorem 7. *(Partial completeness of backward simulations) If A is a forest and $A \leq_{*T} B$, then $A \leq_B B$.*

2.4 History Relations

A pair (h, n) is a *normed history relation* from A to B if (h, n) is a normed forward simulation from A to B and h^{-1} is a step refinement from B to A. Write $A \leq_H B$ if there exists a normed history relation from A to B.

Thus $A \leq_H B$ implies $A \leq_F B$ and $B \leq_R A$. Through these implications, the preorder and soundness results for forward simulations and refinements carry over to history relations. In fact, if (h, n) is a normed history relation from A to B then h^{-1} is just a functional *branching bisimulation* between A and B in the sense of Van Glabbeek and Weijland [9]. Hence, history relations preserve behavior of automata in a very strong sense.

The following theorem is a variant of a result proved by Sistla [17].

Theorem 8. *(Completeness of history relations and backward simulations) If* $A \leq_{*T} B$ *then there exists a forest* C *such that* $A \leq_H C \leq_B B$.

Theorem 9. $A \leq_F B \Leftrightarrow (\exists C : A \leq_H C \leq_R B)$.

2.5 Prophecy Relations

A pair (p, n) is a *normed prophecy relation* from A to B if (p, n) is a normed backward simulation from A to B and p^{-1} is a step refinement from B to A. Write $A \leq_P B$ if there exists a prophecy relation from A to B, and $A \leq_{iP} B$ if there is an image-finite prophecy relation from A to B. Thus $A \leq_{iP} B$ implies $A \leq_{iB} B$ and $A \leq_P B$, and $A \leq_P B$ implies $A \leq_B B$ and $B \leq_R A$. Moreover, if all states of A are reachable, B has finite invisible nondeterminism and $A \leq_P B$, then $A \leq_{iP} B$. Through these implications, the preorder and soundness results for backward simulations and refinements carry over to prophecy relations.

Theorem 10. *(1)* $A \leq_B B \Leftrightarrow (\exists C : A \leq_P C \leq_R B)$. *(2)* $A \leq_{iB} B \Leftrightarrow (\exists C : A \leq_{iP} C \leq_R B)$.

We can now state variants of the well-known completeness result of Abadi and Lamport [1].

Theorem 11. *(Completeness of history+prophecy relations and refinements) Suppose* $A \leq_{*T} B$. *Then (1)* $\exists C, D : A \leq_H C \leq_P D \leq_R B$. *(2) If* B *has finite invisible nondeterminism then* $\exists C, D : A \leq_H C \leq_{iP} D \leq_R B$.

2.6 Decidability

Fix an assertion language $\mathcal{L}$ that includes first-order predicate logic and interpreted symbols for expressing the standard operations and relations. If automata A and B, and a conjectured simulation relation R and norm function n can all be expressed within a fragment of $\mathcal{L}$ for which tautology checking is decidable and if the transition relations of A and B can be specified using a finite number of deterministic transition predicates (as defined, for instance in, [7]), then it is decidable whether the pair (R, n) is a normed forward or normed backward simulation. It is not hard to prove that this result does not hold for the refinements, forward and backward simulations presented in [13], nor for the prophecy variables of [1].

2.7 Reachability

When proving simulations one often restricts the automata to the reachable sub-automata, in order to be able to use invariants. In backward simulations this is not convenient, therefore a slightly adapted version of the backward simulation is presented below. The predicate Q on states of B can be used as induction hypothesis.

The adapted *normed backward simulation* from A to B consists of a total relation b over $states(A) \times states(B)$ and a function $n : (steps(A) \cup start(A)) \times states(B) \to S$, for some well-founded set S, such that

1. If $s \in start(A) \wedge u \in b[s] \wedge Q(u)$ then
   - $u \in start(B)$, or
   - $\exists u' \in b[s] : u' \xrightarrow{\tau}_B u \wedge n(s, u') < n(s, u) \wedge Q(u')$.
2. If $s' \xrightarrow{a}_A s \wedge u \in b[s] \wedge reachable(s') \wedge Q(u)$ then
   - $u \in b[s'] \wedge a = \tau$, or
   - $\exists u' \in b[s'] : u' \xrightarrow{a}_B u \wedge Q(u')$, or
   - $\exists u' \in b[s] : u' \xrightarrow{\tau}_B u \wedge n(s' \xrightarrow{a}_A s, u') < n(s' \xrightarrow{a}_A s, u) \wedge Q(u')$.

3 Example: IEEE 1394

In this section we illustrate the notions of step refinements and normed (forward and backward) simulations through the verification of a fragment of IEEE 1394 [12], a high performance serial multimedia bus protocol. The specific algorithm that we analyze is an abstract version of the tree identify phase (TIP) of the IEEE 1394. We present the TIP protocol at three levels of abstraction, and prove, via refinements and simulations, that these three specifications are trace equivalent. The three automata are described in the IOA language of [7], and the relations that will be established between them are depicted below.

$$
\boxed{\text{TIP1}} \quad \begin{array}{c} \geq_R \\ \leq_B \end{array} \quad \boxed{\text{TIP2}} \quad \begin{array}{c} \geq_R \\ \leq_F \end{array} \quad \boxed{\text{TIP3}}
$$

IOA contains the basic type **Bool** with its standard operators, such as $\wedge$, $\vee$ and $\neg$. In addition type constructors **Array**, **Seq** (finite sequences) and **Set** (finite sets) are part of the language. The notation _[__] is used for array subscripting, an array with a value **e** in all cells is denoted by **const(e)**. The operation _ ⊢_ appends an element at the end of a sequence.

The task of the TIP is to check whether the finite and connected network topology is cycle free, and (if this is indeed the case) to elect a leader amongst the nodes. In Figure 2, a simple example network is displayed, with *devices* **A**, **B** and **C**, and *ports* **p**, **q**, **r** and **s**. It is assumed that each port is connected to exactly one other port, which is called its *peer*. A network may contain a loop, and devices even can be connected to themselves. So, in the example port **q** also could have been connected to **r**, but then **q** and **r** could not have been connected to **p** and **s**, respectively.

```
automaton TIP1
  signature
    output root(d : Dev),
           loopdetect(d : Dev)
  states
    root, lpd: Array[Dev,Bool] := const(false)
  transitions
    output root(d)
      pre ¬∃ e: Dev (oncycle?(e) ∨ root[e])
      eff  root[d] := true
    output loopdetect(d)
      pre oncycle?(d) ∧ ¬ lpd[d]
      eff  lpd[d] := true
```

Fig. 3. Automaton TIP1.

In Figure 3, automaton TIP1 is presented. This simple automaton has two action schemas root(d:Dev) and loopdetect(d:Dev). Specification TIP1 says that if the network is cycle free exactly one node will perform a root action. Otherwise, no root action will occur, but instead each node that lies on a cycle will perform a loopdetect action.

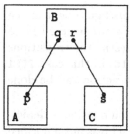

Fig. 2. A network

Automaton TIP2, presented in Figure 4, is an implementation of TIP1. The states contain an extra variable child: Set[Port]. If port p is in child then we say that its device dev(p) has a child, namely dev(peer(p)). When all but one neighbours of a device are its children it can become a child itself. Besides the loopdetect and root actions, TIP2 has an addchild action, which adds a port to the child set. If we consider the connections with a port in the child set to be the branches of a tree, then this tree grows with each addchild action from the leaves in the direction of the root. If all the ports of a device are in the child set then this device will become the root.

Automaton TIP3, presented in Figure 6, is an implementation of TIP2. It extends TIP2 with a state variable mq, which gives a queue of outgoing messages per port. Furthermore, some status bits per device (init, rc) are added. For a detailed description of the protocol we refer to [6] and the full version of this paper. Next the relations between the automata will be discussed.

(TIP2 $\leq_R$ TIP1) The function b from states of TIP2 to states of TIP1 is defined as the projection on the state variables of TIP1, in IOA notation: b([child,root,lpd]) == [root, lpd]. It is quite simple to prove that b is a step refinement (see Section 2.1) from TIP2 to TIP1.

The simulation from TIP1 to TIP2 illustrates the usefullness of backward simulations. A (traditional) forward simulation exists, but no *normed* forward

```
automaton TIP2
  signature
    internal addchild(d: Dev,p: Port),
    output   root(d: Dev),
             loopdetect(d: Dev)
  states
    child: Set[Port] := {},
    root,lpd: Array[Dev,Bool] := const(false)
  transitions
    internal addchild(d,p) where d = dev(p)
      pre  p ∉ child ∧
           ports(dev(peer(p))) - child = {peer(p)}
      eff  child := insert(p,child)
    output root(d)
      pre  ¬root[d] ∧ ports(d) ⊆ child
      eff  root[d] := true
    output loopdetect(d)
      pre  oncycle?(d) ∧ ¬lpd[d]
      eff  lpd[d] := true
```

Fig. 4. Automaton TIP2.

simulation. The reason for this can be seen in Figure 5. This figure depicts the transition systems of TIP1 and TIP2, for a network with only two devices (d and e) and a single link connecting these. The solid arrows represent the transitions of the systems, r is a shorthand for root and a for addchild. In this case TIP1 only can do a root(d) or a root(e) action. Before a root action can be done in TIP2 an addchild action has to be done.

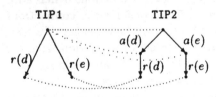

TIP1   TIP2

Fig. 5. Transition systems

A possible simulation relation is depicted by the dotted lines. This is not a normed *forward* simulation because the start state of TIP1 is related to a state where only a root(d) action can happen and not a root(e) action.

However the dotted lines depict a normed *backward* simulation from TIP1 to TIP2. The norm is defined on the states of TIP2 as the number of ports in the child set. Note that the only internal action of TIP2 is addchild, so the norm only needs to decrease when an addchild is simulated backwards (is 'undone').

In general, backward simulations can be useful when the implementation 'makes a decision' with internal steps. In TIP2 the decision who becomes root device is made by the internal action addchild.

(TIP2 $\leq_B$ TIP1) The inverse of function b is used as simulation relation. A predicate Q on the states of TIP2 is used to restrict the statespace.

$$Q(u) = \forall d.u.\texttt{root}[d] \rightarrow \texttt{ports}(d) \subseteq u.\texttt{child} \land$$
$$\forall d.u.\texttt{lpd}[d] \rightarrow \texttt{oncycle?}(d) \land$$
$$\texttt{GDT}(u.\texttt{child})$$

The first two conjucts are trivial consequences of the specification. $\texttt{GDT(S)}$ is a predicate on ports stating that the net obtained by deleting all links without a port in the set $\texttt{S}$ is a Growing Directed Tree. This means that it contains no cycles and each device has at most one parent and when a device has a parent all its other neighbours are its children. The norm function only depends on the state of $\texttt{TIP2}$, it is defined as the cardinalty of the set $\texttt{child}$.

($\texttt{TIP3} \leq_R \texttt{TIP2}$) The function $\texttt{f}$ from states of $\texttt{TIP3}$ to states of $\texttt{TIP2}$ is the projection on the state variables of $\texttt{TIP2}$. In IOA notation :
$\texttt{f([child,mq,init,rc,root,lpd]) == [child,root,lpd]}$

In the routine proof of $\texttt{TIP3} \leq_R \texttt{TIP2}$ an invariant $\texttt{I}$ is proved at the same time, where $\texttt{I == oncycle?(d) --> init(d)}$.

($\texttt{TIP2} \leq_F \texttt{TIP3}$) The proof that $\texttt{f}^{-1}$ is a normed forward simulation from $\texttt{TIP2}$ to $\texttt{TIP3}$ will be discussed in more detail. The condition for start states holds trivially. Next the three actions of $\texttt{TIP2}$ must be simulated, they will be discussed each. The norm function is defined per action schema and the result type is the natural numbers with the usual ordering. For convenience actions of $\texttt{TIPx}$ are subscripted with $\texttt{x}$. The states $\texttt{s}$ and $\texttt{t}$ are states of $\texttt{TIP2}$ before and after a transition respectively, similarly $\texttt{u}$ and $\texttt{v}$ are states of $\texttt{TIP3}$.

The $\texttt{loopdetect}_2$ action of $\texttt{TIP2}$ has the same precondition as the action $\texttt{loopdetect}_3$ of $\texttt{TIP3}$, and mentions only state variables that the automata have in common. Thus if the precondition of $\texttt{loopdetect}_2$ holds on a state $\texttt{s}$ then the precondition of $\texttt{loopdetect}_3$ also holds on states in $\texttt{f}^{-1}(\texttt{s})$. Because the $\texttt{loopdetect}_2$ action can be simulated directly, the norm function for $\texttt{loopdetect}_2$ is irrelevant.

The precondition of the the $\texttt{root}_2$ action is similar to the precondition of $\texttt{root}_3$, the latter has only a single extra conjunct: $\neg\texttt{init[d]}$. The norm function for $\texttt{root(d)}_2$ is defined to be 1 when $\texttt{init[d]}$ holds and 0 otherwise.

If $\texttt{root(d)}_2$ is enabled and $\texttt{f(u) = s}$ then $\texttt{root(d)}_3$ or $\texttt{childrenknown(d)}_3$ are enabled in $\texttt{u}$. A case distinction on $\texttt{u.init[d]}$ is made. Suppose $\texttt{u.init[d]}$ holds then the action $\texttt{childrenknown(d)}_3$ is enabled. This action reduces the norm, and the state after this action, is also related to $\texttt{s}$. Suppose $\neg\texttt{u.init[d]}$ then $\texttt{root(d)}_3$ is enabled in $\texttt{u}$ and $\texttt{root(d)}_3$ can be simulated directly.

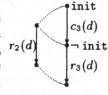

The proof that $\texttt{addchild}_2$ is simulated is similar to the proof for $\texttt{root}_2$ but longer. Where the $\texttt{root}_2$ simulation had two cases, we have seven cases for $\texttt{addchild}_2$. The case distinction is on whether init holds or not and whether the message queues of the port that is added and its peer are empty or contain a parent request.

343

Notice that the relations used in the simulations are the inverses of the functions (**b** and **f**) used in the step refinements, so in fact we have proved a stronger result, namely: TIP1 $\leq_{iP}$ TIP2 and TIP2 $\leq_H$ TIP3.

A drawback of the use of normed simulations instead of 'traditional' simulations could be that one has to find a suitable norm function. In our experience the norm functions were obvious. We expect this to be the case in general, because the norm function is 'local', only for a specific transition in one automaton the internal step in the other should decrease this measure.

References

1. M. Abadi and L. Lamport. The existence of refinement mappings. *Theoretical Computer Science*, 82(2):253–284, 1991.
2. S. Bensalem, Y. Lakhnech, and H. Saidi. Powerful techniques for the automatic generation of invariants. In *Proc. CAV'96*, LNCS 1102, pp 323–335. Springer, 1996.
3. M. Browne, E. Clarke, and O. Grümberg. Characterizing finite Kripke structures in propositional temporal logic. *Theoretical Comp. Sci.*, 59(1,2):115–131, 1988.
4. R. De Nicola and F. Vaandrager. Three logics for branching bisimulation. *Journal of the ACM*, 42(2):458–487, 1995.
5. M. Devillers, W. Griffioen, and O. Müller. Possibly infinite sequences: A comparative case study. In *Proc. TPHOLs'97*, LNCS 1275, pp 89–104. Springer, 1997.
6. M. Devillers, W. Griffioen, J. Romijn, and F. Vaandrager. Verification of a leader election protocol — formal methods applied to IEEE 1394. Technical Report CSI-R9728, University of Nijmegen, 1997.
7. S. Garland, N. Lynch, and M. Vaziri. IOA: A language for specifiying, programming, and validating distributed systems, September 1997. Available through http://larch.lcs.mit.edu:8001/~garland/ioaLanguage.html.
8. R. Gawlick, R. Segala, J. Søgaard-Andersen, and N. Lynch. Liveness in timed and untimed systems. In *Proc. 21th ICALP*, LNCS 820. Springer, 1994. A full version appears as MIT Technical Report MIT/LCS/TR-587.
9. R. van Glabbeek and W. Weijland. Branching time and abstraction in bisimulation semantics. *Journal of the ACM*, 43(3):555–600, 1996.
10. J. Groote and J. Springintveld. Focus points and convergent process operators — a proof strategy for protocol verification. Report CS-R9566, CWI, 1995.
11. L. Helmink, M. Sellink, and F. Vaandrager. Proof-checking a data link protocol. In *Proc. TYPES'93*, LNCS 806, pp 127–165. Springer, 1994.
12. IEEE Computer Society. IEEE Standard for a High Performance Serial Bus. Std 1394-1995, August 1996.
13. N. Lynch and F. Vaandrager. Forward and backward simulations, I: Untimed systems. *Information and Computation*, 121(2):214–233, 1995.
14. K. Namjoshi. A simple characterization of stuttering bisimulation. In *Proc. FST & TCS'97*, LNCS 1346, pp 284–296. Springer, 1997.
15. T. Nipkow and K. Slind. I/O automata in Isabelle/HOL. In *Types for Proofs and Programs*, LNCS 996, pp 101–119. Springer, 1995.
16. S. Owre, J. Rushby, N. Shankar, and F. von Henke. Formal verification for fault-tolerant architectures: Prolegomena to the design of PVS. *IEEE Transactions on Software Engineering*, 21(2):107–125, 1995.
17. A. Sistla. Proving correctness with respect to nondeterministic safety specifications. *Information Processing Letters*, 39(1):45–49, 1991.

18. J. Søgaard-Andersen, S. Garland, J. Guttag, N. Lynch, and A. Pogosyants. Computer-assisted simulation proofs. In *Proc. CAV'93*, LNCS 697, pp 305–319. Springer, 1993.
19. J. Søgaard-Andersen, N. Lynch, and B. Lampson. Correctness of communication protocols – a case study. Report MIT/LCS/TR-589, MIT, Cambridge, MA, 1993.

```
automaton TIP3
  signature

  states
    child: Set[Port] := {}
    mq: Array[Port,Seq[Mes]] := const({})
    init: Array[Dev,Bool] := const(true)
    rc, root, lpd: Array[Dev,Bool] := const(false)
  transitions
    internal childrenknown(d)
      pre init[d] ∧ size(ports(d) - child) ≤ 1
      eff init[d] := false;
          for p in ports[d] do if p ∈ child
                                 then mq[p] := mq[p] ⊢ ack
                                 else mq[p] := mq[p] ⊢ parent fi od
    internal addchild(d,p) where d = dev(p)
      pre init[d] ∧ head(mq[peer(p)]) = parent
      eff child := insert(p, child); mq[peer(p)] := tail(mq[peer(p)])
    internal receivemes(d,p,mes) where d = dev(p)
      pre ¬init[d] ∧ ports(d) - child = {p} ∧ head(mq[peer(p)]) = mes
      eff if mes = parent then rc[d] := true fi;
          mq[peer(p)] := tail(mq[peer(p)])
    internal solverootcontent(d,p) where d = dev(p)
      pre rc(d) ∧ rc(dev(peer(p)))
      eff child := insert(p,child);
          rc(d) := false; rc(dev(peer(p))) := false
    output root(d)
      pre ¬init[d] ∧ ¬root[d] ∧ ports(d) ⊆ child
      eff root[d] := true
    output loopdetect(d)
      pre oncycle?(d) ∧ ¬lpd[d]
      eff lpd[d] := true
```

Fig. 6. Automaton TIP3.

An Experiment in Parallelizing an Application Using Formal Methods

Computer Aided Parallelization

Raphaël Couturier and Dominique Méry

UMR n°7503 LORIA CNRS
Université Henri Poincaré
BP 239, 54506 Vandœuvre-lès-Nancy
France
email: couturie,mery@loria.fr

Abstract. Scientists and engineers have successfully developed much useful sequential code using classical programming languages, such as Fortran, and highly performant computers can help them to model problems whilst improving their results of simulation. However, great skill and care are required to design *correct* parallel code from sequential code. We focus our work on 3 aspects of producing correct parallel code from sequential code. First, we use a theorem prover, namely PVS, as a practical tool for asserting proof obligations and for stating programs and properties. Secondly, we build an abstraction from some sequential code in order to derive a postcondition. Finally, we characterize the "glueing condition" that will ensure the correctness of the final parallel code. Our method does not need any new notation but reuses proof theoretical notations together with the composition of postconditions with respect to the glueing condition.

1 Introduction

Parallel program design is a very challenging topic that requires formal techniques for guaranteeing both safety and liveness properties; furthermore, parallel programming poses questions with regards to the efficiency of the designed programs and on the relationship of the designed program to a given architecture. The design of parallel programs has been greatly influenced by the seminal framework of Chandy and Misra, namely UNITY [2], where a new perspective was suggested: a general framework for stating programs, properties and mapping shows how formal techniques could be put together in a uniform notation. The concept of refinement is a very crucial point in the UNITY philosophy: a "text" refines another "text" when what is true for the first "text" is also true for the second text. The formal interpretation of this statement is founded on the notion of predicate transformers [4, 5] and the choice of a language for specifying properties such as invariance or eventuality. Our paper tackles the question of parallelization of sequential code provided by non-computer scientists[1], under

---

[1] Physics, Chemistry

extra assumptions for preserving semantics through transformations by analyzing the code with a theorem prover, namely PVS [10], and by reasoning with a formal notation integrating proof methods. Moreover, our case study, has produced parallel executable code for a high peformance parallel computer[2], in our laboratory, which is actually used by the original scientists.

Before stating the method we have used in the parallelization of a Monte Carlo simulation of a grid of spins, we review different critical points related to the use of a formal method. We are not proposing an implementation of the UNITY notation in PVS but we do use the UNITY philosophy to separate a formal reasoning into an intermediate notation, namely PVS, together with the implementation in a parallel programming language (a parallel version of Fortran). We want to avoid the myth of the universal theorem prover and try to convince our non-computer scientists colleagues that tools may improve their work and help them to build parallel programs. The underlying model for stating algorithmic notations is based on UNITY but can also be related to TLA [8], VDM [6] and Z [13], where actions are also expressed using post-states with primed notation. We are interested by properties stating that when the program halts a postcondition holds, and this requires the use of invariants and the generation of proof obligations. The main problem is to derive a global property from local properties of pieces of the global program when it is parallelized. We limit our study to programs that are supposed to terminate in the manner of Chandy and Taylor [3]. Our problem is to organize the computations to preserve the total correctness of the initial program.

Our method consists of abstracting from an existing sequential code using the specification language of a prover, namely PVS [10]. The specification must explicily state the postconditions of the parallel parts. Our aim is to use postconditions and to prove, with the help of a prover, that postconditions obtained with the parallel program imply postconditions resulting from the sequential program, under an extra *glueing* condition, which ensures that pieces of programs cooperate properly. This condition is either given by the user or stated by the system. We apply this method to a Monte Carlo simulation of a grid of spins [11]. Our problem has a large number of iterations (about one million) and uses a huge number of random numbers (about 10^{14}). During each iteration, there are four steps. Three steps are easy to parallelize, but the fourth requires more attention because it involves the creation of graphs which may be on the whole grid. It is difficult to argue without a formal approach that the transformed code is correct with respect to the initial specification.

The paper is organized as follows. Section two describes our method. Section three explains the Monte Carlo simulation. Section four parallelizes the application. Section five proves, with the help of PVS, that our parallelization concerning the graphs is correct. Section six explains how a prover can be used to discover postconditions guaranteeing a correct program parallelization, and to state the glueing condition. Section seven presents other work related to our problem. Section eight concludes our paper.

---

[2] The Silicon Graphics Origin 2000 of the Charles Hermite Center

2 Using postconditions and a prover to parallelize an algorithm

The proof of a parallel program is a hard task, which can be done in at least two ways. On the one hand, we can develop the program and then prove it. Or, on the other hand, we can specify it, prove it and then develop it using the specification. The technique we are proposing can be used with both these methods.

In general when we parallelize a program, we already have the sequential version and the parallel code is founded on this. With more or less abstraction, the parallel parts of the code are fragments of the sequential code. Thus, the postcondition of a sequential code part is the same as the equivalent part in the parallel code, if this postcondition is well defined.

Next, given suitably defined postconditions, we must define the postcondition of the *glue* code which assembles all parts computed in parallel. If all these postconditions are well defined with a good level of abstraction[3], it is possible to prove that the postconditions of parallel code plus the postconditions of the glueing code implies the postconditions of the equivalent sequential code. This first method is schematized in Fig1(a).

The alternative method consists of first realizing an abstraction of the sequential algorithm and thus specifying the postconditions of the algorithm. Then, when we try to prove that postconditions of the parallel code without any glue conditions, all the proof obligations may not be proven. This is normal because the postcondition of the glue code is not specified. However, all the failed proof obligations are the required postconditions of the glue code. This second method is schematized in Fig1(b).

3 The Monte Carlo simulation

In this section, we explain briefly the simulation of Monte Carlo we use to validate our method, and describe the problems this parallelization implies. We take sequential code, developed in the Laboratoire de physique des Matériaux, by B. Berche, P.E. Berche and C. Chatelain [11]. This application is based on a large number of interdependent iterations, but each iteration is not time consuming (less than one second). We dispose spins on nodes of a rectangular net. The initial net was a grid 100*100. These spins follow a Markov law, that is to say that their evolution is based on a given probabilistic transition of a current configuration to the next one. At each iteration, thousands or millions of random numbers are generated (depending on the size of the given problem).

Now we present the 4 different steps involved in each iteration. The first step consists of randomly destroying links of the grid with a given probability. Next, the second step consists of exploring the grid to create graphs using existing

---

[3] If the level of abstraction is too high, the proof would be very difficult; and, if it is too low, the postcondition would not be useful.

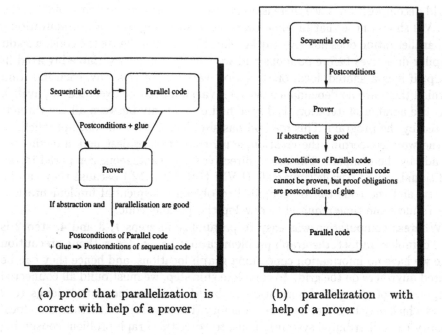

(a) proof that parallelization is correct with help of a prover

(b) parallelization with help of a prover

Fig. 1. The two methods we are proposing

links (there are either horizontal links or vertical links). Then links must be updated using graphs obtained during step two. Finally, we must calculate physical measures modeled by the system.

One of the most difficult problems to parallelize with this application is that we always want to generate the same random numbers with the parallel code as with the sequential code; but the random number generator, namely RANDAR [15], used for its properties (weak correlation...), cannot be parallelized, except by making time consuming concessions, because it is a combination of two generators. We overcome this constraint by generating the same random numbers for the initialization of the simulation process and then using different generators with different seeds.

Using this approach, we obtain converging results using sequential and parallel simulation after several iterations.

4 Parallelization of the simulation

In this section we present the parallelization which was made on the Silicon Graphics Origin 2000 at the Charles Hermite Center, LORIA, in Nancy. This machine possesses 64 processors with a distributed shared memory. The initial code is written in Fortran 77, so we keep this language and we use its parallel version on the Origin. Steps 1, 3 and 4 can be parallelized quite easily using band or grid decomposition, since there is no interaction between different points of the grid. We should note that in some cases, corresponding to small computations, the parallelization does not give any acceleration. To parallelize the code, we add compiler directives before DO loops and we specify, for each variable involved in a loop, if it is a shared, local or reduction variable. In this way, each iteration in which there are no dependance between variables can be executed in parallel. Thus the number of iterations is dispatched dynamicaly between all the threads created by the program. This method has similitudes with the data-parallelism. All the work concerning the creation, synchronisation or destruction of threads is made by the compiler. The use of directives is advantageous compared to the traditional way of parallelizing code (PVM [14], MPI [12]) because they can be ignored and the code can be compiled to obtain a sequential implementation. This reduces the time required to develop the parallel code.

Whereas computation was easy to parallelize in steps 1, 3 and 4, step 2 is more complex. In fact, the graph problem cannot be divided without precaution since we have no information concerning graph locations, and hence they can be located anywhere on the grid. To complete this step, we must build all connected components of the grid. Information to build these components belongs to 2 arrays which may be either in shared memory (in our case) or distributed on local memory (in a distributed system). Thus, to solve this graph problem consuming as little time as possible, we split the initial grid into sub-grids. Then, using the same algorithm as in the sequential case, we can build partial graphs on sub-grids in parallel. When all the partial graphs are built, an assembly step (we call this the glue step), is required in order to obtain the same graphs as would be seen in the sequential computation (this last step is realized sequentially because we do not want to use critical sections, which are time consuming in our case). The figure Fig2 shows how an example of two partial graphs which are glued and the resulting graph.

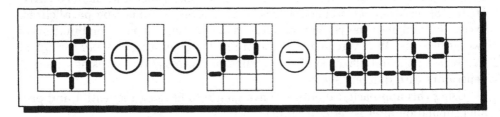

Fig. 2. Glueing of two graphs obtained in sequential

Previously, we stated that the random number generator we used could not be parallelized even though the generation of random numbers is a crucial task in this simulation. Thus the substitute method used, consisting of generating the same initial numbers with the same generator and then using different generators with different seeds, must provide, at the end of the simulation, a result very close to the sequential one. This property can be observed in our case, but some applications may exist which would require another method to parallelize the random number generator. This was beyond the scope of this paper.

The performance gains we obtain are given below. The time is expressed in seconds.

Here is the resume of the used steps:
step 1: destruction of links
step 2: graphs construction
step 3: links updates
step 4: measures

- 100000 iterations on a 200*200 grid

nb proc	step 1	step 2	step 3	step 4	an iteration	speed up
1	3397	3581	767	432	0.082	1
4	892	1051	234	536	0.027	3

- 10000 iterations on a 600*600 grid

nb proc	step 1	step 2	step 3	step 4	an iteration	speed up
1	3046	3323	686	536	0.76	1
4	965	877	223	745	0.28	2.7
9	423	651	94	281	0.14	5.4
16	230	598	57	117	0.10	7.6

Despite the overload of work, it is amazing to see that the graphs creation step is fast. We must say that only the fact of splitting the grid allows a performance gain even in the sequential case (due to the cache memory of the machine). The overal speedup is between 2.7 and 3 with 4 processors. With more processors, the efficiency gains are less attractive. This relatively bad performance with more processors is explained by the use of frequent synchronisations inherent in the programming model. The Fortran compiler synchronises all the threads or processes after each DO loop and, in the present computation, there are several short loops.

5 Proof that the "graph parallelization" is correct

In this section we prove, with the help of the PVS prover, that the parallelization of the graphs creation step is correct. For this we use the method described in Fig1(a). We consider the case where we have only 4 processors and so we decompose the initial grid into 4 sub-grids. We start by establishing the postcondition of the sequential code concerned with this step.

In the Fortran code, we use 2 arrays, HLink and VLink, containing horizontal and vertical links for each point of the grid. After the graphs creation step, results are returned in another array called Spin.

Using the formalism of PVS [10], we define 2 types for arrays of `nat` and `bool`. The variable `Spinp` is the array containing all the graphs in the sequential case, whereas `Spin2p` contains all graphs in the parallel case (we use the letter p in reference to the concept of primed variable in TLA [8]).

```
Array2_nat : TYPE = [nat,nat->nat]
Array2_bool : TYPE = [nat,nat->bool]
Spinp,Spin2p : Var Array2_nat
HLink,VLink : Var Array2_bool
```

Now, we define the postcondition obtained after the execution of the sequential algorithm. As we use the same algorithm in the parallel code, this postcondition is also verified after each computation on the sub-grids. The variables `off_x` and `off_y` represent, respectively, an x and an y offset of the grid from which we apply the algorithm. We use offsets to be able to apply the same algorithm at different locations on the grid, and so parallelize this step.

```
Algo_seq(HLink,VLink,off_x,off_y,width,height,Spinp) : bool =
(FORALL x,y: x>=off_x and x<off_x+width-1 and y>=off_y and
   y<=off_y+height-1 =>
     FORALL a:(Spinp(x,y)=a and (HLink(x,y) => Spinp(x+1,y)=a))
)
and
(FORALL x,y: x>=off_x and x<=off_x+width-1 and y>=off_y and
   y<off_y+height-1 =>
     FORALL a:(Spinp(x,y)=a and (VLink(x,y) => Spinp(x,y+1)=a))
)
```

In this formula, we specify that for all well defined x and y, if after the execution of the algorithm we obtain a value a in `Spinp(x,y)` and if there is a `HLink` in `(x,y)`, then we have `Spinp(x+1,y)=a`. We have a similar property with `VLink`. We quantify a because we do not know in advance the value of this variable.

Then we specify the glue condition. The `VerticalGlueing` for instance, says that for x and y belonging to the boundary, if `Spin2p(x,y)` contains a value in the right grid and if `Spin2p(x+1,y)` contains another value, then if there is a `HLink` in `(x,y)` then this implies that both the values are equal.

```
VerticalGlueing(HLink,VLink,off_x,width,height,Spin2p): bool =
FORALL x,y: (x=off_x and y>=0 and y<height-1 =>
  FORALL a,b: (Spin2p(x,y)=a and Spin2p(x+1,y)=b) =>
    HLink(x,y) => a=b)
```

```
HorizontalGlueing(HLink,VLink,off_y,width,height,Spin2p) : bool =
FORALL x,y: (y=off_y and x>=0 and x<width-1 =>
  FORALL a,b: (Spin2p(x,y)=a and Spin2p(x,y+1)=b) =>
    VLink(x,y) => a=b)
```

Now, we just have to specify what exactly we want to prove. We have the specification of the sequential algorithm (which is the same as the parallel one), and we have the glue postconditions. As we use only 4 sub-grids (for this proof), we must prove that:

```
EQUIVALENCE : THEOREM FORALL k1,k2 : k1=width/2
and k2=height/2 and width>=2 and height>=2 =>
(
 (
 Algo_seq(HLink,VLink,0,0,width,height,Spinp) and
 Algo_seq(HLink,VLink,0,0,k1,k2,Spin2p) and
 Algo_seq(HLink,VLink,k1,0,k1,k2,Spin2p) and
 Algo_seq(HLink,VLink,0,k2,k1,k2,Spin2p) and
 Algo_seq(HLink,VLink,k1,k2,k1,k2,Spin2p) and
 VerticalGlueing(HLink,VLink,k1-1,width,height,Spin2p) and
 HorizontalGlueing(HLink,VLink,k2-1,width,height,Spin2p)
 )
 =>
 (
 (FORALL x,y: x>=0 and y>=0 and x<width-1 and y<height-1 =>
  (FORALL a,b,c:
   (
    (Spinp(x,y)=a and Spin2p(x,y)=b and Spin2p(x+1,y)=c ) =>
    (HLink(x,y) => (Spinp(x+1,y)=a and Spin2p(x+1,y)=b) )
   )
  )
 ) and
 (FORALL x,y: x>=0 and y>=0 and x<width-1 and y<height-1 =>
  (FORALL a,b,c:
   (
    (Spinp(x,y)=a and Spin2p(x,y)=b and Spin2p(x,y+1)=c ) =>
    (VLink(x,y) => (Spinp(x,y+1)=a and Spin2p(x,y+1)=b) )
   )
  )
 )
 )
)
```

In this theorem, we start by giving values to variables k1 and k2. These variables define, respectively, half of the width and half of the height of the grid. With these conditions, we want to prove that after the execution of both the sequential codes (specified by the first call to the formula Algo_seq on the whole grid), and the parallel one (specified by the four last calls to the same formula with different parameters) and the glue conditions (specified by the calls of VerticalGlueing and HorizontalGlueing) we have the same graphs. The grid obtained in the sequential case is Spinp, and the grid obtained in all the parallel processes is Spin2p. All the sub-grids work on a different location. They all have a width equal to k1 and a height equal to k2. But they all have a different offset, respectively equal to (0,0), (k1,0), (0,k2) and (k1,k2). The glue postcondition modifies the value of Spin2p by assembling partial graphs linked by either a HLink if x=k1-1 or a VLink if y=k2-1.

Then the second part of the theorem corresponds to the equivalence between the sequential and the parallel code of each point of the grid. We prove that we obtain the same graphs in the two versions of our algorithm. We do not attempt to prove that all the points have the same value, since we do not use the same random number generator.

We have two parts corresponding respectively to the horizontal and the vertical case. In the first case, for all points (x,y) of the grid, if the value of Spin, obtained after the sequential code, equals a, if the value of the parallel code is b and the value in (x+1,y) is equal to c another value, then in presence of a HLink in (x,y), the value of the left neighbour (in (x+1,y)) is, in the sequential case, a and, in the parallel case, b. The second case is considered symmetrically.

The proof of this theorem is obvious for all points not on these boundaries. For the others, we use the formula of the glue code and the proof is not difficult.

How can we verify that the specification we express corresponds to the code we abstract from? If we try to prove that the specification is correct we must prove it using known proof methods and we must prove the algorithm. In our case, we do not want to do that because we are interested in proving only that the parallelization is correct. We suppose that the sequential code is correct. Nevertheless, we can verify easily that our specification is valid during the execution of the program by injecting all formulas specified in the PVS language into the Fortran code. Of course this method can not guarantee that our specification is correct but with it we can have a good intuition of the correctness. Moreover, if we choose a too simple postcondition we could do nothing concerning the parallelization into PVS. Thus this injection of code seems us to be the appropriate way to convince ourselves of the relevance of our specification.

6 Discovery of the glue postcondition using PVS

We have seen that an important point of our methodology consists of proving that a parallel program is correct with respect to the sequential one from which it is developed. But our method also provides a good way of finding the glue condition to parallelize a program. For that, we define the postcondition of the sequential algorithm. Then we partition data in the Monte Carlo simulation this consists of defining sub-domains that are sub-grids where we can apply the sequential algorithm. If we try to prove that the sequential program is implied or equivalent, this depends from which point of view we take. From the parallel point of view, the prover cannot prove all the proof obligations since some data on the boundaries are not computed. But the unproven obligation proofs define the postcondition of the glue code if the specification is well designed. Unfortunately, in most cases, it is difficult to conclude that a specification is correct if we have not proved it. Nevertheless, with some experience, the intuition of correctness of a specification can be achieved.

We give an example with the Monte Carlo simulation glueing code search. Suppose we have no idea of the glue postcondition needed to assemble all the graphs given by the sequential algorithm applied on the sub-grids. If we try to prove the theorem EQUIVALENCE, in section 5, without the two lines VerticalGlueing and HorizontalGlueing specifying the glue code, using PVS, we obtain many unproven proof obligations. Consider the following fragment, in which we hide all the non-relevant formulas.

```
[-1]    Spin2p!1(x!1, y!1) = b!1
[-2]    Spin2p!1(x!1, y!1 + 1) = c!1
[-3]    VLink!1(x!1, y!1)
  |-------
[1]     y!1 < k2!1 - 1
[2]     y!1 >= k2!1
[3]     Spin2p!1(x!1, y!1 + 1) = b!1
```

In this sequent, we have 3 formulas preceded by a negative number, these are antecedent formulas (formulas with a positive number are consequent formulas). Formulas [1] and [2] express negation of y!1 >= k2!1 - 1 and y!1 < k2!1. That is why we could obtain the following equivalent sequent in which we introduce a new formula [-1] which expresses the same fact that y!1 >= k2!1 - 1 and y!1 < k2!1.

```
[-1]    y!1 = k2!1 - 1
[-2]    Spin2p!1(x!1, y!1) = b!1
[-3]    Spin2p!1(x!1, y!1 + 1) = c!1
[-4]    VLink!1(x!1, y!1)
  |-------
[1]     Spin2p!1(x!1, y!1 + 1) = b!1
```

Then, if we try to compare this second sequent with the HorizontalGlueing formula, we can see the similarity between both of them. In the sequent, all variables are suffixed by !1 (by PVS). If we instanciate a and b of Horizontal-Glueing by b and c of the second sequent, we can conclude with this formula that b=c. The second sequent allows us to conclude that b=c: the hypothesis of sequent and formula are equivalent. Thus, without specifying the formula HorizontalGlueing, this unproven proof obligation expresses the same fact; so we can build the postcondition expressing the horizontal glueing in PVS.

7 Related work

The characterization of our approach is the combination of a formal approach with practical considerations, especially the use of a theorem prover to help in the parallelization of existing codes. UNITY [2] is a way to define abstraction in a language of action systems; correctness properties are expressed in a fragment of the linear temporal logic. Properties are then proven using the proof system, where several systems have been developed to assist the proof of UNITY programs (see, for example, HOL-UNITY [1] and UV [7]). UNITY is oriented towards the refinement of specifications and programs and we use the refinement together with the abstraction; results from UNITY may be reused in our framework and be applied on real case studies. PCN [3] is an approach that is probably related to our experiment, since it provides a way to combine different pieces of codes with respect to combinators and under the *definitional* variables. In PCN, the key concept is the *definitional* variables used for communicating values between processes or for synchronizing concurrent activities. A PCN specification states a precondition and a postcondition over variables and provides rules for composing specifications. The strong requirement over the non-sharing of common variables between processes makes proofs easier and aids the design of code. Our experiment is another viewpoint onto the same process, and it emphasizes the process itself directly using PVS. There is no *definitional* variable in our approach but mathematical variables may play the role of *definitional* variables.

8 Conclusion

The use of a theorem prover, such as PVS, to parallelize a real and existing problem probably appears to be an unusual way to re-engineer existing code. The main advantage is to obtain correct code and to justify the way to compose pieces of programs. Furthermore, the decomposition was driven by the shape of the domain but parallelization patterns can be extracted from our case study and reused in other problems. The decomposition of our example was very simple but we have really developed a new parallel code for this kind of problem, in cooperation with physicists who do not take care over the correctness of programs but do require efficiency.

Another point is related to the efficiency of the produced code. First of all, the abstraction allows us to reason at the heart of the parallelization problem. Secondly, the abstraction can be used to define a measure for the complexity.

Future work will explore other case studies, and will develop a library of proved patterns for parallelizing existing codes through the abstraction mechanism and using PVS for the validation. The approach is very similar to the works of Lindsay [9], but on a class of problems for scientific applications.

References

1. F. Anderson. *A theorem prover for UNITY in Higher Order Logic*. PhD thesis, Technical University Denmark, 1992.
2. K. M. Chandy and J. Misra. *Parallel Program Design A Foundation*. Addison-Wesley Publishing Company, 1988. ISBN 0-201-05866-9.
3. K.M. Chandy and S. Taylor. *An Introduction to Parallel Programming*. Jones and Bartlett, 1992.

4. J.-P. Gibson and D. Méry. A Unifying Model for Specification and Design. In D. Galmiche J.P. Bashoun, J. Fiadeiro and A. Yonezawa, editors, *Proceedings of the Workshop on Proof Theory of Concurrent Object-Oriented Programming*, Linz, July 1996.

5. J.-P. Gibson and D. Méry. A unifying framework for multi-semantic software development. In Max Mühlhäuser, editor, *Special Issues in Object-Oriented Programming*. Dpunkt, 1997.

6. C. B. Jones and R. C. Shaw. *Case Studies in Systematic Software Development*. Prentice-Hall International Series in Computer Science. Prentice-Hall, 1990. ISBN0-13-116088-5.

7. M. Kaltenbach. Model checking for unity. Technical Report TR94-31, Department of Computer Sciences, The University of Texas at Austin, December 1994.

8. Leslie Lamport. A temporal logic of actions. *ACM Transactions on Programming Languages and Systems*, 16(3):872–923, May 1994.

9. D. Hemer P. A. Lindsay. Reuse of verified design templates through extended pattern matching. Technical report, Queensland, 1997.

10. S. Owre, N. Shankar, and J. M. Rushby. The PVS specification language. Technical report, SRI International, June 14, 1993 1993.

11. B. Berche P.E. Berche, C. Chatelain. Aperiodicity-induced second-order phase transition in the 8-state potts model. *Physical Review Letters*. To appear.

12. W. Gropp E. Lusk A. Skjellum. *Using MPI : portable parallel programming with the message passing interface*. MIT Press, 1994.

13. J. M. Spivey. *Understanding Z : a specification language and its formal semantics*. Cambridge University Press, 1987.

14. A. Geist A. Beguelin J. Dongarra W. Jiang R. Manchek V. Sunderam. *PVM : A Users' Guide and Tutorial for Networked Parallel Computing*. MIT Press, 1994.

15. I. Vattulainen. *News tests of random numbers for simulations in physical systems*. PhD thesis, University of Helsinki, Finland, 1994.

Efficient Symbolic Detection of Global Properties in Distributed Systems

Scott D. Stoller and Yanhong A. Liu

Computer Science Dept., Indiana University, Bloomington, IN 47405, USA
{stoller,liu}@cs.indiana.edu.

Abstract. A new approach is presented for detecting whether a computation of an asynchronous distributed system satisfies **Poss** Φ (read "possibly Φ"), meaning the system could have passed through a global state satisfying property Φ. Previous general-purpose algorithms for this problem explicitly enumerate the set of global states through which the system could have passed during the computation. The new approach is to represent this set symbolically, in particular, using ordered binary decision diagrams. We describe an implementation of this approach, suitable for off-line detection of properties, and compare its performance to the enumeration-based algorithm of Alagar & Venkatesan. In typical cases, the new algorithm is significantly faster. We have measured over 400-fold speedup in some cases.

1 Introduction

A history of a distributed system can be modeled as a sequence of events in their order of occurrence. Since execution of a particular sequence of events leaves the system in a well-defined global state, a history uniquely determines a sequence of global states through which the system has passed. In an asynchronous distributed system,[1] no process can determine in general the order in which events on different processors actually occurred. Therefore, no process can determine in general the sequence of global states through which the system passed. This leads to an obvious difficulty for detecting whether a global property (*i.e.*, a predicate on global states) held.

Cooper and Marzullo's solution to this difficulty involves two modalities, which we denote by **Poss** (read "possibly") and **Def** (read "definitely") [CM91]. These modalities are based on logical time as embodied in the *happened-before* relation, a partial order that reflects causal dependencies [Lam78]. A history of an asynchronous distributed system can be approximated by a *computation*, which comprises the local computation of each process together with the happened-before relation. Happened-before is useful for detection algorithms because, using vector clocks [Mat89], it can be determined by processes in the system.

---

[1] An *asynchronous* distributed system is characterized by lack of synchronized clocks and lack of bounds on processor speed and network latency.

Happened-before is not a total order, so it does not uniquely determine the history. But it does restrict the possibilities. Histories *consistent* with a computation c are exactly those sequences of the events in c that correspond to total orders containing the happened-before relation. A *consistent global state* (CGS) of a computation c is a global state that appears in some history consistent with c. A computation c satisfies **Poss** Φ iff, in *some* history consistent with c, the system passes through a global state satisfying Φ. A computation c satisfies **Def** Φ iff, in *all* histories consistent with c, the system passes through a global state satisfying Φ.

Cooper and Marzullo give centralized algorithms for detecting **Poss** Φ and **Def** Φ for an arbitrary predicate Φ [CM91]. A stub at each process reports the local states of that process to a central monitor. The central monitor incrementally constructs a lattice whose elements correspond to CGSs of the computation. **Poss** Φ and **Def** Φ are evaluated by straightforward traversals of the lattice.

Unfortunately, these algorithms can be expensive. In a system of N processes, the worst-case number of CGSs is $\Theta(S^N)$, where S is the maximum number of steps taken by a single process. This worst case comes from the (exponential) number of CGSs of a computation in which there is little communication. Any detection algorithm that enumerates all CGSs—like the algorithms in [CM91,MN91,AV97]—has time complexity that is at least linear in the number of CGSs. This time complexity can be prohibitive, so researchers have sought faster alternatives. One approach is to restrict the problem and develop efficient algorithms for detecting only certain classes of predicates [GW94,TG93].[2] Another approach is to modify some aspect of the problem—for example, detecting a different modality [FR97] or assuming that the system is partially synchronous [MN91,Sto97].

This paper presents an efficient and general approach to detecting **Poss** Φ. In this approach, the set of CGSs is represented symbolically, using boolean formulas implemented as ordered binary decision diagrams (BDDs), and **Poss** Φ is detected by testing satisfiability of a formula. This can be much more efficient than explicit enumeration. For simplicity, we consider here only off-line detection, in which the detection algorithm is run after the distributed computation has terminated. The approach can also be applied to on-line detection. Section 2 provides some background. Section 3 describes our detection algorithm. Section 4 gives performance results from using the new algorithm and (for comparison) an enumeration-based algorithm [AV97] to detect violations of invariants in a coherence protocol and a spanning-tree algorithm. For both examples, when the invariant is not violated, the new method is faster by a factor that increases exponentially with the number of processes in the system. We also measure the effects of judiciously applying the two variable-reordering methods. Both methods greatly reduce memory consumption, though at a significant cost in running time. Section 5 compares our work to temporal-logic model checking. Directions for future work include extending our algorithm to support on-line detection, applying our symbolic approach to detection of **Def** Φ, and experimenting with

---

[2] These restricted algorithms do not apply to the examples in Section 4.

the use of a satisfiability checker, such as tableau [CA96], instead of BDDs. Our approach does not involve computation of fixed points, so the use of a canonical form, such as BDDs, is not essential.

2 Background

2.1 System Model

A (distributed) system is a collection of processes connected by an asynchronous, reliable, and FIFO network. Let N denote the number of processes. We use the numbers $0, 1, \ldots, N-1$ as process identifiers, and define $\text{PID} = \{0, 1, \ldots, N-1\}$. A local state s of a process p is a mapping from the local variables of p to values; for example, $s(x)$ is the value of variable x in local state s.

Each process starts in a specified initial state and optionally with its timer set to a specified value. Computations contain only two kinds of events: timer expiration and message reception. As a result of either kind of event, a process can atomically (i.e., without interruption by other events) change its local state, send a set of messages (with specified destinations), and set its timer.[3] Processes can be non-deterministic, i.e., the input event need not uniquely determine the new local state, set of sent messages, and timer setting.

Each process has a timer. For convenience, we assume the timers all run at the same speed, though this assumption is not required for correctness of the example protocols in Section 4.

Each process p has a vector clock vc_p with N components. We regard vc_p as a (special) variable; thus, $s(vc_p)$ is the value of the vector clock in local state s. In the initial state of process p, $vc_p = \langle 0, 0, \ldots, 0 \rangle$. The vector clock is updated after each event, and the updated value is piggybacked on the outgoing messages (if any). Thus, each message m has a vector timestamp $\text{ts}(m)$. The rules for updating the vector clock are: (1) For a timer expiration event of process p, component p of vc_p is incremented by 1; (2) When process p receives a message m, its vector clock vc_p is assigned the component-wise maximum $\max(vc_p, \text{ts}(m))$ and then component p is incremented by 1.

Given a system, a straightforward simulation can be used to generate a possible computation of that system. The intrinsic non-determinism of the asynchronous network is modeled by selecting message latencies from a random distribution. Each running timer and in-transit message corresponds to a pending event. When a pending event is generated, it is timestamped with its (future) time of occurrence. The simulator repeatedly executes the pending event with the lowest timestamp, thereby changing the local state of a process and generating new pending events. Since some protocols are designed to service requests forever, the simulator accepts a parameter *maxlen*, which is the maximum number

---

[3] Thus, in contrast to most models of distributed computation, the sending of a message is not modeled as a separate event. This difference is inessential but simplifies our model slightly.

of events per process. So, the simulation ends either when there are no pending events or when some process has executed *maxlen* events.

A *computation* of a system is represented as a sequence of N local computations, one per process. A *local computation* is a sequence of local states that represents the execution history of a single process. Each local state includes values of all the declared variables of the process and the value of the process's vector clock.

2.2 Consistent Global States and Poss Φ

A *global state* is a collection of local states, one from each process. For a sequence c and natural number i, $c[i]$ denotes the i'th element of c (we use 0-based indexing). A global state of a computation c is a collection of local states $s_0, \ldots, s_{N-1}$ such that, for each process p, s_p is an element of $c[p]$.

Some global states of a computation are uninteresting, because the system could not have been in those global states during that computation. So, we restrict attention to *consistent* global states, *i.e.*, global states through which the system might have passed during the computation. We define consistency for global states in terms of the happened-before relation on local states [GW94]. Intuitively, a local state s_1 happened-before a local state s_2 (of the same or a different process) if s_1 finished before s_2 started. In particular, define $\to$ for a computation c to be the smallest transitive relation on the local states of c such that

1. For all proceses p and all local states s_1 and s_2 of p in c, if s_1 immediately precedes s_2, then $s_1 \to s_2$.
2. For all local states s_1 and s_2 in c, if the event immediately following s_1 is the sending of a message and the event immediately preceding s_2 is the reception of that message, then $s_1 \to s_2$.

Two local states s_1 and s_2 of a computation are *concurrent*, denoted $s_1 \parallel s_2$, iff neither happened-before the other: $s_1 \parallel s_2 \triangleq s_1 \not\to s_2 \wedge s_2 \not\to s_1$. A global state is *consistent* iff its constituent local states are pairwise concurrent.

Vector timestamps are useful because they capture the happened-before relation [Mat89]. Define a partial order $\prec$ on vector timestamps by: $v_1 \prec v_2$ iff $(\forall p \in \text{PID} : v_1[p] \leq v_2[p])$. Then, for all computations c and all processes p_1 and p_2,

$$(\forall i_1 \in \text{dom}(c[p_1])) : (\forall i_2 \in \text{dom}(c[p_2])) : \\ c[p_1][i_1] \to c[p_2][i_2] \equiv c[p_1][i_1](vc_{p_1}) \prec c[p_2][i_2](vc_{p_2}))) \tag{1}$$

where for a sequence σ, $\text{dom}(\sigma) = \{0, 1, \ldots, (|\sigma| - 1)\}$, where $|\sigma|$ is the length of σ. Concurrency of two local states can be tested in constant time using vector timestamps by exploiting the following theorem [FR94]: for a local state s_1 of process p_1 and a local state s_2 of process p_2,

$$s_1 \parallel s_2 \equiv s_1(vc_{p_1})[p_2] \leq s_2(vc_{p_2})[p_2] \wedge s_2(vc_{p_2})[p_1] \leq s_1(vc_{p_1})[p_1] \tag{2}$$

where, for example, $s_1(vc_{p_1})[p_2]$ is component p_2 of the vector timestamp $s_1(vc_{p_1})$.

Now we define **Poss**. A computation c satisfies **Poss** Φ, denoted $c \models$ **Poss** Φ, iff there exists a consistent global state of c that satisfies Φ.

3 Detection Method

To test $c \models \mathbf{Poss}\,\Phi$ efficiently using symbolic methods, we generate a formula b such that b is satisfiable iff $c \models \mathbf{Poss}\,\Phi$. In this formula, we use x_p to denote the local variables (excluding the vector clock) of process p, and we use the variable $vc_{p,q}$ to denote component q of the vector clock of process p (*i.e.*, we treat each vector clock as N separate variables). For convenience, we assume that the sets of local variables of different processes are disjoint. Let x denote the collection of variables $x_0, x_1, \ldots, x_{N-1}$, and let vc denote the collection of all $\Theta(N^2)$ vector-clock variables. Using (2) to express concurrency of local states, it is easy to show that b can be taken to be

$$\Phi(x) \wedge \text{globalState}_c(x, vc) \wedge \text{consis}_c(vc) \tag{3}$$

where

$$\text{globalState}_c(x, vc) = \bigwedge_{p \in \text{PID}} \bigvee_{i \in \text{dom}(c[p])} x_p = c[p][i](x_p) \wedge \bigwedge_{q \in \text{PID}} vc_{p,q} = c[p][i](vc_p)[q]$$

$$\text{consis}_c(vc) = \bigwedge_{p_1 \in \text{PID}} \bigwedge_{p_2 \in (\text{PID} \setminus \{p_1\})} vc_{p_2,p_1} \le vc_{p_1,p_1}$$

Formulas obtained from (3) contain $\Theta(N^2)$ variables for the vector clocks. To reduce the number of variables in the formula, and thereby reduce the cost of testing satisfiability of the formula, we change variables. For each process p, we introduce a new variable idx_p, which contains the "index" of the local state in $c[p]$, *i.e.*, $(\forall i \in \text{dom}(c[p]) : c[p][i](idx_p) = i)$.[4] Re-expressing globalState and consis in terms of these new variables, we take b to be:

$$\Phi(x) \wedge \text{globalState}_c(x, idx) \wedge \text{consis}_c(idx) \tag{4}$$

where

$$\text{globalState}_c(x, idx) = \bigwedge_{p \in \text{PID}} \bigvee_{i \in \text{dom}(c[p])} x_p = c[p][i](x_p) \wedge idx_p = i$$

$$\text{consis}_c(idx) = \bigwedge_{\substack{p_1 \in \text{PID} \\ p_2 \in (\text{PID} \setminus \{p_1\})}} \bigvee_{i_2 \in \text{dom}(c[p_2])} idx_{p_2} = i_2 \wedge c[p_2][i_2](vc_{p_2})[p_1] \le idx_{p_1}$$

where idx denotes the collection of variables $idx_0, idx_1, \ldots, idx_{N-1}$.

For example, consider a system with $N = 2$. Suppose each process p has a single local variable y_p, and that we want to detect $\mathbf{Poss}(y_0 + y_1 = 1)$. Consider the computation c in which each local computation has length 2, and $c[p][i](y_p) = i$, $c[p][0](vc_p) = \langle 0, 0 \rangle$, $c[0][1](vc_0) = \langle 1, 0 \rangle$, and $c[1][1](vc_1) = \langle 1, 1 \rangle$. Instantiating (4) yields the formula

$$(y_0 + y_1 = 1) \wedge \text{globalState}_c(y_0, y_1, idx) \wedge \text{consis}_c(idx)$$

---

[4] We could take idx_p to be $vc_{p,p}$, since the rules for updating vector clocks imply $c[p][i](vc_{p,p}) = i$. However, we find it easier to think of idx_p as a new variable.

where

$$\text{globalState}_c(y_0, y_1, \textbf{\textit{idx}}) = \quad ((y_0 = 0 \wedge idx_0 = 0) \vee (y_0 = 1 \wedge idx_0 = 1))$$
$$\wedge ((y_1 = 0 \wedge idx_1 = 0) \vee (y_1 = 1 \wedge idx_1 = 1))$$
$$\text{consis}_c(\textbf{\textit{idx}}) = \quad ((idx_1 = 0 \wedge 0 \leq idx_0) \vee (idx_1 = 1 \wedge 1 \leq idx_0))$$
$$\wedge ((idx_0 = 0 \wedge 0 \leq idx_1) \vee (idx_0 = 1 \wedge 0 \leq idx_1))$$

3.1 Implementation and an Optimization

We represent the formula defined by (4) using ordered binary decision diagrams (BDDs) [Bry92]. Let true_{bdd} and false_{bdd} denote the BDDs representing true and false, respectively. Let $\wedge_{bdd}$ denote conjunction of BDDs. Let a formula with an overline denote a function that returns the BDD representation of that formula. Formula b is constructed and tested for satisfiability by procedure BDD-detection0 in Figure 1.

The numbers in vector timestamps are encoded as unsigned integers, with a binary variable representing each bit; the number of bits required is easily determined, since we consider here only off-line detection. If $\textbf{Poss}\,\Phi$ holds, it is straightforward to obtain a satisfying assignment for b and (from that) a particular CGS satisfying Φ.

```
procedure BDD-detection0(c, Φ̄)            procedure BDD-detection(c, ⋁_{α∈S} Φ̄_α)
    b := true_bdd                              b := true_bdd
    b := b ∧_bdd globalState_c(x, idx)         b := b ∧_bdd globalState_c(x, idx)
    b := b ∧_bdd consis_c(idx)                 b := b ∧_bdd consis_c(idx)
    b := b ∧_bdd Φ̄(x)                          for each α in S
    if b = false_bdd then                          b1 := b ∧_bdd Φ̄_α(x)
        return("c ⊭ Poss(Φ)")                      if b1 ≠ false_bdd then
    else return("c ⊨ Poss(Φ)")                         return("c ⊨ Poss(Φ)")
                                               return("c ⊭ Poss(Φ)")
```

Fig. 1. Pseudo-code for BDD-detection0 and BDD-detection.

Often (as in both examples in Section 4), Φ is a disjunction: $\Phi = \bigvee_{\alpha \in S} \Phi_\alpha$, for some set S. Procedure BDD-detection0 can be optimized by distributing the conjunctions over the disjunction, yielding procedure BDD-detection in Figure 1. By testing each disjunct of Φ separately, BDD-detection avoids constructing the potentially large intermediate result $\overline{\Phi}$.

4 Examples

We compare the performance of BDD-detection to Alagar & Venkatesan's off-line detection algorithm [AV97], which (to our knowledge) is the most time-

and space-efficient previously known general-purpose algorithm for detecting **Poss**. Their algorithm, which we refer to as DFS-detection, performs a depth-first-search search of the lattice of CGSs. Their algorithm cleverly exploits the presence of vector timestamps to avoid storing the set of explored CGSs.

To characterize the performance of a detection algorithm, it is important to consider cases where $c \models$ **Poss** Φ holds and cases where it doesn't. The most common use of detection algorithms for **Poss** is to check that an invariant I holds, by detecting whether the computation satisfies **Poss** $\neg I$. So, we consider correct and buggy versions of each example protocol.

For each version of each example, we use a simulator to generate a computation, and then we analyze that computation using both BDD-detection and DFS-detection. By default, the simulator selects message delays from the distribution $\rho_1 = 1 + \text{expRand}(1)$, where $\text{expRand}(\mu)$ denotes an exponential distribution with mean μ. To measure the sensitivity of the analysis cost to message latencies, we consider also another (less realistic) distribution, $\rho_0 = \text{expRand}(1)$.

All measurements were made on a SGI Power Challenge with ten 75 MHz MIPS R8000 CPUs and 2GB RAM. The algorithms we measured are sequential, so the use of a parallel machine was irrelevant. We use the BDD library developed by E. M. Clarke's group at CMU [BDD]. The reported running times are "user times" obtained from the UNIX `time` command; thus, they reflect the CPU time consumed.

For BDD-detection, the variable ordering can affect performance. The overall variable ordering is $x_0, x_1, \ldots, x_N, idx_0, idx_1, \ldots, idx_N$, where x_p denotes the sequence of binary variables encoding the local state of process p excluding idx_p and excluding variables not mentioned in the predicate being detected, and idx_p denotes the sequence of binary variables encoding the "index" of the local state.

4.1 Coherence Protocol

We consider a protocol that uses read locks and write locks to provide coherent access to shared data. The protocol allows concurrent reading of shared data, and it prevents a process from reading or writing shared data while another process is writing. Each process repeatedly tries to read or write the implicit shared data. Before starting to write, a process sends WriteReq to all other processes and waits for them to reply with WriteOK. On receiving WriteReq, a process replies immediately with WriteOK unless it is reading or writing or is waiting to write and had started waiting "before" the WriteReq was sent (as indicated by the relevant vector timestamps, compared using lexicographic order). If a process doesn't reply immediately to a WriteReq, it remembers the request and replies later. Before starting to read, a process waits for all processes to which it has sent WriteOK to reply with WriteDone. When a process starts reading or writing, it sets its timer to a value generated by expRand(4).[5] When the timer expires, the

---

[5] The choice of this distribution is arbitrary, in the sense that correctness of the protocol does not depend on it.

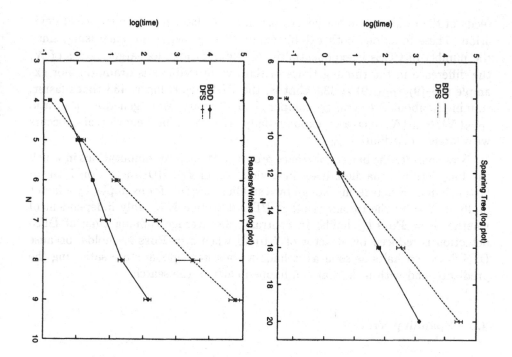

Fig. 2. Left: Logarithm of running time of detection algorithms on coherence protocol. Right: Logarithm of running time of detection algorithms on spanning-tree algorithm.

process stops reading or writing, respectively, and again sets its timer to a value generated by expRand(4). When the timer expires, the process tries to read or write (the choice is random) the shared data. The buggy version of the protocol is the same except that WriteOK is included with every WriteDone.

4.2 Analysis of Coherence Protocol

We use the detection algorithms to find violations of the following invariant Φ_C: when one process is writing, no other process is reading or writing. Formally,

$$\Phi_C = \bigvee_{p_1 \in \text{PID}} \bigvee_{p_2 \in \text{PID} \setminus \{p_1\}} wrtg_{p_1} \wedge (rdg_{p_2} \vee wrtg_{p_2}).$$

where boolean variables rdg_p and $wrtg_p$ indicate whether process p is reading or writing, respectively.

To make the computations of the coherence protocol finite, we take the argument *maxlen* of the simulator to be $8N$; on average, this lets each process read or write the shared data twice during a computation. The left graph in Figure 2 shows $\log_{10}(t_{\text{BDD}}(N))$ and $\log_{10}(t_{\text{DFS}}(N))$ for the coherence protocol, where $t_{\text{BDD}}(N)$ and $t_{\text{DFS}}(N)$ denote the average running times, in seconds, of BDD-detection and DFS-detection, respectively. The average is over 10 different seeds of the random number generator; the error bars show the standard deviation. These functions both exhibit exponential growth—not surprising, since the number of CGSs is exponential in N. Nevertheless, for larger values of N, the difference in the running times of the two procedures is dramatic. For example $t_{\text{DFS}}(9)/t_{\text{BDD}}(9) \approx 433$; that is, the BDD algorithm is 433 times faster, running in about 2.4 minutes, compared to 17 hours. More generally, the ratio $t_{\text{DFS}}(N)/t_{\text{BDD}}(N)$ increases exponentially with N. This behavior also occurs with latency distribution ρ_0.

Now consider the buggy coherence protocol. We ignore computations in which the bug does not manifest itself in a violation of Φ_C. BDD-detection is again faster than DFS-detection, though by a smaller margin—for example, by a factor of 46 at $N = 9$. The running time of BDD-detection is roughly independent of whether $c \models \textbf{Poss}\,\Phi_C$ holds. In contrast, the average running time of DFS-detection is reduced by a factor of 7 to 10 when $c \models \textbf{Poss}\,\Phi_C$ holds, because DFS-detection halts as soon as it finds a consistent global state satisfying the predicate, and with luck, that can happen early in the search.

4.3 Spanning Tree

The following algorithm constructs a spanning tree in a network [Lyn96, Section 15.3]. For convenience, we assume that process 0 always initiates the algorithm and therefore always becomes the root of the spanning tree. Process 0 initiates the algorithm by sending its level in the tree (namely, 0) to each of its neighbors in the network. When a process other than process 0 receives its first message, it takes the sender of that message as its parent, sets its level to one plus the level of its parent, and sends its level to each of its neighbors, except its parent. A process ignores subsequent messages.

To save space in local states, we represent the identity of the parent using relative coordinates rather than absolute coordinates. For example, in a (2-dimensional) grid with N processes, we can represent the parent with 2 bits (0=left neighbor, 1=upper neighbor, etc.), compared to $\log_2 N$ bits to store a PID. The type RC corresponds to these relative coordinates. For a process p and relative coordinate r, PIDofRC(p, r) is the PID of the process with relative coordinate r with respect to process p. If process q is a neighbor of process p, then RCofPID(p, q) is the relative coordinate of q with respect to p. Thus, PIDofRC$(p, \text{RCofPID}(p, q)) = q$.

In the buggy version of the algorithm, process 0 "forgets" to retain its special role, so it accepts the sender of the first message it receives (if any) as its parent. If the initial message from process 0 to a neighbor p has a high latency, then p might receive a message from some other process p_1 before p receives a message from process 0. In that case, process p sends a message to process 0, and (because of the bug) process 0 takes process p as its parent, creating a cycle. To make this error manifest itself more often, when simulating the spanning tree algorithm, we always take the latency of messages from process 0 to process 1 to be 5.

4.4 Analysis of Spanning Tree

We use the detection algorithms to find violations of the following invariant Φ_S: the level of a process is larger than the level of its parent. Formally,

$$\Phi_S = \bigvee_{p_1 \in \text{PID}} hasParent_{p_1} \wedge level_{p_1} \leq level_{\text{PIDofRC}(parent_{p_1})}$$

where boolean variable $hasParent_p$ indicates whether process p has gotten a parent, $parent_p$ is the (relative coordinate of) the parent of process p, and $level_p$ is the level of process p in the spanning tree. Φ_S implies absence of cycles.

Φ_S cannot be expressed directly as a boolean formula using the given variables, because $level_{\text{PIDofRC}(parent_{p_1})}$ is not a particular variable. So, we use DFS-detection to detect Φ_S but use BDD-detection to detect the following logically equivalent predicate:

$$\Phi_S' = \bigvee_{p_1 \in \text{PID}} \bigvee_{p_2 \in \text{PID} \setminus \{p_1\}} hasParent_{p_1} \wedge parent_{p_1} = p_2 \wedge level_{p_1} \leq level_{p_2}.$$

We analyze computations of this algorithm in a network with a grid topology. Each row in the grid contains $m = \lfloor \sqrt{N} \rfloor$ processes. Each process is connected to its neighbors in the grid. Thus, process i is connected to processes $i - 1$ (if $i > 0$), $i + 1$ (if $i < N - 1$), $i - m$ (if $i \geq m$), and $i + m$ (if $i < N - m$).

The right graph in Figure 2 shows $\log_{10}(t_{\text{BDD}}(N))$ and $\log_{10}(t_{\text{DFS}}(N))$ for the spanning-tree algorithm. Again, the average is over 10 different seeds of the random number generator, and the error bars show the standard deviation. BDD-detection is significantly faster for larger values of N; for example, $t_{\text{DFS}}(20)/t_{\text{BDD}}(20) \approx 21.2$. The ratio $t_{\text{DFS}}(N)/t_{\text{BDD}}(N)$ again increases exponentially with N. This behavior also occurs with latency distribution ρ_0.

For the buggy spanning-tree algorithm, DFS-detection is much faster than BDD-detection when **Poss** Φ_S holds and is much slower than BDD-detection when **Poss** Φ_S does not hold. The running time of the BDD algorithm is again roughly independent of whether $c \models$ **Poss** Φ_S holds. In contrast, when **Poss** Φ_S holds, DFS-detection is "lucky" and finds a CGS satisfying Φ_S very early in the search: for $4 \leq N \leq 20$, DFS-detection is approximately 10^5 times faster when $c \models$ **Poss** Φ_S than when $c \not\models$ **Poss** Φ_S.

We also implemented the spanning-tree algorithm using PIDs rather than relative coordinates to indicate a process's parent. The effect on the running time of DFS-detection is negligible. The memory usage and running time of BDD-detection increase by roughly the same percentage as the number of bits per global state (which is the number of variables in the BDD), e.g., for $N = 20$, by approximately 20%.

4.5 Memory Usage

BDD-detection uses significantly more memory than DFS-detection, because DFS-detection never stores any representation of the entire set of CGSs. Let

$m_{\text{BDD}}(N)$ and $m_{\text{DFS}}(N)$ denote the memory used by BDD-detection and DFS-detection, respectively. For the coherence protocol, $m_{\text{BDD}}(N)$ grows exponentially with N, to 28.5 MB at $N = 9$, while $m_{\text{DFS}}(N)$ is linear in N, growing to 2.6 MB at $N = 9$. For the spanning-tree example, the same asymptotic behavior occurs, though $m_{\text{BDD}}(N)$ is much larger in absolute terms. For example, $m_{\text{BDD}}(20) = 914MB$, while $m_{\text{DFS}}(20) = 2.5MB$. The memory usage of BDD-detection can be greatly reduced by variable reordering, as discussed next.

4.6 Effect of Variable Reordering

We also ran BDD-detection using the two variable-reordering methods, called sift and window3, provided by the BDD package [BDD]. Variables were reordered once, immediately after construction of $\overline{\text{globalState}_c}(\boldsymbol{x}, \boldsymbol{idx}) \wedge_{\text{bdd}} \overline{\text{consis}_c}(\boldsymbol{idx})$. According to [BDD], the sift method "generally achieves greater size reductions, but is slower" than window3. For the coherence protocol, the window method is preferable, because the increase in running time is smaller (typically a factor of about 1.5, compared to a factor of about 4 for sift) and, unexpectedly, the the decrease in memory usage is greater (typically a factor in the range 0.2–0.4, compared to 0.3–0.5 for sift). For the spanning-tree example, the sift method is preferable, because the decrease in memory usage is greater (e.g., a factor of 0.05 at $N = 9$, compared to 0.08 for window) and, unexpectedly, the increase in running time is smaller (typically a factor of about 6, compared to 9 for window). For the spanning-tree example, the fractional reduction in memory usage increases with N.

4.7 Comparing Performance of BDD-detection and BDD-detection0

Predicates Φ_C and Φ'_S are disjunctions, so it is interesting to compare procedures BDD-detection and BDD-detection0. For the correct and buggy coherence protocols, the two procedures have the same the running time and same amount of memory used, to within 1%. For the spanning-tree algorithm, BDD-detection is significantly more efficient than BDD-detection0, with benefits that appear to grow exponentially with N. For example, for $N = 12$, so BDD-detection is 493 times faster than BDD-detection0 and uses 0.017 as much memory. Further work is needed to characterize the class of examples for which the optimization in BDD-detection is effective.

5 Comparison with Symbolic Model Checking for CTL

Detection of **Poss** Φ can be reduced to CTL model checking [C+92]: a computation is encoded as a transition system whose runs are the histories consistent with the computation, and a CTL model checker is used to check whether that transition system satisfies the CTL formula $\exists \diamond \Phi$. With this encoding, an BDD-based model checker, such as SMV [SMV], would represent sets of CGSs as BDDs, as we do. However, that approach could still differ appreciably in performance from our algorithm, because different intermediate BDDs would be constructed.

For example, with our method, the iterative calculations in the construction of globalState and consis are independent of Φ. With SMV, the corresponding iterative fixed-point calculation used to evaluate $\exists \diamond \Phi$ depends on Φ (roughly, the effect is as if lines 2 and 4 were swapped in BDD-detection), which might make the BDDs obtained in each iteration larger. Further experiments are needed to determine the performance impact of such differences.

References

[AV97] Sridhar Alagar and S. Venkatesan. Techniques to tackle state explosion in global predicate detection. Submitted to *IEEE Transactions on Software Engineering*, 1997. Preliminary version appeared in *International Conference on Parallel and Distributed Systems* (ICPDS'94), pp. 412–417, 1994.

[BDD] The BDD Library (ver. 1.0). http://www.cs.cmu.edu/ modelcheck/bdd.html.

[Bry92] R.E. Bryant. Symbolic boolean manipulation with ordered binary-decision diagrams. *ACM Computing Surveys*, 24(3), 1992.

[C$^+$92] E. M. Clarke et al. Automatic verification of sequential circuit design. In C. A. R. Hoare and M. J. C. Gordon, editors, *Mechanized Reasoning and Hardware Design*. Prentice-Hall, 1992.

[CA96] James M. Crawford and Larry D. Auton. Experimental results on the crossover point in random 3-SAT. *Artificial Intelligence*, 81(1):31–57, 1996.

[CM91] Robert Cooper and Keith Marzullo. Consistent detection of global predicates. In *Proc. ACM/ONR Workshop on Parallel and Distributed Debugging*, 1991. Appeared as ACM SIGPLAN Notices 26(12):167-174, December 1991.

[FR94] Eddy Fromentin and Michel Raynal. Local states in distributed computations: A few relations and formulas. *Operating Systems Review*, 28(2), April 1994.

[FR97] Eddy Fromentin and Michel Raynal. Inevitable global states: a concept to detect unstable properties of distributed computations in an observer independent way. *Journal of Computer and System Sciences*, 55(3), Dec. 1997.

[GW94] Vijay K. Garg and Brian Waldecker. Detection of weak unstable predicates in distributed programs. *IEEE Transactions on Parallel and Distributed Systems*, 5(3):299-307, 1994.

[Lam78] Leslie Lamport. Time, clocks, and the ordering of events in a distributed system. *Communications of the ACM*, 21(7):558–564, 1978.

[Lyn96] Nancy A. Lynch. *Distributed Algorithms*. Morgan Kaufmann, 1996.

[Mat89] Friedemann Mattern. Virtual time and global states of distributed systems. In M. Corsnard, editor, *Proc. International Workshop on Parallel and Distributed Algorithms*, pages 120–131. North-Holland, 1989.

[MN91] Keith Marzullo and Gil Neiger. Detection of global state predicates. In *Proc. 5th Int'l. Workshop on Distributed Algorithms (WDAG '91)*, volume 579 of *Lecture Notes in Computer Science*, pages 254–272. Springer-Verlag, 1991.

[SMV] SMV. http://www.cs.cmu.edu/ modelcheck/smv.html.

[Sto97] Scott D. Stoller. Detecting global predicates in distributed systems with clocks. In Marios Mavronikolas, editor, *Proc. 11th International Workshop on Distributed Algorithms (WDAG '97)*, volume 1320 of *Lecture Notes in Computer Science*, pages 185–199. Springer-Verlag, 1997.

[TG93] Alexander I. Tomlinson and Vijay K. Garg. Detecting relational global predicates in distributed systems. In *Proc. ACM/ONR Workshop on Parallel and Distributed Debugging*, 1993. ACM SIGPLAN Notices 28(12), December 1993.

A Machine-Checked Proof of the Optimality of a Real-Time Scheduling Policy

Matthew Wilding

The University of Texas at Austin*

Abstract. We describe a mechanically-checked proof of the optimality of earliest-deadline-first (EDF) schedulers on periodic tasks accomplished using the Nqthm theorem prover. We present a formalization of the theorem and discuss why the machine-checked proof is both more complex and more reliable than a corresponding informal proof.

1 Introduction

Real-time applications often have several required functions with different timing constraints. In a seminal paper for building real-time systems, Liu and Layland introduce abstractions that facilitate real-time application development [4]. Using a simple computation model, they exhibit different real-time scheduling policies that choose which of an application's various tasks to assign a processor and argue that these policies have certain useful properties. One scheduling policy is earliest-deadline-first (EDF), which assigns the processor to a task that has earliest deadline among the tasks that are currently running. An EDF scheduler is optimal for tasks requested periodically in the sense that if any schedule can meet the timing constraints on the requests then an EDF schedule will. The original proof of this theorem was flawed [4], but a subsequent published proof developed independently of the machine-checked proof presented in this paper appears correct [9].

EDF schedulers are rarely used because developers generally prefer static priority scheduling policies that ensure that critical tasks not miss a deadline because a less-critical task is selected. However, because EDF schedulers have a higher theoretical CPU utilization, if one is going to guarantee through formal analysis that no deadlines are missed by the tasks of an application it may be preferable to use an EDF scheduling policy.

Formal proofs – proofs constructed in a well-defined proof system where no step in the proof is skipped – are longer and harder to construct than standard proofs, but they allow mechanical checking. A proof checked mechanically by a trusted proof-checking program such as Nqthm [1] is very dependable, but such proofs require absolute precision in the statement of conjectures.

This paper describes a machine-checked proof of the EDF optimality theorem. Section 2 presents Nqthm definitions related to EDF schedules and periodic

---

* author's present address: Rockwell Collins Advanced Technology Center, Cedar Rapids, Iowa USA 52498. email: mmwildin@collins.rockwell.com

tasks used in the theorem. Section 3 presents the optimality theorem and an example of its application. The EDF optimality proof checked using Nqthm is discussed in Section 4.

2 Some Real-Time Scheduling Definitions

We first present some definitions in the Nqthm logic related to the scheduling of a processor to the tasks of a real-time application. The abstractions we define are similar to those in Liu and Layland [4]. A real-time application is composed of tasks each with a unique name. Occasionally there is a request for a task, which has four elements: the requested task's name, the time of the task request, the task request deadline, and the task's duration. Time is modeled with discrete units, tasks are interruptible, and we ignore task switch overhead.

A schedule is a list that represents a processor schedule assignment over time. A task name tk at location n in a schedule indicates that the processor is assigned to task tk at time n, and **nil** indicates that no task is assigned. A schedule fulfills a task request if during the period no earlier than the task request time and before the task request deadline it contains the task name a number of times equal to the requested task duration. A good schedule is one that fulfills each of a set of task requests.

We use functions provided in the Lisp-inspired Nqthm logic: cons (a, l) constructs a new list with a as the first element and l as the rest, car (l) returns the first element of a list, cdr (l) returns all but the first element of a list, listp (l) is true when l is a non-empty list, firstn (n, l) returns the first n elements of list l, nthcdr (n, l) returns all but the first n elements of list l, append (a, b) returns the concatenation of lists a and b, occurrences (v, l) returns the number of occurrences of value v in list l. **t** abbreviates the constant TRUE and **f** abbreviates the constant FALSE. Each of the functions 'name', 'request-time', 'deadline', and 'duration' when applied to a task request returns the appropriate value associated with that request.

The property of being a good schedule s with respect to a request list r is easily formalized using Nqthm. (We use Nqthm infix notation for definitions [2].)

DEFINITION:
good-schedule (s, r)
= **if** listp (r)
   then (occurrences (name (car (r)),
                   firstn (deadline (car (r)) − request-time (car (r)),
                        nthcdr (request-time (car (r)), s)))
        = duration (car (r)))
     ∧ good-schedule $(s,$ cdr $(r))$
   else t endif

Nqthm definitions are executable. In the following examples 'good-schedule' is applied to two example schedules and lists of task requests. Each task request is represented by a list of the task name, request time, deadline, and duration.

```
*(GOOD-SCHEDULE '(A NIL C A B A B C NIL NIL)
                '((A 0 7 3) (B 2 6 2) (C 1 5 1) (C 7 8 1)))
 F
*(GOOD-SCHEDULE '(A NIL C A B B A C NIL NIL)
                '((A 0 7 3) (B 2 6 2) (C 1 5 1) (C 7 8 1)))
 T
```

active-task-requests (*time*, *r*) returns the list of requests that are in *r* and for which *time* is not less than the request time and is less than the deadline.

DEFINITION:
active-task-requests (*time*, *r*)
$=$ **if** listp (*r*)
    then if (*time* $<$ deadline (car (*r*)))
        $\wedge$ (*time* $\geq$ request-time (car (*r*)))
        then cons (car (*r*), active-task-requests (*time*, cdr (*r*)))
        else active-task-requests (*time*, cdr (*r*)) **endif**
    else nil endif

```
*(ACTIVE-TASK-REQUESTS 3 '((A 0 7 3) (B 2 6 2) (C 1 5 1) (C 7 8 1)))
 '((A 0 7 3) (B 2 6 2) (C 1 5 1))
```

unfulfilled (*time*, *s*, *r*) returns the list of requests in *r* for which the task duration is not equal to the number of occurrences of the task name in *s* before *time* but no earlier than the task request time.

DEFINITION:
unfulfilled (*time*, *s*, *r*)
$=$ **if** listp (*r*)
    then if occurrences (name (car (*r*)),
                firstn (*time* $-$ request-time (car (*r*)),
                    nthcdr (request-time (car (*r*)), *s*)))
        $=$ duration (car (*r*)) **then** unfulfilled (*time*, *s*, cdr (*r*))
        else cons (car (*r*), unfulfilled (*time*, *s*, cdr (*r*))) **endif**
    else nil endif

```
*(UNFULFILLED 3 '(A NIL C A B B A C NIL NIL)
                '((A 0 7 3) (B 2 6 2) (C 1 5 1)))
 '((A 0 7 3) (B 2 6 2))
```

least-deadline (*r*) returns a request in *r* with least deadline.

DEFINITION:
least-deadline (r)
$=$ **if** listp (r)
    then if listp (cdr (r))
        then if deadline (car (r)) $<$ deadline (car (cdr (r)))
            then least-deadline (cons (car (r), cdr (cdr (r))))
            else least-deadline (cdr (r)) **endif**
        else car (r) **endif**
    else nil **endif**

```
*(LEAST-DEADLINE '((A 0 7 3) (B 2 6 2)))
 '(B 2 6 2)
```

The term edf (n, r) returns a schedule of length n for requests r such that an unfulfilled active task request with least deadline is chosen at each moment in the schedule if one exists or **nil** if there is no such request.

DEFINITION:
edf $(lengthschedule, r)$
$=$ **if** $lengthschedule \simeq 0$ **then** nil
    else let s **be** edf $(lengthschedule - 1, r)$
        in
        let *unfulfilled* **be** unfulfilled $(lengthschedule - 1, s,$
                               active-task-requests $(lengthschedule - 1,$
                                              r))
        in
        if listp $(unfulfilled)$
        then append $(s,$ list (name (least-deadline $(unfulfilled)$))))
        else append $(s,$ list (nil)) **endif endlet endlet endif**

```
*(EDF 10 '((A 0 7 3) (B 2 6 2) (C 1 5 1) (C 7 8 1)))
 '(A C B B A A NIL C NIL NIL)
```

EDF scheduling would appear to be a sensible way to schedule task requests. Note that the EDF scheduler applied to the task requests of the previous examples generates a good schedule.

```
*(GOOD-SCHEDULE '(A C B B A A NIL C NIL NIL)
               '((A 0 7 3) (B 2 6 2) (C 1 5 1) (C 7 8 1)))
 T
```

Our model for tasks is that they are *periodic*, meaning that task requests for a particular task occur with constant frequency. The function 'periodic-tasksp' identifies valid lists of periodic tasks, each of which is a triple containing a unique name, a positive period, and a positive duration.

```
*(PERIODIC-TASKSP '((A 3 2) (B 0 3)))
 F
*(PERIODIC-TASKSP '((A 3 2) (B 9 3)))
 T
```

The term periodic-tasks-requests (*pts*, *n1*, *n2*) generates task requests from periodic tasks list *pts*. A request is generated for each periodic task at every time less than *n2* that is the sum of *n1* and a multiple of the task's period. The deadline of a periodic task request is the next request of that task.

DEFINITION:
periodic-task-requests (*pt*, *starting-time*, *ending-time*)
= **if** periodic-taskp (*pt*)
  then if *starting-time* < *ending-time*
    then cons (list (tk-name (*pt*), *starting-time*,
         starting-time + tk-period (*pt*), tk-duration (*pt*)),
        periodic-task-requests (*pt*, *starting-time* + tk-period (*pt*),
             ending-time))

     else nil endif
   else nil endif

DEFINITION:
periodic-tasks-requests (*pts*, *starting-time*, *ending-time*)
= **if** periodic-tasksp (*pts*)
  then if listp (*pts*)
    then append (periodic-task-requests (car (*pts*), *starting-time*, *ending-time*),
         periodic-tasks-requests (cdr (*pts*), *starting-time*, *ending-time*))
    else nil endif
   else nil endif

```
*(PERIODIC-TASKS-REQUESTS '((A 3 2) (B 9 3)) 0 18)
'((A 0 3 2) (A 3 6 2) (A 6 9 2) (A 9 12 2)
  (A 12 15 2) (A 15 18 2) (B 0 9 3) (B 9 18 3))
```

Nqthm can reason about rationals [6], but it is simpler to introduce some functions that facilitate expressing the EDF theorem using integer arithmetic. big-period (*pts*) is the product of the task periods in *pts*. cpu-utilization (*pts*, *n*) returns the sum of (*n* * *duration*) ÷ *period* for each task in *pts*.

DEFINITION:
big-period (*pts*)
= **if** listp (*pts*) **then** tk-period (car (*pts*)) * big-period (cdr (*pts*))
  else 1 endif

DEFINITION:
cpu-utilization (*pts*, *bigp*)
= **if** listp (*pts*)
  then ((*bigp* * tk-duration (car (*pts*))) ÷ tk-period (car (*pts*)))
    +   cpu-utilization (cdr (*pts*), *bigp*)
  else 0 endif

```
*(BIG-PERIOD '((A 3 2) (B 9 3)))
 27
*(CPU-UTILIZATION '((A 3 2) (B 9 3)) 27)
 27
```

3 EDF Optimality for Periodic Tasks

We present the optimality theorem about EDF schedules on periodic tasks using the definitions of the previous section. If the *pts* is a list of periodic tasks such that $\sum_{tasks} duration/period \leq 1$ and n is a multiple of big-period(pts), then the EDF schedule satisfies the requests of *pts* through n time units.

$((\text{big-period}(pts) \geq \text{cpu-utilization}(pts, \text{big-period}(pts)))$
$\wedge \quad \text{periodic-tasksp}(pts)$
$\wedge \quad ((n \bmod \text{big-period}(pts)) = 0))$
$\rightarrow \quad \text{good-schedule}(\text{edf}(n, \text{periodic-tasks-requests}(pts, 0, n)),$
$\qquad\qquad\qquad \text{periodic-tasks-requests}(pts, 0, n))$

We call this an optimality theorem since the theorem shows that any set of periodic tasks for which there exists a good schedule can be scheduled using an EDF scheduler. We illustrate the application of this remarkable theorem on a small example. Assume task A has period 16 and duration 4, task B has period 5 and duration 2, and task C has period 3 and duration 1. If we let N be 240 and PTS the tasks described above, each of the hypotheses of the theorem is satisfied.

```
*(BIG-PERIOD PTS)
 240
*(CPU-UTILIZATION PTS 240)
 236
*(NOT (LESSP (BIG-PERIOD PTS) (CPU-UTILIZATION PTS (BIG-PERIOD PTS))))
 T
*(PERIODIC-TASKSP PTS)
 T
*(EQUAL (REMAINDER N (BIG-PERIOD PTS)) 0)
 T
```

Since we have proved the theorem and the hypotheses are satisfied, we know that the EDF schedule is a good schedule for the generated task requests.

```
*(GOOD-SCHEDULE
    (EDF N (PERIODIC-TASKS-REQUESTS PTS 0 N))
    (PERIODIC-TASKS-REQUESTS PTS 0 N))
 T
```

The first few assignments of the EDF schedule are calculated below, and the initial part of the schedule is displayed pictorially in Figure 1.

```
*(EDF N (PERIODIC-TASKS-REQUESTS PTS 0 N))
 '(C B B C A B C B A C B B C A A C B B C A B C B A C B B C A
     A C B B C A B C B A C B B C A A C B B C A B C B A C B B
     C A A C B B C A B C B A C B B C A A C B B C NIL B C B A
     ....
```

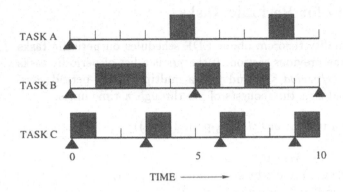

Fig. 1. An Example EDF Schedule

4 EDF Optimality Proof

4.1 An Informal Proof of EDF Optimality

Theorem 1. *Let R be a periodic request history corresponding to a periodic set P of m tasks. Let (tk_i, d_i, p_i) denote the ith element of P. $\sum_{i=1}^{m}(d_i/p_i) \leq 1$ implies the earliest deadline first schedule of R has no overflow.*

Proof: Let c be the product of the periods of P. Let P' be identical to P except let each duration d_i' and period p_i' in P be c times the corresponding values d_i and p_i in P. Let R' be a task request history of P'.

Let S' be a schedule for R' by repeating length(R) times the following:

$$(tk_1)^{d_1'/p_1} (tk_2)^{d_2'/p_2} \ldots (tk_m)^{d_m'/p_m} \, \mathbf{nil}^{c-\sum d_i'/p_i}$$

Since $\sum_{i=1}^{m}(d_i/p_i) \leq 1$, length($R$)*$c$ is the length of S' and S' does not overflow for R'.

We define swap(t, S, R) for time t, schedule S, and request history R as follows. Let tk be the least task with earliest absolute deadline unfulfilled at t. Return a schedule identical to S except that the task name at location t and the task name at the location of the first occurrence of tk no earlier than t are swapped. If schedule S does not overflow for request history R, then neither does swap(i, S, R).

Let $S_0' = S'$ and $S_{n+1}' = $ swap(n, S_n', R'). Let $S'' = S'_{length(S')}$. Note that S'' does not overflow for R' and that the element n in S'' is equal to the $n - (n$ **mod** $c)$ element of S''. Let S''' be composed of the elements of S'' in locations that are multiples of c. S''' is the earliest deadline first schedule of R and does not overflow.

Q.E.D.

4.2 The Nqthm Proof

The Nqthm proof of EDF optimality consists of approximately 500 "events" – not including a previously-proved library of arithmetic theorems upon which this proof depends [7] – that follow the informal proof described above. Nontrivial theorems are proved using Nqthm by proving lemmas that when applied automatically in later proofs lead to the desired proof. Nqthm provides the confidence associated with formal proof without the drudgery of writing the complete formal proof. Most of the 500 events of the EDF proof are lemmas designed to guide Nqthm to the proof of later theorems. The events are listed in [8]. The proof effort took approximately 3 man-months, and a comparison of the informal proof in Section 4.1 and the Nqthm proof in [8] makes obvious that the Nqthm proof required greater effort. Is this effort needed because formal proof is difficult, or is the difference simply due to difficulty using Nqthm?

We believe we faced greater difficulties proving this theorem using Nqthm because of the precision formal mathematics requires. Nqthm merely enforces the requirement that we be precise and not skip any details of the proof. On several occasions during the development of the proof the final theorem appeared nearly proved but was not. The complexity of doing formal mathematics is apparent in the complexity of the lemmas listed in [8]. Formal mathematics requires we be precise, and Nqthm succeeds in enforcing this requirement.

Many of the concepts needed in the proof of this theorem would not be introduced explicitly in an informal proof. As an example we examine 'firstn', which returns the first n elements of a list. This concept is defined in the Nqthm proof of the EDF optimality theorem because it is needed to define some of the notions in the proof, but a mathematician not doing formal proofs would not trouble himself to define it explicitly. In the Nqthm logic we define this concept as follows.

DEFINITION:
firstn $(n,\ list)$
$=$ **if** $n \simeq 0$ **then nil**
    else cons (car $(list)$, firstn $(n - 1,$ cdr $(list)))$ **endif**

In order for Nqthm to reason about schedules and task requests many theorems are proved that "program" the theorem prover [1,8]. Figure 2 presents some of the theorems involving 'firstn' that were proved in order to prove EDF optimality but which would probably be skipped in an informal proof. Each of these lemmas is proved using Nqthm and is applied subsequently in proofs involving 'firstn'. We believe that these facts about 'firstn' are needed in formal proofs involving 'firstn' whether or not one is using Nqthm. If one wishes to prove formally something that involves 'firstn' and 'append', for example, there is no getting around the requirement to prove theorem (2). An Nqthm user is forced to prove something akin to this theorem as a part of the proof of EDF optimality because any formal proof of EDF optimality requires it.

General lemmas like these about 'firstn' can be reused in future Nqthm proofs that involve 'firstn', because the collection of theorems proved about subsidiary

1. length (firstn $(n, list)$) = fix (n)
2. firstn $(n,$ append $(l1, l2))$
    =   **if** length $(l1) < n$ **then** append $(l1,$ firstn $(n -$ length $(l1), l2))$
        else firstn $(n, l1)$ **endif**
3. firstn (length $(x), x$) = plist (x)
4. plist (firstn (n, l)) = firstn (n, l)
5. nthcdr $(n,$ firstn $(n + x, s))$ = firstn $(x,$ nthcdr $(n, s))$
6. firstn $(n,$ replace-nth $(i, v, l))$
    =   **if** $i < n$ **then** replace-nth $(i, v,$ firstn $(n, l))$
        else firstn (n, l) **endif**
7. nth $(n,$ firstn $(n2, s))$
    =   **if** $n < n2$ **then** nth (n, s)
        else 0 **endif**
8. firstn $(a,$ firstn $(b, x))$
    =   **if** $b < a$ **then** append (firstn $(b, x),$ repeat $(a - b, 0))$
        else firstn (a, x) **endif**
9. firstn $(1, s)$ = list (car (s))
10. $(i < j) \rightarrow$ (nth $(i, s) \in$ firstn (j, s))
11. (car $(x) \in$ firstn (n, x)) = $(n \not\simeq 0)$
12. $((i \geq y) \wedge (i < (x + y))) \rightarrow$ (nth $(i, s) \in$ firstn $(x,$ nthcdr (y, s)))
13. $(x \notin l) \rightarrow ((x \in$ firstn $(n, l))$ = $((x = 0) \wedge$ (length $(l) < n)))$
14. firstn $(n1,$ repeat $(n2, v))$
    =   **if** $n2 < n1$ **then** append (repeat $(n2, v),$ repeat $(n1 - n2, 0))$
        else repeat $(n1, v)$ **endif**
15. nthcdr $(n,$ firstn (n, l)) = nil
16. listp (firstn (n, l)) = $(n \not\simeq 0)$
17. (nil = firstn (n, l)) = $(n \simeq 0)$
18. $n \geq$ occurrences $(v,$ firstn $(n, l))$
19. firstn $(a + b, l)$ = append (firstn $(b, l),$ firstn $(a,$ nthcdr (b, l)))

Fig. 2. Some theorems proved about 'firstn'

functions constitutes a strategy for proving theorems about them. This is not necessarily the case when using proof systems that encourage the development of less-automatic proofs, such as PC-Nqthm [3] or PVS [5]. The EDF optimality proof used previously-proved arithmetic facts developed for Nqthm-checked proofs of other theorems [7].

It is our belief that the difficulties we overcame to construct an Nqthm proof of this theorem using the approach presented in this paper result from the complexity and precision of formal mathematics rather than a deficiency in Nqthm.

5 Conclusions

Proofs of this kind lead to precise statements of theorems useful for computer system verification. Informal proofs often make intuitive leaps that are difficult to justify, or omit details that can lead to misinterpretation. The original proof of EDF optimality was flawed because a step in the informal proof was not valid, but if one trusts Nqthm and accepts the formalization presented in this paper one need not examine the proof to conclude that EDF optimality is a theorem.

References

1. R. S. Boyer and J S. Moore. *A Computational Logic Handbook*. Academic Press, Boston, 1988.
2. R. S. Boyer and J S. Moore. *Chapter 14 of A Computational Logic Handbook, 2nd edition*. Academic Press, Boston, 1997. (Distributed in Nqthm-1992 release available from Computational Logic, Inc.).
3. Matthew Kaufmann. A user's manual for an interactive enhancement to the Boyer-Moore theorem prover. Technical Report 19, Computational Logic, Inc., May 1988.
4. C.L. Liu and James W. Layland. Scheduling algorithms for multiprogramming in a hard real-time environment. *Journal of the Association for Computing Machinery*, 20(1):46–61, 1973.
5. S. Owre, N. Shankar, and J. M. Rushby. *User Guide for the PVS Specification and Verification System (Beta Release)*. Computer Science Laboratory, SRI International, Menlo Park, CA, February 1993.
6. Matthew Wilding. A mechanically-checked correctness proof of a floating-point search program. Technical Report 56, Computational Logic, Inc., May 1990.
7. Matthew Wilding. Proving Matijasevich's lemma with a default arithmetic strategy. *Journal of Automated Reasoning*, 7(3), September 1991.
8. Matthew Wilding. *Machine-Checked Real-Time System Verification*. PhD thesis, University of Texas, May 1996. ftp.cs.utexas.edu/pub/boyer/wilding-diss.ps.gz.
9. Zheng Yuhua and Zhou Chaochen. A formal proof of the deadline driven scheduler. *Formal Techniques in Real-Time and Fault-Tolerant Systems, Third International Symposium*, pages 756–775, 1994.

Acknowledgments: I thank Al Mok, Bob Boyer, Mathai Joseph, Matt Kaufmann, and Bill Young for many helpful suggestions about drafts of this paper. The views and conclusions contained in this document are those of the author. This work was supported in part at Computational Logic, Inc., by the Defense Advanced Research Projects Agency, ARPA Order 7406.

A General Approach to Partial Order Reductions in Symbolic Verification (Extended Abstract)

Parosh Aziz Abdulla[1], Bengt Jonsson[1], Mats Kindahl[1,2], and Doron Peled[3]

[1] Uppsala University, Dept. of Computer Systems,
P.O. Box 325, S-751 05 Uppsala, Sweden,
{parosh,bengt,matkin}@docs.uu.se
WWW: http://www.docs.uu.se/~{parosh,bengt,matkin}
[2] IAR Systems AB
Box 23051, 750 23 Uppsala, Sweden
mats.kindahl@iar.se
[3] Bell Laboratories, 700 Mountain Ave., Murray Hill, NJ 07974, USA
doron@research.bell-labs.com

Abstract. The purpose of partial-order reduction techniques is to avoid exploring several interleavings of independent transitions when model checking the temporal properties of a concurrent system. The purpose of symbolic verification techniques is to perform basic manipulations on sets of states rather than on individual states. We present a general method for applying partial order reductions to improve symbolic verification. The method is equally applicable to the verification of finite-state and infinite-state systems. It considers methods that check safety properties, either by forward reachability analysis or by backward reachability analysis. We base the method on the concept of commutativity (in one direction) between predicate transformers. Since the commutativity relation is not necessarily symmetric, this generalizes those existing approaches to partial order verification which are based on a symmetric dependency relation.
We show how our method can be applied to several models of infinite-state systems: systems communicating over unbounded lossy FIFO channels, and unsafe (infinite-state) Petri Nets. We show by a simple example how partial order reduction can significantly speed up symbolic backward analysis of Petri Nets.

1 Introduction

This paper is concerned with applying partial-order techniques to improve symbolic verification methods for state-space exploration.

- The purpose of *partial-order techniques* (e.g., [GP93,GW93,HP94,Pel96,Val90,Val93]) is to avoid exploring several interleavings of independent transitions, i.e., transitions whose execution order is irrelevant, e.g., because they are performed by different processes. When verifying temporal properties, partial order methods often give substantial reductions of the search space.

- The purpose of *symbolic techniques* (e.g., [BCMD92,AČJYK96,BG96]) is to perform the basic manipulations in verification on sets of states rather than on individual states. A basis is some representation of (possibly infinite) sets of states, which can be manipulated conveniently.

We use the term *constraint* to denote some representation of a set of states. Common forms of constraints are BDDs [BCMD92], zones or regions representing infinite sets of clock values of of a timed automaton [ACD90,LLPY97], upward closed sets of states of an infinite state system [AČJYK96] such as a lossy channel system [AJ93] or a Petri Net [Fin90], an infinite set of queue contents [BG96], etc. The effect of a program statement on constraints is represented by a predicate transformer. The state-space of the system is explored by generating new constraints by applying predicate transformers to already generated constraints. In this paper, we consider both forward and backward symbolic state-space exploration. To represent forward symbolic state-space exploration, we include for each statement t of the program the predicate transformer which maps a constraint φ to a constraint representing the set $post(t)(\varphi)$ of states reachable from a state in φ using statement t. To represent backward symbolic state-space exploration (e.g., as in [AČJYK96]), we include the predicate transformer which maps a constraint φ to a constraint representing the set $pre(t)(\varphi)$ of states from which a state in φ can be reached using statement t. Different exploration strategies can be used (depth-first, breadth-first, etc.). Note that standard (non-symbolic) state-based exploration corresponds to the special case where each constraint denotes a single state.

The idea in partial order techniques is to restrict the set of statements that are explored from a given state. The basis for most existing work on partial-order methods is a symmetric dependency relation on program statements, which is used to determine a subset of statements to be explored from a given state. Different criteria for reductions have been presented which are based on the concept of a dependency relation, e.g., *stubborn sets* [Val90], *persistent sets* [GP93] or *ample sets* [Pel96].

In symbolic verification, one should similarly try to reduce the set of predicate transformers that need be applied to a given constraint. As a basis for such a reduction, we have found it useful to employ the notion of *commutativity* (in one direction) between predicate transformers, originally introduced by Lipton [Lip75]. This is a weakening of the dependency relation, in that it need not be symmetric. It is more succinct than the standard definition of the symmetric dependency relation used in the literature on partial order methods.

We use commutativity to present a general definition of partial order reduction for constraint verification systems. We illustrate the applicability of our definition by

- showing that it covers our earlier work on partial order methods for symbolic verification of lossy channel systems, and
- presenting a partial order reduction on symbolic backward reachability analysis for checking the coverability problem in (unbounded) Petri Nets. To our knowledge, this is the first partial-order reduction which applies equally well

to infinite-state Petri Nets as to finite-state Petri Nets. We present a test of the reduction on a simple example.

Related Work Partial-order techniques have been employed in state-space exploration, and the literature is continuously expanding (e.g., [GP93,GW93,HP94,Pel96,Val93]). Most of this work employs a symmetric dependency relation as a basis for defining reduction strategies. Asymmetric relations are present in a few works on automated verification, e.g., [Val90]. The dependency relation can be conditional on the particular state where statements are executed [GP93,KP92]. In our formulation, the commutativity relation can be defined to be dependent on the constraint.

A combination of partial-order and symbolic techniques is also presented by Alur et al [ABH+97]. These approaches differ from ours in that they first define a partial-order reduction of the state-space, similar to the earlier literature, and thereafter explore this symbolically, using BDDs. The paper considers only forward search from initial states. In contrast, our work defines partial order reduction on top of symbolic verification, and is based on a more general assymetric commutativity relation. To our knowledge, no formulation has been given of partial order reduction for algorithms based on backward reachability analysis. Techniques for Petri Nets which exploit partial order semantics [McM95] or partial order reduction [Val90] are based on forward reachability analysis for bounded nets.

This paper is a generalization and simplification of our earlier work, [AKP97], where we considered partial-order reduction in symbolic verification of lossy channel systems [AJ93]. In this paper, we have simplified the definition of partial order reduction, and made it applicable to a range of symbolic verification methods.

Commutativity between actions or predicate transformers was introduced by Lipton [Lip75], and has been used in assertional reasoning by Back [Bac89], Lamport [Lam90], Katz and Peled [KP92], and others.

Outline. In the next section, we introduce basic definitions and constraint verification methods. In Section 3, we present our method of partial-order reductions. In Section 4, we describe how the method can be applied to symbolic verification of lossy channels and of Petri nets. We also show how partial order methods can improve verification times on a simple Petri net.

2 Programs and Symbolic Verification

We assume a program which consists of a (possibly infinite) set Σ of states, and a finite set T of transitions. Each transition $t \in T$ is a binary relation on Σ. In this paper we will consider the problem of checking reachability: given a program, a set $S_I \subseteq \Sigma$ of initial states and a set $S_F \subseteq \Sigma$, of final states, determine whether there is a sequence $\sigma_0 t_1 \sigma_1 t_2 \cdots t_n \sigma_n$ of states and transitions from some initial state $\sigma_0 \in S_I$ to some final state $\sigma_n \in S_F$ such that $\sigma_{i-1} t_i \sigma_i$ for all i with

$1 \leq i \leq n$. The verification of most safety properties can be transformed to the reachability problem by standard techniques.

We consider symbolic verification methods, which manipulate sets of states rather than individual states, and where the effect of transitions is represented by predicate transformers.

A *predicate* over Σ is a subset of Σ. We will often use the term *constraint* for predicates. The set of constraints over Σ forms a lattice with ordering $\sqsubseteq$ taken as set inclusion. We will say that a constraint φ *covers* another constraint φ', if $\varphi' \sqsubseteq \varphi$. Let $\bot$ be the empty constraint and let $\top$ be the set Σ.

A *predicate transformer* τ is a function from 2^Σ to 2^Σ. We will consider only predicate transformers which are monotone and strict (i.e., such that $\tau(\bot) = \bot$). Given predicate transformers $\tau_1, \ldots \tau_n$ we let $\tau_1; \ldots; \tau_n$ denote the predicate transformer τ' such that $\tau'(\varphi) = \tau_n(\cdots(\tau_1(\varphi))\cdots)$ for any constraint φ. Observe the order of application of the predicate transformers. A predicate transformer τ is *enabled* at constraint φ if $\tau(\varphi) \neq \bot$. We will consider symbolic verification algorithms which check the reachability problem either by forward reachability analysis or by backward reachability analysis. In forward analysis, we start from a set of constraints whose union is the set of initial states, and generate new constraints by applying the predicate transformer $post(t)(\varphi) = \{\sigma' : \exists \sigma \in \varphi . \sigma t \sigma'\}$ for each transition t and already generated constraint φ. New constraints which are included in already generated constraints need not be further explored. The search terminates when a constraint containing a final state is generated, or when no more constraints are generated. Backward analysis is analogous, but starts from a set of constraints that represents the set of final states, and applies the predicate transformer $pre(t)(\varphi) = \{\sigma : \exists \sigma' \in \varphi . \sigma t \sigma'\}$, attempting to find a constraint containing an initial state.

For a constraint φ, a set ψ of states, and a sequence $\rho = \tau_1; \ldots; \tau_n$ of predicate transformers in $\mathcal{T}$ we say that ρ *leads from* φ *to* ψ if $\psi \cap \tau_1; \ldots; \tau_n(\varphi) \neq \bot$. We say that ψ is *reachable* from φ if there is a sequence ρ which leads from φ to ψ. We say that ψ is *reachable* from a set Φ of constraints if ψ is reachable from some $\varphi \in \Phi$. analysis to the symbolic case. **Algorithm 1** in Figure 1 is a standard generalization of state-based reachability. The algorithm repeatedly selects constraints from W to be explored. Line 4 checks if the constraint removed from W is already covered by some previously visited constraint, in which case it is redundant and can be discarded. Line 5 checks to see if we have reached a constraint that contains some final state. Line 6 computes the successor constraints to investigate. For this, a function *select* determines the subset of $\mathcal{T}$ which is to be explored from each constraint. Line 7 adds the newly processed constraint to the list of already visited constraints.

Note that at line 6, the algorithms is parameterized by a function *select* which determines the set of predicate transformers to explore from a given constraints. In the next section, we will study how the function *select* can be changed in order to reduce the search space. In this section, we will take $select(\varphi)$ to be the set $\mathcal{T}$ of all predicate transformers. Equivalently, we can let $select(\varphi)$ be the set $enabled(\varphi)$ of all predicate transformers which are enabled at φ (if τ is not

383

Algorithm 1 (Reachability Algorithm)
Input: A finite set $\mathcal{T}$ of predicate transformers, a finite set Φ_0 of initial constraints, and a set ψ of final states.
Output: true if ψ is reachable from Φ_0.
Local Variables: A set V of constraints representing visited constraints and a working set W of constraints yet to be investigated.

1) Let $W = \Phi_0$ and let $V = \emptyset$
2) While W is not empty, repeat steps 3–7
3)   Select and remove a constraint $\varphi \in W$
4)   If there is $\varphi' \in V$ such that $\varphi \sqsubseteq \varphi'$, goto 2
5)   If $\psi \wedge \varphi \not\equiv \bot$, then exit with the result **true**
6)   Add the constraints $\{\tau(\varphi) \; : \; \tau \in select(\varphi)\}$ to W.
7)   Add φ to V
8) If W becomes empty, exit with the result **false**

Fig. 1. Algorithm 1 (Reachability)

enabled at φ, then $\tau(\varphi)$ generates $\bot$ which is trivially discarded). In Section 3, we will investigate how *select* can be made even smaller, without endangering the correctness of the algorithm.

An obvious requirement on the selection of constraints in line 3 is that it is fair in the following sense: Each constraint which is inserted into W at line 6 is eventually removed at line 3 of the algorithm. We will from now on assume that any reachability algorithm under consideration satisfies this fairness condition. Breadth-first is an example of a fair exploration strategy. Depth-first need not be fair if the state-space is infinite. For the class of well-structured infinite-state systems considered in our earlier work using backward analysis [AČJYK96], any strategy is fair, since the algorithm will always terminate with W empty.

We observe that, due to the above fairness requirement, the algorithm is *complete* in the sense that it is guaranteed to return **true** if the set ψ is reachable. If ψ is not reachable. the algorithm may add an infinite sequence of constraints to W, without terminating, since the set of states and the set of constraints may both be infinite.

3 Improving the Reachability Algorithm

In this section we introduce strategies to improve the reachability algorithm presented in Section 2. The idea is to only apply a subset of the predicate transformers to a constraint, resulting in that we only explore a subset of all possible sequences of predicate transformers. Our aim is to substantially reduce the number of different constraints generated during the verification. As a basis for such a reduction, we have found it useful to employ the notion of *commutativity*, originally introduced by Lipton [Lip75].

Definition 1. *Given predicate transformers τ_2, τ_1, and a constraint φ, we say that τ_1 commutes left with τ_2 in φ, denoted $\tau_1 \ll_\varphi \tau_2$, if $\tau_2; \tau_1(\varphi) \sqsubseteq \tau_1; \tau_2(\varphi)$.*

Intuitively, if τ_1 commutes left with τ_2 in φ, then it seems plausible that we need not apply the sequence $\tau_2; \tau_1$ to the constraint φ, since the constraint generated is a subset of the constraint generated by the sequence $\tau_1; \tau_2$.

Definition 2. *Let φ be a constraint ρ a finite sequence of predicate transformers, and τ a predicate transformer. We say that τ is* contributory *to ρ from φ if, for any partition $\rho_1; \tau'; \rho_2$ of ρ we have $\tau \ll_{\rho_1(\varphi)} \tau'$.*

It is easy to see, using the definition of commutativity, that if τ is *contributory* to ρ from φ, then $\rho\tau(\varphi) \sqsubseteq \tau\rho(\varphi)$.

We will now present strategies for reducing the set of predicate transformers that need be explored from a given constraint φ. This is done in a similar spirit as for state-based partial order techniques. In our setting there are some additional differences: the search space may be infinite, and constraints are discarded if they are covered by already explored constraints. The search will be affected by the function *select*, and we are interested in requirements on *select* that guarantee completeness of the algorithm. We will present two sets of requirements, both of which guarantee completeness. The first is inspired by the definition of stubborn sets [Val90], and the second by the ample set technique [Pel96].

Our first set of requirements on *select* consists of the following two conditions.

C1 Every predicate transformer in $select(\varphi)$ is contributory to every sequence $\rho \in (\mathcal{T} \setminus select(\varphi))^*$ of predicate transformers not in $select(\varphi)$ from φ.
C2 There is no sequence $\rho \in (\mathcal{T} \setminus select(\varphi))^*$ of predicate transformers not in $select(\varphi)$ which leads from φ to ψ.

Condition **C1** defines what is usually termed a persistent set [GP93]. It is the reason for why we can exploit commutativity to defer exploration of the predicate transformers outside $select(\varphi)$. Condition **C2** is a simple way of ensuring that this deferral does not sacrifice completeness.

Theorem 1. *If the function select satisfies the conditions **C1** and **C2** for each constraint φ, then Algorithm 1 will return* **true** *if ψ is reachable from Φ_0.*

Proof. We prove by induction on n the following property: For each constraint φ generated by the algorithm which is not discarded at line 4, if some sequence $\rho \in \mathcal{T}^*$ of predicate transformers of length n leads from φ to ψ, then the algorithm will eventually generate a constraint φ' such that $\varphi' \cap \psi \neq \bot$. The case $n = 0$ is trivial. Let φ be a constraint generated by the algorithm which is not discarded, and let $\rho = \tau_1; \ldots; \tau_{n+1}$ be a sequence in $\mathcal{T}^*$ of length $n + 1$ which leads from φ to ψ. By **C2**, there is an i with $1 \leq i \leq n + 1$ such that $\tau_i \in select(\varphi)$. Let i be the least such i. Let $\rho_1 = \tau_i; \tau_1; \ldots; \tau_{i-1}; \tau_{i+1}; \ldots; \tau_{n+1}$. By **C1** and monotonicity of predicate transformers, we have $\rho(\varphi) \sqsubseteq \rho_1(\varphi)$. Thus, if $\tau_i(\varphi)$ is not discarded by the algorithm, the induction hypothesis yields the desired conclusion. If the result $\tau_i(\varphi)$ of applying τ_i to φ is discarded at line 4 because it is covered by some constraint φ_1 already in V, then by monotonicity there is a sequence of predicate transformers of length at most n which leads from the generated and not discarded constraint φ_1 to ψ, which concludes the proof of the property. Finally, letting φ be any of the initial constraints in Φ_0 proves the statement in the theorem.

We note that conditions **C1** and **C2** are both rather abstract, and that some more concrete and restrictive versions must be used in a practical implementation. For instance, condition **C2** could be enforced by finding some necessary change that must present on any sequence from φ to ψ (such as changing a particular state component), and checking that this change can only be effected by the transformers in $select(\varphi)$.

A weaker but more complex version of Theorem 1 can be obtained by replacing **C2** by the following three conditions.

D2 If **C2** does not hold, then there is a $\tau \in select(\varphi)$ such that $\varphi' \cap \psi \neq \bot$ implies $\tau(\varphi') \cap \psi \neq \bot$ for any constraint φ'.

D3 If for some transformer $\tau \in select(\varphi)$, the successor $\tau(\varphi)$ is discarded at line 4, then $select(\varphi) = enabled(\varphi)$ (or equivalently $select(\varphi) = \mathcal{T}$).

D4 If the algorithm generates an infinite path of predicate transformers, none of which is discarded, then each predicate transformer in $\mathcal{T}$ must be explored infinitely often along this path.

An explanation of these conditions should be provided by the proof of the following theorem.

Theorem 2. *If the function select satisfies the conditions* **C1, D2, D3** *and* **D4** *for each constraint φ, then Algorithm 1 will return* **true** *if ψ is reachable from Φ_0.*

Proof. Just as for Theorem 1, we prove by induction on n the following property: For each generated and not discarded constraint φ, if some transformer sequence ρ of length n leads from φ to ψ, then the algorithm will eventually generate a constraint φ' such that $\varphi' \cap \psi \neq \bot$. The case $n = 0$ is trivial. Let φ be a constraint generated by the algorithm which is not discarded, and let $\rho = \tau_1; \ldots; \tau_{n+1}$ be a sequence of length $n+1$ which leads from φ to ψ. If there is an i with $1 \leq i \leq n+1$ such that $\tau_i \in select(\varphi)$, we proceed as in the proof of Theorem 1. Otherwise, by condition **D2** there is a $\tau_1' \in select(\varphi)$ such that $\tau_1; \ldots; ; \tau_{n+1}; \tau_1'(\varphi) \cap \psi \neq \bot$. It follows by **C1**, falsity of **C2**, and monotonicity that $\tau_1'; \tau_1; \ldots; ; \tau_{n+1}(\varphi) \cap \psi \neq \bot$. Let $\varphi_1 = \tau_1'(\varphi)$. By condition **D3**, we infer that τ_1' is not discarded (remember that τ_1 is not explored from φ). Just as for φ we have that ρ leads from φ_1 to ψ. If there is an i with $1 \leq i \leq n+1$ such that $\tau_i \in select(\varphi_1)$, we proceed as in the proof of Theorem 1. Otherwise, we proceed as with φ. In this way, we generate a path $\varphi\varphi_1\varphi_2 \cdots$ of generated and not discarded constraints. The path stops if at some point condition **C2** holds, in which case we are done. If not, the path is infinite. By condition **D4** there is a j such that $\tau_1 \in select(\varphi_j)$. Regardless of whether $\tau_1(\varphi_j)$ is discarded or not, we can use the induction hypothesis to conclude the proof, just as in the previous theorem.

4 Examples

In this section, we apply the results in the previous section to some models of infinite state systems.

4.1 Lossy Channel Systems

A *lossy channel system* consists of a *control part* and a *channel part*. The control part is modeled as a number of finite-state processes communicating via the channels, while the channel part consists of a finite set of channels. Each channel behaves as a FIFO buffer which is unbounded and unreliable in the sense that it can lose messages. A channel is used to perform asynchronous communication between a pair of processes, so for each channel there is unique process sending messages to the channel, and a unique process receiving messages from the channel. A constraint defines the control state of each process, and defines for each channel the contents of the channel as an upward closed set of strings. Predicate transformers correspond to backward performing of send and receive transitions. In [AKP97] we apply a partial order technique for a symbolic backward reachability analysis described in [AJ93]. An algorithm (satisfying **C1** - **C2**) for computing *select* at a particular configuration is given as follows. If there is a process where all its enabled transitions are either send transitions to a non-empty channel, or receive transitions, then select exactly all enabled transitions of the process. If no such process exist, then select the set of enabled transitions of all processes. In [AKP97] we apply the above algorithm to a *go back n* protocol, obtaining time reductions of up to 25%, and to a mutual exclusion protocol, obtaining time reductions of up to 97%.

4.2 Petri Nets

In this section we will apply the techniques to algorithms for checking the coverability problem for Petri Nets. A Petri net is a tuple $\mathcal{N} = \langle P, T, in, out \rangle$, where P is a finite set of *places*, T a finite set of *transitions*, and $in : T \mapsto (P \mapsto \mathcal{N})$ and $out : T \mapsto (P \mapsto \mathcal{N})$ are functions that for each transition $t \in T$ define how many tokens are consumed and produced at each place when t is fired. A *marking* m is a mapping from P to $\mathcal{N}$. A transition t can fire in a marking m if $in(t)(p) \leq m(p)$ for each place $p \in P$. When t fires, the marking is changed from m to the marking m' defined by $m'(p) = m(p) - in(t)(p) + out(t)(p)$ for each $p \in P$. We define $\ominus$ (monus) by $a \ominus b = \max(0, a - b)$. We define the operators $+$ and $-$ on markings in the natural way, and the partial order $\leq$ by point-wise extension, i.e. $m_1 \leq m_2$ iff $m_1(p) \leq m_2(p)$ for every place $p \in P$.

A set φ of markings is *upward closed* if $m \in \varphi$ implies $m' \in \varphi$ for all m' with $m \leq m'$. We will be interested in the coverability problem, which is defined as follows: Given a set M_I of initial markings, and a set M_F of final markings, determine whether there is a set of transitions leading from a marking in M_I to a marking m which covers some marking $m_F \in M_F$ in the sense that $m_F \leq m$. The coverability problem can be checked by backward search as follows. Let our constraints be sets of the form $\varphi_{m_0} = \{m \; : \; m_0 \leq m\}$ for some m_0. Note that $pre(t)(\varphi_m) = \varphi_{m \ominus out(t) + in(t)}$. In **Algorithm 1**, let Φ_0 be a finite set of constraints, whose union is M_F, and let the set $\mathcal{T}$ be the set $\{pre(t) \; : \; t \in T\}$. Let ψ be M_I. **Algorithm 1** then represents a symbolic backward analysis for solving the coverability problem in the case that $select(\varphi) = \mathcal{T}$ for each φ. It can be shown (e.g., [AČJYK96]) that this analysis is guaranteed to terminate.

We can now present a partial order reduction strategy which is based on sufficient (but in general not necessary) criteria for commutativity.

We say that the predicate transformers $pre(t_1)$ and $pre(t_2)$ are in *conflict* if for some place p we have $out(t_1)(p) > 0$ and $out(t_2)(p) > 0$. We say that a transformer $pre(t)$ is *deficient* for p at φ_m if $m(p) < out(t)(p)$. We say that a transformer $pre(t)$ *separates* a marking m from a set M_I of markings if there is a place p with $out(t)(p) > 0$ such that $m(p) > m_I(p)$ for each marking $m_I \in M_I$. We observe that if $pre(t)$ separates m from M_I then any sequence of predicate transformers that leads from φ_m to some φ_{m_I} with $m_I \in M_I$ must contain a predicate transformer $pre(t')$ for a transition with $out(t')(p) > 0$, where p is the place that makes t' separating. It follows that the sequence must contain either $pre(t)$ or a transformer which is in conflict with $pre(t)$.

The following is a procedure to generate a set of predicate transformers $select(\varphi_m)$ to be explored from a constraint φ_m. We assume that the set M_I (corresponding to ψ in Algorithm 1) is given.

- Start with some transformer $pre(t_0)$ which separates m from M_I.
  Let $select(\varphi_m) = \{pre(t_0)\}$ initially.
  Repeatedly add to $select(\varphi_m)$ all transformers $pre(t')$ for which there is a transformer $pre(t) \in select(\varphi_m)$ such that either
  (1) $pre(t)$ and $pre(t')$ are in conflict, or
  (2) there is a place p such that $pre(t)$ is deficient at p and $in(t')(p) > 0$
- If no transformer $pre(t_0)$ can be found which separates m from M_I, let $select(\varphi_m) = \mathcal{T}$, i.e., explore all transformers.

It can be checked that this procedure generates a subset of transitions (i.e., predicate transformers) which satisfies conditions **C1** and **C2**. An intuitive explanation is as follows. By the observation above, if $pre(t_0)$ separates m from M_I then any sequence of predicate transformers that leads from φ_m to some φ_{m_I} with $m_I \in M_I$ must contain a transition in $select(\varphi)$: either $pre(t_0)$ or a transformer which is in conflict with $pre(t_0)$. Thus **C2** is satisfied. To verify **C1**, first note that conditions (1) and (2) imply that $pre(t) \ll_{\varphi_m} pre(t')$ for all $pre(t) \in select(\varphi_m)$ and $pre(t') \notin select(\varphi_m)$. Suppose that after a sequence of transformers we reach a constraint $\varphi_{m'}$ where $pre(t) \not\ll_{\varphi_{m'}} pre(t')$ but $pre(t) \ll_{\varphi_m} pre(t')$. Then the sequence must remove tokens from a place p with $out(t)(p) > 0$ and hence contain a transition which is in conflict with $pre(t)$.

Measurements. we will describe the results from a small experiment with the procedure for generating reduced sets of predicate transformers at the end of Section 4.2 following heuristics to select ample sets.

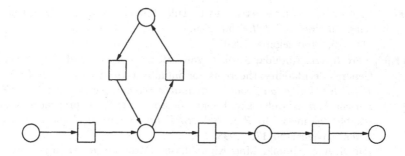

Fig. 2. A Petri Net Buffer

The example we used consists of a Petri net that moves tokens from an initial place (to the left) to a final place (to the right). We also added a loop to the sequence to show that a Petri net which is not a simple directed graph can be handled. The net can be seen in figure 2. The results from executing this Petri net is shown in the following table. The column "Tokens" denotes the number of tokens in the final place at the start of the backward analysis. The running times are in seconds.

Tokens	Standard Algorithm	Partial Order Algorithm
4	0.1	0.0
8	1.5	0.1
12	13.3	0.2
16	78.8	0.3
20	346.3	0.6
24	1239.7	0.9
28	–	1.5
32	–	2.3
36	–	3.3
40	–	4.6

As can be seen, the standard method degenerates very fast, while the partial order method is still well within acceptable running times. The good performance comes from the fact that, using our method for selecting reduced sets of transformers, the partial order method will move one token at a time from the end place to the initial place. The standard algorithm will investigate every interleaving of moving tokens from the end place closer to the start place.

References

[ABH+97] R. Alur, R.K. Brayton, T.A. Henzinger, S. Qadeer, and S.K. Rajamani. Partial-order reduction in symbolic state space exploration. In O. Grumberg, editor, *Proc. 9th Int. Conf. on Computer Aided Verification*, volume 1254, pages 340–351, Haifa, Israel, 1997. Springer Verlag.

[ACD90] R. Alur, C. Courcoubetis, and D. Dill. Model-checking for real-time systems. In *Proc. 5th IEEE Int. Symp. on Logic in Computer Science*, pages 414–425, Philadelphia, 1990.

[AČJYK96] Parosh Aziz Abdulla, Karlis Čerāns, Bengt Jonsson, and Tsay Yih-Kuen. General decidability theorems for infinite-state systems. In *Proc. 11th IEEE Int. Symp. on Logic in Computer Science*, pages 313–321, 1996.

[AJ93] Parosh Aziz Abdulla and Bengt Jonsson. Verifying programs with unreliable channels. In *Proc. 8th IEEE Int. Symp. on Logic in Computer Science*, pages 160–170, 1993.

[AKP97] Parosh Aziz Abdulla, Mats Kindahl, and Doron Peled. An improved search strategy for Lossy Channel Systems. In Tadanori Mizuno, Nori Shiratori, Teruo Hegashino, and Atsushi Togashi, editors, *FORTE X / PSTV XVII '97*, pages 251–264. Chapman and Hall, 1997.

[Bac89] R.J.R. Back. A method for refining atomicity in parallel algorithms. In *Proc. PARLE 89*, volume 366 of *Lecture Notes in Computer Science*, pages 199–216. Springer Verlag, 1989.

[BCMD92] J.R. Burch, E.M. Clarke, K.L. McMillan, and D.L. Dill. Symbolic model checking: 10^{20} states and beyond. *Information and Computation*, 98:142–170, 1992.

[BG96] B. Boigelot and P. Godefroid. Symbolic verification of communication protocols with infinite state spaces using QDDs. In Alur and Henzinger, editors, *Proc. 8th Int. Conf. on Computer Aided Verification*, volume 1102 of *Lecture Notes in Computer Science*, pages 1–12. Springer Verlag, 1996.

[Fin90] A. Finkel. Reduction and covering of infinite reachability trees. *Information and Computation*, 89:144–179, 1990.

[GP93] P. Godefroid, D. Pirottin. *Refining Dependencies Improves Partial-Order Verification Methods*. Proc. 5th Conference on Computer Aided Verification, Lecture Notes in Computer Science 697, Springer, 438–449. Elounda, Greece, 1993.

[GW93] P. Godefroid and P. Wolper. Using Partial Orders for the Efficient Verification of Deadlock Freedom and Safety Properties. In *Formal Methods in System Design*, Kluwer, 2 (1993), 149–164.

[HP94] G.J. Holzmann and D. Peled. An improvement in formal verification. In *Proc. FORTE '94*, pages 197–211, 1994.

[JZ92] W. Janssen and J. Zwiers. From sequential layers to distributed processes. In *Proc. 11th ACM Symp. on Principles of Distributed Computing*, Canada, 1992.

[KP92] Shmuel Katz and Doron Peled. Defining conditional independence using collapses. *Theoretical Computer Science*, 101:337–359, 1992.

[KLM+98] R.P. Kurshan, V. Levin, M. Minea and D. Peled, H. Yenigun,. Static Partial Order Reduction. *TACAS'98, Workshop on Tools and Algorithms for the Construction and Analysis of Systems*, Lisbon, Portugal.

[Lam90] L. Lamport. A theorem on atomicity in distributed algorithms. *Distributed Computing*, 4(2):59–68, 1990.

[Lip75] Lipton. Reduction, a method of proving properties of parallel programs. *Communications of the ACM*, 18(12):717–721, Dec. 1975.

[LLPY97] K.G. Larsen, F. Larsson, P. Pettersson, and W. Yi. Efficient verification of real-time systems: Compact data structure and state-space reduction. In *Proc. 18th IEEE Real-Time Systems Symposium*, pages 14–24, San Francisco, California, Dec. 1997.

[McM95]   K.L. McMillan. A technique of a state space search based on unfolding. *Formal Methods in System Design*, 6(1):45–65, 1995.

[Pel96]   D. Peled. Combining Partial Order Reductions with On-the-fly Model-Checking. *Journal of Formal Methods in Systems Design*, 8 (1996), 39–64.

[Val90]   A. Valmari. Stubborn sets for reduced state space generation. In *Advances in Petri Nets*, number 483 in Lecture Notes in Computer Science, pages 491–515. Springer-Verlag, 1990.

[Val93]   A. Valmari. On-the-fly verification with stubborn sets. In Courcoubetis, editor, *Proc. 5th Int. Conf. on Computer Aided Verification*, number 697 in Lecture Notes in Computer Science, pages 59–70, 1993.

Correctness of the Concurrent Approach to Symbolic Verification of Interleaved Models

Felice Balarin

Cadence Berkeley Laboratories
Berkeley, CA, USA

Abstract. Interleaved models of computations limit the number of system components that can change states simultaneously. This restriction often decreases efficiency of symbolic verification methods based on binary decision diagrams. We propose to ignore this restriction, and allow all components to change states simultaneously. This approach may result in an over-approximation of reachable states. We show that if a system satisfies certain conditions, then the approach computes reachable states exactly. We also show that even if a system does not meet these conditions, it is still possible to compute its reachable states exactly by only partially removing interleaving restrictions. We present experiments that show that the approach improves efficiency of symbolic verification, even when costs of correctness testing are taken into account.

1 Introduction

Finite-state models can be classified based on rules for deriving behaviors of systems from behaviors of components. Roughly, the models are divided into two classes: *interleaved* and *concurrent*. In interleaved models (sometimes also called asynchronous, or disjunctive), a transition of the system corresponds to a transition of a single, or a small number of related components [5, 4, 10, 7]. On the other hand, in concurrent models (sometimes also called synchronous, or conjunctive, or simultaneous), a transition of the system corresponds to transitions of all, or an arbitrary number of components [6, 11, 2]. Traditionally, interleaved models are used for modeling software and asynchronous hardware, while concurrent models are used for synchronous hardware. This distinction is not fundamental: it is quite easy to develop methods for embedding models from one class into another.

The two classes also differ in approaches to their verification. Formal verification tools based on interleaved models typically employ explicit state space search [4, 7], while those based on concurrent models often use symbolic search based on *binary decision diagrams (BDDs)* [11, 2]. While not fundamental, this distinction has some practical justification. On one side, interleaved models are better for explicit search because they require enumerating enabled transitions, while concurrent models require enumerating all subsets of enabled transitions. On the other side, the requirement that only a single component executes at a time, may cause artificial correlation between components, which may decrease the efficiency of the symbolic search [3, 1].

Motivated by excellent performance of symbolic search methods on concurrent models, there have been several attempts to improve symbolic search for interleaved models. They are either based on extending partial-order methods to symbolic search [1, 8], or on changing the order of symbolic search to avoid the artificial-correlation problem [3].

Here, we pursue a different approach, where a system in an interleaved model is analyzed as if its components were composed in a concurrent model. The approach was originally suggested in [3]. It was noted there the approach may produce incorrect results, but rather than exploring the problem further, the authors only remarked that no discrepancies occurred on the set of examples they were considering.

In this paper, we give a characterization of systems for which the concurrent approach is correct. We note that checking exact correctness conditions is hard, and propose several sufficient tests. One of the proposed tests, when it fails, produces a side-result, which may be used to perform correct symbolic search on a model which allows less simultaneous transitions than the concurrent, but still more than the interleaved model. The test is of polynomial complexity, and our experiments indicate that its cost may be more than justified by savings from using the concurrent approach.

In the rest of this paper we first set the context in Section 2. Then, we give the correctness criteria in Section 3, and propose sufficient correctness checks in Section 4. An example is introduced in Section 5, and some experimental results are presented in Section 6. Final comments are given in Section 7.

2 Preliminaries

In this section we present an interleaved model of computation. The details of the model are chosen to simplify the presentation of our approach, but the approach is not specific to the presented model. It is quite straightforward to develop similar approaches for other interleaved models of computation.

A *system* is a finite collection of *processes*. Each process P_i is given by:

- the *present state variable* $\mathbf{ps}_i$ and the *next state variable* $\mathbf{ns}_i$ both ranging over some finite set of *local states*; we use $\mathbf{ps}$ ($\mathbf{ns}$) to denote the vector containing all present (next) state variables, and refer to their valuations as global states,
- the *initial states* predicate $\mathbf{I}_i$ in variable $\mathbf{ps}_i$,
- the *transition relation* predicate $\mathbf{T}_i$ in variables $\mathbf{ps}$ and $\mathbf{ns}_i$.

Note that $\mathbf{T}_i$ can depend on all present state variables in $\mathbf{ps}$, i.e. the processes communicate by observing states of other processes.

An *execution* of the system is any finite sequence $s_0, s_1, \ldots, s_n$ of global states such that:

1. for all processes P_i: $s_{0,i}$ satisfies $\mathbf{I}_i$, and
2. for every $j = 1, \ldots, n$ there exists a process P_i such that $(s_{j-1}, s_{j,i})$ satisfies $\mathbf{T}_i$ and $s_{j-1,k} = s_{j,k}$ for all $k \neq i$.

Given a system consisting of processes P_i, we say that a *composition* of P_i's is any process that has vector **ps** of the present state variables of P_i's as its present state variable, vector **ns** as its next state variable, and the initial states predicate $\bigwedge_i I_i$. In particular, we define the *interleaved composition* $P_\parallel$ to be the composition with the transition relation predicate:

$$\mathbf{T}_\parallel = \bigvee_i \left(\mathbf{T}_i \wedge \bigwedge_{j \neq i} (\mathbf{ps}_j = \mathbf{ns}_j) \right) , \tag{1}$$

and the *concurrent composition* $P_\times$ to be the composition with the transition relation predicate:

$$\mathbf{T}_\times = \bigwedge_i (\mathbf{T}_i \vee (\mathbf{ps}_i = \mathbf{ns}_i)) . \tag{2}$$

Intuitively, while $\mathbf{T}_\parallel$ requires that at every step exactly one process executes, $\mathbf{T}_\times$ allows any number of processes (including zero) to execute in any step. It is not hard to see that a collection of processes has the same executions as their interleaved composition.

A global state of a system is said to be *reachable* if it appears in some execution of the system. Computing reachable states is the crucial step in formal verification of safety properties of systems. It is well known that reachable states can be computed by the following fix-point computation:

Algorithm REACH
1. $\mathbf{R} := \bigwedge_i I_i$;

    repeat
2. $\mathbf{R} := \mathbf{R} \vee [\exists \mathbf{ps} : \mathbf{R} \wedge \mathbf{T}_\parallel]_{\mathbf{ns} \leftarrow \mathbf{ps}}$;
    until convergence

(We use $[\mathbf{P}]_{\mathbf{x} \leftarrow \mathbf{y}}$ to denote the predicate obtained by replacing every occurrence of **x** in **P** with **y**.)

After k iterations, **R** represents exactly those states which appear in some execution of length k or less. This means that even if all P_i's are independent, their present state variables will be correlated in **R** (because they must satisfy the *interleaving constraint* that the sum of number of transitions in individual processes is less or equal to k). This correlation may cause the BDD representation of **R** to grow [3, 1]. In practice, it is often possible to weaken the correlation by computing the fix-point in a somewhat different order, using a partition of $\mathbf{T}_\parallel$ [3].

In this paper, we pursue a different approach where $\mathbf{T}_\parallel$ is replaced with $\mathbf{T}_\times$ in step 2 of algorithm REACH. We refer to this modification of REACH as algorithm CONCUR. Algorithm CONCUR may improve on REACH in several ways:

- $\mathbf{T}_\times$ may have a smaller BDD representation than $\mathbf{T}_\parallel$ ((2) is certainly simpler than (1), however this does not necessarily translate to a smaller BDD representation),
- algorithm CONCUR may require fewer iterations than REACH,
- intermediate representation $\mathbf{R}$ of reachable states may be simpler in CONCUR because the interleaving constraint is removed.

Of course, these are all heuristics, and it is possible to construct examples where REACH is more efficient than CONCUR, but we will show in Section 6 that these heuristics are supported by experiments.

3 Correctness of the Concurrent Approach

Algorithm CONCUR may not compute reachable states correctly. In this section, we will first show that it always computes a superset of reachable states, and then establish some sufficient conditions, such that if a system satisfies them, then CONCUR computes reachable states exactly. Finally, we will show that in case these conditions are not met, it is still possible to construct a composition that is more concurrent than $P_\parallel$ (thus retaining some benefits of $P_\times$), but has the same reachable states as $P_\parallel$.

Proposition 1. *Let P' be some composition of P_i's, and let $\mathbf{T}'$ be its transition relation predicate. If $\mathbf{T}_\parallel \Rightarrow \mathbf{T}'$ is valid, then every execution of $P_\parallel$ is also an execution of P'.*

The proof is straightforward from the definition of an execution.

It is easy to check that $\mathbf{T}_\parallel \Rightarrow \mathbf{T}_\times$ is valid. Thus, the following result holds by Proposition 1.

Corollary 2. *Every state reachable in $P_\parallel$ is also reachable in $P_\times$.*

Before we examine when the opposite holds, we need some definitions. We call a pair of global states a *global transition*. A global transition that satisfies the transition relation of some process P is said to be *enabled* in P. Given a transition (s, q), its set of *active processes* is defined by:

$$\{P_i \mid s_i \neq q_i\} \ .$$

We say that a sequence $s_0, \ldots, s_N$ of global states is a *serialization* of some global transition (s, q) if:

- $s_0 = s$, $s_N = q$, N is the number of active processes of (s, q), and
- there exists an ordering $P_{i_1}, \ldots, P_{i_N}$ of active processes of (s, q) such that for every $j = 1, \ldots, N$:
  - (s_{j-1}, s_{j,i_j}) satisfies $\mathbf{T}_{i_j}$, and
  - for all $k \neq i_j$: $s_{j-1,k} = s_{j,k}$.

A composition of P_i's is *serializable* iff every enabled transition in every one of its reachable states has a serialization.

Proposition 3. *If a composition P' of P_i's is serializable, then every state reachable in P' is also reachable in $P_\parallel$.*

Indeed, if a state s is reachable in P' it must appear in some execution r' of P'. From r', we can construct an execution r of $P_\parallel$, by (i) replacing every transition in r' with its serialization, and (ii) eliminating any adjacent occurrences of the same state. Obviously, s also appears in r, thus it is reachable in $P_\parallel$.

Corollary 4. *If $P_\times$ is serializable, then it has the same reachable states as $P_\parallel$.*

If $P_\times$ is not serializable, algorithm CONCUR can be used to compute an over-approximation of reachable states. Or, the concurrent approach may be modified, as indicated by the following result.

Proposition 5. *If P' is a composition of P_i's such that:*

- *it is serializable,*
- *its transition relation predicate has the form $\mathbf{T}_\times \wedge \neg \mathbf{C}$, where $\mathbf{C}$ is such that any global transition satisfying $\mathbf{C}$ has at least two active processes,*

then, P' has the same reachable states as $P_\parallel$.

By Proposition 3 states reachable in P' are also reachable in $P_\parallel$, because P' is serializable. To prove the opposite, observe that any global transition satisfying $\mathbf{T}_\parallel$ has at most one active process. It follows that $\mathbf{T}_\parallel \wedge \mathbf{C}$ is not satisfiable. From this fact and the validity of $\mathbf{T}_\parallel \Rightarrow \mathbf{T}_\times$, we have that $\mathbf{T}_\parallel \Rightarrow (\mathbf{T}_\times \wedge \neg \mathbf{C})$ is valid, and the desired result is immediate from Proposition 1.

In the following section we will propose a conservative serializability test, which as a side-product computes $\mathbf{C}$ satisfying the conditions of Proposition 5.

4 Checking Serializability

Deciding whether a process is serializable is a hard problem in general. It can be shown that just checking whether a single global transition has a serialization, is NP-complete. Fortunately, we rarely have to solve the general problem. It is possible that some modeling style generate only serializable systems. An example of such a style is the model of asynchronous circuits presented in [5]. It is also well known that any system can be made serializable by refining the granularity of its transitions [10]. However, this may unacceptably increase its size.

Often, it is possible to define simple syntactic sufficient serializability tests. For example, if in our model of computation local state spaces are decomposed into observable and hidden components, and any transition that changes observable states depends only on the local state, then $P_\times$ is serializable. This check can be performed locally on $\mathbf{T}_i$'s. It is similar to a single-reference rule in [10].

Serializability can also be established by analyzing the dependency graph of the system, in which nodes correspond to processes, and there is an edge (i, j) whenever $\mathbf{T}_j$ depends on $\mathbf{ps}_i$. If the graph of the system is acyclic, then the system is serializable. In this case, we may use a fixed serialization order, such that a process is always executed after all the processes that depend on it.

4.1 A test based on disabling

Next, we will present a slightly more complex sufficient serializability test. The complexity of this test is quadratic in the number of processes. If a system is not serializable, the results of the test can be used to modify $P_\times$ as in Proposition 5.

The key concept in the test is transitions disabling one another. First, we formally define a *local transition* of some process P_i as a predicate of the form $\mathbf{ps}_i = s \wedge \mathbf{ns}_i = q$, where s and q are two *distinct* local states of P_i.

We say that a local transition $\mathbf{t}$ *may disable* some other local transition $\mathbf{u}$ in some other process, if there exists a global state in which they are both enabled, but $\mathbf{u}$ is no longer enabled if (only) $\mathbf{t}$ is executed. Formally, the *disable relation* $Dsbl$ contains all pairs $(\mathbf{t}, \mathbf{u})$ such that $\mathbf{t}$ is a local transition of some process P_i, $\mathbf{u}$ is a local transition of some different process P_j, and

$$\mathbf{T}_i \wedge \mathbf{T}_j \wedge \neg [\mathbf{T}_j] \mathbf{ps}_i \leftarrow \mathbf{ns}_i \wedge \mathbf{t} \wedge \mathbf{u}$$

is satisfiable.

Proposition 6. *If the disable relation is acyclic, then $P_\times$ is serializable.*

If the disable relation is acyclic, then it induces a partial order on active process of some transition. To serialize that transition, we may choose any total ordering of active processes that is consistent with the inverse of that partial order. In other words, given a set active processes, we always choose to execute one that may not disable any other still active process. Since the disable relation is assumed to be acyclic, such a choice is always possible.

Proposition 7. *If $Cut \subseteq Dsbl$ is such that $Dsbl - Cut$ is acyclic, then the composition of P_i's with the transition relation predicate:*

$$\mathbf{T}_\times \wedge \neg \bigvee_{(\mathbf{t},\mathbf{u}) \in Cut} \mathbf{t} \wedge \mathbf{u} \tag{3}$$

has the same reachable states as $P_\parallel$.

This result follows from Proposition 5. To apply this proposition, we need to show that:

- any global transition satisfying $\bigvee_{(\mathbf{t},\mathbf{u}) \in Cut} \mathbf{t} \wedge \mathbf{u}$ has at least two active processes,
- the composition of P_i's with the transition relation (3) is serializable.

The former is straightforward, and to show the latter observe that any set of local transitions that form a cycle in *Dsbl* must contain at least one pair of transitions in *Cut*, but (3) ensures that no pair of transitions in *Cut* may appear in the same global transition.

The size of *Dsbl* is at worst quadratic in the total number of local transitions, which is obviously linear in the number of processes. Checking whether *Dsbl* is acyclic can be done in linear time, by a simple traversal of its graph. The same traversal may be used to generate the *Cut* set. It is a reasonable heuristic to keep *Cut* small, but finding the smallest *Cut* is not practical, because it is known to be NP-complete.

In case the number of local transitions is much larger than the number of processes, it may be more efficient to find the cut predicate $\mathbf{C}$ using the following modification of the Floyd-Warshall algorithm [9], which avoids explicit enumeration of local transitions:

Algorithm CUT
1. $\mathbf{C} := \textit{false}$;
    for each pair of processes P_i, P_j such that $i \neq j$
2. $\mathbf{D}^*_{i,j} := \mathbf{D}_{i,j} := \mathbf{T}_i \wedge \mathbf{T}_j \wedge \neg[\mathbf{T}_j]\mathbf{ps}_i \leftarrow \mathbf{ns}_i \wedge \mathbf{ps}_j \neq \mathbf{ns}_j$;
    rof
    for each process P_i $i = 1, 2, \ldots$
        for each process $P_j \neq P_i$
            if $j < i$ **then**
3. $\mathbf{C} := \mathbf{C} \vee \left(\mathbf{D}_{i,j} \wedge \mathbf{D}^*_{j,i} \right)$;
            fi
            for each process $P_k \neq P_i, P_j$
4. $\mathbf{D}^*_{j,k} := \mathbf{D}^*_{j,k} \vee \exists \mathbf{ps}_i, \mathbf{ns}_i : \left(\mathbf{D}^*_{j,i} \wedge \mathbf{D}^*_{i,k} \right)$;
            rof
        rof
    rof

Intuitively, predicate $\mathbf{D}_{i,j}$ characterizes the portion of *Dsbl* corresponding to processes P_i and P_j, and $\mathbf{D}^*_{i,j}$ eventually characterizes its transitive closure. After the i-th pass through the main loop, a pair of local transitions in P_j and P_k satisfies $\mathbf{D}^*_{j,k}$ iff there exists a path between them in *Dsbl* that does not visit any process with index higher than i.

At the end, the cut predicate $\mathbf{C}$ characterizes at most one pair of local transitions per each independent cycle in *Dsbl*. Of course, it is not necessarily the smallest such set.

There may be some cycles in *Dsbl* that are not cut by $\mathbf{C}$, but any such cycle must include two local transitions of the same process. Since transitions of the same process cannot occur simultaneously even in $\mathbf{T}_\times$, it follows that $\mathbf{T}_\times \wedge \neg \mathbf{C}$ still satisfies conditions of Proposition 5.

There is an interesting relation between the proposed algorithm and partial-order reduction methods such as [13]. These methods attempt to accelerate state space search by not executing all enabled transitions in a state. Instead, the so-called *ample* set of transition is chosen to be executed, such that every transition not in the ample set is independent of all the transitions in it. Our approach has similar objectives, except that it attempts to execute in one step as many transitions as possible, rather than trying to execute only a subset of transitions. Since the cut predicate **C** prevents only a subset of transitions in *Dsbl* from executing concurrently, and since all the pairs of transitions in *Dsbl* are dependent, it follows that whenever a partial order method can execute only one transition from a pair, our algorithm will execute both of them in one step.

The disabling based test is less conservative than the test based on decomposing the state space into observable and hidden components. Note that hidden transition can never disable any other transitions (because they are not observable). Also note that observable transitions can never be disabled (because we assume they depend only on the local state). These two observations imply that the disable relation is acyclic.

The disabling based test is also less conservative than the test based on the dependency graph. In fact, the dependency graph may be seen as an abstraction of the disable relation where all transitions of the same process are merged into a single node.

5 An Example

Consider the system shown in Figure 1. A typical process P_i starts in the initial state 0, moves to 1 if its left neighbor is in state 0, then moves to 2 if its right neighbor is in state 1, and finally returns to the initial state to repeat this behavior indefinitely. Boundary processes P_1 and P_N are similar, except that their state changes are unconditional, if their neighbors do not exist.

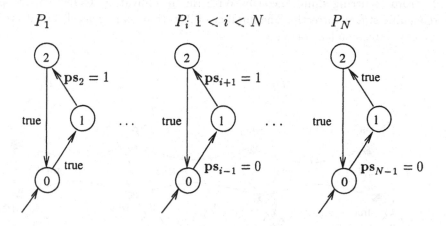

Fig. 1. A system with N processes.

The example in Figure 1 is constructed to highlight circumstances in which the concurrent symbolic verification approach out-performs other approaches. First, observe that partial order methods are of little use in this example because most of the transitions are dependent. For comparison to other symbolic approaches, it is useful to analyze how the system can reach the state in which all processes are in state 2. That state is interesting because it is hard to reach, in the sense that the REACH algorithm reaches it later than any other state. The shortest path to that state requires $2N$ process executions in the following order:

$$P_1, P_2, \ldots, P_N, P_N, P_{N-1}, \ldots, P_1 .$$

Thus, the REACH algorithm requires $2N + 1$ iterations (the last one to ensure that no new states are added). Approaches based on partitioning the transition relation can reduce this number, but since they typically process individual transition relations in a fixed order, at least one half of the sequence above will be in the wrong order, and they will still require $O(N)$ iterations.

On the other hand, the CONCUR requires only 3 iterations, since state $(2, \ldots, 2)$ can be reached in two steps, first by executing concurrently all processes to reach state $(1, \ldots, 1)$, and then executing all of them once more to reach $(2, \ldots, 2)$.

It is not hard to see that the $Dsbl$ relation is acyclic in this case. For example, the graph of the $Dsbl$ relation for the system with 4 processes is shown in Figure 2. However, if P_1 is modified so that it can move from state 0 only if P_N is in state 0, the $Dsbl$ relation would have a cycle containing $0 \to 1$ transitions of all the processes. The CONCUR would now compute a strict superset of reachable states. For example, it would indicate that state $(1, \ldots, 1)$ is reachable, even though in every truly reachable state at least one process must be in state 0. To fix this problem it suffices to choose $Cut = \{(\mathbf{ps}_1 = 0 \wedge \mathbf{ns}_1 = 1, \mathbf{ps}_2 = 0 \wedge \mathbf{ns}_2 = 1)\}$ and to modify $\mathbf{T}_\times$ as in (3). This would prevent $0 \to 1$ transitions in P_1 and P_2 from occurring simultaneously. With this modification, CONCUR computes reachable states correctly. The number of iterations is increased, but it is still a constant independent of N.

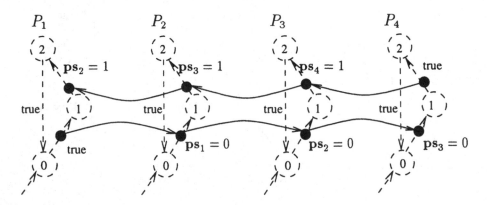

Fig. 2. The graph of the disable relation.

6   Experiments

We have implemented algorithms REACH, CUT, and a modification of algorithm CONCUR where $\mathbf{T}_\times$ has been modified as in Proposition 5, using the cut predicate $\mathbf{C}$ computed by CUT. We have named this algorithm CON_CUT. Of course, if the disable relation is acyclic, CUT will compute $\mathbf{C} = false$, and CON_CUT becomes CONCUR. For comparison purposes, we have also implemented an algorithm we call PART, which is an exact reachability algorithm based on partitioning $\mathbf{T}_\parallel$, similar to those discussed in [3]. All algorithms are implemented on top of the same BDD package [12]. We note that the partitioning approach could also apply to CON_CUT, but we do not have any experimental results for that combination.

We have applied these algorithms to two groups of examples: a cyclic version of the example described in Section 5, and an asynchronous tree arbiter described in [5]. The latter arbitrates access to a shared resource among 2^n processors. It is configured as a binary tree of $2^n - 1$ cells, each arbitrating between two processors, or two cells at a lower level of the tree.

Table 1. Results for the example from Section 5.

alg.	# of processes				
	10	20	30	40	50
CUT	1.3s	10s	34s	82s	160s
CON_CUT	.03s	.07s	.11s	.16s	.23s
REACH	.23s	1.6s	7.9s	17s	98s
PART	.48s	6.5s	50s	225s	719s

Execution times for the example in Section 5 are summarized in Table 1. As expected, the concurrent approach significantly outperforms other approaches. Furthermore, CON_CUT requires only seven iterations, regardless of the number of processes. Also, intermediate sets of reachable states generated by CON_CUT had smaller BDDs than those generated by REACH or PART. In this case, CUT is not an efficient way to check serializability. In fact, it is less expensive to compute reachable states with REACH than to compute the cut predicate $\mathbf{C}$ with CUT. However, with only three transition per process, and the disable relation that grows linearly with the number of processes, this example is well suited for explicit traversal of the disable relation.

Execution times for the tree arbiter are shown in Table 2. Again, CON_CUT outperforms REACH and PART. In this case, the disable relation is acyclic, so CUT serves only as a proof of correctness, but it is not required for computing reachable states. Note that for 16 or more processors combined run times of CUT and CON_CUT are shorter than run times of REACH or PART. Furthermore, the run time of CUT grows slower than run times of other algorithms.

Table 2. Results for the asynchronous tree arbiter.

alg.	# of processors			
	4	8	16	32
CUT	.34s	2.7s	21s	172s
CON_CUT	.05s	.41s	9.9s	695s
REACH	.09s	2s	391s	>5h
PART	.14s	1.9s	81s	1h

7 Conclusions and Future Work

We have shown that relaxing interleaving requirements may improve efficiency of symbolic verification, but it may also lead to incorrect (too conservative, to be precise) verification results. We have proposed several correctness tests, and showed that results of one of these can be used to only partially relax interleaving requirements in a manner that guarantees correctness.

All proposed tests try to establish a priori that the concurrent approach is correct for the system at hand. There is also an alternative where one applies the concurrent approach without any checks. If the computed set of reachable states contains no unsafe states, the system is declared correct. If that is not the case, the verification tool produces a path from some of the initial states to some of the unsafe states. It that path contains only serializable transitions, the system is declared incorrect. Otherwise, the transitions in the path that are not serializable are eliminated from $\mathbf{T}_\times$ as in (3), and the procedure is repeated.

It is not hard to show that the described procedure terminates in a finite number of iterations. However, the provable bound is of little practical use, because the procedure will be competitive to other approaches only if the number of iterations is much smaller than in the worst case.

Results of this paper are applicable to verification of safety properties, but the approach could (and should in the future) be extended to liveness properties as well. The future work should also include more experiments to better understand when the proposed approach is beneficial.

References

1. Rajeev Alur, R. K. BraytonT. A. Henzinger, S. Qadeer, et al. Partial-order reduction in symbolic state space exploration. In O. Grumberg, editor, *Proceedings of Computer Aided Verification: 9th International Conference, CAV'97, Haifa, Israel, 22-25 June*. Springer-Verlag, 1997. LNCS vol. 1254.
2. R.K. Brayton, A. Sangiovanni-Vincentelli, G.D. Hachtel, F. Somenzi, A. Aziz, S.-T. Cheng, S. Edwards, S. Khatri, Y. Kukimoto, S. Qadeer, R.K. Ranjan, T.R. Shiple, G. Swamy, T. Villa, A. Pardo, and S. Sarwary. VIS: A system for verification and synthesis. In Rajeev Alur and Thomas A. Henzinger, editors, *Proceedings of Computer Aided Verification: 8th International Conference, CAV'96, Rutgers, NJ, July, 1996*. Springer-Verlag, 1996. LNCS vol. 1102.

3. J. R. Burch, Edmund M. Clarke, David E. Long, Ken L. McMillan, and David L. Dill. Symbolic model checking for sequential circuit verification. *IEEE Transactions on Computer–Aided Design of Integrated Circuits and Systems*, 13(4):401–24, April 1994.

4. D. L. Dill, A. J. Drexler, A. J. Hu, and C. H. Yang. Protocol Verification as a Hardware Design Aid. In *Proceedings of ICCD*, pages 522–525, October 1992.

5. D.L. Dill. *Trace Theory for Automatic Hierarchical Verification of Speed-Independent Circuits*. The MIT Press, Cambridge, Mass., 1988. An ACM Distinguished Dissertation 1988.

6. Z. Har'El and R. P. Kurshan. Software for analysis of coordination. In *Proceedings of the International Conference on System Science*, pages 382–385, 1988.

7. Gerard J. Holzmann. *Design and validation of computer protocols*. Englewood Cliffs, N.J. : Prentice Hall, 1991.

8. R. P. Kurshan, V. Levin, M. Minea, D. Peled, et al. Verifying hardware in its software context. In *Digest of Technical Papers of the 1997 IEEE International Conference on CAD*, pages 742–9, November 1997.

9. Eugene L. Lawler. *Combinatorial optimization : networks and matroids*. Holt, Rinehart and Winston, 1976.

10. Zohar Manna and Anir Pnueli. Verification of concurrent programs: The temporal framework. In R. Boyer and J. Moore, editors, *Correctness Problem in Computer Science*, pages 215–273. Academic Press, 1981.

11. Kenneth L. McMillan. *Symbolic Model Checking*. Kluwer Academic Publishers, 1993.

12. F. Somenzi. CUDD : CU Decision Diagram Package, June 1996. User's Manual.

13. P. Wolper and P. Godefroid. Partial-order methods for temporal verification. In E. Best, editor, *Proceedings of CONCUR '93. 4th International Conference on Concurrency Theory, Hildesheim, Germany, 23-26 Aug.* Springer-Verlag, 1993.

Verification of Timed Systems Using POSETs *

Wendy Belluomini[1] and Chris J. Myers[2]

[1] Computer Science Department
[2] Electrical Engineering Department
University of Utah
Salt Lake City, UT 84112

Abstract. This paper presents a new algorithm for efficiently verifying timed systems. The new algorithm represents timing information using geometric regions and explores the timed state space by considering partially ordered sets of events rather than linear sequences. This approach avoids the explosion of timed states typical of highly concurrent systems by dramatically reducing the ratio of timed states to untimed states in a system. A general class of timed systems which include both event and level causality can be specified and verified. This algorithm is applied to several recent timed benchmarks showing orders of magnitude improvement in runtime and memory usage.

1 Introduction

The fundamental difficulty in verification is controlling the state explosion problem. The state spaces involved in verifying reasonably sized systems are large even if the timing behavior of the system is not considered. The problem gets even more complex when verification is done on timed systems. However, verification with timing is crucial to applications such as asynchronous circuits and real-time systems.

A number of techniques have been proposed to deal with state explosion. Approaches have been proposed that use stubborn sets [1], partial orders [2], or unfolding [3]. These techniques reduces the number of states explored by considering only a subset of the possible interleavings between events. These approaches have been successful, but they only deal with untimed verification.

The state space of timed systems is even larger than the state space of untimed systems and has been more difficult to reduce. The representation of the timing information has a huge impact on the growth of the state space. Timing behavior can either be modeled continuously (i.e., dense-time), where the timers in the system can take on any value between their lower and upper bounds, or discretely, where timers can only take on values that are multiples of a discretization constant. Discrete time has the advantage that the timing analysis technique is simpler and implicit techniques can be easily applied to improve performance [4, 5]. However, the state space explodes if the delay ranges are large and the discretization constant is set small enough to ensure exact exploration of the state space.

* This research is supported by a grant from Intel Corporation, NSF CAREER award MIP-9625014, SRC grant 97-DJ-487, and a DARPA AASERT fellowship.

Continuous time techniques eliminate the need for a discretization constant by breaking the infinite continuous timed state space into equivalence classes. All timing assignments within an equivalence class lead to the same behavior and do not need to be explored separately. In order to reduce the size of the state space, the size of the equivalence classes should be as large as possible. In the *unit-cube* (or region) approach [6], timed states with the same integral clock values and a particular linear ordering of the fractional values of the clocks are considered equivalent. Although this approach eliminates the need to discretize time, the number of timed states is dependent on the size of the delay ranges and can explode if they are large.

Another approach to continuous time is to represent the equivalence classes as convex *geometric regions* (or zones) [7–9]. These geometric regions can be represented by sets of linear inequalities (also known as *difference bound matrices* or DBMs). These larger equivalence classes can often result in smaller state spaces than those generated by the unit-cube approach.

While geometric methods are efficient for some problems, their complexity can be worse than either discrete or unit-cube methods when analyzing highly concurrent systems. The number of geometric regions can explode with these approaches since each untimed state has at least one geometric region associated with it for every firing sequence that can result in that state. In highly concurrent systems where many interleavings are possible, the number of geometric regions per untimed state can be huge. Some researchers [10–12] have attacked this problem by reducing the number of interleavings explored using the partial order techniques developed for untimed systems. These algorithms reduce verification time by exploring only part of the timed state space, but this may limit the timing properties that can be verified. While reducing the number of interleavings is useful, in [10, 11] one region is still required for every firing sequence explored to reach a state. If most interleavings need to be explored, these techniques could still result in state explosion.

The algorithm presented in [13, 14] significantly reduces the number of regions per untimed state by using *partially ordered sets* (or POSETs) of events rather than linear sequences to construct the geometric regions. Using this technique, untimed states do not have an associated region for every firing sequence. Instead, the algorithm generates only one geometric region for any set of firing sequences that differ only in the firing order of concurrent events. This algorithm is shown in [14] to result in very few geometric regions per untimed state. The entire timed state space is explored, so it can be used to verify a wide range of timing properties. However, it is limited to specifications where the firing time of an event can only be controlled by a single predecessor event (known as the *single behavioral place (or rule) restriction*). This restriction can be worked around with graph transformations, but the graph transformations add $n!$ new rules for each event with n behavioral rules[15, 16]. In [17], we presented an approximate algorithm for exploring the entire state space with POSETs on a general class of specifications, lifting the single behavioral rule restriction. However, it may generate regions that are larger than necessary.

This paper presents a new algorithm for timed state space exploration based on geometric regions and POSETs. This algorithm operates on a very general class of specifications, *timed event/level (TEL) structures* [18], which are capable of directly expressing both event and level causality. Through a straightforward construction (omitted due to space constraints), it can be shown that TEL structures are at least as expressive as 1-safe time Petri nets [19]. TEL structures can also represent some behavior more concisely due to their ability to specify levels which are not directly supported in time Petri nets. While they are not as expressive as timed automata [6], TEL structures represent an interesting class of timed automata sufficient to accurately model timed circuit behavior. Unlike the partial order techniques discussed earlier, the POSET timing algorithm does explore every interleaving between event firings, and therefore explores all states of the system. This new algorithm dramatically improves the performance of geometric region based techniques on highly concurrent systems, making dense-time verification extremely competitive with discrete-time when the delay ranges are small and far superior when the ranges are large. The performance of POSET timing is demonstrated by orders of magnitude improvement in runtime and memory usage on several recent timing verification benchmarks.

2 Timed systems and exploration of their timed states

The process of timing verification begins with a specification of a timed system and properties that it must satisfy. To check if these properties are satisfied, the verification algorithm explores the timed state space allowed by the specification. This section presents our formalism for modeling timed systems and exploring their state spaces.

2.1 Timed event/level structures

The algorithm presented in this paper is applied to specifications in the form of TEL structures [18], an extension of timed event-rule structures [15]. TEL structures are very well suited to describing asynchronous circuits since they allow both event causality to specify sequencing and level causality to specify bit value sampling. This section gives a brief overview of TEL structures. See [18] for a more complete description of their semantics. A TEL structure is a tuple $T = \langle N, s_0, A, E, R, \# \rangle$ where:

1. N is the set of signals;
2. $s_0 = \{0, 1\}^N$ is the initial state;
3. $A \subseteq N \times \{+, -\} \cup \$$ is the set of atomic actions;
4. $E \subseteq A \times (\mathcal{N} = \{0, 1, 2...\})$ is the set of events;
5. $R \subseteq E \times E \times \mathcal{N} \times (\mathcal{N} \cup \{\infty\}) \times (b : \{0, 1\}^N \to \{0, 1\})$ is the set of rules;
6. $\# \subseteq E \times E$ is the conflict relation.

The signal set, N, contains the wires in the specification. The state s_0 contains the initial value of each signal in N. The action set, A, contains for each signal, x, in N, a rising transition, $x+$, and a falling transition, $x-$. The set A also includes a dummy event, \$, which is used to indicate an action that does not result in a signal transition. The event set, E, contains actions paired with occurrence indices (i.e., $\langle a, i \rangle$). Rules represent causality between events. Each rule, r, is of the form $\langle e, f, l, u, b \rangle$ where:

1. e = enabling event,
2. f = enabled event,
3. $\langle l, u \rangle$ = bounded timing constraint, and
4. b = a sum-of-products boolean function over the signals in N.

A rule is *enabled* if its enabling event has occurred and its boolean function is true in the current state. A rule is *satisfied* if it has been enabled at least l time units. A rule becomes *expired* when it has been enabled u time units. Excluding conflicts, an event cannot occur until every rule enabling it is satisfied, and it must occur before every rule enabling it has expired. If a rule's boolean function becomes false after the rule has become enabled, but before its enabled event has occurred, this indicates that the enabled event has a hazard which is considered a failure during verification.

The conflict relation, #, is used to model disjunctive behavior and choice. When two events e and e' are in conflict (denoted $e\#e'$), this specifies that either e or e' can occur but not both. Taking the conflict relation into account, if two rules have the same enabled event and conflicting enabling events, then only one of the two mutually exclusive enabling events needs to occur to cause the enabled event. This models a form of disjunctive causality. Choice is modeled when two rules have the same enabling event and conflicting enabled events. In this case, only one of the enabled events can occur.

If a specification is cyclic, then the TEL structure representing it is infinite. However, due to its repetitive nature, this infinite behavior can be described with a finite model by adding an additional set of rules and conflicts which recursively defines the infinite structure [15].

2.2 Timed state space exploration

The *untimed state* of a TEL structure is composed of two parts: the set of rules whose enabling events have occurred, R_m, and the state, s_c, of all the signals in the system. From this untimed state, the set of enabled rules, R_{en}, can be constructed by including only those members of R_m whose boolean expressions are satisfied by s_c. In order to determine the set of satisfied rules R_s, timing information is needed. It is referred to as *TI* and is included in the *timed state* $(R_m \times s_c \times TI)$.

The state space of a TEL structure is explored using a depth first search. In each state, the algorithm chooses a rule from R_s to fire, and places onto the stack the current state and the remainder of R_s. It then fires the chosen rule, adds it to a set of fired rules, R_f, which is part of the timing information, and determines the new timed state. If R_f contains a set of rules sufficient to fire an event e, the new timed state has a marking in which e has fired. If this timed state has not been seen before, it is added to the state space, and a new R_s is calculated. If a timed state is reached that has been seen before, the algorithm pops off the stack a timed state and the list of rules that have not yet been explored for that state. When a state that has been seen before is reached and the stack is empty, the entire timed state space has been found.

The timing information must be updated at every rule firing during state space exploration. Therefore, it is very important that the procedure for updating it is efficient. The timing analysis algorithm presented here uses geometric regions to represent the timing information within a timed state. Whenever a rule r_i becomes enabled, a clock c_i is created to be used in timing analysis. The minimum and maximum age differences of all the clocks associated with rules in R_{en} are stored in a constraint matrix M. Each entry m_{ij} in the matrix M has the value $max(c_j - c_i)$, which is the maximum age difference of the clocks. A dummy clock c_0 whose age is uniquely 0 is used to allow the inclusion of the minimum and maximum ages of the clocks in M. In other words, the maximum age of c_i is in the entry m_{0i}, and the negative of the minimum age of c_i is in the entry m_{i0}. Note that M only needs to contain information on the timing of the rules that are currently in R_{en}, not on the whole set of rules. This particular way of representing timed regions was first introduced in [7]. This constraint matrix represents a convex $|R_{en}|$ dimensional region. Each dimension corresponds to a rule and the firing times of the rule can be anywhere within the space.

3 Timed state space exploration using POSET timing

While geometric regions are an effective way to represent dense-time state spaces, the number of geometric regions can explode for highly concurrent timed systems [14, 5]. In [14], an algorithm is described that uses *partially ordered sets* (POSETs) of events rather than linear sequences to mitigate this state explosion problem. POSET timing techniques take advantage of the inherent concurrency in the TEL structure and prevent additional regions from being added for different sequences of event firings that lead to the same untimed state. This results in a compression of the state space into fewer, larger geometric regions that, taken together, contain the same region in space as the set of regions generated by the standard geometric technique. Therefore, all properties of the system that can be verified with the standard geometric technique can be verified with the POSET algorithm. This combination of regions could also be done as each region is generated during state space exploration. However the check to see if the combination of two regions is convex takes $O(n^4)$ time in the number of constraints in the matrix. This check must be done between each new region and all the regions that have been generated previously, making this approach prohibitively expensive [13].

The POSET algorithm maintains a *POSET matrix* (also know as a process matrix in [13, 14, 17]), in addition to the constraint matrix. A POSET is a partially ordered set of events created from a TEL structure and a firing sequence. It is constructed from a TEL structure as follows: The POSET is initially empty. Events are added in the same order as they occur in the firing sequence. For an event in the firing sequence, a correspondingly labeled event is added to the POSET. Rules are added to connect the newly enabled event to the events in the POSET that enabled it.

The POSET matrix stores the minimum and maximum possible separations between the firing times of all the events in the POSET that are allowed by the firing sequence currently being explored. At each iteration, the time separations in the POSET matrix are copied into the entries of the constraint matrix that restrict the differences in the enabling times of the rules. Events are projected out of the POSET matrix when their timing information is no longer needed, so the algorithm only needs to retain and operate on local timing information.

3.1 Partially ordered sets without levels

When a new event fires and is added to the POSET matrix, the minimum and maximum time separations between its firing time and the firing times of all other events in the matrix must be determined. This set of separations must be consistent with the rule firing sequence that resulted in the current state. The rule firing sequence often limits the separations between events that are possible. There may be separations between events that are possible over all firing sequences but are not possible given the current one. Therefore, the separations in the POSET matrix must be restricted so that they are reachable given the current rule firing sequence.

The POSET matrix is kept consistent with the current rule firing sequence by ensuring that the time separations in the matrix reflect the causality implied by the current rule firing sequence. An event that is enabled by multiple rules does not fire until all of these rules have fired. The last rule to fire actually causes the event to fire, and is referred to as the *causal* rule. More formally, a rule $r_m = \langle e_c, e, l, u \rangle$ is causal to event e given a rule firing sequence $r_0...r_n$, if the firing sequence $r_0...r_{m-1}$ does not enable e and the firing sequence $r_0...r_m$ does enable e. A set of rules R_f enables event e if $\forall r_i = \langle e_i, e, l, u \rangle \in R : (r_i \in R_f) \vee (\exists r_j = \langle e_j, e, l_j, u_j \rangle \in R_f : e_i \# e_j)$ [15, 17].

The significant difference between the POSET technique described here and the work presented in [13, 14] is the method used to compute the POSET matrix. In [13, 14], it is not necessary to use explicit causality information since the causal rule is always the behavioral rule. With multiple behavioral rules, causality must be considered in order to compute a correct POSET matrix. Assume that I_n is a correct, maximally constraining set of inequalities that relate the firing times of a set of events E_n. When a new event e fires with causal rule $r = \langle e_c, e, l, u \rangle$, a new new set of correct, maximally constraining inequalities I_{n+1} can be computed from I_n. Initially, I_{n+1} is set to equal I_n. Then, I_{n+1} is updated with the inequalities $t(e) - t(e_c) \leq u$ and $t(e_c) - t(e) \leq -l$. These inequalities are always true since no rule can delay the firing of e once its causal rule has fired. Next, for each rule $r_i = \langle e_i, e, l_i, u_i \rangle$ in R_f, the inequality $t(e_i) - t(e) \leq -l_i$ needs to be added because each rule enabling e must be satisfied. These new inequalities may cause other inequalities in I_{n+1} to no longer be maximally constraining. This occurs when there exists a subset of I_{n+1} of the form $\{t(e) - t(e_c) \leq u, t(e_i) - t(e) \leq -l_i, t(e_i) - t(e_c) \leq n\}$ where $u - l_i < n$. All of the inequalities in I_{n+1} can be made maximally constraining by running Floyd's all pairs shortest path algorithm[7].

After the all pairs shortest path algorithm is run, I_{n+1} contains a maximally constraining set of inequalities that includes all the constraints that result from firing e. However, minimum and maximum constraint between e and all of the events in E_n must also be included in I_{n+1}. These additional constraints are immediately derivable from the constraints already in I_{n+1}. The maximum constraints are as follows: $t(e) - t(e_j) \leq u + max(t(e_c) - t(e_j))$. This inequality holds since the maximum separation between e_j and e occurs when e_j happens as much before e's causal event as possible. If there is a rule $r_j = \langle e_j, e, l_j, u_j \rangle$ that relates e_j and e, then the minimum constraint is $t(e_j) - t(e) \leq min(-l_j, -(l - max(t(e_j) - t(e_c))))$. This inequality holds because the minimum separation between e_j and e occurs when e_j happens as much after e's causal event as possible, but must be no less than the minimum on the rule relating e_j and e. The inequalities $t(e_j) - t(e) \leq -l_j$ are added to I_{n+1} before the all pairs shortest path step, and are constrained further to $t(e_j) - t(f) \leq -(l - max(t(e_j) - t(e)))$, if necessary. If there is not a rule $r_j = \langle e_j, e, l_j, u_j \rangle$ that relates e_j and e, the minimum constraint is simply $t(e_j) - t(e) \leq -(l - max(t(e_j) - t(e_c)))$. I_{n+1} now contains a correct, maximally constraining set of inequalities that represent the minimum and maximum separations between all the events in $E_{n+1} = E_n \cup e$. Note that as an optimization, inequalities that are no longer needed to compute future inequalities are removed from I_n. Since the base case is simply $I_0 = \emptyset$, this procedure can be used to construct correct sets of inequalities for an arbitrary rule firing sequence.

A geometric region representing the differences in the ages of a set of clocks associated with a set of enabled rules R_{en} can easily be computed given a POSET matrix using a method similar to the one described in [13, 14]. The maximum difference in the ages of the two clocks c_i and c_j associated with rules $r_i = \langle e_i, f_i, l_i, u_i \rangle$ and $r_j = \langle e_j, f_j, l_j, u_j \rangle$ is simply the maximum difference in the firing times of e_i and e_j which is in the POSET matrix as $t(e_i) - t(e_j) \leq max$. The minimum likewise exists in the POSET matrix as $t(e_j) - t(e_i) \leq -min$. These constraints are simply copied into the matrix representing the geometric region. The minimum and maximum bounds of the rules are used to set the minimum and maximum age differences between c_i and c_0. Floyd's algorithm is then run on the constraint matrix resulting in a maximally constraining set of inequalities. This may further constrain some of the inequalities since the POSET inequalities do not take into account the fact that a clock associated with a rule may not be older than the maximum bound on the rule. Additionally, the normalization algorithm described in[13] is applied to ensure the state space remains finite.

Figure 1 illustrates how the POSET timing analysis algorithm solves two of the problems that occur when using geometric regions for timed state space exploration: region splitting and multiple behavioral rules. In this example, initially the R_{en} set is $\{\langle A, B \rangle, \langle A, C \rangle\}$, indicating that event A has just fired. The POSET matrix contains a single event, A. The constraint matrix shows that the maximum time since A has fired is 5. If more than 5 time units had passed, the rule $\langle A, C \rangle$ would have been forced to fire. Since both the rules in R_{en} are enabled by A, the difference in their enabling times must be 0, and the region in space that shows this is a 45 degree line.

From this timed state, either event B or event C can fire. In this example, B fires next. The POSET matrix now contains the minimum and maximum separations between the firing times of A and B. The values are copied into the constraint matrix. After the all pairs shortest path algorithm is run, the separation of 7 that is possible between the firing of A and the firing of B in the POSET matrix is reduced to 5 in the constraint matrix since rule $\langle A, C \rangle$ has a maximum bound of 5 and therefore its clock cannot be more than 5 time units older than another clock.

In this state event C or rule $\langle B, D \rangle$ can fire next and C is chosen. When C fires, the POSET matrix no longer needs to contain A since all events it has enabled have fired. The POSET matrix shows that B could have fired at most 5 time units after C and C could have fired at most 2 time units after B. Now there are three rules enabled and the region is 3-dimensional. In the figure, a two dimensional projection of the region into the $\langle C, D \rangle, \langle B, D \rangle$ plane is shown. This region shows the advantage of the POSET technique. Even though in this particular firing sequence B fires before C, the region produced here contains timing assignments where C fires before B. Since B and C occur in parallel, all of these timing assignments are allowed by the rule firing sequence that produced this state. The dashed line in the middle of the region shows the two regions that would be generated by standard geometric techniques. The upper region contains timing assignments where B fired first, and the lower region contains timing assignments where C fired first.

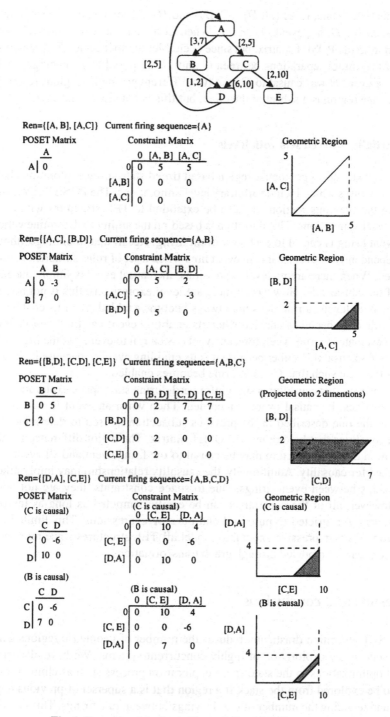

Fig. 1. Example of timing with partially ordered sets.

In this timed state, rules $\langle B, D \rangle$, $\langle C, D \rangle$, and $\langle C, E \rangle$ are enabled. Once both of the rules that enable D fire, event D can fire. When D fires, information on event B can be removed from the POSET matrix, but since C enables another event, E, it remains. Two different maximum separations between C and D are possible depending on whether event C or event B was causal to D, and two different geometric regions result. In this example, one region is a subset of the other, but this is not always the case.

3.2 Partially ordered sets with levels

In [18], we extended a geometric region based timed state space exploration algorithm to TEL structures which include arbitrary level annotations. The POSET algorithm presented in the previous section can also be extended to TEL structures with a limited class of level annotations. The algorithm is based on the ability to determine which previous event firing is causal to each new event firing. Recall that in our algorithm, rules fire independently of events, and an event fires when a set of rules sufficient to enable it have fired. When there are no level expressions, the causal event is simply the enabling event of the causal rule. However, if there are level expressions, this is not necessarily the case. With levels, a rule does not always become enabled when its enabling event fires. A rule only becomes enabled when its enabling event has fired *and* its level expression evaluates to true. Therefore, an event e is causal to event f if the firing of event e enables f's causal rule either because it is its enabling event or because it changes the value of the state such that f's causal rule becomes enabled.

Determining this causality is straightforward during state space exploration. Whenever a rule fires, its causal event is recorded. Then when an event fires, a procedure similar to the one described in the previous subsection is used to determine the new set of inequalities that belong in the POSET matrix. The major difference is that now any event in the TEL structure may be causal to the firing event and all events need to be checked for causality. Additionally, the causality relationship may imply other time relationships between event firings. Due to space constraints, they are not described here. However, all of the constraints can be easily computed as long as the boolean expressions are restricted to pure **and** and pure **or** expressions. This limited class of TEL structures is expressive enough to model all TEL structures since more complex expressions can be modeled through graph transformations.

4   Results and conclusions

The POSET algorithm drastically reduces the number of geometric regions generated during state space exploration of highly concurrent systems. We have also made additional optimizations to the state space exploration process such as eliminating timed states to be explored from the stack if a region that is a superset of previous regions is found, and reducing the number of interleavings between rule firings. This new POSET timing algorithm along with these optimizations has been implemented within the CAD tool ATACS and produce very good results as illustrated with the parameterized timing verification benchmarks in this section.

The first two, the Alpha and Beta examples, are from [5]. Each stage of the Alpha example is composed of a single event which can fire repeatedly at a given interval and is not effected by any other events in the system. In [5], they showed that techniques based on DBMs (i.e., geometric regions) could only handle 5 stages of this highly concurrent example while their symbolic discrete-time technique using numerical decision diagrams (NDDs) could handle 18 stages in 12 hours on a SUN UltraSparc with 256MB of memory. A *loglog* plot of the results from [5] and our results using POSET timing on a SPARC 20 with 128 MB of memory are shown in Figure 2. These results indicate that POSET timing is orders of magnitude faster and more memory efficient. In fact, our techniques found the reachable states space for 512 stages in about 73 minutes using 112 MB of memory. This simple example clearly has only one untimed state regardless of the number of stages, and POSET timing can represent the timed state space using only one geometric region. Our technique does not find the region in its first iteration, however. It first finds a number of smaller regions before finding the final region that is a superset of all the rest. Therefore, although its performance is very good, it does not analyze the example instantaneously.

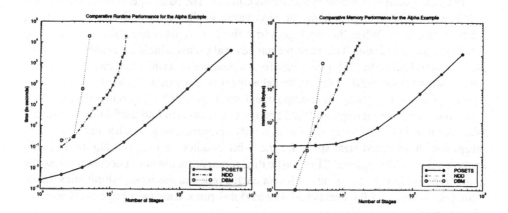

Fig. 2. Comparative performance for the Alpha example.

One stage of the Beta example is composed of one state bit per stage with two events, one to set and one to reset the bit. In [5], they showed that DBMs could only handle 4 stages while their technique could handle 9 stages. A semilog plot of their results and ours are shown in Figure 3. POSET timing can handle 14 stages in 108 MB of memory in just 16 minutes. For the Beta example, the number of states is exactly 2^n where n is the number of stages, so POSET timing could handle an example with 32 times more untimed states than in [5]. Again, POSET timing is able to represent all the timing behavior in this example using one geometric region per state. Clearly, the Alpha and Beta examples are ideally suited to our algorithm, but they are used in [5] to demonstrate the weakness of traditional geometric region based methods.

413

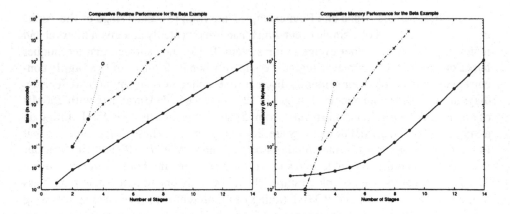

Fig. 3. Comparative performance for the Beta example.

The next example is a n-bit synchronous counter. The basic operation of the counter is that when the clock goes high, the next value of the count is determined in from the previous value. When the clock goes low, the new value is latched and fed back to determine the next count. This example has several events which are enabled by multiple behavioral rules. In [15], graph transformations are described that can create a new specification which satisfies the single behavioral rule restriction allowing verification by Orbits [13, 14]. Using these graph transformations, Orbits could only analyze a 3-bit counter because it required 10,222 geometric regions to find the 64 untimed states. With our new POSET timing algorithm, it only requires 294 geometric regions to represent the entire timed state space for the 3-bit counter. In fact, our algorithm could analyze up to a 6-bit counter. This drastic difference in region count occurs because the graph transformation adds $n!$ new rules for each event that has n behavioral rules. In the 3-bit counter most of the events had 4 behavioral rules, causing a huge combinatorial explosion in the number of regions.

The last example is a STARI communication circuit described in detail in [20, 21]. The STARI circuit is used to communicate between two synchronous systems that are operating at the same clock frequency, π, but are out-of-phase due to clock skew which can vary from 0 to *skew*. The environment of this circuit is composed of a clk process, a transmitter, and a receiver. The STARI circuit is composed of a number of FIFO stages built from 2 C-elements and 1 NOR-gate per stage which each have a delay of l to u. There are two properties that need to be verified: (1) each data value output by the transmitter must be inserted into the FIFO before the next one is output (i.e., $ack(1)-$ precedes $x(0).t-$ and $x(0).f-$) and (2) a new data value must be output by the FIFO before each acknowledgment from the receiver (i.e., $x(n).t+$ or $x(n).f+$ precedes $ack(n+1)-$) [22]. To guarantee the second property, it is necessary to initialize the FIFO to be approximately half-full [21]. In addition to these two properties, we also verified that every gate is hazard-free (i.e., once a gate is enabled, it cannot be disabled until it has fired).

There have been two nice proofs of STARI's correctness [21, 23], but they have been on abstract models. In [22], the authors state that COSPAN which uses the unit-cube (or region) technique for timing verification [24] ran out of memory attempting to verify a 3 stage gate-level version of STARI on a machine with 1 GB of memory. This paper goes on to describe an abstract model of STARI for which they could verify 8 stages in 92.4 MB of memory and 1.67 hours. We first verified STARI at the gate-level with delays from [22] (i.e., $\pi = 12$, $skew= 1$, $l = 1$, and $u = 2$). Using POSET timing, we can verify a 3 stage STARI in 0.74 MB in only 0.40 seconds. For an 8 stage STARI, the verification took 11 MB and only 55 seconds. In fact, POSET timing could verify 10 stages in 124 MB of memory in less than 20 minutes. This shows a nice improvement over the abstraction method and a dramatic improvement over the gate-level verification in COSPAN. For 10 stages, POSET timing found 14,531 untimed states and only needed 14,859 geometric regions to describe the timed state space. This represents a ratio of only 1.02 geometric regions per untimed state.

Finally, the complexity of POSET timing is relatively independent of the timing bounds used. We also ran our experiments using $l = 97$ and $u = 201$, $skew= 101$, and $\pi = 1193$ which found more untimed states. With $l = 102$, we found less untimed states. Both cases with higher precision delay numbers had comparable performance to the one with lower precision delay numbers. This shows that higher precision timing bounds can be efficiently verified and can lead to different behaviors. It would not be possible to use this level of precision with a discrete-time or unit-cube based technique, since the number of states would explode with such large numbers.

Our results clearly show that POSET timing can dramatically improve the efficiency of timing verification allowing larger, more concurrent timed systems to be verified. It does so without eliminating parts of the state space, so it does not limit the properties that can be verified. In the future, we plan to further increase the size and generality of the specifications that can be verified with the POSET method. We believe the abstraction technique from [22] and POSET timing methods are orthogonal, and we are interested in trying to combine them for further improvement. Finally, our algorithm currently represents the state space explicitly, and we are working on applying implicit techniques. Our preliminary results show that this can lead to a significant improvement in memory performance [25].

Acknowledgments

We would like to thank Mark Greenstreet of the University of British Columbia, Brandon Bachman, Eric Mercer, and Robert Thacker of the University of Utah and Tom Rokicki of Hewlett Packard for their helpful comments.

References

1. A. Valmari. A stubborn attack on state explosion. In *International Conference on Computer-Aided Verification*, pages 176–185, June 1990.
2. P. Godefroid. Using partial orders to improve automatic verification methods. In *International Conference on Computer-Aided Verification*, pages 176–185, June 1990.

3. K. McMillan. Using unfoldings to avoid the state explosion problem in the verification of asynchronous circuits. In G. v. Bochman and D. K. Probst, editors, *Proc. International Workshop on Computer Aided Verification*, volume 663 of *Lecture Notes in Computer Science*, pages 164–177. Springer-Verlag, 1992.

4. J. R. Burch. Modeling timing assumptions with trace theory. In *ICCD*, 1989.

5. M. Bozga, O. Maler, A. Pnueli, and S. Yovine. Some progress in the symbolic verification of timed automata. In *Proc. International Conference on Computer Aided Verification*, 1997.

6. R. Alur. *Techniques for Automatic Verification of Real-Time Systems*. PhD thesis, Stanford University, August 1991.

7. D. L. Dill. Timing assumptions and verification of finite-state concurrent systems. In *Proceedings of the Workshop on Automatic Verification Methods for Finite-State Systems*, 1989.

8. B. Berthomieu and M. Diaz. Modeling and verification of time dependent systems using time petri nets. *IEEE Transactions on Software Engineering*, 17(3), March 1991.

9. H. R. Lewis. Finite-state analysis of asynchronous circuits with bounded temporal uncertainty. Technical report, Harvard University, July 1989.

10. T. Yoneda, A. Shibayama, B. Schlingloff, and E. M. Clarke. Efficient verification of parallel real-time systems. In Costas Courcoubetis, editor, *Computer Aided Verification*, pages 321–332. Springer-Verlag, 1993.

11. A. Semenov and A. Yakovlev. Verification of asynchronous circuits using time Petri-net unfolding. In *Proc. ACM/IEEE Design Automation Conference*, pages 59–63, 1996.

12. E. Verlind, G. de Jong, and B. Lin. Efficient parial enumeration for timing analysis of asynchronous systems. In *Proc. ACM/IEEE Design Automation Conference*, 1996.

13. T. G. Rokicki. *Representing and Modeling Circuits*. PhD thesis, Stanford University, 1993.

14. T. G. Rokicki and C. J. Myers. Automatic verificaton of timed circuits. In *International Conference on Computer-Aided Verification*, pages 468–480. Springer-Verlag, 1994.

15. C. J. Myers. *Computer-Aided Synthesis and Verification of Gate-Level Timed Circuits*. PhD thesis, Stanford University, 1995.

16. C. J. Myers, T. G. Rokicki, and T. H.-Y. Meng. Automatic synthesis of gate-level timed circuits with choice. In *16th Conference on Advanced Research in VLSI*, pages 42–58. IEEE Computer Society Press, 1995.

17. W. Belluomini and C. J. Myers. Efficient timing analysis algorithms for timed state space exploration. In *Proc. International Symposium on Advanced Research in Asynchronous Circuits and Systems*. IEEE Computer Society Press, April 1997.

18. W. Belluomini and C. J. Myers. Timed event/level structures. In collection of papers from TAU'97.

19. P. Merlin and D. J. Faber. Recoverability of communication protocols. *IEEE Transactions on Communications*, 24(9), 1976.

20. M. R. Greenstreet. *STARI: A Technique for High-Bandwidth Communication*. PhD thesis, Princeton University, 1993.

21. M. R. Greenstreet. Stari: Skew tolerant communication. unpublished manuscript, 1997.

22. S. Tasiran and R. K. Brayton. Stari: A case study in compositional and heirarchical timing verification. In *Proc. International Conference on Computer Aided Verification*, 1997.

23. H. Hulgaard, S.M. Burns, T. Amon, and G. Borriello. Practical applications of an efficient time seperation of events algorithm. In *ICCAD*, 1993.

24. R. Alur and R. P. Kurshan. Timing analysis in cospan. In *Hybrid Systems III*. Springer-Verlag, 1996.

25. R. A. Thacker. Implicit methods for timed circuit synthesis. Master's thesis, University of Utah, 1998.

Mechanising BAN Kerberos
by the Inductive Method

Giampaolo Bella*   Lawrence C Paulson**

Computer Laboratory – University of Cambridge
New Museums Site, Pembroke Street
Cambridge CB2 3QG (UK)

Abstract. The version of Kerberos presented by Burrows et al. [5] is fully mechanised using the *Inductive Method*. Two models are presented, allowing respectively the leak of any session keys, and of expired session keys. Thanks to timestamping, the protocol provides the involved parties with strong guarantees in a realistically hostile environment. These guarantees are supported by the generic theorem prover Isabelle.

1   Introduction

Although pioneered two decades ago [10], he use of formal methods in the field of security protocols has become common practice only during the 1990s. Two paradigms are dominant.

The seminal paper of Burrows et al. [5] suggested the use of a *belief logic* to reason about properties such as freshness. The limitations of this approach have been widely discussed: for instance, reasoning about secrecy. Many extensions have been developed to enhance expressiveness, but they tend to sacrifice the intuitions. Another approach consists in the exhaustive *enumeration of the states* reachable during the computation of a protocol (e.g. [6]). This method requires keeping the state space at a manageable size, which is achieved by simplifying assumptions. However, belief logics can easily reason about authentication, and state enumeration methods can pinpoint simple flaws quickly.

Deep structural properties that had only informal treatment in the past can now be formally expressed by the *inductive method* [12]. The method relies on an algebraic theory of messages with inductively-defined operators applicable to a set of messages. An attacker with the ability of intercepting all traffic over the network is modelled. The attacker can also exploit the accidental loss of secrets by honest agents. Compared with other work, our model is quite realistic. Meadows's approach [8] is important and has an element of induction.

Promising results have been achieved with nonce-based protocols such as Needham-Schroeder, Otway-Rees, Yahalom [12–14], and a flaw has been discovered on a variant of Otway-Rees. This paper presents results about Kerberos, which is based on timestamps. In spite of this difference, many technical results

* Giampaolo.Bella@cl.cam.ac.uk
** Larry.Paulson@cl.cam.ac.uk

from the previously analysed, nonce-based protocols could be easily reused. We present here two models: a basic one leaking any session keys, and a refined one leaking only session keys that have expired. The latter idealisation seems realistic, as the risk of leaking session keys increases over time. The proof script takes a little longer in the latter model, but provides stronger guarantees.

We pay particular attention to what the agents need to check to infer the results stated by the theorems. If theorems rely on assumptions that require knowledge coming from the network, then their importance might be merely theoretic. One might prove that if the spy never gets hold of a session key, then messages encrypted under such a key are reliable. The importance of this theorem is limited, as no honest agent can check its assumption.

The main concepts of the inductive method are given in Section 2. The formalisation of Kerberos is given in Section 3, and its refinement in Section 4. Related work appears in Section 5. Section 6 concludes the paper.

2   The Inductive Method

Only some guidelines are given here. A complete description is published elsewhere [12].

2.1   Overview

A concrete notion of *event* is borrowed from the state enumeration approach. The traffic over the network is created by agents sending messages to each other. So, the basic event Says A B *msg* formalises an agent A sending a message *msg* to an agent B. A *trace* is a set of events.

Intuitively, a security protocol is a non-deterministic program that should guarantee certain properties during its operation. Security protocols are inductively defined as the set of all possible traces. Given as a base case that the empty trace belongs to the set, the formalisation describes how to extend a trace of the set with a new event, according to the protocol operation.

The model does not force agents to reply to any message. Agents can reply late, or reply more than once, or not reply at all. Interleaved runs are possible because agents can even reply to old messages.

Proving a property of a protocol is done by induction. The property should hold on the base trace and, if it holds on a certain trace, then it should hold on all traces extending it. This is simple induction, but it often involves a number of steps that are difficult to manage without tools. The theorem prover Isabelle [11] provides automation.

2.2 Algebra of Messages

The model formalises the knowledge of the attacker (called *spy* in the sequel) by the operator **spies** as follows:

1. $\text{spies}\,[] = \{\text{shrK}\,A \mid A \in bad\}$
2. $\text{spies}\,(\text{Says}\,A\,B\,X \,\#\, evs) = \{X\} \cup \text{spies}\,evs$

The first rule says that the spy's knowledge over the empty trace — i.e. the initial knowledge — consists in the long-term keys of compromised agents. The second, inductive rule expresses the spy's ability to intercept any message on the network.

Given a set H of messages, which is typically expressed in terms of the **spies** operator, we define inductively the following operators.

- **parts** H is intuitively the set of all components of messages in H. The only items that **parts** can not catch are the encryption keys.
- **analz** H is intuitively the subset of **parts** H that does not break ciphers. Thus, to add the body of an encrypted message, its encryption key must be analysable.
- **synth** H is what the spy can synthesise from H by concatenation and encryption. In particular

$$\text{Agent}\,A \in \text{synth}\,H \qquad\qquad \text{Number}\,T \in \text{synth}\,H$$

These rules allow the spy to synthesise agent names and timestamps, because they can be guessed with no previous analysis. Note that there is no such a rule for nonces, for they are built as non-clashing random numbers by honest agents. This makes a timestamp-based protocol harder to mechanise.

Everything the spy can synthesise from the observation of the traffic over a trace *evs* is formalised by the set

$$\text{synth}(\text{analz}(\text{spies}\,evs))$$

Recall that the long-term keys of compromised agents belong to the set **spies** *evs*. Session keys lost by accident belong to the set **analz**(**spies** *evs*) — this will be explicitly formalised below by the "oops" event. Therefore, such a spy has a potentially infinite behaviour [12].

3 A Model for BAN Kerberos

Kerberos is a cryptographic protocol designed during the mid 1980s at MIT. The BAN version, coming from the paper of Burrows et al. [5], is shown in fig. 1 with lifetimes omitted, as suggested by Bellovin and Meritt [2]. The trusted third party S (called *server* in the sequel) sends A the session key to be shared with B and a ticket that contains the copy of the session key for B. A forwards the

1. $A \rightarrow S : A, B$
2. $S \rightarrow A : \{Tk, B, Kab, \underbrace{\{Tk, A, Kab\}_{Kb}}_{ticket}\}_{Ka}$
3. $A \rightarrow B : \underbrace{\{Tk, A, Kab\}_{Kb}}_{ticket}, \underbrace{\{A, Ta\}_{Kab}}_{authenticator}$
4. $B \rightarrow A : \{Ta + 1\}_{Kab}$

Fig. 1. BAN Kerberos

ticket to B together with an authenticator to assure B that the sender is the same party to whom the ticket had been issued.

Fig. 2 shows the formalisation of Kerberos by the inductive method, with a few mathematical symbols in place of their ASCII equivalents. Rules **Kb1** to **Kb4** describe how to extend a given trace of the set according to the protocol operation. For instance, rule **Kb2** states that if the first message of Kerberos appears on a trace of the set, then the concatenation of the given trace with the second message of the protocol also is a trace of the set. Rule **Fake** models the introduction on the traffic of all fake messages that the spy can build up. Rule **Oops** models the accidental loss of any session key to the spy. The function

$$Ct : event\ list \longrightarrow bool$$

formalises the current time over a given trace. The observation that a trace is extended by any protocol step suggested the definition of the current time as the length of the trace. This simple definition has shown sufficient expressiveness thanks to the monotonicity of the length of traces.

The lifetime of a session key, i.e. the time interval within which the key is accepted as fresh by any party, is formalised by the natural number SesKeyLife. Similarly, AutLife formalises the time interval within which an authenticator is considered recent. Therefore, the predicate Expired Tk evs, expressing that the timestamp Tk has expired over the trace evs, is defined by

$$(Ct\,evs) - Tk > \mathsf{SesKeyLife}$$

The predicate ExpiredAuth Ta evs, expressing that the timestamp Ta has expired over evs, is defined by

$$(Ct\,evs) - Tk > \mathsf{AutLife}$$

Note that in rule **Kb3**, A will only forward a ticket that has come with a non-expired session key, and that B requires the same condition to hold in **Kb4** together with the condition of having received a non-expired authenticator.

Rule **Kb4** does not increment Ta. It could do so, but we believe this is irrelevant.

```
kerberos_ban :: event list set
inductive kerberos_ban

Base   [] ∈ kerberos_ban

Fake   [| evs ∈ kerberos_ban; B ≠ Spy; X ∈ synth(analz(spies evs)) |]
       ⟹ Says Spy B X # evs ∈ kerberos_ban

Kb1    [| evs ∈ kerberos_ban; A ≠ Server |]
       ⟹ Says A Server {|Agent A, Agent B|} # evs ∈ kerberos_ban


Kb2    [| evs ∈ kerberos_ban; A ≠ B; A ≠ Server; Key Kab ∉ used evs;
          Says A' Server {|Agent A, Agent B|} ∈ set evs |]
       ⟹ Says Server A Crypt (shrK A)
                           {|Number (Ct evs), Agent B, Key Kab,
                             Crypt (shrK B)
                                 {|Number (Ct evs), Agent A, Key Kab|}
                           |} # evs ∈ kerberos_ban


Kb3    [| evs ∈ kerberos_ban; A ≠ B;
          Says A Server {|Agent A, Agent B|} ∈ set evs;
          Says S A Crypt (shrK A) {|Number Tk, Agent B, Key K, X|}
          ∈ set evs;
          ¬ Expired Tk evs |]
       ⟹ Says A B {|X, Crypt K {|Agent A, Number (Ct evs)|}|}
          # evs ∈ kerberos_ban


Kb4    [| evs ∈ kerberos_ban; A ≠ B;
          Says A' B {|Crypt (shrK B) {|Number Tk, Agent B, Key K|},
                     Crypt K {|Agent A, Number Ta|}|} ∈ set evs;
          ¬ Expired Tk evs; ¬ ExpiredAuth Ta evs |]
       ⟹ Says B A Crypt K (Number Ta)
          # evs ∈ kerberos_ban

Oops   [| evs ∈ kerberos_ban; A ≠ Spy;
          Says Server A Crypt (shrK A)
                             {|Number Tk, Agent B, Key K, Ticket|}
          ∈ set evs |]
       ⟹ Says A Spy {|Number Tk, Key K|} # evs ∈ kerberos_ban
```

Fig. 2. Formalising BAN Kerberos

3.1 Guarantees about BAN Kerberos

This section presents the main theorems proven about BAN Kerberos. Some proofs were easily adapted from those for the protocols already analysed, others had to be performed from scratch. Confidentiality guarantees are now expressed from the viewpoint of each party involved in the protocol. The authenticity theorems are new.

1. There must be a trace containing the last message of the protocol that involves two given agents different from the trusted third party.

```
[| A ≠ B; A ≠ Server; B ≠ Server |]
==> ∃ Timestamp K. ∃ evs ∈ kerberos_ban.
        Says B A (Crypt K (Number Timestamp)) ∈ set evs
```

This is the main *possibility* property. The proof is straightforward: resolve by all protocol rules, then simplify.

2. Spy never sees another agent's shared key, unless the agent is compromised.

```
evs ∈ kerberos_ban
==> (Key (shrK A) ∈ parts (spies evs)) = (A ∈ bad)
```

The proof exploits the definition of **spies** (see pag. 3) that allows the spy to see the shared keys of agents belonging to **bad**. Then, induction verifies that the protocol messages protect the other shared keys.

3. The server only sends well-formed messages.

```
[| Says Server A (Crypt K' {|Number Tk, Agent B, Key K, X|})
        ∈ set evs; evs ∈ kerberos_ban |]
==> K' = shrK A & K ∉ range shrK &
    X = (Crypt (shrK B) {|Number Tk, Agent A, Key K|})
```

Induction and simplification form the proof. Despite its simplicity, this technical lemma is useful to prove more complicated guarantees, because it expresses the form of the ticket.

4. If a message of the form of the second of the protocol appears on the traffic, then it originated with the server.

```
[| Crypt (shrK A) {|Number Tk, Agent B, Key K, X|}
        ∈ parts (spies evs); A ∉ bad; evs ∈ kerberos_ban |]
==> Says Server A (Crypt (shrK A)
                    {|Number Tk, Agent B, Key K, X|}) ∈ set evs
```

A simple induction proves that the message originated with the server. The spy could not fake it because *A* is uncompromised. When *A* gets hold of such a message, she infers that the session key *K* really was created by the server at time *Tk*. By checking *Tk* against the current time, she is able to decide the *freshness* of *K* .

5. If the ticket appears on the traffic, then it originated with the server.

```
[| Crypt (shrK B) {|Number Tk, Agent A, Key K|}
      ∈ parts (spies evs);
    B ∉ bad;  evs ∈ kerberos_ban |]
 ⟹ Says Server A (Crypt (shrK A) {|Number Tk, Agent B, Key K,
                        Crypt (shrK B) {|Number Tk, Agent A, Key K|}|})
      ∈ set evs
```

The proof follows the same strategy presented for the previous theorem, and *B* gets the same guarantees as *A* does: the session key *K* originated with the server at time *Tk*.

6. The session key uniquely identifies the message sent by the server.

```
[| Says Server A (Crypt (shrK A) {|Number Tk, Agent B, Key K, X|})
      ∈ set evs;
    Says Server A' (Crypt (shrK A')
                       {|Number Tk', Agent B', Key K, X'|})
      ∈ set evs; evs ∈ kerberos_ban |]
 ⟹ A=A' & Tk=Tk' & B=B' & X = X'
```

This is the main *unicity* result, stating that a session key only was generated at one point *Tk* for one specific pair of agents. The proof rests on induction to find out that session keys are only generated by the server, and that the same key is never generated more than once. This result can be applied to show that the agent who forwards *K* to *B* in the third message is the same agent to whom the second message (containing *K*) was addressed. It simplifies several proofs.

7. If a key can be analysed from the traffic and another session key, then either the two keys are the same, or the first key can be analysed from the traffic alone.

```
[| evs ∈ kerberos_ban;  Kab ∉ range shrK |]
 ⟹ Key K ∈ analz (insert (Key Kab) (spies evs)) =
    (K = Kab | Key K ∈ analz (spies evs))
```

The theorem means that session keys are never used to encrypt other keys, so the compromise of one key would not compromise others. It is a crucial rewrite rule for other theorems based on the analz operator. Although the proof requires a number of lemmas about analz [12], it executes in only 20 seconds.

8. Spy can not see the session key sent by the server in the second message if such a key has not been accidentally lost (by an "oops" event), and the two recipients are uncompromised.

```
[| Says Server A (Crypt K' {|Number Tk, Agent B, Key K, X|})
    ∈ set evs;
   (ALL T. Says A Spy {|T, Key K|} ∉ set evs);
   A ∉ bad;  B ∉ bad;  evs ∈ kerberos_ban |]
⟹ Key K ∉ analz (spies evs)
```

This theorem states the *confidentiality* of the session key from the server's viewpoint, because it relies on a **Says** event that only the server can check. The key is obviously required not to have been accidentally leaked, although this can not be checked (this strong assumption is relaxed in the refined model — see next section). The recipients of the session key must be uncompromised, otherwise they would trivially reveal it to the spy. Because *A* is uncompromised, the external encryption of the second message can be proven safe. The ticket forwarded in the third message keeps the session key secure because also *B* is uncompromised.

9. If a message of the form of the second message of the protocol appears on the traffic, and contains a session key for two uncompromised agents that has not been leaked by accident, then the session key can not be seen by the spy.

```
[| Crypt (shrK A) {|Number Tk, Agent B, Key K, X|}
    ∈ parts (spies evs);
   (ALL T'. Says A Spy {|T', Key K|} ∉ set evs);
   A ∉ bad;  B ∉ bad;  evs ∈ kerberos_ban |]
⟹ Key K ∉ analz (spies evs)
```

The theorem expresses the confidentiality of the session key from *A*'s viewpoint, as it rests on conditions that *A* can check when she receives the second message of the protocol, provided that her interlocutor is uncompromised. The proof applies theorem 4 to theorem 8.

10. If the ticket appears on the traffic, and contains a session key for two uncompromised agents that has not been leaked by accident, then the session key can not be seen by the spy.

```
[| Crypt (shrK B) {|Number Tk, Agent A, Key K|}
    ∈ parts (spies evs);
   (ALL T'. Says A Spy {|T', Key K|} ∉ set evs);
   A ∉ bad;  B ∉ bad;  evs ∈ kerberos_ban |]
⟹ Key K ∉ analz (spies evs)
```

This theorem is analogous to the previous one, but expresses the confidentiality of the session key from *B*'s viewpoint. The proof applies theorem 5 to theorem 8.

11. If the fourth message appears, and is encrypted under a safe session key, then it originated with B.

```
[| Crypt K (Number Ta) ∈ parts (spies evs);
    Crypt (shrK A) {|Number Tk, Agent B, Key K, X|}
      ∈ parts (spies evs);
    ALL T. Says A Spy {|T, Key K|} ∉ set evs;
    A ∉ bad;  B ∉ bad;  evs ∈ kerberos_ban |]
⟹ Says B A (Crypt K (Number Ta)) ∈ set evs
```

This theorem expresses the *authentication* of B to A. If B were compromised, the spy could easily impersonate him. The non-trivial case is when B is honest. To assure that the session key is kept secret, theorem 8 about confidentiality is applied. Induction then shows that the fourth message only could originate with B. If A can successfully decrypt by K the message containing the timestamp Ta, then she gets evidence that B shares K with her as a session key. A also infers that B was present after she has issued Ta (this timestamp is actually used as a nonce).

12. If the authenticator appears, and is encrypted under a safe session key, then it originated with A.

```
[| Crypt K {|Agent A, Number Ta|} ∈ parts (spies evs);
    Crypt (shrK B) {|Number Tk, Agent A, Key K|}
      ∈ parts (spies evs);
    ALL T. Says A Spy {|T, Key K|} ∉ set evs;
    A ∉ bad;  B ∉ bad;  evs ∈ kerberos_ban |]
⟹ Says A B {|Crypt (shrK B) {|Number Tk, Agent A, Key K|},
              Crypt K {|Agent A, Number Ta|}|} ∈ set evs
```

This theorem expresses the authentication of A to B and can be discussed as the previous one. The proof follows the same pattern: apply theorem 8 about confidentiality, and then use induction. If B can decrypt the authenticator successfully, he understands that A agrees on the session key K. Then, B can check the timestamp Ta against the current time and infer when A was present. Therefore, the authenticator fulfils the aims for which it was envisaged.

4 Refining the Model

The theorems presented in the previous section support the claim that BAN Kerberos assesses strong goals of confidentiality and of authentication. (Another protocol providing similar authentication goals is Yahalom [14]). However, these guarantees rely on session keys that have not been leaked by accident, a condition that can not be checked by any honest agents.

Since the probability of secrets to become compromised increases over time (the longer they are on the traffic, the higher the risk), it seems realistic to assume that session keys are only leaked when they have expired. The **Oops** rule is refined accordingly by adding to its assumptions the temporal check

Expired Tk evs

The main guarantees can be refined as follows.

8'. Confidentiality of the session key for the sever.

```
[| Says Server A (Crypt K {|Number Tk, Agent B, Key K, X|})
      ∈ set evs;
      ¬ Expired Tk evs; A ∉ bad; B ∉ bad; evs ∈ kerberos_ban |]
 ⟹ Key K ∉ analz (spies evs)
```

9'. Confidentiality of the session key for A.

```
[| Crypt (shrK A) {|Number Tk, Agent B, Key K, X|}
      ∈ parts (spies evs);
      ¬ Expired Tk evs; A ∉ bad; B ∉ bad; evs ∈ kerberos_ban |]
 ⟹ Key K ∉ analz (spies evs)
```

10'. Confidentiality of the session key for B.

```
[| Crypt (shrK B) {|Number Tk, Agent A, Key K|}
      ∈ parts (spies evs);
      ¬ Expired Tk evs; A ∉ bad; B ∉ bad; evs ∈ kerberos_ban |]
 ⟹ Key K ∉ analz (spies evs)
```

11'. Authentication of B to A.

```
[| Crypt K (Number Ta) ∈ parts (spies evs);
   Crypt (shrK A) {|Number Tk, Agent B, Key K, X|}
      ∈ parts (spies evs);
      ¬ Expired Tk evs; A ∉ bad; B ∉ bad; evs ∈ kerberos_ban |]
 ⟹ Says B A (Crypt K (Number Ta)) ∈ set evs
```

12'. Authentication of A to B.

```
[| Crypt K {|Agent A, Number Ta|} ∈ parts (spies evs);
   Crypt (shrK B) {|Number Tk, Agent A, Key K|}
      ∈ parts (spies evs);
      ¬ Expired Tk evs; A ∉ bad; B ∉ bad; evs ∈ kerberos_ban |]
 ⟹ Says A B {|Crypt (shrK B) {|Number Tk, Agent A, Key K|},
                Crypt K {|Agent A, Number Ta|}|} ∈ set evs
```

The proofs for the basic model could be adapted by including some arithmetic reasoning to deal with the temporal checks. However, the new theorems provide stronger guarantees, for the temporal assumptions can be easily checked by any agents.

5   Related Work

Bolignano analyses crypto-protocols by modelling the states of agents, and gives a procedure to decide mechanically whether the spy can see certain items [3]. Although the spy's knowledge is unbounded, the method needs a substantial formal overhead. It is only applied to a trivial protocol that uses neither nonces nor timestamps, and that establishes no secrets. It is not clear to us how the method could handle general protocols.

The mentioned work of Burrows et al. [5] contains the first application of formal methods to BAN Kerberos. Although they provide no confidentiality analysis, they state formally that, at the end of the protocol run, the two parties know they are agreeing on the same session key. The proof is very short, but the whole reasoning has been criticised as too abstract, and the same approach has failed to discover known weaknesses of other protocols.

Brackin [4] extends and mechanises this work using the HOL theorem prover. It is a good attempt of supporting the BAN logic by machine, but it does not enhance the expressiveness of the logic itself.

Lowe has analysed timestamps by state enumeration on a simple two-message protocol [7].

State enumeration has been tested on Kerberos Version IV by Mitchell et al. [9]. They first tackle a system of size three, and find no attacks. Then, they discover and fix a known weakness on a system of size four. However, their analysis omits timestamps, and does not allow multiple runs. Relaxing the last two limitations is promised by the authors as future work.

6   Conclusion

The paper has presented the mechanisation of the BAN Kerberos protocol by the Inductive Method using the theorem prover Isabelle. The work is based on the formalisation of timestamps, and has benefited from the technical results sketched by the authors about Kerberos Version IV [1].

Two models are investigated: the first allows the leak of any session keys, the second only considers the leak of session keys that have expired. The second model only requires some minor modifications to the first. Strong guarantees of freshness, confidentiality, and authentication could be proven in both cases. Confidentiality is now stated from the viewpoint of each party involved in the protocol. Authentication is expressed in a form that is useful to the parties.

Although the second model makes the — fairly realistic — assumption that session keys can only be leaked when they have expired, it provides strong guarantees based on simple temporal checks. The choice of the most realistic model is left to the reader.

The proofs of the theorems require a deep knowledge of Isabelle, and are omitted for space limitations[1]. The entire work (both models) required three

---

[1] Full proof scripts available at http://www.cl.cam.ac.uk/~gb221/BanKerberos/

weeks human time. The proof script of the basic model amounts to 80 commands, and runs in 140 seconds CPU time on a Sun SuperSPARC Model 61. Commands become 90 and execution time rises to 160 seconds for the script of the second model.

References

1. G. Bella, L. C. Paulson. Using Isabelle to Prove Properties of the Kerberos Authentication System. In *Proc. of Workshop on Design and Formal Verification of Security Protocols,* Orman and Meadows (eds.), DIMACS, 1997.
2. S. M. Bellovin, M. Merritt. Limitations of the Kerberos authentication system. *Computer Comm. Review,* 20(5), 119-132, 1990.
3. D. Bolignano. Towards a Mechanization of Cryptographic Protocol Verification. In *Proc. of Conference on Computer Aided Verification,* Springer Verlag, 1997.
4. S. H. Brackin. A HOL Extension of GNY for Automatically Analyzing Cryptographic Protocols. In *Proc. of Computer Security Foundations Workshop,* IEEE Press, 1996.
5. M. Burrows, M. Abadi, R. M. Needham. A logic of authentication. *Proceedings of the Royal Society of London,* 426:233-271, 1989.
6. G. Lowe. Breaking and Fixing the Needham-Schroeder Public-Key Protocol using FDR. In *Tools and Algorithms for the Construction and Analysis of Systems,* Margaria and Steffen (eds.), LNCS1055, Springer Verlag, 147-166, 1996.
7. G. Lowe. Casper: a Compiler for the Analysis of Security Protocols. Oxford University, Computing Laboratory, *Technical Report,* 1996.
8. C. Meadows. The NRL Protocol Analyzer: An Overview. *Journal of Logic Programming,* 26(2), 113-131, 1996.
9. J. C. Mitchell, M. Mitchell, U. Stern: Automated Analysis of Cryptographic Protocols Using Murphi. In *Proc. of Symposium on Security and Privacy,* IEEE Press, 1997.
10. R. M. Needham, M. Schroeder. Using encryption for authentication in large networks of computers. *Communications of the ACM,* 21(12), 993-999, 1978.
11. L. C. Paulson. *Isabelle: A Generic Theorem Prover.* Springer, 1994. LNCS 828.
12. L. C. Paulson. Proving properties of security protocols by induction. In *Proc. of Computer Security Foundations Workshop,* IEEE Press, 1997.
13. L. C. Paulson. Mechanized proofs for a recursive authentication protocol. In *Proc. of Computer Security Foundations Workshop,* IEEE Press, 1997.
14. L. C. Paulson. On Two Formal Analyses of the Yahalom Protocol. Cambridge University, Computer Laboratory, *Technical Report No. 432,* 1997.

Protocol Verification in Nuprl

Amy P. Felty[1], Douglas J. Howe[1], and Frank A. Stomp[2]

[1] Bell Labs, Murray Hill, NJ 07974, USA. {felty,howe}@bell-labs.com
[2] Dept. of Comp. Sci., UC Davis, Davis, CA 95616, USA. stomp@cs.ucdavis.edu

Abstract. This paper presents work directed toward making the Nuprl interactive theorem prover a more effective tool for protocol verification while retaining existing advantages of the system, and describes application of the prover to verifying the SCI cache coherence protocol. The verification is based, in part, on formal mathematics imported from another theorem-proving system, exploiting a connection we implemented between Nuprl and HOL. We have designed and implemented a type annotation scheme for Nuprl's logic that allows type information to be effectively applied by the system's automated reasoning facilities. This is significant because Nuprl's powerful constructive type theory buys much of its expressive power and flexibility at the cost of giving up the more manageable kinds of type system found in other logics.

1 Introduction

Nuprl [2] is an interactive theorem-proving system in the lineage of LCF. One of its main distinguishing characteristics is its highly expressive formal logic, a constructive type theory whose classical variant has expressive power equivalent to conventional set theory (ZFC) [12,6].

Nuprl has been extensively applied, and its expressive power has been shown to be a substantial advantage in a variety of domains, but little work has been specifically directed toward effectiveness for the kind of large-scale practical applications where the bulk of the formal mathematics is highly complicated, but shallow and representationally simple.

This paper describes our work in this direction, and features an application of Nuprl to prove safety properties of the SCI cache coherence protocol [8].

We chose SCI as an example partly because its complexity is representative of the scale of algorithms which can be currently handled by mechanized tools. Model checking systems that have been applied to the protocol suffer from state explosion at a small number of processors, though even so some bugs have been found [11]. A second reason for choosing it is that a proof method and supported invariants have already been worked out [3].

Our work has been to improve Nuprl for these kinds of applications without compromising existing advantages of the system by, *e.g.*, adding restrictions to the logic. There are three parts to this work.

Imported mathematics. Verification using an interactive theorem-prover requires a great deal of basic formal mathematics about elementary data structures and models. Building it is time-consuming, and is largely duplication of effort since these basic facts tend to be similar across systems. To avoid doing this ourselves, we *import* some basic mathematics from HOL [5], a system that has, over the years, accumulated a large corpus of mathematics of the kind useful for software/hardware verification. The paper [7] gives the basic design of the connection between HOL and Nuprl, and [4] gives an extension to it and an application to a moderately difficult problem in metamathematics. Our work, though just a first step, establishes that sharing mathematics can be useful in software/hardware verification.

Type Annotation. Nuprl buys its expressive power at the cost of some traditional aspects of type systems. In particular, the type theory's flexibility is in large part due to the fact that terms are *untyped* in the sense that one cannot determine from the syntax of an expression what, if any, type it is a member of. In this way, Nuprl is similar to set theory, with types being analogous to sets. This is a problem for automation for two reasons. First, it is often important for terms to come with their types; for example, in term rewriting, type information can enable a useful form of conditional rewriting. Second, typing properties require proof, so, for example, every time a lemma is instantiated, the instantiating objects must be proved to have the right types. We have designed and implemented an annotation scheme where terms are decorated with types in such a way that types can (almost always) be efficiently maintained during inference, but no new syntactic restrictions are placed on the logic. We have obtained roughly a factor of 10 speedup in term rewriting (the main workhorse in Nuprl proofs). Unfortunately, the implementation wasn't completed until part-way through the SCI effort, so a good deal of work was done without its benefit.

Tactic support. We represent the protocol and its specification using a familiar kind of embedding of a Unity-like language. We used Nuprl's *tactic* mechanism to implement a suite of automated reasoners specialized to this model.

One might ask why not just use HOL (for example)? The answer is that we are aiming to make Nuprl an effective tool for a wide range of formal problems related to protocol verification. For example, we want to be able to reason about abstraction and refinement methods (see [1] for an example), an area where expressive power can be a great advantage. Of course, there are verification tasks, such as checking that the atomic state transitions of a system preserve a property, where expressive power may be less important and where the speed and effectiveness of basic inference mechanisms, such as term rewriting, is crucial. One goal of our work is to enhance the second kind of reasoning without imposing restrictions that affect the first kind.

Our proof is completely constructive (by choice). While we don't see much application for this fact in this particular case, it is noteworthy that constructivity has not gotten in the way. It may be possible to engineer constructive proofs of protocols from which one can synthesize, for example, programs that track simulations of the protocol and produce interesting data about the current state.

In the rest of the paper we describe the SCI correctness proof and the improvements we made to Nuprl. The proof is not yet finished, though it is nearing completion. A description of what remains to be done is included later in the paper. Details of the completed formalization will be available on the web at www.cs.bell-labs.com/~felty/sci/.

2 SCI Cache Coherence and Its Formalization in Nuprl

This section gives an overview of the SCI cache coherence protocol and its formalization in Nuprl. Before proceeding to the overview, we give a brief description of Nuprl. Formal mathematics in Nuprl is organized in a single library, which is broken into files simulating a theory structure. Library objects can be definitions, display forms, theorems, comments or objects containing ML code. Definitions define new operators, possibly with binding structure, in terms of existing Nuprl terms and previously defined operators. Display forms provide notations for defined and primitive operators. These notations need not be parsable since Nuprl uses structure editors. Theorems have tree structured proofs, possibly incomplete. Each node has a sequent, and represents an inference step. The step is justified either by a primitive rule, or by a *tactic*. Nuprl's notion of tactic is derived from that of LCF, as is HOL's.

Nuprl's type theory has a rich set of type constructors. The following are some example types: $\Pi n \in N . B^n \to B^n$,

$$\{ x \in N \; list \, | \, x \neq nil \}, \quad \Sigma n \in N . B^n, \quad (x, y) : Z \times N^+ // (x_1 y_2 = y_1 x_2).$$

The first of these can be thought of as the type of functions mapping an n and an n-ary bit-vector to an n-ary bit-vector. The second is the type of nonempty list of natural numbers, the third is the collection of pairs (n, b) such that b is an n-ary bit-vector, and the last is a quotient type representing the rational numbers represented as pairs of integers with the usual equivalence relation.

2.1 SCI Cache Coherence

The SCI protocol is an IEEE standard for specifying communication between multiprocessors in a shared memory model [8]. Due to the space limitations we present a very high-level description of our model of the cache coherence part of that protocol. A detailed description of our model can be found in [3].

Processors which try to access the store form a doubly linked list. This list can be thought of as prioritizing processors so that read and write conflicts do not arise. The protocol is distributed; there is no global cache or global data structure for the linked list. Instead each processor p has a set of local variables which keeps track of, for instance, its view of the cache (cv_p), knowledge of whether or not its view is valid (cs_p), and its current successor ($succ_p$) and predecessor ($pred_p$) on the linked list, if any. All communication is via point-to-point message passing. Since a very large number of processors could be on the network, a huge amount of concurrency is present, complicating the understanding of the protocol. (The IEEE standard specifies an upper bound of 64,000 processors. The proof we are formalizing proves the correctness for an arbitrary finite number of processors.)

The protocol is specified as a set of guarded actions. For example, the following is an action executed by the memory controller m.

$buf[m]?read\_cache\_freshQ(p) \longrightarrow$
  if $status_m = Gone$ **then** $buf[p]!read\_cache\_freshR(m, head_m, cv_m, gone)$
  else $buf[p]!read\_cache\_freshR(m, head_m, cv_m, ok)$ **fi**;
  $head_m := p$; **if** $status_m = Home$ **then** $status_m := Fresh$ **fi**

Here, the guard indicates that this action can be executed if the first message in $buf[m]$ (m's message buffer) has type $read\_cache\_freshQ$ which indicates that processor p wants to read. The message is removed from the queue (received) and the body is executed. A message $read\_cache\_freshR(m, head_m, cv_m, gone)$ is sent to processor p, if some processor on the list had issued a write query (indicated by the argument $gone$). Otherwise, response $read\_cache\_freshR(m, head_m, cv_m, ok)$ is sent to p. (Argument ok indicates that no processors are on the list which have requested to modify the store.) Local variable $status_m$ is used by m to record whether some processor is on the list which has issued a write query — its value is then $Gone$; or whether processors on the list have issued read queries only — its value is then $Fresh$; or if no such queries have been issued and hence the list is empty — its value is then $Home$. Finally, local variable $head_m$ is maintained by m to record the head of the list. As shown by this example, bodies can contain assignments, conditionals, and sends. In addition to receives, guards can be boolean conditions.

The protocol is represented as 21 actions: 4 for memory including the one above and 17 for each processor. Communication is via 14 types of messages, made up of 7 pairs of query (Q) and response (R) messages. In addition to the above action, memory has two actions responding to write requests, one from a processor that is already on the doubly linked list because it is reading, and one from a processor that is not yet on the list. It also has an action responding to a processor that wants to go off the list. The 17 actions for each processor include one read request, two write requests, actions for requesting to go on the list or to go off the list (for example, after it has "accessed" the store), an action for purging others off the list when it has been given permission to write the store and decided that it is indeed going to do so, actions for modifying the cache, as well as actions that respond to each kind of request from another processor. This high degree of communication is a main complicating factor in the protocol. Several rounds of messages must be exchanged before a processor is on the list with $succ_p$ and $pred_p$ properly set. Thus, the doubly linked list is constantly modified and constitutes an abstraction of the structure which arises during an actual computation. A variable $status_p$ keeps track of a processor p's state with respect to the list and can take on one of 8 possible values.

2.2 Formalization in Nuprl

Our formalization of correctness follows closely the proof in [3]. Our embedding of the semantics of state transition systems in Nuprl is fairly straightforward. We define a state as a pair where the first component is the usual mapping from identifiers to values. The second component is a *history* variable that records the sequence of messages that have been sent and received during the entire execution. This history variable is important for reasoning about the program's communication behavior. The Nuprl definitions of the components of state are given below. Booleans (B), atoms, integers (Z), and lists are defined in the standard Nuprl libraries.

```
PId  ==  {k:Z| k ≥ 0 }        hist_el ==  B × PId × Z × mesg
id   ==  Atom × PId           hist    ==  hist_el List
mesg ==  Z × Z List           state   ==  (id → Z) × hist
```

For simplicity, the values of all identifiers (`id`) are assumed to be integers. The first component of an identifier is its name (type `Atom`) and the second is the process identifier (type `PId`) to which the variable belongs. The first component of a history element (`hist_el`) is a boolean value indicating whether the message is a send (`tt`) or a receive (`ff`). The remaining components are the sender, receiver, and message (type `mesg`). Message types such as *read_cache_freshQ* are encoded as integers as the first component of a message. The second component encodes the arguments.

Expressions and commands are defined as functions on state. As an example, we give the definition of the assignment command.

```
com  ==  state → state
x:=e ==  λs.<λy.if (x = y) then (e·s) else (y·s), s.h>
```

Nuprl's display forms are used to define := and · as infix operators. The dot is used for evaluation in a state and is overloaded. Here e·s is expression evaluation defined as (e s) and (y·s) maps identifiers to values and is defined as (s.1 y) (where .1 denotes the projection of the first element of a pair). Other commands are defined similarly. Note that the assignment statement updates the first component of the state. The send command updates the second component by simply adding a history element to the front of the history with tt as its first component and the new message as its last component. (Histories and buffers are represented in reverse order.) The receive command also adds a history element to the front of the history, but is more complicated because it computes this element from the contents of the current history h. It uses an operation queue(p;h) which filters out those history elements that contain messages that have been sent and not yet received by process p. It then chooses the last (oldest) element and creates a new copy whose first component is ff. The message buffer of a process p in state s, denoted (buf[p])·s, is also computed using queue. In this case, the message components of the elements of list queue(p;s.2) are projected out.

A program is defined as a pair containing a list of commands and an initial condition which is a predicate on state (of type state → P_1 where P_1 is the type of Nuprl propositions). In our model, a command is enabled if it changes the state when applied. Thus commands whose guards are true but do not change the state are considered disabled. A trace is defined in the usual way as a function from natural numbers to states such that for any n, there is an action (enabled or not) such that when applied to state n results in state $n + 1$.

The correctness of the SCI cache coherence protocol is stated as five linear temporal logic formulas. The first, for example, expresses that there is always a unique cache owner. The notion of cache owner is fairly complex because of the distributed nature of the protocol. If no processor has requested to write to the cache, then memory is the owner. Otherwise, the owner roughly corresponds to the processor p whose variable cs_p has value *dirty*. However, there are various cases where 0 or more than 1 processor has this value. In such cases there is a always a message in some processor's buffer that will cause it to set its value of cs_p to *dirty* or to something else making it or some other processor the unique owner. In order to show that this uniqueness property and the other four properties hold, we prove a series of complex invariants from which these properties follow. These invariants are expressed as 14 lemmas (spanning several pages in [3]), each with several interdependent clauses. There are also many auxiliary concepts that appear in the invariants. For example, there are 6 predicates on processors indicating their degree of progress in getting on or off the doubly linked list. The most complex concept is a function called *rank* whose value reflects how close a process is to getting permission to write.

In related work, Stern and Dill [11] use Murϕ, a verification system that employs explicit state enumeration, to analyze SCI cache coherence. Their largest example included three processors with one cache line each, one memory with one address and two data values, and they reported finding several errors using a smaller example. The model they used was extracted from the C code describing the protocol in [8], whereas our model has been constructed from the informal English explanation. By abstracting at this level, inconsistencies in the lower-level description were removed. Our model also differs from theirs (and from the SCI protocol standard) in that we have assumed that messages sent from one processor to another processor are always received in the order sent. Stern and Dill check for certain safety properties, two of which are formulated as invariants. One of their invariants corresponds to one of our five correctness properties stating that processors in a certain state have a consistent view of the cache. The other is essentially the same as an invariant in one of our supporting lemmas stating at what point a processor is at the head of the linked list.

In [10], Park and Dill use PVS to verify the FLASH cache coherence protocol. Because the protocol uses directories instead of the distributed list of SCI, it seems simpler, and also it seems that the abstraction method they employ may not be applicable to SCI.

3 Imported Mathematics

In this section we describe the connection between HOL and Nuprl, and summarize how it was used in our proof.

3.1 The Importation Mechanism

We believe that much of the mathematics used in practical verification is highly sharable, including theories of basic data types, and also a good deal of the mathematics related to software modeling and semantic connections to external tools. We have taken a first step toward this kind of sharing by borrowing some of the mathematics we needed for our verification from HOL.

Importation of mathematics from HOL into Nuprl is done at the theory level. An HOL theory consists of some type and individual constants, some axioms (usually definitional) constraining the constants, and a set of theorems following from the axioms (and the axioms of ancestor theories). To import a theory, one *interprets* the type constants with Nuprl types and the term constants with members of the appropriate types, and then proves the axioms. When this is done, the theorems can then all be accepted immediately as Nuprl theorems. Typechecking is undecidable in Nuprl, so the well-typedness of interpreting terms must be proven explicitly.

Theorems directly imported from HOL are usually of a form that makes them useless for direct application in Nuprl proofs. It turns out that massaging the theorems into the desired form is possible, and is largely automatable.

To illustrate what kind of transformations are needed on directly imported mathematics, consider an example from list theory. The following is a raw import of a HOL theorem stating that a non-empty list is a cons. Because Nuprl currently has a single flat namespace, the names of all imported constants have an "h" prepended to avoid conflicts with Nuprl objects. The outermost quantifier quantifies over the type S of all (small) non-empty types (this quantifier is implicit in HOL).

```
∀'a:S ↑(hall (λl:hlist('a).
            himplies (hnot (hnull l))
                (hequal (hcons (hhd l) (htl l)) l)))
```

Apart from the outermost quantifier, the logical connectives themselves are imported constants. The transformed, "Nuprl-friendly" theorem generated from the above is

```
∀'a:S. ∀l:'a List.  ¬mt(l) ⇒ hd(l)::tl(l) = l.
```

The logical connectives in HOL are all boolean-valued functions, possibly taking functional arguments, as in the case of the quantifiers. The interpretations of these connectives use boolean logic defined within Nuprl. The boolean connectives are rewritten in the second theorem to Nuprl's normal logical connectives, which are defined using a propositions-as-types correspondence. The operator ↑ in the imported theorem coerces a boolean into a Nuprl proposition. The imported list type is interpreted as Nuprl's list type, and the imported tail function is interpreted as Nuprl's tail function. Note however that htl is *applied*, as a function, to its argument, while the Nuprl tl is a defined operator with a single operand (Nuprl also has an operator for function application, of course). We have used a notational device to suppress type arguments in the (pre-rewrite) imported theorem. Each of the imported constants in the theorem actually has at least one type argument. In the rewritten theorem, there are no hidden type arguments (the Nuprl operations are "implicitly polymorphic").

The most interesting point in this translation is the function for head of a list. In HOL, this is a *total* function on lists. When we import it into Nuprl, we must prove that the interpretation returns a value on every list, empty or not. Since hhd is polymorphic, given an arbitrary type and the empty list as an argument, it must choose some arbitrary member of the type as output. Thus we must give hhd a noncomputable definition in Nuprl. However, we can prove that this function is the same as Nuprl's hd when the list is non-empty. This gives us a conditional rewrite which goes through for this example theorem.

3.2   HOL Math Used in the SCI Verification

The main source of HOL theorems used in the SCI verification is a large body of theorems about lists. Lists are important in two central areas of the proof. First, the definition and proof of properties about the contents of buffers require sophisticated list manipulation since, as mentioned, they are computed from the history component of a state. For example, from the definition of buffer, it fairly is straightforward to prove that when a message M is sent to process p in state s, its buffer becomes M::((buf[p])·s) where :: is the cons operator. The proof that but_last_el((buf[p])·s) is the contents of p's buffer after p receives a message is significantly more complex. The operator but_last_el is defined in an HOL library in terms of the lastn operator (the operation which extracts the last n elements of a list) which is also defined in HOL. The snoc operator, which is the opposite of cons (in particular, the property snoc(x;l) = l @ (x::[])) holds, where @ is the append operator), is also defined in HOL and is useful for reasoning about these operators. The existing HOL theorems about these and a variety of other operators were directly usable in this and other proofs.

The above two theorems are examples of lemmas used as rewrite rules. Nuprl provides powerful automation for the application of rewrite lemmas and good use of this machinery is essential for a large proof such as the SCI verification. We proved and make extensive use of numerous other rewrite lemmas involving histories and buffers. A variety of other theorems about histories and buffers have also been proved and used as support for other kinds of rewrite lemmas.

One invariant (part of Lemma 9 [3]) states that any processor has at most one outstanding message. In particular, for any Q/R pair, there is at most one Q message for which a processor is waiting for the corresponding R message. This means that there is either 0 or 1 Q messages from a processor p in some q's buffer, or there is 0 or 1 R messages in p's buffer, but not both. Our rewrite lemmas along with various other list operators and properties from HOL play a central role in proving this fact.

The second area of the proof in which lists are important is in defining the notion of rank. Rank roughly corresponds to the order in which processors have requested to read or write to the cache. It is only defined for *active* processors, a property of processors that are on or "mostly on" the doubly linked list. An important property is the fact that for any processor, its rank does not increase. This property insures that the list does not contain circularities. As long as a process stays active (and a few other properties hold) its rank will decrease until it becomes 0 at which point it is allowed to write if it has requested to do so. Rank is defined by filtering from the history all read and write requests that memory has received, projecting out the sender, and keeping only the first occurrence of each active processor in the resulting list. The first occurrence corresponds to a processor's most recent request. We prove a variety of lemmas describing how a processor's rank changes with changes in the state. These lemmas are also used as rewrite rules in proving invariants.

4 A Type Annotation Scheme for Nuprl

Our type annotation scheme is a way of attaching type expressions, which we call *annotations*, to all (or only some) of the subterms of a term. Our scheme meets the following goals.

1. Annotations are optional. Terms that do not have annotations attached to them are treated as before by Nuprl's tactics.
2. If a term t is introduced into a proof as a member of a type T, and t occurs somewhere in the current goal with a compatible annotation, then the requirement to prove $t \in T$ is eliminated.
3. Annotations justify rewriting, so that a subterm with an annotation A can be replaced by an equal term (*qua* member of A) without further justification.
4. There are no heuristics in the scheme *per se*. Although type inference and checking are highly heuristic in Nuprl, this is independent of the annotation scheme. Annotations for terms are generated by examining the results of applying Nuprl's existing machinery.
5. Annotations can be effectively maintained. In principal, it is possible for annotations to be lost during inference. For example, the generalized term in the induction rule needs to reannotated (or left without annotations). However, such inference steps form a tiny fraction in practice. For example, annotations are almost never lost during equational rewriting.
6. There are no global tables. We retain the tree-structuring of proofs, with independence of proof branches, that allows us, among other things, to do dependency-directed backtracking, and selective replay of subproofs.
7. Soundness depends only on a fixed set of primitive inference rules that all proofs must reduce to.
8. The scheme is almost entirely invisible to users.

The type theory of the PVS system [9] has some similarities to Nuprl, such as subtypes, (a limited form of) dependent types, and undecidable typechecking. PVS uses a typing discipline that achieves most of the goals above, but it would only be applicable to an insufficiently small subtheory of Nuprl. Some complicating aspects of Nuprl, which aren't present in PVS, are: universe polymorphism; type-indexed equality, so that two terms may both be in two types, but be equal in one type and not in the other; contravariant subtyping, where a function type is enlarged when its domain is shrunk; and general dependent types. In addition, the PVS scheme does not address 7 above.

Nuprl terms have the form $\theta(\overline{x}_1.\,e_1; \ldots; \overline{x}_n.\,e_n)$ where θ is an *operator* and in each operand $\overline{x}_i.e_i$, each of the variables in the sequence $\overline{x}_i$ binds in e_i. Note that no types are associated with the variables in this syntax. An *annotated term* has the form

$$\theta(\ldots; \overline{x}_i.\ e_i : [\phi_i]A_i; \ldots) : B$$

where the e_i are also annotated terms. The expressions $[\phi_i]A_i$ are the *subannotations* of the term, and can be thought of as the expected types for the operands, and B is the annotation type of the term. Informally, $e_i : [\phi_i]A_i$ can be thought of as meaning that under assumption ϕ_i, e_i has type A_i. The ϕ_i can refer to the variables in $\overline{x}_i$, and can contain, for example, assertions of the form $x \in T$. Examples of annotated terms are $fact((3 : Z) : [true]N) : N$, where $fact$, N and Z are factorial, the natural numbers and the integers respectively, and $if(b:B;\ e_1:[b]A;\ e_2:[\neg b]A): A$.

One of the key points is how the annotation type of a term relates to its subannotations and to the subannotations of an immediately surrounding term. We chose the minimal requirement that supports rewriting as described above, and so we require only respect for equality. For example, in $\theta((e : A) : [\phi]A') : B$, where the operand $e : A$ is itself an annotated term, we require, first, that for all $x \in A'$, if $x = e \in A'$ then $\theta(x) = \theta(e) \in B$, and, second, that for all $x \in A$, if $x = e \in A$ then $x = e \in A'$. The generalization of this requirement to the presence of binding variables is straightforward.

As with ordinary typing in Nuprl, the validity of an annotation of a term is undecidable, and must be proven. One possibility would be to generate "type checking conditions" as PVS does, which are side conditions generated whenever a new term is introduced. This is not workable for Nuprl because tactics work by putting together appropriate primitive inference rules, and need an opportunity to assemble proofs of annotation validity at the same time as the proofs justifying the main inference. Rewriting works, for example, by taking a term and producing a rewritten term along with a proof of equality. For annotated terms, it is natural to modify rewriting to take an annotated term, and produce a new term, an equality proof, and *also* a proof that the new term's annotations are correct. We therefore have two kinds of annotations: one kind we can assume are valid during the course of a proof, and the other must be proved to be valid.

The annotation scheme is justified semantically, and requires a re-interpretation of the semantics of sequents. A full report is in preparation.

5   The Correctness Proof in Nuprl

The definition below encodes the formula $\Box P$ from linear temporal logic and is central in proving invariants. A state **s** is in an execution of program **prg**, denoted `in_exec(s;prg)`, if s occurs in some trace of **prg**.

`inv(prg;s.I[s]) == ∀s:state. in_exec(prg;s) ⇒ I[s]`

In a proof of this magnitude, it was essential to provide a high degree of automation. Our automation falls roughly into two categories: tactics that decompose reasoning modularly, and properties expressing equality and equivalence that can be used by Nuprl's rewriting machinery such as those mentioned in Sect. 3.2. Both the decomposition properties and rewrite theorems include general theorems and theorems specific to SCI. The rewrites for message buffers discussed in Sect. 3.2, for example, are not specific to SCI, while the notion of rank is. The decomposition tactics rely on lemmas that we have proven, such as one stating that to show that inv(prg;s.I[s]) holds, it suffices to consider one case for each action of the program and to show that the initial condition holds in the initial state. From this general lemma, we proved decomposition lemmas for SCI which decompose reasoning into 21 cases, one for each memory action and one for each processor action for some arbitrary processor p. We chose to further decompose conditional statements into cases so that each case contains only send, receive, and assignment statements. Rewriting operates on these simplified cases. Although these decomposition properties are specific to SCI, we automated the generation of their statements — as well as a variety of other properties specific to SCI — from the definitions of the actions. Their proofs were often largely automatic also. We also automated the application of many of these lemmas by writing tactics which apply them and solve various subgoals automatically.

Of the 14 lemmas expressing invariants, the first 8 (roughly 2.5 pages in [3]) are fairly simple and express properties about the values that various variables can take on during execution. For example, we prove:

$$read\_cache\_freshR(p, r, cv, arg) \in buf[p] \Rightarrow$$
$$[p = m \land q \in \mathcal{P}(n) \land (r = nil \lor r \in \mathcal{P}(n)) \land (arg = ok \lor arg = gone)].$$

Here $\mathcal{P}(n)$ denotes the set of processors involved in the protocol, with process identifiers $1, \ldots, n$.

The 9th lemma contains five statements which together express the property of outstanding messages described in Sect. 3.2 as well as eight statements expressing which kind of outstanding message a processor p has depending on the value of $status_p$. Lemmas 10 and 11 express a variety of properties of the form $\Box(P \ W \ Q)$ (where W is the weak until operator). We proved a general decomposition theorem for formulas of this form which makes the structure of these proofs similar to those for the other invariants. Lemma 12 expresses some basic properties about rank including two which follow directly from the definition (which is slightly different but equivalent to the one given in [3]) and two which must be proven as invariants. While the invariants up to this point are large and detailed, they are fairly straightforward to prove. The main difficulty in the proof is found in the 13th and 14th lemmas. Lemma 13 has 17 clauses and one assumption which later gets discharged and Lemma 14 has 7 clauses. They state the complex invariants about rank that are required to prove correctness of the protocol.

The proofs up through and including Lemma 11 are completed, as well as the two properties of Lemma 12 that follow from the definition of rank. We have also proven 5 and nearly completed 2 more of the 17 clauses of Lemma 13. For example, we have proven the invariant:

$$purgeQ(q) \in buf[p] \Rightarrow (visiting(p) \land rank(q) = rank(p) + 1)$$

where *visiting* processors are a subset of the *active* ones. In doing so, we have developed all of the rewrite lemmas about the rank function and all other auxilliary predicates that we need to complete the remainder of Lemmas 12, 13, and 14. The reasoning needed to complete the proof by showing that the desired safety properties follow from these invariants will be detailed but straightforward.

Because we started from a proof of correctness [3], we did not expect to find errors in the protocol. However, we have found two errors in the proof. Two of the conjuncts of the first clause of Lemma 13 could not be proved using the assertions we had formulated, although they are true. To prove these conjuncts, we had to add and prove some additional clauses. One is an invariant explicitly stating that two particular messages sent from one processor to another are received in the order sent.

References

1. C.-T. Chou and D. Peled. Verifying a model-checking algorithm. In *Tools and Algorithms for the Construction and Analysis of Systems*, volume 1055 of *Lecture Notes in Computer Science*, pages 241–257. Springer-Verlag, 1996.

2. R. L. Constable, et al. *Implementing Mathematics with the Nuprl Proof Development System*. Prentice-Hall, Englewood Cliffs, New Jersey, 1986.

3. A. Felty and F. Stomp. A correctness proof of a cache coherence protocol. 1997. Available at www.cs.bell-labs.com/~felty/sci/. An earlier version appears in *Proceedings of the 11th Annual Conference on Computer Assurance*, 1996.

4. A. P. Felty and D. J. Howe. Hybrid interactive theorem proving using Nuprl and HOL. In *Fourteenth International Conference on Automated Deduction*, volume 1249 of *Lecture Notes in Computer Science*, pages 351–365. Springer-Verlag, 1997.

5. M. J. C. Gordon and T. F. Melham. *Introduction to HOL: A Theorem Proving Environment for Higher Order Logic*. Cambridge University Press, 1993.

6. D. J. Howe. On computational open-endedness in Martin-Löf's type theory. In *Proceedings of the Sixth Annual Symposium on Logic in Computer Science*, pages 162–172. IEEE Computer Society, 1991.

7. D. J. Howe. Importing mathematics from HOL into Nuprl. In *Theorem Proving in Higher Order Logics*, volume 1125 of *Lecture Notes in Computer Science*, pages 267–281. Springer-Verlag, 1996.

8. IEEE-P1596-05Nov90-doc197-iii. *Part IIIA: SCI Coherence Overview*, 1990. Unapproved Draft. Approved standard is described in IEEE Std. 1596-1992 "The Scalable Coherent Interface".

9. S. Owre and N. Shankar. The formal semantics of PVS. Technical report, SRI, August 1997.

10. S. Park and D. L. Dill. Verification of FLASH cache coherence protocol by aggregation of distributed transactions. In *8th ACM Symposium on Parallel Algorithms and Architectures*, 1996.

11. U. Stern and D. L. Dill. Automatic verification of the SCI cache coherence protocol. In *Correct Hardware Design and Verification Methods*, 1995.

12. B. Werner. Sets in types, types in sets. In *International Symposium on Theoretical Aspects of Computer Software*, volume 1281 of *Lecture Notes in Computer Science*. Springer-Verlag, 1997.

You Assume, We Guarantee: Methodology and Case Studies*

Thomas A. Henzinger   Shaz Qadeer   Sriram K. Rajamani

EECS Department, University of California at Berkeley, CA 94720-1770, USA
Email:{tah,shaz,sriramr}@eecs.berkeley.edu

Abstract. Assume-guarantee reasoning has long been advertised as an important method for decomposing proof obligations in system verification. Refinement mappings (homomorphisms) have long been advertised as an important method for solving the language-inclusion problem in practice. When confronted with large verification problems, we therefore attempted to make use of both techniques. We soon found that rather than offering instant solutions, the success of assume-guarantee reasoning depends critically on the construction of suitable abstraction modules, and the success of refinement checking depends critically on the construction of suitable witness modules. Moreover, as abstractions need to be witnessed, and witnesses abstracted, the process must be iterated. We present here the main lessons we learned from our experiments, in form of a systematic and structured discipline for the compositional verification of reactive modules. An infrastructure to support this discipline, and automate parts of the verification, has been implemented in the tool MOCHA.

1 Introduction

Formal verification is a systematic approach for detecting logical errors in designs. The designer uses a language with mathematical semantics to describe the design, which is then analyzed for correctness with respect to a specification. We refer to the design being analyzed as the implementation. The verification problem is called *refinement checking* when the specification is a more abstract design. For a trace semantics, the refinement-checking problem is PSPACE-hard in the size of the implementation description and in the state space of the specification. Not surprisingly, algorithms for refinement checking are exponential in the size of the implementation description and doubly exponential in the size of the specification description.

There are two general classes of techniques for combating this state-explosion problem. Type-1 techniques focus on improving algorithms, often developing heuristics that target specific application domains, such as symbolic methods for synchronous hardware designs, and partial-order methods for asynchronous communication protocols. Type-2 techniques focus on dividing the verification task at hand into simpler tasks, often making use of the compositional structure of both implementation and specification, such as assume-guarantee methods for proof decomposition. While type-1 techniques can be applied fully automatically and improve the efficiency of formal verification, they need to be complemented by type-2 techniques in order to make the approach fully scalable. Type-2 techniques, however, require substantial assistance from human verification experts, and their systematic application in nontrivial situations remains somewhat of a black art.

We are developing a formal-verification tool, called MOCHA [AHM+98], which is based on the system description language of *reactive modules* [AH96]. Reactive modules permit the modular and hierarchical description of heterogeneous systems, and have been designed explicitly to support type-2 techniques such as assume-guarantee reasoning. In this paper, we present the

---
* This work is supported in part by ONR YIP award N00014-95-1-0520, by NSF CAREER award CCR-9501708, by NSF grant CCR-9504469, by ARO MURI grant DAAH-04-96-1-0341, and by the SRC contract 97-DC-324.041.

experiences and results of our attempts to make use of type-2 techniques within MOCHA in a disciplined and systematic way. We report on a methodology that has led us to success in verifying a hardware circuit that implements Tomasulo's algorithm, and a sliding-window communication protocol. Since the description of these examples would require more space than is available in these proceedings, we illustrate our methodology, instead, on a circuit that implements a simple three-stage pipeline.

We now briefly outline our methodology, which approaches a refinement-checking problem of the form $P_1 \| P_2 \preceq Q$ (where $\preceq$ is the trace-containment relation) by introducing abstraction and witness modules. Suppose that the state space of the implementation $P_1 \| P_2$ is too large to be handled by exhaustive search algorithms. A naive compositional approach would attempt to prove both $P_1 \preceq Q$ and $P_2 \preceq Q$, and then conclude $P_1 \| P_2 \preceq Q$. Though sound, the naive approach often fails in practice, because P_1 usually refines Q only in a suitable constraining environment, and so does P_2. Hence we construct a suitable constraining environment A_2 for P_1, and similarly A_1 for P_2. Since A_1 describes the aspects of P_1 that are relevant to constraining P_2, and similarly A_2 is an abstract description of P_2, the two new modules A_1 and A_2 are called *abstraction modules*. By assume-guarantee reasoning, we conclude $P_1 \| P_2 \preceq Q$ from the two proof obligations $P_1 \| A_2 \preceq A_1 \| Q$ and $A_1 \| P_2 \preceq Q \| A_2$.

Traditionally, the size of the implementation has been viewed as the main source of complexity for the refinement-checking problem. In our approach, we shift the focus to the size of the *gap* between the implementation and the specification. As an extreme case, if we are given two identical copies of a design, we ought to be able to verify that one is a valid refinement of the other, no matter how large the designs. We want the success rate of our methodology to increase if the designer invests effort in structuring the implementation and specification so as to expose more commonality between them. Abstraction modules form an intermediate layer between the implementation and the specification, and thus provide a systematic way of reducing the gap. In our case studies, we found that abstraction modules generally take the form of abstract definitions for hidden implementation variables. When composed with the original specification, which often specifies only relationships between primary inputs and outputs, the abstraction modules yield a richer specification that is closer to the implementation. Constructing good abstraction modules requires manual effort. Once constructed, our methodology automatically makes effective use of the abstraction modules to decompose the refinement check.

Even if the state space of the implementation becomes manageable as a result of proof decomposition, each remaining refinement check, say $P' = P_1 \| A_2 \preceq A_1 \| Q = Q'$, is still PSPACE-hard in the size of the specification state space. However, for the special case that all variables of Q' are also present in P' (in this case, we say that Q' is *projection refinable* by P'), the refinement check reduces to a transition-invariant check, which verifies that every move of P' can be mimicked by Q'. The complexity of this procedure is linear on the state spaces of both P' and Q'. If Q' is not projection refinable by P', our methodology advocates the introduction of a *witness module* W, which makes explicit how the hidden variables of the specification Q' depend on the state of the implementation P'. Then Q' is projection refinable by $P' \| W$, and it suffices to prove $P' \| W \preceq Q'$ in order to conclude $P' \preceq Q'$. The construction of witness modules also requires manual effort, but whenever the specification Q' simulates the implementation P', a suitable witness can be found.

Related work. The individual pieces of our methodology are not new; we simply advocate their disciplined use within the framework of reactive modules. In particular, assume-guarantee rules for various formalisms can be found in [Sta85,CLM89,GL94,AL95,McM97]; the rule used in this paper has been taken from [AH96]. Witnesses have appeared in various guises and forms (homomorphisms, refinement mappings, simulation relations, etc.) in different works [Lam83,LT87,AL91,BBLS92,CGL92,Kur94,LV95,McM97]. Also our choice of case studies is not new. Other correctness proofs for Tomasulo's algorithm can be found in [DP97,McM98]; the sliding-window protocol is taken from [Tan92].

2 A Verification Problem

Reactive modules. Reactive modules is a formalism for the modular description of systems with heterogeneous components. The definition of reactive modules can be found in [AH96]; here we give only a brief introduction. The state of a reactive module is determined by the values of three kinds of variables: the *external variables* are updated by the environment and can be read by the module; the *interface variables* are updated by the module and can be read by the environment; the *private variables* are updated by the module and cannot be read by the environment. The external and interface variables are called *observable*; the interface and private variables, *controlled*.

The state of a reactive module changes in a sequence of rounds. The first round is called the *initial round*, and determines initial values for all variables. Each subsequent round is called an *update round*, and determines new values for all variables. For external variables, the values in the initial and update rounds are left unspecified (i.e., chosen nondeterministically). For controlled variables, the values in the initial and update rounds are specified by (possibly nondeterministic) guarded commands. In each update round, the new value of a controlled variable may depend on the (latched) values of some variables from the previous round. In addition, in each round, the initial (or new) value of a controlled variable may depend on the initial (or new) values of some other variables from the same round; such a dependency between the values of variables within a single round is called an *await dependency*. In order to avoid inconsistent specifications, the await dependencies must be acyclic. In reactive modules, the acyclicity restriction is enforced statically, by partitioning the controlled variables into *atoms* that can be ordered such that in each round, the initial (or new) values for all variables of an atom can be determined simultaneously from the initial (or new) values of the external variables and the variables of earlier atoms.

Each round, therefore, consists of several subrounds—one for the external variables, and one per atom. Each atom has an *initial command*, which specifies the possible initial values for the variables of the atom, and an *update command*, which specifies the possible new values for the variables of the atom within each update round. In the update command, unprimed occurrences of variables refer to the latched values from the previous round; in both the initial and update commands, primed occurrences of variables refer to the initial (or new) values from the same round.

Example 1. Consider the simple instruction set architecture defined by the reactive module *ISA* of Figure 1. The module *ISA* has five external variables (inputs)—the operation *op*, the immediate operand *inp*, the source registers *src1* and *src2*, and the destination register *dest*. There are two interface variables (outputs)—the value *out* of a *STORE* instruction, and a boolean variable *stall*, which indicates if the current inputs have been accepted. If the value of *stall* is *true* in a round, then no instruction is processed in that round, and the environment is supposed to produce the same instruction again in the next round. Finally, there is one private variable—the register file *isaRegFile*.

A round of the module *ISA* consists of four subrounds. In the first subround of each update round, the environment chooses an operation, operands, and a destination, by assigning values to the external variables. In the second subround, the atom *ISAStall* decides nondeterministically if the current inputs are processed, by setting *stall* to *true* or *false*. The third subround belongs to the atom *ISARegFile*. If the updated value of *stall* is *false*, then the current instruction is processed appropriately. If the operation is *AND* or *OR*, it is performed on the source registers and the result is placed into the destination register. If the operation is *LOAD*, the immediate operand is assigned to the destination register. The fourth subround belongs to the atom *ISAOut*. If the

```
module ISA
    external op, inp, src1, src2, dest
    interface out, stall
    private isaRegFile
    atom ISAStall controls stall
        init update
            [] true → stall' := nondet
    atom ISARegFile controls isaRegFile
        init
            [] true → forall i do isaRegFile'[i] := 0
        update
            [] ¬stall' ∧ op' = LOAD → isaRegFile'[dest'] := inp'
            [] ¬stall' ∧ op' = AND  → isaRegFile'[dest'] := isaRegFile[src1'] ∧ isaRegFile[src2']
            [] ¬stall' ∧ op' = OR   → isaRegFile'[dest'] := isaRegFile[src1'] ∨ isaRegFile[src2']
    atom ISAOut controls out
        init update
            [] ¬stall' ∧ op' = STORE → out' := isaRegFile[dest']
```

Fig. 1. Instruction set architecture

updated value of *stall* is *false* and the current operation is $STORE$, then *out* is updated to the contents of the destination register from the previous round. Since both atoms *ISARegFile* and *ISAOut* wait, in each update round, for the new value of *stall*, they must be executed *after* the atom *ISAStall*, which produces the new value of *stall*. However, there are no await dependencies between the atoms *ISARegFile* and *ISAOut*, and therefore the third and fourth subrounds of each update round can be interchanged. □

Parallel composition. The composition operation combines two reactive modules into a single module whose behavior captures the interaction between the two component modules. Two modules P and Q are *compatible* if (1) the controlled variables of P and Q are disjoint, and (2) the await dependencies between the variables of P and Q are acyclic. If P and Q are two compatible modules, then the *composition* $P\|Q$ is the module whose atoms are the (disjoint) union of the atoms from P and Q. The interface variables of $P\|Q$ are the (disjoint) union of the interface variables of P and Q, and the private variables of $P\|Q$ are the (disjoint) union of the private variables of P and Q. The external variables of $P\|Q$ consist of the external variables of P that are not interface variables of Q, and the external variables of Q that are not interface variables of P.

Example 2. The module *ISA* from Figure 1 can be seen as the parallel composition of three modules. The module *ISAStall* has the interface variable *stall*; the module *ISARegFile* has the external variables *op*, *inp*, *src1*, *src2*, *dest*, and *stall*, and the interface variable *isaRegFile*; the module *ISAOut* has the external variables *op*, *dest*, *stall*, and *isaRegFile*, and the interface variable *out*. The operation **hide** makes the interface variable *isaRegFile* private:

$$ISA = \text{hide } isaRegFile \text{ in } ISAStall\|ISARegFile\|ISAOut \qquad □$$

Refinement. The notion that two reactive modules describe the same system at different levels of detail is captured by the refinement relation between modules. We define refinement as trace containment. A *state* of a module P is a valuation for the variables (external, interface, and private) of P. A state is *initial* if it can be obtained at the end of the initial round. Given two states s and t, we write $s \rightarrow_P t$ if when the state at the beginning of an update round is s, then the state at the end of the update round may be t. A *trajectory* of P is a finite sequence $s_0, \ldots, s_n$ of states such that (1) s_0 is an initial state of P, and (2) for $i \in \{0, 1, \ldots, n-1\}$,

444

```
module Opr1
    interface opr1
    external stall, pipe1.op, pipe2.op, pipe1.inp, wbReg, regFile, src1
    atom Opr1 controls opr1
        update
        []  ¬stall' → opr1' :=
            if src1' = pipe1.dest ∧ pipe1.op ≠ NOP ∧ pipe1.op ≠ STORE
            then if pipe1.op = LOAD then pipe1.inp else aluOut'
            else if src1' = pipe2.dest ∧ pipe2.op ≠ NOP ∧ pipe2.op ≠ STORE
                then wbReg else regFile[src1']

module Opr2
    interface opr2
    external stall, pipe1.op, pipe2.op, pipe1.inp, wbReg, regFile, src2
    "Same as Opr1 with src1 replaced by src2"

module Pipe1
    interface pipe1.op, pipe1.inp, pipe1.dest
    external stall, inp, op, dest
    atom Pipe1 controls pipe1.op, pipe1.dest, pipe1.inp
        init
        [] true → pipe1.op' := NOP
        update
        [] true → pipe1.op' := if stall' then NOP else op';
                  pipe1.dest' := dest'; pipe1.inp' := inp'
```

Fig. 2. Pipeline stage 1

we have $s_i \rightarrow_P s_{i+1}$. The states that lie on trajectories are called *reachable*. An *observation* of P is a valuation for the observable variables (external and interface) of P. If s is a valuation to a set of variables, we use $[s]_P$ to denote the set of valuations from s restricted to the observable variables of P. For a state sequence $\bar{s} = s_0, \ldots, s_n$, we write $[\bar{s}]_P = [s_0]_P, \ldots, [s_n]_P$ for the corresponding observation sequence. If $\bar{s}$ is a trajectory of P, then the projection $[\bar{s}]_P$ is called a *trace* of P. The module Q is *refinable* by module P if (1) every interface variable of Q is an interface variable of P, and (2) every external variable of Q is an observable variable of P. The module P *refines* the module Q, written $P \preceq Q$, if (1) Q is refinable by P, and (2) for every trajectory $\bar{s}$ of P, the projection $[\bar{s}]_Q$ is a trace of Q.

Example 3. Consider the three-stage pipeline defined by the reactive module *PIPELINE* shown in Figures 2 and 3. In the first stage of the pipeline, the operands are fetched; in the second stage, the operations are performed; in the third stage, the result is written into the register file. The *PIPELINE* module is the parallel composition of seven modules. The first stage consists of the modules *Pipe1*, *Opr1*, and *Opr2*. Forwarding logic in *Opr1* and *Opr2* ensures that correct values are given to the second stage, even if the value in question has not yet been written into the register file. The second stage consists of the module *Pipe2*, which has an *ALU* atom that processes arithmetic operations using the operands from the first stage and writes the results into a write-back register called *wbReg*. The third stage is consists of the module *RegFile*, which copies *wbReg* into the appropriate register. The *PipeOut* module outputs a register value in response to a *STORE* instruction. The *Stall* module controls the *stall* signal, which is set to *true* whenever a *STORE* instruction cannot be accepted due to data dependencies.

Our goal is to show that *PIPELINE* is a correct implementation of the instruction set architecture *ISA*. This is the case if every sequence of instructions given to *PIPELINE* produces a sequence of outputs (and stalls) that is permitted by *ISA*. The module *ISA* is refinable by *PIPELINE*, so it remains to be shown that every trace of *PIPELINE* is a trace of *ISA*. □

3 Our Methodology

Witness modules. The problem of checking if $P \preceq Q$ is PSPACE-hard in the state space of Q. However, the refinement check is simpler in the special case in which all variables of Q are observable. The module Q is *projection refinable* by the module P if (1) Q is refinable by P, and (2) Q has no private variables. If Q is projection refinable by P, then every variable of Q is observable in both P and Q. Therefore, checking if $P \preceq Q$ reduces to checking if for every trajectory $\bar{s}$ of P, the projection $[\bar{s}]_Q$ is a *trajectory* of Q. According to the following proposition, this can be done by a transition-invariant check, whose complexity is linear in the state spaces of both P and Q.

Proposition 1. *[Projection refinement] Consider two modules P and Q, where Q is projection refinable by P. Then $P \preceq Q$ iff (1) if s is an initial state of P, then $[s]_Q$ is an initial state of Q, and (2) if s is a reachable state of P and $s \to_P t$, then $[s]_Q \to_Q [t]_Q$.*

We make use of this proposition as follows. Suppose that Q is refinable by P, but not projection refinable. This means that there are some private variables in Q. Define Q^u to be the module obtained by making every private variable of Q an interface variable. If we compose P with a module W whose interface variables include the private variables of Q, then Q^u is projection refinable by the composition $P \| W$. Moreover, if W does not constrain any external variables of P, then $P \| W \preceq Q^u$ implies $P \preceq Q$ (in fact, P is simulated by Q). Such a module W is called a *witness* to the refinement $P \preceq Q$. The following proposition states that in order to check refinement, it is sufficient to first find a witness module and then check projection refinement.

Proposition 2. *[Witness modules] Consider two modules P and Q such that Q is refinable by P. Let W be a module such that (1) W is compatible with P, and (2) the interface variables of W include the private variables of Q, and are disjoint from the external variables of P. Then (1) Q^u is projection refinable by $P \| W$, and (2) $P \| W \preceq Q^u$ implies $P \preceq Q$.*

Furthermore, it can be shown that if P does not have any private variables, and P is simulated by Q, then a witness to the refinement $P \preceq Q$ does exist. In summary, the creativity required from the human verification expert is the construction of a suitable witness module, which makes explicit how the private state of the specification Q depends on the state of the implementation P.

Assume-guarantee reasoning. The state space of a module may be exponential in the size of the module description. Consequently, even checking projection refinement may not be feasible. However, typically both the implementation P and the specification Q consist of the parallel composition of several modules, in which case it may be possible to reduce the problem of checking if $P \preceq Q$ to several subproblems that involve smaller state spaces. The assume-guarantee rule for reactive modules [AH96] allows us to conclude $P \preceq Q$ as long as each component of the specification Q is refined by the corresponding components of the implementation P within a suitable environment. The following proposition gives a slightly generalized account of the assume-guarantee rule.

Proposition 3. *[Assume-guarantee rule] Consider two composite modules $P = P_1 \| \cdots \| P_m$ and $Q = Q_1 \| \cdots \| Q_n$, where Q is refinable by P. For $i \in \{1, \dots, n\}$, let Γ_i be the composition of arbitrary compatible components from P and Q with the exception of Q_i. If $\Gamma_i \preceq Q_i$ for every $i \in \{1, \dots, n\}$, then $P \preceq Q$.*

module *Pipe2*
   interface *pipe2.op, pipe2.dest, wbReg, aluOut*
   external *pipe1.op, pipe1.inp, pipe1.dest, opr1, opr2*
   atom *ALU* **controls** *aluOut*
      update
         $[]$ *pipe1.op = AND* → *aluOut'* := *opr1* ∧ *opr2*
         $[]$ *pipe1.op = OR* → *aluOut'* := *opr1* ∨ *opr2*
   atom *Pipe2* **controls** *pipe2.op, pipe2.dest*
      init
         $[]$ *true* → *pipe2.op'* := *NOP*
      update
         $[]$ *true* → *pipe2.op'* := *pipe1.op*; *pipe2.dest'* := *pipe1.dest*
   atom *WbReg* **controls** *wbReg*
      update
         $[]$ *pipe1.op = AND* ∨ *pipe1.op = OR* → *wbReg'* := *aluOut'*
         $[]$ *pipe1.op = LOAD* → *wbReg'* := *pipe1.inp*

module *RegFile*
   interface *regFile*
   external *pipe2.op, pipe2.dest, wbReg, aluOut*
   atom *RegFile* **controls** *regFile*
      init
         $[]$ *true* → **forall** *i* **do** *regFile'[i]* := 0
      update
         $[]$ *pipe2.op = AND* ∨ *pipe2.op = OR* ∨ *pipe2.op = LOAD* →
         forall *i* **do** *regFile'[i]* := **if** *pipe2.dest = i* **then** *wbReg* **else** *regFile[i]*

module *PipeOut*
   interface *out*
   external *op, regFile, dest*
   atom *Out* **controls** *out*
      update
         $[]$ ¬*stall'* ∧ *op' = STORE* → *out'* := *regFile[dest']*

module *Stall*
   interface *stall*
   external *op, dest, pipe1.op, pipe1.dest, pipe2.op, pipe2.dest*
   atom *Stall* **controls** *stall*
      update
         $[]$ *op' = STORE* ∧ *pipe1.op* ≠ *NOP* ∧ *pipe1.op* ≠ *STORE* ∧ *dest' = pipe1.dest* →
         stall' := *true*
         $[]$ *op' = STORE* ∧ *pipe2.op* ≠ *NOP* ∧ *pipe2.op* ≠ *STORE* ∧ *dest' = pipe2.dest* →
         stall' := *true*
         $[]$ **default** → *stall'* := *false*

Fig. 3. Pipeline stages 2 and 3, output, and stall

We make use of this proposition as follows. First we decompose the specification Q into its components $Q_1\|\cdots\|Q_n$. Then we find for each component Q_i of the specification a suitable module Γ_i (called an *obligation module*) and check that $\Gamma_i \preceq Q_i$. This is beneficial if the state space of Γ_i is smaller than the state space of P. The module Γ_i is the parallel composition of two kinds of modules—*essential modules* and *constraining modules*. The essential modules are chosen from the implementation P so that every interface variable of Q_i is an interface variable of some essential module. There may, however, be some external variables of Q_i that are not observable for the essential modules. In this case, to ensure that Q_i is refinable by Γ_i, we need to choose constraining modules from either from the implementation P or from the specification Q (other than Q_i). Once Q_i is refinable by Γ_i, if the refinement check $\Gamma_i \preceq Q_i$ goes through, then we are done. Typically, however, the external variables of Γ_i need to be constrained in order for the refinement check to go through. Until this is achieved, we must add further constraining modules to Γ_i.

It is preferable to choose constraining modules from the specification, which is less detailed than the implementation and therefore gives rise to smaller state spaces (in the undesirable limit, if we choose $\Gamma_i = P$, then the proof obligation $\Gamma_i \preceq Q_i$ involves the state space of P and is no simpler than the original proof obligation $P \preceq Q$). Unfortunately, due to lack of detail, the specification often does not supply a suitable choice of constraining modules. According to the following simple property of the refinement relation, however, we can arbitrarily "enrich" the specification by composing it with new modules.

Proposition 4. *[Abstraction modules] For all modules P, Q, and A, if $P \preceq Q\|A$ and Q is refinable by P, then $P \preceq Q$.*

So, before applying the assume-guarantee rule, we may add modules to the specification and prove $P \preceq Q\|A_1\|\cdots\|A_k$ instead of $P \preceq Q$. The new modules $A_1,\dots,A_k$ are called *abstraction modules*, as they usually give high-level descriptions for some implementation components, in order to provide a sufficient supply of constraining modules. In summary, the creativity required from the human verification expert is the construction of suitable abstraction modules, which on one hand, need to be as detailed as required to serve as constraining modules in assume-guarantee reasoning, and on the other hand, should be as abstract as possible to minimize their state spaces.

While witness modules are introduced "on the left" of a refinement relation, abstraction modules are introduced "on the right." So it may be necessary to iterate both processes, providing witnesses for abstractions, and abstractions for witnesses. An example of this will appear in the next section.

4 Our Solution

We prove that $PIPELINE \preceq ISA$ using Propositions 1, 2, 3, and 4. We note that ISA is refinable by $PIPELINE$, but not projection refinable. This is because $isaRegFile$ in ISA is a private variable. We claim that the module $ISARegFile$ is a witness module for $isaRegFile$. We then use Proposition 2 to reduce the proof obligation $PIPELINE \preceq ISA$ to $ISARegFile\|PIPELINE \preceq ISA^u$. This proof obligation can be expanded in terms of component modules to

$$ISARegFile\|RegFile\|Opr1\|Opr2\|\atop Pipe1\|Pipe2\|PipeOut\|Stall \preceq ISARegFile\|ISAOut\|ISAStall.$$

Let us start by identifying $ISAOut$ with Q_1. We need to find an obligation module Γ_1, such that $\Gamma_1 \preceq ISAOut$. There is only one interface variable for $ISAOut$, namely out. The component of $PIPELINE$ that generates out is $PipeOut$. Thus $PipeOut$ is the only essential module for Γ_1. However, the proof obligation

$$\Gamma_1 = PipeOut \preceq Q_1 = ISAOut$$

fails trivially, because *ISAOut* is not refinable by *PipeOut*. The module *ISAOut* has an external variable *isaRegFile* that is not present in *PipeOut*. To achieve refinability, we add *ISARegFile*, the module controlling *isaRegFile*, to Γ_1 and try to prove

$$\Gamma_1 = ISARegFile \| PipeOut \preceq Q_1 = ISAOut.$$

This fails because the input *regFile* to *PipeOut* is not constrained. We add *RegFile* to constrain *regFile*, but in vain, because the check

$$\Gamma_1 = ISARegFile \| RegFile \| PipeOut \preceq Q_1 = ISAOut$$

also fails. The reason now is that the inputs to *RegFile* are not constrained. We add *Pipe2* for this purpose, and then *Pipe1*, *Opr1*, *Opr2*, and *Stall* to constrain the inputs to *Pipe2*. At last, we are able to prove the proof obligation

$$\Gamma_1 = ISARegFile \| RegFile \| Pipe1 \| Pipe2 \| Opr1 \| Opr2 \| Stall \| PipeOut \preceq Q_1 = ISAOut.$$

Now, according to Proposition 3, the assume-guarantee proof looks as follows:

$$\frac{\begin{array}{c} ISARegFile \| RegFile \| Pipe1 \| Pipe2 \| \\ Opr1 \| Opr2 \| Stall \| PipeOut \end{array} \preceq ISAOut \\ ISARegFile \preceq ISARegFile \\ Stall \preceq ISAStall}{\begin{array}{c} ISARegFile \| RegFile \| Pipe1 \| Pipe2 \| \\ Opr1 \| Opr2 \| Stall \| PipeOut \end{array} \preceq ISAOut \| ISARegFile \| ISAStall}$$

However, notice that the biggest module on the left side above the line is exactly the same as the module on the left side below the line. Hence, the compositional approach did not yield much advantage.

So let us return to the *PIPELINE* module with the intent of adding abstraction modules. We will add three abstraction modules—*AbsOpr1*, *AbsOpr2*, and *AbsRegFile*, corresponding to *Opr1*, *Opr2*, and *RegFile*. Notice that whenever the required operand specified by *src1* is currently being produced by *ALU* or is in *wbReg*, module *Opr1* looks ahead and finds it. Otherwise, it gets the operand from the register file in *PIPELINE*. It is observed that the specification variable $isaRegFile[src1']$ contains the same value that will be produced by the forwarding logic. This observation can be used to write the following abstraction module for *Opr1*.

> **module** *AbsOpr1*
> **external** *isaRegFile*, *src1*, *stall*
> **interface** *opr1*
> **atom** *AbsOpr1* **controls** *opr1*
> **update**
>   [] $\neg stall' \rightarrow opr1' := isaRegFile[src1']$

Note that the abstraction module leaves the value of *opr1* unspecified if *stall* is *true*. The implementation module *Opr1*, on the other hand, specifies a value for *opr1* in every round. Such incomplete specification is an essential characteristic of abstraction modules. A similar abstraction module *AbsOpr2* can be written for *Opr2*.

To write an abstraction module for the implementation register file, *regFile*, observe that the value of *regFile* in every round must be equal to the value of *isaRegFile* from two rounds earlier. Thus, we can write the abstraction module for *RegFile* as $AbsRegFile \| ISARegFile_d$, where *AbsRegFile* and $ISARegFile_d$ are given below.

> **module** $ISARegFile_d$
> **atom** $ISARegFile_d$ **controls** $isaRegFile_d$
> **init**
>   [] $true \rightarrow$ **forall** i **do** $isaRegFile_d'[i] := 0$
> **update**

$[]\ true \rightarrow$ **forall** i **do** $isaRegFile'_d[i] := isaRegFile[i]$

module $AbsRegFile$
    atom $AbsRegFile$ **controls** $regFile$
      init
        $[]\ true \rightarrow$ **forall** i **do** $regFile'[i] := 0$
      update
        $[]\ true \rightarrow$ **forall** i **do** $regFile'[i] := isaRegFile_d[i]$

On composing $AbsRegFile$ and $ISARegFile_d$ with ISA, we find that the new specification is not projection refinable by $ISARegFile \| PIPELINE$, because of the new specification variable $isaRegFile_d$. To regain projection refinability, a witness module needs to be written for the abstraction module $isaRegFile_d$, and composed with $PIPELINE$. A suitable witness is simply the module $ISARegFile_d$. After adding the abstraction modules, according to Proposition 3, we obtain the following assume-guarantee proof:

$$
\begin{array}{c}
\dfrac{PipeOut\|Pipe1\|Pipe2\|Stall\|}{AbsRegFile\|ISARegFile_d\|ISARegFile} \preceq ISAOut \\[2ex]
\dfrac{Opr1\|AbsOpr2\|Pipe1\|Pipe2\|}{AbsRegFile\|ISARegFile_d\|ISARegFile} \preceq AbsOpr1 \\[2ex]
\dfrac{Opr2\|AbsOpr1\|Pipe1\|Pipe2\|}{AbsRegFile\|ISARegFile_d\|ISARegFile} \preceq AbsOpr2 \\[2ex]
\dfrac{AbsOpr1\|AbsOpr2\|Pipe1\|Pipe2\|}{RegFile\|ISARegFile_d\|ISARegFile\|Stall} \preceq AbsRegFile\|ISARegFile_d \\[2ex]
Stall \preceq ISAStall \\[1ex]
ISARegFile \preceq ISARegFile \\
\hline
\begin{array}{c} ISARegFile\|ISARegFile_d\|RegFile\| \\ Pipe1\|Pipe2\|Opr1\|Opr2\|PipeOut\|Stall \end{array} \preceq \begin{array}{c} ISARegFile\|ISAOut\|ISAStall\|AbsOpr1\| \\ AbsOpr2\|AbsRegFile\|ISARegFile_d \end{array}
\end{array}
$$

All proof obligations above the line satisfy projection refinability, and involve smaller state spaces than the conclusion of the proof. Following Proposition 1, they can be discharged by a transition-invariant check. Let us now focus on the modules below the line. Notice that the composite module on the left side is $PIPELINE \| ISARegFile \| ISARegFile_d$, and the composite module on the right side is $ISA^u\|ISARegFile_d\|AbsOpr1\|AbsOpr2\|AbsRegFile$. By Proposition 4, we can remove $ISARegFile_d\|AbsOpr1\|AbsOpr2\|AbsRegFile$ from the right side to obtain the refinement $PIPELINE\|ISARegFile\|ISARegFile_d \preceq ISA^u$. The module $ISARegFile \| ISARegFile_d$ is a witness for the refinement $PIPELINE \preceq ISA$. Hence, by Proposition 2, we conclude that $PIPELINE \preceq ISA$.

5 Discussion

In the previous section, we presented an assume-guarantee proof of the fact that $PIPELINE$ refines ISA. In this section, we would like to touch upon some of the issues and finer points that came up while we were developing this methodology.

Projection refinability. Our definition of projection refinability is stronger than necessary. A variable is *history-free* if no atom uses the (latched) value of the variable from the previous round. Otherwise, the variable is said to be a *latch variable*. For module Q to be projection refinable by module P, it is sufficient to require that every latch variable of Q is observable in both P and Q.

Trivial witnesses. An atom is *deterministic* if two distinct guards of the initial command cannot be true in any given round, and the same is true for the update command. A module is *deterministic* if all its atoms are deterministic. If a private variable of the specification is controlled by a deterministic module, and all variables on which it depends are already present in the implementation, then the witness module for this variable can be easily constructed by copying the initial and update commands of the controlling module. This phenomenon can be noticed in the case study of Section 4, where we claimed *ISARegFile* as the witness for the variable *isaRegFile*. Notice also that this simplicity comes at a price. The module *ISARegFile* has latch variables, and so we have increased the number of state bits in the module over which we perform the transition-invariant check. Alternatively, a more complex witness for *isaRegFile*, which does not have any latch variables, can be produced [HQR98].

Choice of constraining modules. An important problem one faces in a compositional proof is the choice of a mimimal set of constraining modules, preferably with small state spaces. Consider one proof obligation ("lemma") $\Gamma_i \preceq Q_i$ in the compositional proof of $P \preceq Q$ using Proposition 3. Starting from the essential modules, our implementation chooses progressively larger obligation modules Γ_i in two steps. First, sufficient constraining modules are added to make Q_i refinable by Γ_i. Second, additional constraining modules are chosen according to a heuristics that looks at the data dependencies in the specification and implementation, until Γ_i refines Q_i. The constraining modules are chosen preferably from the specification Q, rather than from the implementation P. Alternatively, the user can force specific submodules of P or Q into Γ_i.

Fairness. Though not discussed here, our methodology also supports fairness conditions on the specification and implementation [HQR98].

Refinement Check	Latches
Monolithic	110*
msgP, indexP	35
msgBuffer	39
msgC, indexC	59
windowS	75
seqS	35
seqR	59
ackWait	15
seqX	55
msgX	55
ackX	51
busy	75
recvd	56
msgBufferR	68

Refinement Check	Latches
Monolithic	67*
Data Out	12
Bus valid bit	0
Bus value	32
Bus tag	0
Register[0] valid bit	4
Register[0] tag	4
Register[0] value	20
Reservation Station[0] valid bit	4
Reservation Station[0] aVal valid bit	22
Reservation Station[0] aVal tag	10
Reservation Station[0] aVal value	35

Table 1. Lemmas in the proof of sliding-window protocol (left) and Tomasulo's algorithm (right)

Other case studies. We used the methodology outlined in Section 3 to verify implementations of a sliding-window protocol and of Tomasulo's algorithm. Space does not permit us to describe these case studies in detail; a detailed description can be found in [HQR98]. The results of our experiments are summarized in Table 1. The table on the left gives the results for the sliding-window protocol with window size 12. The table on the right gives the results for Tomasulo's algorithm with 4 registers and 4 reservation stations. The tables enumerate the lemmas that were proved to conclude that the implementation refines the specification. There is a lemma for each component of the specification, and a lemma for each abstraction module that is composed with the specification. The second column gives the number of boolean latch variables that encode the state space of the corresponding obligation module. In all proofs, most obligation modules contained components from the specification or abstraction modules. These components are typically very abstract, with much nondeterminism and small state spaces. The row labeled "monolithic" refers to a noncompositional proof, where the transition-invariant check is performed on the full state space of the implementation. The superscript * indicates an unsuccessful verification attempt.

Acknowledgments

We thank Ken McMillan and Amir Pnueli for inspiring this work.

References

[AH96]   R. Alur and T.A. Henzinger. Reactive modules. In *Proceedings of the 11th Annual Symposium on Logic in Computer Science*, pages 207–218. IEEE Computer Society Press, 1996.

[AHM+98]   R. Alur, T.A. Henzinger, F.Y.C. Mang, S. Qadeer, S.K. Rajamani, and S. Tasiran. MOCHA : Modularity in model checking. In A. Hu and M. Vardi, editors, *CAV 98: Computer Aided Verification*, Lecture Notes in Computer Science. Springer-Verlag, 1998.

[AL91]   M. Abadi and L. Lamport. The existence of refinement mappings. *Theoretical Computer Science*, 82(2):253–284, 1991.

[AL95]   M. Abadi and L. Lamport. Conjoining specifications. *ACM Transactions on Programming Languages and Systems*, 17(3):507–534, 1995.

[BBLS92]   S. Bensalem, A. Bouajjani, C. Loiseaux, and J. Sifakis. Property-preserving simulations. In G. von Bochmann and D.K. Probst, editors, *CAV 92: Computer Aided Verification*, Lecture Notes in Computer Science 663, pages 260–273. Springer-Verlag, 1992.

[CGL92]   E.M. Clarke, O. Grumberg, and D.E. Long. Model checking and abstraction. In *Proceedings of the 19th Annual Symposium on Principles of Programming Languages*, pages 343–354. ACM Press, 1992.

[CLM89]   E.M. Clarke, D.E. Long, and K.L. McMillan. Compositional model checking. In *Proceedings of the 4th Annual Symposium on Logic in Computer Science*, pages 353–362. IEEE Computer Society Press, 1989.

[DP97]   W. Damm and A. Pnueli. Verifying out-of-order executions. In *Proceedings of the IFIP Working Conference on Correct Hardware Design and Verification Methods, CHARME*, 1997.

[GL94]   O. Grumberg and D.E. Long. Model checking and modular verification. *ACM Transactions on Programming Languages and Systems*, 16(3):843–871, 1994.

[HQR98]   T.A. Henzinger, S. Qadeer, and S.K. Rajamani. You assume, we guarantee: Methodology and case studies. Technical report, Electronics Research Lab, Univ. of California, Berkeley, CA 94720, 1998.

[Kur94]   R.P. Kurshan. *Computer-aided Verification of Coordinating Processes*. Princeton University Press, 1994.

[Lam83]   L. Lamport. Specifying concurrent program modules. *ACM Transactions on Programming Languages and Systems*, 5(2):190–222, 1983.

[LT87]   N.A. Lynch and M.R. Tuttle. Hierarchical correctness proofs for distributed algorithms. In *Proceedings of the 6th Annual Symposium on Principles of Distributed Computing*, pages 137–151. ACM Press, 1987.

[LV95]   N.A. Lynch and F. Vaandrager. Forward and backward simulations, Part I: Untimed systems. *Information and Computation*, 121(2):214–233, 1995.

[McM97]   K.L. McMillan. A compositional rule for hardware design refinement. In O. Grumberg, editor, *CAV 97: Computer Aided Verification*, Lecture Notes in Computer Science 1254, pages 24–35. Springer-Verlag, 1997.

[McM98]   K.L. McMillan. Verification of an implementation of Tomasulo's algorithm by compositional model checking. In A. Hu and M. Vardi, editors, *CAV 98: Computer Aided Verification*, Lecture Notes in Computer Science. Springer-Verlag, 1998.

[Sta85]   E. W. Stark. A proof technique for rely/guarantee properties. In *Proceedings of the 5th Conference on Foundations of Software Technology and Theoretical Computer Science*, Lecture Notes in Computer Science 206, pages 369–391. Springer-Verlag, 1985.

[Tan92]   Andrew S. Tanenbaum. *Computer Networks*. Prentice-Hall Inc., 1992.

Verification of a
Parameterized Bus Arbitration Protocol [*]

E. Allen Emerson and Kedar S. Namjoshi

Department of Computer Sciences,
The University of Texas at Austin, U.S.A.

Abstract. Model Checking is well established as a verification technique for finite-state systems. Many protocols, while composed of finite-state processes, are parameterized by the number of such processes, hence Model Checking cannot be applied directly to determine correctness of the inherently infinite-state parameterized system. We present a case study on the verification of such a parameterized protocol, the SAE-J1850 data transfer procotol. This is a standard in the automobile industry, where it is used to transmit data between various sensors and micro-controllers in an automobile. The protocol communicates data over a single-wire bus, and provides on-the-fly arbitration between competing transmissions. Our verification effort is interesting from many aspects : it proves correctness for arbitrary instances, is largely automated, and uses abstraction in an essential way. The abstractions used are exact, in the sense that a property is true of the parameterized protocol if and only if it is true of the finite-state abstraction.

1 Introduction

Model Checking [CE 81] (cf. [QS 82],[CES 86]) is well established as a verification technique for finite-state systems. Many communication protocols, however, are parameterized by the number of processes, which induces an infinite *family* of (usually) finite-state instances. While Model Checking is often used to verify correctness of individual instances, this does not provide any guarantee of correctness for the entire family [1]. Thus an important research task is to develop algorithms and semi-algorithmic procedures to verify parameterized systems. The general problem is known to be undecidable [AK 86]; however, algorithms exist for specific types of systems (cf. [GS 92], [EN 95], [EN 96]), and many semi-algorithmic procedures have been proposed (cf. [CG 87], [SG 89], [KM 89], [WL 89], [PD 95],[CGJ 95]).

We present a case study on the verification of an parameterized industrial standard protocol. The protocol is called the SAE-J1850 protocol [SAE 92], and

---

[*] This work was supported in part by NSF grant CCR 941-5496 and SRC Contract 97-DP-388. The authors may be reached at {emerson,kedar}@cs.utexas.edu.
[1] This situation is, ironically, similar to testing; verifying a few individual instances may help detect bugs, but can never demonstrate their absence for the entire family.

it is an automobile industry standard for transmitting data between various sensors and controllers in an automobile. The system consists of a single-wire bus to which several controllers (units) are attached. Since the bus is a single wire, symbols **0** and **1** are transmitted by encoding them by both the length and the value of a bus pulse. For instance, a **0** may be sent with either a long high or a short low pulse.

Several units may transmit concurrently; the protocol incorporates a *distributed, on-the-fly* arbitration mechanism which ensures that only the units transmitting the highest priority message succeed. Priority between messages (strings over $\{0, 1\}$) is determined by lexicographic order, given that the symbol **0** has priority over the symbol **1**. The protocol is correct if it ensures that the arbitration mechanism functions correctly. We should note here that the protocol as described in [SAE 92] has other higher-level functionality, which we have not considered in order to concentrate our attention on the core arbitration question. The protocol is further complicated by the presence of arbitrary but bounded delays in the units while detecting a change in the bus state. These delays have an electrical origin; they arise from delays in the detection circuitry, and the presence of different bias voltages at the units. To accommodate these delays, "long" and "short" are actually time *intervals*, whose length is proportional to the maximum delay. Thus the protocol is parameterized both by the maximum delay and by the number of units taking part in it.

The verification of the protocol proceeds by two applications of abstraction, one for each parameter. The first abstraction theorem shows a *delay independence* property of the protocol : an instance of the protocol with n units and maximum delay Δ is correct iff the instance with n units and maximum delay 2 is correct. Thus, correctness need be proved only for the family of instances with maximum delay 2. The second abstraction uses the algorithm in [EN 96] to handle the parameterization over the number of units in a *fully* automated manner; the algorithm constructs a *finite* "abstract graph" which represents the entire family of instances exactly, over which properties can be model-checked. A simple version of this protocol, without the complexity introduced by the delays, was verified in [EN 96]. The modeling of the delay not only introduces complexity into the behavior of the units, but also introduces additional parameterization into the protocol, which is dealt with by the delay independence theorem.

The success of this effort leads us to believe that careful specification of the computational model underlying other protocols will expose constraints that can be utilized, as in this case, for developing decision procedures for other classes of parameterized protocols. It also exposes a dire need for developing and popularizing notation for expressing such protocols. Remarkably, the SAE-J1850 document does not contain a succinct protocol description; the development of such a description was a major component of this project. The successful verification of the protocol using symbolic methods, despite the theoretical result on PSPACE-completeness of the procedure used [EN 96], is reason to believe that fully automated parameterized verification is feasible for reasonably sized protocols.

The rest of the paper is structured as follows: Section 2 describes the various components of the protocol in more detail. Section 3 discusses the abstractions used for handling the parameterizations. In Section 4, we describe the implementation of the [EN 96] algorithm, and its application to this protocol. Section 5 concludes the paper and provides comparisons with related work.

2   Protocol Description

The SAE-J1850 protocol is a data transfer protocol over a single wire bus, which is intended to be used for communication between various sensors and controllers in an automobile. The restriction to a single wire bus reduces wiring complexity. An instance of the parameterized system consists of several *units* connected to a single *bus*. The operation of the protocol can be described at the "interface" and "implementation" levels.

At the interface level, the units communicate by broadcasting messages (sequences of symbols from the set $\{0, 1\}$) over the bus. Units may transmit concurrently; arbitration takes place during transmission. The arbitration mechanism is defined in terms of priority among symbols; the symbol 0 has higher priority than 1. The priority order among symbols is extended to messages by lexicographic ordering. The key correctness property of this protocol is that the arbitration mechanism works as follows : whenever several units are sending messages concurrently, the message with the highest priority is placed on the bus.

At the implementation level, since the bus is a single wire, symbols are encoded by pulses of differing length and the bus value during the pulse. For instance, the 0 symbol is encoded by either a "long" high pulse, or by a "short" low pulse. The high and low states on the bus are referred to as *Dominant* and *Passive* respectively in the SAE-J1850 document [SAE 92], so we will use this terminology in the rest of the paper. The state of the bus is an "or" of the bus states desired by the units. The protocol is further complicated by non-deterministic, but bounded delays in the units while detecting a change in bus value. This delay is caused either by bias voltages, or by delays in the detection circuitry. To account for these delays, "long" and "short" are not fixed numbers, but are instead non-empty intervals, whose length is proportional to the maximum delay parameter, which we term Δ.

We will continue to use the symbolic names "long" and "short". There are four parameters associated with a symbolic length l : $Txmin(l)$, $Trmin(l)$, $Txmax(l)$, $Trmax(l)$. Their values are based on a nominal value $Tnom(l)$ and are given by the formulae : $Txmin(l) = Tnom(l) - \Delta/2$, $Txmax(l) = Tnom(l) + \Delta/2$, $Trmin(l) = Tnom(l) - 3\Delta/2$, $Trmax(l) = Tnom(l) + 3\Delta/2$. $Tnom(l)$ is itself proportional to Δ. $Tnom(Long) = 8 * \Delta$, and $Tnom(Short) = 4 * \Delta$. The values are given explicitly in the table below:

Note that the interval $[Txmin(l), Txmax(l)]$ is properly contained in the interval $[Trmin(l), Trmax(l)]$, and that the least *Long* value exceeds the largest *Short* value by Δ. The core of the protocol is the following procedure followed by each

Length	$Trmin$	$Txmin$	$Txmax$	$Trmax$
Short	2.5Δ	3.5Δ	4.5Δ	5.5Δ
Long	6.5Δ	7.5Δ	8.5Δ	9.5Δ

Fig. 1. Interval Lengths

unit to transmit a symbol with symbolic length l at a bus value of b (e.g., **0** as a *Short*, *Passive* pulse). At the entry to this procedure, $request = b$, $localbus = b$, and $counter = 1$.

```
var localbus (* the bus value perceived by the unit *)
var request (* the bus value desired by the unit at the next cycle *)
var counter (* the number of cycles elapsed for this transmission *)

do
   counter ∈ [0, Trmin(l)) ⟶
      if
            localbus = b ⟶request, counter := b, counter + 1
      []   localbus ≠ b ⟶counter := 1; signal FAILURE(* pulse too short *)
      fi
[] counter ∈ [Trmin(l), Txmin(l)) ⟶
      if
            localbus ≠ b ⟶counter := 1; signal SUCCESS
      []   localbus = b ⟶request, counter := b, counter + 1
      fi
[] counter ∈ [Txmin(l), Txmax(l)) ⟶
      if
            localbus ≠ b ⟶counter := 1; signal SUCCESS
      []   localbus = b ⟶request := ¬b
      fi
[] counter ∈ [Txmax(l), Trmax(l)] ⟶
      if
            localbus ≠ b ⟶counter := 1; signal SUCCESS
      []   localbus = b ⟶request, counter := Passive, counter + 1
      fi
[] counter > Trmax(l) ⟶signal FAILURE (* pulse too long *)
od
```

Fig. 2. Algorithm to transmit a symbol with length l and bus value b.

Informally, the procedure above attempts to maintain the bus at value b for $Txmin(l)$ time units. If this attempt succeeds, then it attempts to change the bus value to $\neg b$ within $Txmax(l)$ time units so as to terminate the pulse. If that fails, then the procedure switches to a *Passive* request and waits for some other unit to change the bus value. As the names indicate, $[Trmin(l), Trmax(l)]$ is the interval for successful "reception" of the symbol while $Txmin(l)$ and $Txmax(l)$

are the time bounds for attempting "transmission" of the symbol. **0** is encoded as either a *Short Passive* pulse or as a *Long Dominant* pulse, while **1** is encoded by the other two combinations. The asymmetry between *Passive* and *Dominant* is used to enforce the priority order $1 \preceq 0$.

2.1 Correctness Properties

The correctness property is stated informally in the protocol document [SAE 92] as: *Whenever several units are transmitting messages concurrently, the message with the highest priority is the one placed on the bus.*

This property can be stated precisely in *CTL* as follows: Consider n units connected to the bus, indexed by i, ($i \in [1, n]$). Let $\mathcal{M}(k)$ denote the set of message strings (over $\{0, 1\}$) of length k. For each i in $[1, n]$, let msg_i denote the fixed message string that is associated with unit i. Let B denote the message that is transmitted on the bus (this may be defined as an auxiliary variable that records symbols as they are transmitted on the bus). Let tr_i be a boolean auxiliary variable that records if unit i is transmitting. Let max be the function that determines the maximum message of a set of messages, according to the lexicographic priority $\preceq$ on messages. If the set is empty, max has value ϵ, the empty string. The following *CTL* formula expresses the property above:

(C0) $(\forall m : m \in \mathcal{M}(k) : \mathsf{AG}(maxT = m \wedge B = \epsilon \Rightarrow \mathsf{A}(B \preceq m \;\mathsf{U}\; B = m)))$,

where $maxT = max\{i : i \in [1, n] \wedge tr_i : msg_i\}$

This expression is of finite length for fixed k. Verification of this property for a fixed k requires adding state to each unit to store message contents, which makes the state space intractably large. To solve this problem, we modify the environment of the protocol so that the message sent by a unit is generated on the fly. At any state, let $sent_i$ denote the message sent by a unit. The modified correctness property is as follows :

(C1) $\mathsf{AG}(maxS = \epsilon \wedge B = \epsilon \Rightarrow \mathsf{AG}(B = maxS))$, where $maxS = max\{i : i \in [1, n] \wedge tr_i : sent_i\}$

Informally, this property states that starting at any state where both the message on the bus and that at the units is empty, at any point of time the message on the bus is equal to the lexicographic maximum of the messages sent by the currently transmitting units. This implies that B must increase (lexicographically) as long as there is a transmitting unit.

While the new environment is simpler, the statement of the property still involves several unbounded auxiliary variables. Instead of checking this property, which refers to the history of a computation, we check several properties that deal with the transmission of a single symbol. We show in Lemma 1 that their conjunction implies (C1). The statement of these properties requires some auxiliary propositions : *insym* holds at states where $B = \epsilon$, or the state is at least Δ time units from the last bus state change; *E0sender* holds iff there is a transmitting unit with current symbol **0**; *E1sender* holds iff there is a transmitting unit with current symbol **1**.

Let $before(x) \equiv \mathsf{A}(insym \;\mathsf{U}\; (insym \wedge x))$, $at(x) \equiv \mathsf{A}(insym \;\mathsf{U}\; (\neg insym \wedge x))$, and $after(x) \equiv \mathsf{A}(insym \;\mathsf{U}\; (\neg insym \;\mathsf{U}\; (insym \wedge x)))$. Informally, $before(x)$ holds iff x holds before every next bus change, $at(x)$ holds iff x holds at the following bus change, and $after(x)$ holds iff x holds just after the bus change is complete.

A *stable state* on an execution sequence is one where $B = \epsilon$, or the state is at Δ time units after the last bus value change. By the protocol definition, in this state every unit perceives the new bus value. A stable state is the first state for which *insym* is true after a bus change.

(C2a) In any global state where symbol transmission is in progress, and there is a unit sending **0**, the next bus value is **0**. In *CTL*, this is specified as

$AG(insym \wedge E0sender \Rightarrow at(value = 0))$

(C2b) In any global state where symbol transmission is in progress, if there is a unit sending **1** and no unit sending **0**, the next bus value is **1**.

$AG(insym \wedge \neg E0sender \wedge E1sender \Rightarrow at(value = 1))$

The properties above are global properties. The following are properties of every unit, expressed in an indexed temporal logic (cf. [RS 85],[BCG 89]):

(C2c) In any global state where symbol transmission is in progress, every unit transmitting **0** succeeds and continues to transmit until the next *insym* state.

$\bigwedge_i AG(insym \wedge tr_i \wedge (sym_i = 0) \Rightarrow after(tr_i))$

(C2d) In any global state where symbol transmission is in progress, and there is a unit sending **0**, every unit transmitting **1** fails before the bus symbol is determined.

$\bigwedge_i AG(insym \wedge E0sender \wedge tr_i \wedge (sym_i = 1) \Rightarrow before(\neg tr_i))$

(C2e) In any global state where symbol transmission is in progress and there is no unit sending **0**, every unit transmitting **1** succeeds and continues to transmit until the next *insym* state.

$\bigwedge_i AG(insym \wedge \neg E0sender \wedge tr_i \wedge (sym_i = 1) \Rightarrow after(tr_i))$

Lemma 1. *Properties (C2a)-(C2e) imply Property (C1).*

Proof. We show by induction on the number of stable states on any computation from a state with $B = \epsilon$ and $maxS = \epsilon$ (the 0th stable state) that the following property holds:

(IH) At the the kth stable state, B is the maximum of the messages sent by units that were transmitting at the start of previous stable bus state if $k > 0$, otherwise it is ϵ. Every transmitting unit has sent B.

Basis : $k = 0$. The message on the bus as well as the message at every transmitting unit are both ϵ, so the claim holds.

Inductive step : Assume that (IH) holds at the kth stable state. If some unit transmits **0** at this state, by (C2a) the next symbol on the bus is **0**. By (C2c), any unit transmitting **0** is transmitting at the next stable state. By (C2d), all units transmitting **1** fail before the next stable state.

If some unit transmits **1** at this state and no unit transmits **0**, then by (C2b), the next bus symbol is **1**, and by (C2e) every unit transmitting **1** is still transmitting at the next stable state. By (IH), at the kth stable state, all units transmit the lexicographic maximum among the sent messages, hence, at the next stable state, the value of B is still the maximum among the messages sent. In either case, the inductive hypothesis holds. $\square$

3   Abstractions

The procotol as described is parameterized by both the maximum delay parameter Δ, and the number of units N. Let $P(N, \Delta)$ stand for the instance of the protocol with N units and delay Δ. This parameterization makes the protocol infinite-state, hence Model Checking cannot be applied directly to determine its correctness. We apply two abstractions that reduce the protocol to an *equivalent* finite-state system. The first abstraction demonstrates a *delay insensitivity* property of the protocol : for every N, $P(N, \Delta)$ is correct iff $P(N, 2)$ is correct. Hence, protocol correctness need be checked only for the set of instances with maximum delay 2. However, this is still a parameterized, infinite-state protocol. This parameterization can be handled with the algorithm presented in [EN 96]. This algorithm abstracts away the number of units, constructing a *finite* "abstract graph" which encodes all instances of the system. Model Checking the abstract graph created by this unit is thus equivalent to checking the doubly parameterized SAE-J1850 protocol. Experimental details are presented in the following section.

3.1   Delay Insensitivity

As noted in the protocol description, the timing parameters are proportional to the parameter Δ. In an underlying dense time model, each test of a clock variable x is of the form $x \in \langle l * \Delta, r * \Delta \rangle$ (the angled brackets indicate either a open or a closed end to the interval), and each reset of x is of the form $x := \textbf{choose}\langle l * \Delta, r * \Delta \rangle$, which assigns to x a nondeterministically chosen value from the interval. It is then straightforward to show that if the intervals $\langle l * \Delta, r * \Delta \rangle$ are changed to $\langle l, r \rangle$ (dividing through by Δ), the resulting unparameterized system has the same computations w.r.t. the non-clock variables as the original one. This is so since global states with identical non-clock values and clocks related by scaling with Δ are bisimilar. This class of systems thus forms a decidable instance of parameterized real-time reasoning (cf. [AHV 93]).

Since our model of the bus system is over integer time (each transition takes 1 time unit), we cannot use this result. The protocol, however, satisfies additional properties that make a similar reduction possible. We show that any execution of $P(n, d)$ (d even and at least 2) can be simulated by an execution of $P(n, 2)$, in the sense that the sequence of symbols on the bus is the same.

Lemma 2. *Let σ be an execution of $P(n, d)$ (d even and at least 2). Let l be the symbolic length of the time interval between successive stable bus states in σ. Then*

1. *Every unit sending a symbol with a different length is aborted by the start of the next stable state, and*
2. *Every unit sending a symbol with the same length is transmitting at the start of the next stable state.*   □

Theorem 1. *Let σ be an execution of $P(n,d)$ (d even and at least 2) from a stable state. There is an execution γ of $P(n,2)$ such that the sequence of symbols on the bus is identical in σ and γ.*

Proof. We construct γ inductively. For each i, γ_i ends in the ith stable state, the symbols on the bus in γ_i and in the subsequence of σ up to and including the ith stable state are identical, and the local states of corresponding units in the ith stable states are the same except for, possibly, the *counter* values. The *counter* values, must however, satisfy the relationship : for any pair of units p, q, $counter_p \leq counter_q$ in the ith stable state in σ implies that $counter_p \leq counter_q$ in the ith stable state in γ.

Let γ_0 equal σ_0. Let p be the unit that determines the bus change that results in the $(i+1)$st stable state. For a *Passive* to *Dominant* change, p is the first unit to request a *Dominant* bus state, and for a *Dominant* to *Passive* change, p is the last unit to request a *Passive* bus state. At each stable state, all units begin transmission of their symbol with request identical to the current bus value. Thus, the change by unit p can occur only at $counter_p = Txmin(l)$, where l is the length that p sends its symbol at. $Txmin(l) = (a/2) * \Delta$, for some a.

The order of *counter* values is the same in the ith stable state in γ. As the *counter* value in each unit does not decrease until a bus change or a termination of transmission, in every execution starting at the ith stable state in γ, unit p still is one of the units that determine the bus change. As the change of bus state occurs at the same multiple of Δ, the symbolic length, and hence the symbol on the bus is the same. From the previous Lemma, the units un-aborted at the $(i+1)$st stable states in γ and σ are the same. There exists a execution where within Δ units after the bus change, *counter* values for unaborted units are chosen in the order of *counter* values at the $(i+1)$th stable state of σ. Hence, the inductive hypothesis holds. □

We obtain the following theorem as a corollary:

Theorem 2. (Delay Insensitivity) *$P(n,d)$ is correct for every even d, $d \geq 2$, iff $P(n,2)$ is correct.*

Proof. The direction from left to right follows by instantiating d with 2. For the direction from right to left, note that if $P(n,d)$ is incorrect for some d, then it contains a computation where the sequence of symbols on the bus is not the maximum of the sent messages. By the previous theorem, this computation can be simulated by one in $P(n,2)$, so $P(n,2)$ is incorrect. □

Proof of Lemma 2:

Note that at a stable state, all units have the same requested bus state, although they may be transmitting different symbols with differing lengths. In the interval between stable states, for any pair of units p, q, $|counter_p - counter_q| \leq \Delta$.

(i) The length of the interval is *Long*. Let p be the unit determining the new symbol. As the bus change occurs when p's *counter* value equals $Txmin(Long)$,
$Txmin(Long) - \Delta \leq counter_q \leq Txmin(Long) + \Delta$, for any unit q, i.e., $6.5\Delta \leq counter_q \leq 8.5\Delta$.

If q sends a symbol by a short pulse, as $Trmax(Short) < 6.5\Delta$, q aborts by the time that the bus changes state. If q sends by a long pulse, its *counter* value remains in the interval $[Trmin(Long), Trmax(Long)]$ up to the next stable state, by which time the new bus state is perceived by q.

(ii) The length of the interval is *Short*. Let p be the unit determining the new symbol. As the bus change occurs when p's *counter* value equals $Txmin(Short)$,
$$Txmin(Short) - \Delta \leq counter_q \leq Txmin(Short) + \Delta, \text{ for any unit } q, \text{ i.e.,}$$
$2.5\Delta \leq counter_q \leq 4.5\Delta$.

If q sends by a long pulse, then as $Trmin(Long) = 6.5\Delta$, q aborts by the next stable state (which occurs in the interval $[3.5\Delta, 5.5\Delta]$). If q sends by a short pulse, its *counter* value remains in the interval $[Trmin(Short), Trmax(Short)]$ up to the next stable state, by which time the new bus state is perceived by q.

Hence, every unit sending a different length aborts, and every unit sending a symbol with the same length is live at the next stable state. □

3.2 Many-Process Verification

The delay insensitivity theorem (Theorem 2) shows that it is both necessary and sufficient to check every instance with delay 2 in order to check correctness for instances over all other delay values. While this eliminates consideration of the delay parameter, the reduced system is still infinite-state, as it is parameterized by the number of units taking part in the protocol.

Verification of this parameterized system can be carried out fully automatically using the algorithm described in [EN 96]. This algorithm is based on a synchronous *control-user* model, where the instances of the parameterized system consist of a fixed control process C, and many copies of a fixed user process U. The n-process instance can thus be described by $C \parallel U_1 \parallel \ldots \parallel U_n$, where $\parallel$ denotes synchronous composition. In the SAE-J1850 protocol, the control process models the behavior of the bus, while the user process models the behavior of a single unit, together with some machinery for modeling the delays in detecting bus value changes.

The algorithm of [EN 96] constructs a finite-state "abstract graph" for such a control-user parameterized system which is an abstraction of the entire *family* of instances. The states of the abstract graph record only the state of the control process, and for each local user state, whether there exists at least one user process in that state. The Lemma below gives a way of checking safety properties of the family. Liveness properties may be checked in two ways : (a) As the abstract graph simulates every instance, if the liveness property holds of the abstract graph, then it holds of the family, (b) An algorithm is provided in [EN 96] for exactly determining whether the liveness property holds of every instance.

Lemma 3. *[EN 96] The abstract graph simulates every instance of the family. Every finite path in the abstract graph corresponds to a finite computation of some instance.*

The paper also shows how to check properties of the form $\bigwedge_i \mathsf{A}g(i)$ by reducing them, using symmetry arguments (cf. [ES 93],[CFJ 93]) to checking a property $\mathsf{A}g(0)$ of the control process in a modified control-user system, which has the same user process, but has $C' = C \parallel U$ as the new control process.

4 Implementation Details

The behavior of the bus and the units as specified in the protocol is coded as a SMV [McM 92] program. The transition relation of the abstract graph is generated automatically by a program which takes the specification of control and user processes (in C), and generates SMV code describing the *transition relation* of the abstract graph. This is done by enumerating the reachable local states for a single user process, then generating each transition of the abstract graph by inspection of the local transitions in the unit. States of the abstract graph are represented by subsets of the local user state space. Each subset indicates the presence of at least one user process in that local state, as discussed in the previous section. Thus, for a local user transition $s \to t$, the corresponding abstract graph transition adds t as a member of a abstract state following one that has s as a member.

For the singly parameterized system with $\Delta = 2$, each unit has 254 reachable states; thus, the number of Boolean variables needed to encode an abstract state is also 254 (subsets are encoded as a boolean membership vector). The correctness properties C2(a) - C2(e) were checked together on the abstract graph. Since some of these properties are liveness properties, they were checked on the abstract graph using the fact that it simulates every instance. Every property succeeds on the abstract graph, so that we can infer that properties C2(a) - C2(e) hold of the parameterized system with delay 2, which by Theorem 2 implies that they hold of the completely parameterized system. By Lemma 1, this implies that the desired correctness property, (C1), holds of the completely parameterized system. We did not have to invoke the potentially expensive but exact method for checking liveness properties.

These checks take about 8 MB and 35 seconds on an Intel Pentium 133 with 32 MB of main memory. Conjunctive partitioning of the transition relation and pre-computation of the reachable states (the strongest invariant) is used. 24 iterations are needed to compute the reachable state space. Incidentally, checking a 15 unit instance takes roughly the same amount of time but less space.

5 Conclusions and Related Work

Verification of parameterized systems is often done by hand, or with the guidance of a theorem prover (cf. [MC 88], [MP 94], [HS 96]). Several methods have been proposed that, to various degrees, automate this verification process. Methods based on manual construction of a process invariant are proposed in [CG 87], [SG 89], [KM 89], [WL 89], [LSY 94], and have been applied for the verification of the Gigamax cache consistency protocol in [McM 92]. These constructions have been partially automated in [RS 93], [CGJ 95] (cf. [V 93],[PD 95],[ID 96]); however, as the general problem is undecidable [AK 86], it is not in general possible to obtain a finite-state process invariant. For classes of parameterized systems obeying certain constraints, [GS 92], [EN 95], [EN 96] give algorithms (i.e., decision procedures) for model checking the parameterized system. These papers demonstrate the methods on simple verification examples; we believe that our case study is one of the few examples of verification of a large and complex parameterized protocol. It is likely that the delay insensitivity theorem is an instance of a general theorem for such types of systems; given such a theorem, the verification of this protocol could be indeed fully automated.

We believe that careful specification of the computational model underlying other protocols will expose constraints that can be utilized, as in this case, for developing decision procedures for large classes of protocols. There is also a need for developing and popularizing notations for expressing such protocols. Remarkably, in the SAE-J1850 document (over 100 pages), there is no succinct protocol description; the description given in Section 2 had to be culled from the entire text. The successful verification of the protocol, despite the theoretical result on PSPACE-completeness of the procedure [EN 96], is reason to believe that fully automated parameterized verification is feasible for reasonably sized protocols.

Acknowledgements We thank Dr. Carl Pixley for suggesting the verification of the SAE-J1850 protocol and for helpful remarks.

References

[AHV 93] Alur, R., Henzinger, T., Vardi, M. Parametric Real-Time Reasoning, *STOC*, 1993.

[AK 86] Apt, K., Kozen, D. Limits for automatic verification of finite-state concurrent systems. *IPL 15*, pp. 307-309.

[BCG 89] Browne, M. C., Clarke, E. M., Grumberg, O. Reasoning about Networks with Many Identical Finite State Processes, *Information and Computation*, vol. 81, no. 1, pp. 13–31, April 1989.

[CE 81] Clarke, E. M., Emerson, E. A. Design and Synthesis of Synchronization Skeletons using Branching Time Temporal Logic. in *Workshop on Logics of Programs*, Springer-Verlag LNCS 131.

[CES 86] Clarke, E. M., Emerson, E. A., and Sistla, A. P., Automatic Verification of Finite-State Concurrent Systems using Temporal Logic, *ACM Trans. Prog. Lang. and Syst.*, vol. 8, no. 2, pp. 244-263, April 1986.

[CFJ 93] Clarke, E. M., Filkorn, T., Jha, S. Exploiting Symmetry in Temporal Logic Model Checking, *5th CAV*, Springer-Verlag LNCS 697.

[CG 87] Clarke, E. M., Grumberg, O. Avoiding the State Explosion Problem in Temporal Logic Model Checking Algorithms, *PODC*, 1987.

[CGJ 95] Clarke, E.M., Grumberg, O., Jha, S. Verifying Parameterized Networks using Abstraction and Regular Languages, *CONCUR*, 1995.

[Em 90] Emerson, E. A. Temporal and Modal Logic, in *Handbook of Theoretical Computer Science*, (J. van Leeuwen, ed.), Elsevier/North-Holland, 1991.

[EN 95] Emerson, E. A., Namjoshi, K. S. Reasoning about Rings, *POPL*, 1995.

[EN 96]   Emerson, E. A., Namjoshi, K. S. Automatic Verification of Parameterized Synchronous Systems, *CAV*, 1996.

[ES 93]   Emerson, E. A., Sistla, A. P. Symmetry and Model Checking, *5th CAV*, Springer-Verlag LNCS 697.

[GS 92]   German, S. M., Sistla, A. P. Reasoning about Systems with Many Processes. *J.ACM*, Vol. 39, Number 3, July 1992.

[HS 96]   Havelund, K., Shankar, N. Experiments in Theorem Proving and Model Checking for Protocol Verification, *FME*, 1996.

[ID 96]   Ip, N., Dill, D. Verifying systems with replicated components in Murϕ, *CAV*, 1996.

[KM 89]   Kurshan, R. P., McMillan, K. A Structural Induction Theorem for Processes, *PODC*, 1989.

[LSY 94]   Li, J., Suzuki, I., Yamashita, M. A New Structural Induction Theorem for Rings of Temporal Petri Nets. *IEEE Trans. Soft. Engg.*, vol. 20, No. 2, February 1994.

[Lu 84]   Lubachevsky, B. An Approach to Automating the Verification of Compact Parallel Coordination Programs I. *Acta Informatica* 21, 1984.

[McM 92]   McMillan, K., Symbolic Model Checking: An Approach to the State Explosion Problem, Ph.D. Thesis, Carnegie-Mellon University, 1992.

[MC 88]   Misra, J., Chandy, K. M. **Parallel Program Design : A Foundation**, Addison-Wesley Publishers, 1988.

[MP 94]   Manna, Z., Pnueli, A. Verification of Parameterized Programs. In **Specification and Validation Methods** (E. Borger, ed.), Oxford University Press, pp. 167-230, 1994.

[Pn 77]   Pnueli, A. The Temporal Logic of Programs. *FOCS*, 1977.

[PD 95]   Pong, F., Dubois, M. A New Approach for the Verification of Cache Coherence Protocols. *IEEE Transactions on Parallel and Distributed Systems*, August 1995.

[QS 82]   Queille, J.P., J. Sifakis, Specification and Verification of Concurrent Systems in CESAR, *Proc. of the 5th International Symposium on Programming*, LNCS#137, Springer–Verlag, pp. 337–350, April 1982.

[RS 85]   Reif, J., Sistla, A. P. A multiprocess network logic with temporal and spatial modalities. *JCSS* 30(1), 1985.

[RS 93]   Rho, J. K., Somenzi, F. Automatic Generation of Network Invariants for the Verification of Iterative Sequential Systems, *CAV*, 1993.

[SAE 92]   SAE J1850 Class B data communication network interface. Society of Automotive Engineers, Inc., 1992.

[SG 89]   Shtadler, Z., Grumberg, O. Network Grammars, Communication Behaviours and Automatic Verification. In J.Sifakis (ed), *Automatic Verification Methods for Finite State Systems*, Springer-Verlag, LNCS 407.

[VW 86]   Vardi, M., Wolper, P. An Automata-theoretic Approach to Automatic Program Verification, *LICS*, 1986.

[V 93]   Vernier, I. Specification and Verification of Parameterized Parallel Programs. *Proc. 8th Intl. Symp. on Computer and Information Sciences*, Istanbul, Turkey, pp. 622-625.

[WL 89]   Wolper, P., Lovinfosse, V. Verifying Properties of Large Sets of Processes with Network Invariants. In J.Sifakis (ed), *Automatic Verification Methods for Finite State Systems*, Springer-Verlag, LNCS 407.

The 'Test Model-Checking' Approach to the Verification of Formal Memory Models of Multiprocessors*

Ratan Nalumasu, Rajnish Ghughal,
Abdel Mokkedem and Ganesh Gopalakrishnan

Department of Computer Science, University of Utah,
Salt Lake City, UT 84112–9205
Contact email: ratan,ghughal,mokkedem,ganesh@cs.utah.edu

Abstract. We offer a solution to the problem of verifying formal memory models of processors by combining the strengths of model-checking and a formal testing procedure for parallel machines. We characterize the formal basis for abstracting the tests into test automata and associated memory rule safety properties whose violations pinpoint the ordering rule being violated. Our experimental results on Verilog models of a commercial split transaction bus demonstrates the ability of our method to effectively debug design models during early stages of their development.

1 Introduction

The fundamentally important problem [1] of verifying whether a given *memory system model* (or "a memory system") provides a *formal memory model* (or "memory model") appears in a number of guises. CPU designers are interested in knowing whether some of the aggressive execution techniques such as speculative issue of memory operations violate sequential consistency; I/O bus designers are interested in knowing the exact semantics of shared accesses provided by split I/O transactions [9]; even language designers of multi-threaded languages such as Java that support shared updates [14] are interested in this problem. Formal verification methods are ideally suited for this problem because: (i) the semantics of memory orderings are too subtle to be fathomed through informal reasoning alone; (ii) *ad hoc* testing methods cannot provide assurance that the desired memory model has been implemented. Unfortunately, despite the central importance of this problem and the large body of formal methods research in this area, there is still no single formally based method that the designer of a realistic multiprocessor system can use on his/her detailed design model to *quickly* find violations in the design. In this paper we describe such a method called *test model-checking*.

---

* Supported in part by ARPA Order #B990 Under SPAWAR Contract #N0039-95-C-0018 (Avalanche), DARPA under contract #DABT6396C0094 (Utah Verifier), and NSF MIP MIP–9321836.

Test model-checking formally adapts to the realm of model-checking a formally based architectural testing method called ARCHTEST. ARCHTEST has been successfully used on a number of commercial multiprocessors [7] by running a suite of test-programs on them. ARCHTEST is an *incomplete* testing method in that it does not, under all circumstances, detect violations of memory orderings [8]. Nevertheless, its tests have been shown to be incisive in practice [7]. Most importantly, the formal theory of memory ordering rules developed by Collier in [8] forms the basis for ARCHTEST, which means that whenever a violation is detected by ARCHTEST, there is a formal line of reasoning leading back to the precise cause.

Being based on ARCHTEST, test model-checking is also incomplete. However, none of the (presumed) complete alternatives to date have been shown to be practical for verifying large designs. For example [25] involves the use of manually guided mechanical theorem proving. Even approaches based on *conventional* model-checking are impossibly difficult to use in practice. For example, the assertions pertaining to the sequential consistency of lazy caching [11], a simple memory system, expressed in various temporal logics (by [15] in $\forall$CTL* [6] and [19] in TLA [21]) are highly complex. We do not believe that descriptions of this style will scale up. On the other hand, the test model-checking method has not only been able to comfortably handle the memory system defined by the symmetric multiprocessor (SMP) bus called *Runway* [4] used by Hewlett-Packard in their high-end machines, but also it discovered many subtle bugs in early models describing this bus that *we created*. Our Utah Runway Model(URM) includes a number of details such as split transactions, out of order transaction completions, and even an element of speculative execution. The errors we made in capturing these details could well have been made in an actual industrial context. We believe that with growing system complexity, the role of debugging methods that are effective and are formally based will only grow in significance, regardless of whether the methods are complete or not.

Our specific contributions in this paper are: (i) the adaptation of a formal testing method for memory models to model-checking, that can be applied during the design of modern microprocessors whose memory systems are very complex; (ii) a formal characterization (accompanied by proofs) of *how* the tests of the testing method are abstracted and turned into a fixed set of safety properties that are then model-checked; and (iii) experimental results on three examples using the VIS model-checker, the last example being much larger than any previously reported in this context.

Related Work

A technique very similar to test model-checking was proposed in [22] under the section heading 'Sequential Consistency'. To give a historic perspective, our test model-checking idea originated in our attempt to answer the following two questions: (i) which memory ordering rule(s) is [22] really verifying? (ii) is this a general technique? *i.e.* can other memory ordering rules be verified in the same fashion? We still have not found a satisfactory answer to the first question because the test in [22] uses only one location which then couldn't make it a test for *sequential consistency*; it could plausibly be a test for coherence—which again does not correspond to what Collier formally proves in [8]. One of our contributions is that we answer these questions by elaborating on the theoretical as well as practical aspects of test model-checking.

Alur et al [3] showed that the problem of finding if there is a sequentially consistent string σ in a regular expression r is undecidable. The problem is undecidable as the actions that follow a read instruction can depend on the value returned by a read instruction. This result is not applicable in our case, because the models we consider do not make decisions based on the value returned by a read instruction. This is detailed in Section 3.1.

In [25], the authors use a method called *aggregation* on a distributed shared memory coherence protocol used in an experimental multiprocessor, to arrive at a simplified model of system behavior. Their technique involves manual theorem proving. The work in [17] as well as [10] are aimed at verifying that synchronization routines work correctly under various memory models, where the memory models themselves are described using finite-state operational models. They do not address the problem of establishing the memory models provided by detailed memory subsystem designs, which is our contribution. In [13], the authors analyze the problem of deciding whether a given set of traces are sequentially consistent. Our approach differs in that we prove properties about design level models of memory system rather than traces (presumably obtained from actual machines) and hence designers can use our approach in early stages of design cycle.

2 Overview of ARCHTEST

ARCHTEST is based on the theory presented in [8] that formally defines and characterizes architectural *rules* obeyed by memory subsystems of multiprocessors. Although these rules are *elemental*, in realistic memory systems the rules manifest in *compound* form. Obeying a compound rule is tantamount to obeying *all* the constituent elemental rules; violating a compound rule is tantamount to violating *any* of the constituent elemental rules. Some of the elemental ordering rules are:

Rule of Computation (CMP): This is a basic rule defining how the terminal value of each operand is calculated from the initial values of the operands. Though most of the literature on memory architectures implicitly assumes this rule, we will often keep it explicit in our discussions.

Rule of Read Order (RO): For any pair of read events a and b in the same process, if a comes before b in program order then a happens before b.

Rule of Write Order (WO): Same as RO with 'write' substituted for 'read'.

Rule of Program Order (PO): For any pair of events a and b in the same process, if a comes before b in program order than a happens before b. Event a or b can be either read or write events. So, both RO and WO are special

$$\text{Initially } A = 0$$

P_1	P_2
$L_1 : A := 1;$	$X[1] := A;$
$L_2 : A := 2;$	$X[2] := A;$
$L_3 : A := 3;$	$X[3] := A;$
$\cdots$	$\cdots$
$L_k : A := k$	$X[k] := A;$

(a) $Test_{\text{ROWO}}$ of ARCHTEST

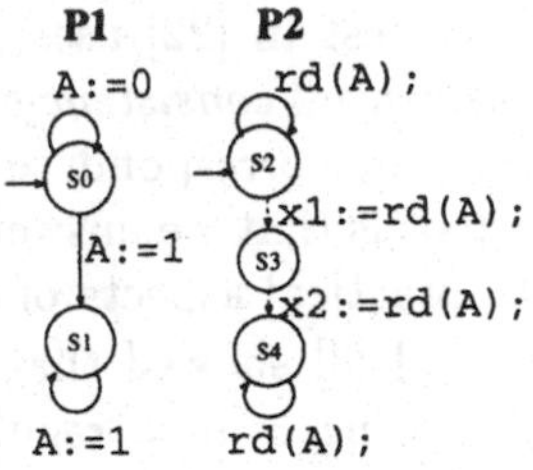

(b) Test automata for $Test_{\text{ROWO}}$

Fig. 1. $Test_{\text{ROWO}}$- ARCHTEST test and test automata for $A(CMP, RO, WO)$

$$\text{Initially } A = B = 0$$

P_1	P_2	P_3	P_4
$L_1 : A := 1;$	$L_{A_1} : U[1] := A;$	$L_{B_1} : X[1] := B;$	$L_1 : B := 1;$
$L_2 : A := 2;$	$L_{B_1} : V[1] := B;$	$L_{A_1} : Y[1] := A;$	$L_2 : B := 2;$
$\cdots$	$L_{A_2} : U[2] := A;$	$L_{B_2} : X[2] := B;$	$\cdots$
$L_k : A := k;$	$L_{B_2} : V[2] := B;$	$L_{A_2} : Y[2] := A;$	$L_k : B := k;$
	$\cdots$	$\cdots$	
	$L_{A_k} : U[k] := A;$	$L_{B_k} : X[k] := B;$	
	$L_{B_k} : V[k] := B;$	$L_{A_k} : Y[k] := A;$	

Fig. 2. $Test_{\text{WA}}$: ARCHTEST test for $A(CMP, RO, WO, WA)$

cases of PO. This is one of the strongest ordering rules and is essential for sequential consistency.

Rule of Write Atomicity (WA): A write operation becomes visible to all processes instantaneously. More precisely, one conceptual *store* S_i is associated with each processor node P_i. Then, for each write operation W, one write event W_i is defined per store S_i. Then, WA guarantees that there are no i, j and no event e such that e is before W_i and is after W_j.

$Test_{\text{ROWO}}$: ARCHTEST test for $A(CMP, RO, WO)$ The test of ARCHTEST for the *compound* rule consisting of the elemental rules CMP, RO, and WO, denoted $A(CMP, RO, WO)$, is shown in Figure 1(a). (Figure 1(b) will be discussed later.) Process P_1 executes a sequence of write instructions (intended to check for WO), and P_2 executes a sequence of read instruction (intended to check for RO). If the memory system correctly realizes $A(CMP, RO, WO)$, then Condition 1 produces a positive outcome:

Condition 1 (Monotonic) *The sequence of X values is monotonically increasing, i.e.:* $\forall i, j : 1 \le i \le j \le k : X[i] \le X[j]$ *or equivalently*
$$\forall i : 1 \le i \le k - 1 : X[i] \le X[i+1].$$

If MONOTONIC condition is violated then at least one of the CMP, RO and WO rules is violated.

$Test_{\text{WA}}$: ARCHTEST test for $A(CMP, RO, WO, WA)$ $Test_{\text{WA}}$, shown in Figure 2 tests for $A(CMP, RO, WO, WA)$, with the conditions checked being: (i) the MONOTONIC condition (suitably modified for arrays U, V, X, Y), and (ii) ATOMIC, which is:

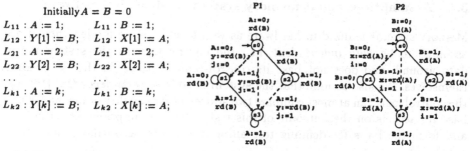

Initially $A = B = 0$

$L_{11} : A := 1;$ $L_{11} : B := 1;$
$L_{12} : Y[1] := B;$ $L_{12} : X[1] := A;$
$L_{21} : A := 2;$ $L_{21} : B := 2;$
$L_{22} : Y[2] := B;$ $L_{22} : X[2] := A;$
...   ...
$L_{k1} : A := k;$ $L_{k1} : B := k;$
$L_{k2} : Y[k] := B;$ $L_{k2} : X[k] := A;$

(a) $Test_{PO}$ of ARCHTEST   (b) Test automata for $Test_{PO}$

Fig. 3. $Test_{PO}$: ARCHTEST test for $A(CMP, PO)$

Condition 2 (Atomic) $\forall i, j : 1 \leq i, j \leq k : V[i] \geq X[j] \vee Y[j] \geq U[i].$

ATOMIC watches for the possibility that a write operation from P_1 and a write operation from P_4 became visible in different orders to P_2 and P_3.

$Test_{PO}$: ARCHTEST **test for** $A(CMP, PO)$ $Test_{PO}$, shown in Figure 3(a) tests for $A(CMP, PO)$, with the conditions checked being: (i) the MONOTONIC condition (suitably modified for arrays X, Y), and (ii) PO_CROSS, which is:

Condition 3 (PO_Cross) $\forall i, j : 1 \leq i, j \leq k : (X[i] \geq j \vee Y[j] \geq i) \wedge (X[i] \leq j \vee Y[j] \leq i).$

All ARCHTEST test programs such as $Test_{WA}$, $Test_{PO}$ etc. are meant to be run on real machines and there cannot be any real guarantees that the particular interleavings that reveal violations (such as for memory ordering rule WA watched by condition ATOMIC in $Test_{WA}$) will indeed happen. To allow for as many interleavings as possible, ARCHTEST recommends that its tests be run for large values of k. With test model-checking, we effectively run the tests for $k = \infty$, as will be elaborated shortly.

3 Test model-checking

Test model-checking converts the tests of ARCHTEST to corresponding *memory rule test automata* ("test automata") that drive the model of the memory system being examined. In our experiments, we use the Verilog language supported by VIS [26] to capture the memory system models as well as the test automata. Precisely, the automata are modeled as (Verilog) processes which run in parallel with the memory system and simply enqueue test automata instructions in the instruction stream of the processors. The CONDITIONS corresponding to each compound memory rule being tested are turned into corresponding *memory rule safety properties* that are checked by the VIS tool.

3.1 Assumptions about memory systems realized in hardware

Memory systems realized in hardware as well as finite-state models thereof are assumed to be *data independent*; *i.e.*, the control logic of the system moves data around, and does not base its control-point settings on the data values themselves. We also assume that the system is address *semi-dependent* [16], *i.e.* the control logic can at most compare two addresses for equality or inequality and base its actions on the outcome of this test. These assumptions are standard, and form the basis for defining test automata as well as memory rule safety properties.

3.2 Creation of test automata

As illustrated in Figure 1(b), we obtain test automata for various memory models by finitely abstracting the data used in ARCHTEST tests, using non-determinism to justify the abstraction. For example, we abstract the specific activities of process P_1 of Figure 1(a) into that of (non-deterministically) writing *all possible* ascending values over $\{0,1\}$, as shown in P_1 of Figure 1(b). Also, since we cannot store infinite arrays in creating process P_2, we turn P_2 and the corresponding memory rule safety property into an automaton that checks that the array values read are monotonically increasing. This, in turn, can be performed using just two *consecutive* array values $x1$ and $x2$ that are nondeterministically recorded by P_2. Hence, the memory rule safety property we model-check for is: P_2 *in final state* $\Rightarrow x2 \geq x1$.

We now provide a justification that these abstractions preserve the memory rule safety properties, i.e., for the same memory system model, a violation of a condition occurs in a test of ARCHTEST for $k = \infty$ iff the same violation will occur in model-checking the corresponding memory rule safety property when test automata are used to drive the memory system model. To keep the presentation simple, we formally argue how the test automata finds every violation present in the test of ARCHTEST with $k = \infty$; the opposite direction of *iff*, i.e. how a test of ARCHTEST with $k = \infty$ finds violations found by the test automata is easy to see because the test automata just appears as a "stuttering" of the test of ARCHTEST. For example, the actions of P_1 in Figure 1(a) can be viewed as repeating the initialization and then repeating the instruction at label L_1 of P_1 of Figure 1(a). Our proof sketches are illustrated on the three tests presented in Section 2.

3.3 Abstracting $Test_{\text{ROWO}}$

We show that if the test program in $Test_{\text{ROWO}}$ shows that MONOTONIC is violated, then the test automata also reveals the error. Since MONOTONIC is violated,

$$\exists i : \quad 1 \leq i < k : X[i] > X[i+1]$$
$$\Longleftrightarrow \quad \exists i, \alpha : 1 \leq i < k : (X[i] > \alpha) \wedge (X[i+1] \leq \alpha)$$
$$\Longleftrightarrow \quad \exists i, \alpha : 1 \leq i < k : (X[i] > \alpha) \wedge \neg(X[i+1] > \alpha)$$

<table>
<tr><td colspan="2">Initially $A = 0$</td><td colspan="2">Initially $A = (0 > \alpha)$</td><td colspan="2">Initially $A = 0$</td></tr>
<tr><td>P_1</td><td>P_2</td><td>P_1</td><td>P_2</td><td>P_1</td><td>P_2</td></tr>
</table>

P_1 column (a):
$L_1 : A := 1;$ $X[1] := (A > \alpha);$
$L_2 : A := 2;$ $X[2] := (A > \alpha);$
$L_3 : A := 3;$ $X[3] := (A > \alpha);$
$\ldots$
$\ldots$
$L_k : A := k$ $X[k] := (A > \alpha);$

(b):
$L_1 : A := (1 > \alpha);$ $X[1] := A;$
$L_2 : A := (2 > \alpha);$ $X[2] := A;$
$L_3 : A := (3 > \alpha);$ $X[3] := A;$
$\ldots$
$L_k : A := (k > \alpha)$ $X[k] := A;$

(c):
$L_1 : A := 0;$ $X[1] := A;$
$\ldots$
$L_\alpha : A := 0$ $X[\alpha] := A$
$L_{\alpha+1} : A := 1$ $X[\alpha + 1] := A$
$L_{\alpha+2} : A := 1$ $X[\alpha + 2] := A$
$\ldots$
$L_k : A := 1$ $X[k] := A;$

(a)   (b)   (c)

Fig. 4. Abstraction of $Test_{\text{ROWO}}$

Since, the last formula compares $X[i]$ and $X[i+1]$ only to α, we can rewrite the test program as shown in Figure 4(a) *assuming data independence*, and rewrite the last formula as $\exists i : 1 \leq i < k : X[i] = 1 \wedge X[i + 1] = 0$. Note that in Figure 4(a) all reads of A occur in the expression $A > \alpha$. Hence, we can replace every $A := v$ with $A := (v > \alpha)$ and $X[i] := (A > \alpha)$ with $X[i] := A$ without affecting MONOTONIC again, *if data independence holds*, to obtain Figure 4(b). Figure 4(c) is obtained by simplifying Figure 4(b): each $v > \alpha$ evaluates to 0 for $v \leq \alpha$ and 1 otherwise. This figure is generalized to obtain the test automata in Figure 1(b). Intuitively the automata finds the violation as follows. P_1 remains in the initial state for α iterations (executing A:=0) and then switches to second state (executing A:=1). Also, P_2 remains in the initial state for $i-1$ iterations and then switches to second state recording $x1$ and then $x2$ (dashed edges show when these variables are recorded). Thus the test automata's execution is identical to that in Figure 4(c) except that the test automata gives the effect of taking k to ∞. Also notice that $x1$ and $x2$ get the values corresponding to $X[i]$ and $X[i+1]$. Also, corresponding to $X[i] = 1 \wedge X[i + 1] = 0$, we have $x1 = 1 \wedge x2 = 0$. Hence the memory rule safety property corresponding to condition MONOTONIC is found violated by the test automata exactly when $Test_{\text{ROWO}}$ for $k = \infty$ detects a violation. Note that the nondeterminism employed in constructing test automata enables P_1 and P_2 to *guess* the right value of α and i corresponding to the violation.

3.4   Abstracting $Test_{\text{WA}}$

Test automata for $Test_{\text{WA}}$ is shown in Figure 5. In this automata P_1 and P_4 write all possible ascending sequences of $\{0, 1\}$ in A and B respectively. Each processor *independently* and *nondeterministically* decides to switch from writing 0 to writing 1. Modifications similar to those in $Test_{\text{ROWO}}$ are applied to P_2 and P_3 also, to (nondeterministically) decide which $U[i], V[i]$ pair and $X[j], Y[j]$ pair are recorded in u, v and x, y. The memory rule safety property corresponding to condition ATOMIC is: P_2 *and* P_3 *in their final states* $\Rightarrow v \geq x \vee y \geq u$. As was explained in Section 3.2 for $Test_{\text{ROWO}}$, our abstraction avoids having to

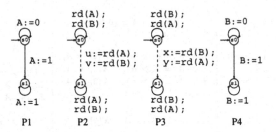

Fig. 5. $Test_{WA}$ test automata : Test Automata for $A(CMP, RO, WO, WA)$

remember the entire extent of the arrays U, V, X, and Y. (In $Test_{WA}$, one has to check for MONOTONIC also; this is done similarly to $Test_{ROWO}$.)

To show that the abstraction preserves ATOMIC, let ATOMIC be violated in $Test_{WA}$ of ARCHTEST. Hence

$$\exists i, j : \qquad U[i] > Y[j] \wedge X[j] > V[i]$$
$$\Longleftrightarrow \exists, i, j, \alpha, \beta : \qquad Y[j] = \alpha \wedge U[i] > \alpha \wedge V[i] = \beta \wedge X[j] > \beta$$

Similar to $Test_{ROWO}$, assuming *data-independence*, we have an execution of the test automata (Figure 5) in which P_1, P_2, P_3, P_4 iterates for $\alpha, i-1, j-1, \beta$ times (respectively) in their initial states before switching to their final states. This test automata execution detects violations of ATOMIC exactly when $Test_{WA}$ for $k = \infty$ would. A violation of ATOMIC happens exactly when $u = 1 \wedge v = 0 \wedge x = 1 \wedge y = 0$.

3.5 Abstracting $Test_{PO}$

We now discuss $Test_{PO}$ for the elemental ordering rule Program Order (PO), which is somewhat more complex than the previous two tests.

We obtain the test automata and the memory rule safety property for $Test_{PO}$ of Figure 3(a) as illustrated in Figure 3(b). P_1 executes a pair of instructions: write to A followed by read from B, infinitely often. The value written to A is 0 for some iterations and is nondeterministically changed to 1. P_2 runs similarly. P_1 nondeterministically selects a pair of write instruction followed by read instruction. It assigns the value written to A to j and the value read from B to y. Similarly, P_2 updates i and x. The dashed edges in Figure 3(b) show when x, y, i, j are updated. The memory rule safety property corresponding to condition PO_CROSS is: P_1 *and* P_2 *in their final states* $\Rightarrow (x \geq j \vee y \geq i) \wedge (x \leq j \vee y \leq i)$. We can show that this abstraction preserves PO_CROSS by an argument similar to that for $Test_{ROWO}$ and $Test_{WA}$.

4 Case Studies

To demonstrate the effectiveness of our approach, we verified three different memory systems, namely serial memory, lazy caching, and URM, all using a symbolic model-checker VIS (See [26] for more information on VIS). These three

Event	Action or condition
Ri(d, a)	if Mem[a] = d
Wi(d, a)	Mem[a] := d

Fig. 6. Serial memory transaction rules

memory systems are described in some detail below, along with some of the subtle bugs that we could detect using test model-checking. Details of all our experiments can be obtained from the Web [23] or by contacting the authors.

4.1 Sequential Consistency

A sequentially consistent memory system [20] requires that there be a single self-consistent trace t of memory operations that when projected onto the memory operations of each individual processor P_i ($R_i(a,d)$ and $W_i(a,d)$ for processor i) is according to program order for P_i. As suggested in [8], one's intuition about sequential consistency matches the behaviour described by $A(CMP, PO, WA)$.

As [8] does not list a single compound test to check for $A(CMP, PO, WA)$, we can use the following two tests that are available: $Test_{WA}$ which tests for $A(CMP, RO, WO, WA)$ and $Test_{PO}$ which tests for $A(CMP, PO)$. This combination is exactly equivalent to testing for sequential consistency because PO implies RO and WO (as formally defined in [8]). While sequential consistency matches the behavior described by $A(CMP, PO, WA)$, successful test model-checking outcomes are only necessary but not sufficient conditions to ensure sequential consistency. As part of our future work, we are exploring the ways to arrive at sufficient conditions for such tests. For every memory system we consider, these two tests are model-checked separately and summarized in Figure 7.

4.2 Serial memory and Lazy caching

The **serial memory** protocol for n processors and a memory is shown in Figure 6. Serial memories are often used to define sequential consistency(SC) operationally. The **lazy caching** protocol [2, 11], (Figure 4 in [11] describes the transition system of the protocol), also implements sequential consistency, and is geared towards a bus based architecture. The memory interface still consists of reads and writes; however, caches C_i are interposed between the shared memory Mem and the processors P_i. Each cache C_i contains a part of the memory Mem and has two queues associated with it: an out-queue Out_i in which P_i write requests are buffered and an in-queue IN_i in which the pending cache updates are stored. These queues model the asynchronous behavior of write events in a sequentially consistent memory. A write event $W_i(a,d)$ doesn't have an immediate effect. Instead, a request (d,a) is placed in Out_i. When the write request is taken out of the queue, by an internal memory-write event $MW_i(a,d)$, the memory is updated and a cache update request (d,a) is placed in every in-queue. This cache update is eventually removed by an internal cache update event $CU_j(a,d)$ as a result of which the cache C_j gets updated. Cache evictions are modeled by internal cache invalidate events: CI_i can arbitrarily remove locations from cache C_i. Caches are filled both as the delayed result of write events and through internal memory-read events, $MR(a, d)$. The latter events model the effect of a cache-miss: in that case the read event stalls until the location is copied from the memory. A read event $R_i(a, d)$, predictably, stalls until a copy of location a is present in C_i but also until the copy contains a correct value in the following sense: SC demands that a processor P_i reads the value at a location a that was recently written by P_i unless some other processor updated a in the meantime. Hence, a read event $R_i(a, d)$ cannot occur unless all pending writes in Out_i are processed as well as the cache updates requests from In_i that corresponds to writes of P_i. For this reason, such cache update requests are marked (with a $\star$).

4.3 Utah Runway Model (URM)

Our third example, called URM, is modeled after a commercial bus used to interconnect processors and memory controller together to form a multiprocessor system. The behavior of this memory system is described in some detail in [4, 5, 18]. The complexity of this protocol stems from many sources, a few of which are elaborated here (see [24] for more details). First, the queues in the clients introduce decoupled execution, leading to a large number of "otherwise equivalent" states. Next, the control mechanism is very complex, owing to many reasons, including: (i) lines can be obtained in various sharing modes such as read-shared-private and read-private; (ii) line states can be eagerly promoted to *private* before the data actually arrives (concurrent dirtying are merged into when the data arrives); (iii) hit after miss situations can be speculatively processed and unrolled when invalidated. Though we did not try to model each of these features in their full glory, we *did* include a modicum of these aggressive features into our URM, which in fact occupies more than 2,000 lines of VIS Verilog code[23].

4.4 Verification results

The tables in figure 7 show execution time for model-checking our Serial memory, Lazy caching and URM models for tests of A(CMP, PO) and A(CMP,RO,WO,WA) (recall that A(CMP, PO, WA) implies SC). The three models running separately the two tests $Test_{WA}$ and $Test_{PO}$ are model-checked for the following conditions: (Figure 3(b) does not show some of these states)

$Test_{WA}$: MONOTONIC: $\land (P_2.inS_2) \Rightarrow (P_2.U_1 \leq P_2.U_2) \land (P_2.inS_2) \Rightarrow (P_2.V_1 \leq P_2.V_2)$
$\land (P_3.inS_2) \Rightarrow (P_3.X_1 \leq P_3.X_2) \land (P_3.inS_2) \Rightarrow (P_3.Y_1 \leq P_3.Y_2)$
ATOMIC: $(P_2.inS_1 \land P_3.inS_1) \Rightarrow (P_2.V \geq P_3.X \lor P_3.Y \geq P_2.U)$
$Test_{PO}$: PO_CROSS: $(P_1.inS_3 \land P_2.inS_3) \Rightarrow$
$(P_1.Y \geq P_2.I \lor P_2.X \geq P_1.J) \land (P_1.Y \leq P_2.I \lor P_2.X \leq P_1.J)$

As can be seen, all these conditions are safety properties, and independent of the model itself, which is a distinct advantage over other methods.

A(CMP,PO)	#states	#bdd nodes	conditions verified	runtime (mn:sec)
serial memory	7229	7145	Vacuity	00:02
			PO_CROSS	00:09
lazy caching	7.80248e+06	306692	Vacuity	01:12
			PO_CROSS	36:33
URM	953675	1657308	Vacuity	14:23
			PO_CROSS	27h28:30

A(CMP,WO,RO,WA)	#states	#bdd nodes	conditions verified	runtime (mn:sec)
serial memory	21242	10084	Vacuity	00:04
			MONOTONIC, ATOMIC	00:34
lazy caching	1.90736e+06	513655	Vacuity	02:02
			MONOTONIC, ATOMIC	59:33
URM	985236	1695092	Vacuity	17:24
			MONOTONIC, ATOMIC	40h17:33

Vacuity: Antecedent of $\Rightarrow$ is not always false

Fig. 7. Verification results using VIS on a SPARC ULTRA-1 with 512 MB Memory

The size of the state space and number of nodes in BDDs are also reported. Note that lazy caching has more states than URM due to the queues present in the model. However, the complexity of the URM protocol is much higher, which results in large BDD size and higher run time. However, in all our experiments, whenever there was any memory ordering rule violation in our model, test model-checking detected it quickly (in the order of minutes). A very desirable feature one can provide in a tool based on test model-checking is a *menu* of previously generated test automata for the various compound rules in [8], using which designers can probe their model.

Our Verilog models captures quite faithfully the cache coherence protocol and the ordering rules of the three memory systems. After an extensive debugging using test model-checking driven by $Test_{PO}$ and $Test_{WA}$, we have a high confidence that the memory systems built based on the Lazy caching model or URM would be sequentially consistent.

Description of a Bug found in a preliminary model of lazy caching: The following bug in our model of Lazy Caching was caught by a violation of PO_CROSS in $Test_{PO}$. The bug was in the queues used by Lazy Caching, which were implemented as shift registers. We forgot to shift the $\star$-bit in In_i when the processor P_i receives a cache-update from In_i queue. With this bug it is possible that In_i queue is not $\star$-ed when it should be, and consequently reads in P_i may bypass writes. This results in a violation of PO. This is a difficult bug to catch because its detection involves understanding the complex feedback from all components of the protocol to each other (queues, memory, and caches). Moreover, this bug is interesting because it violates PO but doesn't violate WA. This is so because only write-read (WR) order is affected by this bug. Our technique effectively caught this bug: the PO_CROSS condition does not pass when we model-checked the model for $Test_{PO}$. However, $Test_{WA}$ (note that it doesn't involve PO) *passes!* This shows the futility of *ad hoc* testing methods:

one could apply subjective criteria to consider a test similar to $Test_{WA}$ to be sufficiently incisive, when in fact it fails to account for a crucial ordering relation such as PO.

We found a more complex bug in URM. Details are too involved to report here, but can be easily obtained from the web site [23, 12].

5 Conclusion and Future Plans

We presented a new approach to verify multi-processors for formal memory models, which combines two existing powerful techniques: model-checking, and the testing method of ARCHTEST. From our results, we conclude that test model-checking can be of great value in detecting bugs during early stages of the design cycle of modern microprocessors whose memory subsystems are complex. Our results on our URM of the HP PA/Runway bus attest to this.

So far we have identified the rules and corresponding tests for sequential consistency. We are currently working on identifying similar rules and tests for other well-known formal memory models such as TSO, PSO, and RMO [1] that are described in the SPARC V9 architecture manual [27]. This work may involve considering memory barrier operations and defining new rules as well as new tests. We are currently working to formulate some reasonable assumptions about the memory system model under which the tests administered by our test automata can be rendered complete. Also, for a limited class of models, model-checking the test for some small value of k might actually be sufficient. Our initial attempts in this direction are encouraging.

Acknowledgments: We would like to thank W.W. Collier for his help in explaining his work, his very informative emails and providing ARCHTEST, Dr. Narendran for many fruitful discussions, and Dr. Al davis and his Avalanche team for offering us the unique opportinuty to work on state-of-art processors and busses.

References

1. Sarita V. Adve and Kourosh Gharachorloo. Shared memory consistency models: A tutorial. *Computer*, 29(12):66–76, December 1996.
2. Yehuda Afek, Geoffrey Brown, and Michael Merritt. Lazy caching. *ACM Transactions on Programming Languages and Systems*, 15(1):182–205, January 1993.
3. Rajeev Alur, Ken McMillan, and Doron Peled. Model-checking of correctness conditions for concurrent objects. In *11th Annual IEEE Symposium on Logic in Computer Science*, pages 219–228, July 1996.
4. William R. Bryg, Kenneth K. Chan, and Nicholas S.Fiduccia. A high-performance, low-cost multiprocessor bus for workstations and midrange servers. *Hewlett-Packard Journal*, pages 18–24, February 1996.
5. Albert Camilleri. A hybrid approach to verifying liveness in a symmetric multi-processor. In *Theorem Proving in Higher Order Logics, 10th International Conference, TPHOLs'97, Murray Hill, NJ*, pages 49–67, August 1997. Springer-Verlag LNCS 1275.

6. E. M. Clarke, E. A. Emerson, and A. P. Sistla. Automatic verification of finite-state concurrent systems using temporal logic specifications. *ACM TOPLAS*, 8(2):244–263, 1986.
7. W. W. Collier. Multiprocessor diagnostics. http://www.infomall.org/diagnostics/archtest.html.
8. W. W. Collier. *Reasoning About Parallel Architectures*. Prentice-Hall, Englewood Cliffs, NJ, 1992.
9. Francisco Corella, April 1997. Invited talk at Computer Hardware Description Languages 1997, Toledo, Spain, on Verifying I/O Systems.
10. David L. Dill, Seungjoon Park, and Andreas Nowatzyk. Formal specification of abstract memory models. In Gaetano Borriello and Carl Ebeling, editors, *Research on Integrated Systems*, pages 38–52. MIT Press, 1993.
11. Rob Gerth. Introduction to sequential consistency and the lazy caching algorithm. *Distributed Computing*, 1995.
12. R. Ghughal, A. Mokkedem, R. Nalumasu, and G. Gopalakrishnan. Using "test model-checking" to verify the Runway-PA8000 memory model. In *Tenth Annual ACM Symposium on Parallel Algorithms and Architectures*, Puerto Vallarta, Mexico, June 1998.
13. Phillip B. Gibbons and Ephraim Korach. Testing shared memories. *SIAM Journal on Computing*, 26(4):1208–1244, August 1997.
14. James Gosling, Bill Joy, and Guy Steele. *The Java^{TM} Language Specification*. Sun Microsystems, 1.0 edition, August 1996.
15. S. Graf. Verification of a distributed cache memory by using abstractions. *Lecture Notes in Computer Science*, 818:207–220, 1994.
16. R. Hojati and R. Brayton. Automatic datapath abstraction of hardware systems. In *Conference on Computer-Aided Verification*, 1995.
17. R. Hojati, R. Mueller-Thuns, P. Loewenstein, and R. Brayton. Automatic verification of memory systems which service their requests out of order. In *CHDL*, pages 623–639, 1995.
18. Gerry Kane. *PA-RISC 2.0 Architecture*. Prentice Hall, 1996.
19. P. Ladkin, L. Lamport, B. Olivier, and D. Roegel. Lazy caching in TLA. *Distributed Computing*, 1997.
20. Leslie Lamport. How to make a correct multiprocess program execute correctly on a multiprocessor. Technical report, Digital Equipment Corporation, Systems Research Center, February 1993.
21. Leslie Lamport. The temporal logic of actions. *ACM Transactions on Programming Languages and Systems*, 16(3):872–923, May 1994. Also appeared as SRC Research Report 79.
22. Kenneth L. McMillan. *Symbolic Model Checking*. Kluwer Academic Press, 1993.
23. A. Mokkedem. Verification of three memory systems using test model-checking. http://www.cs.utah.edu/~mokkedem/vis/vis.html.
24. R. Nalumasu, R. Ghughal, A. Mokkedem, and G. Gopalakrishnan. The 'test model-checking' approach to the verification of formal memory models of multiprocessors. Technical Report UUCS-98-008, University of Utah, 1998. also available in http://www.cs.utah.edu/~mokkedem/frames/tr98.ps.gz.
25. Seungjoon Park and David L. Dill. Verification of FLASH cache coherence protocol by aggregation of distributed transactions. In *SPAA*, pages 288–296, Padua, Italy, June 24–26, 1996.
26. Vis-1.2 release. http://www-cad.eecs.berkeley.edu/Respep/Research/vis/.
27. David L. Weaver and Tom Germond. *The SPARC Architecture Manual – Version 9*. P T R Prentice-Hall, Englewood Cliffs, NJ 07632, USA, 1994.

Design Constraints in Symbolic Model Checking

Matt Kaufmann*, Andrew Martin, and Carl Pixley

Motorola, Inc.
P.O. Box 6000, MD: F52
Austin, TX 78762
carl_pixley@email.mot.com

Abstract. A time-consuming and error-prone activity in symbolic model-checking is the construction of environments. We present a technique for modeling environmental constraints that avoids the need for explicit construction of environments. Moreover, our approach supports an assume/guarantee style of reasoning that also supports simulation monitors. We give examples of the use of constraints in PowerPC^{TM}[1] verification.

1 Introduction

This work addresses the problem of providing a convenient way for designers to specify environments for symbolic model-checking, while supporting assume/guarantee reasoning.

CTL model-checking [1] is defined with respect to a closed system, that is, a system without primary inputs. In practice, however, one wishes to perform model-checking on circuits that have inputs, and hence are not closed. To accomplish this goal, one combines a model of the subject circuit with an enclosing model of its environment.

The most general enclosing environment is an independent, nondeterministic assignment of zeros and ones to the input pins of the circuit on each clock edge. Many circuits, however, are designed to work correctly only under specific environmental assumptions. Thus, in practice, the enclosing environment must model the actual environment in which the circuit will operate.

There are at least two problems with the environment modeling approach. The construction of such environments can be a difficult and time-consuming procedure. Moreover, there is no clear methodology for ensuring that the environment model is a true abstraction of the actual environment in which the subject circuit will operate.

---

* Matt Kaufmann's current address is: EDS CIO Services, 98 San Jacinto Blvd. Suite 500, Austin, TX 78701

[1] PowerPC is a trademark of the International Business Machines Corporation, used under license therefrom.

Constraints, as implemented in Motorola's Verdict model-checker, address these two problems. They provide a simple way to model environments. Moreover, they support an assume/guarantee methodology for ensuring that the environment models created are conservative abstractions of the actual environment in which the circuit will operate. Constraints can be used easily as properties to monitor during simulation of large units.

A constraint is a boolean formula involving any signals occurring in a design, including inputs to the design. If a monitor is used, constraints may involve signals of the monitor. Conceptually, constraints can be described in three levels of generality. The simplest constraints involve only input signals. For example, a constraint that inputs A, B and C are one-hot is expressed by the following formula:

$$(A + B + C)\&!(A\&B)\&!(A\&C)\&!(B\&C); \tag{1}$$

A second, more general, type of constraint involves signals that may depend upon the internal state of the design. A simple example from a microprocessor bus interface unit (BIU) is the assertion that if the BIU's address state machine is not in state "address idle" then its transaction-start input is not asserted, that is, if a transaction start input is asserted then the address state machine must be in the idle state:

$$\texttt{\$constraint(ts} \rightarrow \texttt{(addr\_state = 'ADDR\_IDLE));} \tag{2}$$

In this more general case of constraints, the inputs of the design, which determine the "next" state, may depend combinationally upon the current signals of the design but *only* on the current signals in the design, not past signals. It is a fundamental insight of the constraint approach that often a design under verification already contains sufficient information to determine what its input should be. Empirically, it was observed that environments being constructed replicated state already present in the design itself.

In the most general case of constraints, the inputs of a design depend not only on the current state of the design but also upon the history of reactions of the design to its inputs. In this case, it is necessary to instantiate a finite-state machine typically referred to as a *monitor* to "watch" the reaction of the design to its inputs and record information necessary to determine what the next input should be. Informally it is clear that, with the addition of monitors, constraints are as expressive as enclosing environment models.

One might imagine that by simply latching design inputs, one could just restrict model checking to the constrained state space. However, the constrained set of states may not be a Kripke model. In particular, it may be possible that some state s_0 is reachable from an initial constrained state through constrained states but such that s_0 does not have a next state that satisfies the constraints. It is our assumption that a state is valid if it is reachable from a valid input using constrained inputs for each step of the reachability calculation. If a "dead-end" state such as s_0 is encountered, this is evidence by itself that either the design or the constraints are incorrect.

This use of constraints has three key advantages over the use of enclosing environments. First, they are generally easier to write, and thus simplify the model-checking process. Second, a constraint, which is an assumption at one level of design hierarchy, automatically converts to an AG property, which is a proof obligation to verify at a higher level of hierarchy. For example, the BIU constraint converts directly into an AG property:

$$AG(\texttt{ts} \rightarrow (\texttt{addr\_state} = \text{'ADDR\_IDLE})); \tag{3}$$

Even in the case in which model checker capacity fails at a higher level, the constraint provides an invariant to monitor during simulation, the failure of which is evidence of faulty design or at least faulty specification. Thus, in a sense, use of constraints can be viewed as an assume/guarantee methodology. Finally, constraints document interface assumptions about design blocks in a set of simple formulas easily understood by designers. By contrast, environment modules constitute an awkward, unreadable, unmaintainable and unverifiable documentation of interface assumptions.

In [2], Long describes a very general method for doing compositional reasoning in the context of CTL model checking. In this work, Long presents a framework based on tableau construction. A procedure is given that constructs a model $T(\psi)$ for an arbitrary formula ψ. that allows one to verify properties of the form $< \psi > M < \phi >$, meaning that the composition of M with any environment satisfying ψ will satisfy ϕ, where M is an arbitrary Kripke structure, and ψ and ϕ are arbitrary ACTL formulas. ACTL is the subset of CTL in which all quantifiers are in essence universal.

The method involves the construction of a tableau, $T(\psi)$, that is a Kripke structure that represents the maximal environment that satisfies ψ. The composition $M\|T(\psi)$ is then checked using standard model-checking algorithms.

The method presented here can be viewed as a special case of Long's work that is of practical interest. Instead of considering assumptions $< \psi >$ with the full generality of ACTL, we restrict attention to assumptions of the form $AG(P)$, where P is an elementary formula, i.e. a (boolean) formula free from temporal operators and path quantifiers. In such cases, as we shall show, it is possible to avoid constructing a tableau explicitly, so that no additional state is introduced into the model provided no state is introduced explicitly on behalf of a monitor.

2 The Methodology

2.1 Methodology basics

Constraints are combinational boolean properties specified by the user at the top level of the a design module, using the $constraint keyword. For example, the constraint below says that signals s1 and s2 cannot both be high. Verdict uses the Verilog expression language.

```
$constraint(!(s1 & s2));
```

Constraints that appear in the top-level module are called *assumptions*. Those that appear in instantiated modules are called *guarantees*.

- All model-checking is performed by considering only those computation paths that globally satisfy the assumptions specified by constraints in the top level module.
- In addition to checking the specifications supplied by the user, the model-checker will also check that all guarantees, specified by constraints in the instantiated modules, hold for all reachable states.

2.2 Assume/guarantee reasoning

Constraints form the basis for automated assume/guarantee reasoning. Suppose one wishes to verify a property, called m_1-spec, of a module m_1 that is instantiated inside a module m_0.

One first treats m_1 as the top-level design, using constraints within it to model an abstraction of its environment. Let these be called the m_1-constraints. Since m_1 is being treated as the top-level design, the m_1-constraints will be treated as assumptions. Specifications within m_1, the m_1-specs, will be verified only for those paths that globally satisfy these assumptions.

Next, one instantiates m_1 within the module m_0, treating m_0 as the top-level design. It is not necessary to re-verify the m_1-specs. Since m_1 is now an instantiated module, the m_1-constraints are treated as guarantees, not as assumptions. When verifying m_0, the model-checker will also verify that the m_1-constraints do, in fact, hold globally: for each constraint C, it checks the CTL formula AG(C). In this way, the assumptions (m_1-constraints) that were made while verifying m_1 are discharged in the verification of m_0.

2.3 Monitors

Monitors allow constraints to specify sequential properties in addition to combinational properties. A monitor is generally a (Verilog) module instantiated within the top-level module of the design under test. Such a monitor has multiple inputs, and a single output. Conceptually, it monitors its inputs to ensure that they are behaving as expected. For example, it could monitor the input signals and selected state of the design under test to ensure that the environment that is driving them is following a given protocol. As long as things are behaving as expected, it continues to assert its output. However, if a protocol violation is detected its output is lowered.

By using the output of a monitor as the input to a constraint in the top-level module, a monitor can be used to restrict attention to state sequences that conform to the protocol. For example, a monitor within module m_1 could be used to restrict verification of the m_1-specs to the assumption that the inputs to m_1 have a certain sequential behavior.

When m_0 is subsequently verified, with m_1 instantiated within it, the same monitor can be used to discharge this assumption. The constraint that was previously treated as an assumption, is now treated as a guarantee. The model-checker will automatically check that the environment provided by m_0 fulfills this guarantee.

Of course, one can implement a monitor using in-line code, rather than an instantiated module, to achieve the same effect.

3   Semantics

A user view of constraints is explained above. Before giving the implementation we discuss the foundations.

Below, "constraint" refers to any constraint in the top-level module. Again, the constraints in other modules are turned into AG specs, automatically.

Notation. For a binary relation R and a set S. $Image(R, S)$ is the image of S by relation R, $\{t \in \text{range}(R): \text{ for some } s \in S, R(s, t)\}$.

Definition. Fix a Kripke structure M with transition relation TR, and fix a Boolean constraint C. Let CI be the set of initial states of M that satisfy C; we assume that CI is not empty. Define M_C to be the Kripke structure obtained from M by replacing the initial state set with CI, and restricting the set of states to the set CR of states *reachable via* C, defined as follows. CR is the least set S of states containing CI such that for every pair of state $< s, s' >$ in TR for which $s \in S$ and s' satisfies C, then s' belongs to S. In other words, CR is the least fixed point of the following monotone functional F, where $C(S)$ is the set of states in S satisfying C:

$$F(S) = CI \cup [Image(TR, S) \cap C(S)].$$

The following describes the kind of structures appropriate for model-checking. The first restriction rules out vacuous models. The second restriction is standard for CTL semantics, and although it is automatically true for for traditional hardware models, it can of course fail in the presence of constraints.

Definition. A Kripke structure is *model-checkable* if (1) it has at least one initial state, and (2) every state has at least one successor state.

Our task at hand is as follows. We are given a Kripke structure M, at least implicitly, and a Boolean constraint C. In fact, what we have in hand is the transition relation derived from a given RTL or gate-level description, using for example Verilog or DSL.[2] We need to verify that M_C is model-checkable. If so, we want to do model-checking on M_C. In other words, the semantics of constraints (in the top module) are to cause the CTL model-checking to be done on the restricted Kripke structure described above, but with a check that model-checking is appropriate according to (1) and (2) above.

4   The Algorithm

There are two ways in which CTL formulas involving constraints can be evaluated: with forward reachability and without. For ease of explanation, consider

---

[2] DSL is an IBM proprietary RTL level description language.

the model in which all inputs are latched, i.e., assigned present-state ps and next-state ns BDD variables, in addition to the usual present- and next-state variables for the latches. In both cases, let $T(ps, ns)$ be the transition relation built without regard to constraints. It is assumed that the set CI of initial states is non-empty and that all its members satisfy the constraints C. (Actually, we form CI by intersecting the set of user-designated initial states with those that satisfy the constraint C.)

4.1 "Without Forward Reachability" Method

Using the full model M, evaluate the CTL formula AG(C -> EX(C)). If the formula is false, then the "without reachability" method fails and the user is notified to use the option to verify with reachability. The model-checker could have simply gone on using the reachability method at such a point, but users often do not notice warnings, and because reachability is expensive it seems safer to give the user the chance to review the situation before proceeding.

Otherwise, create a new transition relation whose range and domain satisfy constraints C. Let this new model be M_C. The rest of the evaluation is the same as Section 4.2 of the "with reachability" method below.

4.2 "With Forward Reachability" Method

Performing Forward Reachability Analysis Using the transition relation T evaluate the formula EX(C). Perform forward reachability analysis with T in the following way. Each time a T-forward-image is calculated, the result is intersected with C. Check that the formula EX(C) holds for the set of newly created image states. If the check fails, Verdict quits with an error message about reaching a "dead-end" state. A feature that is not yet implemented would be to report a trace from an initial state satisfying C, through a set of states all satisfying C to a state that has no "next-state" satisfying C. This trace would show the user how the design can get into a "dead-end" state through valid transitions satisfying C.

Assuming that the EX(C)-check holds for each new frontier, the model checker has a set of states M_C in hand containing the initial states CI and such that for any state in M_C all of its T-next states satisfying C are in M_C.

Evaluating CTL Formulas Using M_C, evaluate the fair states and quit if there are no fair initial states. Modify the model again further restricting to fair states and check CTL specifications.

It should be pointed out that there are numerous variations and optimizations that can be made to the above algorithms. For example, one need not latch all of the inputs to create the transition relation T — just the inputs involved in the constraints and the CTL properties.

Furthermore, by existentially quantifying out inputs from C one can create C' which is the set of states which satisfy C for some input. Then one can cofactor each component of the relation T with C'. Likewise, one can cofactor the range of T as well.

It is important during model checking to make sure that all images and pre-images satisfy C, intersecting with the set of states satisfying C when necessary.

5   Examples

The use of constraints is illustrated by an example, derived from a PowerPC microprocessor design. The example is the controller for an instruction queue. The queue holds instructions that are waiting for operands, prior to being issued to one of several execution units. The controller performs the following tasks:

- When it has space, and instructions are available that are destined for the units served by this queue, it loads the instructions into the queue from the main instruction dispatch queue.
- When an instruction is ready for execution, and an execution unit is available, it issues the instruction to that execution unit.
- It tracks which queue entries have valid instructions.
- It tracks the relative age of instructions in the queue. This age information is used in the process of deciding whether an instruction is ready to execute.

The original module, as it existed in the PowerPC design, had several hundred primary inputs and outputs, and over a hundred internal latches. For the purpose of this presentation, the design has been simplified substantially by omitting some functionality, by shortening the queue, and by reducing the number of dispatch and issue ports. The clocking scheme has also been simplified from two-phase non-overlap, to a simple positive-edge-triggered synchronous design. However, the original design was indeed verified, and in spite of these simplifications, the basic verification issues remain unchanged from the original.

The module presented here is a queue with three entries, numbered 0, 1, and 2. It can receive up to two instructions from the main instruction dispatch queue per cycle, and issue up to two instructions, one to each of two execution units.

It has the following primary inputs

clk Internal latches update on the rising edge of this global clock.

iq_loads[0 : 1] A two bit input from the instruction dispatch queue. An asserted value indicates that data is available from the corresponding port.

our_op[0 : 2] Each bit indicates whether the corresponding instruction queue entry contains an operation that should be executed by one of the execution units serviced by this queue.

exe0_ready is asserted when by execution unit 0 when it is ready to receive a new instruction to execute.

exe1_ready is asserted by execution unit 1 when it is ready to receive a new instruction to execute.

ops_ready[0 : 2] Each bit is asserted when all the operands for the corresponding queue entry are available.

flush[0 : 2] For various reasons, such as branch mis-prediction, it is sometimes necessary to flush instructions from the queue. A queue entry will be flushed (by resetting its valid bit) when the corresponding flush input is asserted.

and the following primary outputs

load0[0 : 1] (resp. load1[0 : 1], load2[0 : 1]) The controller asserts load$i$[j] to load queue element i from dispatch port j.

issue0[0:2] (resp. issue1[0:2]) The controller asserts issue$i$[j] to issue an instruction from queue element j to execution unit i.

valid[0:2] The controller asserts valid[i] when queue entry i has a valid entry.

The specifications that we wished to verify were straightforward. There were a number of safety specifications, of the form AG(p) where P is a (non-temporal) boolean formula expressed in terms of the inputs, outputs, and some internal signals of the module. Some were single cycle specifications, of the form AG(P → AX Q). There were also three liveness specifications of the form AG AF P.

As it turned out, to verify even relatively simple properties about this design required some non-trivial assumptions about the design's environment. The environmental assumptions needed to verify the safety and single-cycle specifications were easily expressed using constraints that referenced only internal signals, primary inputs, and primary outputs. That is, no additional state was required. To verify the liveness specifications, however, it was necessary to introduce some additional state in order to constrain the inputs adequately.

One of the simplest constraints referred only to the primary inputs of the design under analysis. It simply required that no instructions be dispatched while a flush was in progress. Here and below, a vertical bar ("|") represents the or-reduction operator, true of a multi-bit signal when at least one bit is on.

$$\$constraint(\neg(|flush[0 : 2] \ \& \ |iq\_loads[0 : 1])) \qquad (4)$$

Of primary concern to the designer of this block was the verification of the valid bits, and the age tracking mechanism. There are state bits, q_age[0 : 2] associated with age tracking. The bit, q_age[0] is asserted if entry 0 is older than entry 1. Bit q_age[1] is asserted if entry 0 is older than entry 2. Bit q_age[2] is asserted if entry 1 is older than entry 2. Should two entries arrive simultaneously, the entry with the smaller index is considered older. An empty queue slot is considered "newer" than an occupied queue slot.

The age bits were verified using several CTL specifications. Here we illustrate only age bit q_age[0]. The specifications for the other bits are completely analogous. Notice that in the case when one or both of valid[0] and valid[1] is de-asserted, the value of q_age[0] is fully determined by the values of valid[0] and valid[1]. This combinational part of the specification is captured by the following CTL formulas. Formula 5 gives the value of q_age[0] when valid[0] is low. Formula 6 gives the value when valid[0] is high but valid[1] is low.

$$AG(\neg valid[0] \rightarrow \neg q\_age[0]) \qquad (5)$$

$$AG(\text{valid}[0] \ \& \ \neg\text{valid}[1] \rightarrow \text{q\_age}[0]) \tag{6}$$

When both valid[0] and valid[1] are asserted, the value of q_age depends on history. The following table shows only the possible transitions to a state in which valid[0] and valid[1] are both high. Transitions to states in which one or both of valid[0] and valid[1] are low are also possible, but the resulting value of q_age[0] in such a state has been determined by formulas 5 and 6 above.

Current State			Next State		
valid[0]	valid[1]	q_age[0]	valid[0]	valid[1]	q_age[0]
0	1	0	1	1	0
1	1	0	1	1	0
0	0	0	1	1	1
1	0	1	1	1	1
1	1	1	1	1	1

This set of transitions is expressed by the following two CTL formulas.

$$AG((\text{valid}[1] \ \& \ \neg\text{q\_age}[0]) \rightarrow$$
$$AX((\text{valid}[0] \ \& \ \text{valid}[1]) \rightarrow \neg\text{q\_age}[0])) \tag{7}$$

$$AG((\neg\text{valid}[1]|\text{q\_age}[0]) \rightarrow$$
$$AX(\text{valid}[0] \ \& \ \text{valid}[1]) \rightarrow \text{q\_age}[0])) \tag{8}$$

One might reasonably hope that the circuit would work correctly for all sequences of input stimulus but, unfortunately, this is not the case. In the chip environment, it turns out that a queue entry is never flushed unless all of the newer entries are flushed as well. The designer took advantage of this knowledge by omitting some (redundant under this assumption) flush information from the equations updating the age information. To verify this circuit, it is necessary to provide an environment that behaves according to these assumptions.

To accomplish this, the environment must know the relative age of the entries in the queue. One could, of course, construct an environment module that keeps track of this information. But to do so would add considerable additional state to the system. In our verification, we have capitalized on the fact that this information is already present *in the design under analysis.* Thus, we use the q_age bits themselves in the environment:

$$\$\text{constraint}(\neg(\text{flush}[0] \ \& \ \neg\text{flush}[1] \ \& \ \text{valid}[0] \ \& \ \text{valid}[1] \ \& \ \text{q\_age}[0])) \tag{9}$$

$$\$\text{constraint}(\neg(\text{flush}[1] \ \& \ \neg\text{flush}[0] \ \& \ \text{valid}[0] \ \& \ \text{valid}[1] \ \& \ \neg\text{q\_age}[0]))$$
$$\tag{10}$$

On the surface, there might appear to be an alarming circularity in using the q_age bits to constrain the environment in order to verify the correctness of the q_age bits. However, the informal reasoning is valid. In this example, we are assuming the correctness of q_age *now* in order to establish the correctness of q_age *next cycle.* Note, however, that this (admittedly informal) reasoning would not be valid if q_age were combinationally dependent upon flush. For a more general treatment of this problem, in the context of abstraction, the reader is referred to [3]

Formally, however, the constraints do nothing more than restrict the scopes of path quantifiers in the CTL formulas to paths that globally satisfy the constraints. Correctness has thus been verified, under the assumption that sequences that violate the constraints will not occur. This assumption can be discharged formally, by model-checking the circuit within its enclosing environment, verifying the spec $AG(C)$, where C is the conjunction of the constraints above. In practise, this circuit was already at the limits of our model-checker's capacity. Nonetheless, the assumption can be validated informally, by checking that no constraint is violated during unit or full-chip simulation.

Finally, we wished to verify that, under certain fairness assumptions, every instruction queue element is eventually dispatched. These properties were easily expressed by the CTL specifications:

$$\text{AG AF}\neg\text{valid}[0] \tag{11}$$

$$\text{AG AF}\neg\text{valid}[1] \tag{12}$$

$$\text{AG AF}\neg\text{valid}[2] \tag{13}$$

As is typical with such specifications, these will only hold under certain fairness assumptions. In particular, we must assume that, for each queue element, there are both arguments and an execution unit available infinitely often. These assumptions alone, however, are not sufficient to verify the desired properties. The problem has to do with barriers. Some instructions are barriers, enforcing in-order execution. A barrier cannot be issued until all the instructions that precede it have completed. Furthermore, no instruction that follows a barrier can execute until the barrier has begun execution.

One could force the specifications to pass, by requiring that both execution units become free *simultaneously* infinitely often. However, this fairness constraint is really too strong. What is required is that once an execution unit becomes free, it does not become busy again until an instruction is issued to it.

To express this property using constraints requires some additional state, beyond that which is present explicitly in the design. The monitor must remember previous values, both of the exe0_ready and exe1_ready signals and of the issue0 and issue1 signals. Let p_exe0_ready, p_exe1_ready, p_issue0, and p_issue1 be the previous values of the corresponding signals. Such values can be obtained easily in Verilog, by constructing a simple latch. The desired constraints are simply:

$$\$\text{constraint}(\neg(\neg\text{exe0\_ready}\ \&\ \text{p\_exe0\_ready}\ \&\ \neg\text{p\_issue0})) \tag{14}$$

That is, it should never be the case that

- execution unit 0 is not ready now,
- execution unit 0 was ready last cycle,
- and nothing was issued to unit 0 last cycle.

Similarly, it is necessary to constrain the signal `barrier[0 : 2]` so that each of its bits changes only when the corresponding queue entry is invalid — being a "barrier" is a static property of an instruction.

With these constraints, and the additional fairness constraints that require each execution unit (independently) to be available infinitely often, it was possible to establish the desired liveness properties.

6 Summary

Our approach to handling constraints is new in several ways.

- Constraints free the user from writing environment models to generate inputs.
- In many cases, constraints accomplish what environments accomplish with fewer BDD variables.
- Constraints allow the automated restriction of computation paths, for example using monitors. Because the restriction can depend on internal state, environment models alone cannot easily be used to accomplish this restriction.
- The algorithm handles input constraints that depend on the state of the design being verified.
- An assume/guarantee methodology allows both the assumption and verification of constraints. Constraints as verification properties can be used with conventional simulation validation.
- Constraints provide a convenient, easily understood method for documenting module interfaces, which can be used to catch errors during simulation as well as model checking.

References

1. E.M. Clarke and E.A. Emerson, *Design and Synthesis of Synchronization Skeletons using Branching Time Temporal Logic*, Proceedings of the Workshop on Logics of Programs, York town Heights, NY, Springer-Verlag LNCS no. 131, pp. 52 – 71, May 1981.
2. D.E. Long, "Model Checking, Abstraction, and Compositional Verification," School of Computer Science, Carnegie Mellon University publication CMU-CS-93-178, July 1993.
3. K. L. McMillan, "A Compositional Rule for Hardware Design Refinement," Orna Grunberg (Ed.) *Computer Aided Verification*, Proceedings of the 9th International Conference, Haifa, Israel, Springer-Verlag LNCS no. 1254, pp. 24 – 35, June 1997.

Verification of Floating-Point Adders **

Yirng-An Chen and Randal E. Bryant
yachen+@cs.cmu.edu, bryant+@cs.cmu.edu
Computer Science Dept., Carnegie Mellon Univ., Pittsburgh, PA 15213

Abstract. In this paper, we present a "black box" version of verification of FP adders. In our approach, FP adders are verified by an extended word-level SMV using reusable specifications without knowing the circuit implementation. Word-level SMV is improved by using Multiplicative Power HDDs (*PHDDs), and by incorporating conditional symbolic simulation as well as a short-circuiting technique. Based on a case analysis, the adder specification is divided into several hundred implementation-independent sub-specifications. We applied our system and these specifications to verify the IEEE double precision FP adder in the Aurora III Chip from the University of Michigan. Our system found several design errors in this FP adder. Each specification can be checked in less than 5 minutes. A variant of the corrected FP adder was created to illustrate the ability of our system to handle different FP adder designs. For each adder, the verification task finished in 2 CPU hours on a Sun UltraSPARC-II server.

1 Introduction

The floating-point (FP) division bug [10] in Intel's Pentium processor and the overflow flag erratum of the FIST instruction (FP to integer conversion) [12] in Intel's Pentium Pro and Pentium II processors have demonstrated the importance and the difficulty of verifying FP arithmetic circuits and the high cost of an arithmetic bug. FP adders are the most common units in FP processors. Modern high-speed FP adders [17] are very complicated, because they require many types of modules: a right shifter for alignment, a left shifter for normalization, a leading zero anticipator (LZA), an adder for mantissas, and a rounding unit.

Formal verification or exhaustive simulation can be used to ensure the correctness of FP adders. However, it is impossible to perform exhaustive simulations for a floating-point adder. Formal verification techniques such as theorem proving and model checking have been used to verify arithmetic circuits. Most of the IEEE FP standard has been formalized by Carreño and Miner [4] for the HOL and PVS theorem provers. To verify arithmetic circuits, theorem provers require users to guide the proof which is structured as series of lemmas describing the effect of circuit modules and their interactions [1]. Thus, the verification process is very tedious and implementation-dependent. After the famous Pentium division bug [10], Intel researchers applied word-level SMV [9] with Hybrid Decision Diagrams (HDDs) [8] to verify the functionality of the FP unit in one of Intel's processors [7]. Due to the limitations of HDDs, the FP adder was partitioned into several sub-circuits to be verified. The correctness of the overall circuit had to be ascertained manually from the verified specifications of the sub-circuits. This partitioning approach requires user intervention and thus could be error prone. Moreover, the specifications for the partitions are highly dependent on the circuit implementation.

** This research is sponsored by the Defense Advanced Research Projects Agency (DARPA) under contract number DABT63-96-C-0071.

To the best of our knowledge, only two types of arithmetic circuits can be verified by treating them as *black boxes* (i.e., the specifications contain only the inputs and outputs). First, an integer adder can be verified by using Binary Decision Diagrams (BDDs) [2]. Second, Hamaguchi *et al* [13] presented the verification of integer multipliers without knowing their implementations using Multiplicative Binary Moment Diagrams (*BMDs) [3]. However, their approach does not work for incorrect designs, because the *BMDs explode in size and counterexamples can not be generated for debugging. None of the previous approaches can verify FP adders without knowing their circuit implementations.

In this paper, we present a black box version of verification of FP adders. In our approach, a FP adder is treated as a black box and is verified by an extended version of word-level SMV with reusable specifications. Word-level SMV is improved by using Multiplicative Power HDDs (*PHDDs) [5] to represent the FP functions, and by incorporating *conditional symbolic simulation* as well as a *short-circuiting* technique. The FP adder specification is divided into several hundred sub-specifications based on the sign bits and the exponent differences. These sub-specifications are implementation-independent, since they use only the input and output signals of FP adders.

The concept of conditional symbolic simulation is to perform the symbolic simulation of the circuit with some conditions to restrict the behavior of the circuit. This approach can be viewed as dynamically extracting circuit behavior under the given conditions without modifying the actual circuit. Can we verify the specifications of FP adders using conditional symbolic simulation, avoiding any use of circuit knowledge? We identify a conflict in variable orderings between the mantissa comparator and mantissa adder, which causes the BDD explosion in conditional symbolic simulation. A short-circuiting technique to overcome this ordering conflict problem is presented and integrated into word-level SMV package. In general, this short-circuiting technique can be used when different parts of the circuit are used under different operating conditions.

We used our system and these specifications to verify the FP adder in the Aurora III Chip [14] at the University of Michigan. This FP adder is based on the design described in [17], and supports IEEE double precision and all 4 IEEE rounding modes. In this verification work, we verified the FP adder only in the round-to-nearest mode, because we believe that this is the most challenging rounding mode for verification. Our system found several design errors. Each specification can be checked in less than 3 minutes or 5 minutes including counterexample generation. A variant of the corrected FP adder was created and verified to illustrate the ability of our system to handle different FP adder designs. For each FP adder, verification took 2 CPU hours. We believe that our system and specifications can be applied to directly verify other FP adder designs and to help find design errors.

The overflow flag erratum of the FIST instruction (FP to integer conversion) [12] in Intel's Pentium Pro and Pentium II processors has illustrated the importance of verification of the conversion circuits which convert the data from one format to another format (e.g., IEEE single precision to double precision). Since these circuits are much simpler than FP adders and only have one input operand, we believe that our system can be used to verify the correctness of these circuits.

2 *PHDD Overview

Chen and Bryant [5] introduced a representation, called Multiplicative Power HDDs (*PHDDs), to provide a compact representation for integer and floating-point functions. For expressing function g from Boolean variables to integer or floating-point values, *PHDDs use one of three decompositions of a function with respect to an input variable x:

$$g = \langle w, f \rangle = \begin{cases} c^w \cdot ((1-x) \cdot f_{\overline{x}} + x \cdot f_x) & (Shannon) \\ c^w \cdot (f_{\overline{x}} + x \cdot f_{\delta x}) & (Positive\ Davio) \\ c^w \cdot (f_x + (1-x) \cdot f_{\delta \overline{x}}) & (Negative\ Davio) \end{cases}$$

where $\langle w, f \rangle$ denotes $c^w \cdot f$, and $\cdot$, $+$ and $-$ denote multiplication, addition and subtraction, respectively. Term f_x ($f_{\overline{x}}$) denotes the 1- (0-) cofactor of f with respect to variable x, i.e., the function resulting when the constant 1 (0) is substituted for x. Term $f_{\delta x} = f_x - f_{\overline{x}}$ is called the linear moment of f with respect to x. This terminology arises by viewing f as a linear function with respect to its variables, and thus $f_{\delta x}$ is the partial derivative of f with respect to x. Similarly, Term $f_{\delta \overline{x}}$ is $f_{\overline{x}} - f_x$.

In general, the constant c can be any positive integer. Since the base value of the exponent in the IEEE floating-point (FP) format is 2, we will consider only $c = 2$ for the remainder of this paper. Observe that w can be negative, allowing the representation of rational numbers. The power edge weights enable us to represent functions mapping Boolean variables to FP values. To the best of our knowledge, *PHDD is the only decision diagram that can represent integer or floating-point functions efficiently. Readers can refer to [5] for more details of FP representation using *PHDDs. In this verification work, the output Boolean vector of a FP adder are converted into word-level functions represented by *PHDDs using a method similar to one described in [3]. Thus, the specifications of FP adders can be expressed in word-level functions using *PHDDs.

3 Floating-Point Adders

Let us consider the representation of FP numbers by IEEE standard 754. Double-precision FP numbers are stored in 64 bits: 1 bit for the sign (S_x), 11 bits for the exponent (E_x), and 52 bits for the mantissa (N_x). The exponent is a signed number represented with a bias (B) of 1023. The mantissa (N_x) represents a number less than 1. Based on the value of the exponent, the IEEE FP format can be divided into four cases:

$$\begin{cases} (-1)^{S_x} \times 1.N_x \times 2^{E_x - B} & If\ 0 < E_x < All\ 1\ (normal) \\ (-1)^{S_x} \times 0.N_x \times 2^{1-B} & If\ E_x = 0\ (denormal) \\ NaN & If\ E_x = All\ 1\ \&\ N_x \neq 0 \\ (-1)^{S_x} \times \infty & If\ E_x = All\ 1\ \&\ N_x = 0 \end{cases}$$

where NaN denotes Not-a-Number and ∞ represents infinity. Let $M_x = 1.N_x$ or $0.N_x$. Let m be the number of mantissa bits including the bit on the left of the binary point and n be number of exponent bits. For IEEE double precision, $m=53$ and $n=11$.

Due to this encoding, an operation on two FP numbers cannot be rewritten as an arithmetic function of the two inputs. For example, the addition of two FP numbers X (S_x, E_x, M_x) and Y (S_y, E_y, M_y) can not be expressed as $X + Y$, because of special cases when one of them is NaN or $\pm\infty$. Table 1 summarizes the possible results of the FP addition of two numbers X and Y, where F represents a normalized or denormalized number. The result can be expressed as $Round(X + Y)$ only when both operands have normal or denormal values. Otherwise, the result is determined by the case. When one operand is $+\infty$ and the other is $-\infty$, the adder should raise an invalid arithmetic operand exception.

		Y			
+	$-\infty$	F	$+\infty$	NaN
$-\infty$	$-\infty$	$-\infty$	*	NaN
X $\quad$ F	$-\infty$	$Round(X+Y)$	$+\infty$	NaN
$+\infty$	*	$+\infty$	$+\infty$	NaN
NaN	NaN	NaN	NaN	NaN

Table 1. Summary of the FP addition of two numbers of X and Y. F represents the normal and denormal numbers. * indicates FP invalid arithmetic operands.

Figure 1.a shows the block diagram of the SNAP FP adder designed at Stanford University [17]. As an alternative to the SNAP design, the ones complementer after the mantissa adder can be avoided, if we ensure that input C (shown in Figure 1.a) of the mantissa adder is smaller than or equal to input A (shown in Figure 1.a), when the exponent difference is 0 and the operation of mantissa adder is subtraction. To ensure this property, a mantissa comparator and extra circuits are needed to swap the mantissas correctly. Figure 1.b shows a variant of the SNAP FP adder with this modification (the *compare* unit is added and the ones complementer is deleted). This *compare* unit exists in many modern high-speed FP adder designs and makes the verification harder as described in Section 5.2. Figure 2 shows the detailed circuit of the *compare* unit which generates the signal to swap the mantissas. The signal $E_x < E_y$ comes from the exponent subtractor. When $E_x < E_y$ or $E_x = E_y$ and $M_x < M_y$ (i.e., $h =1$), A is M_y (i.e. the mantissas are swapped). Otherwise, A is M_x.

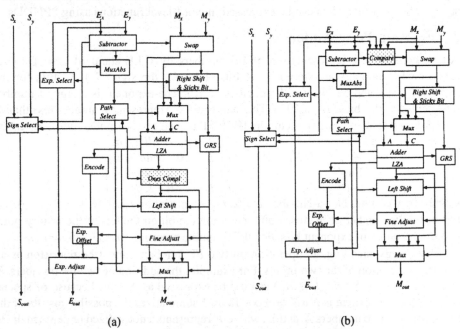

(a)   (b)

Fig. 1. The Stanford SNAP FP adder (a) and its variant (b).

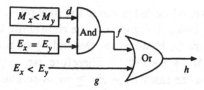

Fig. 2. Detailed circuit of the compare unit

4 Specifications of FP Adders

In this section, we focus on the general specifications of the FP adder, especially when both operands have denormal or normal values. In cases where at least one of the operands is a NaN or ∞, the specifications can be easily written at the bit level. For example, when both operands are NaN, the expected output is NaN (i.e. the exponent is all 1s and the mantissa is not equal to zero). This specification can be expressed as the "AND" of the exponent output bits is 1 and the "OR" of the mantissa output bits is 1.

4.1 Specifications

When both operands have normal or denormal values, the ideal specification is $OUT = Round(X + Y)$. However, the *PHDD representation of FP addition grows exponentially with the size of the exponent. Thus, the specification must be divided into several sub-specifications for verification. According to the signs of the operands, the function $X + Y$ can be rewritten as Equation 1. Similarly, for FP subtraction, the function $X - Y$ can be also rewritten as true addition when the operands have different signs and true subtraction when the operands have the same sign.

$$X + Y = (-1)^{S_x} \times \begin{cases} (2^{E_x-B} \times M_x + M_y \times 2^{E_y-B}) & S_x = S_y (true\ addition) \\ (2^{E_x-B} \times M_x - M_y \times 2^{E_y-B}) & S_x \neq S_y (true\ subtraction) \end{cases} \quad (1)$$

The *PHDDs for the true addition and subtraction still grow exponentially. Based on the sizes of the two exponents, the function $X + Y$ for true addition can be rewritten as:

$$X + Y = (-1)^{S_x} \times \begin{cases} 2^{E_x-B} \times (M_x + (M_y >> i)) & E_y \leq E_x \\ 2^{E_y-B} \times (M_y + (M_x >> i)) & E_y > E_x \end{cases}, \text{where } i = |E_x - E_y|.$$

When $E_y \leq E_x$, the exponent is E_x and the mantissa is the sum of M_x and M_y right shifted by i bits ($M_y >> i$ in the equation). $|E_x - E_y|$ can range from 0 to $2^n - 2$, but the number of mantissa bits in FP format is only m bits.

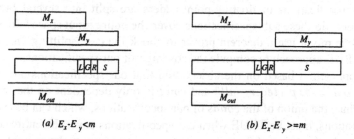

(a) E_x-E_y<m   (b) E_x-E_y>=m

Fig. 3. Cases of true addition for the mantissa part.

Figure 3 illustrates the possible cases of true addition for $E_y \leq E_x$ based on the values of $E_x - E_y$. In Figure 3.a, for $0 \leq E_x - E_y < m$, the intermediate (precise) result contains more than m bits. The right portion of the result is denoted as L, G, R and S, where L is the least signification bit of the mantissa. The rounding mode will use these bits to perform the rounding and generate the final result (M_{out}) in m-bit format. When $E_x - E_y \geq m$ as shown in Figure 3.b, the right shifted M_y only contributes to the intermediate result in the G, R and S bits. Depending the rounding mode, the output mantissa will be M_x or $M_x + 1 * 2^{-m+1}$. Therefore, we only need one specification in each rounding mode for the cases $E_x - E_y \geq m$. A similar analysis can be applied to the case $E_y > E_x$. Thus, the specifications for true addition with rounding can be written as:

$$\begin{cases} C_{a1}[i] \Rightarrow OUT = Round((-1)^{S_x} \times 2^{E_x-B} \times (M_x + (M_y >> i))) \ 0 \leq i < m \\ C_{a2} \Rightarrow OUT = Round((-1)^{S_x} \times 2^{E_x-B} \times (M_x + (M_y >> m))) \ \ i \geq m \\ C_{a3}[i] \Rightarrow OUT = Round((-1)^{S_x} \times 2^{E_y-B} \times (M_y + (M_x >> i))) \ 0 < i < m \\ C_{a4} \Rightarrow OUT = Round((-1)^{S_x} \times 2^{E_y-B} \times (M_y + (M_x >> m))) \ \ i \geq m \end{cases}$$

where $C_{a1}[i]$, C_{a2}, $C_{a3}[i]$ and C_{a4} are the conditions $Cond\_add \& E_x = E_y + i$, $Cond\_add \& E_x \geq E_y + m$, $Cond\_add \& E_y = E_x + i$, and $Cond\_add \& E_y \geq E_x + m$, respectively. $Cond\_add$ represents the condition for true addition and exponent range (i.e. normal and denormal numbers only). OUT is composed from the outputs S_{out}, E_{out} and M_{out}. While building BDDs and *PHDDs for OUT from the circuit, the conditions on left side of the $\Rightarrow$ will be used to simplify the BDDs automatically by conditional symbolic simulation.

The number of specifications for true addition is $2m + 1$. Since the value of m for IEEE double precision is 53, the number of specifications for true addition is 107. Since the specifications are very similar to one another, they can be generated by a looping construct in the word-level SMV specification language.

Similarly, the specification of true subtraction can be divided into several hundred of sub-specifications. The specification of true subtraction is divided into two cases: *far* ($|E_x - E_y| > 1$) and *close* ($E_x - E_y$=0,1 or -1). For the *far* case, the result of mantissa subtraction does not require a massive left shift (i.e., LZA is not active). For the *close* case, the result of mantissa subtraction requires a massive left shift (i.e., LZA is active), which makes the verification harder. Thus, the specifications of the *close* case must be divided further based on the number of bits to be left shifted. Readers can refer to [6] for the details of these specifications.

4.2 Specification Coverage

Since the specifications of floating-point adders are split into several hundred sub-specifications, do these sub-specifications cover the entire input space? To answer this question, one might use a theorem prover to check the case splitting. In contrast, we propose a BDD approach to compute the coverage of our specifications.

Our approach is based on the observation that our specifications are in the form "*cond* $\Rightarrow$ *out* = *expected_result*" and *cond* is only dependent on the inputs of the circuits. Thus, the union of the *cond*s of our specifications, which can be computed by BDD operations, must be TRUE when our specifications cover the entire input space. In other words, the union of the *cond*s can be used to compute the percentage of input space covered by our specifications and to generate the missing cases.

5 Verification System: Extended Word-Level SMV with *PHDDs

To verify integer arithmetic circuits, SMV [16] was extended using HDDs [8] to handle word level expressions in the specification formulas [9]. For verification of FP circuits, we replaced the HDDs in word-level SMV with *PHDDs and introduced relational operators for FP numbers. As in word-level SMV, only the word-level functions are represented by *PHDDs while the rest of the functions are represented by BDDs.

5.1 Conditional Symbolic Simulation

We have introduced a conditional symbolic simulation technique into word-level SMV. Symbolic simulation performs a simulation with inputs having symbolic values (i.e., Boolean variables or Boolean functions). The simulation process builds BDDs for the circuits. If each input is a Boolean variable, this approach may cause a explosion of the BDD size in the middle of the process, because it tries to simulate the entire circuit for all possible inputs at once. The concept of conditional symbolic simulation is to perform the simulation process under restricted conditions, expressed as a Boolean function over the inputs.

In [15], Jain and Gopalakrishnan encoded the conditions together with the original inputs as new inputs to the symbolic simulator using a parametric form of Boolean expressions, but it is hard to incorporate this approach into word-level SMV. Our approach is to apply the conditions directly during the symbolic simulation process. After building the BDD for a circuit gate, the condition is used to simplify the BDD using the *restrict* [11] algorithm. Then, the simplified BDD is used as the input function for the gates connected to this one. This process is repeated until the outputs are reached. This approach dynamically extracts the circuit behavior under the specified condition without modifying the actual circuit.

5.2 Short-Circuiting Technique

Can we verify the specifications of FP adders by conditional symbolic simulation? In our experience, all the specifications for the FP adder design without a mantissa comparator, as in Figure 1.a, can be verified by conditional symbolic simulation, but not so for the FP adder containing a mantissa comparator, as in Figure 1.b. This is caused by a conflict in variable orderings for the mantissa adder and the mantissa comparator, which generates the signal $M_x < M_y$ (i.e. signal d in Figure 2). The best variable ordering for the comparator is to interleave the two vectors from the most significant bit to the least significant bit (i.e., $x_{m-1}, y_{m-1}, ..., x_0, y_0$). Table 2 shows the CPU time in seconds and the BDD size of the signal d under different variable orderings, where ordering offset represents the number of bits offset from the best ordering. For example, the ordering is $x_{m-1}, ..., x_{m-6}, y_{m-1}, x_{m-7}, y_{m-2}, ..., x_0, y_5, ..., y_0$, when the ordering offset is 5. Clearly, the BDD size grows exponentially with the offset. In contrast to the comparator, the best ordering for the mantissa adder is $x_{m-1}, ..., x_{m-k-1}, y_{m-1}, x_{m-k-2}, y_{m-2}, ..., x_0, y_k, ..., y_0$, when the exponent difference is k. We observed that the best ordering for the specification represented by *PHDDs is the same as the best ordering for the mantissa adder. Thus, extended word-level SMV can not build the BDDs for both the mantissa comparator and mantissa adder by conditional symbolic simulation, when the exponent difference is large.

Let us examine the *compare* unit carefully. We find that the signal d is used only when $E_x = E_y$. In other words, it is not necessary to build the BDDs for it, when $|E_x - E_y|$ is greater than 0. Based on this fact, we introduce a short-circuiting technique to eliminate unnecessary computations as early as possible. The word-level SMV system is modified to incorporate this technique. In the *PHDD package, the BDD operators, such as *And* and *Or*, are modified to abort the operation and return a *special token* when the number of newly created BDD nodes within this BDD call is greater than a size threshold. In word-level SMV, for an *And* gate with two inputs, if the first input evaluates 0, 0 will be returned without building the BDDs for the second input. Otherwise, the second input will be evaluated. If the second input evaluates to 0 and the first input evaluates to a *special token*, 0 is returned. Similar rules are applied to *Or* gates with two inputs. *Nand(Nor)* gates can be decomposed into *Not* and *And* (*Or*) gates and use the same technique to terminate earlier. For other logic gates with two inputs, the result is a *special token* if either of the inputs evaluates to a *special token*. If the *special token* is propagated to the output of the circuit, then the size threshold is doubled and the output is recomputed. This process is repeated until the output BDD is built. For example, when the exponent difference is 30, the size threshold is 10000, the ordering is the best ordering of mantissa adder, and the evaluation sequence of the *compare* unit shown in Figure 2 is d, e, f, g and h, the values of signals d, e, f, g and h will be *special token*, 0, 0, 1, and 1, respectively, by conditional symbolic simulation. With these modification, the new system can verify all of the specifications for both types of FP adders by conditional symbolic simulation. We believe that this short-circuiting technique can be generalized and used when different parts of the circuit are used under different operating conditions.

Ordering Offset	BDD Size	CPU Time (Sec.)
0	157	0.68
1	309	0.88
2	608	1.35
3	1195	2.11
4	2346	3.79
5	4601	7.16
6	9016	13.05
7	17655	26.69
8	34550	61.61
9	67573	135.22

Table 2. Performance measurements of a 52-bit comparator with different orderings.

6 Verification of FP Adders

We use the FP adder in the Aurora III Chip [14], designed by Dr. Huff as part of his PhD dissertation at the University of Michigan, as an example to illustrate the verification of FP adders. This adder is based on the same approach as the SNAP FP adder [17] at Stanford University. This FP adder only handles operands with normal values. When the result is a denormal value, it is truncated to 0. This adder supports IEEE double precision format and the 4 IEEE rounding modes. Dr. Huff found several errors with the approach described in [17]. In this verification work, we verify the adder only in round to nearest mode, because we believe that the round to nearest mode is the hardest one to verify. All experiments were carried out on a Sun 248 MHz UltraSPARC-II server with 1.5 GB memory.

The FP adder is described in the Verilog language in a hierarchical manner. The circuit was synthesized into flattened, gate-level Verilog by Dr. John Zhong at SGI. Then, a simple Perl script was used to translate the circuit from gate-level Verilog to SMV format and to perform latch removal.

6.1 Latch Removal

Huff's FP adder is a pipelined, two phase design with a latency of three clock cycles. We handled the latches during the translation from gate-level Verilog to SMV format. Figure 4.a shows the latches in the pipelined, two phase design. In the design, the phase 2 clock is the complement of the phase 1 clock. Since we only verify the functional correctness of the design and the FP adder does not have any feedback loops, the latches can be removed. One approach is to directly connect the inputs and the outputs of latches. This approach would eliminate some logic circuits related to the latch enable signals as shown on the right side of the latches in Figure 4.a. With this approach, the correctness of these circuits can not be checked. For example, a design error in the circuit, always generated 0s for the enable signals of latches, can not be found if we use this approach to remove the latches.

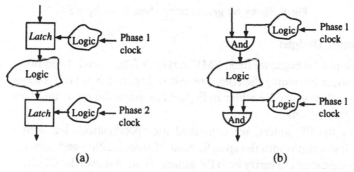

Fig. 4. Latch Removal. (a) The pipelined, two phase design. (b) The design after latch removal.

Our approach for latch removal is based on this observation: the data are written into the latches when the enable signals are 1. To ensure the correctness of the circuits for the enable signals, the latches can be replaced by *And* gates, as shown in Figure 4.b, without losing the functional behavior of the circuit. Since phase 2 clock is the complement of the phase 1 clock, we must replace the phase 2 clock by the phase 1 clock. Otherwise the circuit behavior will be incorrect. With this approach, we can also check the correctness of circuits for the enable signals of the latches.

6.2 Design with Bugs

During the verification process, our system found several design errors in Huff's FP adder. These errors were not caught by random simulations performed by Dr. Huff. The first error we found is the case when $A + C = 01.111...11$, $A + C + 1=10.000...00$, and the rounding logic decides to add 1 to the least significant bit (i.e., the result should be $A + C + 1$), but the circuit design outputs A+C as the result. This error is caused by incorrect logic in the *path select* unit, which categorized this case as a no shift case instead of a right shift by 1. While we were verifying the specification of true addition, our system generated a counterexample for this case in around 50 seconds. To ensure that this bug was not introduced by when translating the circuits, we have used Cadence's Verilog simulation to verify this bug in the original design by simulating the input pattern generated by our system.

Another design error we found is in the sticky bit generation. The sticky bit generation is based on the table given in page 10 of Quach's paper describing the SNAP FP adder [17]. The table only handles cases when the absolute value of the exponent difference is less than 54. The design sets the sticky bit to 1 when the absolute value of the exponent difference is greater than 53 (for normal numbers only). The bug is that the sticky bit should not always be 1 when the absolute value of the exponent difference is equal to 54. Figure 5 shows the sticky bit generation when $E_x - E_y = 54$. Since N_x has 52 bits, the leading 1 will be the Round (R) bit and the sticky (S) bit is the OR of all of N_y bits, which may be 0. Therefore an entry for the case $|E_x - E_y| = 54$ is needed in the table of Quach's paper [17].

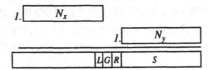

Fig. 5. Sticky bit generation, when $E_x - E_y = 54$.

6.3 Corrected Designs

After identifying the bugs, we fixed SMV version of the circuit. In addition, we created another FP adder by adding the *compare* unit in Figure 1.b to Huff's design. This new adder is equivalent to the FP adder in Figure 1.b, since the *ones complement* unit will not be active at any time.

To verify the FP adders, we combined the specifications for both addition and subtraction instructions into the specification of true addition and subtraction. We use the same specifications to verify both FP adders. Table 3 shows the CPU time in seconds and the maximum memory required for the verification of both FP adders. The CPU time is the total time for verifying all specifications. The FP adder II can not be verified by conditional symbolic simulation without the short-circuiting technique. The maximum memory is the maximum memory requirement of verification of these specifications. For both FP adders, the verification can be done within two hours and requires less than 55 MB. Each individual specification can be verified in less than 3 minutes. The verified specifications cover 99.78% of the input space for FP adders in IEEE round-to-nearest mode. The reason for uncovered input space (0.22%) is that the circuit does not implement the cases where either operand with denormal, NaN or ∞ values, and where the result of true subtraction is a denormal value.

Case	CPU Time (Sec.)		Max. Memory(MB)	
	FP adder I	FP adder II	FP adder I	FP adder II
True addition	3283	3329	49	55
True subtraction (*far*)	2654	2668	35	35
True subtraction (*close*)	994	1002	53	48

Table 3. Performance measurements of verification of FP adders. FP adder I is Huff's FP adder with the bugs fixed. FP adder II is FP adder I with the *compare* unit in Figure 1.b. For true subtraction, *far* represents the cases $|E_x - E_y| > 1$, and *close* represents the cases $|E_x - E_y| \leq 1$.

In our experience, the choice of decomposition type of the subtrahend's variables for true subtraction cases is very important to the verification time. The best decomposition type of the subtrahend's variables is *negative* Davio decomposition. If the subtrahend's variables use the *positive* Davio decomposition, the *PHDDs for OUT can not be built after a long CPU time (> 4 hours).

7 Conversion Circuits

The overflow flag erratum of the FIST instruction (FP to integer conversion) [12] in Intel's Pentium Pro and Pentium II processors has illustrated the importance of verification of conversion circuits [14] which convert the data from one format to another. These circuits perform conversions between any of the three number formats: integer, IEEE single precision, and IEEE double precision.

We believe that the verification of conversion circuits is much easier than the verification of FP adders, since these circuits are much simpler than FP adders and only have one operand (i.e. less input variables). For example, the specification of the double-to-single operation, which converts data from double precision to single precision, can be written as *"(overflow_flag = expected_overflow) & (not overflow_flag ⇒ (output = expected_output))"*, where *overflow_flag* and *output* are directly from the circuit, and *expected_overflow* and *expected_output* are computed in terms of the inputs. *Expected_output* is computed by $Round((-1)^S \times M \times 2^{E-B})$. Similarly, *expected_overflow* can be computed from the inputs. This specification covers double precision values which cannot be represented in single precision. For another example, the specification of the single-to-double operation can be written as *"output = input"*, since every number represented in single precision can be represented in double precision without rounding (i.e. the output represents the exact value of input).

8 Conclusions and Future Work

We presented a black box version of verification of FP adders with reusable specifications using extended word-level SMV, which was improved by using the Multiplicative Power HDDs (*PHDDs), and by incorporating conditional symbolic simulation as well as a short-circuiting technique. Based on case analysis, the specifications of FP adders are divided into several hundred implementation-independent sub-specifications. Conditional symbolic simulation and a short-circuiting technique make these specifications reusable in any implementation. We used our system and reusable specifications to verify a FP adder from the University of Michigan. Our system found several bugs in Huff's FP adder. Each specification was checked in less than 3 minutes or 5 minutes including counterexample generation. A variant of the corrected FP adder was created and verified to demonstrate the ability of our system to handle different implementations. For each FP adder, verification finished in 2 CPU hours on a Sun UltraSPARC-II server. We believe that our system and specifications can be applied to directly verify FP adders and to help find errors.

The overflow flag erratum of the FIST instruction [12] in Intel's Pentium Pro and Pentium II processors has illustrated the importance of verification of conversion circuits which convert data from one format to another. Since these circuits are much simpler than FP adders and have only one operand, we believe that our system can verify the correctness of these circuits. We plan to verify the conversion circuits in the Aurora III chip.

Acknowledgements

We thank Prof. Brown, Dr. Huff and Mr. Riepe at University of Michigan for providing us with Huff's FP adder and valuable discussions. We thank Dr. John Zhong at SGI for helping us to synthesize the FP adder into flattened, gate-level Verilog. We also thank Bwolen Yang and Henry A. Rowley for proofreading this paper.

References

1. BROCK, B., KAUFMANN, M., AND MOORE, J. S. ACL2 theorems about commerical microprocessors. In *Proceedings of the Formal Methods on Computer-Aided Design* (November 1996), pp. 275–293.
2. BRYANT, R. E. Graph-based algorithms for boolean function manipulation. In *IEEE Transactions on Computers* (August 1986), pp. 8:677–691.
3. BRYANT, R. E., AND CHEN, Y.-A. Verification of arithmetic circuits with binary moment diagrams. In *Proceedings of the 32nd ACM/IEEE Design Automation Conference* (June 1995), pp. 535–541.
4. CARREÑO, V. A., AND MINER, P. S. Specification of the IEEE-854 floating-point standard in HOL and PVS. In *High Order Logic Theorem Proving and Its Applications* (September 1995).
5. CHEN, Y.-A., AND BRYANT, R. E. *PHDD: An efficient graph representation for floating point circuit verification. In *Proceedings of the International Conference on Computer-Aided Design* (November 1997), pp. 2–7.
6. CHEN, Y.-A., AND BRYANT, R. E. Verification of floating-point adders. Tech. Rep. CMU-CS-98-121, School of Computer Science, Carnegie Mellon University, 1998.
7. CHEN, Y.-A., CLARKE, E. M., HO, P.-H., HOSKOTE, Y., KAM, T., KHAIRA, M., O'LEARY, J., AND ZHAO, X. Verification of all circuits in a floating-point unit using word-level model checking. In *Proceedings of the Formal Methods on Computer-Aided Design* (November 1996), pp. 19–33.
8. CLARKE, E. M., FUJITA, M., AND ZHAO, X. Hybrid decision diagrams overcoming the limitations of MTBDDs and BMDs. In *Proceedings of the International Conference on Computer-Aided Design* (November 1995), pp. 159–163.
9. CLARKE, E. M., KHAIRA, M., AND ZHAO, X. Word level model checking – Avoiding the Pentium FDIV error. In *Proceedings of the 33rd ACM/IEEE Design Automation Conference* (June 1996), pp. 645–648.
10. COE, T. Inside the Pentium Fdiv bug. *Dr. Dobbs Journal* (April 1996), pp. 129–135.
11. COUDERT, O., AND MADRE, J. C. A unified framework for the formal verification of sequential circuits. In *Proceedings of the International Conference on Computer-Aided Design* (November 1990), pp. 126–129.
12. FISHER, L. M. Flaw reported in new intel chip. *New York Times* (May 6 1997), D, 4:3.
13. HAMAGUCHI, K., MORITA, A., AND YAJIMA, S. Efficient construction of binary moment diagrams for verifying arithmetic circuits. In *Proceedings of the International Conference on Computer-Aided Design* (November 1995), pp. 78–82.
14. HUFF, T. R. Architectural and circuit issues for a high clock rate floating-point processor. *PhD Dissertation in Electrical Engineering Department, University of Michigan* (1995).
15. JAIN, P., AND GOPALAKRISHNAN, G. Efficient symbolic simulation-based verification using the parametric form of boolean expressions. In *IEEE Transactions on Computer-Aided Design of Integrated Circuits and Systems* (August 1994), pp. 1005–1015.
16. MCMILLAN, K. L. *Symbolic Model Checking.* Kluwer Academic Publishers, 1993.
17. QUACH, N., AND FLYNN, M. Design and implementation of the SNAP floating-point adder. Tech. Rep. CSL-TR-91-501, Stanford University, December 1991.

XEVE, an ESTEREL Verification Environment

Amar Bouali

INRIA, B.P. 93, F-06902 Sophia-Antipolis cedex
amar@sophia.inria.fr

Abstract. We describe the verification methods and tools we are currently developing around the language ESTEREL. This language is dedicated for the development of synchronous reactive systems such as hardware or software controllers for which the control handling aspects are predominant. The language has a strong mathematical semantics in terms of Finite State Machines. Automatic verification is then possible on this model in which we represent exhaustively all the possible behaviors of a system. Our methods are based on model minimization coupled with unrelevant behaviors masking and model checking techniques to verify correctness properties like safety and liveness ones by means of synchronous observers

1 Introduction

ESTEREL [1] belongs to the family of synchronous languages, dedicated for the development of reactive systems. ESTEREL syntax is based on a set of primitives to express sequencing, parallelism, instantaneous broadcast, exceptions and watchdogs. It is defined by a mathematical semantics that relies on the *perfect synchrony hypothesis* that assumes a program reacts to its environment fast enough to be considered as instantaneous. The language compiles into two main formalisms according to its mathematical semantics: *explicit* Finite State Machines (FSMs) or *implicit* FSMs as a set of boolean equations with latches. In the first case, the compiler generates the FSM in some internal format, then translated in FC2[1]. In the second case, the compilers generates the equations in BLIF[2]. The FSM model allows automatic analysis and exhaustive verification of the control part of ESTEREL programs. This activity, called model-checking, is becoming ever more popular in the hardware community, [5, 6]. We shall describe in this paper our own approaches to the problem, some partially borrowed from similar work on our part in asynchronous process algebras, [2], some original and dedicated to the synchronous model. Roughly, they shall be split amongst: (compositional) *reduction* techniques, and (side) *observer* monitoring.

2 The ESTEREL Language

ESTEREL programming style allows to describe a systems as a set of parallel interacting modules, which in turn may be composed of interacting submodules.

---

[1] This is a textual format for graph-like object used to interface our verification tools
[2] *Berkeley Logical Interchange Format* for boolean sequential circuits

A module has an input/output interface which is declared on top of it. The example below is a small program for a synchronous bus arbiter, a simplified version described in [8]: users (Cell modules) try to access a bus concurrently by setting a request (RequestIn signals) and obtain the access when the arbiter emits a corresponding acknowledge (AckOut signals).

```
% The Init module
module Init
output Token;

emit Token;
end.

% The cell module
module Cell:
input Req, GrantIn, TokenIn;
output GrantOut, TokenOut, Ack;

every immediate [GrantIn or TokenIn] do
   present Req then emit Ack
   else emit GrantOut end
end
||
every immediate TokenIn do
   pause; emit TokenOut
end.
```

```
% The main module
module Arbiter4:
input Req1, Req2, Req3;
output Ack1, Ack2, Ack3;

signal G1, G2, G3, G4, T1, T2, T3, T4 in
   run Init [signal T1/Token]
|| run Cell [signal Req1/Req, Ack1/Ack,
                    G1/GrantIn, G2/GrantOut,
                    T1/TokenIn, T2/TokenOut]
|| run Cell [signal Req2/Req, Ack2/Ack,
                    G2/GrantIn, G3/GrantOut,
                    T2/TokenIn, T3/TokenOut]
|| run Cell [signal Req3/Req, Ack3/Ack,
                    G3/GrantIn, G4/GrantOut,
                    T3/TokenIn, T4/TokenOut]
|| run Cell [signal Req4/Req, Ack4/Ack,
                    G4/GrantIn, G1/GrantOut,
                    T4/TokenIn, T1/TokenOut]
end.
```

The protocol consists in putting the desired number of cells (4 in the example) in parallel, connecting them to form a ring. The run instruction calls an instance of a sub-module: the signal declaration that follows is a renaming instruction, that renames the sub-modules proper signals into signals of the environment they are put in. More details on the ESTEREL programming can be found at http://www.inria.fr/meije/esterel/.

3   The Verification Methods

Verification is based on the FSM model. Due to the state space explosion problem (the FSM size may be exponential with respect to the size of the program sources), our approach consists first is reducing as much as possible the state and transition spaces while keeping the structure and the behaviors of the system. This is achieved by using compositional methods. When this method fails, the compiler can still produce the circuit representation. In this case, we use symbolic representation to represent the state and transition spaces using BDDs.

Verification consists in analyzing the system behaviors to detect deadlock or livelocks, and perform model checking of properties we express through *synchronous observers*. We now describe each in turn:

FSM Minimization: Reduction consists in quotienting the model by state equivalence (bisimulation [9]), after a prior abstraction of signals due to the property checked (unconcerned signals are simply hidden, which can introduce non-determinism). Still, FSMs either deterministic or not, can be minimized canonically using bisimulation. In practice, the original algorithm for coarsest (state) partitioning [7,4] has to be refined, due to the particular symbolic representation of input events mentioned above. Now *sets* of outgoing transitions have to be matched against *sets* of similar transitions for states to remain equivalent. Strong bisimulation remains a congruence for synchronous product, so that compositional reduction can be performed. The FC2SYMBMIN tool takes a FC2 explicit description of the FSM, minimizes it, and generates the minimal FSM in a new FC2 file. BLIFFC2 works on BLIF files where an FSM is described implicitly as a set of boolean equations with latches. It exploits the TIGER system library[3] to manipulate symbolically the FSM. It first computes the reachable state space (RSS) of the FSM, minimizes the FSM states and transitions symbolically using BDDs. The minimized FSM is generated explicitly in a FC2 file.

Compositional Minimization: Roughly, compositional minimization consists in reducing sub-modules first separately before composing them in parallel. In a hierarchical description, a node module is obtain by composing smaller sub-modules. FC2SYMBMIN can perform the synchronous product of two sub-modules given as reactive automata in the same way the ESTEREL compiler makes it when we put them in parallel. This method is a way to tackle the state space explosion avoiding the evaluation of the full global FSM. It reduces drastically the size of the FSM to store when combined with signal hiding.

Termination Status and Liveness: An important information when dealing with continuously interacting systems is to know if the system is able to stop reaching a deadlock, or to behave silently infinitely (while it change states inside a loop, no visible output can be emitted). This check can be done *modulo* a subset of input signals set to off and output signals not considered as visible. We use this feature to verify some liveness properties expressed in a *always eventually* style. Indeed, we verify it by checking that there's no silent loops before the behavior expressed in the eventually part, if we mask all the signals not concerned with the property. Diagnostic paths are extracted in case.

Verification by Observers: Observers are simply new reactive components set in parallel with the main program, and monitoring some of its outputs while feeding it inputs at times to exercise it towards desired configurations. Then observers usually testify of their results by specific new signals *Success* or *Failure*. We try to use observers to check *safety* properties, but also a growing number of *liveness* properties, and also to develop a range of properties inherent to synchronous languages (and in particular ESTEREL) that are of constant use (as *deadlocks* and *livelocks* in usual asynchronous systems). Treatment of fairness is also an exciting issue in such context (although we shall not deal with it here), especially if one consider that programs are now issued from a "real" language, and not an ad-hoc formalism kept close to the verification model. The CHECKBLIF tool takes a BLIF description of an observed program as input and a set of observer output to check for emission. For each output that can be emitted, one (of the shortest) example path leading to a state from which the

---

[3] Developed at DEC by O.Coudert, J-C.Madre and H.Touati, it offers data structures for BDDs and FSM manipulations, starting from circuits described in BLIF

output is emitted is extracted and saved in an ascii format called `csimul`. This kind of files are loadable in the ESTEREL graphical simulator called XES.

4 The Toolset

We described the list of software modules we have developed for the analysis and the verification of ESTEREL programs:

XEVE [3] is a graphical panel allowing file selection and application of verification methods, as well as signal (de)selections when they play a parameter role. Programs are supposed to come in BLIF syntax for boolean equation form, and FC2 syntax for explicit FSMs.

CHECKBLIF verifies simple properties from specific signals in a product machine, following the observer paradigm;

BLIFFC2 performs reduction of implicit FSM relative to bisimulation, and provide an explicit (small) FSM as result;

FC2SYMBMIN performs reduction of explicit FSM relative to bisimulation, and allows parallel composition of such FSMs so that it is compatible with the observer approach, allowing compositional verification;

ATG is a graphical display system used in our context to visualize Mealy machines, usually after reduction.

XES is the ESTEREL graphical simulator used in our setting to play counter-example sequences generated from verification failures.

XEVE is available by anonymous ftp and is largely diffused. It is also used in an industrial context, particularly at Dassault Aviation where ESTEREL has been chosen to implement critical pieces of embedded softwares.

Figure 1 shows the software architecture of the XEVE environment. Figure 2 shows its main graphical panel and some of result windows.

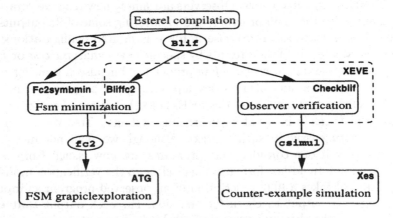

Fig. 1. Xeve internal and external tool modules

504

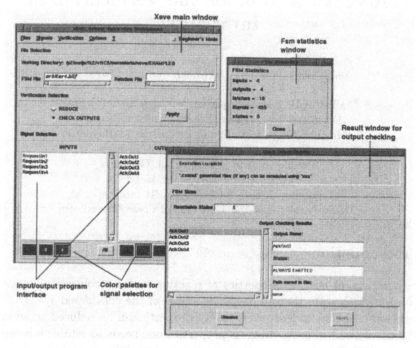

Fig. 2. Xeve graphical interface

References

1. G. Berry, and G. Gonthier The Esterel Synchronous Programming Language: Design, Semantics, Implementation *Science Of Computer Programming*, 19(2):87–152, 1992.
2. A. Bouali, A. Ressouche, V. Roy, and R. de Simone. The FC2Tools set. In *Proceedings of CAV'96* vol. 1102 of *LNCS*, 1996.
3. A. Bouali. XEVE: an ESTEREL Verification Environment (Version v1_3). Technical Report 214, INRIA, December 1997. http://ftp-sop.inria.fr/pub/rapports/RT-214.ps.
4. A. Bouali and R. de Simone. Symbolic bisimulation minimisation. In *Fourth Workshop on Computer-Aided Verification*, volume 663 of *LNCS*, pages 96–108, Montreal, 1992. Springer-Verlag.
5. J.R. Burch, E.M. Clarke, K.L. McMillan, D.L. Dill, and L.J. Hwang. Symbolic model checking 10^{20} states and beyond. *Information and Computation*, 98(2):142–170, June 1992.
6. O. Coudert, C. Berthet, and J.C. Madre. Verification of synchronous sequential machines based on symbolic execution. In *Automatic Verification Methods For Finite State Systems*, Grenoble, France, 1989. LNCS 407, Springer-Verlag.
7. P.C. Kanellakis and S.A. Smolka. CCS expressions, finite state processes, and three problems of equivalence. *Information and Computation*, 86:43–68, 1990.
8. Mc Millan. *Symbolic Model Checking.* Kluwer Academic Publishers, 1993.
9. D.M.R. Park. Concurrency and automata on infinite sequences. In P. Deussen, editor, 5th *GI Conference*, vol. 104 of *LNCS*, 1981.

InVeSt : A Tool for the Verification of Invariants[*]

S. Bensalem[1], Y. Lakhnech[2] and S. Owre[3]

[1] VERIMAG, Centre Equation – 2, avenue de Vignate,
F-38610 Giéres, France. Email: Bensalem@imag.fr
[2] Institut für Informatik und Praktische Mathematik,
Christian-Albrechts-Universität zu Kiel,
Preußerstr. 1-9, D-24105 Kiel, Germany.
Email: yl@informatik.uni-kiel.de
[3] Computer Science Laboratory, SRI International,
Menlo Park, CA 94025, USA. Email : owre@csl.sri.com

1 Introduction

A very important class of properties of reactive systems consists of *invariance* properties which state that all reachable states of the considered system satisfy some given property. Indeed, every safety property can be reduced to an invariance property and to prove progress properties one needs to establish invariance properties [15]. Proving invariance properties is especially crucial for infinite and large finite state systems which escape algorithmic methods. In this paper we present the tool InVeSt which supports the verification of invariance properties of infinite state systems. InVeSt integrates deductive and algorithmic verification principles for the verification of invariance properties as well as abstraction techniques.

2 Methodology

There are basically two approaches to the verification of reactive systems, the *algorithmic* approach on one hand and the *deductive* approach on the other hand. The algorithmic approach is based on the computation of fix-points, on effective representations of sets of states, and on decision procedures to solve the inclusion problem of sets of states. For example the *backward procedure* is an instance of this approach. To prove that a set of states P is an invariant of a system S, the backward procedure computes the largest set Q of states satisfying $Q \subseteq P$ and $Q \subseteq \text{WP}(\tau, Q)$, for every transition $\tau \in T$ of S. Here $\text{WP}(\tau, Q)$ is the weakest pre-condition of τ with respect to Q. Then, P is an invariant of S if and only if every initial state of S satisfies Q. In general, the algorithmic approach is based on an effective representation $\mathcal{R}$ for sets of states, effective boolean operations, a procedure for deciding inclusion in $\mathcal{R}$, effective predicate

[*] This work has been partly performed while the first two authors were visiting the Computer Science Laboratory, SRI International. Their visits were funded by NSF Grants No. CCR-9712383 and CCR-9509931.

transformers to guarantee recursiveness of the method, and convergence of fix-points to guarantee completeness.

In general, in case of infinite state systems, first-order logic with Peano arithmetic is considered as representation $\mathcal{R}$. In fact, it can be proved that any weaker logic is not expressive enough (e.g. [8]), when the considered system contains variables that range over infinite domains. Thus, one has effective boolean operations and can define predicate transformers, but inclusion is undecidable. Moreover, convergence of fix-points is not guaranteed. Consequently, the algorithmic approach cannot be applied in general to infinite state systems. On the other hand, the deductive approach is very powerful and gives a complete method even for infinite state systems. It relies upon finding *auxiliary invariants* and proving validity of first-order formulas, called *verification conditions*. The deductive approach is, however, in contrast to the algorithmic approach, difficult to apply. Indeed, it is in general a hard task to find suitable auxiliary invariants and time consuming to discharge all generated verification conditions. Therefore, there is a strong need for tools that support both tasks. InVeSt is such a tool as it supports the verification of invariance properties of infinite state systems.

The salient feature of InVeSt is that it combines the algorithmic with the deductive approaches to program verification in two different ways:

1) It integrates the principles underlying the algorithmic (e.g. [4, 20]) and the deductive methods (e.g. [16]) in the sense that it uses fix-point calculation as in the algorithmic approach but also the reduction of the invariance problem to a set of first-order formulas as in the deductive approach.
2) It integrates the theorem prover PVS [19] with the model-checker SMV [17] through the automatic computation of finite abstractions. That is, it provides the ability to automatically compute finite abstractions of infinite state systems which are then analyzed by SMV or, alternatively, by the model-checker of PVS.

InVeSt supports the proof of invariance properties using the method based on induction and auxiliary invariants (e.g. [16]) as well as the method based on abstraction techniques [5, 13, 7, 11, 12, 6].

InVeSt's approach to finding auxiliary invariants. We use calculation of pre-fix-points by applying the body of the backward procedure a finite number of times and use techniques for the automatic generation of invariants (cf. [16, 14, 1]) to support the search for auxiliary invariants. The tool provides strategies which allow to derive *local invariants*, that is, predicates attached to control locations and which are satisfied whenever the computation reaches the corresponding control point. InVeSt includes strategies for deriving local invariants for sequential systems as well as a composition principle that allows to combine invariants generated for sequential systems to obtain invariants of a composed system.

InVeSt's approach to computing abstractions. InVeSt provides also a module that allows to compute an abstract system from a given concrete system and an abstraction function. The method underlying this module is presented in [2]. The main features of this method is that it is automatic and compositional. Moreover, it generates an abstract system which has the same structure as the concrete one. This gives the ability to apply further abstractions and techniques to reduce the state explosion problem and facilitates the debugging of the concrete system. The computed abstract system is optionally represented in the specification language of PVS or in that of SMV. A graphical interface allows to interact with InVeSt and SMV in a uniform way.

Finally, it is important to understand that our use of the theorem-prover PVS is limited to discharging the verification conditions. This shows a difference of our approach to the approach followed in most of the work using theorem-proving for verifying invariance properties (e.g. [9, 10]). That is we do not encode the invariance problem in the specification language of the considered theorem-prover and then use the theorem-prover to solve it, but we use the deductive approach to reduce the problem to a set of first-order formulas whose validity is proved using the theorem-prover. Moreover, the construction of the verification conditions as well as the generation of an auxiliary invariant are performed outside the theorem-prover.

3 Design Principles

The structure of InVeSt is motivated by a number of design decisions. These decisions are :

- **Minimization of user's intervention.** This decision is motivated by our belief that the success of the algorithmic approach is partly due to the fact that it does not require user's intervention. To support this choice we have
  - developed techniques for the generation of auxiliary invariants,
  - implemented the strengthening method and its refined version,
  - investigated strategies for proving first-order predicates, and
  - developed a method for computing abstractions of infinite state systems.
- **Use of an existing theorem-prover.** We build on an existing theorem-prover for the following reasons. The first is that we want to rely on a widely used tool; this increases our trust and confidence in the prover. Our particular choice is to use PVS, since PVS gives us the possibility to combine decision procedures and interactive proofs (see [18]). The examples we have considered show that this feature is a prerequisite to reach a high level of automation.
- **Theorem-prover as a "Decision Procedure".** Most of the theorem-provers, including PVS, are general purpose provers. This means that they have general specification languages and if they include pre-defined strategies, then these are in general not tuned to a particular application. This is often a source of inefficiency and prevents a higher level of automation. There is always a trade off between generality on one side and efficiency and automation on the other side. We use the theorem-prover in a particular way and for a particular task, namely to discharge the verification conditions. This should be seen in contrast to the alternative approach where one

encodes the verification problem within the specification language of PVS and tries to solve it completely within this theorem-prover, usually by expanding the definitions of the semantics of the programs and the definition of invariance and using an induction argument. Our approach is different, since we use deductive rules to reduce the invariance problem to a set of first-order formulas whose validity is proved using PVS. This design decision allows us to implement the components of our tool outside PVS.

- **Modularity with respect to the theorem-prover.** Our tool builds on PVS in two different ways. The first obvious point is that it uses PVS to discharge verification conditions as explained above. There is another, less transparent dependency, which lies in the fact that we use the internal representations of PVS of all objects constructed by the PVS type-checker including programs, actions, formulas, expressions, etc.. In order to be modular with respect to PVS, the interface between the components of the tool and PVS itself has to be defined precisely. As interface, we use a module which contains functions that allow to access internal PVS variables. This ensures that even when the data structure used in PVS is modified, the functioning of our tool is still guaranteed as long as the accessor functions maintain their semantics.

4 Tool structure

The main components of InVeSt are: a front-end that translates guarded command-like programs into a PVS-theory, a module of functions for generating invariants, a module of proof strategies, and a module for computing abstractions. In the sequel, we discuss each of these components.

- **Front-end:** As formalism for describing systems we consider a language similar to Unity. Variables are allowed to be of any type of the specification language of PVS. The role of the front-end consists of translating the extended transition system into a PVS-theory that can be type-checked. The components of the system are translated into PVS-constants of type "Program" consisting of a list of actions. An action can be a function or a relation between states. When the PVS-theory corresponding to the system is type-checked a list of LISP-objects corresponding to the declarations in the PVS-theory is constructed. By accessing to the elements of this list, we have at our disposal PVS-representations corresponding to the relevant syntactic objects of the system. Our tool works with these representations. Accessors functions have been implemented that allow to access these representations and their components. For instance, there is a function GET-GUARD that is used to extract the guard of an action, and a function GET-AFFECTED-VARIABLES to extract the list of variables to which a value is assigned by the action.
- **Generation of Invariants:** A central component in the tool is a module consisting of functions that implement strategies used to automatically generate invariants. Basically, we implemented the strategies presented in [1]

which allow us to derive *local invariants*, that is, predicates attached to control locations such that these predicates are satisfied whenever the computation reaches the corresponding control point. We have strategies for deriving local invariants for sequential systems and a composition principle that allows to combine invariants generated for sequential systems to obtain an invariant of a composed system.

- **Proof strategies:** A proof strategy determines which verification conditions are constructed and how to handle failed proofs. The choice of a strategy is determined by:

  1 whether auxiliary invariants are generated automatically,

  2 whether in case the proof of a verification condition fails, the strengthening method [16] or its refined version [3] is applied.

In case auxiliary invariants are generated, verification conditions are weakened by taking the generated predicate as assumption in the left-hand side of the implication. Thus, if φ is the generated invariant, then to prove that P is preserved by a transition τ it suffices to prove $(\varphi \wedge P) \Rightarrow \text{WP}(\tau, P)$. We implemented a function that takes as arguments two predicates φ and ψ, a transition τ, and a PVS-proof strategy *str* and which calls the PVS-prover on the formula $(\varphi \wedge P) \Rightarrow \text{WP}(\tau, \psi)$ with the strategy *str*.

- **Computing Abstractions:** The abstraction module implements the method presented in [2] for computing abstractions of infinite state systems. For a given concrete system and a given abstraction function, it computes an abstraction of the concrete system compositionally and automatically. The process of generation of the abstract system does not depend on the assumed semantics of the parallel operator; it works for the synchronous as well as for the asynchronous computation model. The generated abstract system has the same structure as the concrete one and there is a clear correspondence between the transitions of both systems. This does not only allow to apply further abstractions and techniques to mitigate the state explosion problem but also facilitates the debugging of the concrete system.

References

1. S. Bensalem and Y. Lakhnech. Automatic generation of invariants. Accepted in Formal Methods in System Design. To appear.
2. S. Bensalem, Y. Lakhnech, and S. Owre. Computing abstractions of infinite state systems automatically and compositionally. Accepted in CAV'98, 1998.
3. S. Bensalem, Y. Lakhnech, and H. Saidi. Powerful techniques for the automatic generation of invariants. In *CAV'96*, volume 1102 of *LNCS*. Springer-Verlag, 1996.
4. E.M. Clarke, E.A. Emerson, and E. Sistla. Automatic verification of finite state concurrent systems using temporal logic specifications: A practical approach. In *10th ACM symp. of Prog. Lang.* ACM Press, 1983.
5. E.M. Clarke, O. Grumberg, and D.E. Long. Model checking and abstraction. *ACM Transactions on Programming Languages and Systems*, 16(5), 1994.
6. D. Dams. *Abstract interpretation and partition refinement for model checking.* PhD thesis, Technical University of Eindhoven, 1996.

7. D. Dams, R. Gerth, and O. Grumberg. Abstract interpretation of reactive systems: Abstractions preserving ACTL*, ECTL* and CTL*. In *PROCOMET*. IFIP Transactions, North-Holland/Elsevier, 1994.

8. J.W. de Bakker. *Mathematical Theory of Program Cortrectness*. Prentice-Hall, NJ., 1980.

9. K. Havelund and N. Shankar. Experiments in theorem proving and model checking for protocol verification. In *FME'96*, volume 1051 of *LNCS*. Springer-verlag, 1996.

10. J. Hooman. Verifying part of the access.bus protocol using PVS. In *Proc. 15th Conference on the Foundations of Software Technology and Theoretical Computer Science*, volume 1026 of *LNCS*. Springer-Verlag,, 1995.

11. R.P. Kurshan. *Computer-Aided Verification of Coordinating Processes, the automata theoretic approach*. Princeton Series in Computer Science. 1994.

12. C. Loiseaux, S. Graf, J. Sifakis, A. Bouajjani, and S. Bensalem. Property preserving abstractions for the verification of concurrent systems. *Formal Methods in System Design*, 6(1), 1995.

13. D. E. Long. *Model Checking, Abstraction, and Compositional Reasoning*. PhD thesis, Carnegie Mellon, 1993.

14. Z. Manna, A. Anuchitanukul, N. Bjøner, A. Browne, E. Chang, M. Colon, L. de Alfaro, H. Devarajan, H. Sipma, and T. Uribe. STeP : The Stanford Temporal Prover. Technical report, Stanford Univ., Stanford, CA, 1994.

15. Z. Manna and A. Pnueli. Completing the temporal picture. *Theoretical Computer Science*, 83(1):97–130, 1991.

16. Z. Manna and A. Pnueli. *Temporal Verification of Reactive Systems: Safety*. Springer-Verlag, 1995.

17. K.L. McMillan. *Symbolic model checking*. Kluwer Academic Publishers, Boston, 1993.

18. S. Owre, S. Rajan, J.M. Rushby, N. Shankar, and M. Srivas. PVS: Combining specification, proof checking, and model checking. volume 1102 of *LNCS*, pages 411–414. Springer-Verlag, 1996.

19. S. Owre, J. Rushby, N. Shankar, and F. von Henke. Formal verification for fault-tolerant architectures: Prolegomena to the design of PVS. *IEEE Transactions on Software Engineering*, 21(2):107–125, Feb. 1995.

20. J. P. Queille and J. Sifakis. Specification and verification of concurrent systems in CESAR. In *Proc. 5th Int. Sym. on Programming*, volume 137 of *Lecture Notes in Computer Science*, pages 337–351. Springer-Verlag, 1982.

Verifying Mobile Processes in the HAL Environment[*]

G. Ferrari[1], S. Gnesi[2], U. Montanari[1], M. Pistore[1], and G. Ristori[1,2]

[1] Dipartimento di Informatica, Università di Pisa
[2] Istituto di Elaborazione dell'Informazione - C.N.R., Pisa

> *Gioia Ristori has recently left this for a better world. She will however remain with us for ever.*

1 Introduction

The *HD Automata Laboratory* (HAL) is an integrated tool set for the specification, verification and analysis of concurrent and distributed systems. A basic notion for the HAL environment is that of *history-dependent automata* (HD-automata) [11]. As ordinary automata, they are composed of states and of transitions between states. However, states and transitions of HD-automata are enriched with sets of local names. In particular, each transition can refer to the names associated to its source state but can also introduce new names, which can then appear in the destination state. Hence, names are not global and static entity but they are explicitly represented within states and transitions and can be dynamically created. HD-automata have shown to be appropriate to model systems whose behaviours are *history dependent*, i.e., systems where the observable behaviour of a step of a computation may depend on what has been done in the past steps of the same computation. An interesting example of history dependent behaviours is provided by mobile processes as specified in the π-calculus [6]. Its primitives are simple but expressive: channel names can be created, communicated (thus giving the possibility of dynamically reconfigurating process acquaintances) and they are subjected to sophisticated scoping rules. In the π-calculus history dependency manifests itself as the ability of referring names created at run-time by previous communications. In [7] a procedure is described which allows *finitary* π-calculus agents to be represented by finite-state HD-automata. Similar mappings have been defined for CCS with causality and for CCS with localities [10]. Moreover, finite HD-automata have been also obtained for history-preserving semantics of Petri nets [8, 9].

The HAL environment includes modules which implement decision procedures to calculate behavioural equivalences, and modules which support verification of behavioural properties expressed as formulae of suitable temporal logics. In

[*] Work partially founded by CNR Integrated Project *Metodi e Strumenti per la Progettazione e la Verifica di Sistemi Eterogenei Connessi mediante Reti di Comunicazione*, CNR Integrated Project *Modelli e Metodi per la Matematica e l'Ingegneria* and Esprit Working Group *CONFER2*.

this note we provide an overview of the current implementation of the HAL environment. The environment has been successfully applied in the specification and verification of mobile processes defined as π-calculus agents. Two major case studies of mobile agents (the handover protocol for mobile telephones, and a web browser specification) were carried out within the HAL environment. A fuller account of the case studies may be found in [4, 5].

2 System Overview

Figure 1 presents an overview of the HAL environment. The dashed boxes indicate work-in-progress, i.e., modules which are under development. The HAL environment allows π-calculus agents to be translated into ordinary automata, so that existing equivalence checkers can be used to calculate whether the π-calculus agents are bisimilar. The environment also supports verification of logical formulae expressing desired properties of the behaviour of π-calculus agents. To this purpose, we found convenient to exploit a logic with modalities indexed by π-calculus actions, and to implement a translation of this π-logic into a logic for ordinary automata. Hence, existing model checkers can be used to verify whether or not a formula holds for a given π-calculus agent.

In the current implementation the HAL environment consists essentially of five modules: three modules perform the translations from π-calculus agents to HD-automata, from HD-automata to ordinary automata, and from π-logic formulae to ordinary ACTL formulae. The fourth module provides routines that manipulate the HD-automata. The fifth module is basically the JACK system [1] which works at the level of ordinary automata and performs the standard operations on them like behavioural verification and model checking. The idea behind the JACK environment is to combine different specification and verification tools, independently developed, around a common format for representing ordinary automata: the FC2 file format [2]. FC2 makes it possible to exchange automata between JACK tools. Indeed, the fifth module in HALis simply a filter that calls the already existing functionalities of JACK. Hence, the JACK bisimulation checker MAUTO is used to verify (strong and weak) bisimilarity of π-calculus agents. Automata minimization, according to weak bisimulation is also possible, by using the functionalities offered in JACK by the HOGGAR tool. Moreover, the ACTL model checker AMC is used for verifying properties of mobile processes, after that the π-logic formulae expressing the properties have been translated into ACTL formulae.

The HAL environment supports a textual user interface to invoke the commands in the modules of the system. For instance the command *"hdaut :=* buildHD *agent"* is used to to generate the HD-automaton *hdaut* associated to the π-calculus agent *agent*. The command *"aut :=* buildFC2 *hdaut"* generates the ordinary automaton *aut* from *hdaut*. Appropriate diagnostic information is returned to the user. We are currently working on a graphical user interface.

513

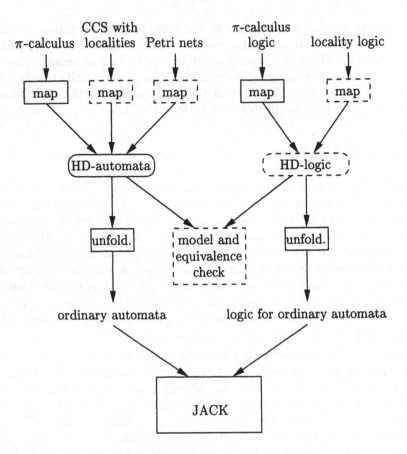

Fig. 1. The HAL environment: an overview.

The HAL environment is written in C++ and compiles with the GNU C++ compiler. It is currently running on SUN stations (under SUN-OS) and on PC stations (under Linux).

3 A Case Study: The Handover Protocol

As a case study we consider the specification of the core of the handover protocol for the GSM Public Land Mobile Network proposed by the European Telecommunication Standards Institute. The specification is borrowed from [12]; it consists of four modules:

- a *Mobile Station*, mounted in a car that moves through two different geographical areas (cells); it provides services to an end user;
- a *Mobile Switching Centre*, that is the controller of the radio communications within the whole area composed by the two cells;
- two *Base Station* modules, one for each cell, that are the interfaces between the Mobile Station and the Mobile Switching Centre.

Table 1. Performance issue

command	states	transitions	time
hdaut := buildHD *handover.pi*	11015	21774	4473 sec.
aut := buildFC2 *hdaut*	32263	62990	442 sec.
min-aut := minimize *aut*	49	91	10 sec.
verify *no-loss-of-messages* on *min-aut*	—	—	6 sec.

The observable actions performed by the Mobile Switching Centre are the input of the messages transmitted from the external environment through an *input* channel. The observable actions performed by the Mobile Station are the transmissions, via an *output* channel, of the messages to the end user. The communications between the Mobile Switching Centre and the Mobile Station happen via the base corresponding to the cell in which the car is located. When the car moves from one cell to the other, the Mobile Switching Centre starts a procedure to communicate to the Mobile Station the names of the new transmission channels, related to the base corresponding to the new cell. The communication of the new channel names to the Mobile Station is done via the base that is in use at the moment. All the communications of messages between the Mobile Switching Centre and the Mobile Station are suspended until the Mobile Station receives the names of the new transmission channels. Then the base corresponding to the new cell is activated, and the communications between the Mobile Switching Centre and the Mobile Station continue through the new base.

There are two kinds of correctness verification that can be done in the environment. One is the checking that the specification of the system is bisimilar to a more abstract service specification in which the system is simply seen as a particular buffer from the input channel to the output channel. The other one is the checking of properties expressed as π-logic formulae, that the specification must satisfy to meet the desired behaviour: for instance, no message can be lost from the input to the output channel and the order of the messages must be preserved. Both these kinds of verification have been successfully performed in our verification environment.

In Table 1 we report the time spent in the different steps of a typical session of verification (performed on a SUN Ultra workstation) for the handover protocol, as well as the number of states and transitions of the automata that are built in the different steps.

4   Concluding Remarks and Future Works

The current implementation of the HAL environment works just on π-calculus agents and on π-logic formulae. As future developments we plan to extend the environment in several directions. The implementation of translation modules from other history dependent calculi to HD-automata is under development.

Moreover, we plan to include in HAL a verification module which implements decision procedures for behavioural equivalences and model checkers directly on HD-automata; this is convenient since ordinary automata have often dramatically more states and transitions than the corresponding HD-automata.

The *Mobility Workbench* (MBW) [13] is another existing tool for verifying properties of π-calculus agent. In the MWB the verification of bisimulation equivalence made *on the fly*, that is the state spaces of the agents are built during the construction of the bisimulation relation. The model checking functionality offered by the MWB is based on the implementation of a tableau-based proof system [3] for the *propositional μ-calculus with name-passing*. The main difference between our approach and that adopted in the MWB is that in HALthe state space of a π-calculus agent is built once and for all. Hence, it can be minimized with respect to some minimization criteria and then used for behavioural verifications and for model checking of logical properties.

References

1. A. Bouali, S. Gnesi and S. Larosa. The integration project for the JACK environment. *Bullettin of the EATCS*, 54, 1994. Detailed information about JACK are also available at http://rep1.iei.pi.cnr.it/Projects/JACK.
2. A. Bouali, A. Ressouche, V. Roy and R. de Simone. The FC2Tools set. In *Proc. CAV'96*, LNCS 1102. Springer Verlag, 1996.
3. M. Dam. Model checking mobile processes. In *Proc. CONCUR'93*, LNCS 715. Springer Verlag, 1993.
4. G. Ferrari, G. Ferro, S. Gnesi, U. Montanari, M. Pistore and G. Ristori. An automata-based verification environment for mobile processes. In *Proc. TACAS'97*, LNCS 1217. Springer Verlag, 1997.
5. S. Gnesi and G. Ristori. A model checking algorithm for π-calculus agents. In Proc. ICTL'97. Kluwer Academic Publishers, 1997.
6. R. Milner, J. Parrow and D. Walker. A calculus of mobile processes, Part I and II. *Information and Computation*, 100(1):1–77, 1992.
7. U. Montanari and M. Pistore. Checking bisimilarity for finitary π-calculus. In *Proc. CONCUR'95*, LNCS 962. Springer Verlag, 1995.
8. U. Montanari and M. Pistore. History dependent verification for partial order systems. In *Partial Order Methods in Verification*, DIMACS Series, Vol. 29. American Mathematical Society, 1997.
9. U. Montanari and M. Pistore. Minimal transition systems for history-preserving bisimulation. In *Proc. STACS'97*, LNCS 1200. Springer Verlag, 1997.
10. U. Montanari, M. Pistore and D. Yankelevich. Efficient minimization up to location equivalence. In *Proc. ESOP'96*, LNCS 1058. Springer Verlag, 1996.
11. U. Montanari and M. Pistore. History-Dependent Automata. To appear as Technical Report, Department of Computer Science, University of Pisa, 1998.
12. F. Orava and J. Parrow. An Algebraic Verification of a Mobile Network. *Formal Aspects of Computing*, 4:497–543, 1992.
13. B. Victor and F. Moller. The Mobility Workbench — A tool for the π-calculus. In *Proc. CAV'94*, LNCS 818. Springer Verlag, 1994.

MONA 1.x: New Techniques for WS1S and WS2S

Jacob Elgaard[1], Nils Klarlund[2], and Anders Møller[3]

[1] BRICS, University of Aarhus (elgaard@brics.dk)
[2] AT&T Labs–Research (klarlund@research.att.com)
[3] BRICS, University of Aarhus (amoeller@brics.dk)

Abstract. In this note, we present the first version of the MONA tool to be released in its entirety. The tool now offers decision procedures for both WS1S and WS2S and a completely rewritten front-end. Here, we present some of our techniques, which make calculations couched in WS1S run up to five times faster than with our pre-release tool based on M2L(Str). This suggests that WS1S—with its better semantic properties—is preferable to M2L(Str).

1 Introduction

It has been known for a couple of years that Monadic Second-order Logic interpreted relative to finite strings (M2L(Str)) is an attractive formal and practical vehicle for a variety of verification problems. The formalism is generally easy to use, since it provides Boolean connectives, first and second-order quantifiers and no syntactic restrictions, say, to clausal forms. However, the semantics of the formalism is the source of definitional and practical problems. For example, the concept of a first-order term doesn't even make sense for the empty string since such terms denote positions.

So, it is natural to investigate whether the related logic WS1S (Weak Second-order theory of 1 Succesor) can be used instead. This logic is stronger in that it captures a fragment of arithmetic, and its decision procedure is very similar to that of M2L(Str). Similarly, we would like to explore the practical feasibility of WS2S (Weak Second-order theory of 2 Successors).

In this note, we present some new techniques that we have incorporated into the first full release of the MONA tool. The MONA tool consists of a front-end and two back-ends, one for WS1S and one for WS2S. The front-end parses the MONA program, which consists of predicates (subroutines that are compiled separately), macros, and a main formula. Each back-end implements the automata-theoretic operations that are carried out to decide the formula corresponding to the program.

Since our earlier presentation of the MONA tool [1], we have completely rewritten the front-end, this time in C++ (the earlier version was written in ML). In the old version, the front-end produces a *code tree*, whose internal nodes each describe an automata-theoretic operation—such as a product or subset construction—and whose leaves describe automata corresponding to basic formulas. We implemented optimization techniques (unpublished) based on rewriting of formulas according to logical laws. In this note, we report on an alternative optimization technique, based on building a code DAG instead of a code tree. (A DAG is a directed, acyclic graph.) Experiments show that this technique together with a more efficient handling of predicates yields up to five-fold improvements in compilation time over the old tool.

We also briefly discuss how a M2L(Str) formula can be translated into an essentially equivalent WS1S formula, and we discuss important problems to be addressed.

2 M2L(Str) and WS1S

M2L(Str) A formula of the logic M2L(Str) is interpreted relative to a number $n \geq 0$, which is best thought of as defining the set of positions $\{0, \ldots, n-1\}$ in a string of length n. The core logic consists of first-order terms, second-order terms, and formulas. A *first-order term* t is a variable p, a constant 0 (denoting the position 0, which is the first position in w) or \$ (denoting $n-1$, which is the last position in the string), or of the form $t' \oplus 1$ (denoting $i+1 \mod n$ when t' is a first-order term denoting i). A *second-order term* is either a variable P or of the form $T' \cup T''$. A formula ϕ is either a basic formula of the form $t \in T$ or $T \subset T'$, or of the form $\psi \wedge \chi$, $\neg \psi$, $\exists p : \psi$ (first-order quantification), or $\exists P : \psi$ (second-order quantification). In addition, we allow formulas involving $=$ (between first-order or second-order terms); $<, \leq, >, \geq$ (between first-order terms); Boolean connectives $\Rightarrow, \Leftrightarrow$ and $\vee$; set operations $\cap, \backslash$, and $\complement$; $\forall$ quantifiers; etc.

The automaton-logic connection (see [5]) allows us to associate a regular language over $\mathbb{B}^k$, for some $k \geq 0$, to each formula ϕ as follows. We assume that there are k variables that are ordered and that include the free variables in ϕ. Now, a string w of length n over the alphabet $\mathbb{B}^k$ can be viewed as consisting of k *tracks* (or rows), each of length n. The kth track is a bit-pattern that defines the interpretation of the kth variable, assumed to be second-order, as the set of positions i for which the ith bit is 1. Note that a first-order variable can be regarded as a second-order variable restricted to singleton values, so the assumption just made that variables are second-order is not a serious one. The *language* associated with formula ϕ is now the set of all strings that correspond to a satisfying interpretation of the formula. As an example, the formula $P \subseteq Q$ is associated with the regular language

$$\left(\binom{0}{0} + \binom{0}{1} + \binom{1}{1} \right)^*$$

where the upper track of a string denotes the value of P and the lower track denotes the value of Q. Any language corresponding to a formula is regular, since the languages corresponding to basic formula can be represented by automata, and $\wedge$, $\neg$, and $\exists$ correspond to the automata-theoretic operations of product, complementation, and projection. In the case of a closed formula with no free variables, the regular language degenerates to a set of strings over a unit alphabet. Thus a closed formula essentially denotes a set of numbers.

The proof of regularity just hinted at forms the basis for the decision procedure: each subformula is compiled into a minimum deterministic automaton, see [5]. An automaton representation based on BDDs is at the core of the MONA implementation as discussed in [5]. For each state p in the state space S, a multi-terminal BDD whose leaves are states represents the transition function $a \mapsto \delta(p,a) : \mathbb{B}^k \to S$ out of p. Each BDD variable corresponds to a first or second-order WS1S variable, and the BBDs are shared among the states. Thus the resulting data structure is a DAG with multiple sources.

The automaton-logic connection (see [5]) allows us to associate a regular language over $\mathbb{B}^k$ to each formula ϕ that has k variables.

WS1S WS1S has the same syntax as M2L(Str) except that there is no C operator and $\oplus 1$ is replaced with $+1$. This logic is interpreted in a simpler manner: first-order terms denote natural numbers, and second-order terms denote finite sets of numbers. The automata-theoretic calculations are similar to that of M2L(Str) except for the existential quantifier (see [5]).

From M2L(Str) to WS1S In principle, it is easy to translate a quantifier free M2L(Str) formula ϕ to a formula ϕ' in WS1S with essentially the same meaning: ϕ' is gotten from ϕ by the following steps.

- A conjunct $p \leq \$$, where $\$$ now is a variable, must be added to any subformula of ϕ containing a first-order variable p.
- Each second-order variable P is left untouched, so that the translated formula will not depend on whether P has any elements greater than $\$$. However, occurrences of $\emptyset$ must be taken into account; for example, the formula $P = 0$ is translated into $\forall p \leq \$: \neg(p \in P)$ so that the translated formula does not depend on the membership status of numbers in P that are greater than $\$$. Any use of set complement operator C must also be carefully replaced.
- Any occurrence of a subformula involving $\oplus$ such as $p = q \oplus 1$ must be replaced by something that captures the modulo semantics (here: $q < \$ \Rightarrow p = q + 1 \land p = \$ \Rightarrow p = 0$).

With such a scheme it can be shown that $\mathcal{I}$ for length $n > 0$ satisfies ϕ if and only if $\mathcal{I}$, augmented by interpreting $\$$ as $n - 1$, satisfies ϕ'. Unfortunately, in order to preserve this property for all subformulas, we need to conjoin extraneous conditions onto every original subformula. A simpler solution is to conjoin them only for certain strategic places, such as for all basic formulas and all formulas that are directly under a quantifier. We have implemented such heuristics in a tool, S2N, that automatically translates M2L(Str) formulas to WS1S formulas.

3 DAGs for compilation

Code trees can be of the form (among others) mk-basic-less(i,j), mk-product (C,C',op), or mk-project(i,C), where i and j are BDD variable indices, *op* is a Boolean function of two variables, and C and C' are code trees. For example, consider the formula $\exists q : p < q \wedge q < r$. If variable p has index 1, i.e., if it is the 1st variable in the variable ordering, variable q has index 2, and variable r has index 3, then this formula is parsed into a code tree `mk-project(2,mk-product(mk-less(1,2), mk-less(2,3), ∧))`. This tree contains a situation that we would like to avoid: essentially isomorphic subtrees are calculated more than once. In fact, the automaton A for `mk-less(1,2)` is identical to the automaton A' for `mk-less(2,3)` modulo a renaming of variables. In general, we would like to rename the indices in A whenever we need A', since this is a linear operation (whereas building A or A' from the code tree is often not a linear operation).

So, we say that a code tree C is *equivalent* to C' if there is an order-preserving (i.e., increasing), renaming of variables in C' such that C' becomes C. Our goal is produce the DAG that arises naturally from the code tree by collapsing equivalent subtrees. Unfortunately, it takes linear time to calculate the equivalence class of any subtree, and so the total running time becomes quadratic. Therefore, the collapsing process is limited to subtrees for which the number of variable occurrences is less than a user definable parameter ℓ.

MONA offers both pre-compiled subroutines, called *predicates*, and typed macros. A use *name*($\mathbf{X}$) of a predicate, where $\mathbf{X}$ is a sequence of actual parameters, is translated to a special node of the form `mk-call(name, X)`. The predicate is then compiled separately given the signature of the call node. The actual parameters are bound to the resulting automaton using a standard binding mechanism: introduction of temporary variables and projection. Additional call nodes with the same signature can then reuse the separately compiled automaton. Call nodes act as leaves with respect to DAGification.

4 Experimental results

We have run a MONA formula, **reverse**, of size 50KB (an automatically generated formula from [3]) through our old MONA (using optimizations) and our new WS1S version with and without DAGification ($\ell = 200$). We also did the experiment on **reverse2**, a version of the formula where all defined predicates were replaced by macros. And, we have run a comparison on a formula representing a parameterized hardware verification problem. The results are (in seconds):

Program	Old MONA	MONA 1.1	w. DAGs	DAG Hits	DAG Misses
reverse	17	8.5	3.0	20513	2725
reverse2	51	90	45	327328	14320
hardware	6.6	5.4	4.7	3284	633

In some cases (like in **reverse2**), the old Mona tool is faster than the new one run without DAGification, since the figures reported for the old apply to the version that carries out formula simplification. The experiments support our claim that WS1S can be as an efficient formalism as M2L(Str). (The underlying BDD-package in the two tools is the same.) Moreover, our DAGs and predicate uses offer substantial benefits, up to a factor five. The hardware example runs only slightly faster, and the improvement is due to the new front-end being quicker.

5 Related and Future Work

There are at least three similar tools reported in the literature: [2] reports on an implementation of WS1S that is not based on BDDs and that therefore is likely not to be as efficient as our tool. The tool in [4] implements M2L(Str) using a different BDD representation, and the tool in [6] implements a decision procedure for WS2S (in Prolog and without BDDs).

There are still several problems and challenges not addressed in the current MONA tool: 1) the semantics of formulas with first-order terms is not appealing, for example, the MONA formula $x1 < x2 \wedge \ldots \wedge x_{n-1} < x_n$ is translated in linear time whereas its negation, $x1 \geq x_2 \vee \ldots \vee x_{n-1} \geq x_n$, is translated in exponential time; 2) there is no reuse of intermediate results from one automaton operation to the next (a general solution to this problem seems to require identification of isomorphic subgraphs, a problem that appears computationally expensive); 3) the automatic translation from M2L(Str) to WS1S by S2N sometimes makes formulas unrunnable for reasons similar to 1), namely that the restrictions a formula is translated under are wrapped into subformulas in unfortunate ways unless the restrictions are reapplied for each intermediate result; 4) the use of formula rewriting (as we did in the earlier MONA version) should be combined with our DAG techniques.

The MONA tool, currently in version 1.2, can be retrieved from http://www.brics.dk/~mona, along with further information.

References

1. M. Bichl, N. Klarlund, and T. Rauhe. Mona: decidable arithmetic in practice (short contribution). In *Formal Techniques in Real-Time and Fault-Tolerant Systems, 4th International Symposium, LNCS 1135*. Springer Verlag, 1996.
2. J. Glenn and W. Gasarch. Implementing WS1S via finite automata. In *Automata Implementation, WIA '96, Proceedings*, volume 1260 of *LNCS*, 1997.
3. J.L. Jensen, M.E. Jørgensen, N. Klarlund, and M.I. Schwartzbach. Automatic verification of pointer programs using monadic second-order logic. In *SIGPLAN '97 Conference on Programming Language Design and Implementation,*, pages 226–234. SIGPLAN, 1997.
4. P. Kelb, T. Margaria, M. Mendler, and C. Gsottberger. Mosel: a flexible toolset for Monadic Second-order Logic. In *Computer Aided Verification, CAV '97, Proceedings*, LNCS 1217, 1997.
5. N. Klarlund. Mona & Fido: the logic-automaton connection in practice. In *CSL '97 Proceedings*, 1998. To appear in LNCS.
6. F. Morawietz and T. Cornell. On the recognizability of relations over a tree definable in a monadic second order tree description language. Technical Report SFB 340, Seminar für Sprachwissenschaft Eberhard-Karls-Universität Tübingen, 1997.

MOCHA: Modularity in Model Checking*

R. Alur[1], T.A. Henzinger[2], F.Y.C. Mang[2], S. Qadeer[2], S.K. Rajamani[2], and S. Tasiran[2]

[1] Computer & Information Science Department, University of Pennsylvania, Philadelphia, PA 19104.
Computing Science Research Center, Bell Laboratories, Murray Hill, NJ 07974.
alur@cis.upenn.edu
[2] Electrical Engineering & Computer Sciences Department, University of California, Berkeley, CA 94720.
{tah,fmang,shaz,sriramr,serdar}@eecs.berkeley.edu

1 Introduction

We describe a new interactive verification environment called MOCHA for the modular verification of heterogeneous systems. MOCHA differs from many existing model checkers in three significant ways:

- For modeling, we replace unstructured state-transition graphs with the heterogeneous modeling framework of *reactive modules* [AH96]. The definition of reactive modules is inspired by formalisms such as Unity [CM88], I/O automata [Lyn96], and Esterel [BG88], and allows complex forms of interaction between components within a single transition. Reactive modules provide a semantic glue that allows the formal embedding and interaction of components with different characteristics. Some modules may be synchronous, others asynchronous, some may represent hardware, others software, some may be speed-independent, others time-critical.
- For requirement specification, we replace the system-level specification languages of linear and branching temporal logics [Pnu77,CE81] with the module-level specification language of *Alternating Temporal Logic* (ATL) [AHK97]. In ATL, both cooperative and adversarial relationships between modules can be expressed. For example, it is possible to specify that a module can attain a goal regardless of how the environment of the module behaves.
- For the verification of complex systems, MOCHA supports a range of *compositional and hierarchical verification methodologies*. For this purpose, reactive modules provide assume-guarantee rules [HQR98] and abstraction operators [AHR98]; MOCHA provides algorithms for automatic refinement checking, and will provide a proof editor that manages the decomposition of verification tasks into subtasks.

In this paper, we describe the toolkit MOCHA in which the proposed approach is being implemented. The input language of MOCHA is a machine readable variant of reactive modules. The following functionalities are currently being supported:

- Simulation, including games between the user and the simulator
- Enumerative and symbolic invariant checking and error-trace generation
- Compositional refinement checking
- ATL model checking
- Reachability analysis of real-time systems

* This research was supported in part by the ONR YIP award N00014-95-1-0520, by the NSF CAREER award CCR-9501708, by the NSF grant CCR-9504469, by the ARO MURI grant DAAH-04-96-1-0341, and by the SRC contract 97-DC-324.041.

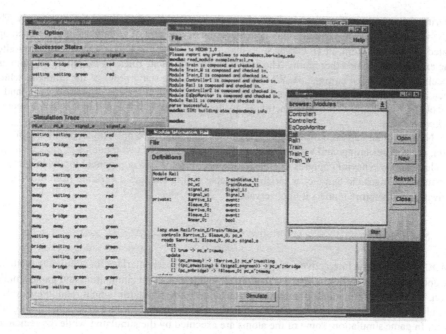

MOCHA is intended as a vehicle for the development of new verification algorithms and approaches. It adopts a software architecture similar to VIS [BHS+96], a symbolic model-checking tool from UC Berkeley. Written in C with Tcl/Tk and Tix [Exp97], MOCHA can be easily extended in two ways: designers and application developers can customize their application or design their own graphical user interface by writing Tcl scripts; algorithm developers and researchers can develop new verification algorithms by writing C code, or assembling any verification packages through C interfaces. For instance, MOCHA incorporates the VIS packages for image computation and multi-valued function manipulation, as well as various BDD packages, to provide state-of-the-art verification techniques.

2 Reactive Modules

A formal definition of reactive modules can be found in [AH96]; here we give only a brief introduction. Unlike simple state-transition graphs, reactive modules is a compositional model in which both states and transitions are structured. The state of a reactive module is determined by the values of three kinds of typed variables: the *external variables* are updated by the environment and can be read by the module; the *interface variables* are updated by the module and can be read by the environment; the *private variables* are updated by the module and cannot be read by the environment. The *observable* variables of a module are its external and interface variables.

The state of a reactive module changes in a sequence of rounds. In the first round (the initialization round), the initial values of the interface and private variables are determined. In each subsequent round (an update round), new values of the interface and private variables are determined, possibly dependent on the old values of some variables from the previous round, and possibly dependent on the new values of some variables from the current round. The external variables are initialized and updated nondeterministically.

Value dependencies between variables within an update round are resolved statically. In each update round, some interface and private variables are updated simultaneously, and some sequentially. Variables that are updated simultaneously are grouped together and controlled by an *atom*.

During the execution of an atom (called subround), its variables are updated simultaneously. The new values of the atom variables may depend on the new values of variables that have been updated, by another atom, in an earlier subround. Hence, some atoms can be executed only after the execution of some other atoms. The initialization and update rules for executing an atom are specified via guarded commands. We require that there is a static order of the atoms in which they can be executed in every update round, and that always at least one guarded command is enabled. This ensures that the interaction of an atom with the other atoms (and the environment) is *nonblocking*.

New modules can be built from existing modules using three operations: parallel composition, variable renaming, and variable hiding. The composition of two modules produces a single module whose behavior captures the interaction between the two component modules. Variable renaming changes the name of a variable. Variable hiding changes a variable from interface to private, and therefore renders it unobservable.

3 Simulation

MOCHA provides an interactive simulator with a graphical user-interface for simulating modules. It operates in three different modes: random simulation, manual simulation, and game simulation. In random simulation, all atoms are executed by the simulator, which randomly resolves nondeterminism. In manual simulation, all atoms are executed according to the directions of the user. In game simulation, some of the atoms are executed by the simulator, while the remaining atoms are executed by the user. Each such simulation can be viewed as a game between the user and the simulator, hence the name game simulation.

4 Invariant Checking

MOCHA provides support for checking both state and transition invariants on finite-state modules. For this purpose, we have implemented both symbolic and enumerative state-exploration algorithms:

Symbolic. We represent the transition relation and the set of reached states of a reactive module as binary decision diagrams (BDDs) [Bry86]. We keep the transition relation of a reactive module in a conjunctively partitioned form. Each conjunct is the transition relation of an atom. The image computation routines have been leveraged off VIS, which provides a heuristic [RAP+95] for image computation based on early quantification that has been shown useful in practice.

Enumerative. The current implementation of the enumerative state-exploration routines is rather naive and does not perform any optimizations. It is used primarily by the simulator.

Both the symbolic and enumerative invariant checkers have the capability to produce error traces. The error traces can be displayed graphically with a Tk widget.

5 Compositional Refinement Checking

We briefly describe what it means for one module to refine another. A *trajectory* of a module P is a finite sequence of states obtained by executing P for finitely many rounds. A *trace* of P is obtained by projecting each state of a trajectory of P onto the observable variables. The module P *refines* another module Q, denoted $P \preceq Q$, if every trace of P is also a trace of Q (in addition to some technical side conditions). We have implemented a compositional methodology for refinement checking. The details of the method are explained in an accompanying paper [HQR98].

To illustrate the main aspects of our methodology that deal with the explosion of the implementation state space, consider the refinement check $P_1 \| P_2 \preceq Q$, where $\|$ denotes the parallel composition operation. Suppose that the state space of $P_1 \| P_2$ is too large to be handled by exhaustive state exploration. Typically, Q specifies the behavior of only those variables that are visible at the boundary of $P_1 \| P_2$. Therefore, to obtain suitable constraining environments for P_1 and P_2, we need to construct *abstraction modules* A_1 and A_2 that specify the behavior of the boundary variables and the interface variables between P_1 and P_2. We can then decompose the proof into lemmas using the following assume-guarantee rule:

$$\frac{\begin{array}{c} P_1 \| A_2 \preceq A_1 \| Q \\ A_1 \| P_2 \preceq Q \| A_2 \end{array}}{P_1 \| P_2 \preceq A_1 \| A_2 \| Q \preceq Q}$$

Even if the implementation state space becomes manageable as a result of decomposition, each lemma of the form $P' \preceq Q'$ is still PSPACE-hard in the description of P' and EXPSPACE-hard in the description of Q'. However, for the special case that Q' is *projection refinable* by P' (i.e., all variables of Q' are observable by both P' and Q'), the refinement check reduces to a transition-invariant check on P'—namely, checking whether every move of P' can be mimicked by a move of Q'. The complexity of this procedure is linear in the state spaces of P' and Q'. When Q' is not projection refinable by P', our methodology advocates the use of a *witness module* that, when composed with P', leads to projection refinability.

An assume-guarantee rule very similar to the one described above has been proved sound also for *fair* refinement checking [AH96]. Hence, our methodology applies to fair modules as well.

6 ATL Model Checking

Alternating Temporal Logic (ATL) is a temporal logic designed for specifying requirements of open systems [AHK97]. Consider a set of agents that correspond to different components of a system and its environment. Then, the logic ATL admits formulas of the form $\langle\!\langle A \rangle\!\rangle \Diamond p$, where p is a state predicate and A is a subset of the agents. The formula $\langle\!\langle A \rangle\!\rangle \Diamond p$ asserts that the agents in A can cooperate to reach a p-state no matter how the remaining agents behave. The semantics of ATL is formalized by defining games such that the satisfaction of an ATL formula corresponds to the existence of a winning strategy.

The model checking problem for ATL is to determine whether a given module satisfies a given ATL formula. The symbolic model-checking procedure for CTL [BCM92] generalizes nicely to yield a symbolic model-checking procedure for ATL. For a set A of agents and a set U of states, let $Pre_A(U)$ be the set of states from which the agents in A can force the system into some state in U in one move. Then, the set of states satisfying the ATL formula $\langle\!\langle A \rangle\!\rangle \Diamond p$ is the least set that contains all states satisfying p and is closed under the operator Pre_U. This set can be easily computed by an iterative symbolic procedure. The time complexity of ATL model checking is, like CTL model checking, linear in the size of both the state space and the formula. Thus, the added expressiveness of ATL over CTL comes at no extra cost.

We plan to integrate the game simulator described in Section 3 with the ATL model checker to provide counter-examples. When an ATL specification fails, the ATL model checker synthesizes and outputs a winning strategy as a counter-example, according to which the simulator will play a game with the user. The user tries to win the game by finding an execution sequence that satisfies the specification. We believe that by being forced into playing a losing game, the user can be convinced that the model is incorrect and can be led to the error.

7 Real-Time Modules

MOCHA supports the reachability analysis of real-time systems that are described in the form of *timed modules* as defined in [AH97]. In addition to the discrete-valued variables of reactive modules, a timed module makes use of real-valued *clock variables*. All clock variables increase at the same rate, and keep track of the time elapsed since they have been assigned a value by a guarded command. The guards of later transitions can depend on the values of clocks. The reachability analysis of timed modules is performed by automatically synthesizing a monitor process that restricts the state exploration to only those trajectories that satisfy the timing constraints on the clock variables, as in the analysis of timed automata [AD94].

References

[AD94] R. Alur and D.L. Dill. A theory of timed automata. *Theoretical Computer Science*, vol. 126, pages 183–235, 1994.

[AH96] R. Alur and T.A. Henzinger. Reactive modules. In *Proc. 11th IEEE Symposium on Logic in Computer Science*, pages 207–218, 1996.

[AH97] R. Alur and T.A. Henzinger. Modularity for timed and hybrid systems. In *Proc. 8th International Conference on Concurrency Theory*, LNCS 1243, pages 74–88. Springer-Verlag, 1997.

[AHK97] R. Alur, T.A. Henzinger, and O. Kupferman. Alternating-time temporal logic. In *Proc. 38th IEEE Symposium on Foundations of Computer Science*, pages 100–109, 1997.

[AHR98] R. Alur, T.A. Henzinger, and S.K. Rajamani. Symbolic exploration of transition hierarchies. In *TACAS 98: Tools and Algorithms for Construction and Analysis of Systems*, LNCS 1384, pages 330–344, 1998.

[BCM92] J.R. Burch and E.M. Clarke and K.L. McMillan and D.L. Dill and L.J. Hwang. Symbolic model checking: 10^{20} states and beyond. *Information and Computation*, Vol 98, No 2, pages 142–170, 1992.

[BG88] G. Berry and G. Gonthier. The synchronous programming language ESTEREL: design, semantics, implementation. Technical Report 842, INRIA, 1988.

[BHS+96] R. Brayton, G. Hachtel, A. Sangiovanni-Vincentelli, F. Somenzi, A. Aziz, S. Cheng, S. Edwards, S. Khatri, Y. Kukimoto, A. Pardo, S. Qadeer, R. Ranjan, S. Sarwary, T. Shiple, G. Swamy, and T. Villa. VIS: A system for verification and synthesis. In *Proc. 8th International Conference on Computer Aided Verification*, LNCS 1102, pages 428–432. Springer-Verlag, 1996.

[Bry86] R.E. Bryant. Graph-based algorithms for boolean-function manipulation. *IEEE Trans. on Computers*, C-35(8), 1986.

[CM88] K.M. Chandy and J. Misra. *Parallel program design: A foundation*. Addison-Wesley, 1988

[CE81] E.M. Clarke and E.A. Emerson. Design and synthesis of synchronization skeletons using branching time temporal logic. In *Proc. Workshop on Logic of Programs*, LNCS 131, pages 52–71. Springer-Verlag, 1981.

[Exp97] Expert Interface Technologies. *Tix Home Page.* http://www.xpi.com/tix/index.html.

[HQR98] T.A. Henzinger, S. Qadeer, and S.K. Rajamani. You assume, we guarantee: Methodology and case studies. In *Proc. 10th International Conference on Computer Aided Verification*. Springer-Verlag, 1998.

[Lyn96] N.A. Lynch. *Distributed Algorithms*. Morgan Kaufmann, 1996.

[Pnu77] A. Pnueli. The temporal logic of programs. In *Proc. 18th IEEE Symposium on Foundations of Computer Science*, pages 46–77, 1977.

[RAP+95] R.K. Ranjan, A. Aziz, B. Plessier, C. Pixley, and R.K. Brayton. Efficient formal design verification: data structures + algorithms. In *Proc. International Workshop on Logic Synthesis*, 1995.

SCR*: A Toolset for Specifying and Analyzing Software Requirements*

Constance Heitmeyer, James Kirby, Bruce Labaw and Ramesh Bharadwaj

Naval Research Laboratory, Code 5546, Washington, DC 20375, USA

Abstract. A controversial issue in the formal methods community is the degree to which mathematical sophistication and theorem proving skills should be needed to apply a formal method and its support tools. This paper describes the SCR (Software Cost Reduction) tools, part of a "practical" formal method—a method with a solid mathematical foundation that software developers can apply without theorem proving skills, knowledge of temporal and higher order logics, or consultation with formal methods experts. The SCR method provides a tabular notation for specifying requirements and a set of "light-weight" tools that detect several classes of errors automatically. The method also provides support for more "heavy-duty" tools, such as a model checker. To make model checking feasible, users can automatically apply one or more abstraction methods.

1 Introduction

Given the high frequency of requirements errors, the serious accidents they may cause, and the high cost of correcting them, tools that aid software developers in the early detection of requirements errors are crucial. To be effective, the tools must be usable by software developers on industrial-strength projects and should be based on a formal model of requirements. The formal model provides a solid basis for formal analysis of the specification, which detects many classes of errors automatically.

For a requirements tool to be useful to software developers, the tool must be part of a development method that provides guidance on those decisions the requirements specification should record and those it should not (i.e., the method distinguishes requirements decisions from design decisions) and guidance on making, evaluating, and recording the decisions. The development method should also provide notations that software developers can apply easily in constructing a requirements specification. Finally, the method should not require the developers to be experts in the formal model underlying the tool.

The SCR (Software Cost Reduction) requirements method is a formal method based on tables for specifying the requirements of safety-critical software systems. Designed for use by engineers, the method has been applied to a variety of practical systems, including avionics systems, telephone networks, and nuclear power plants. Originally formulated by NRL researchers to document the

---

* This work was supported by the Office of Naval Research and SPAWAR.

requirements of the Operational Flight Program (OFP) of the US Navy's A-7 aircraft [11, 1], SCR has been used in practice by a number of industrial organizations, such as Grumann, Bell Laboratories, Ontario Hydro, and Lockheed, to specify software requirements. For example, in 1993-94, Lockheed used SCR tables to specify the complete requirements of the C-130J OFP [5], a program containing more than 230K lines of Ada code.

Introduced in 1995 [8, 9], SCR* is an integrated suite of tools supporting the SCR requirements method. Figure 1 illustrates SCR*, which includes a *specification editor* for creating a requirements specification, a *dependency graph browser* for displaying the variable dependencies in the specification, a *consistency checker* for detecting well-formedness errors (e.g., type errors and missing cases), a *simulator* for validating the specification, and a *model checker* for checking application properties. Currently, more than 50 organizations in the US, Canada, UK, and Germany, including industrial and government organizations as well as universities, are experimenting with SCR*.

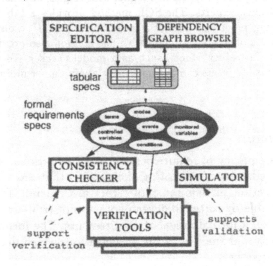

Fig. 1. SCR*: Tools supporting the SCR requirements method

To date, SCR* has been applied successfully in three external pilot projects. In the first, researchers at NASA's IV&V Facility used SCR* to detect missing cases and nondeterminism in the prose requirements specification of software for the International Space Station [4]. In the second project, engineers at Rockwell-Collins used SCR* to expose 24 errors, many of them serious, in the requirements specification of an example flight guidance system [14]. Of the detected errors, a third were uncovered in constructing the specification, a third in running the consistency checker, and the remaining third in executing the specification with the simulator. In a third project, researchers at the JPL (Jet Propulsion Laboratory) used SCR* to analyze specifications of two components of NASA's Deep Space-1 spacecraft for errors [13].

In a fourth pilot project, NRL applied the SCR tools, including a newly integrated model checker [3], to a sizable contractor-produced requirements specification of the Weapons Control Panel (WCP) for a safety-critical US military system [10]. The tools uncovered numerous errors in the contractor specification, including a serious safety violation. Translating the contractor specification into the SCR tabular notation, using SCR* to detect specification errors, and building a working prototype of the WCP required only one person-month, thus demonstrating the utility and cost-effectiveness of the SCR method.

2 The SCR Requirements Model

An SCR requirements specification describes the required system behavior as the composition of a nondeterministic environment and a (usually) deterministic system [7]. The system environment contains *monitored* and *controlled quantities*, quantities that the system monitors and controls. The environment nondeterministically produces a sequence of input events, where an *input event* is a change in some monitored quantity. Beginning in some initial state, the system responds to each input event in turn by changing state and possibly changing one or more controlled quantities. In SCR, the system behavior is assumed to be *synchronous*—the system completely processes one input event before processing the next input event.

The SCR formal model, a special form of the classic state machine model, represents a system Σ as a 4-tuple, $\Sigma = (S, S_0, E^m, T)$, where S is a set of states, $S_0 \subseteq S$ is the initial state set, E^m is the set of input events, and T is the transform describing the allowed state transitions [7]. In the formal model presented in [7], the transform T is deterministic, a composition of smaller functions called *table functions*, derived from the tables in an SCR specification. The formal model requires the information in each table to satisfy certain properties. These properties guarantee that each table describes a total function.

In SCR, two relations, NAT and REQ, describe the required system behavior. NAT specifies the natural constraints on the system behavior—constraints imposed by physical laws and the system environment. REQ specifies the relation that the system must enforce between the monitored and controlled quantities. To specify REQ concisely, the SCR method uses mode classes, conditions, and events. A *mode class* organizes the system states into equivalence classes, each called a *mode*. The SCR model includes a set RF containing the names of all variables (e.g., monitored and controlled variables, mode classes) in a given specification and a function mapping each variable in RF to a set of values. In the model, a *state* is a function mapping each variable in RF to its value, a *condition* is a predicate defined on a system state, and an *event* is a predicate defined on two system states when any state variable changes.

3 The SCR Tools

Specification Editor. To create, modify, or display a requirements specification, the user invokes the specification editor [8]. Each SCR specification is organized into dictionaries and tables. The dictionaries define the static information in the specification, such as the names and values of variables and constants, the user-defined types, etc. The tables specify how the variables change in response to input events. One important class of tables specifies the behavior of controlled variables.

Dependency Graph Browser. Understanding the relationship between different parts of a large specification can be difficult. To address this problem, the Dependency Graph Browser (DGB) represents the dependencies among the variables in a given SCR specification as a directed graph [9]. By examining this graph, a user can detect errors such as undefined variables and circular definitions. The user can also use the DGB to display and extract subsets of the dependency graph, e.g., the subgraph containing all variables upon which a selected controlled variable depends.

Consistency Checker. The consistency checker [7, 9] analyzes a specification for properties derived from the SCR requirements model. It exposes syntax and type errors, variable name discrepancies, missing cases, unwanted nondeterminism, and circular definitions. When an error is detected, the consistency checker provides detailed feedback to facilitate error correction. A form of static analysis, consistency checking is performed without execution of the specification or a reachability analysis and is hence more efficient than model checking. In developing an SCR specification, the user normally invokes the consistency checker first and postpones more heavy-duty analysis such as model checking until later. By exploiting the special properties guaranteed by consistency checking (e.g., determinism), later analyses can be more efficient [3].

Simulator. To validate a specification, the user can run the simulator [9] and analyze the results to ensure that the specification captures the intended behavior. Additionally, the user can define invariant properties believed to be true of the required behavior and, using simulation, execute a series of scenarios to determine if any violate the invariants. To provide input to the simulator, the user either enters a sequence of input events or loads a previously stored scenario.

The simulator supports the construction of front-ends, tailored to particular application domains. One example is a customized front-end for pilots to use in evaluating an attack aircraft specification (see Figure 2). Rather than clicking on monitored variable names, entering values for them, and seeing the results of simulation presented as variable values, a pilot clicks on visual representations of cockpit controls and sees results presented on a simulated cockpit display. This front-end allows the pilot to move out of the world of requirements specification and into the world of attack aircraft, where he is the expert. Such an interface facilitates customer validation of the specification. A second customized front-end, part of the WCP prototype mentioned above, has also been developed.

Model Checker. Recently, the explicit state model checker Spin [12] was integrated into SCR* [3]. After using SCR* to develop a formal requirements specification, a developer can obtain an automatic translation of the specification into *Promela*, the language of Spin, and then invoke Spin within the toolset to check properties of the specification. Currently, the model checker analyzes invariant properties. The user can use the simulator to demonstrate and validate any property violation detected by Spin.

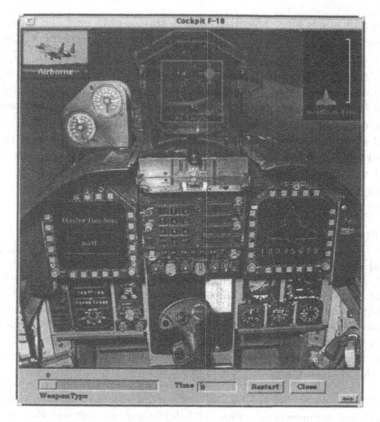

Fig. 2. Customized simulator front-end for an attack aircraft specification

The number of reachable states in a state machine model of real-world software is usually very large, sometimes infinite. To make model checking practical, we have developed sound methods for deriving abstractions from SCR specifications [3]. The methods are practical: none requires ingenuity on the user's part, and each derives a smaller, more abstract model automatically. Based on the property to be analyzed, these methods eliminate irrelevant variables as well as unneeded detail from the specification. For example, prior to invoking Spin to check the WCP specification for a safety property, we used our abstraction methods to automatically reduce the number of variables from 258 to 55 and to replace several real-valued variables with finite-valued variables, thus making model checking feasible [10].

4 Comparison with Other Tools

The method most closely related to SCR is the Requirements State Machine Language (RSML) and associated tools [6]. In [2], Anderson et al. describe the use of the model checker SMV to analyze a component of the TCAS-II specification expressed in RSML. Unlike our approach to limiting state explosion which reduces the specification by applying sound abstraction methods, Anderson et al. propose a more efficient encoding for the BDD representation of the

RSML specification. More recently, Park et al. [15] have used the Stanford Validity Checker (SVC) to check the consistency of RSML specifications. Their approach is similar to that used by the consistency checker in SCR* [7, 9].

SCR* can be distinguished in three major ways from other tools. First, unlike most commercial tools for requirements specification, SCR* has a solid mathematical foundation, thus allowing sophisticated analyses, such as consistency checking and model checking, largely unsupported by current tools. Second, the SCR tools, unlike most research tools, have a well designed user interface, are integrated to work together, and provide detailed feedback when errors are detected to facilitate their correction. Finally, users of SCR* can do considerable analysis *without* interaction with application experts or formal methods researchers, thereby providing formal methods usage at low cost.

References

1. T. A. Alspaugh et al. Software requirements for the A-7 aircraft. Report 9194, Naval Research Lab, Wash. DC, 1992.
2. R. J. Anderson et al. "Model checking large software specifications." *Proc. 4th ACM SIGSOFT Symp. Foundations of Software Eng.*, October 1996.
3. R. Bharadwaj and C. Heitmeyer. "Model checking complete requirements specifications using abstraction." *Journal of Automated Software Eng.* (to appear).
4. S. Easterbrook and J. Callahan. "Formal methods for verification and validation of partial specifications: A case study." *Journal of Systems and Software*, 1997.
5. S. Faulk et al. "Experience applying the CoRE method to the Lockheed C-130J." *Proc. 9th Annual Computer Assurance Conf. (COMPASS '94)*, June 1994.
6. M. P. E. Heimdahl and N. Leveson. "Completeness and consistency analysis of state-based requirements." *Proc. 17th Int'l Conf. on Software Eng. (ICSE'95)*, Seattle, WA, Apr. 1995.
7. C. Heitmeyer, R. Jeffords, and B. Labaw. "Automated consistency checking of requirements specifications." *ACM Trans. Software Eng. and Method.* 5(3), 1996.
8. C. Heitmeyer et al. "SCR*: A toolset for specifying and analyzing requirements." *Proc. 10th Annual Conf. on Computer Assurance (COMPASS '95)*, June 1995.
9. C. Heitmeyer, J. Kirby, and B. Labaw. "Tools for formal specification, verification, and validation of requirements." *Proc. 12th Annual Conf. on Computer Assurance (COMPASS '97)*, June 1997.
10. C. Heitmeyer, J. Kirby, and B. Labaw. "Applying the SCR requirements method to a weapons control panel: An experience report." *Proc. 2nd Workshop on Formal Methods in Software Practice (FMSP'98)*, St. Petersburg, FL, March 1998.
11. K. L. Heninger. Specifying software requirements for complex systems: New techniques and their application. *IEEE Trans. on Software Eng.* SE-6(1), Jan. 1980.
12. G. J. Holzmann. *Design and Validation of Computer Protocols.* Prentice-Hall, 1991.
13. R. R. Lutz and H.-Y. Shaw. "Applying the SCR* requirements toolset to DS-1 fault protection." Report D15198, Jet Propulsion Lab, Pasadena, CA, Dec. 1997.
14. S. Miller. "Specifying the mode logic of a flight guidance system in CoRE and SCR." *Proc. 2nd Workshop on Formal Methods in Software Practice (FMSP'98)*, St. Petersburg, FL, March 1998.
15. D. Y. W. Park et al. "Checking properties of safety-critical specifications using efficient decision procedures." *Proc. 2nd Workshop on Formal Methods in Software Practice (FMSP'98)*, St. Petersburg, FL, March 1998.

A Toolset for Message Sequence Charts

Doron A. Peled

Bell Laboratories
700 Mountain Ave.
Murray Hill, NJ 07974, USA
email: doron@research.bell-labs.com

Abstract. Message Sequence Charts (MSCs) are a popular graphical notation for describing communication protocols. MSCs enjoy an international standard (ITU-Z120) and a growing number of tools include an MSC interface for either displaying simulation or verification results, or testing the inclusion of a particular scenario in the design. We describe here a toolset that was developed to help designing a system using the MSC notation. The toolset allows creating an MSC description of a design for communication systems, and performing some verification tasks on the design.

The MSC notation is becoming a popular notation for describing communication protocols. It enjoys an international standard called ITU-Z120 [4]. MSCs are among the standard description techniques used for designing communication systems [2], and a growing number of tools include an MSC interface [8].

Each MSC describes a scenario where some processes communicate with each other. Such a scenario includes a description of the messages sent and received and the ordering between them. Each process is represented by a vertical line, while a message is represented by a horizontal or slanted arrow from the sending process to the receiving one (see Figure 1). Since a communication system usually includes many such protocols, a high level description allows combining MSC scenarios together. This description consists of a graph, where each node contains one MSC. Each path in this graph, starting from a designated initial state, corresponds to a single scenario.

In this paper, we describe a toolset that allows performing the early design of a communication system using the notation of message sequence charts. These tools allow applying simple verification tasks to the MSC design. Since the early design is quite abstract, often avoiding detailed information such as the value of particular process variables, the need for further verification at later stages is not eliminated. However, finding design errors early in the development process is very cost-effective and is rather efficient.

The first tool, called Msc [1], supports representing message sequence charts. It allows both a graphical description of the MSCs, and its standard textual representation [4]. Thus, an MSC can be obtained by either drawing it using the graphical interface, or by typing it in its standard syntax. This approach has the

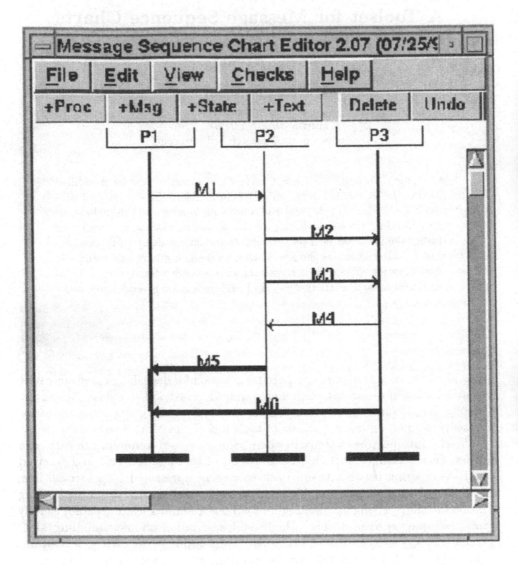

Fig. 1. A Message Sequence Chart

advantage that the graphical representation of an MSC is related to some formal representation. We assign to each MSC its semantics denotation as a partially ordered set of *send* and a *receive* event.

The semantics of an MSC depends on some architectural parameters; it can differ between architectures with fifo or non-fifo queues, or between architectures with one or multiple incoming message queue. This results in a slightly different behavior under each such choice. In our implementation, the user is required to select the desired semantics (using a choice menu), and the analysis is done according to this selection. Under fifo with one input queue semantics, the following pairs of events are ordered:

- A send p and its corresponding receive q.
- Two sends p, q of the same process, where p appears above q on the process line.
- A receive p and a send q of the same process, where p appears above q on the process line.
- Two receives p, q of the same process corresponding to sends from some mutual process, where the send corresponding to p appears above the send corresponding to q.

Notice that in general, two receives p and q of the same process of messages corresponding to sends from different processes, are not ordered. Similarly, a send p that appears above a receive q in the same process line is unordered with q.

We apply some simple verification algorithms to MSCs. One such check is whether the MSCs contain *race conditions*. A race condition can result in from the fact that in most cases, time progresses within each MSC process line downwards; however, this is not always the case, due to some limited control we have over concurrently executed events. For example, the MSC in Figure 1 contains two receive events of process $P1$ (of messages $M5$ and $M6$). Since each process line is one dimensional, the MSC notation forces choosing one of the receive events to appear above the other. However, these two messages were sent from different processes, $P2$ and $P3$, and the chart imposes no order between these sending events. Thus, there is no reason to believe that these messages would indeed arrive in the particular order depicted using the MSC. In Figure 1, the lines corresponding to the two messages in that race appear emphasized. This is a result of applying the race detection algorithm.

Finding races is done as follows [1]: we translate the MSC syntax into its semantical representation as a partially ordered set of events. We calculate the transitive closure $\sqsubseteq$ of this order using the Floyed-Warshall algorithm [9]. Another order that is constructed from the syntax of the MSC is the *visual order* $<$. This includes pairs of events $p < q$, where p is a send and q is a receive, or p appears above q on a process line. Then a race is reported for each pair of events where $p < q$ but it is not the case that $p \sqsubseteq q$. In our example, the two receive events p, q of messages $M5$ and $M6$, we have $p < q$, since p appears above q on process $P1$ line. But it does not hold that $p \sqsubseteq q$.

In a similar way, the tool allows checking for time inconsistencies. One can assign lower and upper time limits to intervals between send and receive events. The consistency between these timing constraints are checked and inconsistencies are reported [1].

The MSC standard allows combining simple MSCs using *hierarchical message sequence charts*. These are graphs, where each node is a single MSC. Each path of this graph, starting from some designated initial state, corresponds to a simple concatenation of the MSCs that appear on it. The POGA tool [3] allows to design hierarchical MSCs. With this capability, one can describe a large or even infinite set of scenarios, each one of them can be finite or infinite (due to loops in the hierarchical graph). The tools MSC and POGA together allow for the creation, debugging, organization, and maintenance of systems of message sequence charts.

The tool TEMPLE [6, 7] adds the ability of searching a hierarchical MSC design for a paths that match a given specification. The specification is also written as an MSC or a hierarchical, using the MSC or **Poga** tools. The specification MSC is called a *template* and denotes a set of events (sending and receiving of messages) and their relative order. A specification *matches* any scenario that contains at least those events that appear in the template, while preserving the order between them. The matching path of the design can have additional events besides the ones appearing in the template. At the conclusion of the search, TEMPLE either provides a matching scenario, or the fact that no matching scenario exists in the checked hierarchical graph.

The use of template matching allows one to mechanize such searches. The match can be used for determining whether MSCs with unwanted properties exist in the design. Another use is for determining whether a required feature is already included in the design or remains to be added.

An example of a template and a matching MSC scenario appears in Figure 2. In both charts, there are three processes, P_1, P_2 and P_3. The result of this match is that s_2 is paired with σ_1, r_2 with ρ_1, s_1 with σ_3, and r_1 with ρ_3.

The user interface for MSC and POGA was written in TCL/Tk, and the algorithms were implemented in the language C. The implementation of the template matching was done by translating the hierarchical graph and the template into two COSPAN [5] processes (COSPAN is an automata-based model-checking tool). A third process represents some collected matching information. Then, the automata intersection is performed. If the intersection is not empty, the resulting counter example is translated back into an MSC and displayed. A new implementation was recently written directly in the language SML.

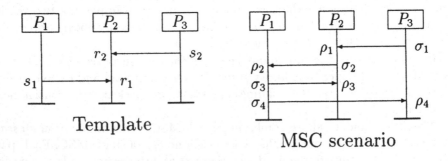

Fig. 2. A template and a matching scenario

536

Acknowledgements

The tools described in this short paper are a result of collaborations with Rajeev Alur, Brian Kernighan, Gerard Holzmann, Bob Kurshan, Vladimir Levin, Anca Muscholl and Zhendong Su.

References

1. R. Alur, G.J. Holzmann, D. Peled. An Analyzer for Message Sequence Charts. *Software Concepts and Tools*, Vol. 17, No. 2, pp. 70–77, 1996.
2. A. Ek, J. Grabowski, D. Hogrefer, R. Jerome, B. Kosh, M. Schmitt, SDL'97, Time for testing: SDL, MSC and Trends, Proceedings of the 8th DSL Forum, Elsevier, France, 23–26, 1997.
3. G.J. Holzmann, Early Fault Detection Tools, *Software Concepts and Tools*, Vol. 17, No. 2, pp. 63–69, 1996.
4. ITU-T Recommendation Z.120, Message Sequence Chart (MSC), March 1993.
5. R.P. Kurshan, *Computer-Aided Verification*, Princeton University Press, 1994.
6. V. Levin, D. Peled. Verification of Message Sequence Charts via Template Matching, *TAPSOFT (FASE)'97, Theory and Practice of Software Development*, Lille, France. *Lecture Notes in Computer Science*. Springer, 1997.
7. A. Muscholl, D. Peled, Z. Su, Deciding Properties for Message Sequence Charts, *FoSSaCS, Foundations of Software Science and Computation Structures*, Lisbon, Portugal.
8. B. Selic, G. Gullekson, P.T. Ward, Real-Time Object-Oriented Modeling, Wiley, 1994.
9. S. Warshall. A theorem on boolean matrices. *Journal of the ACM*, 9 (1962), pp. 11-12.

Real-Time Verification of STATEMATE Designs

Udo Brockmeyer and Gunnar Wittich *

OFFIS, Escherweg 2, 26121 Oldenburg, Germany
{Brockmeyer,Wittich}@OFFIS.Uni-Oldenburg.de

Abstract. This paper presents a toolset for real-time verification of STATEMATE[1] designs. STATEMATE is a widely used design tool for embedded control applications. In our approach designs including all timing information are translated into untimed finite state machines (FSMs) which are verified by symbolic model-checking. Real-time requirements are expressed by TCTL formulae interpreted over discrete time. A reduction from TCTL model-checking to CTL model-checking is implemented in order to use a CTL model-checker for the verification task. Some experimental results of the toolset are given.

1 Introduction

In this paper we present a toolset for real-time verification of STATEMATE designs [8–10]. STATEMATE is a widely used graphical specification tool for embedded control applications. The STATEMATE toolset captures the phases of specification, analysis, design and documentation of real-time systems. To cope with the complexity of real life applications, a system under development may be described graphically from three different viewpoints within STATEMATE. They cover structural (*Module-Charts*), functional (*Activity-Charts*) and behavioral (*Statecharts* [7]) aspects of a system.

For the real-time verification of STATEMATE designs we use the technique of model-checking. Model-checking is an automatic method for proving that a given implementation of a design meets its requirement specification represented by a temporal logic formula. As specification language, we use TCTL as introduced in [2] restricted to a discrete time domain. Our TCTL model-checking procedure aims at reuse of an industrial CTL model-checker [6] and contains two major new components: first a translation of STATEMATE designs into untimed FSMs and second an embedding of the discrete time TCTL model-checking problem into CTL model-checking.

The semantical foundation of our translation from STATEMATE designs into untimed FSMs [3], as required by the model-checker [6], can be found in [5]. Our

* Part of this work has been funded by the Commission of the European Communities under the ESPRIT project 20897, SACRES and the German BMBF project KORSYS, grant number 01-IS-519-E-0
[1] STATEMATE is a registered trademark of i-Logix Inc.

toolset supports real-time verification for the synchronous (step) semantics as well as for the asynchronous (super-step) semantics provided by the STATEMATE simulator and therefore for both of the semantics given in [9]. Furthermore, in addition to almost the complete language of Statecharts, the language of Activity-Charts is also covered by our toolset.

In this tool-paper we demonstrate the feasibility of our approach to real-time model-checking on some case studies. Two of them are industrial sized applications provided by our project partners. The first one originates from the SACRES project and is provided by British Aerospace. It is a Storage Management System of an aircraft. The second one was provided by ESG[2] in the KORSYS project. This case study is a Helicopter Monitoring System which monitors engine and fuel parameters.

2 Modeling Real-Time Features of STATEMATE

STATEMATE distinguishes between the synchronous simulation semantics (*step semantics*) and the asynchronous simulation semantics (*super-step semantics*). In the step semantics, each step of a design corresponds to exactly one discrete time unit, time increases uniformly and the environment can influence the valuation of variables at every step. In contrast, in the super-step semantics a system performs a chain of internal steps until a stable state (no more internal steps are possible) is reached. Only in a stable state time progresses and the system accepts new stimuli.

In order to perform real-time verification of STATEMATE, designs have to be translated into a format interpretable by the model-checker. Our toolset translates designs in two steps. A STATEMATE design is first translated into an intermediate language called SMI (STATEMATE *InterMediate*). We defined SMI as a language for the translation of high-level formalisms into FSMs[3]. In a second phase, the generated SMI code is translated into a FSM for model-checking.

SMI is a simple imperative programming language containing concepts to model hierarchy, parallelism, and nondeterminism of STATEMATE designs. The data-types and expression language of SMI are powerful enough to cover a wide range of STATEMATE types. The cyclic behavior of a STATEMATE design is represented as a non-terminating loop in SMI code. One execution of this loop corresponds to exactly one step of the design. In SMI all control information, all variables and all events of the STATEMATE design are encoded by variables.

STATEMATE provides two ways to introduce explicit timing information into a Statechart which both relate events and actions to the discrete virtual simulation clock. The first alternative allows to trigger transitions by *timeout events*. The second alternative for introducing timing information into a Statechart allows to delay the execution of actions for some time units by a *scheduled action*. To cope with timing aspects of a design the translation process introduces clock variables

---

[2] Elekronik Systeme GmbH, Munich, Germany

[3] In other projects, we translate VHDL, a subclass of Petri-Nets, and a subclass of OCCAM into SMI

for timeout events and scheduled actions. All clocks are running synchronously. Because we require all time expressions to evaluate to a constant at compile time, finite domains for the clocks can be determined.

Because after the translation of a STATEMATE design into SMI all necessary clocks are represented by a finite number of bounded variables, untimed FSMs can be generated out of the code. The construction is such that one step of the FSM corresponds to one execution of the complete loop-body of the SMI code. Thus, in step semantics in each state of the FSM timers are increased by one. In super-step semantics, timers are increased only in certain states, while they remain unchanged in all other states.

3 Real-Time Model Checking

As specification logic we use TCTL as introduced in [2] interpreted over discrete time. Verification is performed by translating TCTL into CTL automatically and model-checking a suitable extended model against the resulting formulae with a slightly enhanced CTL model-checker.

To model-check a TCTL formula with a CTL model-checker, we transform the FSM by adding an additional specification clock. The upper bound of this clock is determined out of the given TCTL formula. This specification clock is incremented whenever time progresses. According to the selected semantics, these states are characterized by a time condition given as a SMI expression.

A similar reduction for a derivate of dense time TCTL is given in [11]. Unlike as in the approach in [11], where additional time transitions between transitions of the system are introduced, we can avoid this blow up by extending CTL (and thus the model-checker, too). Thus, we reduce the number of steps performed by the model-checker while doing its work significantly.

4 Experimental Results

In this section we present some experimental results obtained with our tools. Figure 1 gives a coarse overview of our toolset. STATEMATE designs are translated by STM2SMI into SMI code out of which FSMs are generated by the tool SMI2FSM. FSM2FSM-T serves to add the specification clock to a FSM. Finally, TCTL2CTL realizes the reduction from TCTL to CTL. The model-checker (MC) we use is the ROBDD [1] based assumption/commitment style CTL model-checker provided by our project partner SIEMENS [6].

Table 1 overviews the results for three examined case studies[4]. The TLC is the well known traffic light controller enhanced by timing information modeling the delay of changing the lights. The second example is a component of a Storage Management System (SMS) of an aircraft. This industrial sized application was provided by our project partner British Aerospace. Finally, we model-checked a Helicopter Monitoring System (HMS) which was provided by our project partner

---

[4] All results were evaluated on a Sun SPARC 20 running at 60 MHz

540

ESG. The second column contains the times needed for the translation from
STATEMATE into SMI. For the TLC we chose super-step semantics, while the
other two designs were translated for step semantics. The third column shows
the times to generate FSMs. Column four and five are indicating the complexity
of the studies. Finally, in the MC column, times for model-checking of relevant
real-time properties on the given models are presented.

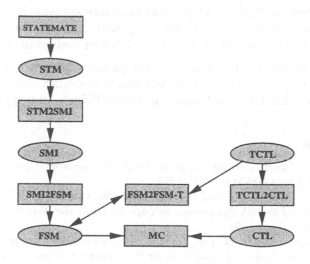

Fig. 1. The Toolset

Beyond these experiences with verifying moderately sized STATEMATE designs against TCTL formulae, we already have very encouraging results on verifying substantially larger STATEMATE designs against CTL formulae. Some of
these results are presented in [3, 4]. There we have shown, that our tools are
very powerful in generating FSMs and performing CTL model-checking. Industrial sized applications with several hundred state bits could be handled. These
models already contain all clocks that model timeouts and scheduled actions
of STATEMATE designs. Because for TCTL model-checking only the additional
specification clock has to be added, we will apply our toolset on these designs,
too, and we expect to be able to verify relevant real-time properties for them.

Model	stm2smi in s	smi2fsm in s	# of bits input/state	# of BDD nodes	MC in s
TLC	2.56	0.45	18/33	2485	12.1
SMS	4.82	6.41	13/53	3284	11.6
HMS	6.78	1.60	32/103	4195	87.4

Table 1. Experimental Results

5 Conclusions and Future Work

In this paper a toolset for real-time verification of STATEMATE designs against TCTL formulae has been presented and its usability on some case studies was demonstrated. Because of the complexity of STATEMATE, there are some rare used features not yet covered by the tools. Our future work is about closing this gap in order to support even these features. Also, we have a lot of ideas for optimizations that can be performed in order to generate smaller FSMs out of STATEMATE designs. Some of these ideas have already been implemented and results have been presented in [3]. Applying these optimizations, we expect to be able to verify real-time properties of much bigger designs in the near future.

Acknowledgment. We thank our project partners British Aerospace, ESG, SIEMENS and i-Logix for providing the tools, case studies and for discussions. Furthermore we thank Werner Damm and Martin Fränzle for helpful discussions.

References

1. S.B. Akers. Binary decision diagrams. In *Transactions on Computers* , No. 6 in Vol. C-27, pages 509-516, IEEE, 1978
2. R. Alur, C. Courcoubetis and D. Dill. Model-Checking for Real-Time Systems. In *Proceedings of the 5th Symposium on Logic in Computer Science*, pages 414-425, Philadelphia, June 1990.
3. U. Brockmeyer and G. Wittich. Tamagotchis need not die – Verification of STATE-MATE Designs. *Tools and Algorithms for the Construction and Analysis of Systems (TACAS'98)*, March 1998
4. W. Damm, U. Brockmeyer, H.J. Holberg, G. Wittich and M. Eckrich. Einsatz formaler Methoden zur Erhöhung der Sicherheit eingebetteter Systeme im KFZ. VDI/VW Gemeinschaftstagung, 1997
5. W. Damm, H. Hungar, B. Josko and A. Pnueli. A Compositional Real-Time Semantics of STATEMATE Designs. In Proceedings of COMPOS 97, edt. H. Langmaack and W.P. de Roever, Springer Verlag, to appear 1998
6. T. Filkorn, SIEMENS AG. Applications of Formal Verification in Industrial Automation and Telecommunication. In Proceedings, *Workshop on Formal Design of Safety Critical Embedded Systems*, April 1997
7. D. Harel. Statecharts: A Visual Formalism for Complex Systems. *Science of Computer Programming 8*, 1987.
8. D. Harel, H. Lachover, A. Naamad, A. Pnueli, M. Politi, R. Sherman, A. Shtull-Trauring and M. Trakhtenbrot. STATEMATE: A working environment for the development of complex reactive systems. In *IEEE Transactions on Software Engineering* , 16:403 – 414, 1990
9. D. Harel and A. Naamad. The STATEMATE Semantics of Statecharts. In *ACM transactions on software engineering and methodology, Vol 5 No 4* , 1996
10. D. Harel and M. Politi. Modeling Reactive Systems with Statecharts: The STATE-MATE Approach. *i–LOGIX INC., Three Riverside Drive, Andover, MA 01810*, June 1996. Part No, D–1100–43
11. T. A. Henzinger and O. Kupferman. From Quantity to Quality. In *Proceedings of Hybrid and Real-Time Systems (HART'97)*, March 1997

Optikron: A Tool Suite for Enhancing Model-Checking of Real-Time Systems

Conrado Daws *

VERIMAG
Centre Équation, 2 avenue de Vignate, 38610 Gières, France.

Abstract. OPTIKRON is a tool suite implementing a set of efficient techniques which can be combined to reduce the number of clock variables of a timed system specification without changing its behavior. Thus, the performance of the model–checking procedures can be improved, both in memory space and running time, as we show for the reachability analysis.

Introduction

The most commonly used techniques for the automatic verification of real–time systems [2, 6], based on model–checking, suffer from the state-space explosion problem. That is, their cost grows drastically not only with the number of components, as in the untimed case, but also with the number of clock variables used in the specification of the system [1, 3, 5].

OPTIKRON offers a set of efficient techniques that can be combined to reduce the number of clocks of a timed system specification without changing its behavior. Using OPTIKRON as the first step of the verification process can improve the performance of the model-checking procedures of the verification tools, whenever a global reduction of the number of clocks is possible, that is, a model with the same behavior and less clocks can be found.

Moreover, even when there is no global reduction, local reductions are always important, because all of the clocks are not needed for the representation of the time constraints of a timed system. OPTIKRON shows how an encoding of the clock-space based on the local reduction results always lead to an important gain, both in time and space, for the computation of the set of reachable states of the system. The efficiency of the model-checking procedures should also be improved if they take into account the local reduction information.

To our knowledge, this is the first succesfull attempt in applying techniques of variable optimization to the case of real-time systems. Related work can be found in [7] where the problem of minimization of timed systems is studied from a theoretical point of view, and in [5] where linear relations between clocks are detected while computing the set of reachable states, with a more expensive algorithm than ours.

---

* WWW: http://www-verimag.imag.fr/PEOPLE/Conrado.Daws/

Clock Reduction Techniques

The main clock-reduction techniques implemented in OPTIKRON, namely the *activity* and the *equality* reduction, are techniques of *static analysis of real-time systems* based on fix-point computations [4].

The first one consists in detecting *active* clocks, that is, clocks that are relevant to the behavior of the system in a given control location. Thus, inactive clocks can be removed without affecting the system behavior. The second one consists in detecting clocks that are always *equal* in a given location. Thus, they can be collapsed into a unique clock without loss of information[1]. Furthermore, since the activity reduction and the equality reduction are orthogonal, they can be combined and their combination can lead to a better reduction.

Verification

Although OPTIKRON can not be considered a verification tool on its own, its main goal is to provide useful information on the clock variables of the model a system, in order to reduce the size of the clock–space and, thus, improve the efficiency of the real–time model–checking procedures implemented in tools like KRONOS [2] and UPPAAL [6].

Moreover, OPTIKRON can compute more efficiently the set of reachable states of a real–time system optimizing the size of the clock–space with respect to the results on the local clock–reductions. This can be useful enough in order to verify *safety* properties of the system.

Experimental Results

Table 1 shows the results of the application of the reduction techniques of OP-TIKRON to several case studies of real–time systems, coming from a wide range of application areas: communication protocols (FDDI, CSMA-CD, Fischer, Tick-Tock), control systems (PLANT, MODUL, ROBOT), and circuits (MOS).

The first three columns of the table give the size of the timed automaton modeling the example. Central columns give the clock-reduction obtained with OPTIKRON(number of iterations and clocks) by applying just the activity or the equality reduction technique, and by combining both of them. Last column shows the memory saving by representing the time constraints of the timed automaton with a data structure of variable size based on the local clock–reduction information.

It is worth noticing that even when there is no global reduction, as for CSMA, FISC, and MODUL, the memory saving obtained with the time constraints representation with variable size is really important (from 45% to 95%).

---

[1] Although the algorithm for detecting equal clocks has recently been adapted to cope with general *linear* relations between clocks, it turns out that in practise the only linear relation between clocks are equality relations.

Table 1. Clock–reduction and memory saving

	Automaton			*Activity*		*Equality*		*Comb.*	*Saving*
Example	*loc*	*trans*	*clo*	*iter*	*clo*	*iter*	*clo*	*clo*	*% Mem*
FDDI 50	150	200	101	100	51	3	101	51	74.2
CSMA 5	918	4590	6	2	6	2	6	6	46.8
FISC 5	2402	5850	5	2	5	2	5	5	79.2
TICK	72	240	6	1	5	2	6	4	70.0
PLANT	236	602	5	1	4	2	5	4	64.2
MOS	769	2683	12	1	10	2	11	6	87.5
MODUL	1421	5809	5	1	5	2	5	5	59.6
ROBOT	106	12816	11	1	5	3	6	2	95.2

Tool Architecture and Distribution

OPTIKRON consists of a module implementing the clock-reduction techniques, optikron, and a module for computing the set of reachable states of the system, simulakro, with a representation of variable size of the time constraints. Figure 1 presents the architecture of the tool.

The optikron module

The current version of the optikron module takes as input a timed system specified as a timed automaton in the *timed graph* format of KRONOS (.tg files)[2]. The output of this module is a binary file .opt containing the information on the local clock–reductions.

Additional information on these reductions can be obtained, by specifying the corresponding options, in the output text files .act (for the list of the set of active clocks in each automaton location), .equ (for the list of equal clocks in each location), and .lin (for the list of the linear relations between clocks in each location).

The clock reduction of the automaton is obtained by renaming its clocks. The local renamings (mappings from the set of original clocks to a set of new clocks) are given in the .ren file. The corresponding renamed timed automaton can be obtained in the file .opt.tg. Clearly, whenever a global reduction is possible, the verification of this model will be more efficient.

The simulakro module

The module for computing the set of reachable states takes as input the .opt.tg file containing the global reduction of the system and the .opt file containing the local clock–reduction information, previously computed. The output is the text file .reach containing a representation of the reachable states.

---

[2] An extension for handling files in the UPPAAL format of *timed automata* (.ta files) is currently in work.

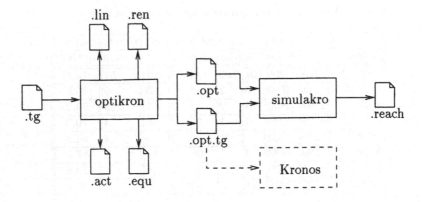

Fig. 1. OPTIKRON 2.2 architecture

Availability

A prototype of OPTIKRON (version 2.2) is freely available for universities and any other non-profit organisms. The distribution package includes executables and a man page. Instructions on how to obtain it, as weel as some additional information on the tool, can be found through the OPTIKRON web page[3].

References

1. R. Alur and D.L. Dill. A theory of timed automata. *Theoretical Computer Science*, 126:183–235, 1994.
2. C. Daws, A. Olivero, S. Tripakis, and S. Yovine. The tool KRONOS. In *Hybrid Systems III, Verification and Control*, pages 208–219. Lecture Notes in Computer Science 1066, Springer-Verlag, 1996.
3. C. Daws and S. Tripakis. Model–checking of real–time reachability properties using abstractions. In B. Steffen, editor, *Proc. of TACAS'98*, Lisbon, Portugal, 31 march - 2 April 1998. Springer Verlag, LNCS 1384.
4. C. Daws and S. Yovine. Reducing the number of clock variables of timed automata. In *Proc. 1996 IEEE Real-Time Systems Symposium, RTSS'96*, Washington, DC, USA, December 1996. IEEE Computer Society Press.
5. K. Larsen, F. Larsson, P. Pettersson, and W. Yi. Efficient verification of real-time systems: Compact data structure and state-space reduction. In *Proc. of the 18th IEEE Real-Time Systems Symposium*, 1997.
6. K. Larsen, P. Pettersson, and W. Yi. Uppaal: Status & developments. In *Proceedings of CAV'97*, Haifa, Israel, 22-25 June 1997.
7. J. Springintveld and F. Vaandrager. Minimizable timed automata. In B. Jonsson and J. Parrow, editors, *Proc. of the 4th International Symposium on Formal Techniques in Real Time and Fault Tolerant Systems (FTRTFT'96)*, volume 1135 of *Lecture Notes in Computer Science*, pages 130–147, Uppsala, Sweden, 1996. Springer-Verlag.

---

[3] http://www-verimag.imag.fr/PEOPLE/Conrado.Daws/optikron.html

Kronos: A Model-Checking Tool for Real-Time Systems*

Marius Bozga[1], Conrado Daws[1], Oded Maler[1],
Alfredo Olivero[2], Stavros Tripakis[1] and Sergio Yovine[3] **

[1] VERIMAG, Centre Équation, 2 avenue de Vignate, 38610 Gières, France.
e-mail: {bozga, daws, maler, tripakis}@imag.fr
[2] Instituto de Computación, Universidad de la República, Montevideo, Uruguay.
e-mail: alfredo@ungs.edu.ar
[3] VERIMAG, currently visiting California PATH, UC Berkeley.
e-mail: yovine@imag.fr, sergio@path.berkeley.edu

General Presentation

KRONOS [9, 11, 8, 21, 17, 4, 3, 10] is a software tool aiming at assisting designers of real-time systems to develop projects meeting the specified requirements.

One major objective of KRONOS is to provide a verification engine to be integrated into design environments for real-time systems in a wide range of application areas. Real-time communication protocols [9, 11], timed asynchronous circuits [17, 4], and hybrid systems [19, 11] are some examples of application domains where KRONOS has already been used.

KRONOS has been also used in analyzing real-time systems modeled in several other process description formalisms, such as ATP [18], AORTA [5], ET-LOTOS [9], and T-ARGOS [16]. On the other direction, the tool itself provides an interface to untimed formalisms such as *labeled-transition systems* (LTS) which has been used to exploit untimed verification techniques [21].

Theoretical Background

The system-description language of KRONOS is the model of *timed automata* [2], which are communicating finite-state machines extended with continuous real-valued variables (*clocks*) used to measure time delays. Usually a system is modeled as a *network* of automata. Communication is achieved by label synchronization à la CCS or CSP (binary or *n-ary rendez-vous*), or shared variables (of bounded integer or enumeration type).

System requirements can be specified in KRONOS using a variety of formalisms, such as the real-time logic TCTL [1, 15], timed Büchi automata, or untimed LTS. These formalisms are useful for expressing most interesting classes of (timed or untimed) properties about systems, namely, *safety* properties (for

---

* KRONOS is developed at VERIMAG, a joint laboratory of UJF, Ensimag and CNRS.
http://www-verimag.imag.fr/TEMPORISE/kronos/.
** C. Daws, A. Olivero and S. Yovine partially supported by European Contract KIT 139 HYBSYS.

example, absence of deadlock, invariant, bounded-delay response, etc), as well as *liveness* properties (for example, time progress, regular occurrence of certain events, etc) [1].

The main verification engine of the tool is based on the *model-checking* approach which comprises both *analysis*: (a) checking whether requirements are satisfied, (b) providing *diagnostic trails* (i.e., execution sequences) demonstrating why a property holds or does not hold; and *synthesis*: adjusting the system (for instance, by computing a restricted sub-system) so that it meets its requirements.

Model-checking is done using two methods: (a) the *fixpoint* method, which, given a timed automaton and a TCTL formula, performs a nested fixpoint computation starting from an initial set of states and iterating a *precondition operator* until stabilization (the operator depends on the type of the formula); (b) the *explorative* method, which, given a network of timed automata and a specification (in terms of a TCTL formula or a timed Büchi automaton), generates the reachability graph of the system while checking at the same time whether the property holds.

In the case of safety properties a simple (depth-first or breadth-first) search of the reachability graph suffices. In the case of general properties, specified as timed Büchi automata, a double search is performed, refining parts of the graph whenever necessary. Both methods are interesting: the main advantage of the fixpoint method is that it can be implemented in a purely *symbolic* manner, using structures like BDD for efficiency (see below); on the other hand, the explorative method is more suitable for *on-the-fly* verification (see below) and can also provide diagnostic trails.

Apart from model-checking, KRONOS offers the possibility to (a) generate the system's reachable state space (to check, for instance, whether an error state can be reached), and (b) compute the coarsest partition of the state space with respect to the *time-abstracting bisimulation*, an equivalence relating states which lead to the same untimed behavior regardless the exact time delays. This method provides an interface to LTS and verification by bisimulation or simulation equivalences [21] using the ALDEBARAN tool suite [14].

Supported Verification Techniques

The main obstacle in the applicability of model-checking is the so-called *state-explosion problem* reflecting the fact that the size of the system's state space is often huge. In order to tackle this, KRONOS offers a number of efficient verification techniques, each of which is best suited for different applications.

- *Symbolic* representation of states means dealing with *predicates* representing sets of states rather than individual states. This results into a much more compact representation and storage. In the current KRONOS implementation,

---

[1] To our knowledge, KRONOS is the only real-time verification tool which can handle liveness properties.

sets of clock values are represented using the *difference bounds matrix* (DBM) structure introduced in [13], whereas discrete variables are encoded as *binary decision diagrams* (BDD) [6].

- *On-the-fly* model-checking means dynamically building the state space during the model-checking process, as directed by the model-checking goal (for instance, the property to be verified); this results in saving up space and time, as well as in giving diagnostics as soon as possible.
- *Abstractions* are used for the exploration of a coarser state space than the "real" (*concrete*) one; they result into space and time savings, at the cost of loosing information, so that sometimes definite conclusions cannot be made.
- *Forward* or *backward* techniques: in the former (typically used in the explorative method) the exploration starts from initial states and tries to reach some target, while in the latter (typically used in the fixpoint method) it is the inverse that happens. Combined with various *search algorithms* (such as depth-first or breadth-first) implemented in the model-checking engine of the tool, these alternative techniques result in a large flexibility with respect to the different application needs.
- *Minimization*: it is used to generate the time-abstracting *minimal model* of the system, which can then be visualized as an untimed graph, compared or further reduced with respect to untimed equivalences, or checked using untimed temporal logics.

Apart from the above techniques which are internal to KRONOS, other tools can be used to preprocess the input timed automata, in order to reduce their size. For example, OPTIKRON [7, 12] can be used to reduce the number of redundant clocks, and ALDEBARAN can be used to minimize the input automata with respect to a bisimulation relation (applied only to the syntactic structure of the automata).

Case Studies

KRONOS has been used to verify various industrial communication protocols, such as an audio-transmission protocol by Philips [11] (where errors have been found to the previously hand-made proofs) or an ATM protocol by CNET [20] (where a bug was also found relative to the consistency of the network components). Other communication protocols modeled and verified by KRONOS include the carrier-sense multiple-access with collision detection (CSMA-CD) protocol [9] and the fiber-optic data-interface (FDDI) protocol [10]. Well-known benchmark case studies verified by KRONOS include Fischer's real-time mutual-exclusion protocol [10] and a production-plant case study [11]. Finally, the tool has been also applied to the verification of the STARI chip [4] and to the synthesis of real-time schedulers [2].

The most recent enhancements of KRONOS include the implementation of different abstraction mechanisms [10], the implementation of a symbolic on-

---

[2] Unpublished work.

the-fly algorithm for checking timed Büchi automata emptiness [3] and a BDD-based implementation oriented towards the timing analysis of circuits [4]. Table 1 presents some typical experimental results extracted from the cited papers. The measurements were taken on a Sparc Ultra-1 with 128 Mbytes of main memory. Time is given in seconds. The size of the state space (when available) is given in symbolic states (i.e., control location plus DBM), BDD nodes, or states and transitions. "OTF" stands for "on-the-fly".

Table 1. Some performance results.

Case study	Method	Time	State space
Production plant	Fixpoint	26	not available
CNET	Forward	3	not available
Philips	Forward	2	not available
Fischer (5 processes)	Minimization	32	3000 states & trans.
Fischer (6 processes)	OTF	2783	164935 symb. states
Fischer (9 processes)	OTF & Abstractions	17098	1096194 symb. states
FDDI (7 stations)	OTF & Büchi aut.	4813	57500 symb. states
FDDI (12 stations)	Forward	1123	13000 symb. states
FDDI (50 stations)	Forward & Abstractions	3900	4000 symb. states
STARI (17 stages)	Fixpoint & BDD	100000	1000000 BDD nodes

It is worth noting that the entire machinery of KRONOS has been useful for handling the above examples. In particular, the fixpoint method has been used in earlier versions of the tool for liveness properties, as well as for synthesis (see, for instance, [11], where initial constraints have been tightened so that the system behaves correctly). Forward model-checking using timed Büchi automata has been recently used for checking liveness on the FDDI protocol for up to 7 processes, as well as to provide diagnostics in the real-time scheduling problem. Minimization has been used for visualizing the behavior of timed automata. On-the-fly techniques have been used whenever syntactic parallel composition could not be applied due to state explosion. Abstractions and clock-reduction techniques have been essential to the verification of the FDDI example for up to 50 processes, and Fischer's protocol for up to 9 processes [10].

Availability

KRONOS is freely available for universities or any other non-profit organisms. It can be obtained through the web at:

        http://www-verimag.imag.fr/TEMPORISE/kronos/

or by anonymous ftp at:

        host: ftp.imag.fr, directory: VERIMAG/KRONOS/tool/.

The distribution package includes executables for various architectures (Sun5, Linux, Windows NT), documentation and examples.

References

1. R. Alur, C. Courcoubetis, and D.L. Dill. Model checking in dense real time. *Information and Computation*, 104(1):2–34, 1993.
2. R. Alur and D.L. Dill. A theory of timed automata. *Theoretical Computer Science*, 126:183–235, 1994.
3. A. Bouajjani, S. Tripakis, and S. Yovine. On-the-fly symbolic model checking for real-time systems. In *Proc. of the 18th IEEE Real-Time Systems Symposium*, 1997.
4. M. Bozga, O. Maler, A. Pnueli, and S. Yovine. Some progress in the symbolic verification of timed automata. In *CAV'97*, 1997.
5. S. Bradley, W. Henderson, D. Kendall, and A. Robson. Validation, verification and implementation of timed protocols using AORTA. In *Proc. 15th PSTV*, 1995.
6. R.E. Bryant. Symbolic boolean manipulation with ordered binary decision diagrams. Technical report, Carnegie Mellon University, 1992.
7. C. Daws. Optikron: a tool suite for enhancing model-checking of real-time systems. 1998. TO appear in CAV'98.
8. C. Daws, A. Olivero, S. Tripakis, and S. Yovine. The tool KRONOS. In *Hybrid Systems III*, 1996.
9. C. Daws, A. Olivero, and S. Yovine. Verifying ET-LOTOS programs with KRONOS. In *FORTE'94*, 1994.
10. C. Daws and S. Tripakis. Model checking of real-time reachability properties using abstractions. In *TACAS'98*, 1998.
11. C. Daws and S. Yovine. Two examples of verification of multirate timed automata with KRONOS. In *RTSS'95*, 1995.
12. C. Daws and S. Yovine. Reducing the number of clock variables of timed automata. In *RTSS'96*, 1996.
13. D. Dill. Timing assumptions and verification of finite-state concurrent systems. In *CAV'89*, 1989.
14. J.Cl. Fernandez, H. Garavel, L. Mounier, A. Rasse, C. Rodriguez, and J. Sifakis. A tool box for the verification of lotos programs. In *14th International Conference on Software Engineering*, 1992.
15. T.A. Henzinger, X. Nicollin, J. Sifakis, and S. Yovine. Symbolic model checking for real-time systems. *Information and Computation*, 111(2):193–244, 1994.
16. M. Jourdan, F. Maraninchi, and A. Olivero. Verifying quantitative real-time properties of synchronous programs. In *CAV'93*, 1993.
17. O. Maler and S. Yovine. Hardware timing verification using KRONOS. In *Proc. 7th Israeli Conference on Computer Systems and Software Engineering*, 1996.
18. X. Nicollin, J. Sifakis, and S. Yovine. Compiling real-time specifications into extended automata. *IEEE TSE Special Issue on Real-Time Systems*, 18(9):794–804, September 1992.
19. A. Olivero, J. Sifakis, and S. Yovine. Using abstractions for the verification of linear hybrid systems. In *CAV'94*, 1994.
20. S. Tripakis and S .Yovine. Verification of the fast-reservation protocol with delayed transmission using Kronos. Technical Report 95-23, Verimag, 1995.
21. S. Tripakis and S. Yovine. Analysis of timed systems based on time–abstracting bisimulations. In *CAV'96*, 1996.

Author Index

Lecture Notes in Computer Science

For information about Vols. 1–1340

please contact your bookseller or Springer-Verlag